THE BRUMBACK LIBRARY

IN MEMORY OF:

Helen (Susie) Dickman

PRESENTED BY:

The Director & Staff
of the
Brumback Library

AMERICA'S
HISTORIC SITES

America's Historic Sites

Volume 3

North Carolina—Wyoming

913-1272

Indexes

from **The Editors of Salem Press**

Managing Editor
Tracy Irons-Georges

SALEM PRESS, INC.

Pasadena, California   Hackensack, New Jersey

Editor in Chief: Dawn P. Dawson

Managing Editor: Tracy Irons-Georges *Acquisitions Editor:* Mark Rehn
Research Supervisor: Jeffry Jensen *Photo Editor:* Philip Bader
Research Assistant: Jeff Stephens *Layout:* Ross E. Castellano
Production Editor: Joyce I. Buchea *Design and Graphics:* James Hutson

Maps in this volume are adapted from Cartesia's MapArt™ Geopolitical Deluxe v2.0 (1998)

Library of Congress Cataloging-in-Publication Data

America's historic sites / the Editors of Salem Press; managing editor, Tracy Irons-Georges.
    p. cm.
  Vol. 1-3.
  Includes bibiographical references and index.
  ISBN 0-89356-122-3 (set : alk. paper) —ISBN 0-89356-123-1 (vol. 1 : alk. paper) — ISBN 0-89356-124-X (vol. 2 : alk. paper) — ISBN 0-89356-147-9 (vol. 3 : alk. paper)
  1. Historic sites—United States—Encyclopedias. 2. United States—History, Local—Encyclopedias. I. Irons-Georges, Tracy. II. Editors of Salem Press.

E159 .A45 2000
973'.03—dc21

                                                                00-056337

First Printing

Contents

AMERICA'S HISTORIC SITES

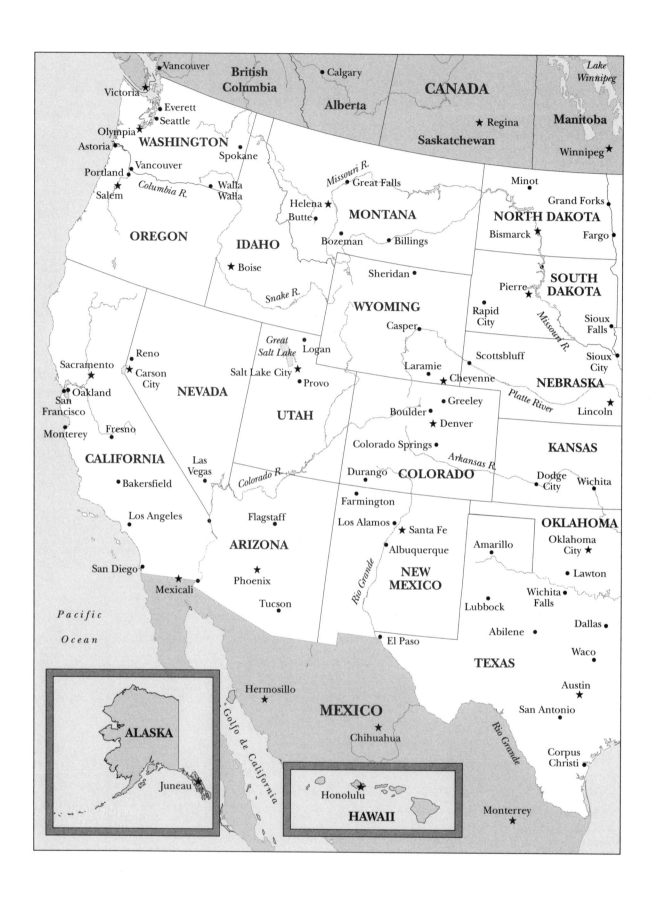

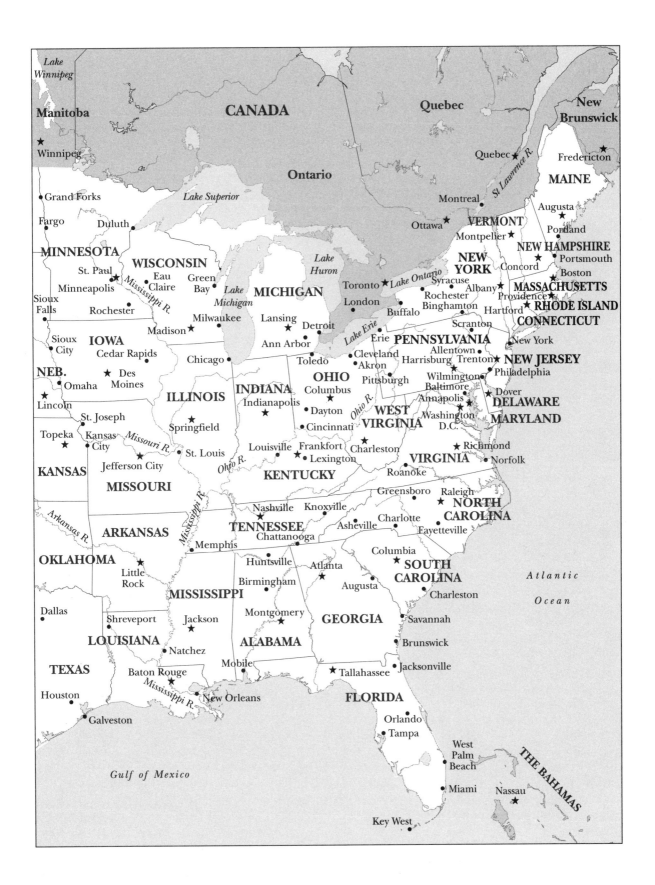

North Carolina

The State Capitol Building in Raleigh. (North Carolina Travel & Tourism)

History of North Carolina

Although sometimes historically overshadowed by its neighbors Virginia and South Carolina, North Carolina has contributed much to the development of the United States. A relatively narrow state, it stretches from the Great Smoky Mountains, a part of the Appalachian system, through the Piedmont Plateau to the coastal plain, which terminates at the long, narrow islands known as the Outer Banks, where Europeans first attempted to settle the land in the late 1500's.

Native Americans and Early Europeans

Sometime around 8000 B.C.E., Native Americans began settling what is now North Carolina. By the period 500 B.C.E., what is known as the Woodland culture had developed throughout much of the area, with cultivation of corn, beans, and squash and the hunting of game. By the time Europeans arrived there were around thirty tribes in the area belonging to three basic linguistic groups, the Algonquian, Iroquoian, and Siouan. The five most powerful and important tribes were the Hatteras (also known as Croatoan), Chowanoe, Tuscarora, Catawba, and Cherokee. The relationship between these Native Americans and the Europeans, especially the English, would have a major impact on the development of North Carolina.

Giovanni da Verrazano, an Italian explorer in the service of France, was the first European to chart the Carolina coast. He was followed by the Spanish in 1526 with an unsuccessful attempt at settlement and in 1540 with Spanish explorer Hernando de Soto's travel through the state. The first serious attempts at European settlement came through England's Sir Walter Raleigh, who had been granted land by Queen Elizabeth. In 1585 and 1586 the first two expeditions sponsored, but not led, by Raleigh were unsuccessful. However, in 1587 a third group established itself on Roanoke Island on the Outer Banks. A few weeks after the colony was founded, Eleanor Dare gave birth to a daughter named Virginia, the first English child born in the New World. John White, father of Eleanor Dare and the colony's governor, sailed to England for supplies. Hostile Spanish fleets prevented his return until 1590, when he found the colony deserted and the word "Croatoan" carved into a tree. Although this may have signaled the community's move to Croatoan Island, south of Cape Hatteras, the mystery of the so-called Lost Colony was never solved.

English Settlement and Revolution

In 1663 King Charles II of England granted a charter to eight Lord Proprietors for a colony to be called Carolina, after himself. A northern county, known as Albemarle, became the foundation of North Carolina. Settlers came from England and Virginia. Initial growth was slow, marked by frequent disputes, sometimes breaking into open rebellion, between settlers and representatives of the Proprietors. The colony faced numerous dangers, including the ravages of pirates, such as Edward Teach or Blackbeard, and the colony was hard-pressed during the Tuscarora War with that tribe, which raged from 1711 through 1715. However, it overcame these difficulties, and in 1712 North and South Carolina were officially recognized as two separate and distinct colonies. In 1731 North Carolina became a royal colony.

After an initially slow start, North Carolina's population grew steadily, and its economy prospered from the production of naval staples such as turpentine and tar. It was during this period that "Tarheel" became a popular nickname for the state and its residents, because of the abundance of that material. As British high taxes and unfair treatment pushed the colonies toward rebellion, North Carolina joined the movement for independence and took a dramatic step in advance of other American colonies: In 1775 citizens of Mecklenburg County adopted a set of "resolves," which declared North Carolina independent of Great Britain. In Halifax in April, 1776, a provincial congress again voted in favor of independence.

Revolution and Statehood

The only two battles during the Revolution fought in North Carolina were those of Moore's Creek Bridge in 1776 and Guilford Courthouse in 1781.

However, there was a vicious partisan struggle during the Revolution between loyalists and rebels, as well as uprisings by Cherokee Indians in the mountain areas throughout the conflict.

North Carolina initially rejected the proposed U.S. Constitution from fear of a strong central government but ratified it in 1789, after the Bill of Rights was proposed. Until the mid-1830's, it lagged behind the new nation in economic development, educational initiatives, and overall prosperity. During this time, North Carolina was sometimes scornfully referred to as the "Rip Van Winkle State" because of its stagnation. However, state leaders pushed through important changes, writing a new state constitution and making the state capital Raleigh, near the center of the state. Railroads, canals, public schools, and other civic improvements led to economic development and population growth.

Civil War

When the Civil War was brewing, North Carolina resisted joining other Southern states in seceding from the Union. There was strong antislavery and pro-Union sentiment in North Carolina, especially in the western portion of the state, and efforts were made to find a peaceful solution to the conflict. It was not until Confederate forces fired on Fort Sumter and President Abraham Lincoln issued a call for troops to put down the rebellion that North Carolina left the Union, in 1861.

Despite coming late to the conflict, North Carolina sent more troops to the Confederate army than any other Southern state, and more than one-quarter of its soldiers were killed. During the war, Union forces quickly captured the Outer Banks and much of the coastline, with only the port of Wilmington remaining open for Confederate blockade runners until the spring of 1865. The last major battle of the war was fought at Bentonville on March 19-21, 1865, between the forces of Union general William Tecumseh Sherman and Confederate Joseph E. Johnston. Johnston's defeat and surrender to Sherman shortly after Confederate general Robert E. Lee's effectively ended the Civil War.

Reconstruction

The Reconstruction period in North Carolina was one of intense struggle between defenders of the old order against newly freed African Americans and whites who had not been slave owners before the war. Under a new constitution, North Carolina was readmitted to the Union in 1868, and a series of reforms were enacted, which benefited both whites and blacks. However, conservative forces regained power in the state legislature in 1870, and in 1876, when federal troops left and Reconstruction ended, blacks and poor whites found themselves again under the domination of landlords and the rich.

Antebellum North Carolina's economy had relied primarily upon agriculture, with the state split between larger farms and plantations dependent upon slave labor in the east and smaller farms in the west. Following the Civil War, small farms leased out to sharecroppers became a dominant pattern, with tobacco and cotton the primary cash crops. Textile mills, many of them using the water power abundant in the state's Piedmont area, were established. Tobacco became a major crop, and North Carolina a major manufacturer of tobacco products. In 1890, James B. Duke founded the American Tobacco Company, and his rival, Richard Joshua Reynolds, made his company, R. J. Reynolds, one of the nation's leading industries. Meanwhile, the abundant forests and water power of western North Carolina and the wood-working technology it powered caused furniture making to become a growth industry that remained important throughout the twentieth century. Technology of another kind was literally launched on December 17, 1903, when Wilbur and Orville Wright made the first powered flight of an aircraft at Kitty Hawk on the windswept Outer Banks.

Modern North Carolina

North Carolina, like so much of the South, was hard hit by the Great Depression, but Franklin Roosevelt's New Deal and the economic mobilization brought about by World War II began massive changes in the state. By offering tax breaks and other incentives, North Carolina was highly successful in recruiting new business, including high-technology firms. Research Triangle Park, located in the Raleigh-Durham-Chapel Hill area, became the site of research and development efforts by many national and international companies, often in conjunction with North Carolina's colleges and universities. During the 1980's, North Carolina became a major player in the financial world as regional and national banks located their headquarters in the state.

Under Governor Terry Sanford, from 1961 to 1965, North Carolina developed a progressive attitude toward education and the arts. Many community and technical colleges were established to provide training and education for workers in high-tech industries, and the nation's first state-supported school for the performing arts was launched in Winston-Salem. During this time North Carolina's institutions of higher education, such as the University of North Carolina at Chapel Hill, Duke University, and Wake Forest, became recognized as among the finest in the United States.

However, economic development and academic achievement were not always evenly matched by social progress. The nation's first sit-in to protest racial segregation occurred in Greensboro in 1960 and provoked reactions from the Ku Klux Klan and other white supremacist groups, including the murder of five protesters at an anti-Klan rally in 1979. At the same time, the Republican Party grew in strength in North Carolina, at times by appealing to the "white backlash" vote. In 1972 Jesse Helms became the first Republican elected to the U.S. Senate from North Carolina in the twentieth century.

The state was also battered by natural disasters in the 1980's and 1990's. In March, 1984, a series of tornadoes in the state's eastern counties killed forty-four people. Only six months later, Hurricane Diana caused more than $65 million in damage. In 1989 Hurricane Hugo, one of the strongest storms ever to come ashore in the United States, caused millions of dollars of damage in Charlotte, hundreds of miles inland. In 1996 two hurricanes, Bertha in July and Fran in September, left massive destruction behind them, and twenty-one people died in Fran's fury. With potential prosperity and growth on the one hand, and unresolved racial tensions on the other, North Carolina is ever more mindful of its motto, *Esse quam videri*—"To be rather than to seem."
—*Michael Witkoski*

Carl Sandburg Home

Date: Farm purchased by Sandburg in 1945; acquired by the National Park Service shortly after his death in 1967

Relevant issues: Cultural history, literary history, social reform

Significance: Sandburg chose this site as the place where he could find both solitude and inspiration for his multifaceted examination of American life. The Carl Sandburg Home National Historic Site preserves Connemara, the 245-acre farm where Carl Sandburg and his family lived the last twenty-two years of his life. The farm consists of a twenty-two-room house, barns, sheds, pastures, woods, trails, two small lakes, a trout pond, flower and vegetable gardens, and an orchard.

Location: Connemara is a farmhouse located on 245 acres atop a hill twenty-five miles south of Asheville, via Interstate 26; the park is five miles south of Hendersonville

Site Office:
Carl Sandburg Home National Historic Site
1928 Little River Road
Flat Rock, NC 28731
ph.: (828) 693-4178
Web site: www.nps.gov/carl/

Perhaps the best way to get both an idea of the literary approach of Carl Sandburg and a glimpse of pre-World War II America is to visit Sandburg's chosen home in North Carolina.

Sandburg's Childhood and Early Life
Carl Sandburg was born in Galesburg, Illinois, on January 6, 1878. His father, August Johnson, emigrated to America from Sweden and, upon encountering several August Johnsons in Galesburg, changed the family name to Sandburg. The Sandburgs were not rich, and only Carl's mother, Clara, could read and write. Because of the economic needs of the family, Carl Sandburg went to work at the age of thirteen after only eight years of schooling. For the next few years, Sandburg worked at several odd jobs ranging from selling fruit on street corners to shining shoes and sweeping floors at a local barbershop. He later fondly recalled the barbershop job because it taught him the art of storytelling and familiarized him with the idiomatic phrases of the Midwest.

The year 1896 proved to be an important one in Sandburg's life: He first heard the compelling oratory of William Jennings Bryan and began a lifelong commitment to populist ideas; he witnessed the celebration of the anniversary of an Abraham Lincoln-Stephen A. Douglas debate which had taken place in Galesburg forty years before, thus commencing a lifetime fascination with Lincoln memorabilia; and he made his first visit to Chicago, a city with which his name always would be identified. The following year, Sandburg traveled westward across the United States, riding the rails with hoboes, pitching wheat in Kansas, and keeping an informal notebook of his travels and of the songs and stories that he heard along the way. He returned to Galesburg, where he enlisted in the Illinois state militia and fought in a few skirmishes in the Spanish-American War.

Sandburg's Literary Development
Sandburg's experiences in the Spanish-American

War marked an important stage in his literary development. While he was stationed in the Caribbean, Sandburg sent home long letters that were published in the Galesburg *Evening Mail*. Upon his return, with discharge money in his pocket and the right to a year's free tuition at Lombard, a local college, Sandburg enrolled as a special college student. Although he never graduated, he participated fully in assorted campus activities: He sang in the glee club, belonged to the debate club, captained the basketball team, was coeditor of the 1901 yearbook, and served as editor-in-chief of *The Lombard Review*.

By far the most important influence on his life at Lombard was Professor Philip Green Wright. Wright, who taught economics and math as well as English, encouraged Sandburg to continue his insatiable reading (Ivan Turgenev, Rudyard Kipling, Karl Marx, and others) and also encouraged him to perfect his writing and critical skills on Sunday afternoons in a group Wright dubbed "The Poor Writers Club." Wright would be the first to publish a Sandburg collection, a small thirty-nine-page pamphlet titled *In Reckless Ecstasy* (1904). The title and the content of the pamphlet clearly revealed Sandburg's literary signature; he always attempted to write sensibly, he wrote, but if that did not work, he would write with "reckless ecstasy."

Sandburg's Contribution to American Literature
Sandburg inexplicably left the Lombard campus in 1902 and once more began to roam the United States, this time confining himself mainly to the northeast coast of the United States. He again rode the rails with the hoboes, getting arrested at one point and spending several days in a Pennsylvania county jail, but he also visited some of the large cities on the East Coast. He returned to Galesburg in 1904 and spent the next two years at various jobs, including stints as a police reporter and a town fireman. More important, however, was the renewal of his contact with Professor Wright. He left Galesburg in 1906 (returning for occasional visits over the years) and moved to Chicago.

For the next twenty-five years Sandburg's life was interwoven with the threads of political and cultural life in the Midwest, with its nexus in Chicago. He began to give lectures, sponsored by a lyceum based in Chicago, and he became the associate editor of *The Lyceumite*. While in Chicago he met a state organizer for the Wisconsin Social-Democratic party and was soon deeply involved in the reform politics of that group. He also met Lillian Steichen, with whom he discussed the ideas of Victor Berger, the leading socialist in Wisconsin, and soon an intellectual encounter blossomed into romance. Lillian, whom he called "Paula," was a member of Phi Beta Kappa and a graduate of the University of Chicago and would act as a profound influence upon Sandburg's literary as well as political decisions. It was she who encouraged him to write without worrying about a label, including the free verse poetry that flowed from his pen, noting that others could worry about labels while he should simply write. Sandburg returned to Chicago in 1912 after three years as private secretary to Emil Seidel, socialist mayor of Milwaukee, and took a job with the *Day Book*, an E. W. Scripps daily. Chicago was in the midst of a literary renaissance, and the "Chicago Group" included such notables as Sandburg, H. B. Fuller, Ben Hecht, Sherwood Anderson, and Edgar Lee Masters. Harriet Monroe, in whose little magazine, *Poetry*, Sandburg's first

widely acclaimed writing was published, and Margaret Anderson, whose *Little Review* served as a vehicle for young writers, were prominent sponsors of the writings of the Chicago Group. Monroe published Sandburg's poem *Chicago*, the opening lines of which at first shocked readers but soon became the anthem of his people's verse.

> Hog Butcher for the World,
> Tool Maker, Stacker of Wheat,
> Player with Railroads and the
> Nation's Freight Handler;
> Storm, husky, brawling,
> City of the Big Shoulders. . . .

Two years later, in 1916, Sandburg's first book of poetry, *Chicago Poems*, was published. Many of the reviews were not favorable; one reviewer called Sandburg's free-verse the work of a "mystical mobocrat." His reputation and popularity, however, continued to grow, and the scope of his literature continued to broaden.

Following work in Sweden for the Newspaper Enterprise Association, Sandburg returned to Chicago in 1919 as special reporter for the *Chicago Daily News*. He served in that capacity for thirteen years and enjoyed the freedom to choose the topics about which he wished to write. His interests ranged from serving as a motion-picture editor to acting as observer and commentator on the Chicago race riots of 1919. The freedom to choose his topics also gave him more time to pursue other, non-newspaper interests, and he published the *Rootabaga Stories* (1922), a collection of children's stories he had written for his daughters, took to the college lecture circuit, pieced together the lyrics and music to songs that he sang at his public appearances in *The American*

Connemara, Carl Sandburg's Home. (Carl Sandburg Home National Historic Site)

Songbag (1927), and continued to collect material about his favorite interest, Abraham Lincoln.

His success as a lecturer, poet, newspaper reporter, writer of children's stories, and, finally, author of a popular biography of the pre-presidential life of Abraham Lincoln called *The Prairie Years* (1926, two volumes), made it possible for Sandburg, his wife, and his extended family to purchase a farm in Harbert, Michigan, which served as a summer residence from 1926 to 1932 and a permanent residence from 1932 to 1945.

Sandburg at Connemara, North Carolina

The activities that he pursued at Harbert from 1932 to 1945 were similar to the ones that he experienced in North Carolina during the last twenty-two years of his life; the literary productivity of those last years, however, was slightly more curtailed. His wife Paula became interested in raising goats and named the place Chicaming Goat Farm. The farm produced milk and yogurt for family and friends, and Sandburg's life, if not his poetry, became more bucolic. Sandburg's interest in Lincoln continued, culminating in *Abraham Lincoln: The War Years* (1939; 2 vols.), which won the Pulitzer Prize in 1940, and his public performances and literary awards continued.

In 1945, at the age of sixty-seven, Sandburg moved with his wife, daughters, grandchildren, Lincoln material, furniture, and Chicaming goats (which were shipped by express) to Flat Rock, North Carolina. There, at a 245-acre farm which had been named Connemara by its previous owner, Sandburg hoped to escape the harsh climate of Michigan and gain a semblance of the privacy he felt that he needed to complete his life. This would be the place where Sandburg would spend, as biographer Richard Crowder described, the "harvest years" of his life.

The farmhouse, a twenty-two-room white clapboard two-story structure which originally had been built in 1838, sits on a hill surrounded by pastures, woods, trails, small lakes, a trout pond, gardens, and an orchard. The National Park Service, which purchased the farm shortly after Sandburg's death in 1967, has successfully preserved the house and its contents to closely resemble the appearance it had when Sandburg was alive. The downstairs consists of several rooms, the most notable of which is the twelve-foot by fifteen-foot living room with a grand piano, overstuffed chairs, bookcases, and magazines to which Sandburg subscribed. Downstairs there is also a library, a farm office, and a bedroom. Upstairs are two bedrooms and Sandburg's workroom. The workroom contains the tools of his trade: reference works, books, a green eyeshade that he always used when he wrote, and an old typewriter.

Connemarra has something for every member of the family. Children will enjoy the goats, which still roam the farm, the family will enjoy the trails, and those interested in getting a glimpse of the people's bard will not be disappointed.

—*Robert L. Patterson*

For Further Information:

Crowder, Richard. *Carl Sandburg*. Boston: Twayne, 1964. A brief biography that summarizes most of the events of Sandburg's life.

Niven, Penelope. *Carl Sandburg: A Biography*. New York: Charles Scribner's Sons, 1991. The result of fourteen years of research, this biography concludes that Sandburg's life was probably more important than his literary output.

Sandburg, Carl. *Abraham Lincoln: The Prairie Years*. 2 vols. New York: Harcourt, Brace, 1926. The first major biographical work on Lincoln, originally contracted as a children's book and expanded into an adult biography.

_____. *Abraham Lincoln: The War Years*. 4 vols. New York: Harcourt, Brace, 1939. A continuation of the life of Lincoln, these volumes follow his career as president. It was awarded the 1940 Pulitzer Prize in Biography.

_____. *Always the Young Strangers*. New York: Harcourt, Brace, 1953. An autobiographical account of the first twenty years of Sandburg's life.

_____. *The American Songbag*. New York: Harcourt, Brace, 1927. Songs, both the words and music, which were often sung by Sandburg at his public lectures.

_____. *Complete Poems*. 6 vols. New York: Harcourt, Brace, 1950. Also contains a "New Section."

_____. *The New American Songbag*. New York: Broadcast Music, 1950. A collection of forty of the songs from the 1927 publication and an addition of several other songs collected since that book.

_____. *Rootabaga Country*. New York: Harcourt, Brace, 1929. A selection of several of the fantastic stories that Sandburg had improvised for his daughters and later formally written.

Kitty Hawk

Date: First successful flight of machine-powered aircraft on December 17, 1903

Relevant issues: Aviation history, science and technology

Significance: From 1900 to 1903, Wilbur and Orville Wright traveled several times from their home in Dayton, Ohio, to the Outer Banks to experiment with gliders and finally a machine-powered aircraft. The National Park Service administers the site and has reconstructed the camp, which includes a hangar and workshop with living quarters. Also on display are replicas of the 1903 Wright flyer and a 1902 glider model.

Location: Memorial on the Outer Banks of North Carolina in the town of Kill Devil Hills, midway between Kitty Hawk and Nags Head on U.S. Highway 158

Site Office:
Wright Brothers National Historic Site
National Park Service
P.O. Box 2539
Kill Devil Hills, NC 27948
ph.: (252) 441-7430
Web site: www.nps.gov/wrbr/

In 1903, two young brothers from Dayton, Ohio, named Wilbur and Orville Wright, profoundly changed the course of human history. In September of that year Wilbur booked a train ride for what was one of several trips the brothers had made during a four-year period to the pristine tiny fishing village of Kitty Hawk on North Carolina's picturesque Outer Banks. In preparation for the historic journey, Orville helped his brother load a biplane into the boxcar at the rear of a train. Despite many unsuccessful attempts during the previous three years, the two brothers remained determined to do something no one had done before: fly.

Early History of Manned Flight

If history was the gauge, the odds were long against the Wright brothers achieving their dream. Indeed, for more than a hundred years before the Wrights left for Kitty Hawk, man was earnestly trying to learn the secrets of flight. By the early twentieth century, however, a series of disasters had convinced many that there would never be such a thing

as a flying machine. In 1894, for example, one noted inventor named Sir Hiram Maxim spent the princely sum of twenty thousand dollars on a four-ton machine equipped with several wings and a 360-horse power engine, but it never got off the ground. In the fall of 1903, the world watched as Professor Samuel Pierpont Langley, head of the Smithsonian Institution, built and tested a steam-powered, fixed-wing "aerodrome" that failed twice, the last nearly killing the pilot as the airplane plunged into the Potomac River.

The Wrights were aware of all of these abortive attempts at flight, but the fear of failure was not a part of their character. Wilbur Wright wrote, "I have been afflicted with the belief that flight is possible to man." Still there was nothing in the Wright brothers' backgrounds to indicate they would be history-making pioneers. Their parents were simple, hard-working, God-fearing midwesterners. As historians Ronald Geibert and Patrick Nolan note, the brothers inherited some important traits from their father that would shape their lives: "intellectual openness and curiosity, a willingness to engage in scientific and human inquiry, a delight in intellectual speculation, a fondness for reading."

The Wright Brothers

Wilbur Wright was born on a farm near Millsville, Indiana, on April 16, 1867; Orville on August 19, 1871, in Dayton, Ohio. From an early age the brothers were inseparable. According to legend, the two would often start humming or whistling the same song at exactly the same moment when working together in the bicycle shop they owned. The two lifelong bachelors, who neither smoked nor drank, shared a passion for flying machines.

Later, people were amazed to learn that neither of the Wright brothers had any special training in science or engineering; in fact, they had left high school before receiving a diploma. At an early age, however, their father bought the young boys a toy—a flying machine that looked like a helicopter and was powered by a rubber band. It would spark their lifelong interest in flight.

In 1892, the year bicycling became a national passion, the brothers opened the Wright Cycle Shop in Dayton, where they built, fixed, rented, and sold bicycles. It was a successful business, but the young men began to take notice of the sensa-

Orville and Wilbur Wright making the first successful powered flight at Kitty Hawk in 1903. (Library of Congress)

cated could trace its history back to the first settlement in American history. Across the Bay from the village was Roanoke Island, the site of the first English colony in the New World.

The experimental aircraft Wilbur brought with him by train to Kitty Hawk was a biplane glider, based on a smaller prototype with a five-foot wingspan, which the Wrights had designed to be flown as a kite. Before Wilbur left for North Carolina, the brothers had tested this prototype in an open field and were satisfied with the results. When Orville joined Wilbur several weeks later, they launched their experiments, which began by flying gliders as kites and then as manned aircraft.

The Wrights pitched their tent about a half mile south of the Kitty Hawk village at a location known as Kill Devil Hills. In a letter to his sister dated October 18, 1900, Orville Wright graphically described the setting:

> About two or three nights a week we have to crawl up at ten or eleven. We hold the tent down.... The wind shaking the roof and sides, the tent sounds exactly like thunder. When we crawl out of the tent to fix things outside, the sand blinds us. It blows across the ground in clouds. We certainly can't complain of the place. We came down here for wind and sand, and we have got them.

It is not certain when the Wrights made their first trial run, but historians generally believe it happened on October 3, 1900, the day before they had set up their camp. A week later, they had just completed a test flight and were adjusting their control lines when a gust of wind caught the glider and smashed it to the ground twenty feet away. They spent the next three days repairing their

tional flights of the German Otto Lilienthal, history's first true glider pilot. When Lilienthal died in a crash in 1896, the brothers took up the challenge and began studying what they described as "flying problems."

The Wrights read everything they could find about flight. In spring 1899, Wilbur wrote to the Smithsonian Institution in Washington, asking for a selection of pamphlets and a list of available books on the subject. As they studied the infant science of aeronautics, they began to build their own glider. In the meantime, they wrote the Weather Bureau in Washington, D.C., for information about places that had steady winds and soft sands for landings. The bureau's answer: Kitty Hawk, North Carolina.

Kitty Hawk

At the turn of the century, Kitty Hawk was an isolated settlement, a small fishing village containing a few weatherbeaten houses scattered around a bay. The coastal region in which Kitty Hawk was lo-

The Wright Brothers Monument at Kitty Hawk. (PhotoDisc)

airfoils. As their knowledge grew, so did their confidence, and in 1902 they perfected their design with their biggest glider yet: one with a thirty-two foot wingspan and two six-foot-high vertical fins, designed to stabilize the machine during turns.

The First Controlled Flight

That summer at Kitty Hawk, they achieved the first controlled flight in history. The brothers went on to complete one thousand successful glides from Big Kill Devil Hill before deciding they were ready to build a powered flying machine.

The 1903 Wright Flyer was a two-wing biplane design with a wingspan of almost 40 feet. There was no suitable lightweight commercial engine available, so the brothers built their own—a four-cylinder, twelve-horse power, two hundred-pound gasoline engine. The biplane's two propellers—the result of their earlier wind tunnel experiments—were the first true aerial propellers ever built. The combined weight of the aircraft and pilot was almost 750 pounds.

When the Wrights arrived in Kitty Hawk on September 25, 1903, after the two-day trip from Dayton, they learned that a severe hurricane had damaged their camp. Nature had delayed what would have been the beginning of their powered flight experiments. It took almost a month for the Wrights to assemble the flyer, and even after it was finished more problems dogged their efforts. Chain sprockets continued to come loose; then the freezing cold cracked a tubular shaft and Orville had to return to Dayton to repair it. He did not return to Kitty Hawk until December 11.

Three days later, the Wrights were ready for their first trial flight. Wilbur won a coin toss to fly the machine, but he oversteered on elevating from the launching rail and the flyer climbed too steeply, stalled, and then crashed into the sand. More repairs were necessary. Finally, on December 17, the Wrights were ready for another attempt. It was a bitterly cold day with near-freezing temper-

craft and trying to keep their tent from blowing away. They made additional flight tests designed to provide a detailed record of the performance of the craft in a wide range of wind and land conditions.

At the same time, they conducted an exhaustive study of birds in flight. According to historian Aycock Brown, "there were times when the natives . . . stared in amazement at Wilbur and Orville as they walked along the beach, observing gulls in flight and imitating them with a wing-like motion of their arms." During that first trip to Kitty Hawk, Wilbur's time aloft in free flight totaled only ten seconds; the Wrights returned to Dayton discouraged. "It will be a thousand years before man learns to fly," Wilbur told his brother on the train ride home.

The Wrights returned to Kitty Hawk during the late summers of 1901 and 1902 and continued to develop their aircraft control system while increasing their knowledge of gliding and wing construction. They undertook precise, systematic experiments and built a wind tunnel, an eight-foot-long structure in which they tested the efficiency of hundreds of different wing shapes.

The new data they collected with their wind tunnel experiments added to their understanding of

atures and strong winds blowing at about twenty-seven miles per hour. The Wrights waited for two hours for the wind to drop and the temperature to rise. Weather conditions were not going to improve, the Wrights realized, and so they decided to make another attempt immediately.

The Wrights' chances of making history did not look good, for the strong headwinds threatened to slow their groundspeed to a crawl. Using a sheet they signaled the volunteers of a nearby lifesaving station that they were ready to try to go airborne. Since Wilbur had made the first attempt on December 14, the two brothers agreed that Orville should now have his turn. At 10:35 A.M. Orville steered the machine into the strong wind. It scudded down the rail as Wilbur steadied the wings, then rose about six feet in the air. The flyer pitched up and down, as Orville overcompensated with the controls, and then swooped down to earth about 120 feet from the takeoff point. Later, Wilbur Wright commented, "Though the flight took only twelve seconds, nevertheless, it was the first time in history that a piloted machine rose into the air under its own power, moved forward in the air without losing speed, and finally landed at a point as big as that from which it took off."

That historic morning, the Wrights made three additional flights. The last one—Wilbur's second—extended an impressive 852 feet and lasted 59 seconds. A strong gust of wind, however, caught the plane after its last flight, flipping it over and damaging it beyond easy repair. It never flew again.

That was merely postcript, for the two brothers had achieved their dream. In less than ten years, without spending more than five thousand dollars they accomplished what eminent scientists had failed to do in a lifetime of work with unlimited funds. The Wrights had ushered in the era of humanity's conquest of the skies.

Early History

Today, Kill Devil Hills is the site of the Wright Brothers National Memorial. A granite boulder marks the spot of the first takeoff, and numbered markers measure the distances of each of the Wrights' four powered flights in 1903. Also at the monument are replicas of the 1902 glider and 1903 flyer, a replica of the brothers' campsite, a public airstrip to accommodate visitors arriving in small planes, and a sixty-foot granite pylon memorial to Wilbur and Orville Wright.   —*Ron Chepesiuk*

For Further Information:

Brown, Aycock. *The Birth of Aviation.* Salem, N.C.: Collins, 1953. An excellent source.

Crouch, Tom D. *The Bishop's Boys: A Life of Wilbur and Orville Wright.* New York: W. W. Norton, 1989. One of many books about the Wrights and their remarkable achievement at Kitty Hawk. A thorough, scholarly biography that puts the Wrights in the context of the times.

Freedman, Russell. *The Wright Brothers: How They Invented the Airplane.* New York: Holiday House, 1991. Will appeal primarily to older children, although it is sophisticated enough that adults can enjoy it too.

Geibert, Ronald R., and Patrick B. Nolan. *Kitty Hawk and Beyond: The Wright Brothers and the Early Years of Aviation.* Dayton, Ohio: Wright State University, 1990. A handsomely illustrated volume with over one hundred fascinating photographs of the Wrights at Kitty Hawk.

Howard, Fred. *Wilbur and Orville: A Biography of the Wright Brothers.* Reprint. Mineola, N.Y.: Dover, 1998. Another thorough, scholarly biography.

Wescott, Lynanne. *Wind and Sand: The Story of the Wright Brothers at Kitty Hawk.* New York: Harry N. Abrams, 1983. A lavishly illustrated text that has depth and insight.

Roanoke Island

Date: First settled in 1585

Relevant issues: Colonial America, European settlement

Significance: Roanoke Island was the site of the first English colony in the Americas. It was first visited by English explorers in 1584 and settled by two English colonizing expeditions, in 1585 and 1587. The latter colony vanished mysteriously. In 1941, one hundred fifty acres in the area were named a National Historic Site.

Location: In the outer banks of North Carolina, sixty-seven miles southeast of Elizabeth City; on U.S. Interstate 64-264 between the Albemarle and Pamlico Sounds, three miles north of Manteo, North Carolina, and ninety-two miles southeast of Norfolk, Virginia

Site Office:
Fort Raleigh National Historic Site
Outer Banks NPS Group
Route 1, Box 675
Manteo, NC 27954
ph.: (252) 473-5772, 473-2111
Web site: www.nps.gov/fora/

Known as the Lost Colony, Roanoke Island was the site of the first attempted English settlement in America. Two groups of English settlers unsuccessfully attempted to colonize the outer banks of North Carolina. The second group of colonists intended to establish a permanent colony in 1587 but was never heard from again.

Sir Walter Raleigh

Between 1584 and 1587, Sir Walter Raleigh sponsored three voyages to America. These voyages were known as the Roanoke Voyages. The aim of the first voyage was to explore and investigate the area while the aims of the second and third voyages were to establish a colony and to found a settlement. England was eager to claim land in North America before it could be claimed by Spain, which had a substantial head start in the race to explore the Americas. Another motive for the colonization was to establish a base from which to raid Spanish ships carrying gold and other riches back from the New World.

Raleigh inherited the project from his half brother Sir Humphrey Gilbert, who sparked British interest in colonizing the Americas when he obtained a charter from Queen Elizabeth "to inhabit and possess . . . all remote and heathen lands not in actual possession of any Christian prince." In 1578, he made the first of two attempts to reach what is today Newfoundland. Gilbert died in 1583 during the second voyage, however, and Raleigh obtained his own grant from the queen to establish a colony in North America. In 1584 he dispatched a reconnaissance expedition under the direction of Philip Amadas and Arthur Barlowe to investigate the territory.

On July 4, 1584, Amadas and Barlowe landed on Roanoke Island. Accompanying the 1584 expedition were Thomas Hariot and John White. Hariot was an astronomer, a mathematician, and a navigator. He was chosen to observe and chronicle the voyage and expedition. He also became the liaison between the colonists and Algonquin Indians, who inhabited the island. In 1588 he wrote *A brief and true report of the new found land of Virginia*, in which he described Native American life and the region's flora and fauna. The second edition of Hariot's book was illustrated with engravings based on watercolor paintings by White, who would be the official artist on the 1585 expedition. His paintings portrayed the Native Americans neither as base savages nor as noble innocents, but as members of a culture that was worthy of attention and respect.

Virginia Colony

Reports from the expedition in 1584 sang the praises of the rich land. Amadas and Barlowe returned with two Native Americans named Manteo and Wanchese, as well as tobacco, potatoes, and other crops. Based on Amada's and Barlowe's report, Raleigh persuaded English investors, including Queen Elizabeth, to finance a colony in North America. The new colony was called "Virginia," after the Virgin Queen. In April, 1585, Raleigh dispatched seven ships and 500 men, 108 of them colonists, for Roanoke Island. He appointed his cousin Sir Richard Grenville as captain and Ralph Lane as governor of the colony. The journey took three months. The colonists reached Port Fernando at Roanoke Island on June 29, 1585. The colony was to serve as a lookout for Spanish and French ships. The colonists built a fort on the island. The initial relations between the colonists and the Native Americans were good.

The colonists arrived with few provisions because of the loss of their flagship at sea, but most of the colonists were soldiers who knew little about land cultivation. It was too late to plant crops, and Lane, who was most interested in exploring for gold and pearls, had little interest in learning native fishing techniques. The colonists therefore relied on the natives for food and were supplied with fish and maize. Grenville returned to England, promising to return with supplies by Easter.

As winter approached, food became scarce and relations between the Native Americans and the colonists had began to sour. The colonists began pilfering the Native Americans' food supplies, and European epidemics such as measles and smallpox swept through the Indian population.

By 1586, the colonists were anxious to resettle in

Sir Walter Raleigh, who sponsored the settlement at Roanoke. (Library of Congress)

the Chesapeake Bay area. After further exploration of the region, Lane concluded that Roanoke was a poor base for privateering. He was also drawn by tales of gold and a possible northwest passage. He led a small expedition up the Moratuc (Roanoke) River to search for precious metals and took Choanoke Indians as hostages in order to ensure their cooperation. Having only a few days' supply of food left, Lane assumed he could get more from Native Americans living in the area. However, Chief Wingina of Roanoke warned inland groups that Lane had planned to raid them. Forewarned, they took their supplies and deserted their villages. Lane and his men survived by eating their guard dogs and returned to the colony, but by late spring there was open warfare.

Peace had been maintained until this point largely through the efforts of Wingina's father, Ensinore. When he died, relations deteriorated rapidly. Wanchese, one of the two Indians who had traveled with Amadas and Barlowe to England and returned with Lane, sided with the Indians. Lane soon learned that Wanchese and Wingina were planning an attack on the colonists, and so arranged a ruse whereby he could launch a preemptive strike. At a meeting called ostensibly to air grievances between the two sides, Lane and his men attacked the Indians, burned their village to the ground, and killed Wingina.

Sir Francis Drake Offers Aid

One week later, Sir Francis Drake, who had been raiding Spanish ports in the Caribbean, arrived at Roanoke Island. Drake offered Lane one month's food supply and a ship, the *Francis*, to transport the colonists back to England. The disappointed colonists eagerly accepted. They were to set sail for England after Lane had finished his explorations. However, a strong storm forced the *Francis* to leave the harbor and sank the smaller ships. Drake offered Lane another ship, the *Bonner*, but could no longer wait for Lane to finish his explorations. On June 18, 1596, Lane abandoned the colony, in his haste leaving behind three men who were off on an expedition. Also, a large group of African and West Indian slaves, who had been liberated by Drake from Spanish control, were left behind in the hurry to create space on the ships for the boarding colonists.

Two days later, a supply ship sent by Raleigh arrived in Roanoke. Grenville arrived two weeks later with supplies and four hundred men ready to fortify the colony and found the place deserted. He left fifteen men on the island and returned to England. The men were left with two years' supply of rations and instructions to "hold" the colony until a new group of colonists arrived.

The Second Colony

More planning went into the second colony. Raleigh appointed White governor of the colony, and the two decided that the colony's success depended on a commitment to the land. It was to be an agrarian colony rather than a base of operations against the Spanish. The inclusion of 17 women and 9 children among the 110 colonists to be sent there was a direct attempt to make the colony a long-term, self-perpetuating settlement. Each settler was deeded a five hundred-acre plot and promised a voice in the government. The colony was given a coat of arms and the name "Cittie of Ralegh." A location was chosen on the lower end of the Chesapeake Bay.

When the ships sailed in May, 1587, the plan was to stop briefly at Roanoke Island to resupply Grenville's party and settle in Chesapeake. When they arrived at Roanoke in July, the ship's captain and his crew were eager to travel to the Caribbean and begin privateering, and refused to sail to Chesapeake. The colonists were left to resettle on Roanoke Island.

Like the first attempt, the beginning of the second colony was unfavorable. The colonists had failed to pick up salt and fruit as planned in Haiti. The fifteen men left by Grenville had been attacked and killed; the new settlers found only the bones of one of the men. Relations with the Native Americans were still uneasy. The colonists attacked an Indian village after a misunderstanding over the date of a peace conference led the settlers to believe their peace offer had been rejected.

Accompanying the second group was Manteo, the Roanoke man who had returned from England with the settlers. He aided in restoring cordial relations with the Native Americans. Manteo was baptized on August 13, 1587, and given the title "Lord of Roanoke." The baptism was the first recorded celebration of a Christian sacrament by English-speaking people in America. Also accompanying the colonists was Governor White's daughter, Eleanor Dare, who on August 25, 1587, gave birth to Virginia Dare, the first child of English parentage born in America.

Although crops were planted, White decided to return to England for relief supplies the next week. White and the colonists had agreed that, if relocation became necessary during his absence, the colonists would leave the name of their new location carved on a tree, with a cross carved above the name if they moved under attack. White departed for England on August 27, 1587, leaving the colonists behind. He arrived as England was preparing to meet the Spanish Armada in war and was unable to return for three years.

The Abandoned Colony

Returning on board a privateering ship, the *Hopewell*, on August 18, 1590, White found the colony abandoned. He saw no sign of the colonists except the letters, "CRO" carved on a tree and the word "CROATOAN," the Algonquin name for the nearby island of Hatteras, carved on a post. Neither a cross nor bodies were found. The houses had been taken down, a palisade constructed, and White's armor lay rusting in the sand. White wanted to sail to Croatoan to search for the colonists, but the privateers were anxious to begin their raids, and supplies were running low. He returned to England in November, 1590, without discovering their fate.

The search for those who have become known as the "lost colonists" did not end with John White. In the first years following their arrival at Jamestown in 1607, Captain John Smith and the other settlers made repeated efforts to locate them. In January, 1608, Jamestown settlers sent a search party upon hearing rumors that some of the colonists were still living. They later tried again to locate them in the Chowan River area.

Theories About the Lost Colonists

Although no one knows what happened to the lost colonists, there are many theories about their fate. The two prevailing theories are that the colonists traveled to Chesapeake and were killed by followers of Powhatan (chief of the Algonquins), and that the colonists moved to Hatteras Island and intermarried with the Croatoans. In 1959 the three foremost scholars on Roanoke—C. Christopher Crittenden, William S. Powell, and David Beers Quinn—met to discuss their views on the lost colonists. They all agreed that the some of the colonists left Roanoke and moved to Hatteras Island, and others moved to the interior. It was also agreed that the colonists' destination was the southern area of Chesapeake Bay, that some of them were killed by Powhatan, and finally, that some of the colonists were still living with the natives shortly before the arrival of the Jamestown colony.

According to David Beers Quinn, the failure of the colonies was due more to poor organization and the conduct of the expeditions than to the failings of the colonies themselves. Nevertheless,

Roanoke Island proved a valuable training ground for English colonization. The Virginia Company of 1607-1624 emerged directly out of the Roanoke ventures. For the native inhabitants of the Northeast, the events at the Roanoke colonies proved only too prophetic. The same patterns of greed, violence, and disease would be played out again and again as Europeans penetrated the continent. According to Quinn, "the Roanoke colonies can be seen as striking the first blow at [the native] culture in eastern North America."

Roanoke During the Civil War

Roanoke Island again came to historical prominence, if much less dramatically, several times since the disappearance of the lost colonists. The island was the site of a naval battle during the Civil War. After Hatteras fell to Union forces, Roanoke Island became the last Confederate stronghold defending Albemarle Sound. The Confederates under Colonel Henry M. Shaw engaged the Union army but were forced to retreat and surrender on December 7, 1862.

Forty years later, at Weir Point on the tip of Roanoke Island, Reginald A. Fessenden, of the U.S. Weather Bureau, successfully communicated with a ship off the coast, using a wireless station he had constructed and would shortly patent.

Modern Preservation Efforts

In 1941, the U.S. government created the Fort Raleigh National Historic Site, which spans one hundred fifty acres and includes a reconstruction of the small earthen fort built by the colonists. Exhibits at the site explore the history of the colony and depict Elizabethan life. The Elizabethan Gardens were created as a memorial to the first colonists and as an example of the gardens of the wealthy investors of the colony. Lost Colony, the Pulitzer Prize-winning play by Paul Green, is produced during the summer in the Waterside Theater by the Roanoke Island Historical Association. The play retells the story of the ill-fated 1587 Roanoke colony.   —*Tabitha R. Oglesby*

For Further Information:

Hume, Ivor Noel. *The Virginia Adventure: Roanoke to James Towne, an Archaeological and Historical Odyssey.* Charlottesville: University Press of Virginia, 1997. A history of the Roanoke Colony and Jamestown.

McCarty, Laura P. "New Findings at the Lost Colony." *National Parks* 6, nos. 7-8 (1993). One of the more recent accounts of the Roanoke experience, focusing on archaeological efforts.

Quinn, David Beers. *Set Fair for Roanoke: Voyages and Colonies, 1584-1606.* Chapel Hill: University of North Carolina Press, 1984. A comprehensive history of the settlements, based on extensive research.

Robinson, Blackwell P., ed. *The North Carolina Guide.* Chapel Hill: University of North Carolina Press, 1955. Although somewhat outdated, provides excellent geographical and historical descriptions of Roanoke Island and the surrounding area.

Stick, David. *Roanoke Island: The Beginnings of English America.* Chapel Hill: University of North Carolina Press, 1983. Fills the void between scholarly and fictionalized treatments of the events at Roanoke.

Other Historic Sites

Bentonville Battlefield

Location: Along state routes 1008 and 1009, Newton Grove and Bentonville, Johnston County

Relevant issues: Civil War, military history

Web site: www.ah.dcr.state.nc.us/sections/hs/bentonvi/bentonvi.htm

Statement of significance: The Battle of Bentonville, where two military titans of the Civil War— Generals William Tecumseh Sherman and Joseph E. Johnston—faced each other for the final time in a major battle, was the last occasion on which Confederate army troops mounted an all-out offensive during the Civil War. The loss here was the Confederates' death knell, for it fatally weakened their last mobile field army.

Bethabara

Location: 2147 Bethabara Road, Winston-Salem, Forsyth County

Relevant issues: Colonial America, European settlement

Statement of significance: Bethabara was the first colonial townsite established in the Carolina Piedmont. It was intended to be a temporary town from which the central Moravian town of Salem and outlying farming communities would be developed within the Moravian lands of Wachovia. However, Bethabara continued in operation as a Moravian community long after Salem was established. Bethabara was the only "House of Passage" built by the Moravians at any of their colonial settlements in the New World. Archaeological investigations have demonstrated that the Bethabara archaeological remains at the townsite are intact and this work has contributed to a significant understanding of the Moravian culture, in particular the manufacture of Moravian pottery.

Biltmore Estate

Location: Biltmore Plaza, Asheville, Buncombe County

Relevant issues: Science and technology

Statement of significance: In 1888, George W. Vanderbilt (1862-1914) began the purchase of over 125,000 acres of farms, woodlands, and forested mountains. In 1892, Vanderbilt appointed as superintendent of his forest Gifford Pinchot (1865-1946), who proved for the first time that scientific forest management was profitable. In 1898, Vanderbilt established the Biltmore Forest School, the first of its kind. On the estate is Biltmore House, designed by Richard Morris Hunt (1827-1895) who was immensely popular among the wealthy families then building great estates in the manner of late Gothic French chateaux. It is now a house museum still owned by the original family.

Blackwell and Company Tobacco Factory

Location: Durham, Durham County

Relevant issues: Business and industry

Statement of significance: From 1874 to 1957, this factory was the home of Bull Durham Smoking Tobacco, the first truly national tobacco brand. W. T. Blackwell and Company introduced production, packaging, and marketing techniques that made Bull Durham a part of American industrial history and folklore.

Cape Hatteras Light Station

Location: Cape Hatteras, Buxton, North Carolina

Relevant issues: Naval history

Web site: www.nps.gov/caha/

Statement of significance: Cape Hatteras is a prominent projection on North Carolina's famous Outer Banks—the long, low stretches of sandy beaches that protect the state's mainland, but that have been the bane of existence for mariners for centuries. Protection was provided at the "Graveyard of the Atlantic," as the cape has been known for years, in 1803, when the first lighthouse was built. In 1854, it was heightened to 150 feet, and in 1870, the current brick tower was erected. Its height of 208 feet makes it the tallest lighthouse in the nation, and its well-known black-and-white spiral bands, its daymark, make it a prominent landmark during daylight hours. In addition to the lighthouse, supporting structures—including the oil house and both the principal and assistant keeper's dwellings—also survive. All are popular daytime visitor attractions at the Cape Hatteras National Seashore, but at night the lighthouse continues to serve its prime purpose, guiding navigators around the cape.

Daniels House

Location: Raleigh, Wake County

Relevant issues: Naval history

Statement of significance: This was the residence (1920-1948) of Josephus Daniels, secretary of the Navy (1913-1921) under President Woodrow Wilson. Daniels reformed policies by introducing schooling for illiterate sailors, instituting vocational training, opening the Naval Academy to enlisted men, and reforming the naval prison system.

Duke Homestead and Tobacco Factory

Location: Durham, Durham County

Relevant issues: Business and industry

Statement of significance: In 1890, Washington Duke's son, James B. Duke, organized the American Tobacco Company, preeminent in its time. The family's frame house, reconstructed small tobacco factory of log construction, and frame third factory (c. 1852-1874) remain.

Fort Fisher

Location: Wilmington, New Hanover County

Relevant issues: Civil War, military history

Statement of significance: This earthen Confederate stronghold created an impassable barrier for the blockading Union fleet. Its fall, in January, 1865, helped spell the collapse of the Confederacy.

Hardaway Site

Location: Badin, Stanly County

Relevant issues: American Indian history

Statement of significance: During the Paleo-Indian to Early Archaic Periods (12,000-6,000 B.C.E.), prehistoric Indian populations came here to exploit the lithic resources of the area to manufacture projectile points and stone tools; these activities created stratified cultural deposits as much as four feet in depth. This site has played a significant role in the development of archaeological method and theory, by advancing knowledge and understanding of the sequential development of prehistoric cultures in the eastern United States, particularly with regard to the earliest periods of human occupation.

Hayes Plantation

Location: Edenton, Chowan County

Relevant issues: Political history

Statement of significance: This plantation was built from 1790 to 1802 by Samuel Johnston, a major political leader of North Carolina during the War for Independence. He served as governor and then senator, as well as president of the North Carolina Convention which ratified the U.S. Constitution. He lived here until his death in 1816.

Helper House

Location: Mocksville, Davie County

Relevant issues: Political history

Statement of significance: This was the residence (1829-1849) of Hinton Rowan Helper (1829-1909), author of *The Impending Crisis of the South* (1857), a book which condemned the institution of slavery for economic, though not moral, reasons. The publication was used for political

purposes by the Republicans in the 1860 elections. Helper lived here for the first twenty years of his life, and returned in later years. The original log structure is now clapboarded and has modern frame additions.

Monitor

Location: Cape Hatteras, Dare County

Relevant issues: Civil War, military history, naval history

Statement of significance: The USS *Monitor* (1862), famous for its Civil War battle with the CSS *Merrimac* (*Virginia*), was the prototype of a class of ironclad, turreted warships which significantly altered both naval technology and marine architecture in the nineteenth century. Designed by Swedish engineer John Ericsson, the vessel contained all the nascent innovations which helped to revolutionize warfare at sea.

North Carolina

Location: Wilmington, New Hanover County

Relevant issues: Military history, naval history, World War II

Statement of significance: First and namesake of a modern class of American battleships built just prior to World War II, USS *North Carolina* set a standard for new shipbuilding technology that combined high speeds with powerful armament. Its superior performance during the Battle of the Eastern Solomons in August, 1942, established the primary role of the fast battleship as the protector of the aircraft carrier. It has the best war record of any surviving American battleship serving in the Pacific during World War II, earning fifteen battle stars for its service.

North Carolina Mutual Life Insurance Company

Location: Durham, Durham County

Relevant issues: African American history, business and industry

Statement of significance: Built in 1921, this building was the second home office of the North Carolina Mutual Life Insurance Company, which was founded in 1898. This company evolved out of a tradition of mutual benefit societies and fraternal organizations which by the twentieth century had become the most important social institutions in African American life, with the exception of the church. From the beginning, the Mutual symbolized racial progress and is an institutional legacy of the ideas of racial solidarity and self-help.

Old East

Location: Chapel Hill, Orange County
Relevant issues: Education
Statement of significance: This was the first building constructed (1795) on the campus of the first state university in the United States to open its doors, the University of North Carolina, which was chartered in 1789.

Pinehurst Historic District

Location: Pinehurst, Moore County
Relevant issues: Cultural history
Statement of significance: The Pinehurst Historic District, a planned recreational resort community, comprises a network of curvilinear roads embracing the village green; late Victorian, Colonial Revival and Bungalow-style hotels, cottages, stores, and churches; golf courses, tennis courts, bowling greens, and croquet courts; and horse stables and a racetrack. From its founding in 1895, the captains of American commerce, finance, and industry, and their families and friends, sought recreational pleasures at Pinehurst, which become the model for a subsequent generation of like resorts. Its creation and integrity today as a remarkably intact recreational resort reflect the genius of the Tufts family of Boston, the designers, and Donald James Ross, who designed and refined the resort's golf courses.

Reed Gold Mine

Location: Concord, Cabarrus County
Relevant issues: Business and industry
Statement of significance: Nuggets found here in 1799 set off the first gold rush in the United States. North Carolina mines furnished much of the gold minted in Philadelphia before 1829. The mines were largely depleted by 1860.

Salem Tavern

Location: Winston-Salem, Forsyth County
Relevant issues: Cultural history, European settlement, religion
Statement of significance: The first brick building in Salem, erected in 1784 by the Moravian congregation that established the town. The Moravians, a devout Germanic people, set about to construct a planned, congregation town in which the church directed the economic as well as spiritual affairs of the residents. The tavern was considered a necessity for the town's development as a trading center.

Union Tavern

Location: Milton, Caswell County
Relevant issues: African American history, business and industry
Statement of significance: Workshop of Thomas Day, early nineteenth century free African American cabinetmaker who achieved recognition for the superior quality of his craftsmanship.

Wolfe House

Location: Asheville, Buncombe County
Relevant issues: Literary history
Web site: www.ah.dcr.state.nc.us/sections/hs/wolfe/Main.htm
Statement of significance: Thomas Wolfe (1900-1938), a major American novelist, used his boyhood experiences in this rambling frame house in his novels, the first of which was *Look Homeward, Angel* (1929). Wolfe's mother bought the house in 1906, and he lived here until 1916.

North Dakota

The State Capitol Building in Bismarck. (North Dakota Tourism Department)

History of North Dakota

With a 1997 population of approximately 641,000, North Dakota ranked forty-eighth among the fifty states in population. Its total area of 71,000 square miles makes it the seventeenth largest state in land mass. Its population density of 9.3 people per square mile is among America's lowest.

Bordered on the north by the Canadian provinces of Saskatchewan and Manitoba, on the east by Minnesota, on the south by South Dakota, and on the west by Montana, North Dakota runs 360 miles from east to west and 210 miles from north to south.

Early History

North Dakota had human inhabitants more than ten thousand years ago. Millions of years earlier, dinosaurs and mastodons roamed the area. During the Ice Age, the Dakotas were covered by glaciers, which melted around 10,000 B.C.E., leaving a huge lake in what is now the Red River Valley in eastern North Dakota. Topsoil trapped in the glacier was deposited in the lake as the ice melted. When the lake evaporated, that topsoil created fertile fields.

Prehistoric settlers lived beside the Red and Missouri Rivers. The Mandan Indians around 1300 C.E. were the earliest of the Native American settlers, followed some three hundred years later by the Hidatsa and Arikara, all groups that created settlements and engaged in farming, growing mostly squash, sunflowers, corn, and beans. They hunted indigenous animals, particularly bison, for their meat and fur.

The more migratory Sioux and Chippewa entered the area in pursuit of the bison. Other tribes lived in North Dakota for short periods, notably the Assiniboine, Cheyenne, Cree, and Crow. The first Europeans in the area were Pierre Gaultier de Varennes, Sieur de La Vérendrye, his sons, and a nephew, who visited Mandan villages in 1738.

The Fur Trade

Relations between North Dakota's Native Americans and visiting Europeans were amicable initially. The American Indians had an abundance of furs, and the European traders had ready markets for these furs. By the 1780's, a thriving fur trade flourished in the region, largely stimulated by the Hudson's Bay Company, headquartered in Manitoba. In 1801, Alexander Henry established a fur-trading post at Pembina, the first European settlement in the area.

In 1713, the French gave England the northern part of North Dakota, which bordered Canada. In 1812, a group of Canadians started a town at the Pembina trading post, building a school and some permanent buildings. In 1818, however, the United States, through a treaty with Great Britain, was given Britain's section of North Dakota, establishing the territory's northern border. Canadians living there returned to Canada.

Early Growth

Few people other than American Indians came to North Dakota in its early days, although Congress established the Dakota Territory in 1861. By 1870, the territory had 2,405 inhabitants. By 1880, however, the population had ballooned to about 37,000.

Three major factors brought this increase. The Homestead Act of 1862, designed to encourage settlement of the sparsely inhabited territory west of the Mississippi, permitted people to stake claims for the 160 acres allotted to each homesteader, to improve the land and live on it for five years, and then to receive a clear title to that land. Although homesteading became more prevalent in the 1870's, there was no immediate rush of homesteaders to the Dakotas.

Homesteading was difficult. In a land bereft of forests, timber was scarce, forcing early settlers to build sod houses made by cutting square chunks of sod from the prairie for roofs and walls. Sod houses extended below ground; these small houses offered adequate shelter and were warm in winter but were quite unlike the dwellings to which homesteaders were accustomed.

The establishment of towns in the area also spurred population growth. Fargo and Grand Forks were established in 1871, and the following

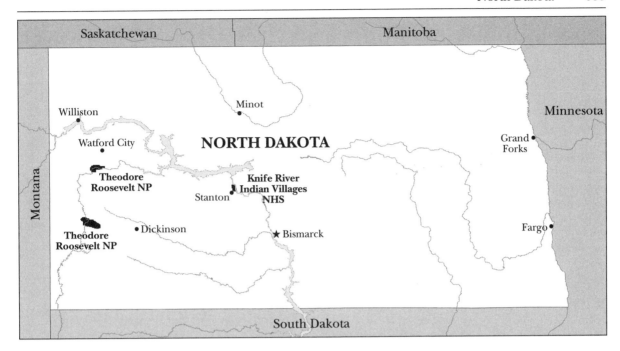

year Bismarck was founded in the middle of the state. By 1874 Bismarck was publishing its own newspaper, the Bismarck *Tribune.* Concurrent with the establishment of towns was the spread of railroads, first from Minnesota to Fargo in 1872 and, in 1873, to Bismarck. Railroad service enabled farmers and cattle ranchers to send their products to eastern markets.

By 1875 farmers in the Red River Valley of eastern North Dakota were producing huge amounts of wheat on their fertile soil. North Dakota is second only to Kansas in the amount of wheat it produces, and it ranks first in its production of sunflower seed and barley. Long, hot summer days and abundant topsoil make the eastern half of the state agriculturally productive.

In 1878 large-scale cattle ranching began in the western Dakota Territory, whose stubby grasses proved perfect for grazing. Growing railroad service made it easy to transport cattle to markets in Chicago, St. Louis, and Kansas City.

American Indian Relations

Although North Dakota's Native Americans generally had amicable relations with the early European traders, relations became strained when the federal government reneged on treaties it had entered into with Native Americans. In 1875, when the government permitted white settlement on American Indian lands in abrogation of the 1868 Fort Laramie Treaty, major Indian uprisings occurred.

The following year, in neighboring Montana, the Sioux killed many American settlers, including Lieutenant Colonel George Custer, in the Battle of the Little Bighorn. In 1877, the federal government confiscated Sioux lands in the Dakotas. Within a year, most of the Native American population was deployed to reservations.

Achieving Statehood

The Dakotas were growing and moving irrevocably toward statehood, although Congress resisted admitting the entire territory as a single state. Between 1880 and 1900, North Dakota's population increased tenfold to about 320,000. In 1883 the territorial capital was moved from Yankton in the southeast to Bismarck.

In 1889 the Enabling Act passed by Congress divided the Dakota Territory into two separate states and guaranteed statehood as soon as each territory submitted acceptable constitutions. North Dakota drew up a constitution that the electorate approved, and late in 1889 President Benjamin Harrison signed papers admitting North Dakota as the thirty-ninth state and South Dakota as the fortieth.

The Early Twentieth Century

Between 1900 and 1915, inequities existed for North Dakota's farmers and cattle ranchers. Their labors were enriching the state's banks, flour mills, and railroads, but life was difficult for those providing the basic labor. In 1915, discouraged by these inequities, thirty thousand farmers joined the Nonpartisan League, which helped to elect Lynn Frazier, a reform candidate, governor.

Frazier helped establish the Bank of North Dakota in Bismarck in 1919. This state-operated bank offered farmers and cattle ranchers low-interest loans. In 1922 the state opened the North Dakota Mill and Elevator, in which wheat farmers could store their crops until they could sell them at favorable prices. Farmers' taxes were lowered, and an increased percentage of state revenues was earmarked for rural schools, which extended educational opportunities to farm children.

During World Wars I and II, North Dakota provided produce to feed members of the armed forces. Although North Dakota opposed entry into both of these wars, the citizens served valiantly in the armed forces.

During the 1920's, agriculture boomed in North Dakota. Sugar beets and red potatoes became profitable crops. The upsurge in agriculture caused the population to more than double between 1900 and 1930.

No state was more severely damaged by the Great Depression than North Dakota. During most of the 1930's, widespread droughts and dust storms that blew away precious topsoil plagued the state. By 1936 half the state's citizens required public assistance. A third of North Dakota's farmers lost their farms. Nearly forty thousand people had left the state by 1940.

In 1937, realizing the need for water conservation, North Dakota established the Water Conservation Commission. All its fifty-three counties embarked upon water-conservation projects. It was not until 1960, however, that the Garrison Dam was completed, creating Lake Sakakawea, which provides irrigation and whose dam generates hydroelectric power.

Recovery

During the 1950's, many farmers moved to cities, entering new walks of life. The state's first television station opened in Minot in 1953. Interstate Highway 94 crossed the state in 1956. Air transportation too became more accessible, and North Dakota, which had suffered from isolation, was now linked more closely to mainstream America.

Oil was discovered in Tioga in 1951, but not until 1978 did an enormous oil boom begin around Williston. In the same general area is substantial mining of lignite, which is burned to fuel electrical generating plants.

North Dakota again experienced an upsurge in population near the end of the twentieth century. People are drawn to it from more populous states by its fine schools, which boast the lowest dropout rate in the nation, its clean air and water, and its low crime rate.

—*R. Baird Shuman*

Knife River Indian Villages

Date: Established in 1974

Relevant issues: American Indian history, western expansion

Significance: An important hub of intertribal and later international trade, the Knife River Indian Villages also played an important role in Plains Indian agricultural and cultural development. Many archaeological sites are preserved at the site. A reconstructed earth lodge re-creates aboriginal life. In addition, the site preserves important native prairie and riverine habitats.

Location: One-half mile north of Stanton

Site Office:

Knife River Indian Villages National Historic Site

P.O. Box 9

Stanton, ND 58571-0009

ph.: (701) 745-3309

Web site: www.nps.gov/knri/

Although prehistoric nomadic peoples exploited the resources of the Knife River region for thousands of years, sedentary life, associated with semipermanent earth lodge villages and well-developed horticulture, belongs to the Plains Village period, beginning about 1000 C.E. Firmly established in the Knife River region by 1200 C.E., this way of life dominated the area until the middle of the nineteenth century. Chiefly associated with the

Mandan and Hidatsa peoples, the Knife River Indian Villages represent the peak of Plains Village period cultural and horticultural development.

Traditional Village Life

The Mandans and Hidatsas shared a village and horticultural tradition particularly adapted to conditions in the upper Missouri River Valley. Summer villages, found along natural terraces above the river, could consist of as many as 120 earth-covered lodges, each holding between ten to thirty members of an extended family. Defensive considerations often played a role in village location, with the river and constructed wooden palisades affording protection. In the winter, the people relocated to smaller lodges along the wooded river bottomland.

In general, matrilineally related women built, maintained, and owned the earth lodges. A number of related lodge families made up a clan whose members provided mutual aid and support. Vehicles for individual expression, age-grade societies for both men and women cut across clan and village lines and often performed important ceremonial and social tasks. Village life observed a sexual division of labor, with women oriented toward agriculture and men toward hunting.

Although the hunting of wild game supplemented village subsistence, horticulture constituted the basis of village life. Cultivated by women, garden plots in the rich river floodplain produced corn, squash, beans, and other crops. Villagers traded their surpluses with nomadic hunting peoples in exchange for hides, dried meat, and other products. Eventually, the peoples of the Knife River became important middlemen in the trade of the upper Missouri, keying into larger complex trading networks far beyond their homes. Food products, locally quarried flint, mineral, and shell products, and later, after European contact, horses, guns, and metal items, made up the increasingly varied trading inventory of the villagers. With the Arikaras to the south, these groups played an important economic role in the region until changes ushered in as a result of European and American contact undermined village life and culture.

European American Contact and Its Aftermath

The villagers' contact with European Americans began in the eighteenth century and accelerated in the nineteenth century as an increasing number of fur traders and travelers penetrated the area, ushering in profound changes. Trading patterns shifted to accommodate the fur trade, dependence on European manufactured items increased, intertribal warfare intensified, and, most significant, epidemic diseases caused drastic population losses. Increasingly vulnerable, Knife River Indian Village peoples shifted and consolidated their village sites a number of times, culminating in the establishment of Like-a-Fishook village, some sixty miles upriver, in 1845. In 1885, this village, also, was abandoned as the federal government relocated the Mandan, Hidatsa, and Arikara peoples to the Fort Berthold Reservation. Notable visitors to the Knife River Indian Villages included the explorers Meriwether Lewis and William Clark and the artists Karl Bodmer and George Catlin, who painted detailed images of village life in the 1830's.

Visiting the Site

Wishing to preserve the archaeological richness and ecological diversity of the area, the federal government set aside 1,759 acres to establish the Knife River Indian Villages National Historic Site in 1974. Administered by the National Park Service, the site is open year-round. Facilities include a museum and visitors' center featuring exhibits and books and a fully furnished, reconstructed earth lodge. In addition, a network of trails takes visitors to a number of archaeological sites, including Big Hidatsa Village, Lower Hidatsa Village, and Sakakawea Village, as well as to protected stretches of prairie and riverine habitats. Near the site, visitors may also visit the remains of Fort Clark, established by the American Fur Company in 1831, and the reconstructed Fort Mandan, winter headquarters of Lewis and Clark.

—*Joseph C. Jastrzembski*

For Further Information:

Ahler, Stanley A., Thomas D. Thiessen, and Michael K. Trimble. *People of the Willows: The Prehistory and Early History of the Hidatsa Indians.* Grand Forks: University of North Dakota Press, 1991. Discusses in detail the archaeological record at Knife River.

Gilman, Carolyn, and Mary Jane Schneider. *The Way to Independence: Memories of a Hidatsa Indian Family, 1840-1920.* St. Paul: Minnesota Historical

Society Press, 1987. An exhibition catalog, this book contains illustrations and photographs of artifacts relevant to Plains Indian village life.

Holder, Preston. *The Hoe and the Horse on the Plains: A Study of Cultural Development Among North American Indians.* Reprint. Lincoln, Nebr.: Bison Books, 1974. Cross-cultural examination of the village way of life. Also discusses village relations with equestrian nomads.

Meyer, Roy W. *The Village Indians of the Upper Missouri: The Mandans, Hidatsas, and Arikaras.* Lincoln: University of Nebraska Press, 1977. Detailed overview of the culture and history of the village Indians closely associated with Knife River.

Peters, Virginia Bergman. *Women of the Earth Lodges: Tribal Life on the Plains.* North Haven, Conn.: Archon Books, 1995. Explores life in the earth lodge villages from the perspective of American Indian women.

Schneider, Mary Jane. *North Dakota's Indian Heritage.* Grand Forks: University of North Dakota Press, 1990. Discusses the history, culture, and contemporary situation of the Mandans, Hidatsas, and Arikaras.

Theodore Roosevelt National Park

Date: Received National Park status on November 10, 1978

Relevant issues: Business and industry, political history, western expansion

Significance: Consisting of two geographically separate units and founded initially as a memorial to the twenty-sixth president of the United States, the park is home to several species of plants and animals that characterize the Great Plains glorified in writings about the Old West. The North Unit represents the natural beauty and remoteness of the Badlands of North Dakota. The South Unit possesses much of the same natural beauty of the North Unit and contains the pioneer town of Medora and most of the historical evidence of early settlement in the area.

Location: In the southwest corner of the state of North Dakota; North Unit is 15 miles (24.1 km) south of Watford City on U.S. Highway 85, and South Unit is 35 miles (56.4 km) west of Dickinson along Interstate 94

Site Office:
Theodore Roosevelt National Park
P.O. Box 7
Medora, ND 58645-0007
North Unit ph.: (701) 842-2333
North Unit fax: (701) 842-3101
South Unit ph.: (701) 623-4466
South Unit fax: (701) 623-4840
Web site: www.nps.gov/thro/

The concept of Theodore Roosevelt National Park, to be created as a memorial to Theodore Roosevelt, originated shortly after his death in 1916. A committee chosen by Sylvane Ferris, a friend and business associate of Roosevelt's, was appointed to investigate the feasibility of such a memorial. It officially became a National Park in 1978.

The Personalities: Roosevelt and de Mores

Roosevelt came to the Dakota Territory as a young man seeking adventure. He arrived in 1883, stepping off a Northern Pacific passenger train at what was the settlement of Little Missouri. Roosevelt, in poor health as a youngster, quickly discovered adventure and found the dry climate of the Badlands beneficial to his health. In fact, most historians credit Roosevelt's time in the Dakota Territory for giving him the stamina and ideologies for his future achievements. In 1884 Roosevelt, smarting from a political defeat and grieving the deaths of both his wife and his mother, returned to the area, seeking solitude. On his previous visit he had entered the cattle business by purchasing an interest in the Maltese Cross Ranch. Unlike many ranchers of the late 1800's, Roosevelt was not the owner and financial entrepreneur running things from afar. He enjoyed the life of a working cowboy. He later sold his interest in the Maltese Cross Ranch and set up a permanent ranch of his own called the Elkhorn Ranch. Roosevelt's original Maltese Cross cabin and the site of the Elkhorn Ranch are parts of the park today.

Roosevelt was not the only rancher or entrepreneur who shaped the character of the area. Indeed, the most flamboyant was the Marquis de Mores. De Mores was a wealthy Frenchman who founded a number of businesses in the area, including a ranch, a stagecoach line, and a grandiose venture into the meat packing business. The de Mores fortune waxed and waned several times. When a more permanent town was created to replace the settlement of Little Missouri, it was named Medora in honor of the Marquis's beautiful red-haired wife. Medora serves as the park's main headquarters. Other remnants of the de Mores presence in the area are the Château de Mores, the luxurious home built by the Marquis, and a tall brick chimney marking the spot where de Mores's last venture, a meat packing plant, was consumed by fire in 1907.

Natural Beauty

Aside from the presence of historical figures, Theodore Roosevelt National Park is full of natural treasures. The park is the core of the North Dakota Badlands and has a unique and complex geologic history. Located in what is geologically called the "slope region" of North Dakota, the park's territory is in an area that was not covered by glaciers during the last Ice Age. Since the layers of sediments were undisturbed by the glaciers, they remained to be removed gradually by the effects of wind and rain erosion. The result is a fantastic landscape of canyons, spires of rock, buttes, and mesas. The wildlife of the area also contributes to the natural wonder. From the tiny prairie dogs living in their "towns" to the herds of massive bison, the wildlife has been preserved or restored to a state representing what once was natural to the area. The bison and the elk, reintroduced in 1956 and 1985, respectively, are examples of successful reintroduction of species nearly hunted to extinction by humans. The park preserves large tracts of grasslands and the unique woodlands of the Little Missouri River bottomlands.

Theodore Roosevelt National Park. (American Stock Photography)

Politics, the Dust Bowl, and a New Park

Though the effort to create this park began shortly after Theodore Roosevelt's death, it took until 1949 for the area to be designated as a state park. The lobbying to make it a part of the National Park system took over sixty years. Ironically, it was the economic and ecological catastrophe of the Dust Bowl that made the park possible. The land for the park and the surrounding Little Missouri National Grasslands were purchased by the state during the 1930's at a mere two dollars per acre. Today the park is renowned for natural beauty, conservation efforts, and tourism. Medora is a town frozen in time, with original buildings including the Château de Mores, intact and open for tours. The park hosts the Medora Musical, a variety show celebrating the state, the land, and the personalities of the area's history. Both units of the park offer excellent camping and wilderness experiences.

—*Paul R. Sando*

For Further Information:

Brands, H. W. *T. R.: The Last Romantic.* New York: Basic Books, 1997.

Collins, Michael L. *That Damned Cowboy: Theodore Roosevelt and the American West, 1883-1898.* New York: Peter Lang, 1989.

Goplen, Arnold O. *The Career of the Marquis De Mores in the Bad Lands of North Dakota.* 2d ed. Bismarck: State Historical Society of North Dakota, 1979.

Miller, Nathan. *Theodore Roosevelt: A Life.* New York: William Morrow, 1992.

Tweton, D. Jerome. *The Marquis de Mores: Dakota Capitalist, French Nationalist.* Fargo: North Dakota Institute for Regional Studies, 1972.

Other Historic Sites

Fort Union Trading Post

Location: Williston, Williams County

Relevant issues: Business and industry, western expansion

Statement of significance: This was the principal fur-trading depot in the upper Missouri River region from 1829 to 1867.

Huff Archaeological Site

Location: Huff, Morton County

Relevant issues: American Indian history

Statement of significance: By 1500 C.E., the Middle Missouri agricultural villages were the principal focus for social organization of the Mandan people, who had developed extensive trading networks over the previous two hundred years. The Huff Village is one of the best-known and best-preserved sites of this period. Its bastioned fortification system, dense and regular arrangement of houses, and wide variety in material culture attest to the extraordinary regional impacts of their way of life. The remains of a large central house facing an open plaza preserve evidence about the ritual space, which corresponds to the complex spiritual and ideological world that the Mandan have maintained since historic times.

Menoken Indian Village Site

Location: Menoken, Burleigh County

Relevant issues: American Indian history

Statement of significance: This site shows certain structural and artifactual similarities to historic and prehistoric earthlodge villages along the upper Missouri River. Pottery and projectile point styles are indicative of the prehistoric period, and the cultural/temporal affinity is suggested to be Initial Middle Missouri Tradition from about 950 to 1300 C.E.

Ohio

Cincinnati. (Ohio Division of Travel & Tourism)

History of Ohio

Located between previously settled eastern states and newer territories in the Midwest, Ohio was one of the first states to be established after the creation of the United States. Ease of transportation, supplied by Lake Erie along the northern border and the Ohio River along the southern border, quickly made Ohio one of the most populous states in the Union. Ohio's rich soils and abundant natural resources have made it one of the most important areas of agricultural and industrial activity in the nation.

Early History

About eleven thousand years ago, the earliest humans to reside in the area used stone tools to hunt bison as well as extinct species such as mammoths and mastodons. About 2,500 years ago, the people of the Adena culture, located in southern Ohio, built mounds, lived in villages, made pottery, and subsisted by hunting, fishing, and gathering wild plant foods. About five hundred years later, the people of the Hopewell culture, living in the same area, established agriculture with the growing of corn. They also produced the most advanced metal artifacts, mostly made from copper, found in North America until the Europeans arrived. About fifteen hundred years ago, the Hopewell culture began to decline. By the time Europeans first arrived in the region in the late seventeenth century, Ohio was mostly uninhabited.

Before Europeans were established in the area, however, Native Americans returned to Ohio in the early eighteenth century. The Wyandot, originally residing in Ontario, were driven south into northern Ohio by the devastation caused by newly introduced European diseases and by their enemies, the Iroquois League, a powerful confederation of eastern Native Americans. The Delaware, originally residing along the Atlantic coast, were driven west into northern Ohio by the Iroquois League and European settlers. The Miami, originally residing in eastern Wisconsin, expanded south and east into many areas, including southern Ohio. The Shawnee, who had originally resided along the Ohio River, were driven out by the Iroquois League but returned to southern Ohio in 1725.

Exploration and Settlement

The first European known to have visited the area was the French explorer René-Robert Cavelier, Sieur de La Salle, who journeyed southwest from Canada along the Saint Lawrence River, past Lake Ontario and Lake Erie, and into Ohio in 1670. During the first half of the eighteenth century, French traders from Canada and British traders from eastern colonies provided manufactured goods to the Native Americans in the area in exchange for deer and beaver skins. The lucrative fur trade led both sides to attempt to win control of the area. In 1749 the French sent an expedition led by Celeron de Bienville from Canada into Ohio, in order to make trade agreements with the inhabitants. The next year, the British sent a similar expedition, led by Christopher Gist, from Virginia to Ohio.

The conflict between France and England for control of North America led to the French and Indian War, which ended with the British in control of the area. During the American Revolution, American forces led by George Rogers Clark seized British outposts in Ohio. Clark also destroyed villages of the Shawnee, who were allied with the British. The war ended with the United States in control of the region. It became part of the newly created Northwest Territory in 1787.

The first permanent settlement in Ohio was founded in 1788 at Marietta by veterans of the Revolutionary War. The next year, settlers from New Jersey led by John Cleves Symes established a settlement at the future site of Cincinnati. These and other early settlements, located along the Ohio River, caused conflicts with the Native Americans inhabiting the region. On August 20, 1794, American forces led by Anthony Wayne defeated an alliance of Native Americans under Shawnee leader Bluejacket at the Battle of Fallen Timbers. The next year Wayne negotiated a treaty that resulted in

England, Ireland, and Germany arrived in large numbers after 1830. Advances in transportation contributed to this growth. Steamboats appeared on the Ohio River as early as 1811. The opening of the Erie Canal in 1825, linking the Hudson River with Lake Erie, improved transportation to Ohio and the territories beyond it. From 1825 to 1841, a series of canals linked the Ohio River and Lake Erie. The first railroad in the state was established in 1832. Between 1825 and 1838, the federal government extended the National Road across Ohio, linking the state to Pennsylvania and Maryland. By 1850, Ohio was the third most populous state in the Union.

At this time, agriculture was the most important part of the state's economy. In 1850 Ohio had a larger agricultural output than any other state. Coal was discovered in Ohio in 1808 and was later of great importance to the iron and steel industry. Other important mineral resources developed at this time included limestone, sandstone, clay, shale, and rock salt.

The Civil War

During the Civil War, Ohio was divided in loyalty. The strongest support for the Union was found in northern Ohio. Southern Ohio, bordering on Kentucky and Virginia, was more sympathetic to the Confederacy. Ohio supplied 320,000 volunteers for the Union. Three of the Union's most important generals, Ulysses S. Grant, William Tecumseh Sherman, and Philip H. Sheridan, were from Ohio.

Ohio was an important center of the Peace Democrats, known to their opponents as Copperheads. The Peace Democrats advocated an end to the war through negotiation with the Confederacy. Clement L. Vallandigham, a leader of the Peace Democrats, was nominated for governor of Ohio in

Native Americans ceding much of their land in Ohio to the United States.

Statehood

Settlements continued to be located almost entirely in the southern part of Ohio until 1796, when settlers from Connecticut arrived in northeast Ohio. By 1802 Ohio had the sixty thousand white adult male residents required for statehood, and it became the seventeenth state the next year. The capital was located at Chillicothe until 1810, when it was briefly moved to Zanesville. After returning to Chillicothe in 1812, the capital was moved to the newly founded city of Columbus in 1816.

During the early years of statehood, Shawnee leader Tecumseh organized an alliance of Native Americans that attempted to win back control of the region from the United States. During the War of 1812 Tecumseh was allied with the British against the Americans. Tecumseh and British general Henry A. Proctor led an invasion of Ohio in 1812 but were driven back into Canada the next year.

After the war, the population of Ohio grew rapidly. In addition to settlers from eastern and

1863 but was defeated by Union supporter John Brough. The same year, Confederate soldiers led by John Hunt Morgan raided southern Ohio, reaching farther north than any other Confederate forces.

Industry and Immigration

The demand for manufactured goods during the war led to the growth of industry in Ohio, particularly in the northern part of the state. Iron ore from states to the northwest was transported via the Great Lakes to the steelmaking cities of Toldeo, Cleveland, and Youngstown. During the 1870's, Akron became a center of the rubber industry. Oil and natural gas were discovered in 1860. The Standard Oil Company, founded in Cleveland in 1870, soon controlled almost all oil production in the United States.

Immigrants from Italy, Poland, Hungary, and Russia arrived in large numbers after 1880. Cleveland was particularly diverse in the ethnic origins of its new residents, with immigrants arriving from Austria, the Netherlands, Portugal, Greece, China, Japan, Turkey, and Mexico. A large number of African Americans moved into the state at this time also, increasing the black population from about twenty-five thousand in 1850 to more than sixty-three thousand in 1870.

The Twentieth Century

Ohio was dominant in national politics during the turn of the century. Of the twelve U.S. presidents who held office from 1869 to 1923, seven were born in Ohio. Ohio was also the birthplace of Victoria Woodhull, who became the first woman to run for president, in 1872.

The state's economy expanded during World War I. The increase in automobile manufacturing after the war strengthened Ohio's oil, rubber, and glass industries. The Great Depression of the 1930's led to widespread unemployment, and the economy did not recover until World War II. Although economic conditions were generally favorable until the late 1970's, Ohio faced serious problems, including pollution in Lake Erie, race riots in Cleveland, poverty in the cities, and a decline in the quality of education.

A recession in the late 1970's and 1980's led to Ohio having 14 percent unemployment in 1982. During the 1980's and 1990's, Ohio shifted much of its economy away from manufacturing to the service and technology industries. The state also took steps to encourage new businesses, provide vocational training, and protect the environment.

—*Rose Secrest*

Kent State University

Date: University was founded in 1910; antiwar protest on May 4, 1970, led to the deaths of four students and the wounding of nine others

Relevant issues: Disasters and tragedies, education, political history, Vietnam War

Significance: The killing and wounding of students at Kent State University called the world's attention to vehement objections to the Vietnam War. It also revealed the split in opinion over the war and over war protest, as Americans took opposing sides in the aftermath of the shootings. Some saw the killings as justified; others perceived the dead and wounded as martyrs to the causes of freedom of expression and antiwar protest.

Location: In the city of Kent, which is twenty-five miles southeast of Cleveland, ten miles northeast of Akron, and thirty-five miles west of Youngstown

Site Office:
Kent State University
Office of University Relations and Marketing
P.O. Box 5190
Kent, OH 44242
ph.: (330) 672-2727
fax: (330) 672-2047
Web sites: www.kent.edu; www.may4.net

During the Vietnam War, many people questioned whether U.S. involvement was appropriate. College students were often involved in the antiwar effort. Kent State did not have a reputation as a hotbed of unrest, yet student demonstrations there in May of 1970 led to a confrontation with National Guardsmen armed with M-1 rifles. Some guardsmen shot into a crowd of demonstrators and onlookers. The incident brought worldwide attention to antiwar protest. Reactions to the incident highlighted cavernous divisions in the nation over not only the war, but also the appropriateness of protest.

Setting the Stage

Kent State University began in 1910 as Kent Normal School, a teacher-training facility. Accredited as a university in 1937, Kent State grew rapidly in the years following World War II. By 1970 its rolling campus served almost twenty thousand students. Some Kent students opposed the Vietnam War and demonstrated against it, but the campus did not have a reputation for protest like many schools elsewhere in the country.

When President Richard Nixon announced the invasion of Cambodia on April 30, 1970, Kent State protesters announced plans for antiwar rallies on the University Commons (a central, open field) for May 1 and May 4. The evening of Friday, May 1, there was extensive vandalism and looting in Kent's downtown bar area. Kent's mayor declared a state of emergency. On Saturday night, May 2, vandals burned down the old Army Reserve Officer Training Corps (ROTC) barracks building on campus. Later that night units of the Ohio National Guard were summoned by Ohio governor James Rhodes. Many of the guardsmen who came to Kent State were sleep-deprived, having come directly from maintaining order at a wildcat trucker strike. They came to campus in trucks, tanks, and helicopters, and they carried loaded weapons.

The reactions of governmental leaders to the student protest were very strong. Governor Rhodes promised to use any means necessary against the protesters, whom he compared to Adolf Hitler's Brownshirts. President Nixon had previously referred to campus protesters in general as "bums on campus."

Throughout the day on Sunday, May 3, there was a carnival atmosphere on the campus. Relaxed sightseers, some bringing their young children, came to look at the military vehicles. One coed placed a flower in the muzzle of a guardsman's rifle. Early Sunday evening a crowd gathered by the Victory Bell on the Commons. (The bell was ordinarily used to announce sports victories.) That group was dispersed, but later demonstrators reassembled in an intersection beside the campus and tear gas was used to disperse them. Many students were very angry and intent on holding the scheduled noon rally on May 4, despite the fact that any public meeting, violent or nonviolent, had been banned by the authorities.

May 4, 1970

The noon rally on the Commons was attended by two to three thousand students. In all the ensuing events that day, onlookers outnumbered demonstrators and were in very close proximity to active protesters. There was no violence until guard officers told the crowd to disperse. Then some demonstrators reacted with verbal abuse. Both the guardsmen and the students felt that they had a legitimate right to be on the Commons. The guardsmen perceived that they were there to prevent the prohibited gathering. The students felt that they had a right to protest the National Guard's occupation of their campus. Guardsmen fired tear gas canisters, and

A student at Kent State University lays flowers on a memorial to Jeffrey Miller, one of four students killed there on May 4, 1970. (AP/Wide World Photos)

some protesters threw them back. Some protesters also threw rocks at the guardsmen. Marching with fixed bayonets, the guardsmen pushed the active group of protesters up Taylor Hall hill and down onto a practice football field on the other side of the hill. The guardsmen then marched back up to the top of the hill. Standing in a line near the Pagoda (an eight-foot-tall concrete structure), twenty-eight guardsmen fired their weapons in a thirteen-second blast. The firings consisted of fifty-one steel-jacketed M-1 bullets, five pistol shots, and a shotgun blast. Some guardsmen shot skyward, but others shot directly into the crowd of students and onlookers. It was never established conclusively that there had been an order to fire.

Jeffrey Miller was 265 feet from the National Guard. He was shot full in the face and his head was blown apart. Allison Krause was standing 343 feet from the National Guard. She died later of a hit to her torso. William Schroeder was 382 feet from the guardsmen and died later of a bullet that passed through his back, lung, and shoulder. Sandra Scheuer was 390 feet from the National Guard and on her way to class when she received a fatal hit to the neck. The nine wounded victims were hit at distances of 71 to 745 feet from the guardsmen. One of them was permanently paralyzed from a spinal cord injury.

The onlooking students experienced disbelief, followed by rage. Two to three hundred gathered on a slope below Taylor Hall. Many wanted another confrontation with the National Guard. However, further tragedy was averted when faculty marshals, headed by Professor Glenn Frank, persuaded the students to leave peacefully. Later that day the university was closed by order of university president Robert I. White and the Portage County prosecutor.

The Aftermath

Kent State University did not reopen until the 1970 summer term. Enrollment was low due to the May 4 incident and remained at a lowered level for several terms. The university established many traditions and created many entities commemorating May 4. A granite memorial was built in 1990. The university created scholarships in the names of the four students who were killed. The university also set aside a permanent collection of materials in its library (the May 4 Archives) and established a campus center for teaching conflict resolution and peaceful change (the Center for Applied Conflict Management). Each year the anniversary of the shootings is marked with many programs including candlelight vigils and prominent speakers, performers, and artists. In July, 1977, some students objected to the university's plan to build a gymnasium annex over a section of the May 4 confrontation area (the practice football field). Protesters erected a tent city to block the construction. Eventually they were arrested, and the gymnasium annex was built.

In the aftermath of the shootings there was much confusion about exactly what had happened, with rumors rampant. For example, there were unproven allegations that guardsmen had conspired to shoot, that the FBI had planted a provocateur, and that snipers had fired at guardsmen. The general public took polarized positions on the shootings. Some felt that the killings were justified; others sympathized deeply with the killed and wounded students. A national Gallup poll taken a week after the incident found that 58 percent felt the students were primarily responsible, 11 percent blamed the National Guard, and 31 percent had no opinion.

Investigations were conducted by the university itself and by many bodies, including the U.S. President's Commission on Campus Unrest (Scranton Commission), the Federal Bureau of Investigation (FBI), and the Ohio State Highway Patrol. While there was no total consensus, most investigators concluded that the authorities had overreacted to the early student protests, that the National Guard acted with ineptness and a lack of professionalism, that no known radical group had staged the protest or manipulated the demonstrators, and that the shootings were unnecessary.

The nine wounded students and the parents of the four who died brought civil damage suits for wrongful death and injury against guardsmen, guard officers, and others. The cases were blocked until the U.S. Supreme Court in *Scheuer v. Rhodes* ruled in 1975 against the state's claim of sovereign immunity. The first trial ended in a mistrial. A retrial concluded with an out-of-court settlement of $675,000 and "statement of regret" by the defendants.

In October of 1975 a state grand jury ordered by Governor Rhodes exonerated the guardsmen and indicted twenty-five persons (the "Kent 25"), the majority of whom were students, on charges such as second degree riot. The charges against all but five of these defendants were eventually dismissed.

A federal grand jury indicted eight guardsmen in March of 1974. The prosecution began in October of that year on charges that guardsmen had deprived students of their constitutional right to due process. Eventually these charges were dropped for lack of evidence by the federal judge hearing the cases.

Kent State University continues to urge a healing of misunderstandings concerning May 4, as evidenced by the motto inscribed on the memorial: "Inquire, learn, and reflect."

Things to See
Most of the sites are close to Taylor Hall, which is near the center of the Kent State campus. These include the May 4 Memorial, designed by Chicago architect Bruno Ast. The memorial consists of black granite disks and four standing pylons on a seventy-foot-wide granite plaza. Informative pamphlets are available at the memorial. The memorial is surrounded by over fifty thousand daffodil plants representing the American Vietnam War dead. Downhill from the memorial on the Commons is the Victory Bell, which was used to summon students to meetings that fateful week and many times before and since. On the opposite side of Taylor Hall is the Pagoda, near which the guardsmen stood as they fired, and a metal sculpture with a three-eighths-inch-thick steel plate in which a bullet hole is visible. Markers in the Prentice Hall parking lot show where the four students were killed. At the Kent Library is a special collection of May 4 materials. Visitors may also wish to see the historic Federal-style buildings on the front campus, the Kent State Museum (which displays fashions in apparel), and the university Ice Arena.

—*Nancy Conn Terjesen*

For Further Information:
Casale, Ottavio M., and Louis Paskoff, eds. *The Kent Affair: Documents and Interpretations.* Boston: Houghton Mifflin, 1971. Two Kent State English professors compiled documents including political cartoons and news stories which show the polarization of opinion.

Hensley, Thomas R., and Jerry M. Lewis. *Kent State and May Fourth: A Social Science Perspective.* 2d ed. Dubuque, Iowa: Kendall/Hunt, 2000. Kent professors collected published and unpublished essays, detailed the gym annex controversy, and included an extensive bibliography.

Lewis, Jerry M. "A Study of the Kent State Incident Using Smelser's Theory of Collective Behavior." *Sociological Inquiry* 15 (August, 1974): 542-547. A Kent professor and eyewitness to the shootings analyzed the events leading up to the shootings.

Michener, James. *Kent State: What Happened and Why.* New York: Random House, 1971. The noted author lived in Kent for several months in 1970 to interview participants for this account. Contains photos and biographies of those killed and wounded.

Stone, Isidor F. *The Killings at Kent State University: How Murder Went Unpunished.* New York: A New York Review Book, 1971. Stone's book contains reprints of his columns, as well as a summary of the FBI report.

U.S. President's Commission on Campus Unrest Report. Washington, D.C.: Government Printing Office, 1970. This is the "Scranton Report" which relates FBI information and concludes that the killings were unwarranted.

Other Historic Sites

Cincinnati Observatory
Location: Cincinnati, Hamilton County
Relevant issues: Science and technology
Statement of significance: In the late nineteenth century, the Cincinnati Observatory was known worldwide for its endeavors in the fields of proper motions, gravitational studies, and sidereal astronomy, including double stars, nebulas, and clusters. It is nationally significant for the publication of *Stellar Proper Motions*, which provided data important in determining the structure and rotation of the Milky Way, and provided data utilized in modern cosmological theories, such as the big bang. It is also signifi-

cant for its association with internationally renowned astronomer Paul Herget, who was director of the observatory from 1946 to 1978.

Cincinnati Zoo Historic Structures

Location: Cincinnati, Hamilton County
Relevant issues: Cultural history
Statement of significance: The second oldest zoo in the United States, it opened to the public in September, 1875. Significant for the antiquity and richness of its collections and for its efforts in the propagation and nurture of rare and endangered species, it was well known as the home of "Martha," the last passenger pigeon. The Aviary, where Martha lived, and the original Monkey House and Herbivore (Elephant) House are the zoo's earliest surviving structures.

Cooke Home

Location: Gibraltar Island, Ottawa County
Relevant issues: Business and industry, Civil War
Statement of significance: From 1865 until his death, this Hight Victorian structure was the summer home of Jay Cooke (1821-1905), the "Napoleon of Finance." During the Civil War, bond sales by financier Cooke were an important source of financial support for the Union. The failure of his banking firm caused the Panic of 1873.

Dunbar House

Location: Dayton, Montgomery County
Relevant issues: African American history, literary history
Statement of significance: From 1903 until his death, this modest two-story red brick structure was the residence of Paul Laurence Dunbar (1872-1906), the distinguished African American poet. His poetic use of black dialect to convey both the joys and the sorrows of an oppressed people brought him national acclaim.

Edison Birthplace

Location: Milan, Erie County
Relevant issues: Science and technology
Statement of significance: This small brick cottage was the birthplace of Thomas Alva Edison (1847-1931), one of America's most illustrious inventors. Although he left here in 1854, Edison cherished the memory of this house; in 1906, he acquired it from his sister.

Fallen Timbers Battlefield

Location: Maumee, Lucas County
Relevant issues: American Indian history, military history, western expansion
Statement of significance: On August 20, 1794, General "Mad Anthony" Wayne's victory here over the Indians at Fallen Timbers asserted American sovereignty in the Old Northwest and made possible the Treaty of Green Ville. The battle and treaty insured a period of peaceful settlement in the Ohio Country long enough for the new nation to consolidate its hold on the Northwest Territory.

Fort Ancient

Location: Lebanon, Warren County
Relevant issues: American Indian history
Statement of significance: This hilltop area with large surrounding earthworks was built and inhabited by people of the Hopewell culture (c. 300 B.C.E.-250 C.E.). Hundreds of years after the site had been abandoned by the Hopewell, the Fort Ancient people (1200-1600 C.E.) settled in the area, establishing villages on the south fort of the earthworks and the Anderson Village site.

Fort Meigs

Location: Perrysburg, Wood County
Relevant issues: Military history
Statement of significance: Built by General William Henry Harrison during the War of 1812, the fort withstood a British siege the next year. It was abandoned in 1815, after the signing of the Treaty of Ghent.

Garfield Home

Location: Mentor, Lake County
Relevant issues: Political history
Statement of significance: From 1876 until his death at the hands of an assassin, Lawnfield was the residence of James A. Garfield (1831-1881), twentieth president of the United States. In 1880, Garfield was selected by the Republican Party as its candidate for the presidency after thirty-six ballots; Garfield ran his campaign from this house, composing many of his campaign speeches in the second-floor study.

Giddings Law Office

Location: Jefferson, Ashtabula County

Relevant issues: Legal history, social reform

Statement of significance: For most of his professional life, this small, two-room frame structure was the law office of Joshua Reed Giddings (1785-1864), abolitionist and congressman (1838-1859). While in Congress, he made his unwavering objective the elimination of slavery by every conceivable political measure—nonextension of slavery to the territories, abolition of the slave trade, even the use of the president's war powers to emancipate the slaves.

Grant Boyhood Home

Location: Georgetown, Brown County

Relevant issues: Military history, political history

Statement of significance: From 1823, when he was brought here as an infant, until he left to enter the U.S. Military Academy in 1839, this was the home of Ulysses S. Grant (1822-1885), one of the great captains in Western military history and the eighteenth president of the United States.

Harding Home

Location: Marion, Marion County

Relevant issues: Political history

Statement of significance: From 1890 until his death, this two-story clapboard house was the residence of Warren G. Harding (1865-1923), twenty-ninth president of the United States (1921-1923). Harding spent most of his adult life in this house, which he and his wife planned before their marriage. He conducted his 1920 "front porch" presidential campaign from here.

Hawthorn Hill

Location: Oakwood, Montgomery County

Relevant issues: Aviation history

Statement of significance: Significant for its association with Wilbur and Orville Wright, inventors of the airplane, Hawthorn Hill (1914) represents the direct expression of the wealth and fame reaped by the Wright Brothers as a result of their accomplishment. Many of the mechanical features of the house were designed by Orville Wright and reflect his creative genius. For thirty-four years, this house was the gathering place for the greats and near greats in the history of American aviation.

Hotel Breakers

Location: Sandusky, Erie County

Relevant issues: Cultural history, sports

Statement of significance: Constructed in 1905, this is one of the few remaining major resort hotels from the turn-of-the-century age of the resort hotel in America. A large, late Victorian chateau-like structure, it is a rare instance of a resort hotel that survives in conjunction with an amusement park. The grounds were the site of events of historic interest such as the perfecting of the forward pass by Knute Rockne and Gus Dorais.

Huffman Prairie Flying Field

Location: Fairborn, Greene County

Relevant issues: Aviation history

Statement of significance: The Huffman Prairie Flying Field is the site used by the Wright Brothers from 1904 to 1905 to develop and test the world's first practical airplane, the Wright Flyer III. It was on this field that the Wright Brothers continued their quest to conquer the air after their return from Kitty Hawk, North Carolina, in 1903. During these years, the Wright Brothers perfected the technique of flying and developed a powered airplane completely controllable by the pilot: able to bank, turn, circle, and make figure eights; withstand repeated takeoffs and landings; and remain airborne trouble-free for more than half an hour.

John Rankin House

Location: 6152 Rankin Road, Ripley, Brown County

Relevant issues: African American history, social reform

Statement of significance: This was the home of Presbyterian minister John Rankin, who is reputed to have been one of Ohio's first and most active "conductors" on the Underground Railroad. In addition, he wrote *Letters on American Slavery*, first published in book form in 1826 and among the first clearly articulated antislavery views printed west of the Appalachians. Rankin, along with his wife and children, assisted hundreds of escaped slaves in their trek to freedom. Located on the Ohio River, Rankin's home (and Ripley, Ohio, in general) were considered one of the first stations on the Underground Railroad. It was here that Harriet Beecher Stowe heard the escaping slave's story which became the basis for part of her famous work *Uncle Tom's Cabin* (1852).

Johnson's Island Civil War Prison

Location: Danbury, Ottawa County

Relevant issues: Civil War, military history

Statement of significance: Johnson's Island, the site of an important Union camp for Confederate prisoners of war during much of the Civil War, is located 2.5 miles northwest of Sandusky, Ohio, in Sandusky Bay. Johnson's Island was chosen because of its size (large enough to house the facility and yet small enough to be easily manageable), wood resources (mostly for fuel), and proximity to Sandusky, which would make provisioning possible. Because of its mission as the major depot for the confinement of Confederate general, field, and company grade officers, Johnson's Island assumes particular significance as a critical element in the war of attrition that brought victory to the Union. Although plots and conspiracies by Confederate agents operating from Canadian sanctuaries and by Northern Copperheads to foment mass escapes came to naught, they compelled the Lincoln administration to divert needed resources of men and materiel from more important theaters of the war.

Kirtland Temple

Location: Kirtland, Lake County

Relevant issues: Religion

Statement of significance: Built in 1834 by members of the Church of Jesus Christ of Latter-day Saints during their brief sojourn in Ohio, this structure combines Federal and Gothic Revival design elements. The result is individualistic and typical of those Mormon structures that were the beginning of a series of exotic structures in wood and stone.

Langston House

Location: Oberlin, Lorain County

Relevant issues: African American history, political history

Statement of significance: From 1856 to 1867, this simple clapboard structure was the home of John Mercer Langston (1829-1897), the man who became the first African American elected to public office when he was elected township clerk in 1855. He later served in the Freedman's Bureau and was the first dean of the Howard University Law School, U.S. representative from Virginia (1890-1891), and minister to Haiti.

Lundy House

Location: Mt. Pleasant, Jefferson County

Relevant issues: African American history, social reform

Statement of significance: In 1820, this was the residence of the abolitionist Benjamin Lundy (1789-1839). Here, in this brick rowhouse, Lundy established his influential antislavery newspaper *Genius of Universal Emancipation*, one of the germinal chronicles of the antislavery movement in America.

McGuffey Boyhood Home Site

Location: Coitsville Township, Mahoning County

Relevant issues: Education

Statement of significance: From 1802 to about 1817, this was the home of William H. McGuffey (1800-1873), college professor and author, whose elementary school texts—the *Eclectic Readers*—were used for more than seventy years in schools in every part of the United States.

McKinley Tomb

Location: Canton, Stark County

Relevant issues: Political history

Statement of significance: This large, circular, domed mausoleum is the resting place of William McKinley (1843-1901), the twenty-fifth president of the United States (1897-1901). His election in 1896 began an era of Republican dominance and also of American expansion in the Caribbean and Far East.

Majestic

Location: Cincinnati, Hamilton County

Relevant issues: Cultural history, naval history

Statement of significance: Built in 1923, *Majestic* is one of two showboats to survive, the other being *Goldenrod*. Perhaps the most extraordinary American adaptation of barges, more than fifty showboats carried circuses and dramatic productions to large and small towns on the rivers of America between 1831 and the 1920's.

Oberlin College

Location: Oberlin, Lorain County

Relevant issues: African American history, education, women's history

Statement of significance: Founded in 1833, Oberlin Collegiate Institute developed into a socially and politically influential college during the years immediately preceding the Civil War. Oberlin made the education of African Americans and women a matter of institutional policy. The admittance of four women in 1837 marked the beginning of coeducation on the collegiate level in the United States; free blacks were admitted on the same basis as whites.

Pendleton House

Location: Cincinnati, Hamilton County

Relevant issues: Political history

Statement of significance: From 1879 until his death, this was the residence of George Hunt Pendleton (1825-1889), lawyer and politician. As a U.S. senator (1879-1885), Pendleton spearheaded civil service reform. He and his committee met here in 1882 to draft the Pendleton Act, creating the Civil Service Merit System. The Civil Service Commission met here for the first two years of its existence.

Plum Street Temple

Location: Cincinnati, Hamilton County

Relevant issues: Religion

Statement of significance: Built in 1865-1666 for B'nai Yeshurun, this is one of the best-preserved Moorish Revival buildings of the nineteenth century. The rabbi at the time of construction was Dr. Isaac Mayer Wise (1819-1900), an important figure in American Judaism. His leadership made Cincinnati a center for Reform Judaism in America.

Rickenbacker House

Location: Columbus, Franklin County

Relevant issues: Aviation history

Statement of significance: From 1895 to 1922, this simple dwelling was the residence of Edward V. Rickenbacker (1890-1973). A leading race car driver prior to World War I, Rickenbacker became a hero as an aviator. His feat of shooting down twenty-six German aircraft in less than six months established him as "American Ace of Aces" and made him the idol of a whole generation of American youth. After the war, Rickenbacker devoted his energies to the developing commercial airline industry.

Serpent Mound

Location: Locust Grove, Adams County

Relevant issues: American Indian history

Statement of significance: This giant, earthen snake effigy, the largest and finest in America, probably dates from the Adena period (1000 B.C.E.-200 C.E.). The site is one of the first in the United States to be set aside because of its archaeological value.

Sherman Birthplace

Location: Lancaster, Fairfield County

Relevant issues: Military history, political history

Statement of significance: This is the birthplace of Senior Republican Senator John Sherman (1823-1900), who wrote the Sherman Anti-Trust Act (1890), the first attempt by the federal government to regulate industry. He also served in the U.S. House and as secretary of state. His older brother, William Tecumseh Sherman, Union Army general, was also born here.

Spiegel Grove

Location: Fremont, Sandusky County

Relevant issues: Political history

Statement of significance: Completed in 1863 and later enlarged, Spiegel Grove was built as a summer home for Rutherford B. Hayes (1822-1893), nineteenth president of the United States (1877-1881). Both Hayes and his wife are buried here. A library and museum in a separate structure preserve family memorabilia.

Sunwatch Site

Location: Dayton, Montgomery County

Relevant issues: American Indian history

Statement of significance: Sunwatch, formerly known as the Incinerator Site, is located on the west bank of the Great Miami River within the city limits of Dayton. Ceramics, radiocarbon dates, and other evidence indicate that this open village site is a discrete Fort Ancient period, Anderson phase village probably occupied for not more than twenty-five years during the late twelfth and early thirteenth centuries. The site is one of the best preserved and most completely excavated and analyzed archaeological village sites associated with the Post Archaic Eastern Farmers.

Taft Home

Location: 2038 Auburn Avenue, Cincinnati, Hamilton County

Relevant issues: Legal history, political history

Statement of significance: This is the birthplace and boyhood home of William Howard Taft (1857-1930), twenty-seventh president of the United States (1909-1913), a distinguished jurist who also served as chief justice of the United States. This building is now within the National Park System as the William Howard Taft National Historic Site.

Upton House

Location: Warren, Trumbull County

Relevant issues: Political history, social reform, women's history

Statement of significance: From 1883 to 1931, this was the home of Harriet Taylor Upton, an important figure in both the woman suffrage movement and the Republican Party; in addition, the house was also the national headquarters of the National American Woman Suffrage Association (NAWSA) from 1903 to 1909, a pivotal period in the organization's history. Upton, whose father was a prominent congressman, joined the NAWSA in 1890 and put her political resources at the disposal of the organization, where her congressional connections and her astute organizational skills ensured her rapid rise through the ranks.

Wright Cycle Company, Wright and Wright Printing

Location: Dayton, Montgomery County

Relevant issues: Aviation history, business and industry

Statement of significance: This building is the site where, from 1895 to 1897, Wilbur and Orville Wright began to manufacture their own brand of bicycles. This activity contributed the know-how and financial resources critical to their experiments in aviation. Their years of working with sprockets, spokes, chain drives, tires, metals, lathes, drills, and engines were of great value to the pair in designing and building their first gliders and flying machines. The Wright Brothers also operated the Wright Printing Shop on the second floor of the building during these years.

Young House

Location: Wilberforce, Greene County

Relevant issues: African American history, military history

Statement of significance: This two-story brick structure was the residence of Colonel Charles Young (1864-1922), the third African American to graduate from West Point and the highest-ranking black officer of World War I. Young also served as the first black military attache in American history. A distinguished soldier and teacher of military courses, he was nationally known by the time of his death.

Oklahoma

The State Capitol Building in Oklahoma City. (Fred W. Marvel/Oklahoma Tourism)

History of Oklahoma

Oklahoma is almost square except for its northwestern extreme, called the Panhandle, a strip about forty miles wide and one hundred twenty miles long that reaches to Colorado, which, with Kansas, forms the state's northern border. To the west lie New Mexico and Texas, which also forms its southern boundary. On the east are Missouri and Arkansas. Although some geographers consider Oklahoma a southwestern state, along with New Mexico, Arizona, and Nevada, others call it a south central state.

Early History

The first humans probably settled in the Oklahoma region more than twenty thousand years ago, living in caves, where their drawings have been discovered on cave walls near Kenton. These early dwellers lived on roots and berries as well as the meat they obtained from the animals they hunted.

When Spanish explorer Francisco Vásquez de Coronado first came to the area in 1541, he found a place in which few people lived, although a few Native American tribes, notably the Plains Indians, eked out an existence there. Chief among these were the Apache, Comanche, and Kiowa, although the area also had some village-dwelling Indians, notably the Caddo, Pawnee, and Wichita, who had inhabited the area prior to 1500. These Native American groups were joined between 1815 and 1840 by the Cherokee, Chickasaw, Choctaw, Creek, and Seminole Indians, known as the Five Civilized Tribes. The federal government had driven them from their homes and forcibly relocated them in large enclaves in Oklahoma and other nearby areas, called Indian Territory.

The Earliest Explorers

It has been speculated that Vikings from Greenland reached Oklahoma as early as 1012. The evidence for this, however, a huge stone found at Heavener in eastern Oklahoma with the date carved into it in the kind of runic letters used by the Vikings, has not been authenticated. It is known that Spanish explorers crossed the Oklahoma Panhandle in 1541, coming from Mexico in search of gold. In the same year, Hernando de Soto, also seeking gold, came into the area from the east, traveling along the Arkansas River. All explorers claimed the area for Spain.

In 1682 René-Robert Cavelier, Sieur de La Salle, explored the Mississippi River, claiming for France all the lands drained by the Mississippi and naming it Louisiana in honor of his king, Louis XIV. The vast area he claimed included most of present-day Oklahoma. The early explorers traded trinkets with the native dwellers for furs.

The Louisiana Territory changed hands several times. In 1762 Spain took it from France. In 1800, Spain returned it to France, and in 1803, the United States, in the Louisiana Purchase, bought it from France for fifteen million dollars. It must be remembered that at the time of the Louisiana Purchase, fewer than five hundred Europeans lived in the entire area called Louisiana, which included parts of Texas, Oklahoma, Arkansas, Kansas, and Missouri.

The first non-Indian settlement in Oklahoma, near present-day Salina, was established in 1823 by Auguste Pierre Chouteau, whose trading post served the area's fur traders. In 1830 the U.S. Congress passed the Indian Removal Act, under which the government was permitted to relocate Indians from the East Coast of the United States. Between 1830 and 1842, around seventy-five thousand Native Americans were deployed to the area, many dying en route. Those who survived lived much as white people in the east did, creating villages, building schools and churches, farming, and raising cattle and poultry. Some became so affluent that they owned slaves.

The government promised the relocated Indians that the land they were given in the eastern and southern parts of the area, known as the Indian Territory, would always be theirs. The various tribes set up their own governments and functioned as separate nations.

The Civil War

Because the Indian Territory had not achieved statehood, it could not secede from the Union dur-

ing the Civil War. Many of the Native Americans who dwelled there owned slaves, and about six thousand of the Indians fought for the Confederacy during the war, although some joined the Union forces. Most of these people held a grudge against the federal government for having taken them from their native lands and relocated them. This caused many who were not slave owners to side with the South.

After the war, in 1866, representatives of the Indian Territory were forced to sign the Reconstruction Treaty. The government retaliated against the Native Americans for their support of the Confederacy by taking back much of their land and by forcing them to permit railroads to cross their property.

Land Disputes

In the 1870's, Texan cattle men drove their herds to Kansas railroad towns from which livestock could be shipped to market, crossing Oklahoma. Irritated, Kansans tried to pressure the government into opening more land in the area to white settlement. The Missouri-Kansas-Texas Railroad crossed eastern Oklahoma by 1872 and brought many people into the region.

Many white farmers rented the land they tilled from the Native Americans. In time the federal government bought five thousand square miles of the Indian Territory and, in 1889, opened it to settlers on a first come, first served basis. Each family could claim 160 acres merely by placing themselves upon it. About fifty thousand land-hungry people arrived. At noon on April 22, the Oklahoma Land Rush of 1889 began, marking an important phase in Oklahoma's development. A tent city in Guthrie housed fifteen thousand people temporarily. On that single day, the settlements of Kingfisher, Norman, Oklahoma City, and Stillwater were started.

After development started there, the U.S. Congress established the Oklahoma Territory, which lay west of the Indian Territory. The two areas were called the Twin Territories. The federal purchase of more Indian land was followed by more land runs, so that by the early 1900's, the area had a substantial white population. The Native Americans wanted to establish their own state, but their desires were overlooked. In 1907 the Twin Territories were admitted to the Union as the state of Oklahoma, the forty-sixth of the United States, with Guthrie as its capital. Three years later, the capital was moved to Oklahoma City.

The Discovery of Oil

In 1901, Oklahoma began its journey toward affluence. Oil was discovered near Tulsa. An oil rush began, with many petroleum companies establishing offices in Tulsa. As oil was discovered in other parts of the state, many boomtowns grew, and the entire state experienced an economic upsurge.

The decade following World War I was a time of considerable prosperity for the state. Oil fueled the economy, but agriculture was also important. The state's prosperity, based on these two enterprises, was not to last, however.

Dust Bowls and the Great Depression

The economic chaos following the collapse of the stock market in 1929 affected the entire United States. Oklahoma, however, suffered more than most other states because, combined with a national economic downturn that devastated the oil industry, a continued drought resulted in huge dust storms and reduced agriculture production to below the subsistence level.

The Great Depression was so devastating to Oklahoma that more than sixty thousand of its citizens, labeled "Okies," left the state, many of them heading for the West Coast, particularly to California.

World War II and After

World War II brought renewed prosperity to Oklahoma. The weather improved to the point that agriculture again contributed significantly to the economy. War industries came into the state, notably aeronautical and munitions factories. The state's oil wells produced much-needed petroleum products for the war effort. Some 200,000 Oklahomans served in the nation's armed forces.

Shortly after the war, in 1947, the McClellan-Kerr Arkansas River Navigation Project was begun. When it was completed in 1970, the Arkansas River had been made navigable by widening and deepening. The system of dams and locks on the river made it possible for large ships to navigate it. Muskogee and Tulsa became important port cities once the waterway was opened.

Other dams were built on rivers throughout Oklahoma as a means of flood control and irrigation. The lakes these dams formed offer visitors extensive recreational facilities and attract many tourists. The hydroelectric power the dams generate stimulated industrial growth.

This industrial growth, mainly in companies that make airplanes, rockets, automobile parts, and computers, brought an influx of new people into the state, which, from 1970 to 1980, attracted 466,000 new residents. During the 1970's, three groups of Oklahoma Indians, the Cherokee, the Choctaw, and the Chickasaw, regained ninety-six miles of the Arkansas River, increasing their prosperity.

In 1971 the voters of Oklahoma City elected Patience Latting mayor, making her the first female mayor of a major metropolis. Three years later, the state selected thirty-three-year-old David Boren as governor, making him the youngest governor in the United States.

The Federal Building Bombing

The 1990's were marked by tragedy in Oklahoma. In a horrible act of domestic terrorism, on April 19, 1995, Timothy McVeigh loaded a rental truck with explosives, parked it outside the Alfred P. Murrah Federal Building in Oklahoma City, retreated a safe distance, and detonated the explosives.

The Murrah Building collapsed, killing 168 people and seriously injuring scores of others, among them many young children in a day care center housed in the building. The city and state were devastated by this crime and erected a memorial on the site of the demolished building. McVeigh, granted a change of venue for his court case, was tried in Denver, Colorado. He was convicted of first-degree murder, for which he received the death sentence. The Oklahoma City National Memorial now stands at the former site of the Murrah Building.   —*R. Baird Shuman*

Oklahoma City National Memorial

Date: Construction of the Alfred P. Murrah Federal Building began in 1974; opened to the public in 1977; bombed on April 19, 1995; memorial dedicated on April 19, 2000

Relevant issues: Disasters and tragedies, political history

Significance: The bombing of the Alfred P. Murrah Federal Building was the worst act of domestic terrorism to its time in the United States.

Location: Downtown Oklahoma City

Site Office:

Oklahoma City National Memorial Foundation
Leadership Square

211 N. Robinson Avenue, Suite 150
Oklahoma City, OK 73102
Mailing address:
P.O. Box 323
Oklahoma City, OK 73101
ph.: (888) 542-HOPE [542-4673]; (405) 235-3313
fax: (405) 235-3315
Web site: connections.oklahoman.net/memorial
e-mail: okcmem@ionet.net

The Alfred P. Murrah Federal Building was graven into the collective memory of Americans through the images of its violent destruction in the worst act of domestic terrorism to that date. However, before that day it had seen nearly two decades of routine service as the home of a number of federal offices in the capital of Oklahoma.

The Murrah Building stood in downtown Oklahoma City, on the corner of northwest Fifth Street and Harvey Avenue. It was named for Alfred P. Murrah, who was the youngest person to be appointed a federal judge and who served on the Tenth Circuit Court from 1940 to 1970. Construction on the building had begun in 1974, and it first opened to the public in 1977. It housed fifteen federal agencies, several defense department offices, and a federally operated day-care center that was used by many parents who worked in the Murrah Building and in other downtown offices.

The Blast

April 19, 1995, started as a routine day for the employees at the Murrah Building and in surrounding buildings. Visitors came into various offices to take care of various matters. In the day care center, the children were just sitting down to their breakfast juice. Nobody paid any particular attention to the large Ryder rental truck parked in front, although a few people knew that delivery trucks were not supposed to park there. Unknown to them, this truck contained a 4,000-pound (1,800-kilogram) bomb made by combining racing fuel with ammonium-nitrate fertilizer.

At 9:02 A.M., everything changed with a flash and a thunderous roar. An explosion tore through the nine-story building, ripping away the entire facade over the front entrance and collapsing parts of all nine floors. Many people within the building suddenly saw their colleagues vanish in a haze of smoke as the floors gave way beneath them. The explosion left a crater eight feet deep and thirty feet across. It also severely damaged several nearby buildings, causing additional injuries. The rear axle of the Ryder truck, thrown several hundred feet by the blast, nearly killed a family when it struck a small passenger car.

People in nearby buildings wondered why thunder should be coming from a clear blue sky, until they saw the smoke rising from the blast site. Others thought that a gas main had exploded. People as far as thirty miles away felt the effects of the blast, and many thought they were feeling an earthquake.

Oklahoma governor Frank Keating was at his desk at the state capitol building at the time of the blast. He heard the explosion, and moments later an aide arrived to tell him of the destruction of the Murrah Building. Keating immediately called for a disaster declaration and ordered the head of the Oklahoma National Guard to take charge of the rescue efforts.

However, people in the area had not waited for any official direction to begin rescue efforts of their own. Survival had often been a matter of merest chance, and many people who had not been seriously hurt immediately began helping their colleagues escape the wreckage. One employee of the Bureau of Alcohol, Tobacco, and Firearms (ATF) survived a six-floor free fall in an elevator and immediately went to work looking for evidence in what he knew would be a major case. Another federal law enforcement officer, trapped within the wreckage, used a portable tape recorder to preserve his own immediate impressions in the hope that they would help identify and convict the perpetrators.

This spontaneous reaction was not limited to the Murrah Building itself. People from nearby buildings, even individuals with no emergency training whatsoever, hurried to offer any help they could. Parents who worked elsewhere hurried back in the hope of rescuing their children from the day care center, which exhibited some of the worst damage.

Soon the professional rescue workers arrived, bringing equipment and trained dogs who could sniff out people trapped within the wreckage. Over the following hours the world watched them pull survivors, many badly injured, from the broken concrete and twisted steel.

Workers assemble the chairs that are part of the Oklahoma City National Memorial. Behind them is one of the Gates of Time, marked 9:01 for the moment before the bomb exploded. (AP/Wide World Photos)

Over the next several days the heroism of rescue workers and medical personnel riveted the attention of the nation as these professionals sifted through the rubble to rescue any remaining survivors. For many of the victims it was already too late, and the sight of firefighters carrying the broken bodies of children from the day care center aroused the indignation of the entire world. Meanwhile, federal investigators were also sifting the rubble for clues to the identity of the perpetrators of this atrocity.

On May 23, over a month after the blast, the recovery efforts were terminated. The ruined structure had become so unstable that continuing to dig for remains would endanger the living. The wreckage was then demolished with dynamite in a controlled explosion, permanently entombing the unrecovered human remains. A total of 168 people had lost their lives in the bombing, and many oth-

ers had been permanently disabled by their injuries.

There were calls for harsher penalties for terrorist acts, as well as more stringent controls on materials that could be used in terrorist activities. Others expressed concern that increased security measures could end up destroying cherished civil liberties for law-abiding citizens without producing any substantial increase in public safety.

The Investigation and Trial

In the first few hours after the blast, many commentators jumped to the conclusion that this had to be the work of foreign terrorists, perhaps Islamic Fundamentalists, who had previously caused an explosion in the World Trade Center in New York City. However, investigators soon traced the axle from the destroyed Ryder truck to a rental agency in Florida. When they interrogated the rental agent, they discovered that this was not the work of foreign terrorists; the perpetrators had been white Americans, quite probably with backgrounds in the armed forces. This was the work of a homegrown terrorist organization.

Further investigation revealed that the primary suspect was already in custody on an unrelated charge. Timothy McVeigh, a veteran of the Persian Gulf War, who had become a drifter after his discharge from the Army, had been stopped for driving an unlicensed vehicle and was awaiting a bail hearing. Federal investigators then contacted the county jail where he was being held and had him transferred to a federal prison to be arraigned on charges of having bombed the Murrah Building and murdered the people who died in the explosion.

This arrest, as well as the arrest of Terry Nichols as a possible accomplice, focused attention on the various antigovernment extremist organizations with which these two men had been connected. Many of these groups actively opposed the federal government as having exceeded its constitutional authority. Many subscribed to various theories that the government was involved in a vast conspiracy to deprive the American people of their traditional liberties and create a police state. They argued that the government had become a tyranny, to the extent that they considered themselves justified in acts of violence against it. These groups had become militant after a 1992 confrontation with federal agents at white supremacist Randy Weaver's Idaho home left his wife and son dead. After the ATF's siege of the Branch Davidian compound in Waco, Texas, on April 19, 1993, turned into a deadly firestorm, many decided it was time to take action.

McVeigh was tried in 1997 for the bombing. Due to the extensive publicity regarding the bombing, the trial was held in Denver rather than in Oklahoma City. During the trial, many of the survivors testified about their experiences. McVeigh was convicted of having bombed the Murrah Building and subsequently was sentenced to death. Nichols was tried separately, and while he was convicted of the lesser charge of having conspired with McVeigh to bomb the Murrah Building, he was not convicted of having used the bomb.

The Memorial

Even while rescue and recovery efforts were still in progress, people began to create their own informal memorial to the victims. Cards, poems, and teddy bears were left along the chain-link fence that surrounded the site. This continued even after the wreckage was demolished.

There was considerable debate as to the long-term future of the site. Some wanted to rebuild the Murrah Building, to have it rise like a phoenix from the ashes as a way of saying that life went on in spite of human evil. Governor Keating firmly rejected this idea, saying that this site was now hallowed ground and should not be put back to mundane bureaucratic purposes. Instead it should be set aside for a permanent memorial that would enshrine the names of the victims and provide hope for a future in which the sort of hatred that had created this destruction would be wiped away.

In 1997, a plan was unveiled for a permanent memorial park featuring 168 empty stone-and-glass chairs, each inscribed with the name of one of the slain victims of the bombing. It also preserved the Survivor Tree, a small tree on the edge of the grounds that had become strongly associated with the survivors of the blast. The plan also included the creation of the Oklahoma City National Memorial Institute for the Prevention of Terrorism and the Oklahoma City Memorial Center. The memorial center would be in the nearby Journal Record Building, containing exhibits explaining the meaning behind the symbolic memorial. This building suffered extensive damage from the blast, and its restoration would be done in such a way as to preserve the appearance of damage to the south facade. The memorial center would also contain a special exhibit designed particularly for children, which would teach them about the bombing while still conveying the message that the good in humanity generally outweighs the bad. Ground was broken for the memorial park in 1998, and it was completed two years later. The Oklahoma City National Memorial was dedicated on April 19, 2000, the fifth anniversary of the bombing.

—Leigh Husband Kimmel

For Further Information:

Hamm, Mark S. *Apocalypse in Oklahoma: Waco and Ruby Ridge Revenged.* Boston: Northeastern University Press, 1997. Concentrates primarily on the politics behind the bombing, in particular the right-wing conspiracy theories held by the bombers.

Hoffman, David. *The Oklahoma City Bombing and the Politics of Terror.* Venice, Calif.: Feral House, 1998. A discussion of the politics behind the bombing and the rationales of terrorists for their acts.

Irving, Clive, ed. *In Their Name: Dedicated to the Brave and the Innocent, Oklahoma City, April, 1995.* New York: Random House, 1995. Focuses on the rescue efforts immediately after the bombing.

Lamb, Nancy. *One April Morning: Children Remember the Oklahoma City Bombing.* New York: Lothrop, Lee, & Shepard Books, 1996. An illustrated book in which children who survived the bombing tell their own stories.

Rappoport, Jon. *Oklahoma City Bombing: The Suppressed Truth.* Santa Monica, Calif.: Blue Press, 1996. Alleges that the Oklahoma City bombing was not the work of Timothy McVeigh, but of a secret government cabal whose actions were covered up by the FBI.

Ross, Jim, and Paul Meyers, eds. *We Will Never Forget: Eyewitness Accounts of the Oklahoma City Federal Building Bombing.* Austin, Tex.: Eakin, 1996. A compilation of eyewitness accounts of people who survived the bombing or participated in the rescue of the survivors.

Serrano, Richard A. *One of Ours: Timothy McVeigh and the Oklahoma City Bombing.* New York: W. W. Norton, 1998. A study of McVeigh's life and how he decided to bomb the Murrah Building, including information on the bombing and the rescue effort.

Sod House Museum

Date: House built in 1894

Relevant issues: Art and architecture, western expansion

Significance: This museum is found in the only extant original sod house in Oklahoma. Built by a homesteader, it gives a glimpse of what Plains living was like in the late nineteenth century. The Sod House Museum contains a display of contemporary implements and furniture typical of 1907, the year that Oklahoma achieved statehood.

Location: On Highway 8, one mile east and two and a half miles south of Aline

Site Office:
Sod House Museum
Rural Route 3
Box 28
Aline, OK 73716
ph.: (580) 463-2441

The sod house is an enduring part of American heritage and a unique component of architecture during the westward expansion of the United States into the Great Plains. Solomon Butcher emigrated to Nebraska but found photography more to his liking than farming. He made a name and career for himself by recording the sodbusters, sod houses, and daily life on homesteaders' farms. His remarkable images immortalized the innovative building methods, adaptations, and ingenious forms that were incorporated into the structures built by the farmers who settled and struggled to live on the Great Plains.

The best lands were occupied early, leaving most to deal with the lack of timber and trees elsewhere. The only remaining available building material was sod. It was easy to use and durable. The sod house, despite its problems, was warm in winter and cool in summer. During some periods of extreme weather or fire, only those living in sod houses would survive. The sod house protected early American settlers and made life on the Great Plains possible.

Historical Background

When the first of modern Americans made their way out of the eastern woodlands and onto the empty Great Plains, they encountered endless seas of waving grass with little in the way of useful building materials in evidence. The prairies of the Midwest had few wooded areas and streams, or protected areas. The land was easy to travel across, the soil was fertile and free of rocks, stumps, and seedlings, and the vista was unlimited, but housing materials were nearly absent, and the weather was very harsh.

In 1862, President Abraham Lincoln signed the Homestead Act, giving eligible U.S. citizens 160 acres of free land out west in return for a ten-dollar filing fee. This land was in the Great Plains, sometimes referred to as the "Great American Desert," a misnomer for the fertile but treeless region in the middle of the north American continent.

Settlers at first trickled into the area, intimidated by the native peoples who were willing to protect their territories, until the military removed most of the Indians to reservations by 1890. After the Civil War, from 1865, nearly fifty thousand African Americans, called "Exodusters," contributed to the increased flow of the human river. Once the railroads were completed, the Indians subdued, and the buffalo destroyed, the flow of the river became a vast tide that washed across the continent, made up of immigrants, emigrants, and all types of people from all over the world.

The continuing exodus of homesteading farmers pushed west by the expansionist powers of Manifest Destiny, were called "sodbusters." They faced, on arrival, land receiving only twenty inches of rain a year, tortured by extreme temperatures and natural disasters, and nearly lacking trees, wood, water, and fuel. They responded to the brutal environmental demands by building houses from the earth itself. Sod houses, or "soddies" as they were often called, are a reflection of the persistence and hardiness of the American pioneers.

Such houses had been in use by plains Indian tribes, such as the Mandan, who may have provided

Homesteaders gather at Lawton on August 6, 1901, ready for another land rush. Many would build sod houses after staking a claim. (AP/Wide World Photos)

settlers with examples of effective housing adaptations, for many thousands of years. The use of subterranean and freestanding dwellings covered with earth has been a universal human response to difficult and demanding environmental conditions since prehistoric times. It was natural to use the earth, as it was the only building material available.

Sod houses were a demonstration of the incredible creativity and resilience of the people who settled the Great Plains states, such as Oklahoma, Nebraska, and the Dakotas. They were inexpensive, easy to build, often well crafted, very durable, and built well into the twentieth century, when wooden frame houses began to dominate the midwestern landscape.

Materials

The sodbusters responded to their unique situation and demanding environment by constructing their houses of sod. Sod is a mixture of soil and grass held together by an intricate root system that makes it both strong and flexible. When farmers broke the sod with the recently developed John Deere grasshopper plow, the soil turned over in long strips about eighteen inches wide and four inches thick, which were then chopped into three- to four-foot lengths and stacked after the fashion of bricks into walls, sometimes three or four bricks deep. The "bricks" were stacked with the root systems facing up. As the roots grew into the bricks above, the layers of bricks were locked more firmly together. Such walls, built properly, could endure for many years.

The interior floor was patted down until it was nearly rock hard. Sod brick walls were built, doors and windows of oil paper or glass were added, then the interior was divided into rooms using tarps, blankets or other materials, usually brought along by the family from the east. A layer of mud or clay could be spread over the interior walls like plaster and whitewashed, or even covered with newspaper or wallpaper to lighten and brighten the subterranean interior. Heat was easily provided by a small wood- or dung-burning stove.

Montgomery Ward was marketing windows and frames for just over one dollar in 1872. Ready-made accessories became popular items as they helped the homesteaders continue to improve their sod houses so as to fulfill the legal requirement that they continue with ongoing improvements to retain title to their land.

Lean-tos, outbuildings, and even barns were built of this versatile material and added onto the house or remained freestanding. In the event of tornado, hail, fire, or grasshopper plague, protection was assured. Some such disasters would strip the land of all exposed plant and animal life. Farmers and their families brought seedlings, animals, tools, and anything else of value into the secure interior until the danger had passed. Fireproof and weatherproof, if not waterproof, the sod house was a perfect expression of early American populist utilitarian architecture.

Types

Some sod houses were freestanding, some were built into the sides of hills or streambeds. Door and window frames were singular or multiple, depending on how well off the owners were. Roofs were made of twigs, thin branches, or whatever supporting material could be found, then piled with straw or grass and covered with a final layer of sod. More fortunate home owners used difficult-to-obtain lumber to build a roof that they could shingle. Such homes were a safe haven and nearly indestructible.

In size, the sod house ranged from a single room of less than one hundred square feet, more like a cave than a house, up to freestanding homes with several rooms and several hundred square feet of living space appropriate for larger families. Sometimes a small house would be home to a large family, and crowding would lead to rapid deterioration of the structure and add-ons being required. If the house was built too high or not deep enough into the ground, if the walls were not even, thick enough, or tapered properly, the structure would be prone to serious problems and would not last very long.

A more durable type involved using sod for the exterior walls, then using a minimal amount of lumber to build a cubic frame on the interior, which could then be covered with fabric or paper. Care had to be taken to avoid putting holes in the walls.

Other types of sod buildings included schools, stores, churches, hotels, and even a post office, built in diverse styles, using a variety of construction techniques and modifications which indicate the importance of the sod house to America's westward expansion. It was truly shelter from the storms of prairie life.

Problems

Sod houses leaked almost continually during the wet seasons. Tarps were hung to catch water and dirt that rained down during storms. Use of the stove during a rainstorm required an umbrella. The continual erosion led some sod houses eventually to collapse. Wet bedding and clothing were common. The interior would often remain humid for many days after a rain, leading to problems with mold and fungus.

As families grew, so did wear and tear on the sod house, leading to its ever-accelerating breakdown. In addition, snakes, mice, and various kinds of bugs lived with their human companions. Fleas, mites, and bedbugs could become intolerable, sometimes forcing a family to build and move into a new sod house. Most families looked forward to the day that they could afford to build a wood frame house and move out of their durable relic.

The Sod House Museum

The Sod House Museum in Aline, Oklahoma, a small farming community in the northwestern part of the state about one hundred miles from Oklahoma City, was established in a prime example of this architectural form and the only remaining original sod house in Oklahoma. The museum provides the opportunity for visitors to walk through history and imagine what life was like on the Great Plains in the late 1890's and early 1900's. It was built in 1894 by homesteader Marshal McCully, who came to Oklahoma during the Oklahoma Land Rush of 1893. The two-room soddy was used as his family's home until 1909. McCully put in a wood floor soon after building the house and used special alkali clay as plaster on the inside walls to keep out insects. Covers made of flour sacks protected the house from dirt, debris, snakes, and insects that came from the ceiling.

Since 1963, the home has been owned and preserved by the Oklahoma Historical Society. A short tour of the museum and its exhibits helps visitors understand the hardships and rewards of pioneer families such as the McCullys around the state and the nation. Admission is free, and the museum is open Tuesday through Friday from 9:00 A.M. to 5:00 P.M. and Saturday and Sunday from 2:00 P.M. to 5:00 P.M. On Labor Day, the museum features local crafts, and a pioneer Christmas party is held there each year. —*Michael W. Simpson*

For Further Information:

McAlester, Virginia, and Lee McAlester. *A Field Guide to American Houses.* New York: Alfred A. Knopf, 1984.

Morrison, Hugh. *Early American Architecture.* Mineola, N.Y.: Dover, 1988.

Stratton, Joanna L. "Homes of Puncheon, Homes of Sod." In *Pioneer Women: Voices from the Kansas Frontier.* New York: Simon & Schuster, 1981.

Taylor, Sarah, ed. *Exploring Oklahoma with Children! The Essential Parents' Travel Guide.* Rev. ed. Edmond, Okla.: Inprint, 1997.

Upton, Dell, and John Michael Vlach, eds. *Common Places: Readings in American Vernacular Architecture.* Athens: University of Georgia Press, 1986.

Tahlequah

Date: Cherokee Constitution signed on September 6, 1839

Relevant issues: American Indian history

Significance: This is the site where the Eastern and Western branches of the Cherokees came together to sign the Cherokee Constitution. Tahlequah functioned as the Cherokee national capital until the Curtis Act of 1898 abolished tribal authority in the Indian Territory. Following Oklahoma's admission as a state, Tahlequah became the seat of Cherokee County. The town remains the administrative headquarters for the Cherokee tribal government.

Location: Cherokee County in the Ozark plateau area of eastern Oklahoma, sixty-seven miles southeast of Tulsa

Site Office:

Tahlequah Chamber of Commerce
123 E. Delaware Street
Tahlequah, OK 74464
ph.: (918) 456-3742

The Cherokees originally lived in the Southeast, on lands that would form parts of the states of North and South Carolina, Tennessee, and Georgia. After they were forced to embark on the Trail of Tears—the long, hard journey to the Indian Territory of Oklahoma—they made Tahlequah their capital. The Cherokees still influence the town's culture and economy.

White Settlers Displace the Cherokees

As white settlers began moving into the Southeast in the eighteenth and early nineteenth centuries, they displaced increasing numbers of the region's native inhabitants. Initially, these Indians were simply pushed into neighboring areas farther from the encroaching settlers. Eventually, however, the federal government decided on a more systematic and comprehensive approach: All of southeastern tribes were to be moved to Oklahoma, which in 1825 was officially designated Indian Territory and declared off limits to white settlers.

One Cherokee group, called the Western Cherokees, had moved west of the Mississippi in about 1770. They were initially assigned by the federal government to an Arkansas reservation in 1817, but white settlers soon clamored for these lands as well. In 1828, the Cherokees signed a treaty with the federal government exchanging their Arkansas land for the northern third of Oklahoma Territory.

Conditions of the Cherokees in Georgia

Meanwhile, most of the remaining Cherokees east of the Mississippi had been squeezed into northwestern Georgia. Life was made increasingly difficult for these Cherokees, as it was for the Choctaws, Creeks, Chickasaws, and Seminoles—the other members of the Five Civilized Tribes (so called because they had adopted many European customs). Pioneers were trespassing on their land, and the governments of Georgia, Florida, Alabama, and Mississippi were threatening to confiscate it. In Georgia, the state legislature enacted laws abolishing the Cherokee tribal government. The state even arrested some missionaries working among the tribe when it was suspected that they were encouraging the Cherokees not to move west.

Indian Removal Act and the Trail of Tears

In 1830, Congress passed the Indian Removal Act,

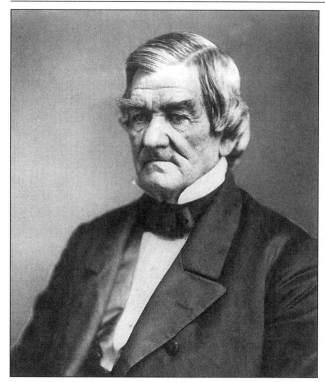

Cherokee leader John Ross. (Smithsonian Institution)

ported large herds of cattle and horses, they also worked the local salt springs. The Cherokees sold many of their products to nearby military posts.

The Western Cherokees had established a new government in Oklahoma, and they invited the Eastern Cherokees to join them. The Eastern Cherokees had more members, however, and John Ross, their chief, convinced the Western Indians to join his government.

Reuniting of the Cherokees in Oklahoma

On September 6, 1839, the Eastern and Western Cherokees met at Tahlequah, on land that would become the town's public square, to sign a new constitution reuniting the two groups. The constitution created a national council to make the laws and also a judicial branch. It contained a bill of rights and gave a vote to every male tribe member over the age of seventeen. The Cherokees made Tahlequah their capital and elected John Ross their first chief under the new constitution. Ross was repeatedly reelected and held the office until his death in 1866.

increasing the government's control over the Indians. The Cherokee leaders now believed that the tribe would suffer further losses unless they agreed to move to Oklahoma. So in 1835 they signed the Treaty of New Echota, which surrendered eight million acres of land in Georgia for a payment of five million dollars. The federal government then began escorting the Cherokees to Indian Territory, where they were to join the Western Cherokees already settled there.

Because the Cherokees and the other southern tribes endured such great suffering on their march to Oklahoma, their journey is called the Trail of Tears. They were stricken by cholera, smallpox, and measles epidemics, and many had to travel in freezing temperatures. They had few wagons, and most of them walked the entire route. About one-fourth of the southern Indians died en route.

The Eastern Cherokees lost most of their livestock and belongings on their journey, but the Western Cherokees gave them food and shared their homes. Soon, aided by their black slaves, they established new farms, plantations, and ranches that produced corn and other grains and sup-

Initially, the main structure in Tahlequah was a shed, around which were the camping grounds for council delegates. The Cherokee government soon decided to create a more elaborate capital for their nation, however, and on January 8, 1845, the council passed an ordinance calling for the removal of all existing buildings on the public square, the laying out of new streets, and the erection of government buildings. Among the earliest of these structures were the Cherokee Supreme Court Building and the Cherokee National Capitol. The former was home not only to the tribal court, but also to the *Cherokee Advocate*, the government's official newspaper, published both in English and in Cherokee. The paper, which began publication in 1844, was edited by William Ross, nephew to Principal Chief John Ross. In 1846, two Cherokee high schools were built near Tahlequah: the Male Seminary just south of town and the Female Seminary in nearby Park Hill.

The Murrell Mansion, one of the finest residences in the area and a center of local social activities, was built around 1843 by George Murrell, a prosperous white merchant who had married a niece of John Ross. Typical of the antebellum style, the mansion was built from local materials, but most of its furnishings came from France and New Orleans.

The Cherokees During the Civil War

With the coming of the Civil War in 1861, the Cherokee authorities in Tahlequah, like the other tribal governments, were forced to choose between retaining their alliance with the Union or throwing their lot with the Confederacy. The Confederacy actively courted the governments of Indian Territory. The Southern states, which grew mostly cotton, tobacco, and rice, saw Indian Territory as a new source of supplies to replace those previously imported from the North. The Confederacy also saw Indian Territory as strategically important: Its acquisition would connect the Confederate States to the territories of the far West, protect Texas against invasion along its northern border, and allow Confederate armies to invade Kansas.

The Union, on the other hand, had all but abandoned Indian Territory. Federal troops were pulled out of forts in the area, and the U.S. government stopped making payments required by the relocation treaties. To make matters worse, many Northern politicians had won office on pledges to open Oklahoma to white settlers.

Despite these disparities between North and South, the debate among the tribal leaders was often fierce, particularly in the Cherokee Nation. Many tribal members favored the Confederacy because they owned slaves; many others wished to remain with the Union. Ultimately, John Ross and the government at Tahlequah sided with the other governments of the Five Civilized Tribes. In 1861, they signed a treaty with the South, making Oklahoma a Confederate territory. Each tribe also agreed to provide troops. Although the Confederacy was supposed to provide guns and supplies for the Indian troops, their own supplies were low and the tribal governments were forced to outfit their own men.

The pro-Union faction among the Cherokees refused to fight for the South, and soon a civil war erupted in Indian Territory itself. With Cherokees fighting on both sides of the conflict, their lands became the site of many battles. In 1862 Union troops entered Tahlequah and captured Chief John Ross. Both sides destroyed Indian homes and tribal buildings and took their crops, livestock, and other belongings. The Cherokee National Capitol was burned to the ground. By the close of the war, the Indian lands were devastated. Many civilians had died in refugee camps and many Indian soldiers, who had served in both the Confederate and Union armies, were killed in battle.

New Treaties with the Federal Government

In 1866 leaders of the Five Civilized Tribes went to Washington to sign treaties with the federal government, which took the western half of Oklahoma from them and settled tribes from other parts of the country on this land. By 1869 the Indians had begun rebuilding their towns, and tribal officials could once again enforce their laws.

One of the first public buildings restored in Tahlequah was the Cherokee National Capitol. The Italianate red-brick structure that replaced the original log capitol was opened in 1870; it housed both the tribal legislature and supreme court. The Cherokee Supreme Court Building had survived the Civil War, but it was gutted by fire in 1874 and needed to be rebuilt. Parts of the original 1845 brick structure are still visible today. While the Supreme Court Building was being renovated, the *Cherokee Advocate* moved its operations to the Cherokee National Prison, which had just been completed. The prison has since been converted to the Tsa-La-Gai Library, which offers children's readings in the former jail cells.

In 1886, Ed Hicks, a Cherokee, built Oklahoma's first commercial telephone line, which ran from Tahlequah to nearby Fort Gibson. The next year the Female Seminary in Park Hill burned to the ground, and it was decided to rebuild the school in the capital. The new building, ornamented with turrets and towers, is now listed in the National Register of Historic Places.

The Opening of Indian Territory to White Settlers

As cattle ranching and lead and coal mining brought prosperity to the area, white settlers pressured the U.S. government to open Indian Territory. Officially, only citizens of the Indian tribes were allowed to live free of restrictions in the territory; whites who wished to settle there needed to purchase an annual five-dollar permit from the tribal government. In order to open more land for these settlers, Congress passed the Dawes Allotment Act of 1887. Prior to this point, lands were held communally by each tribe. The Dawes Act ended this traditional system of ownership by parceling out 160-acre allotments to individual Indians. The millions of acres of remaining lands were declared surplus and opened to white settlers. The Five Civilized Tribes managed to exclude themselves from this treaty until 1893, and even then the allotments were divided such that no surplus land was given to settlers.

Such obstacles created by the tribal governments were overcome with the Curtis Act of 1898, which abolished tribal authority, made Indians subject to federal laws, required surveys of towns and the creation of free public schools for white children in the territory, and extended voting rights to the permit holders, who by 1900 outnumbered Indians. The white settlers now lobbied Congress to admit Oklahoma Territory as a state. In response, the Five Civilized Tribes called for a separate Indian state to be carved out of the eastern half of the territory, which they proposed to call Sequoyah (after the inventor of the Cherokee alphabet). Congress refused their plans, however, and on November 16, 1907, President Theodore Roosevelt signed the proclamation making Oklahoma a state.

Modern Preservation Efforts

Tahlequah was named the seat of Cherokee County, and the buildings once used by the tribal government were given over to county functions. The Cherokee National Capitol, for instance, served as the county courthouse from 1907 to 1979; it is now a National Historic Landmark. The Female Seminary was purchased by the state in 1909 and became the main building of Northeastern State College, now the second-largest employer in Tahlequah. The Male Seminary south of town was destroyed by fire in 1910.

Tahlequah continues to be the administrative headquarters for the Cherokee tribal government, which is the town's largest employer. In 1993 the Cherokee Nation had an annual budget of sixty-eight million dollars and controlled over seven thousand square miles of territory. The tribal government made headlines in 1985 when Wilma P. Mankiller was appointed its first female chief. She was overwhelmingly reelected in 1987 and 1991.

—*Phyllis R. Miller*

For Further Information:

Duvall, Deborah L. *The Cherokee Nation and Tahlequah.* Charleston, S.C.: Tempus, 1999. A largely pictorial history of Tahlequah in the Images of America series.

Gibson, Arrell M. *The Oklahoma Story.* Norman: University of Oklahoma Press, 1978. For young readers, but adults will also be interested in its detailed history, beginning in prehistoric times, and its many maps, drawings, and historical photos.

Wallis, Michael. *Way down Yonder in the Indian Nation.* New York: St. Martin's, 1993. A collection of essays about the people of Oklahoma, including Chief Wilma Mankiller.

Workers of the Writers' Program of the Work Projects Administration in the State of Oklahoma. *Oklahoma: A Guide to the Sooner State.* 1941. Rev. ed. Norman: University of Oklahoma Press, 1957. Part of the WPA's American Guide Series and revised by Kent Ruth and the staff of the University of Oklahoma Press, with special articles contributed by authorities on particular topics.

Other Historic Sites

Boley Historic District

Location: Boley, Okfuskee County
Relevant issues: African American history
Statement of significance: Begun as a camp for African American railroad construction hands, this is the largest of the towns established in Oklahoma to provide African Americans with the opportunity for self-government in an era of white supremacy and segregation.

Camp Nichols

Location: Wheeless, Cimarron County
Relevant issues: Western expansion
Statement of significance: This camp was established

by Kit Carson in 1865 to offer protection to wagon trains using the Cimarron Cutoff of the Santa Fe Trail.

Creek National Capitol

Location: 6th Street and Grand Avenue, Okmulgee, Okmulgee County

Relevant issues: American Indian history, political history

Statement of significance: This Victorian-style structure was used by the Creeks from 1878 to 1907, after their adoption of a representative form of government modeled on the United States Congress.

Fort Gibson

Location: Lee and Ash Streets, Fort Gibson, Muskogee County

Relevant issues: American Indian history, Civil War, military history

Statement of significance: Cherokee, Creek, and Seminole Indians removed from the Southeast by the government were brought here between 1824 and 1840. The fort was abandoned in 1857 and turned over to the Cherokee Nation. During the Civil War, it was reoccupied by federal forces consisting of three Cherokee Regiments, four companies of Kansas Cavalry, and Hopkins Battery. After the war, the post was garrisoned intermittently until it was abandoned as a military post in 1890 and reverted to the Cherokee Nation.

Fort Sill

Location: Fort Sill, Comanche County

Relevant issues: American Indian history, military history

Statement of significance: Troops stationed here were active in campaigns against Southern Plains tribes in the late 1800's. Virtually all the original fort survives; it has expanded and continued to play a significant role for the Army in the twentieth century.

Fort Washita

Location: Nida, Bryan County

Relevant issues: American Indian history, western expansion

Statement of significance: This fort was established in 1842 (reportedly by Zachary Taylor) because of treaty commitments to the Chickasaws and Choctaws and to serve as a way station for travelers on the Southern Overland Trail.

Guthrie Historic District

Location: Bounded by Oklahoma Ave. on the north, Broad St. on the east, Harrison Ave. on the south, and railroad tracks on the west (includes 301 Harrison St.), Guthrie, Logan County

Relevant issues: Western expansion

Statement of significance: Comprising the commercial core of the city of Guthrie, the historic district contains mostly two- and three-story commercial buildings made of red brick and/or sandstone constructed between 1889 and 1910. This outstanding collection of late nineteenth and early twentieth century commercial architecture displays the aspirations of the city's founders to create a city worthy of the distinction as the first and only territorial capital of Oklahoma (1890-1907) and then as the first state capital (1907-1910). Guthrie is also significant for its association with the opening of the last frontier to non-Indian settlement and is representative of the attraction and opportunities that cities held for the thousands of settlers who chose not to make their living from the land.

101 Ranch Historic District

Location: Ponca City, Kay County

Relevant issues: African American history, cultural history

Statement of significance: This large cattle ranch was the home base of the 101 Wild West Show, which toured from 1904 to 1916 and again from 1925 to 1931. The show featured Bill Pickett, the well-known African American cowboy who invented steer wrestling and was elected to the Cowboy Hall of Fame.

Sequoyah's Cabin

Location: Akins, Sequoyah County

Relevant issues: American Indian history, education, literary history

Statement of significance: This frontier house of logs was occupied (1829-1843) by Sequoyah (c. 1770-1843), the teacher who in 1821 invented a syllabary which made it possible to write and read the Cherokee language. The giant California sequoia trees are named for him.

Washita Battlefield

Location: Cheyenne, Roger Mills County

Relevant issues: American Indian history, military history

Statement of significance: This was the scene of an 1868 attack by George Armstrong Custer's troops on the village of Black Kettle, peace chief of the southern Cheyenne. It demonstrated the effectiveness of winter campaigns against Southern Plains Indian groups.

Oregon

The State Capitol Mall in Salem. (Oregon Tourism Commission)

History of Oregon

Oregon's special character, like that of every state, was formed from its geography and geographical position in the nation combined with the formative events of its history. Oregon's character marries the independent spirit of the frontier West inherited from the nineteenth century with modern, urban America, the result of the economic development of the World War II era and the years of steady growth that followed. The cool, wet western portion of the state coexists with a semi-arid eastern segment in whose economy irrigation has played a major role. Oregon's society and politics exhibit a unique blend of liberalism and conservatism, making it a fascinating laboratory of democracy.

Early History

Before the arrival of white settlers, the region of Oregon was inhabited by numerous Native Americans. These included the Clackma, the Multnomah, the Tillamook, and the Kalapuya in the northwest. Also present were the Bannock, Cayuse, Nez Perce, Paiute, and Umatilla, who lived east of the Cascade Mountains. Near today's California border were the Klamath and the Rogue peoples.

Exploration

Oregon was explored by a succession of European nations before Americans arrived. In the sixteenth century, Spanish adventurers first explored the region. Two centuries later English and more Spaniards searched for the Northwest Passage linking eastern North America to the Pacific, eliminating a voyage around South America. In 1774 Juan Pérez sailed the coast, and the following year Bruno Heceta was the first European to find the Columbia River.

In 1778 the famed English navigator Captain James Cook, also searching for the Northwest Passage and the finders' reward of twenty thousand pounds, sailed up the coast to Yaqina Bay. In 1788 the first American ships arrived, including those of John Kendrick and Robert Gray. In 1792 Gray became the first white man to sail up the Columbia River, which he named after his ship. Soon afterward, William Brougham, a lieutenant of British captain George Vancouver, who was exploring the region, sailed into the Columbia and continued well inland. At this time, too, Russian traders were pushing south from posts in Alaska, and British fur traders were exploring the West, since Oregon furs were seen as a promising component of the growing trade with China.

American Exploration and Settlement

Spain abandoned exploration of the area after 1795, leaving it to the British and Americans. In 1805, Meriwether Lewis and William Clark, leading the expedition sent by President Thomas Jefferson to explore the territory of the Louisiana Purchase, arrived at Fort Clatsop, where the Colombia River meets the Pacific Ocean.

A more permanent American presence first appeared in the form of fur trappers and traders, and only later in the form of agricultural settlers. The first American fur company was established in the region by John Jacob Astor, who brought his Pacific Fur Company to Oregon, basing it in Astoria in 1811. Two years later, during the War of 1812, he sold it to the North West Company, which in turn sold it to Hudson's Bay Company in 1821. By then, however, Britain and the United States had signed a treaty establishing joint occupation of the region by both countries.

Joint occupation brought both British and American influence. By the 1820's, Britain's Hudson's Bay Company was a dominant force in the region, guided by Dr. John McLoughlin at Fort Vancouver, on the Columbia River. Americans were also arriving: Mountain men such as Jedediah S. Smith rivaled the trappers of Hudson's Bay Company in the southeast of the region. In 1829, Hall J. Kelley founded the American Society for the Settlement of Oregon Territory. One of his followers, Nathaniel J. Wyeth, attempted to establish a permanent post on the Columbia River.

Missionaries added their numbers to the fur trappers and traders, especially after Marcus Whitman arrived in the region in 1836. The missionaries awakened American interest in the region. Two

years after Whitman, the first Roman Catholic missionaries, François N. Blanchet and Modeste Demers, arrived, and others followed.

The 1840's saw the advent of the "Great Migration" of Americans moving steadily westward in covered wagons across the Great Plains. In 1842 and 1843 enormous wagon trains braved American Indian attacks and hardship to cross the prairies and mountain chains of the Oregon Trail. Friction soon arose between Americans and British. It had not been so long, after all, since Britain had attempted to undo the results of the American Revolution in the War of 1812. American leaders such as Jesse Applegate advocated establishment of an American government in the area. Thus, in 1843 about one hundred settlers, missionaries, and retired fur traders met at Champoeg and created an Oregon provisional government, modeled on American lines, despite objections by the British-oriented among them.

Conflict with Native Americans and Statehood

The national spirit of the young American republic was now sufficiently stirred to demand removal of British authority in its entirely from the area. The 1844 election slogan Fifty-four Forty or Fight expressed American demands for ousting the British up to that latitude. Fighting proved unnecessary, however, since in 1846 the two nations agreed on borders dividing the Oregon Country.

The next year, the slaughter by American Indians of Marcus Whitman and thirteen others near present-day Walla Walla, Washington, brought demands for protection. The massacre led to the Cayuse War of 1847-1848 and the execution in 1850 of five Indians found guilty of its perpetration. Demands for protection from Indians also led to the establishment of Oregon Territory. The Territory embraced far more than the present state but was reduced in 1853 with the creation of a separate Washington Territory. Finally, in 1859 Oregon became the nation's thirty-third state.

The discovery of gold in Oregon's southwest led to fighting with the Rogue Indians, who resisted abuse at the hands of miners. Conflict with Indians often arose on account of settlers' abuse or Native American resistance to their forcible removal to reservations, as occurred with the Medoc tribe in the early 1870's.

Economic Development

The period from 1850 to 1880 was marked by Indian wars. Nevertheless, Oregon's economy was developing. The California gold rush brought thousands of people to nearby Oregon. Discovery of gold in Oregon had a similar effect.

In 1867-1868 a bumper wheat crop made it possible to ship grain to England, beginning a large wheat export industry in the state. The most important stimulus came later in the century, however, with the arrival of the transcontinental railroad. Under the direction of Henry Villard, the North Pacific Railroad was completed in the 1880's, bringing with it new trade and the onset of manufacturing. The lumber industry was already important to the state's economy, much of the timber being shipped overseas. Australian newspapers of the period invariably carried advertisements for Oregon lumber. With the arrival of the transcontinental railroad from the east however, wood could be shipped throughout the United States, and for a time timber dominated the state's economy. The railroad was also extended to California, facilitating transport of Oregon goods to the growing state to the south.

Political Developments

After 1900, with the state's growing prosperity, Oregon's politics tended to conservatism. This conservatism, however, has long been punctuated with a pronounced streak of reformism and a taste for grassroots democracy. The latter is illustrated by a series of measures enacted early in the century, designed to ensure the influence of popular will over government. In 1902 the initiative and referendum were adopted. The former gave the right of citizens to propose laws to be voted upon in general elections. The referendum secured the electorate's right to reject certain laws passed by the state legislature. In 1904 direct primary elections were instituted. These empowered the electorate at the expense of political party organizations, since candidates for office at general elections were to be chosen directly by the electorate at "primary" elections. In 1908 the state adopted the "recall" election, whereby office holders can be voted from office in special elections. Finally, in 1912, woman suffrage was adopted, after a long and difficult struggle led by Abigail Jane Scott Duniway.

Depression and War

Oregon's twentieth century economic and social life saw continued emigration from the East. Electric power and irrigation projects propelled agriculture and manufacturing to the fore. The Great Depression of the 1930's dramatically increased the role of the federal government in economic affairs. Federal law allowed the lumber industry to set production quotas and prices. Farmers were paid to lower crop production. The federal government also completed the Bonneville Dam on the Columbia River in 1938, bringing important economic benefits as well as flood control to the region.

After the economic hardships of the 1930's, World War II saw a tremendous lift to the state's manufacturing industries. The war brought the state an aluminum industry and revitalized Portland's shipbuilding industry. The city also became an important port for shipping war material to U.S. forces and the Soviet Union. Thousands of workers migrated from the East to work in wartime industries, and many stayed after the war. The federal government built and operated an entire city in the Portland-Vancouver, Washington, area to house the huge influx of wartime workers. The city

was not well situated, however, and was washed away in the great Columbia River floods of 1948.

Postwar Developments

Growing prosperity punctuated by a thriving tourist industry marked the postwar era. Visitors flocked to see the state's scenic wonders, including Crater Lake National Park. Cheap hydroelectric power became more plentiful from a series of federally funded dams, such as The Dalles and McNary projects on the Columbia River. By 1956 natural gas became available, adding to the energy supply. Mechanization and diversification of products aided the state's farms and agricultural industries. In the 1960's, forest products also became more diversified, as new uses were found for previously discarded refuse.

The postwar state's population also became predominantly urban. In 1880 only 15 percent lived in towns. In 1910, the figure was 44 percent, but by 1993, 62 percent of the population lived in incorporated cities and towns. These demographic changes were reflected in the state's politics. The state's early history was marked by domination of the Republican Party. With the urbanization of the 1950's and 1960's and the influx of migrants from other parts of the country, the pattern was reversed and a majority of voters were Democrats. From the 1970's to the end of the 1990's reformist politics were prominent. Oregonians, however, showed themselves independent minded, repeatedly electing Independent Wayne Morse, an outspoken critic of the Vietnam War, for U.S. Senate. Indicative of this spirit was Oregon's passage of the nation's first "bottle law," requiring deposits on disposable bottles and cans. The state's centurylong tradition of conservation continued, and in 1998, the nation's first "right to die" law, which passed as an initiative in 1994, went into effect.

—*Charles F. Bahmueller*

Fort Astoria

Date: Established in 1811
Relevant issues: Business and industry, western expansion
Significance: A fur trading post, Fort Astoria was the first permanent settlement in the Northwest by citizens of the United States and came to sym-

bolize the young nation's desire for westward expansion and a commercial empire.

Location: A replica of a guard tower, boundary lines indicating the fort's original layout, and a historical plaque occupy a park on the corner of 15th and Exchange Streets in Astoria

Site Office:
City of Astoria
1095 Duane Street
Astoria, OR 97103
ph.: (503) 325-5821
fax: (503) 325-2017
Web site: www.el.com/To/Astoria

The idea for Fort Astoria came from the dream of empire. The political and commercial currents of the late eighteenth and early nineteenth centuries, never wholly distinct, merged in the Pacific Northwest. Explorers searching for a fabled Northwest Passage linking the Pacific Ocean to the Atlantic discovered a wealth of beaver and sea otter. Both were prized in China, a market having vast promise for intrepid European merchants. Whatever country owned the Northwest would have the best access to lucrative trade routes and a blue chip commodity. Accordingly, British, French, Spanish, and Russian government agents and entrepreneurs schemed to control the Northwest fur trade. None was as able and visionary as John Jacob Astor of the young United States.

Growth Based on Commercial Competition

In 1807, Astor envisioned a series of trading posts from St. Louis to the Pacific Ocean, approximately along the trail blazed two years earlier by Meriwether Lewis and William Clark. He used his immense wealth and political influence to obtain the official backing of the New York state government and the promise of quasi-official support from President Thomas Jefferson for the Pacific Fur Company, created in 1810. He argued that his initial goal, establishment of a trading post at the mouth of the Columbia River, would help the nation dominate the largely unexplored territory while providing a strategic port for the China trade. He also concluded a mutual-support agreement with the Russian-American Fur Company, headquartered in Alaska. Astor needed the help. His main rival in the fur trade, the North West Company of Canada, was backed by the power of the British Empire.

Astor dispatched two expeditions to the Columbia; both were nearly disastrous. The first sailed on the *Tonquin* around Cape Horn. The ship arrived in March, 1811, after its captain and the traders had made enemies of each other. Despite the captain's enmity and the loss of eight men, the traders built a large trading center, dwelling house, blacksmith

John Jacob Astor, founder of the fur trading post Fort Astoria. (Library of Congress)

shop, and storage shed, surrounded by a wooden palisade ninety feet on a side, about ten miles inside the river's mouth on its south side. On April 12, 1811, they named this compound Fort Astoria in honor of Astor. Soon afterward the *Tonquin*, the fort's link to civilization, sank during a battle with Native Americans off Vancouver Island, British Columbia. Meanwhile, an expedition left St. Louis in March, 1811, to establish an overland route. Personnel conflicts, supply problems, and misunderstanding of the topography nearly led to catastrophe. The exhausted party did not reach Fort Astoria until February, 1812.

War Drives Astor Out

After a bad beginning, the Astorians managed to establish satellite trading posts and enjoyed fairly good trading relations with local American Indian tribes. Alarmed that Astorians might monopolize the fur trade, the North West Company rushed to establish posts of its own, and a trade war was in the offing. The United States and England were on the verge of military conflict too. Not long after Congress declared war in 1812, the Astorians learned that a Royal Navy flotilla was on its way to capture the fort. To make the best of a bad situation, the senior partners of the Pacific Fur Company sold Fort Astoria to the North West Company before the British could take it away from them by force. In December, 1813, it was renamed Fort George and flew the Union Jack. Although outraged by the deal, Astor could do little about it until the war ended. Even then an 1818 treaty gave joint control of the area to the British and American governments, and the North West Company retained day-to-day administrative control of the fort. Astor dissolved the Pacific Fur Company and abandoned his dream of a fur-trading empire.

In 1834 British traders moved their headquarters upriver from Fort George to Fort Vancouver, across the Columbia River from present-day Portland, Oregon. Fort George gradually turned into the fishing village of Astoria, and the original trading post fell into decay. Although the fort belonged to Americans for less than two years, its existence was a crucial step for the young republic. According to historian James P. Ronda in *Astoria and Empire* (1990), Fort Astoria came to symbolize its aspiration for commercial and territorial expansion into the West.

—*Roger Smith*

For Further Information:

Dodds, Gordon B. *Oregon: A Bicentennial History.* New York: W. W. Norton, 1977. A general state history with a cogent chapter on fur trading companies, including John Jacob Astor's.

Franchère, Gabriel. *Adventure at Astoria, 1810-1814.* Norman: University of Oklahoma Press, 1967. An account, based upon journals of a member of the *Tonquin* expedition, of the establishment of Fort Astoria.

Irving, Washington. *Astoria.* Portland, Oreg.: Binfords and Mort, 1967. An early, dramatic history of Fort Astoria, written with the help of Astor and some of the original Astorians; originally published in 1836.

Jones, Robert F., ed. *Astorian Adventure: The Journal of Alfred Seton, 1811-1815.* New York: Fordham University Press, 1993. A journal of a voyage to the Columbia River and life at Fort Astoria by a Pacific Fur Company clerk.

O'Donnell, Terence. *That Balance So Rare.* Portland: Oregon Historical Society Press, 1988. A concise history of Oregon that captures the essence of Astor's scheme in a few pages, with abundant illustrations.

Ronda, James P. *Astoria and Empire.* Lincoln: University of Nebraska Press, 1990. A thorough, readable account of the exploitation of the Northwest and its roots in international political-economic rivalry.

Fort Clatsop

Date: Original fort built in December, 1805

Relevant issues: Western expansion

Significance: This unit of the National Park System is the site of the final encampment of the westbound Lewis and Clark Expedition of 1804-1806. Fort Clatsop is a 1955 reconstruction of the original fifty-foot-square log stockade, in which two rows of cabins are separated by a parade ground. Near the compound are a freshwater spring probably used by the party, and a site along the Lewis and Clark River where the explorers presumably first landed their canoes.

Location: Northwestern Oregon, about six miles west of Astoria off U.S. Highway 101

Site Office:

Fort Clatsop National Memorial

92343 Fort Clatsop Road
Astoria, OR 97103
ph.: (503) 861-2471
Web site: www.nps.gov/focl/

In the throes of westward expansion at the beginning of the nineteenth century, the United States had a particularly enlightened president in Thomas Jefferson. His educated sense of curiosity turned toward the continent's remaining frontiers, where the United States might at the least establish commercial interests, and perhaps some day establish new territory. The nation was only thirty years old, after all, and its economy—and prestige—burgeoned with each land acquisition and subsequent settlement. The Americans—along with the British and anyone else who saw the potential for prosperity in the Far West—were especially interested in determining whether there existed the fabled Northwest Passage, a direct water route to the Pacific Ocean that would expedite river transportation.

Need for Information About the Wilderness Regions

Despite years of exploration and trade in the western wilderness, the Spanish and French were reluctant to release information about territories that they considered strategic. The best sources for details were the British (especially after they acquired Canada from the French in 1763) and an occasional American trader. Among the latter was Jonathan Carver of Massachusetts, who wrote *Travels in the Interior Parts of North America* about his journey up the Missouri River to the Sioux in 1766—a book Jefferson later read.

When, in 1792, the American Robert Gray approached the continent from the Pacific Ocean, he discovered a major river flowing from the east into the ocean. This bolstered the notion that there existed a continuous water route that, except for a minor portage through the Shining Mountains (the Indian name for the Rockies), would link the transcontinental rivers—in particular the Missouri—to the ocean. Gray was sailing the *Columbia* at the time, and he named the river accordingly.

Jefferson's Promotion of Exploration

As secretary of state in 1793, Jefferson began to promote efforts toward exploration of the lands northwest of the Mississippi River, and Meriwether Lewis, a Virginia acquaintance, had shown a keen interest in participating in any such expedition. In 1801, the new president asked Lewis—who by then had become a captain in the U.S. Army—to become his private secretary. Lewis had been assigned a post in the Northwest Territory, and the expansionist president desired access to Lewis's knowledge of the western United States up to the Mississippi River.

In a way Jefferson thought, like a missionary, of conversion—but cultural rather than religious. He planned to begin with the Indians along the Mississippi River, hoping to assimilate these tribes by inducing them to become farmers and work in peaceful coexistence with their new white neighbors. Jefferson chose his trusted secretary to make the initial foray in an appropriately sensitive manner.

Planning the Lewis and Clark Expedition

Wilderness explorations were actively competitive. In the two-volume work he published in 1801 about his westward trek across Canada nearly a decade earlier, the Scottish trader Alexander Mackenzie advocated a British policy to monopolize the fur and fishing trades in the Far West. He was determined that the Americans should not have access to the Northwest Passage, if such a direct route to the Pacific existed. Jefferson could not ignore such a challenge. Ironically, Mackenzie's chronicle was a boon for the ambitious Americans: In it, Lewis found an itemized record of all the stores and provisions Mackenzie had taken along, including details about gifts to the Indians. However, Mackenzie's description of the portage through the Rockies—"eight hundred and seventeen paces in length"—that led to a Pacific-bound river (now the Mackenzie River) on the west did not prepare Lewis and partner William Clark for the grueling portage they were to experience.

Uncertainty about eventual ownership of the Louisiana Territory accelerated Jefferson's plans. He would risk sending an expedition across Spanish property, but if Spain were to cede the territory to France, as was rumored, the Americans would be trespassing on Napoleon's property—quite a different matter. For Jefferson, it became crucial that the journey proceed while the territory was still Spanish. However, Spain did indeed cede the Loui-

A replica of Fort Clatsop. (Fort Clatsop National Memorial, NPS)

siana Territory to France, an act which, contrary to Jefferson's initial misgivings, enabled the United States to arrange the propitious Louisiana Purchase from France in 1803. With the transaction all of the lands drained by the Missouri River and its tributaries became part of the United States. In practical terms, this meant that Lewis and Clark would be traveling a good deal of the way on U.S. territory after all.

A major contention remained with England, however, over the northern border of the uncharted territory. Jefferson hoped that Lewis and Clark could establish once and for all where the boundary between the western United States and British Canada lay. Jefferson communicated to Congress on January 18, 1803, his intentions concerning the so-called "voyage of discovery." His message included numerous subterfuges; one reason for secrecy undoubtedly was the fact that the Spanish government, still owner of the territory, would consider such an expedition to be a significant trespass on its territory.

Financing the Expedition

As well, Jefferson strictly interpreted the Constitution, and knew that nothing in it would permit the government to sponsor a voyage of discovery in quest of mere knowledge. So he turned to constitutional provisions that allowed appropriations to encourage foreign commerce. Jefferson also set a ludicrously low cost for the expedition, $2,500 to send ten or twelve men on a year-and-a-half journey to cover a round trip of six thousand to eight thousand miles. The unstated fact was that the War Department would be providing, aside from the men, many nonbudgeted provisions. The actual cost of the expedition, never revealed to the public, was somewhere between $40,000 and $60,000. On February 28, 1803, Congress approved with little fanfare Jefferson's voyage of discovery.

Jefferson arranged for the selection of a special corps of men to undertake this important exploration. He wanted a detailed documentation of the journey, from the terrain to the flora, fauna, and natives. The natives were most important, perhaps, as it was these people who would determine the westward progress of U.S. commerce and settlement. A key difference between this first U.S. exploration and later encroachments was the expedition's desire to learn about the Indians, to understand their respective cultures and interactions with each other. Though Lewis and Clark no doubt considered themselves superior to the natives, theirs was an exploratory journey, not one of conquest. The white men considered themselves diplomats, in effect, unlike the later missionaries, mercenaries, and military forces who sought at the very least to control or, in some cases, even supplant the Indians. Ever the diplomat, Jefferson approached the Indians as he would any foreign nation. He advised Lewis:

> In all your intercourse with the natives treat them in the most friendly and conciliatory manner which their own conduct will admit. Allay all jealousies as to the object of your journey, satisfy them of its innocence, make them acquainted with the position, extent, character, peaceable, and commercial dispositions of the U.S., of our wish to be neighborly, friendly, and useful to them, and of our disposition to a commercial intercourse with them. Confer with them on the points most convenient as mutual emporiums and the articles of most desirable interchange for them and us.

Meriwether Lewis left March 15, 1803, for the federal arsenal at Harpers Ferry, Virginia, where he began ordering provisions. Much of the equipment he chose was standard army fare: shoes, stockings, shirts, coats, woolen overalls, blankets, knapsacks, and hunting shirts. The firearms included flintlock muskets, versatile weapons that could take buckshot, birdshot, or single balls. The rifles he selected were new, short-barreled versions of the legendary Kentucky rifle, and were accurate to at least two hundred yards. He included a heavy blunderbuss for its frightening report.

Finalizing the Expedition's Plans

On June 20, 1803, Jefferson wrote up an explicit plan for the expedition, requiring meticulous charting of the river and surrounding land, and insisting that the travelers adhere to the Missouri River until they reached its source. Lewis was to serve as the party's cartographer, mineralogist, ethnologist, botanist, zoologist, meteorologist, and geographer. The immense sum of these duties probably led to Lewis's invitation to William Clark, younger brother of the Indian fighter George Rogers Clark, to join the expedition as co-captain. In fact, Clark served admirably as resident meteorologist and cartographer. Clark also had the advantage of being well known in the Northwest Territory, whereas Lewis was not. The compatibility of the two personalities ensured the expedition's success, as unified leadership was essential.

The cartographer Nicholas King drew on all available information to map out the journey. Even so, he could locate with certainty only three features on the prospective river route: the mouth of the Missouri River, the site of Mandan Indian villages (near present-day Bismarck, North Dakota), and, toward the West Coast, the lower Columbia River.

On October 15, 1803, Lewis met up with Clark at Clarksville, in the Indiana Territory below the Falls of the Ohio, where the two began offering prospective recruits twelve dollars each to sign up. In addition to Clark's slave, York, the first nine enlistees were William E. Bratton, John Colter, Joseph and Reuben Field, Charles Floyd, Jr., George Gibson, Nathaniel H. Pryor, George Shannon, and John Shields. Lewis and Clark continued to recruit from various military posts along the Ohio. A key addition was George Drouillard, son of a Shawnee mother and French Canadian father. Though he was expert at trapping, hunting, and scouting, the expedition hired him as a civilian interpreter: His knowledge of the "language of gesticulation" would be essential for the white men and Indians to communicate with each other.

The Expedition Begins

On March 31, 1804, Lewis and Clark selected the following enlistees to complete their expeditionary force: John Collins, Patrick Gass, Silas Goodrich, Hugh Hall, Thomas P. Howard, Hugh McNeal, John Newman, John Ordway, John Potts, Moses B. Reed, John B. Thompson, William Werner, Joseph Whitehouse, Alexander H. Willard, Richard Windsor, and Peter M. Wiser. The total party thus consisted of Lewis and Clark, York, Drouillard, twenty-two privates and three sergeants; with few adjustments, this was the party that built Fort Clatsop at the westward journey's end nearly two years later. The corps of discovery departed Camp Wood near St. Louis on May 14, 1804.

The expedition's phenomenal documentation of its travels was the first record, pictorial and written, of the western continent. Lewis was particularly adept at enthusiastically capturing his new discoveries on paper. Page after page of his elk-bound journal documents to the minutest detail animals, plants, and peoples which were exotic to the East. Five journals survive—those of Lewis and Clark, and three by other expedition members. Every day was accounted for by at least one of the journals.

After a testy encounter with the intimidating Teton Sioux, who did not want to let the crew continue up the Missouri, the explorers encountered friendlier peoples. The party met the Mandan, Minitari, and Amahami Indians, a concentrated group of mound-dwelling tribes who occupied five villages on the Missouri River. The party spent a reasonably comfortable winter at Fort Mandan, which they built near the villages. There the party prepared a shipment for Jefferson that shared their discoveries of the first 1,600 miles of their journey, including Clark's map of the Missouri, which was unprecedented in its detail.

Their key task during the winter, however, was to assemble facts about the territory that lay ahead. They projected a series of a major landmarks, from the confluence of the Yellowstone and Missouri Rivers, some 220 miles west of Fort Mandan (and 1,850 miles upriver from St. Louis), through the great falls another 350 miles beyond, then the Rocky Mountains and, finally, the Columbia River to take them to the Pacific coast.

Sacagawea and Her Husband Join the Expedition

While with the Mandan, they met Toussaint Charbonneau, a Frenchman whose young wife, Sacagawea, had been taken captive years before from her native Shoshone Indians on the Pacific coast. Lewis and Clark planned on crucial dealings with those Indians to secure horses necessary for crossing the Rockies, so they let Charbonneau join the party as interpreter; Sacagawea would interpret the Shoshone language for the explorers.

The expedition headed upstream once more on April 7, 1805, with six small canoes and two large pirogues to carry them into the vast, uncharted territory. Persistent headwinds on the Missouri slowed the expedition to an average of fifteen miles a day instead of the twenty to twenty-five Lewis and Clark had hoped to achieve. The party arrived at the Yellowstone River on April 26, 1805, a mere thirty miles from where the Indians had advised them it would be.

Lewis and Clark's charted course served them well until June 2, 1805—Clark noted that voyage of discovery had by then traveled more than 2,500 miles up the Missouri from St. Louis—when the expedition reached an unexpected fork in the river. It was not apparent whether they should follow the branch flowing in from the southwest or the branch from the northwest. After further probings, the captains decided on the southwest branch, which turned out to be the correct choice.

The Expedition Reaches the Rockies

Once they had negotiated the series of great falls on the Missouri, Lewis and Clark sought out the Shoshone Indians to secure horses to help with the impending mountain crossing. While the expedition was among the Shoshone, their chief, Cameahwait (Sacagawea's brother), described how the Nez Perce Indians would traverse the mountains from the west to the plains on the east each year to commence their buffalo hunting. Lewis assumed that if the Nez Perce could cross the Rockies so handily, then his men could meet this task. They even had the advantage of an Indian guide who knew the Nez Perce trail. On September 1, the ascent began. What the expedition actually encountered in the Bitterroot Mountains, a chain of the Rockies on the present Montana-Idaho border, was "high rugged mountains in every direction," freezing temperatures and snow, and near starvation. The party emerged from the mountains three weeks later, on September 20. Fortunately for them, the Nez Perce were in the area to provide food and shelter.

The voyage of discovery left the Indians for the final leg down the Clearwater to the Pacific on October 7, 1805. It was on November 7 that Lewis and Clark and their companions finally achieved their long-sought vision: the ocean (actually the inlet called Gray's Bay). The men were overjoyed at this first sighting. During the next month, as they looked for a site to build a winter fort, the incessantly inclement weather tempered their enthusiasm. Clark wrote in his journal:

The sea, which is immediately in front, roars like a repeated rolling thunder and have roared in that way since our arrival on its borders, which is now twenty-four days since we arrived in sight of the Great Western Ocean—I can't say Pacific as since I have seen it, it has been the reverse. Its waters are foaming and perpetually break with immense waves on the sands and rocky coasts, tempestuous and horrible.

Winter in the Northwest

Unfortunately for the group, it was already winter; they had just spent a year and a half traveling through thousands of miles of wilderness, and their reward was to experience several months of Pacific Northwest winter. They were soggy and disenchanted, and the journals were filled with daily laments about rain, chilly weather, and lack of sunshine. The party diligently sought a site for a winter camp, finally settling on a high, protected site on the south side of Gray's Bay about three miles from the ocean and where they thought elk grazed. There was plenty of timber available, and the men began building Fort Clatsop on December 7, 1805, and were settled in by Christmas.

The Fort Clatsop compound comprised two parallel rows of cabins with a twenty-foot-wide parade ground between. On one side were three cabins for the enlisted men; facing these were four cabins housing the captains' quarters, a guardroom, a meat locker, and a room for Charbonneau, Sacagawea, and their infant son. The whole ensemble was about fifty feet square, with gated, log palisades at each end of the parade ground.

The expedition endured increasingly dismal weather at Fort Clatsop. There were only twelve days when it did not rain, the party was reduced to a diet mostly of lean elk and boiled roots, and there was no tobacco or alcohol left for diversion. There was bountiful game, for despite the rain that ruined gunpowder, the hunting parties shot at least 131 elk and 20 deer during the winter. One major task was collecting water from the Pacific and boiling it to extract salt for preserving the game, which otherwise spoiled quickly. The nearby natives, the friendly Clatsop Indians, also traded fish, berries, and roots to the Fort Clatsop residents for other commodities. While the captains refined their maps and diaries, other members replaced ruined clothing by tanning hides and sewing new garments—including 350 pairs of moccasins alone—boiled the seawater for salt, hunted, and fixed broken weapons and tools.

The Expedition Completes Its Work

Though the physical circumstances at the fort were barely tolerable (most of the party fell ill at one point or another), the explorers remained mindful of their scientific mission, venturing out to chart the nearby coastal region and its exotic flora, fauna, and peoples. In all, Lewis and Clark's geographical, ethnological, mineralogical, zoological, botanical, agronomical, and ornithological studies yielded the discovery of 24 Indian tribes, 178 plants, and 122 animals then unknown to the United States and Europe.

The expedition bade farewell to Fort Clatsop on March 23, 1806, nearly two years after its departure from St. Louis. The homeward-bound crew had few regrets about leaving the dreary Pacific coast; six months later they were back in St. Louis.

After Lewis and Clark abandoned Fort Clatsop, the wood buildings quickly began to rot; by the time a homesteader built a house on the site in 1850, only a few logs remained. Local historians had kept an eye on the site, and in 1901 the Oregon Historical Society purchased three acres there. By then, the overgrown area hid all traces of the buildings that had been Fort Clatsop. Historians' continued efforts resulted in the 1955 reconstruction of Fort Clatsop, and in 1958 Congress designated the Fort Clatsop National Memorial on the site. The historical recreation of the fort—including a series of popular "living history" programs enacted by rangers who have studied the expedition journals—could not compensate for the multiple loggings that had cleared the site of vegetation, however; it will take about two hundred more years for the National Park Service's relatively recent plantings to achieve the forested state of the site as Lewis and Clark knew it.

—*Randall J. Van Vynckt*

For Further Information:

Clark, Ella E., and Margot Edmonds. *Sacagawea of the Lewis and Clark Expedition*. Reprint. Berkeley: University of California Press, 1983. Focuses on one of the peripheral but legendary characters of the expedition, the Native American woman who joined Lewis and Clark when they sojourned with the Mandan villagers.

Dillon, Richard. *Meriwether Lewis: A Biography.* Reprint. Santa Cruz, Calif.: Western Tanager Press, 1988. A lively account of one of the expedition's dominant—and ultimately tragic—personalities; a major enigma about Lewis concerns his violent, mysterious death in 1809, and this author opts for murder over suicide.

Fanselow, Julie. *Traveling the Lewis and Clark Trail.* 2d ed. Helena, Mont.: Falcon, 2000. This guidebook is a revised edition of 1994's *A Traveler's Guide to the Lewis and Clark Trail.*

Hawke, David Freeman. *Those Tremendous Mountains: The Story of the Lewis and Clark Expedition.* New York: W. W. Norton, 1980. A well-documented and compelling account, full of anecdotes and passages from the expedition's journal entries. Illustrations include selections from Lewis's journal, later artists' interpretations of the expedition's botanical and zoological discoveries, and renderings by nineteenth century artists of the encountered landscapes and Indian life and lore.

Lavender, David. *The Way to the Western Sea: Lewis and Clark Across the Continent.* Reprint. New York: Anchor Books, 1990. Provides an evenhanded, authoritative, and detailed narrative with fascinating insights into the many personalities involved with the venture.

Snyder, Gerald S. *In the Footsteps of Lewis and Clark.* Washington, D.C.: National Geographic Society, 1970. Documents the author's personal experience of Lewis and Clark's route. Facts about the original expedition are interspersed with conjecture by the author, his family, and current sources met along the way.

Other Historic Sites

Bonneville Dam Historic District

Location: Columbia River, Bonneville, Multnomah County (also in Washington)

Relevant issues: Science and technology

Statement of significance: Built in the 1930's by the federal government to raise and divert the Columbia River to generate hydroelectric power, the dam represented a unique engineering challenge for a diversion/overflow dam; it was the first major structure built with a "hydraulic drop" capable of developing more than 500,000 kilowatts of electric power. Other structures in the district are the No. 1 Powerhouse, the Navigation Lock, the Fishways, and the Fish Hachery.

Jacksonville Historic District

Location: Jacksonville, Jackson County

Relevant issues: Western expansion

Statement of significance: Founded as a mining town in 1852, Jacksonville is a mid-nineteenth century inland commercial town significant for its magnificent group of surviving unaltered commercial and residential buildings. The town was the principal financial center of southern Oregon until it was bypassed by the railroad.

Lightship Wal-604 "Columbia"

Location: Astoria, Clatsop County

Relevant issues: Naval history

Statement of significance: The 1950 Lightship Wal-604 (*Columbia*), along with its sister Wal-605, is the best representative of the last class of lightships built under the auspices of the U.S. Coast Guard. Although these vessels closely resembled earlier lightships in external appearance, they were a distinct departure in terms of the rest of their construction. Of the lightships built after 1939, Wal-604 retains the best integrity and is associated with the nationally significant station off the Columbia River Bar. It was retired in 1979 as the last Columbia station lightship, as well as the last on the Pacific Coast.

Sunken Village Archaeological Site

Location: Portland, Multnomah County

Relevant issues: American Indian history

Statement of significance: Sunken Village is the archaeological remains of a Chinook settlement (1250-1750 C.E.) which is extraordinarily well preserved. The Chinooks who lived there were a cosmopolitan people and practiced a successful, complex hunter-gatherer economy that permitted densely occupied villages and extensive trade relations.

Wallowa Lake Site

Location: Joseph, Wallowa County
Relevant issues: American Indian history
Statement of significance: This site, commanding an excellent view of a high, glaciated lake and mountain country, preserves a traditional Nez Perce ancestral campground associated with religious and cultural values that have persisted for more than the century that has elapsed since the band of nontreaty Nez Perce led by Young Chief Joseph was driven out.

Pennsylvania

Pittsburgh. (Corbis)

History of Pennsylvania

Even though Pennsylvania is located in the northeastern part of the United States and is called a mid-Atlantic state, it is not on the Atlantic Ocean, as are Delaware, New Jersey, and New York. It has access to the Atlantic Ocean's important shipping routes from the Delaware River, which marks Pennsylvania's eastern boundary. New York is east and north of it, New Jersey east, and Delaware east and south. Maryland borders it to the south, and West Virginia lies both south and west of it. Its western boundary is eastern Ohio.

Located in the middle of the original thirteen colonies, Pennsylvania is known as the Keystone State. The state is quite mountainous, with the Appalachian Mountains running through much of it. In the east are the Pocono Mountains and to the south the Blue Ridge. These mountains have more than two hundred lakes, the largest of which is Lake Wallenpaupack in northeastern Pennsylvania, between Milford and Scranton.

Early History

Humans lived in Pennsylvania as much as twelve thousand years ago, probably drawn there by its network of rivers. Besides the Delaware, Susquehanna, Schuylkill, and Lackawanna Rivers in the east, the Monongahela, Ohio, Juniata, and Allegheny Rivers run through the western part of the state. The northwestern section of Pennsylvania borders on Lake Erie, one of the five Great Lakes. These waterways afforded the earliest settlers mobility, food, and water.

Among the people who originally inhabited the area were Algonquian, Delaware, Erie, Lenape, Monongahela, and Susquehannock Indians. The state's Native American population in the 1990's of about fourteen thousand were mostly descendants of the Algonquians.

The first Europeans in the area were Dutch explorers Cornelius Jacobsen Mey, who sailed into the Delaware River in 1614, and Cornelius Hendrickson, who, in 1615, sailed up the Delaware to its junction with the Schuylkill, near modern Philadelphia. By 1638, Swedish immigrants had built the first European settlement, New Sweden, establishing Fort New Gothenburg on Tinicum Island south of present-day Philadelphia. The Dutch captured New Sweden in 1655. In 1664 the British took it from the Dutch. Shortly thereafter, in 1681, King Charles II of England granted William Penn's father the area which today is Pennsylvania. The following year, William Penn founded the Pennsylvania colony and the city of Philadelphia, after making peace with the American Indians who lived in the region.

The Importance of Philadelphia

Pennsylvania lay midway between the New England colonies and those in the South. When official business was to be transacted, Philadelphia, a well-developed colonial city, was the logical meeting place. Benjamin Franklin had settled there in 1723 and established a library in 1731. The State House, later renamed Independence Hall, provided a good venue for delegates from the other colonies. Its famed bell, later known as the Liberty Bell, was placed in its tower in 1753.

England was engaged in war against France during the period immediately before the Revolutionary War. To finance the war, the English raised the colonies' taxes. The outcry against taxation without representation became strident. Beginning in 1774, the leaders of the thirteen original colonies met in Philadelphia. In 1775, they named George Washington to head the Continental Army, and on July 4, 1776, they approved the Declaration of Independence, which was read publicly four days later.

In effect, this declaration began England's war against the colonies. Although they were clearly the underdogs in this conflict, the colonists ultimately prevailed. England surrendered in 1781 and signed a peace treaty in 1783. A Constitutional Convention was called and met in Philadelphia in 1787, out of which the United States Constitution, ratified on December 12, 1787, evolved. Pennsylvania became the second of the United States. Philadelphia, because of its central location, was the capital of the country from 1790 to 1800.

Pennsylvania's Growth

From 1732, although England laid claim to the whole of Pennsylvania, the French were building forts in the western part of Penn's land grant. Conflicts over the ownership of western Pennsylvania resulted in a war between England and France, and it was the financing of this war that led indirectly to the Revolutionary War.

By 1763 England controlled all of Pennsylvania. The English raised Fort Pitt beside the Monongahela River, where modern Pittsburgh stands. This area, because of its geographical isolation, was slower to develop than the eastern region of Penn's grant, but its rivers and Lake Erie provided it with the potential to grow quickly.

The Pennsylvania colony was quite progressive. It had a circulating library as early as 1731 and a volunteer fire department by 1736. The first hospital in the colonies opened in Philadelphia in 1751. With the discovery of bituminous coal near Pittsburgh in 1759 and anthracite coal in the Wyoming Valley in 1762, ready sources of power became available. This, combined with navigable waterways throughout the state, led to rapid development. The state decreed in 1780 that no black born in Pennsylvania would be a slave. It remained a free state throughout its existence.

By 1812 steamboats transported people and goods down the Ohio River. Canals and roads were being built. In 1829 the state's first commercial railroad was functioning. The state became a trading center. In 1859 the first commercially successful oil well in the United States was drilled at Titusville in western Pennsylvania.

With plentiful oil, coal, and iron ore available in the western part of the state, it was clear that steel manufacturing would become a major enterprise in and around Pittsburgh, where the first steel mill was established in 1873. Later the Bethlehem Steel Company was established in the eastern part of the state.

The Civil War

A free state since its inception, Pennsylvania was a staunch supporter of the Union during the Civil War. Many towns in the state had, since the early 1800's, been significant waystations along the Underground Railroad, an informal complex of safe havens for slaves escaping from the South and heading to either New England or Canada. Safe houses throughout Pennsylvania offered shelter and food to runaway slaves.

Following President Abraham Lincoln's call for volunteers to fight in the war, Pennsylvanians, in

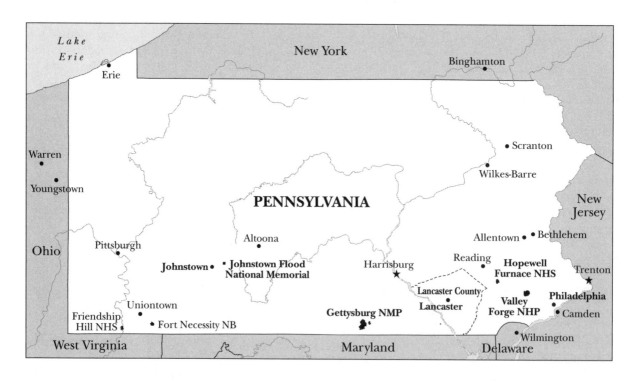

two weeks, created twenty-five regiments to fight against the Confederate forces. A total of more than 340,000 men from Pennsylvania served in the Union forces between 1861 and 1865.

General Robert E. Lee's army invaded Pennsylvania in 1863. As Lee made his incursions into the state, the Army of the Potomac stood between his army and Washington, D.C., in an attempt to protect the nation's capital. On July 1, 1863, the two armies met outside Gettysburg in the southern part of the state and, for three days, engaged in the bloodiest battle of the Civil War, leaving more than fifty thousand dead or wounded soldiers on the battlefield. This battle was the turning point in the war, although before it ended, Confederate forces attacked Chambersburg in July, 1864.

Pennsylvania's People

Most Pennsylvanians are descendants of early settlers from Europe. More than 70 percent of all Pennsylvanians live in cities, chief among them Philadelphia, Pittsburgh, Allentown, Easton, Bethlehem, Scranton, Lancaster, Williamsport, Erie, and Harrisburg, the state's capital since 1812. Nearly four million Pennsylvanians live on farms or in small towns, giving the state the largest rural population in the nation.

The earliest European settlers were from Germany, France, the Netherlands, Scandinavia, and Britain. Immigrants from Ireland arrived in the 1840's. In the 1880's, people began arriving in large numbers from central Europe, notably Czechoslovakia, Poland, and Russia.

Unique among Pennsylvanians are the Pennsylvania Dutch, German immigrants who live mostly in Lancaster County. These Amish farmers lead simple lives, eschewing electricity, telephones, and automobiles.

About 9 percent of Pennsylvanians are of African American descent. Some lived there as free men before the Civil War, but many flooded into Pennsylvania after the war and again during World Wars I and II, when the defense industries offered them ready work.

The Pennsylvania Economy

About four million Pennsylvanians work in such service industries as banking, insurance, and retail. John Wanamaker established the first American department store in Philadelphia in 1876, mostly to serve visitors to the United States Bicentennial Exposition, which was held in Philadelphia's Fairmount Park.

Manufacturing industries, mainly of steel, food products, and chemicals, employ almost one million people. Another hundred thousand work on farms. Mining, which was once a major industry, now, because of mechanization, employs around twenty thousand miners. Philadelphia, Pittsburgh, and Erie are thriving ports that employ many people, and Hershey has the world's largest chocolate factory. Tourism, which brings in ten billion dollars annually, also contributes significantly to the state's economy.

Dairy products are the leading farm product. The state's leading agricultural crop is mushrooms. Pennsylvania also has a large timber industry that produces wood for building.

—*R. Baird Shuman*

Broad Street, Philadelphia

Date: Academy of Music opened in 1857; Pennsylvania Academy of Fine Arts built in 1871

Relevant issues: Art and architecture, cultural history

Significance: First built as a prestigious residential area, Broad Street is now home to several famous cultural and historical institutions, including the Pennsylvania Academy of Fine Arts (the oldest art museum and school in the country) and the Academy of Music (the oldest musical auditorium still in use in the country).

Location: Stretches twelve miles running north-south across the north side of Philadelphia

Site Offices:

Academy of Music
Broad and Locust Streets
Philadelphia, PA 19102
ph.: (215) 893-1935

Pennsylvania Academy of Fine Arts
Broad and Cherry Streets
Philadelphia, PA 19102
ph.: (215) 972-7600

Across the north end of Philadelphia stretches Broad Street, named after its original plan to be one hundred feet wide. In its early days, the street was only a few blocks long, but in the years following the American Revolution, it was extended to reach 12 miles, the second-longest straight street in the country (only topped by Chicago's Western Avenue at 23.5 miles). In the latter half of the nineteenth century, Broad Street was Philadelphia's most glamorous residential area. Since then, it has evolved into a mecca of cultural and historical institutions. Two of its oldest and most important historical sites are the Pennsylvania Academy of Fine Arts and the Academy of Music.

Early History

Although the Pennsylvania Academy of Fine Arts as it stands today was not built until 1871, its origins date back to 1805. At that time, Philadelphia was beginning a transition from rural country town to thriving urban community. During the summer of that year, artist Charles Willson Peale had the idea to build a fine arts center that would display valuable pieces of art, instruct students, and weave the fine arts discipline into the Philadelphia community. He wrote a letter to Thomas Jefferson explaining the need for such an institution, and later that year brought together a group of seventy-one men—only three of them artists—to organize the project. George Clyner, a signer of the Declaration of Independence, was elected academy president, and the group began efforts to raise funds.

The first home to the academy was a building at Philadelphia's Tenth and Chestnut Streets. Designed by architect John Dorsey and opened in 1806, the building was a classical structure that initially displayed mostly European paintings. In these early days, the academy also housed such pieces as Benjamin West's *Death on the Pale Horse* and Washington Allston's *Dead Man Restored to Life by Touching the Bones of the Prophet Elisha*, both of which required the building to be mortgaged for their purchase. Other work on display included paintings by Thomas Scully, William Rush, and Gilbert Stuart.

The Academy's Art School

Although its collections grew rapidly, the academy's art school was slow to start. In 1812, a group of twenty-four distinguished painters, sculptors, architects, and engravers was organized to attract students and establish the art school academia. Just as it is today, the art school's early curriculum was composed of drawing, sculpture, painting, anatomy and perspective, and drawing from casts of ancient sculpture. Especially popular was its portrait class, as portrait painting provided many academy students with their income. In 1844, the academy's board of directors granted women artists exclusive use of the statue gallery at certain times of the day. By the 1880's, women students were considered equal in status to men.

In 1845, the academy suffered from a severe fire that badly damaged its structure and a part of its collection. The building was reconstructed with the same foundation and floor plans and reopened three years later. However, as the academy's collections and student body began to grow, the building became cramped for space. In addition, a severe storm had struck in 1870, damaging many of the gallery skylights. Shortly after, the board decided to sell the building, and for seven years the academy housed its treasures and taught its classes in nearby rented quarters.

In 1871, the architectural firm of Furness and Hewitt was commissioned to design a third building for the academy. One of its principal architects, Frank Furness, had already been credited with the design of most of Philadelphia's civic buildings including libraries, hospitals, banks, churches, university buildings, and railroad stations. Furness had also designed many homes for Philadelphia's notable citizens.

"Fearless" Frank Furness

After serving in the Union army during the Civil War, "Fearless" Frank Furness completed his architectural studies and took permanent residence in his hometown of Philadelphia. He began his career in 1866 with the design of Philadelphia's Unitarian Church of Germantown. Influenced by such contemporaries as Richard Morris Hunt, Violletle Duc, and William Burges, his work was characterized by a wide mixture of styles, colors, forms, scales, textures, and materials. During the time of Philadelphia's great cultural growth, Furness was one of its principal artistic contributors.

Furness, along with his partner, George Hewitt, designed the new Pennsylvania Academy of Fine Arts in a fashionable High Victorian manner on the corner of Broad and Cherry Streets. The spacious structure, built of incombustible construction materials, provided plenty of room for both the museum and art school. The building was made of brick, stone, iron, and glass, with wood added only where necessary. Specially decorated arches, columns, lintels, beams, girders, and trusses stood as a reflection of structural expressionism and a signature of the Furness design. The building was ready to open in 1876, just in time for Philadelphia's celebration of the nation's centennial.

Thomas Eakins

With the grand opening of the third academy building came realist painter and modern thinker Thomas Eakins, who began teaching in 1876. Eakins was appointed director in 1882, whereupon he began several controversial practices that led to his dismissal four years later. Such practices included allowing female students to work from live nude models. (Male students had been required to work with live nudes since the 1850's.) During this period, the academy's collection was upgraded by managing director Harrison S. Morris, who supervised purchases including Winslow Homer's *Fox Hunt* and many fine examples of American Impressionism. Also during this period, the academy instructed such students as Robert Henri, Henry O. Tanner, John Marin, and Mary Cassatt.

Over time, the academy underwent many changes in decor as styles constantly evolved. By the start of the twentieth century, much of its Victorian appearance had been altered. Although its collection grew and improved through the years, the building itself did just the opposite. A hundred years of neglect, dirt, and sloppy stylistic revisions left the academy in poor condition. In 1966, the building underwent a thorough cleaning of the exterior. Then in 1973, the academy's board of trustees decided to close the building for two years in order to modernize it and restore its interior to Furness's original Victorian design.

Modern Restoration of the Academy

The restoration turned out to be much less complicated than anyone thought. Most of the original decor was revealed simply by removing layer after layer of dirt, paint, and wall coverings. The arched ceiling was stripped to expose its original white brick. The grand stone stairhall and the remaining mosaic tile floor underneath it were uncovered and carefully cleaned to reveal a sparkling surface that reflects light and considerably brightens the interior. When Furness designed the academy, he placed much emphasis on natural light. During the restoration, the ceiling was returned to its original design—a huge glass skylight sprinkled with silverleaf stars. Once again, sunlight poured in, flooding the academy with natural brightness.

Along with the restoration, the academy underwent an extensive updating of its facilities. Air-conditioning, air cleaning, and ultraviolet filtration systems were installed, along with electronic security and fire detection devices. New lighting systems were added. The old water-powered freight elevator was replaced with a new passenger elevator, and a museum shop was built. All these modernizations were made without any violation of the building's design. The restoration completed in 1976, the academy once again opened its doors—this time to celebrate the academy's centennial and the nation's bicentennial.

Today, the academy still has one of the largest, most widely known and respected collections of American art. In 1955, over one hundred of its works traveled under the sponsorship of the U.S. Information Agency to Madrid, Florence, Copenhagen, Brussels, Innsbruck, and Stockholm. As a whole, the collection can be seen as a historical expression of Philadelphia's artistic heritage. For example, the earliest American paintings reflect an influence of the newest styles emanating from London. The stylistic demands of the 1790's, when Philadelphia was the nation's capital and portrait painting was highly competitive, are also reflected in art of this time. The collection is also marked by the many gifts, bequests, and purchases made during the prosperous last quarter of the nineteenth century.

The Pennsylvania Academy of Fine Arts is the oldest art institution in the country. Although it has undergone many physical changes and changes in its collection, its founding principles still remain as written in the academy's charter: "to promote the cultivation of the fine arts in the United States of America."

Other Cultural Centers

Another institution of culture and tradition on Broad Street is the Academy of Music. Built on the corner of Broad and Locust Streets, the academy is the oldest musical auditorium still in use in the country. A celebrated historical landmark, the academy remains one of the busiest halls in the world, hosting many community functions and cultural activities.

In the early 1850's, Philadelphia was quickly becoming one of the most important cultural centers in the country. For years, citizens had worried that Philadelphia's lack of an opera hall caused them to lag behind the Europeans culturally. Attempts to build such a hall were made as far back as 1839, but not until 1855 was a stock offering initiated and an official charter drawn up. The charter, in addition to setting construction and management guidelines, led to a national architectural competition for the design assignment. The Philadelphia firm of Napoleon Le Brun and Gustavus Rungé was selected to design the academy.

Although the center of the city would have been an obvious location, the founders decided to build in Philadelphia's residential section. By avoiding the cultural heart of the budding metropolis, the academy would escape the noise from carriage and horse traffic as well as cattle and sheep herding. After careful consideration, the corner of Broad and Locust Streets was chosen as a location. The architects agreed to leave the exterior a simple brownstone; it was designed so a marble facade could be added later, when funds were available, but the brownstone has always remained unaltered. The exterior is embellished with red brick, painted cast iron, reinforcement arches, and rectangular features in the style of an Italian opera house.

The architects paid much more attention to the academy's interior, emphasizing convenience and efficiency, along with a luxurious decor. The auditorium is shaped like an open horseshoe to provide greater visibility for the side balcony seats. The balconies are recessed upward and supported by Corinthian columns; the first balcony is decorated with stylized medallions. A five thousand-pound crystal chandelier, originally lit by two hundred forty gas burners, hangs from a frescoed ceiling. Painted on the ceiling are allegorical figures representing poetry, music, comedy, tragedy, and dance. The hall is decorated with carved and gilded wood sculptures and four elliptical panels containing cherubs that depict the four seasons.

Restoration of the Academy

With the exception of occasional modernizations, the Academy of Music did not undergo a major restoration until the 1950's. To raise funds for the improvements, a Restoration Fund Office was established. The office's biggest project, the Academy of Music Anniversary Concert and Ball, has since become one of the country's most successful annual fund-raisers. Its proceeds have funded such projects as conservation of the academy's wood sculptures and ceiling murals, and the renovation, soundproofing, and carpeting of the ballroom. The academy also installed a new main house curtain and two elevators that make all levels of the auditorium accessible to the handicapped. In 1957, the huge chandelier was rewired and fitted with an electric-powered winch. This change allowed the chandelier to be lowered in five minutes. Before the rewiring, it required four hours and twelve people to lower it by hand.

The main hall of the academy, which seats 2,929 people, has been constantly in use for operas, concerts, ballets, and other events. The ballroom has primarily been the site of the Philadelphia Orchestra's Chamber Music Series, but it is also available for social and civic functions. In fact, many United States presidents have visited the Academy—in 1872, Ulysses S. Grant was nominated there for his second term. Grover Cleveland even held his wedding dinner in the auditorium. In 1889, Philadelphia's first indoor football game was held there also, after the temporary installment of a wooden floor.

The academy's basement has also played a historical role. When the academy first opened in 1857, its basement was an elegant restaurant complete with drawing rooms and Victorian decor. During World War II, the restaurant was turned into the Stage Door Canteen, a gathering place for military men and women. The Canteen, open until October, 1945, served refreshments and presented big-name entertainers including Abbott and Costello, Duke Ellington, Alfred Lunt, and Frank Sinatra.

After the Grand Opening Ball on February 25, 1857, the academy became home to the American premieres of many now-famous operas including

Giuseppe Verdi's *Il trovatore* (1852), *La traviata* (1853), and *Aïda* (1871); Charles Gounod's *Faust* (1859); and Ambroise Thomas's *Hamlet* (1868). Since its founding in 1900, the Philadelphia Orchestra Association has owned and operated the academy. The academy also serves other cultural institutions including the Pennsylvania Ballet, the Opera Company of Philadelphia, and the All Star/Forum. The list of famous artists who have performed there is long: Igor Stravinsky, Gustav Mahler, Peter Tchaikovsky, Aaron Copland, Richard Strauss, Sergei Rachmaninoff, Enrico Caruso, Luciano Pavarotti, Joan Sutherland, Artur Rubenstein, Vladimir Horowitz, Isaac Stern, and many others. The Academy of Music was designated a historical landmark in 1963.

Both the Pennsylvania Academy of Fine Arts and the Academy of Music play an integral part in Philadelphia's cultural history. As the oldest American institutions of their kind still in use, their influence has made Broad Street a cultural catalyst not only for Philadelphia, but for the whole country as well. —*Cynthia L. Langston*

For Further Information:

Alotta, Robert I. *Street Names of Philadelphia*. Philadelphia: Temple University Press, 1975. A unique street-by-street directory of Philadelphia, describing each street, explaining its location, and giving a brief history of it.

Boyle, Richard J. "The Pennsylvania Academy of the Fine Arts: Its Founding and Early Years." *Antiques*, March, 1982. A fairly detailed essay that includes several photos of the academy's famous early paintings.

Burt, Nathaniel. *The Perennial Philadelphians: The Anatomy of An American Aristocracy*. Reprint. Philadelphia: University of Pennsylvania Press, 1999. Includes several references to the academies in its historical discussion of the city.

Goodyear, Frank H., Jr. "American Paintings at the Pennsylvania Academy." *Antiques*, March, 1982. Traces the history of the academy's renowned American collection and includes several photographs.

Klein, Philip S., and Ari Hoogenboom. *A History of Philadelphia*. New York: McGraw-Hill, 1973. Makes many references to both the Pennsylvania Academy of Fine Arts and the Academy of Music.

Myers, Hyman. "The Three Buildings of the Pennsylvania Academy." *Antiques*, March, 1982. Describes the history of each academy building, emphasizing interior decor and exterior design.

Weinberg, Ephraim. "The Art School of the Pennsylvania Academy." *Antiques*, March, 1982. Tells the story of the art school, its curriculum, and its accomplishments.

Edgar Allan Poe National Historic Site

Date: Designated a National Historic Site in August, 1980

Relevant issues: Literary history

Significance: This was the home of Edgar Allan Poe, his wife Virginia, and her mother during part of their stay in Philadelphia. It has been preserved as a memorial to a great American literary genius. It gives visitors a vivid impression of residential architecture and domestic lifestyle in a northern American city in the 1800's.

Location: 530 North 7th Street, near the corner of Spring Garden Street, just north of Philadelphia's Center City and Independence Hall

Site Office:
Edgar Allan Poe National Historic Site
National Park Service
532 North Seventh Street
Philadelphia, PA 19123
ph.: (215) 597-8780
Web site: www.nps.gov/edal/
e-mail: INDE_Poe_House@nps.gov

Edgar Allan Poe is believed to have moved into this house sometime between the fall of 1842 and June of 1843 and lived there until April of 1844. It was chosen by the U.S. Congress as the nation's official memorial to the man many consider to be America's greatest literary genius.

Poe's Tragic Life and Legacy

Edgar Allan Poe's short life was characterized by tragedy, poverty, anxiety, and depression. His father deserted the family when Poe was an infant. His mother, a beautiful actress, died when Edgar was only two. He was raised, but never legally adopted, by John Allan, a wealthy Richmond, Vir-

Edgar Allan Poe National Historic Site. (Independence National Historical Park)

After Virginia died in 1847, Poe became increasingly despondent. He was reputed to have become an alcoholic and died in a delirium in a Baltimore hospital at the age of forty.

Poe lived in Philadelphia for six years (1838-1844), during which time he attained his greatest successes as editor and critic and published some of his most famous tales, including "The Gold Bug," "The Fall of the House of Usher," "The Tell-Tale Heart," and "The Murders in the Rue Morgue." Of Poe's several Philadelphia homes, only the three-story brick house at 7th and Spring Garden Streets has survived.

Poe was a genius who is credited with inventing the detective story, defining the form of the modern short story, and revolutionizing modern poetry through his influence on the French Symbolists. His influence extended worldwide to such famous writers as the creator of Sherlock Holmes, Sir Arthur Conan Doyle (1859-1930), science-fiction writers Jules Verne (1828-1905) and H. G. Wells (1866-1946), French poet and critic Charles Baudelaire (1821-1867), Russian novelists Fyodor Dostoevski (1821-1881) and Vladimir Nabokov (1899-1977), and the surrealistic Austrian writer Franz Kafka (1883-1924), among countless others.

The National Historic Site

The Edgar Allan Poe National Historic Site consists of a complex of three buildings. Two serve as a visitors' center and entrance to the site. Ranger-guided tours begin here. This area contains exhibits, an audiovisual program, and a gift shop. The National Park Service has not furnished the main house because of the absence of information describing the contents during Poe's occupancy. It is easy to imagine that the building is haunted by the ghostly characters of the author's creation. Visitors are shown the gloomy cellar reminiscent of the one depicted in "The Black Cat," a horror story written while Poe lived here.

ginia, businessman whose philistine nature was incompatible with that of his hypersensitive, imaginative, and artistic ward. By the age of eighteen, Poe, accustomed to an environment of culture and comfort, had quarreled with Allan and was forced to fend for himself. For the rest of his life he led a hand-to-mouth existence as editor, critic, lecturer, and freelance writer. He married his first cousin, Virginia Clemm, when she was only thirteen years old; her mother Maria Clemm, who had a small pension, became part of the Poe household.

Poe's hard life and many disappointments undoubtedly affected everything he wrote. His volatile temperament made it difficult for him to hold down editorial jobs, which were poorly paid anyway. He received only one hundred dollars for his famous short story "The Gold Bug" and only ten dollars for "The Raven," which is world-famous and has been called the most perfectly constructed poem ever written. He became a harsh but incisive and influential critic and lecturer. His poems and stories reflect his morbid outlook on life. As an editor, however, he had learned that the public delights in reading about the dark side of human nature, which explains why newspapers are still full of stories about crime and why Poe's stories of murder, insanity, premature burial, and other horrors remain popular today.

The park is open daily from 9:00 A.M. to 5:00 P.M. during the summer months. The rest of the year it is open Wednesday through Sunday from 9:00 A.M. to 5:00 P.M. It is closed on Christmas, Thanksgiving, and New Year's Day. There is no admission charge.

Other Places to Visit

The Poe House is located near the center of Philadelphia, which holds many historical attractions, including Independence Hall, where the Declaration of Independence was signed, and the Liberty Bell pavilion. The National Park Service also maintains the Thaddeus Kosciuszko National Memorial, where Kosciuszko resided during the winter of 1797 to 1798. Kosciuszko (1746-1817), a world-famous Polish patriot, came to assist the Colonials in the Revolutionary War. In 1783, Congress promoted him to brigadier general in the Continental Army and passed a resolution recognizing "his long, faithful, and meritorious service." This typical eighteenth century house is about 1.75 miles from the Poe House.   —*Bill Delaney*

For Further Information:

Baudelaire, Charles. *Baudelaire on Poe.* State College, Pa.: Bald Eagle Press, 1952. Baudelaire, who spent fourteen years translating Poe's tales into French, was the person most influential in spreading Poe's fame throughout Europe.

Meyers, Jeffrey. *Edgar Allan Poe: His Life and Legacy.* New York: Charles Scribner's Sons, 1992. Meyers puts Poe's life and literature in perspective and shows Poe's influence on subsequent writers.

Poe, Edgar Allan. *Complete Tales and Poems of Edgar Allan Poe.* New York: Vintage Books, 1975. Contains all of the imaginative works for which Poe is best known throughout the world.

_____. *Essays and Reviews.* New York: Literary Classics of the United States, 1984. This beautiful book contains the most complete collection of Poe's essays and reviews, including the classic "The Rationale of Verse" and "The Philosophy of Composition."

Silverman, Kenneth. *Edgar A. Poe: Mournful and Never-ending Remembrance.* New York: Harper Collins, 1991. Silverman emphasizes the effect of Poe's mother's untimely death on his literary works. Clarifies many questions about Poe's life and works.

Gettysburg

Date: Battle fought July 1-3, 1863; established as a National Park in 1895

Relevant issues: Civil War, military history

Significance: Gettysburg National Military Park is a 3,802-acre site that includes the entire U.S. Civil War battlefield of Gettysburg.

Location: Manufacturing borough and seat of Adams County in southern Pennsylvania, approximately thirty miles west-southwest of York

Site Office:
Gettysburg National Military Park
97 Taneytown Road
Gettysburg, PA 17325
ph.: (717) 334-1124
Web site: www.nps.gov/gett/

Gettysburg sits at a geographical crossroads, unspectacular to the casual observer passing through. Even so, the quiet town has played a significant role in the history of the United States. For three days in July, 1863, it was the site of a U.S. Civil War clash that most scholars call the greatest battle ever to take place in the Western Hemisphere. Along with the simultaneous fall of Vicksburg, Mississippi, the Battle of Gettysburg marked the beginning of the end for Confederate hopes—the turning point that led to the Union victory in 1865.

The Civil War

The Civil War moved into its third year in 1863, progressing much as it had the previous two years, with a series of Confederate victories over Union forces still trying to find the right combination of leadership and strategy. Things were starting to change on the western front, however, as Union general Ulysses S. Grant had surrounded Vicksburg, threatening to topple the final major Confederate stronghold on the Mississippi River.

Confederate general Robert E. Lee's Army of Northern Virginia remained dominant on the eastern front, defeating Joseph Hooker's Army of the Potomac in early May at Chancellorsville, Virginia, despite being outnumbered. Lee was confident when he met with Confederate president Jefferson Davis in mid-May to discuss the Vicksburg situation. Though Davis wanted to send some of his eastern troops to Mississippi to try to dislodge Grant, Lee had other ideas, instead convincing the Confederate president to allow him to launch an attack into Union territory. The attack would serve two purposes. Hooker's troops still sat on the Rappahannock River threatening the Confederate capital of Richmond, Virginia; Lee wanted to drive him north to defend his own capital. Lee also felt that if he succeeded, Grant would be forced to abandon Vicksburg in order to protect northern soil.

Events Leading to the Battle of Gettysburg

Confederate movements toward the Pennsylvania state line began in June with a series of successful skirmishes led by Jeb Stuart's cavalry. Lee's seventy thousand men moved northward steadily, split into three separate corps: one led by James Longstreet, another by A. P. Hill, and the last by Richard Ewell. Hooker was unsure of Lee's intentions as he marched east of the Confederate forces. He would never have a chance to uncover those intentions, however; U.S. president Abraham Lincoln replaced him on June 27 with George Gordon Meade.

Lee's three corps closed in on Gettysburg as July 1, 1863, dawned. Some of his troops had actually passed through the town four days earlier, but found few supplies. Now, however, a rumor circulated that somewhere in the town was a storehouse of shoes, invaluable to Confederate soldiers who had gone barefoot for months. As the rebel infantry under Harry Heth sat just to the north of the town, Union cavalrymen led by John Buford coincidentally approached from the south. Throughout June, Northern officials were unsure of the exact whereabouts of the main Confederate army—when townspeople told Buford that Confederates were in the area, he sent scouts north and west to assess their forces.

When they returned the scouts told Buford that there were as many as fifty thousand troops in the area; his force of only three thousand could be easily overwhelmed. Alarmed, he sent word to Meade and to the closest infantry unit, led by Major General John F. Reynolds, eleven miles to the south. Meade debated whether to meet Lee at Gettysburg, or to assume a defensive posture and wait. Lee's scouts had been in the area as well; based on their reports, he surmised that the main Union force lay due south of Gettysburg, and decided it would be a perfect place to meet with them. When Meade came to the same decision, the stage was set—some

140,000 troops in various locations headed for the small town of only 2,400.

Contact Between Confederate and Union Forces

The first contact occurred early on July 1—Heth's roughly 7,500 troops met 1,200 of Buford's cavalry at Herr's Ridge north and west of town. Though thoroughly outnumbered, the Northern cavalrymen were equipped with repeater rifles that were faster and easier to load than the muskets of their Southern counterparts. This advantage bought them a little time, but they were eventually driven back a mile to another plot of high ground on McPherson's Ridge. After two more hours, the Union situation was becoming desperate. With no help from Reynolds's infantry, the Union troops were in danger of being completely overrun, effectively ending the battle before it ever started. The reinforcements arrived at 10 A.M., just as the Confederates were beginning to break through; Reynolds himself was killed shortly after his arrival.

Abner Doubleday found himself in control after Reynolds's death, and also in a dangerous situation. Two major portions of the full Confederate force led by Richard Ewell and Jubal T. Early had arrived; after two more hours of stubborn fighting they sent Doubleday retreating. With the town now in rebel hands, Union troops regathered on the heights of Culp's Hill and Cemetery Hill to the south of town. The Confederates had a prime opportunity to crush what remained of the federal force before the rest of the help could arrive. Couriers brought word of another possible Union disaster to Meade, who pressed on with reinforcements.

Lee saw the chance for the kill, and consulted his field generals on whether they were willing to attack the heights. Hill reported that his troops had clashed with the Union cavalry all morning and afternoon; they were exhausted and nearly out of ammunition. Ewell was nervous that some of the Union reinforcements had stationed artillery on the high ground; he too opted against battle. Thus, fighting on the first day ended—casualties totaled 5,400 for the Union and 5,600 for the Confederates.

Throughout the night, reinforcements for both sides arrived in droves. James Longstreet's men completed the reunification of the Confederate forces, while Meade and the rest of the Union army

The Gettysburg Battlefield. (PhotoDisc)

arrived and dug into the hills for another day of fighting. By July 2, there would be 65,000 Confederate and 80,000 Union troops at Gettysburg. By the end of the conflict, more than one-third of them would be casualties.

The Armies Prepare for Battle

By morning, Union troops had settled into a fishhook formation south and east of town. They were surrounded by high ground, hills known as Big and Little Round Tops to their left and Culp's and Cemetery Hills to their right. This time, it was Lee who chose the offensive; he would try to occupy the heights. Lee ordered Ewell to attack the right flank at Culp's Hill, while leaving Longstreet's men to take the Round Tops.

To find his best route of attack, Lee sent a scout toward the Union left flank early in the morning. To his surprise, the scout was able to ride around the south end of the Union line without meeting a single soldier. The area north of the Round Tops was also lightly guarded— if the Confederates gained superiority, they could set up artillery and blast down on the Union troops, destroying them. At 9 A.M., Lee ordered a protesting Longstreet to assemble his troops for an attack.

Normally known for his quick and efficient activity, Longstreet took his time preparing for the attack; some say it was his unwillingness to fight an offensive war that led him to do so. Because of the delay, troops that had not been in place when the scout had ridden through in the early morning were now stationed near areas on the left known as the Peach Orchard and the Devil's Den. By 4 P.M. the attack was ready to begin. John B. Hood, a major general under Longstreet, was informed that the Union far left was still vulnerable to a wider flank attack; he told Longstreet that this would be the best route to take, but Longstreet refused, wanting to stick to Lee's original plan.

Meade readied for the attack, stationing regiments strategically along his line. One of those regiments was led by Daniel Sickles, sent to the left to counter Longstreet. Never known for following orders, Sickles defiantly moved his troops forward from their assigned position onto slightly higher ground to improve their position, in his estimation. What he failed to realize was that this broke the solid Union front and left their flank vulnerable to attack. When he learned of his disobedience, Meade ordered Sickles to move back, but it was too late—with Longstreet's attack launched, Sickles's troops were now pinned beneath enemy fire in the Peach Orchard.

At four o'clock Union major general Gouverneur Warren rode up to the Round Tops. He noticed their strategic importance, and was shocked to find that they were so lightly guarded. To avoid disaster, he sent a courier to contact other field generals to see if they could spare troops for protection. The courier met up with Major General George Sykes, who in turn sent him to gather some of his men. On the way, the courier met up with

Colonel Strong Vincent, who ordered four of his own regiments to climb Little Round Top immediately.

Vincent's men had little time to spare, for as the battle raged farther up the left flank, the Fifteenth and Forty-second Alabama regiments led by William C. Oates had scaled Big Round Top with no resistance. Reaching the summit, Oates looked down at Little Round Top and the battlefield below. He knew that if his men could take Little Round Top, they would have the prime artillery position in the conflict.

Because of the hill's steepness, Vincent ordered his troops to scale Little Round Top on its east side. Simultaneously, Oates's men, exhausted from a morning march without water, climbed the steeper west side. In charge of guarding the Union left at the summit was Joshua Lawrence Chamberlain's Twentieth Maine, numbering fewer than four hundred men. He faced both of Oates's regiments knowing that if he wavered, the Union troops would be flanked and crushed.

Union Troops Repel Confederate Attacks

Four times the Confederates attacked, and four times they were driven back; about one-third of Chamberlain's men were killed or wounded within ninety minutes, often in brutal toe-to-toe combat. As the Alabama regiments prepared for a fifth assault, Chamberlain saw that his men were running out of ammunition. In a final act of desperation and defiance, he ordered his men to fix bayonets and charge down the hill in a seemingly suicidal offensive. Using what little ammunition they had left, the Maine men moved forward. The stunned Alabamians turned and fled as bullets and bayonets seemed to come at them from all sides—the tiny Maine force had held Little Round Top.

The news was not all good for the Union; Sickles's men were still trapped in the Peach Orchard by Longstreet. Making matters worse for Sickles was a second attack by a division led by Lafayette McLaws, a flanking as well as a frontal assault. His men were being destroyed, and Sickles was forced to give up his position and retreat; he himself lost a leg and had to be carried from the field. Meanwhile, the Confederates had also fought for and taken a rocky crag known as Devil's Den, dealing the Union more heavy casualties.

Meade sent reinforcements to spell his thinning ranks, but in doing so created an opening on Cemetery Ridge. There were still a few as yet unused Confederate brigades—another Alabama brigade tried to exploit the weakness. Almost immediately, Union major general Winfield Scott Hancock saw the Confederate push, but he had few troops to spare to stop it. He sent the 262-man First Minnesota against the oncoming 1,600 rebels. The Northerners fixed bayonets immediately and charged, staggering the surprised Confederates. The tiny regiment lost 82 percent of its members in the first five minutes; in the end, only forty-seven were left unhurt, but had they fended off the Confederates long enough for the gap to close; the Union line had held again.

As this bloody fighting raged on the left, Ewell's men sat idle on the right, a diversion so that Meade would not send large numbers of troops to the battle. As the day wore on, heavy losses left Meade no choice—he rushed troops away, leaving Culp's Hill and Cemetery Hill vulnerable to Ewell's attack. Ewell tried to take advantage, but not until nightfall, and was only moderately successful even with superior numbers of troops. Still, he was able to drive some Union troops from their trenches at the base of Culp's Hill; but, with darkness fully set in, the second day of fighting ended.

The Second Day of Fighting

July 2 was in many ways a nightmare for the Union, which lost more than nine thousand men to six thousand for the Confederates; Sickles's brigade was all but obliterated, and many other divisions were decimated. Still, Union forces managed to keep their line of defense intact, despite Ewell's toehold on Culp's Hill. Though the Confederates had fought well, they had little to show for it—Lee sought to change that on the third day.

Confederate Frontal Assault on Day Three

Lee was certain as July 3 dawned that the heavy casualties the Union had suffered rendered them unable to launch any kind of offensive. Early in the morning, Union major general Alpheus Williams decided to try to take back the trenches at Culp's Hill. Williams's men used artillery to soften up the Confederates, then moved in. Throughout the next couple of hours, a series of small battles raged on; by 11 A.M., the Northerners had managed to drive the rebels away. The aid Ewell was supposed to get from Jeb Stuart's cavalry was halted by the Union cavalry led by George Armstrong Custer. Lee's plan to attack the federals on their flanks and collapse their defenses into the middle had failed on both ends.

For Lee, the only option that remained was an all-out assault on the federal center. Lee believed this plan could work because Meade had to use so many troops in the flank attacks; his center was now weak. Longstreet disagreed vehemently; he thought such an operation would result in the same kind of suicide he had watched Union troops commit at Fredericksburg. Lee would not relent; he put together a makeshift force of fifteen thousand, led by General George E. Pickett's men, to make the charge.

Meade once again anticipated Lee's movements, and readied his men. At the center of the Union lines, eerily reminiscent of Fredericksburg, stood a stone wall. This time, it was the Union troops who waited in defense. At 1 P.M. Confederate artillery began shelling the Union positions. Union guns responded for an hour, but then Meade ordered them to stop. Doing so, he thought, would accomplish two goals: save ammunition for the main Confederate charge, and fool Lee into thinking he had destroyed the Union batteries with his shelling.

Meade's plan worked. When Longstreet gave the go-ahead for Pickett's troops, Lee thought they would have an easy time overcoming the Union defenders. Nearly thirteen thousand Confederates marched out of the woods with one goal: to climb over the stone wall and crush the Union center. As they marched, Meade's artillery opened fire again. Shells killed up to ten rebels at once, but still more filled their places.

The federals were instructed not to shoot until the invaders came into range. When the order was given, eleven cannons and more than seventeen hundred rifles fired at once, slaughtering hundreds of Confederates. Despite massive casualties, the Confederates moved on, driving for a section of the wall broken into a right angle. The high point in the Confederate assault came when some were actually able to clamber over the wall, driving the men of the Seventy-first Pennsylvania from their defending positions.

Their success would be short-lived. Though the Confederates still had numerical superiority, their leaders were being killed, and their march was deteriorating into disorganization. Union troops quickly rebounded and then flanked and surrounded the rebels. Every Confederate who had crossed the wall was either killed or captured. The attack had ended up a total failure, forever living in Confederate infamy as the failed Pickett's Charge.

Confederate casualties were horrible; nearly sixty-five hundred men, half of those who charged, had fallen or been taken prisoner. Pickett's division had been completely shattered; all three of his brigade commanders and fourteen of fifteen regimental commanders were lost. Pickett never forgave Lee for sacrificing his men; Longstreet later wrote that he never believed the frontal assault would work.

The Butcher's Bill

In all, twenty-three thousand Union and twenty-eight thousand Confederate soldiers had fallen at Gettysburg. Yet, despite these huge losses, it was not apparent on July 4 that the battle was over. Meade and Lee each thought the other was preparing for another attack, and warily stayed put. The Confederates could ill afford to lose the numbers they did; Lee soon understood that he did not have the manpower to continue northward, and retreated to Virginia the next day, ending the campaign in full by July 13.

Four months later, in his now famous speech, Abraham Lincoln helped to remember the dead at the dedication of a national cemetery in Gettysburg. Today, visitors can travel throughout the battlefield and visit the places where men of both sides gave their lives. Monuments to various regiments dot the countryside and help to commemorate three days that can only be remembered as an American apocalypse. —*Tony Jaros*

For Further Information:

Smith, Carl. *Gettysburg 1863: High Tide of the Confederacy.* London: Osprey Military, 1998. An analysis of the Battle of Gettysburg, illustrated with battlescene plates. Includes bibliographical references.

Symonds, Craig L. *Gettysburg: A Battlefield Atlas.* Baltimore: Nautical and Aviation Publishing, 1992. Provides an overview of all the individual battles in the conflict with detailed and helpful maps.

Ward, Geoffrey C. *The Civil War.* Reprint. New York:

Alfred A. Knopf, 1997. A colorful and complete history of the conflict. The book is the basis for a multipart television program.

Wheeler, Richard. *Witness to Gettysburg*. New York: Harper, 1987. Tells the battle story in narratives from individuals who lived through the conflict.

Hopewell Furnace

Date: Founded in 1771

Relevant issues: Business and industry

Significance: Part of the Hopewell Village National Historic Site, this is a restoration of a typical iron plantation of eighteenth and nineteenth century American ironmaking communities. Such communities were the foundation of the country's later Industrial Revolution.

Location: About six miles south of Birdsboro on Pennsylvania 345 and ten miles from the Morgantown Interchange on the Pennsylvania Turnpike, via Pennsylvania 23 East and Pennsylvania 345 North

Site Office:
Hopewell Furnace
2 Mark Bird Lane
Elverson, PA 19520
ph.: (610) 582-8773
fax: (610) 582-2768
Web site: www.nps.gov/hofu/
e-mail: hofu_superintendent@nps.gov

In 1771, Mark Bird, a colonial ironmaster, entrepreneur, and patriot, opened Hopewell Furnace near French Creek in southern Berks County, Pennsylvania. The furnace was a natural outgrowth of his father's Hopewell Forge near the Schuylkill River at Birdsboro. The elder Bird had become prosperous, owning two forges, a furnace, and more than three thousand acres at his death in 1761.

Like his father and other colonial ironmasters, young Mark Bird operated his furnace in direct defiance of Britain's Iron Act of 1750. The act was designed to curtail the making of finished iron products by the colonists. It demanded that Americans make only pig iron and ship it to England. British ironworks would then make the finished ironware, such as bells and stove plates, and sell it to the colonists at great profit. The colonial ironmasters could

make much more money by ignoring the act and illegally selling the finished products directly to their countrymen.

Early History

Historical records on Hopewell before 1784 are sketchy or nonexistent, but a surviving Franklin stove plate proves that Bird did defy the Iron Act. It has the imprint "Mark Bird—Hopewell Furnace—1772." Hopewell was not the first ironworks on the North American continent. That honor belonged to an ironmaster who attempted to start a forge near Jamestown, Virginia, in 1621. Neither was Hopewell the most successful. It was typical of such iron plantations, and its site lent itself to restoration.

Hopewell was typical because the raw materials—timber, ore, limestone, and water—were close and abundant. There were good roads between Hopewell and its forges and markets. Skilled and unskilled workers were plentiful. Young Bird himself became prosperous. By 1770, he owned thousands of acres of woodland, iron mines, water rights, and eighteen slaves, the single largest slaveholding in Berks County.

The Revolutionary War

By the time the Revolutionary War started, Bird was deeply involved in the war effort as ironmaster, entrepreneur, and patriot. As ironmaster, he saw to it that the cannon, shot, and shell that Hopewell furnished the Continental army were the finest possible. As entrepreneur, he sold such wares to the army, often for Continental Congress IOUs. As patriot, he served as delegate to the Pennsylvania Committee of Correspondence and the Provincial Conference of 1775, as a member of the Pennsylvania Assembly, and as a judge on the Berks County Court. Bird's two brothers-in-law, both ironmasters, were signers of the Declaration of Independence.

Bird was also a colonel in the Berks County Militia and used his own resources to provide three hundred militiamen with clothing, tents, and provisions. During 1778, when he served as deputy quartermaster general, he shipped one thousand barrels of flour to George Washington's starving troops at Valley Forge. Bird knew that route well. He had sent many a shipment of pig iron to that forge. However, Bird died a ruined man, hiding from his creditors in North Carolina. His downfall resulted from bad investments, overexpansion of his operations, and unpaid bills by the Continental Congress.

In 1788, Bird's Hopewell Plantation was auctioned off to James Old and Cadwallader Morris to satisfy debts. It passed through several other hands until finally, in 1800, Hopewell was bought by the partnership of Daniel Buckley and his brothers-in-law Matthew and Thomas Brooke. Those families operated Hopewell for eighty-three years.

The Furnace in Its Heyday

The restored site shows the operations as they were in the furnace's heyday, 1820 to 1840. The cold-blast furnace made iron from ore found in the vicinity. The burning charcoal fuel was kept under control by bellows that fed cold air into the bottom of the furnace through an opening called a tuyere. The bellows was operated by a water wheel that, in prosperous times, ran twenty-four hours a day. Charcoal, iron ore, and limestone were dumped into the top of the furnace in that order. The charcoal fires at temperatures of 2,600 to 3,000 degrees Fahrenheit melted the iron ore into liquid form. The limestone, used as flux, helped remove impurities from the ore.

The molten iron flowed out the bottom of the furnace into sand beds to form ingots or "pig iron." Molten iron also flowed into casts for such things as stove plates, pots, sash weights, and tools. Pig iron bars, anconies (or bars with knobbed ends), or merchant bars were sent to forges, either on site or at places such as Valley Forge, to be hammered into finished ironwork. Blacksmiths made the iron into nails, horseshoes, and wheel rims.

Social Organization and Craftsmen

Hopewell village was a paternalistic, pyramidal society with the ironmaster at the top. Under the master were the clerk and founder (a technician, not an owner). In descending order were keepers, fillers, guttermen, molders and molders' helpers, colliers, miners, teamsters, and woodcutters.

In the Brooke dynasty, the first owner lived in the "Big House," or ironmaster's mansion. At other iron plantations, the ironmaster lived in these luxurious quarters. According to historians W. David Lewis and Walter E. Hugins, an ironmaster was similar to a chief operating officer; he was a "capitalist, technician, market analyst, personnel director, bill collector, purchasing agent, and transportation expert."

Next in line was the company clerk, who often lived in the mansion as well. He was bookkeeper and paymaster, he soothed irate customers, managed the company store, filled orders, and extended credit. He was a wage earner, but the wages were high and he could move up to ironmaster if very good at his job.

The founder's job was to keep the furnace running at top efficiency by maintaining the temperature and knowing when the iron was ready to flow. He did this by keeping an eye on the color of the flame. A founder was usually the highest paid furnace worker. In the mid-1830's, a founder with skill, experience, and judgment made about six hundred dollars a year.

A keeper took over when the founder was off duty. Fillers also aided the founder with the back-breaking work of dumping materials into the furnace. This meant filling and pushing barrow load after barrow load of charcoal, ore, and limestone. The barrows were pushed to the top of the furnace and dumped in. Fillers had to accurately estimate the amount of material in their loads and report it to the founder. According to Lewis and Huggins, they "had to endure the flame, smoke, and cinders at the tunnel head and work in all weather, but were paid little more than common laborers."

Guttermen prepared the sand casting beds for pig iron. Guttermen, often boys, also stacked the ingots outside the cast house and carried cinders to the slag, or waste, heap.

Molders were highly skilled craftsmen and much more highly paid than fillers and guttermen. They received about ten dollars a ton for castings in 1836. Molders made curved stove plates with a technique called flask casting. It was a long task, both mentally and physically demanding. It involved two boxes that could be clamped together and nine steps that required steady hands when working with sand of varying consistencies and ladles of molten ore.

Colliers made charcoal from timber in the forests surrounding Hopewell. The task always involved sleepless nights watching the fire—they were paid to produce charcoal, not ashes. Using hardwood billets, short pieces of fire wood supplied by woodcutters, colliers built hearths in

Hopewell Furnace National Historic Site. (American Stock Photography)

cleared areas in the woods, some thirty to forty feet in diameter. The billets were stacked around a central chimney, and the resulting cone-shaped structure was then covered with thin slats. The slats, in turn, were covered by leaves and charcoal dust to keep out excess air. Kindling was dropped down the chimney and ignited. The workers tended the pit night and day for two weeks and then raked out the charcoal, cooled it, and loaded it into furnace-bound wagons. Colliers worked from April to November, so they were outdoors in weather that was sometimes severe. Colliers worked as contractors. They were paid by the bushel of charcoal produced, minus the cost of the wood consumed. A good collier could produce thirty-five to forty bushels from a cord of wood. Annual incomes for colliers in 1825 could run from $150 to nearly $350.

Iron Mining

Iron ore mining at first was done from open pits with pick and shovel. Later, as the pits were exhausted, shafts and tunnels were used. Miners were not wage earners but were paid according to the weight of the ore brought to the furnace. They were not badly paid; they averaged more than half the income of skilled furnace workers.

Teamsters drove the vehicles, such as Conestoga wagons, the sole means of transporting large or heavy goods until the canals and railroads were built. They hauled ore, charcoal, and limestone, and most important, took finished products to market. They were paid by the load, plus expenses. Yearly pay was usually less than $100, but one David Hart averaged $475 a year from 1818 to 1840.

Woodcutters, a large segment of the workforce, were at the bottom of the pyramid. From 1835 to 1837, woodcutters accounted for 112 out of 213 Hopewell employees. Much of the work was done during the winter by part-time employees. They cut about two cords a day and were paid by the cord, the distance it was hauled, and the quality of the wood. The awful appetite of the furnaces helped in Hopewell's later decline. Ecologically speaking, the strip ore mines ruined land and the furnace consumed an acre of hardwood trees a day. The owners used the clear-cutting method, which left the land bare and unable to grow new trees for thirty years.

African American, Women, and Child Workers

After the abolition of slavery in Pennsylvania in 1780, African Americans were employed at Hopewell. Many places in southeastern Pennsylvania were stops on the Underground Railroad. Hopewell was close to the Mason-Dixon Line and probably hired fugitive blacks from the South. Most of them held menial, low-paying jobs and eventually moved on to safer areas. Some, however, stayed on as laborers, teamsters, or semiskilled workers. Black workers were paid the same wages as white workers and neither housing nor schools were segregated.

All the jobs were hard and the hours long by today's standards. The men had their outlet. Tradition says that to make a ton of iron required 2.5 tons of ore, 180 bushels of charcoal, and a gallon each of beer and whiskey.

Women and children also were employed at Hopewell, although the furnace site was described as "Heaven for horses but Hell for women." Most of the women supplemented family incomes by selling needlepoint, eggs, and home-cooked or home-preserved products. Other sources of additional income included boarding single men and sewing, repairing, or laundering for both company and workers.

Some skilled women earned regular wages for seamstressing, cooking, or candle-dipping in the ironmaster's mansion. Others had their own furnace-related businesses, dealing in ore, stoves, or farm products.

Not all women were restricted to home activities. Hopewell records indicate that in the early 1830's, two widows were paid seventy-five cents an hour for cleaning sand off stove plate castings. Although most "men's work" at the time called for considerable physical strength, some women worked as miners, farm laborers, and woodcutters.

Children were also employed, such as the boy guttermen. Many learned a furnace trade by apprenticeship, most often with their fathers. They were also apprenticed out to various tradesmen. Indenture as a servant was also common. Clement Brooke once signed an agreement to take a five-year-old boy as an apprentice for sixteen years. Wives and children of workers were also hired as household staff for the ironmaster's mansion. At Hopewell, the company provided a school and a company store. The company store was run for the employees' convenience, not for profit, like later corporate company stores.

All worked a six-day week when times were good and the furnace was in constant use. When the furnace was down for lack of business or for repairs, no one was paid. There were no unemployment payments; those who had savings lived off them. Others had to scrabble.

On Sunday, the only day off, the main activity was churchgoing, a very important emotional, social, and intellectual experience. Some Hopewell workers went to Episcopal churches in Warwick, Douglasville, or Morgantown. Others attended the Bethesda Baptist Church. Forms of entertainment included "frollicks," which were more like work than play. The host would provide whiskey for those willing to help in some mundane task, such as cutting firewood. There were also the timeless forms of entertainment at Hopewell—whiskey, dancing, and fighting.

Technological Improvements over the Years

Over the years, the Buckley-Brooke management team made capital improvements. One of these was the replacement of the outmoded leather bellows with devices called wooden piston tubs. Still using water-wheel power, the tubs forced air through leather valves and into the furnace. The valves allowed closer control of the air flow and increased the efficiency of the operation. Their usefulness was enhanced by a Hopewell innovation called "patent elastic piston springs." To further increase profits, the plant decreased the production of pig iron and made more castings of finished products. The partnership also built a wheelhouse to protect the machinery and a stamping mill to recover iron from slag.

Hopewell's prosperity in the 1830's and 1840's was due largely to the business acumen of Clement Brooke, son of one of the men who bought Mark Bird's furnace. He inherited one-sixth of the property from his father in 1831. Two years later, he and his brother, Charles, bought a share of the Buckley holding. Clement Brooke was not just an owner's son taking over a business his father helped build. He learned the business by working at the furnace part-time and as clerk, and he soon became an ironmaster in his own right. He had a reputation as one of the best in Pennsylvania.

Clement Brooke retired in 1848, after supervising the most prosperous period for Hopewell. The ironworks then started its decline, but not simply because he was no longer in charge. Times and technology were changing. The hot-blast furnace, the invention of the Bessemer steel-making process, the change from wood fuel to anthracite coal, and the depletion of nearby raw materials all played a role. An attempt to build an anthracite furnace on the site in 1853 proved abortive. The paternalistic, family-owned business approach was also doomed by the rise of corporate business, which required large amounts of capital unavailable to small businesses and strangled competition through monopolies. In 1883, the Hopewell Furnace was shut down for the last time.

Modern Preservation Efforts
Restoration began in 1935, when the federal government bought the property from Louise Clingan Brooke. The furnace stack, the ironmaster's mansion, four tenant houses, spring house, company store, the blacksmith shop, and several other buildings were still standing. Initially, the government did not realize Hopewell's historic value, and the Civilian Conservation Corps was assigned to make Hopewell into a recreation area. Thanks to historian Roy Appleman, it was named a National Historic Site in 1938 and restoration began.

Today's visitors can see eighteen restored areas and workers in period garb doing tasks such as blacksmithing, gardening, cooking, weaving, candlemaking, and soapmaking.

The restored areas are the village roads, charcoal hearths, charcoal house and cooling shed, anthracite furnace, furnace bank, water wheel and its headraces, company store, cast house, furnace, cleaning shed, blacksmith shop, tenant house, schoolhouse, barn, spring house, smoke house, ironmaster's mansion, and ironmaster's garden. The Bethesda Baptist Church near Baptizing Creek can also be seen. Visitors can also view furnace products and wheeled vehicles like a two-wheel dump cart, freight wagon, and charcoal wagon.
—*James Lahey*

For Further Information:
Hindle, Brooke. "Mechanizing a Nation." In *Visiting Our Past: America's Historylands.* Wash-ington, D.C.: National Geographic Society, 1986. Provides interesting sidelights.

Lewis, W. David, and Walter E. Hugins. *Hopewell Furnace: A Guide to Hopewell Village National Historic Site, Pennsylvania.* Washington, D.C.: National Park Service, 1983. A ninety-five-page, fully illustrated book that provides in-depth coverage of the furnace, the people, the times, and the technology. It also includes tour information.

Independence National Historical Park

Date: Established as a National Historical Park in 1948
Relevant issues: Colonial America, political history, Revolutionary War
Significance: This National Historical Park is the original area of Philadelphia, the first capital of the United States of America and the site of the writing and adoption of the Declaration of Independence and the drafting of the U.S. Constitution.
Location: Central Philadelphia; bounded roughly by Arch Street on the north, Front Street on the east, Spruce Street on the south, and 6th Street on the west, with a few sites outside of these boundaries
Site Office:
Independence National Historical Park
313 Walnut Street
Philadelphia, PA 19106
ph.: (215) 597-8974
Web site: www.nps.gov/inde/

Just west of the Delaware River in the oldest section of Philadelphia, Independence National Historical Park encompasses twenty-six buildings and sites where the Founding Fathers of the United States created the new nation. In the park's Independence Hall, George Washington, Thomas Jefferson, Benjamin Franklin, and other leading citizens of the thirteen colonies debated and signed the Declaration of Independence and the U.S. Constitution. The Liberty Bell rang in Independence Square, on the first public reading of the Declaration of Independence.

Early History

Philadelphia was founded in 1682 by the Quaker William Penn. When Benjamin Franklin, destined to become the city's most famous resident, arrived there in 1723 as a teenager, it was still a small Quaker town on the edge of the wilderness and the Delaware River. Franklin later established a printing business and started the *Pennsylvania Gazette* newspaper. He founded the American Philosophical Society and organized the first firefighting company in the colonies, saw to it that streets were lighted and paved, started the local militia, and founded Philadelphia's first hospital.

The restored Market Street houses, three of which were built by Franklin, serve as a reminder of his presence. Just behind them is the site of the only home Franklin ever owned. A steel frame marks the site, as there was not enough information available about the home to do an authentic reconstruction. Beneath it is an underground museum and architectural/archaeological exhibit and an operating eighteenth century print shop. Franklin is buried nearby at Christ Church Cemetery.

By 1774 Philadelphia had grown into the colonies' largest, wealthiest, and most cosmopolitan city, with nearly thirty thousand residents occupying six thousand houses and three hundred shops clustered along the Delaware River, in what is now the site of Independence National Historical Park. At this time, the city was a melting pot of English, German, and Scotch-Irish who were Lutherans, Jews, Catholics, Moravians, Methodists, and Presbyterians as well as Quakers, and it was home to the genteel as well as the ordinary laborer.

The colonies also were growing, and colonists were tired of paying taxes to England while having no representation in the English Parliament. Philadelphia, the American focal point of the ideals of the Enlightenment, the intellectual awakening that swept Europe in the mid-eighteenth century, was a natural base for radicals seeking change.

Growing Friction with British Rule

To circumvent Pennsylvania's conservative provincial assembly, Benjamin Franklin and other liberal leaders began meeting at Philadelphia's City Tavern to discuss revolutionary measures combining mass involvement and economic tactics. On May 20, 1774, Paul Revere arrived at the tavern with the news that the English had closed the port of Boston. An extensive discussion followed inside, with the group coming to the conclusion that they would convey their sympathies to Boston and adhere firmly to the cause of American liberty.

Such discussions laid the groundwork for a revolution in Pennsylvania, and soon radical committees were operating in every county in Pennsylvania, with the de facto popular government's "headquarters" in City Tavern. This Philadelphia Committee of Observation, Inspection, and Correspondence decided to convene a Congress of the Thirteen Colonies in September, 1774, in Philadelphia to formulate statements on colonial rights and grievances.

The First Continental Congress

The First Continental Congress delegates to arrive from twelve colonies (Georgia declined to attend) met at City Tavern and walked over to inspect the newly constructed, roomy but private Carpenters' Hall, and decided to hold the Congress there. To the Congress came such men as George Washington, John Adams, Samuel Adams, Patrick Henry, and John Jay. The Adamses were warned by other delegates, including some Philadelphians, "You must not utter the word independence, or give the least hint or insinuation of the idea. No one dares to speak of it here." Revolution was still an idea only the radicals seriously considered, and many believed the outspoken Adams cousins were agitators for independence.

Joseph Galloway, speaker of the Pennsylvania Assembly, had offered the State House (now Independence Hall) for the delegation, and considered the rejection of it in favor of Carpenters' Hall as a slap at the conservative assembly. To make matters worse, the delegates next chose Charles Thomson, "the Sam Adams of Philadelphia," as secretary of the Congress. Although most of the Congress delegates were moderates, these decisions lent a radical tone to the rest of the proceedings.

During the first week, a report that the British had killed some colonists while seizing gunpowder supplies in Boston and had fired their cannon on Boston riled the Congress to the point of wanting war. The report turned out to be a hoax, but it let Samuel Adams test the mood of the delegates in light of an outbreak of violence. The news had caused many to change their moderate positions.

Resolutions and Declarations

A week had not passed before Paul Revere arrived with the Suffolk Resolves, a list of resolutions drawn up by residents of Suffolk County, Massachusetts. The resolves called for formation of a colonial army, disobedience to acts of Parliament, and the funneling of taxes to an independent provincial government. A motion to endorse the measures passed by a voice vote that was recorded as unanimous, although Galloway and his allies sat in stunned silence. Galloway called the vote "tantamount to a complete declaration of war," and believed Samuel Adams was behind the Suffolk Resolves and the author of the Boston hoax. Hoping to counter Adams and the radicals, Galloway presented his "Plan of Union," which proposed a colonial council that would become a branch of the British Parliament. The council would have control over intercolonial commercial, civil, and criminal matters, requiring only the approval of Parliament to validate its actions.

A terrific debate between conservatives and radicals ensued, but the die had been cast. The revolutionary radical faction won a victory when delegates voted down Galloway's plan, and the Congress formulated and sent a Declaration of Rights and Grievances to King George III. They also agreed to boycott English goods, forming the Continental Association to enforce this decision.

The men decided to gather again the following spring if England did not rectify the colonies' grievances. England did not act, and the Second Continental Congress met at the Pennsylvania State House (Independence Hall) on May 10, 1775. Fighting against the British had already broken out at Lexington and Concord in Massachusetts, and the Congress reluctantly moved from ethereal theories of government to armed resistance. George Washington was appointed commander in chief of all American armed forces. The Continental Congress also assumed authority over provincial troops at Boston. During these first months of the revolution, people in colony after colony transferred their allegiance from their legal governmental institutions to extralegal revolutionary committees, state conventions, and the Continental Congress.

On May 1, 1776, the moderates won a referendum against independence in the Pennsylvania Assembly. The radicals in the Second Continental Congress were proceeding toward independence, however, and waited only for the assurance of popular support before making their proclamation. Throughout May and June, the Pennsylvania Assembly met on the second floor of the State House, debating the issue of independence, while the Continental Congress sat below on the first floor waiting. Meanwhile, Thomas Paine, newly arrived in Philadelphia, published *Common Sense*, a persuasive pamphlet on why the colonies should break from England.

The Declaration of Independence

On May 15, 1776, the Congress, in a document written by John Adams, urged the colonies to set up their own governments as states. This decision, however, still fell short of a formal, collective declaration of independence by all the colonies. Before recessing on June 10, the Congress appointed a five-man committee to draft such a declaration. The task of writing the first draft fell mainly to Thomas Jefferson. Working in a second-floor parlor of Jacob Graff's house, Jefferson completed the draft of the Declaration of Independence in two weeks, basing the document on broad universal rights. He submitted it to the committee, and Benjamin Franklin and John Adams made small alterations. The Congress still was not unanimous on independence, and there followed a nine-hour debate on July 1. The Congress adopted the Declaration of Independence on July 4, 1776.

On July 6, the declaration was published in the *Pennsylvania Evening Post* and the term "United States of America" used for the first time. The declaration was first read in public in the State House yard (now Independence Square) outside Independence Hall, on July 8, 1776. The British royal coat of arms was torn down and burned and not one, but two Liberty Bells were rung.

The Liberty Bell

The first Liberty Bell had been cast in 1752 to commemorate the fiftieth anniversary of the Pennsylvania Charter of Privileges, the democratic constitution William Penn had granted the colony in 1701. It cracked while being tested, and the colonists got tired of waiting for a new bell from London, so they recast the original bell in Philadelphia. The mended bell was hung in the tower of the Pennsylvania State House, but because of the copper used

Independence Hall, Philadelphia. (PhotoDisc)

Thaddeus Kosciuszko

In August, 1776, Thaddeus Kosciuszko, a Pole who had studied military engineering, arrived in Philadelphia and applied to the Continental Congress for a commission in the army. Although he had no formal military experience, Kosciuszko's request was granted, and the thirty-year-old became a colonel. Kosciuszko distinguished himself near Saratoga, contributing greatly to the surrender of six thousand troops under General John Burgoyne at Bemis Heights, overlooking the Hudson River. Many consider the surrender of Burgoyne on October 17, 1777, the turning point of the Revolutionary War. It was the colonies' first major victory over the British, and led France to join the colonies' fight.

Kosciuszko next was entrusted with the defense of the Hudson River at West Point, beginning in March, 1778, and continuing for twenty-eight months. The fortifications he planned and built were so imposing that the British never attacked. In 1780, Kosciuszko began serving in the southern campaign where he remained until the war ended. He was promoted to brigadier general in 1783. He returned to Poland in 1784 and became involved in the Polish resistance to Czarist Russia. He wrote the Act of Insurrection, a document strongly resembling the American Declaration of Independence. The resistance movement was defeated, and Kosciuszko was banished from Poland. He returned to Philadelphia to a hero's welcome in 1797, and stayed at a boardinghouse at Third and Pine Streets. Here he recuperated from his war wounds and became close friends with Thomas Jefferson, the two sharing many political beliefs. The second-floor bedroom where Kosciuszko stayed has been restored to look much as it did when he was there and is dedicated as the Thaddeus Kosciuszko National Memorial.

The Articles of Confederation

On November 17, 1777, the Second Continental Congress adopted the Articles of Confederation in

during repairs, the tone was not good. When its replacement arrived from London, it was decided to use both bells together, so both bells tolled during the first public proclamation of the Declaration of Independence. When British troops entered Philadelphia the next year, the bells were sent to Allentown for safekeeping and returned when the troops left.

The first bell next cracked during the funeral of Chief Justice John Marshall in 1835. It last rang formally in 1846 during the observance of George Washington's birthday, and now remains on display in Liberty Bell Pavilion. Antislavery groups coined the bell's name in the nineteenth century, inspired by its inscription, "Proclaim Liberty thro' all the Land to all the Inhabitants thereof." The second bell is at Villanova University.

Philadelphia and presented the document to the states for approval. Under the Articles, the central government's authority rested in the member states. The document was ratified on March 1, 1781. The Articles did not provide for a direct link to the people; instead the Congress had to try to enforce its laws through the states, which from the end of the Revolutionary War were increasingly becoming embroiled in quarrels and going their separate ways. Furthermore, the Congress had no capacity to raise money or regulate commerce, no executive to carry out its laws, and no judiciary to enforce them. Foreign nations treated the American Confederation with contempt, refusing to recognize it fully until the national government compelled the states to cooperate.

Calls for a New Constitution

The nationalists in Congress, including Alexander Hamilton and James Madison, began to believe that a total restructuring was necessary to restore the dream of the American Revolution. Others simply wanted reform to enable the central government to pay its war debts and spur economic revival. All wanted to make the central government adequate to its tasks and to command more respect from the rest of the world.

In September, 1786, New York, New Jersey, Delaware, Pennsylvania, and Virginia sent delegates to the Annapolis Convention to discuss commercial matters. Because delegates from four other states arrived too late, it was impossible for those present to come to conclusions on commerce. Instead the men adopted a resolution by Hamilton that asked that all states send delegates to a new convention set for May, 1787, in Philadelphia. Besides commercial matters, the new convention would address issues necessary "to render the constitution of the Federal Government adequate to the exigencies of the Union." A few weeks later, the Congress of the Confederation endorsed the meeting at Philadelphia "for the sole and express purpose of revising the Articles of Confederation and reporting to Congress and the several legislatures such alterations and provisions therein."

Before the delegates could meet, Shays's Rebellion occurred. Indebted farmers in Massachusetts revolted against the high taxes that the state levied as a means to pay its war debt. The armed resistance was the final indicator that change was necessary.

The Constitutional Convention

To the Philadelphia convention in May came delegates from twelve states, including such distinguished men as George Washington (who was presiding officer), James Madison, Benjamin Franklin, George Mason, Gouverneur Morris, James Wilson, Roger Sherman, and Elbridge Gerry. Of fifty-five participants, more than half were lawyers and twenty-nine had attended college. After less than a month of debate, the convention decided that a new national government, not simply a revisal of the Articles, was necessary.

The debate next centered on the question of proportional versus equal representation of the states in Congress, pitting small states against large. In July, the convention agreed that representation in the lower house would be proportional to a state's population while representation in the upper house would be equal. In the next major compromise, the South agreed to grant Congress the authority to pass navigation acts that the North wanted in return for the North's agreeing that Congress would not interfere with the slave trade for twenty years. In September, after a great debate, the convention agreed to grant Congress the right to regulate foreign trade and interstate commerce.

It was then that Franklin said of the chair in which George Washington had been sitting, one with a sun with outstretched rays on its back:

> I have often and often in the course of the session and vicissitudes of my hopes and fears as to its issue, looked at that behind the president without being able to tell whether it was rising or setting. But now at length I have the happiness to know that it is a rising and not a setting sun.

The resulting document, the Constitution, was approved on September 17, 1787, ratified by the requisite nine states on July 2, 1788, and took effect on March 4, 1789, in New York City, which had become the home of the national government after mutinous Pennsylvania soldiers had surrounded the Pennsylvania State House in 1783, demanding back pay.

Philadelphia as Temporary Capital

Philadelphia became a temporary capital in 1790 as a result of a compromise, while a new permanent site was being planned in what would become Washington, D.C. Many Philadelphians hoped to persuade the new national government to remain. They built a new County Courthouse (now Congress Hall) on the west side of the State House, for the U.S. Congress, which met there from 1790 to 1800, and a new City Hall on the east side for the Supreme Court; the court met there from 1791 to 1800. The First Bank of the United States was constructed. President Washington and his family moved into Robert Morris's mansion in the city.

Philadelphia remained the capital until 1800. During these ten years in Philadelphia, Washington's second inauguration took place in Congress Hall, the Bill of Rights was officially added to the Constitution, and three new states were admitted to the union. After the national government moved to Washington, D.C., Philadelphia never regained its prominence as the country's principal city.

Creation of the Historic Park
Independence National Historical Park was founded by an act of Congress in 1948 to preserve Independence Hall (originally Pennsylvania's State House) and a few surrounding buildings. In 1950 the park took over the area's preservation and administration and bought other sites owned by the city of Philadelphia. The National Park Service began a restoration of the area, which it completed in the 1970's.

This historic square mile also contains the sites where the first and second Continental Congresses convened and where the U.S. Supreme Court and U.S. Congress first met, when Philadelphia was capital of the newly formed United States from 1790 to 1800. Colonial middle-class and upper-middle-class homes, as well as businesses and churches, most of them restored originals, show how the residents of the time lived. George Washington dined at City Tavern before going off to lead the Continental army.   —*Sharon Bakos*

For Further Information:

American Political Science Association, American Historical Association. *This Constitution: Our Enduring Legacy.* Washington, D.C.: Congressional Quarterly, 1986. A collection of twenty-one essays by scholars in history, law, and government. Focuses on the roots and philosophies behind the Constitution, its framing, its meaning, and its evolution, including modern-day issues.

Brands, H. W. *The First American: The Life and Times of Benjamin Franklin.* New York: Doubleday, 2000. A biography of Franklin that discusses politics in the colonial era.

Clark, Ronald W. *A Biography of Benjamin Franklin.* New York: Random House, 1983. Takes readers on a journey with Franklin from his arrival in Philadelphia as a teenager to his involvement in the revolution and his success in the court of Louis XV of France.

National Park Service. Division of Publications. *Independence: A Guide to Independence National Historical Park, Philadelphia, Pennsylvania.* Washington, D.C.: National Park Service, U.S. Department of the Interior, 1982. Provides a historical perspective on the park, and discusses such places of interest as Congress Hall, the Liberty Bell Pavilion, and Graff House, where Jefferson wrote the Declaration of Independence.

Secor, Robert, ed. *Pennsylvania 1776.* University Park: Pennsylvania State University Press, 1975. An excellent account of life, ideas, the arts, politics, and war in Pennsylvania during 1776. Written by a variety of specialists, the book provides insight into the events of 1776 in Philadelphia and the crucial state of Pennsylvania.

Johnstown Flood National Memorial

Date: Flood occurred on May 31, 1889

Relevant issues: Business and industry, disasters and tragedies, political history, science and technology

Significance: The Johnstown Flood of 1889 was a combination of natural disaster and the effects of human greed, neglect, error, and complacency.

Location: Allegheny Plateau section of the Appalachian Mountains in western Pennsylvania

Site Office:
Johnstown Flood National Memorial
733 Lake Road
South Fork, PA 15956
ph.: (814) 495-4643
Web site: www.nps.gov/jofl/

A death toll of over 2,200 people, destruction of 1,600 homes and 280 businesses, and $17 million in property damage ensured a place for the Johnstown Flood in history. It was the media event of its day, brought nearly $4 million in contributions from people in eighteen countries, and was the first major disaster relief effort for the Red Cross, organized by Clara Barton only eight years before.

An Early Outpost

The first white settlers came to the valley surrounding Johnstown about 1771, and, after being abandoned several times, the area became a backwoods trading center. The population began growing significantly when the canal system from Philadelphia to Pittsburgh was finished. By 1889, ten thousand people lived in Johnstown proper, built on a nearly level flood plain at the confluence of the Little Conemaugh and Stony Creek Rivers in Cambria County, while a total of thirty thousand crowded into the narrow valley.

When completed, Pennsylvania's canal system had too little water in the summer to be usable, so in 1836 the state legislature appropriated funds for a reservoir dam on the South Fork River. Completed in 1852, the canal system was made obsolete six months later by the new Pennsylvania Railroad.

Although the dam had originally been constructed according to the best engineering knowledge of the day, a series of alterations weakened it. In 1862 fire destroyed a tower that controlled five cast-iron sluice pipes set into the base of the dam. In 1875, Congressman John Reilly purchased the reservoir, removed the pipes and sold them for scrap, then resold the property four years later to Benjamin F. Ruff. In 1879, Ruff persuaded fifteen Pittsburgh men to form the South Fork Fishing and Hunting Club. Members included Andrew Carnegie, Henry Clay Frick, Andrew Mellon, and railroad magnate Robert Pitcairn. Named president, Ruff continued the weakening of the dam: boarding up the holes left by the pipes, lowering the height several feet so two carriages could drive abreast on its top, and installing a bridge over the spillway and under it a screen of iron rods to keep in the fish with which the lake was to be stocked. Lake Conemaugh, was a mile across and two miles long, drained sixty square miles of mountainside, was seventy feet deep in the spring and contained water weighing twenty million tons.

The alterations to the dam apparently caused concern to no one except downstream industrialist Daniel J. Morrell of the Cambria Iron Works. He sent his own engineer to inspect the altered dam and offered to help pay for making it safe. The offer was declined. Morrell died in 1885, Ruff in 1887, and two years later, retired hotel owner Elias J. Unger was named club president and manager, and he took up fulltime residence at the lake.

A Flood Zone

The first recorded flood was in 1808, when a small dam across Stony Creek, put in as a millrace for one of the first forges, was breached. As the years went by, floods became more serious because timber was being stripped off the mountainsides to provide lumber, and the river channels were narrowed to make room for buildings and bridges. Thus, a smaller volume for the river had to handle more runoff.

In 1881 heavy rains caused serious damage to the dam, and later, during a flash flood, rumors flew that it was about to break. These rumors were renewed each year, but the dam held, and in spite of repeated floods, an attitude of complacency developed.

The spring of 1889 brought a heavy snowfall followed by frequent and heavy rains. On May 29 at the South Fork Club seven inches fell. On May 30 the sky was lighter, the wind had lessened, and people who lived in areas which had been flooded assumed the storm was over and the waters would recede. However, during the night, heavy rains and high winds returned, and the heavy storm water tore big holes in the saturated ground. By morning rivers were rising faster than one foot per hour, and men arriving for their shifts at the Cambria mills were told to go home and take care of their families. By 10:00 A.M. schools had closed. At noon the water level in Johnstown was at a record high, and after Stony Creek ripped out the Poplar Street and Cambria City bridges, George T. Swank, editor and proprietor of the *Johnstone Tribune* started a running log of events.

Meanwhile, at the lake, workers were trying without success to throw up a ridge of earth to increase the height of the dam. Local onlookers advised Unger to tear out the bridge and the iron mesh spillway, but he did not want to lose the fish. At noon, when he finally ordered the spillway

The Johnstown Flood Cemetery. (American Stock Photography)

cleared, it was too late: the debris was jammed in. By 2:00 P.M. the water was running over the center of the dam, which at 3:10 P.M. "just moved away."

As the water smashed down the valley it took out everything in its path, including soil down to bedrock. Those people who had not fled to high ground in time either were killed instantly or went racing downstream on their own rooftops. Where the river curved, the water would slam against the hillside and create a backwash; several strong railroad bridges briefly dammed the water and then released it to flow more violently; the debris and the friction with the hillside also caused the top water to travel more rapidly, so that a "surf" effect developed, pounding debris and bodies deep into the mud and making later retrieval difficult.

In Johnstown, the floodwaters had actually begun to recede. Most people, perched in upper stories, never saw the water coming, but they heard it. The water hit Johnstown harder than anything it had encountered in its one-hour, four-teen-mile course from the dam. It bounced off the mountain in its path and washed back up two miles, carrying debris and people with it. The devastation took just ten minutes.

The massive stone-arched Pennsylvania Railroad bridge on the downriver side of Johnstown had been protected by a curve in the river and held. Debris piled up forty feet high in a forty-acre area, and as night came on it caught fire. Editor Swank, who had been watching everything from his *Tribune* office window, wrote that the fire burned "with all the fury of the hell you read about—cremation alive in your own home, perhaps a mile from its foundation; dear ones slowly consumed before your eyes, and the same fate yours a moment later." Rescue parties worked through the night to free people trapped alive in the burning pile, but still an estimated eighty died. The finest and newest hotel in town, the Hulbert House, had been used by many people seeking a safe refuge. It collapsed almost the instant it was hit by the flood. Of the sixty people inside the building only nine survived.

Roads were impassable. The railroad had been destroyed. Every telegraph and telephone line to the outside was down. There was no drinkable water, little food, and no stores from which to obtain either. However, townspeople organized and mobilized at dawn, and newspaper reporters, the first of whom arrived that morning by foot, publicized the tragedy, bringing aid from all over the country. In two days more than one thousand people came to help the twenty-seven thousand who needed aid.

By June 4 thousands more had arrived, including Clara Barton and her newly organized American Red Cross, which set up tent hospitals, six hotels with hot and cold running water, kitchens, and laundries. In five months she distributed nearly a half million dollars' worth of blankets, clothing, food, and cash. Upon her departure she was presented with a diamond locket by the people of Johnstown, and was later feted in Washington at a dinner attended by President and Mrs. Benjamin Harrison.

By the end of the month a book on the disaster had been published, and within six months, a dozen would appear. Newspapers carried sensational stories for weeks and published extra editions, all of which sold out. Songs were written, several of which became best-sellers. Sightseers with picnic baskets arrived and bought souvenirs. Cash contributions from around the world would total more than $3.7 million.

Those bodies not identified were numbered, their descriptions recorded, and buried; one out of every three bodies would never be identified. Hundreds of people who were lost would never be found; it is supposed that some simply walked away and never came back. Not for months would there be any realistic count of the dead, and there would never be an exact, final count. Two bodies would be found as late as 1906. Ninety-nine whole families had been wiped out; ninety-eight children had lost both parents; hardly a family had not suffered a death. The flood had killed about one out of every nine people. In spite of assiduous cleanup, including the sprinkling of four thousand barrels of quicklime over the area, typhoid broke out, affecting 461 people and killing 40.

The faults of the dam were made public. In Pittsburgh, members of the South Fork Club met and officially decided that it would be best to say nothing. Lawsuits were brought, but the club had no assets except the now worthless site, and, widespread negative publicity notwithstanding, no one was awarded anything. Cyrus Elder, who had lost his wife and daughter and his home, and who was the only local member of the club, concluded, "If anybody be to blame I suppose we ourselves are among them, for we have indeed been very careless in this most important matter and most of us have paid the penalty of our neglect."

New Beginnings

Everyone took it for granted that Johnstown would be rebuilt, and so it was. Some of the mills have closed, but the Gautier Mills, built by Cambria Iron Company and then rebuilt after the flood, have been continuously used since their construction. They were sold to Bethlehem Steel in 1923, more recently sold again, and now form a part of the Johnstown America Corporation's steel making facilities. Redevelopment has eliminated some of the historic buildings, but many remain, and have become part of the area's tourist attractions. During the Depression in the 1930's, a multimillion-dollar project to build river walls to protect the city from future floods was designed by the U.S. Army Corps of Engineers and constructed by unemployed steel workers and coal miners. Still, another serious flood occurred in 1977.

Places to Visit

The Johnstown Flood National Memorial is located in historic St. Michael, the site of the former South Fork Fishing and Hunting Club. The visitors' center features exhibits, the film *Black Friday*, and walking tours of the dam site. Every May 31, over 2,209 candles are lit in commemoration of those who died in the flood.

The exhibits at the downtown Johnstown Flood Museum include a twenty-four-foot relief map with fiberoptic light and sound, as well as extensive exhibits and artifacts of and from the disaster and rebuilding. The telephone number for the museum is (814) 539-1889.

The Allegheny Portage Railroad National Historic Site atop Cresson Mountain, commemorates the first crossing of the Allegheny Mountains in 1834. This pioneer railroad ran for twenty years and is a part of the nation's transportation heritage. The telephone number for this National Historic Site is (814) 886-6150.

The Inclined Plane, built in 1891, is advertised as the steepest vehicular inclined plane in the world. Cars carry passengers and vehicles up a 71.9-degree grade to a visitors' center, restaurant, and observation deck. The telephone number for the Inclined Plane is (814) 536-1816.

Grandview Cemetery, located in the Westmont neighborhood, typifies nineteenth century cemetery design and includes a monument, erected in 1892, to the unknown victims of the flood.

Point Park and the stone bridge, the seven-arch stone bridge which withstood the flood, today form a background for an eternal flame commemorating the victims. Pasquerilla Performing Arts Center, located on the campus of the University of Pittsburgh in Johnstown, also houses the Southern Alleghenies Museum of Art. It can be reached at (814) 269-7200.

The Community Arts Center of Cambria County, located in the oldest original log house in the Johnstown area, is located in Westmont and includes a gift shop and art gallery. Its telephone number is (814) 255-6515.

Fort Necessary National Battlefield commemorates George Washington's first military action and his only surrender. The park also manages the Mount Washington Tavern, a museum that once was a popular stagecoach stop along the National Road. The park is located along U.S. Route 40 in Farmington. The phone number for the park is (814) 329-5512.

Friendship Hill National Historic Site tells the story of statesman Albert Gallatin. It is located fifteen miles south of Uniontown along Pennsylvania Route 166. The telephone number is (814) 725-9190.   —*Erika E. Pilver*

For Further Information:

Degen, Paula, and Carl Degen. *The Johnstown Flood of 1889: The Tragedy of the Conemaugh.* Philadelphia: Eastern Acorn Press, 1984. Primarily a photographic history, this illustrated text tells the story of the flood through period photography. Available from the Johnstown Flood Museum.

McCullough, David. *The Johnstown Flood.* New York: Simon & Schuster, 1968. The author is a well-known historian, and this work remains the definitive history of the flood. An extensive bibliography is included. McCullough is also author of an article, "Run for Your Lives!" published in *American Heritage Magazine* (16, no. 4, 1966, pp. 5-11; 66-75) and available from the museum.

Walker, James Herbert. *The Johnstown Horror: Or, Valley of Death.* Philadelphia: H. J. Smith, 1889. Although obviously no longer available except by chance in libraries or antique bookstores, the book has provided information for this entry.

Pennsylvania Dutch Country

Date: First permanent European settlement founded about 1719

Relevant issues: Cultural history, religion

Significance: The city and county of Lancaster attracted many German immigrants, especially members of minority religions, beginning in the eighteenth century. Known overall as the "Pennsylvania Dutch," these settlers have had a great impact on the agricultural and industrial development of the area. Many persons of the Amish faith still farm in Lancaster County, using traditional, nonmechanical methods.

Location: In southeastern Pennsylvania sixty-six miles west of Philadelphia in the middle of Lancaster County, which is bordered on the west by the Susquehanna River, on the east by the town of Gap, on the north by the city of Reading, and on the south by Maryland

Site Office:

Pennsylvania Dutch Convention and Visitors Bureau
501 Greenfield Road
Lancaster, PA 17601
ph.: (717) 299-8901

The earliest permanent European settlement in Lancaster County was established around 1719 by a group of Swiss Mennonites led by Hans Herr. The Mennonites, established in Emden, Germany, in 1530, were one of the many Protestant sects that had arisen in Europe as a result of the Reformation. In 1683, a group of Mennonites had founded Germantown, Pennsylvania, and became quickly established in the state. Heavily taxed and persecuted in Europe, sects such as the Mennonites were attracted to William Penn's "Holy Experiment" in religious freedom. Penn had extended an invitation to the Quakers and other sects to settle in his state. The Mennonites were particularly attracted to the frontier of a new land because their religious beliefs precluded following secular authority. They would not take oaths and had a distrust of wealth, the arts, and science.

The Amish

In 1693, the Old Order Amish had split from the Mennonites. The Amish, who began arriving in the Lancaster area about 1760, favored religious services conducted in German in their homes and were committed to a simple, frugal life without modern conveniences and with no books other than the Bible. The Amish virtues of order, self-sufficiency, and peace and their values of family, farming, and faith are still evident in Amish settlements in Lancaster County. Another minority sect to settle in the area was the Ephrata Society. In 1732, the Ephrata Cloister was established by Conrad Beissel as one of the first religious commu-

Ephrata Cloister. (Pennsylvania Dutch Convention & Visitors Bureau)

nal societies in America. This sect stressed celibacy, even for married couples. New members, therefore, had to be constantly recruited. The actual cloister was built between 1728 and 1733 in northern Lancaster County, and the sect itself disbanded in 1814.

The Ephrata Cloister did not long outlast its founder's death in 1768, but it produced more than one thousand hymns during its lifetime. The cloister is now a tourist attraction and is an important example of the kind of "Old World" architecture favored by the sects.

German Immigration

The many German immigrants who came to Lancaster County during the eighteenth century were attracted to the level land and rich soil of the area—assets which are still considered the county's most important resources. The majority of the five thousand Hessian soldiers who fought for the British crown during the Revolutionary War settled in Pennsylvania, including Lancaster. Waves of immigration from Europe continued until World War I.

Because the German immigrants kept their native tongue, they referred to themselves as Pennsylfawnisch Deitsch (Deutsch in the more formal High German). To English ears, the word sounded like Dutch, and the term Pennsylvania Dutch was coined early in the colonial era.

Founding of Lancaster

George Gibson in 1721 opened a tavern in what is now Penn Square in the center of the town of Lancaster and is its first recorded resident. In 1730, the town of Lancaster was established by John Wright, who named it for his home in Lancashire, England. By the time of the American Revolution, Lancaster was one of the largest and most important inland towns in the colonies.

In the mid-1700's German immigrants in Lancaster County's Conestoga Creek Valley began making large wagons. These "Conestoga" wagons were sixteen feet long, four feet high and deep, and perched on top of four-foot high wheels with iron tires four inches wide. They were capable of carrying up to six tons and were therefore pulled by specially bred horses. Because of their wide wheels, the wagons were able to travel easily on the dirt roads of the day.

Conestoga wagons originally were used to carry crops to market. Flour and iron ore were typical products carried from Lancaster to Philadelphia, where they were exchanged for tools, clothing, and furniture. As word of the huge, sturdy wagons spread, settlers began using them for their westward journeys and the Conestoga wagon's ultimate fame rested on the fact that it was the vehicle of choice for carrying pioneers and material westward to the Pacific coast.

Lancaster also became the first American center for the production of rifles. Based on German designs and much more accurate than English-style muskets, these guns became known as Pennsylvania rifles and were widely used during the young nation's early years. Iron ore furnaces and glassmaking also were important early Lancaster industries.

On September 27, 1777, Lancaster served for a day as the colonies' capital when the Continental Congress fled Philadelphia during the British occupation. However, Lancaster also was felt to be unsafe, and the colonial capital was moved across the Susquehanna River to York, where it remained for nine months. From 1799 to 1812, Lancaster was the capital of Pennsylvania.

The nation's fourteenth oldest college, Franklin and Marshall College, was established in Lancaster in 1787. Three of its buildings today are on the National Register of Historic Places: Old Main, Goethean Hall, and Diagonothian Hall.

Lancaster County has an important place in transportation development. It was the site of the nation's first turnpike—a sixty-five-mile road built between 1792 and 1794 linking Philadelphia and Lancaster. Funding for the Lancaster Pike, the first paved road in Pennsylvania, was raised by William Bingham of Philadelphia. In order to pay back the debt, each traveler on the road had to stop every ten miles and pay a toll in order to open a gate. These gates

had long shafts known as pikes, and the term "turning the pike" was eventually shortened to turnpike. The inventor of the first successful steamboat, Robert Fulton, was born in southern Lancaster County. In 1807 he launched his boat on the Hudson River in New York.

Abolitionist Movement and the Civil War
During the 1840's and 1850's, as the slavery issue began to tear the nation apart, Lancaster County was the site of numerous stations on the Underground Railroad, the path to freedom for escaping slaves. An incident in Lancaster County in which Edward Gorsuch was killed as he attempted to retrieve his runaway slaves in 1851 is considered by some to be the first skirmish of the Civil War.

Because Lancaster was in the heart of the industrial North, Confederate troops invaded the surrounding area in search of supplies during the fall of 1862 and the summer of 1863. This was as far north as the Confederates ever penetrated and this activity culminated in the famous Battle of Get-

In Lancaster County, the Amish still ride in horse-drawn buggies. (Pennsylvania Dutch Convention & Visitors Bureau)

tysburg—only eighty-six miles from Lancaster County's northern border. Many Union army regiments were composed largely of Pennsylvania Dutch.

The only Pennsylvanian to occupy the White House was elected while living just west of Lancaster. James Buchanan retired to his Pennsylvania estate, Wheatland, after his term ended in 1861 and died there in 1868. He had bought the home in 1848.

Lancaster's Commercial Development

The city of Lancaster grew into an important commercial and industrial center. It is home to the first successful Woolworth's variety store. F. W. Woolworth opened the store in 1879 after his initial effort failed in Utica, New York. The store and others that followed originally sold only items costing five and ten cents and were a retail innovation at the time. The largest stockyards east of Chicago operated in Lancaster until the late twentieth century. Today, the Lancaster area remains the site of several well-known businesses, including Armstrong World Industries, maker of floor and ceiling coverings, and Hamilton Watch, one of the few watch factories left in the United States.

The Modern Amish

It is still farming and tourism that are the main industries of the area. The Amish are a strong presence in Lancaster County. They still eschew tractors and most other farm machinery, instead tilling their fields with teams of Clydesdale horses and bringing their crops to the barns in Conestoga wagons.

Many of the Amish still grow tobacco in their impeccably tilled fields. They practice crop rotation almost religiously. In fact, an Amish farmer who does not properly care for his fields is brought before the church for censure.

The Amish are not totally opposed to mechanical improvements when it comes to farming. In the 1920's they were advised to obey new laws regarding the hygiene of milk products, and now many Amish dairy farms feature refrigeration units run by diesel engines. Cow stalls have been modified to meet modern specifications, and trucks from large dairy cooperatives arrive at Amish farms daily to pick up milk.

Population Growth and Tourism

During the last decades of the twentieth century, threats to the Amish way of life came in the form of population growth in Lancaster County. During this period, more than four thousand new residents a year arrived—making Lancaster one of Pennsylvania's fastest-growing counties. Some of the world's richest farmland has been lost forever to suburban sprawl. In 1984 the Lancaster Farmland Trust was established to encourage sensitive planning and preservation. The 1,500-member private, not-for-profit organization is made up mostly of Lancaster County residents committed to maintaining economic growth while preserving resources.

Tourism, too, has had its impact on the Amish. A long-standing Amish taboo against photography has been noticeably eroded by years of contact with camera-toting tourists. Young people, especially, become attracted to the "worldly" ways with which they come into increasing contact.

Lancaster and Lancaster County hold much for the tourist. The town is easily walkable, with most of the historic places located near Penn Square. The original F. W. Woolworth store (1879) and the Fulton Opera House (built in 1852 and one of the oldest theatres in the country) are of particular interest.

In Lancaster County, the 20 buildings of the Ephrata Cloister are open for touring. Tours of several Amish farms are also available. The Strasburg Railroad, the oldest short line in the United States, gives rides using the railroad's original steam equipment, and a multitude of farmers' markets, craft shops, and antique fairs are found throughout the area.

—*Linda J. King*

For Further Information:

Curran, Alfred A. *German Immigration to Pennsylvania 1683-1933*. Columbus, Ga.: Brentwood University Press, 1986. A fascinating scholarly look at how the Pennsylvania Dutch came to be. It covers German influence in Pennsylvania, but there are sections specific to Lancaster. It is short and fairly easy to read and offers insight into Lancaster history not found in other books.

Hoffman, William N. *Going Dutch*. Lancaster, Pa.: Spring Garden, 1991. An excellent guidebook that covers the whole of Pennsylvania Dutch

Country. It provides phone numbers, visitor information, and schedules of events. It is particularly good in describing the history of each county, town, and attraction.

Parsons, William T. *The Pennsylvania Dutch: A Persistent Minority*. Boston: Twayne, 1976. Difficult to read, as it tends to go off on tangents, but overall it presents solid information on the influence the Pennsylvania Dutch have had on Lancaster history. It is particularly effective in its discussion of the present state of this culture and the pressures now upon it.

Steinbicker, Earl. *Daytrips Pennsylvania Dutch Country and Philadelphia: Fifty One-Day Adventures from the Philadelphia and Lancaster Areas*. Norwalk, Conn.: Hastings House, 2000. A guidebook to Pennsylvania Dutch Country.

Valley Forge

Date: Created as a National Historical Park in 1976

Relevant issues: Military history, Revolutionary War

Significance: This is the site of the historic encampment of General George Washington's Continental army during the winter of 1777-1778. The park today covers about three thousand acres on both sides of the Schuylkill River.

Location: Eighteen miles northwest of Philadelphia, near exit 24 on the Pennsylvania Turnpike at the junction of Pennsylvania Routes 23 and 363

Site Office:
Valley Forge National Historical Park
P.O. Box 953
Valley Forge, PA 19482
ph.: (610) 783-1077
Web site: www.nps.gov/vafo/

Valley Forge, the winter quarters of General George Washington's Continental army in 1777-1778, has been called the most celebrated encampment in the history of the world. It was there that Washington and his ragged and exhausted army of twelve thousand men lived for six months, enduring brutal cold and severe privation. Although no battles were fought there, several thousand men died of malnutrition, exposure, and dis-

ease. Despite that terrible winter of hardship, Valley Forge has been called the turning point of the Revolutionary War. It transformed Washington's "rabble in arms" into a disciplined fighting force that in the spring emerged to win the key Battle of Monmouth Courthouse and went on to win several other important battles, culminating with the victory at Yorktown.

Although General Washington's troops had achieved significant victories at Trenton and Princeton in the winter of 1776-1777, the fortunes of the American army took a turn for the worse after Sir William Howe, commander in chief of the British forces in North America, landed his experienced army at the upper end of the Chesapeake Bay. His objective was the capture of the American capital in Philadelphia.

Washington was able to maneuver his army into position to defend the city, but a combination of Howe's skillful tactics and several blunders by Washington led to a British victory at Brandywine and a draw at Germantown. The Continental Congress fled Philadelphia, and the British occupied the city. With winter rapidly approaching and prospects of further military actions unpromising, Washington turned his attention to obtaining winter quarters for his men.

Selection of Valley Forge for Winter Quarters

Several sites were proposed, but his selection, Valley Forge, was perhaps the best of those considered. Named for an iron forge on Valley Creek, Valley Forge was close enough to the British to prevent their raiders from sweeping into the Pennsylvania interior, yet far enough away to prevent surprise attacks. The area's high ground between Mount Joy and Mount Misery, with the Schuylkill River to the north, made it easily defensible.

It was snowing on the day Washington led his twelve thousand exhausted men up Guelph Road into the encampment. Included in the ranks were boys as young as twelve and men in their fifties and sixties. Some of the soldiers were blacks; others, Indians. They presented a truly sorry picture as they trudged wearily into camp. According to historian Joan Marshall-Dutcher, "Many a soldier's shoes had been destroyed by the long marches, and clothing and blankets were tattered almost beyond serviceability. Hundreds of men were declared unfit for duty. . . . "

Conditions in the Camp

The most pressing problem was shelter for the men. Brigadier General Louis du Portail, chief of the French engineers, was assigned the monumental task of building approximately one thousand cabins or huts for the troops as quickly as possible. The huts were to measure fourteen by sixteen feet, to house twelve men each, and to be grouped by military unit into streets and sections. Although hampered by several shortages, including nails, tools, and boards for doors and roofs, du Portail and his units had built nearly all the huts by the third day in camp, a feat undoubtedly helped by Washington's having offered several prizes to the units that finished their huts first.

Although very cramped, and with roofs that leaked more or less constantly, the huts were nevertheless satisfactory for men accustomed to the hardships of army life. Even so, after months of sheltering unwashed men and food waste, these huts were major sources of disease and contagion. Soldiers, frequently ill and inadequately dressed for the cold, were not inclined to trek all the way to the camp latrines. Small wonder that General Anthony Wayne reportedly said he would rather go into battle than on an inspection tour of the huts.

One of the greatest problems was the acute shortage of food and supplies. According to the rations determined by the Continental Congress for the troops, the men were to receive daily "a pound and a half of flour or bread, a pound of pork, and a gill [four ounces] of spirits, with an occasional half pint of peas or beans in place of flour . . . "

The disparity between these generous rations and what the men actually received was shocking and a source of great dissension among the troops. When the army arrived at Valley Forge, they had had no fresh food for several days, and none would arrive for several days thereafter. Although foraging parties had found enough mutton and rum for all in limited quantities on Christmas Day, shortages continued for most of the winter and often left the men near starvation. On some days, many of the troops had no rations at all. At other times they had nothing but flour, to which they added water before roasting it over the coals to create "firecake."

These shortages were the result of poor organization, limited forage for the horses, devaluation of the Continental currency, and the behavior of the wagoners. According to historian Noel F. Busch, the wagoners charged high wages but did little to earn them. For example, they emptied flour barrels into open carts and poured the brine off of salt meat, causing it to spoil. Washington was moved to write, "To see men without clothes to cover their nakedness, without blankets to lie on, without shoes . . . without a house or hut to cover them until those could be built, and submitting without a murmur, is a proof of the patience and obedience, which in my opinion, can scarcely be paralleled."

Even so, desertions ran into the thousands—many men returned home only to rejoin under another name and secure the bounty for enlistment. Worse, an estimated one thousand men joined the British at Philadelphia of their own free will. Many

George Washington's headquarters at Valley Forge. (American Stock Photography)

of them were so-called Old-country men, English immigrants less dedicated to the rebel cause than native-born Americans.

To deal with this problem, Washington, like other commanders of the time, relied on corporal punishment. For instance, the original punishment for desertion was thirty-nine lashes on the bare back, but by 1776 Congress had lifted the limit to one hundred, and it soon increased. Other harsh penalties were meted out for trading with the enemy, embezzling, theft, dueling, drunkenness, and gambling.

Disease Takes a Heavy Toll

By far the worst scourge to face the soldiers was death from disease, which during the encampment took an estimated 2,500 lives, or 25 percent of the force that had arrived at Valley Forge in December. One of the worst killers was typhus, or "camp fever," spread mainly by body lice. The remedy was to burn a spoonful of sulfur or gunpowder in the hut of the stricken man every day. Needless to say, few were saved by this treatment. Another devastating disease was smallpox. Although the benefits of inoculation were understood at the time (if only imprecisely), there were also chronic shortages of medical supplies, and it took months to treat the entire camp. Typhus and smallpox were often mistaken for one another in their early stages of development, and sufferers of the two diseases were not separated, so that those who caught the one disease were likely to catch the other as well.

Most of the afflicted were quartered at hospitals in or near camp. The biggest one, at Yellow Springs, had formerly been a local health spa. Each row of huts in camp was equipped with its own sick bay. These bays were frequently the site of amputations necessitated by frostbite. Other common ailments were "the itch," a type of scabies that often led to serious infection, and, of course, the common cold, which could lead to pneumonia. The unsanitary conditions at camp contributed to a high rate of food poisoning and dysentery.

Unsanitary conditions were the result not only of the soldiers' behavior, but of the rotting bodies of horses that had died of exposure or starvation. "Removing their carcasses was obviously a task of the first magnitude," writes historian Noel F. Busch, "but burying them in the frozen ground was even more difficult, and the graves were often shal-low. After a heavy rain or thaw, the rotting remains would then be exposed so that the job had to be done a second or third time."

Von Steuben Takes Charge of Discipline

On February 23, Friedrich Wilhelm Ludolf Gerhard Augustin von Steuben, formerly a captain in the Prussian army, arrived in Valley Forge. Von Steuben was a drillmaster without peer, and he was able to transform the ragtag forces he found into a disciplined army. Upon his arrival, he had been given the task of creating, from scratch, a practical training program. Von Steuben began by training a core group of soldiers selected from various state armies. Once trained, these men would themselves teach what they had learned to the other troops in their units. To aid in the training von Steuben wrote a manual eventually published as *Regulations for the Order and Discipline of the Troops of the United States* (but better known as the Blue Book), which would be used as the basic training guide for the U.S. Army for more than fifty years. Each night he wrote a training plan in French; it was immediately translated into English and copied for all the individual regiments and companies.

The men learned to march, charge with bayonets, and load and fire muskets. Von Steuben also introduced the latest European maneuvers, designed to allow regiments to move rapidly and to develop maximum firepower. but perhaps his greatest accomplishment was to instill in the Continental officers a new spirit of military discipline based, in the Prussian manner, on mutual trust—a spirit of respect that held a company, a regiment, or an army together.

Spring's arrival saw a decided uplift in the spirit of the men encamped at Valley Forge. Under Von Steuben, the army had gained a new sense of unity. There were new arrivals almost daily from South Carolina, Maryland, and New York. General Nathanael Greene, one of of Washington's most trusted lieutenants, was appointed quartermaster general and began to remedy supply problems. Morale grew steadily. Then on May 5, 1778, the government announced a formal alliance with France.

Washington's Army Moves Out

On June 19, 1778, six months to the day after it had marched into Valley Forge, the newly resolute Continental army, led by its commander, General

Washington, moved out of Valley Forge. Washington led his troops to Monmouth Courthouse, where just nine days later they won a significant victory against the British. The newly forged army then marched on to eventual victory at Yorktown.

Today Valley Forge and the surrounding area, consisting of several thousand acres of rolling hills and forest overlooking the Schuylkill River, is known as Valley Forge National Historical Park and is administered by the federal government. Several of the original huts and buildings are still intact. Also on view at the park are the Memorial Arch, a 1917 replica of the Arch of Triumph in Paris; a bronze equestrian statue of General Anthony Wayne; General Washington's headquarters, located in the Isaac Potts House; several redoubts important in the defense of the area; and Washington Memorial Chapel.   —*Terence J. Sacks*

For Further Information:

Busch, Noel F. *Winter Quarters: George Washington and the Continental Army at Valley Forge.* New York: Liveright, 1974. Provides a detailed look at the incredible privations and suffering of the men at Valley Forge, and how Washington and Von Steuben managed to convert this demoralized group into an effective fighting force.

Eastby, Allen G. "The Baron." *American History Illustrated*, November/December, 1990. Presents an insightful and fascinating picture of the man entrusted by General Washington to instill discipline into the Continental army.

Marshall-Dutcher, Joan. "Winter at Valley Forge." *American History Illustrated*, November/December, 1990. Marshall-Dutcher, official historian at the park, presents a concise and stirring description of the events there.

Treese, Lorett. *Valley Forge: Making and Remaking a National Symbol.* University Park: Pennsylvania State University Press, 1995. Discusses the history of Valley Forge and recent efforts toward restoration and conservation.

Other Historic Sites

Acheson House

Location: Monongahela, Washington County
Relevant issues: Science and technology
Statement of significance: From 1890 to 1895, this was the home of Edward G. Acheson (1856-1931), inventor. This is also the site where in 1891 he invented carborundum, at the time the hardest known artificial substance, widely used in industry since its invention.

American Philosophical Society Hall

Location: Philadelphia, Philadelphia County
Relevant issues: Science and technology
Web site: www.amphilsoc.org
Statement of significance: Since 1789, this two-story, late Georgian brick building has been the home of one of America's oldest and most honorable learned societies. The society traces its origins back to 1743, when Benjamin Franklin publicly urged the creation of a society to stimulate interest in learning. The society publishes the oldest scholarly journal in America, its *Transactions*.

Andalusia

Location: Philadelphia, Bucks County
Relevant issues: Business and industry, political history
Statement of significance: From 1821 to 1844, this was the residence of Nicholas Biddle (1786-1844), head of the Second Bank of the United States (1823-1836), famous as President Andrew Jackson's opponent. To the original house, whose north front is an outstanding example of the Regency style in the United States, he added a wing modeled on a Greek temple.

Becuna

Location: Philadelphia, Philadelphia County
Relevant issues: Naval history, World War II
Web site: www.subnet.com/fleet/ss319.htm
Statement of significance: An example of the standard fleet-type Balao Class submarines which could operate at a test depth of four hundred feet, *Becuna* was commissioned in 1944 and served in World War II as the submarine flagship of the

Pacific Fleet under the command of General Douglas MacArthur. It is credited with sinking 3,888 tons of Japanese shipping and received four battle stars for its World War II service.

Bedford Springs Hotel Historic District

Location: Bedford, Bedford County

Relevant issues: Cultural history, health and medicine, political history

Statement of significance: Significant as one of the nation's finest remaining examples of the mineral springs resort phenomenon of the nineteenth and early twentieth centuries, this district presents a vivid picture of resort spa architecture and lifestyle. With its grand buildings and many mineral springs, the Bedford Springs Hotel became renowned among society's elite as a fashionable place for recuperation, relaxation, and leisure. It was also an important political gathering place during the mid-nineteenth century, due to its proximity to Washington and its half century-long association with Pennsylvanian James Buchanan, the fifteenth president of the United States, who used the resort as a summer White House during his administration.

Boathouse Row

Location: Philadelphia, Philadelphia County

Relevant issues: Sports

Statement of significance: Situated in Fairmount Park, the private boat and barge clubs and skating club were created to serve the recreational needs of Philadelphians. The clubs' parent organization, the Schuylkill Navy, formed in 1858, is the oldest amateur governing body in the United States. National and international champions, including many Olympic participants and winners, have come from these clubs. Included are the oldest continuously existing club in the United States and the oldest women's club.

Bost Building

Location: Homestead, Allegheny County

Relevant issues: Business and industry, political history

Statement of significance: Between June 29 and November 21, 1892, much of the nation followed the events of a labor strike outside Pittsburgh that pitted the Carnegie Steel Company against one of the strongest labor unions at the time. During the strike at the Homestead Steel Works, the Bost Building served as the local headquarters for the Amalgamated Association of Iron and Steel Workers and as the base for American and British newspaper correspondents reporting the events. The confrontation turned bloody when Pinkerton guards approached Homestead on barges in a failed attempt to reclaim the steel works from the striking workers and their supporters. The Bost Building is the best surviving structure associated with this important strike.

Bradford House

Location: Washington, Washington County

Relevant issues: Political history

Statement of significance: Constructed in 1788, this well-decorated two-and-a-half-story stone house was the residence of David Bradford, the most prominent leader of the rebels in the Whiskey Rebellion (1794). Bradford, a lawyer in Washington, D.C., led the rebels in a march on Pittsburgh; after the suppression of the rebellion, Bradford fled the United States. His house is a museum owned by the Commonwealth of Pennsylvania.

Brandywine Battlefield

Location: Brandywine Battlefield Park, Chadds Ford, Delaware County

Relevant issues: Military history, Revolutionary War

Statement of significance: On September 11, 1777, George Washington's Continentals met the British forces under Lord Richard Howe in the only major clash during the British campaign which resulted in the capture of Philadelphia. Although the battle was an American defeat, the Continentals demonstrated a newly won ability to withstand the determined attack of British regulars, even while sustaining heavy losses.

Buck House

Location: Dublin, Bucks County

Relevant issues: Literary history

Statement of significance: From 1933 until her death, this was the principal residence of noted American novelist Pearl S. Buck (1892-1973), the first American woman to win the Nobel Prize in

Literature (1938). Buck purchased this farm with royalties from her novel *The Good Earth* (1931).

Bushy Run Battlefield

Location: Harrison City, Westmoreland County
Relevant issues: American Indian history, colonial America, military history
Statement of significance: Fought in 1763, the Battle of Bushy Run was a decisive British victory during Pontiac's Rebellion, the best-organized eighteenth century campaign by Native Americans against Anglo-American frontier settlements.

Cambria Iron Company

Location: Johnstown, Cambria County
Relevant issues: Business and industry
Statement of significance: Founded in 1852, the Cambria Iron Company was considered one of the greatest of the early modern iron and steel works. In the 1850's, 1860's, and 1870's, Johnstown attracted some of the best engineers, innovators, and managers in the industry and was the technological leader in the manufacture of iron and steel rail. The plant's history is a continuum reflecting the evolution of the industry nationwide.

Carlisle Indian School

Location: Carlisle, Cumberland County
Relevant issues: American Indian history, education
Statement of significance: Founded in 1879 by Brigadier General Richard H. Pratt (1840-1924), a Civil War officer and veteran of the Indian campaigns in the West, the school pioneered federal programs for Indian education and was a model for similar schools built elsewhere.

Cliveden

Location: Philadelphia, Philadelphia County
Relevant issues: Military history, Revolutionary War
Web site: www.cliveden.org
Statement of significance: Completed in 1764, this Georgian-style house with handsome pediments, cornices, and a fine doorway was the home of Benjamin Chew, attorney general of Pennsylvania. It is the most important surviving landmark of the Battle of Germantown (October 4, 1777) which, combined with the American victory at Saratoga in the same month, helped to secure the alliance of the United States with France.

Colonial Germantown Historic District

Location: Germantown Avenue, between Windrum Avenue and Upsal Street, Philadelphia, Philadelphia County
Relevant issues: Colonial America, European settlement
Statement of significance: This district was founded in 1683 by Germans fleeing religious persecution who were invited to Pennsylvania by William Penn. The district exemplifies the successful settlement of a non-British group in one of the thirteen original British colonies.

Drake Oil Well

Location: Drake Well Memorial Park, 3 miles southeast of Titusville, Venango County
Relevant issues: Business and industry
Statement of significance: On August 27, 1859, Edwin L. Drake (1819-1880) struck oil here, the site of the world's first successful oil well. Its establishment resulted in an oil boom that made the region the oil center of the United States for twenty-five years. It is now Drake Well Memorial State Park.

Eakins House

Location: Philadelphia, Philadelphia County
Relevant issues: Art and architecture
Statement of significance: From the age of two until his death, this was the home of Thomas Eakins (1844-1919), one of America's greatest painters.

Eisenhower Farmstead

Location: Gettysburg, Adams County
Relevant issues: Political history
Web site: www.nps.gov/eise/
Statement of significance: This farm served Dwight D. Eisenhower (1890-1969), thirty-fourth president of the United States (1953-1961), as a retreat during his presidential years and as his principal residence during retirement.

Esherick House and Studio

Location: Malvern, Chester County

Relevant issues: Art and architecture

Web site: www.craftsreport.com/august96/esherick
.html

Statement of significance: From 1926 to 1966, this was the home and workplace of Wharton Esherick (1887-1970), an artist and craftsman who applied the principles of modern sculpture to all his work, including furniture and architectural designs. In doing so, he bridged the gap between the fine arts and the decorative arts. His impulse to produce hand-done works with great respect for the material is also rooted in the Arts and Crafts movement which swept England and America at the end of the nineteenth century.

Fallingwater

Location: Mill Run, Fayette County

Relevant issues: Art and architecture

Statement of significance: A summer house built for a Pittsburgh millionaire, Fallingwater (1937) has been called the most famous modern house in the world. The house, cantilevered over a waterfall, is one of Frank Lloyd Wright's masterworks.

Friends Hospital

Location: Philadelphia, Philadelphia County

Relevant issues: Health and medicine

Statement of significance: Friends Hospital was the first private, nonprofit, exclusively mental hospital in the United States and is the oldest continuing such institution. The social and medical concerns which Quakers held regarding psychiatric problems guided Friends Hospital in its physical site plan, the methodology of treatment, and even the manner of its original fundraising. These approaches became the model which was studied throughout the nineteenth and early twentieth centuries by others wishing to found similar facilities. The hospital's design, based upon William Tuke's York Retreat in England, but with better ventilation and light as suggested by Philadelphia Friend Thomas Scattergood, became a model for other American mental facilities.

Fulton Birthplace

Location: Quarryville, Lancaster County

Relevant issues: Naval history, science and technology

Statement of significance: This stone house was the birthplace of Robert Fulton (1765-1815), artist, civil engineer, and inventor. Fulton worked on the development of canal systems and engineering; he is perhaps best remembered for designing the *Clermont*, the first commercially successful American steamboat, launched in 1807.

Germantown Cricket Club

Location: Philadelphia, Philadelphia County

Relevant issues: Sports

Statement of significance: Founded in 1855, this is the second-oldest cricket club in the United States. Its part in the sport of cricket was of international rank in the nineteenth century. Early in the twentieth century, tennis gained prominence over cricket at the club. The most noted member was William T. ("Big Bill") Tilden (1893-1953), an international tennis star of the 1920's.

Harmony Historic District

Location: Harmony, Butler County

Relevant issues: Social reform

Statement of significance: The Harmony Society, three hundred followers of George Rapp, established a utopian settlement here in 1805. It developed into a prosperous agricultural and manufacturing community, which was sold when the society decided to move to Indiana in search of more fertile land.

Harper House

Location: Philadelphia, Philadelphia County

Relevant issues: African American history, social reform, women's history

Statement of significance: From 1870 to her death, this was the home of Frances E. W. Harper (1825-1911), an African American writer and social activist who participated in the abolitionist, black rights, woman suffrage, and temperance movements.

Hershey Mansion

Location: Hershey, Dauphin County

Relevant issues: Business and industry

Statement of significance: From 1908 to 1945, this was the residence of Milton S. Hershey (1857-1945), originator of the Hershey Bar. In the first half of the twentieth century, Hershey's company became the world's largest manufacturer of chocolate.

Hill-Keith-Physick House

Location: Philadelphia, Philadelphia County
Relevant issues: Health and medicine
Statement of significance: From about 1815 until his death, this was the home of Philip Syng Physick (1768-1837), the late eighteenth and early nineteenth century Philadelphia physician who has been called the founder of American surgery.

Institute of the Pennsylvania Hospital

Location: Philadelphia, Philadelphia County
Relevant issues: Health and medicine
Statement of significance: Completed in 1859, this hospital for the mentally ill introduced innumerable innovations for its day and influenced similar institutions throughout America. Its basic plan was the work of Dr. Thomas Story Kirkbride (1809-1883), who believed that insanity should be treated as an illness.

John Coltrane House

Location: Philadelphia, Philadelphia County
Relevant issues: African American history, cultural history
Statement of significance: This house was the home of tenor saxophonist and American jazz pioneer John Coltrane (1926-1967) from 1952 until his death, including the critical years during which he developed his characteristic musical language. A musician and composer, Coltrane is a principal figure in twentieth century American music who played a central role in the development of jazz during the 1950's and 1960's. He took the American jazz tradition as it had developed by the late 1940's, with its established forms and harmonies, and radically transformed it, pioneering modal harmonies and incorporating influences from a variety of international sources. He is also, along with Louis Armstrong and Charlie Parker, one of the most influential performing soloists in the history of jazz.

Johnson House

Location: 6306 Germantown Avenue, Philadelphia, Philadelphia County
Relevant issues: African American history, social reform
Web site: www.cr.nps.gov/nr/underground/pa6.htm
Statement of significance: Philadelphia was a center of the nineteenth century American movement to abolish slavery, and the Johnson House was one of the important stations on the Underground Railroad that helped lead so many to freedom. From 1770 to 1908, five generations of the Quaker Johnson family, leading abolitionists and reformers, lived in this colonial stone house. Among the oldest structures in Germantown, it later served as a women's club and is now a historic house museum. The house is within the Colonial Germantown National Historic District.

Kennywood Park

Location: West Mifflin, Allegheny County
Relevant issues: Cultural history
Web site: www.kennywood.com/index2.html
Statement of significance: Opened to the public in 1899, this is the best-preserved survivor of the "trolley park" era when street railway companies built suburban amusement parks linked to center cities by trolley. Kennywood has been called the Roller Coaster Capital of the World and America's Greatest Traditional Amusement Park; it retains rare, exceptional, and highly representative historic amusements.

Laurel Hill Cemetery

Location: 3822 Ridge Avenue, Philadelphia, Philadelphia County
Relevant issues: Art and architecture, cultural history
Statement of significance: Designed by noted Scottish-American architect John Notman in 1836, Philadelphia's Laurel Hill Cemetery is the second major rural cemetery in the United States, and Notman's first known commission. Its romantic landscape, commemorative monuments, and eclectic architecture made it a popular tourist attraction in the nineteenth and early twentieth centuries. Laurel Hill is a landmark in American social and cultural history, an essay in the evolution of the nation's architecture, landscape design, and funerary art.

Lukens Historic District

Location: South First Street, Coatesville, Chester County

Relevant issues: Business and industry, women's history

Statement of significance: This district is associated with Rebecca Lukens (1794-1854), who played a leading role in the nineteenth century American iron industry, and her family legacy. The firm she owned and managed—Brandywine Ironworks (later Lukens Steel Company)—was one of the industry's major firms in the decades before the Civil War. She was the only woman in the antebellum period to head a heavy industry that had interstate and international interests. Lukens prefigures a pattern which would become more common in the late nineteenth and early twentieth centuries, in which family business gave women entree to management or ownership of large concerns. Rebecca Lukens served as matriarch of this industrial dynasty; her family continued her commitment of fairness to workers, innovative technology, and personal interest in fine architecture.

M. Carey Thomas Library

Location: Bryn Mawr, Montgomery County

Relevant issues: Education, women's history

Statement of significance: Completed on the campus of Bryn Mawr College in 1907, this library illustrates the achievements of M. Carey Thomas (1857-1935), who broke new ground in women's education by establishing at Bryn Mawr academic opportunities for women that paralleled the highest standards in male higher education. As president of Bryn Mawr, Thomas was instrumental in making her college a pioneer among women's colleges in all aspects of higher education. Additionally, Thomas pursued a far-reaching building campaign that resulted in building the first in the United States of what would become known as the Collegiate Gothic Style.

Merion Cricket Club

Location: Haverford, Montgomery County

Relevant issues: Sports

Statement of significance: Founded in 1865 and at this site since 1892, Merion Cricket Club is among the handful of U.S. properties that illustrate the history of cricket, which was a major sport in the nineteenth century, contending with baseball for supremacy. After 1900, the members assumed a vigorous role in lawn tennis. This is a work of one of Philadelphia's premier Victorian-era architects, Frank Furness.

Merion Friends Meeting House

Location: Merion Station, Montgomery County

Relevant issues: European settlement, religion

Statement of significance: Merion Friends Meeting House is the building most closely associated with the "Merioneth Adventurers," a group of Welsh Quakers who came to Pennsylvania in 1682 as part of the earliest-known migration of Celtic-speaking Welsh people in the Western Hemisphere. They came in response to the egalitarian policies that William Penn practiced in his colony. The building is the second-oldest Friends meeting house in the country, having been started c. 1695 and completed by 1714. The stone-walled church, now stuccoed, is in the form of a T and is a rare survivor of Welsh-inspired vernacular architecture.

Mill Grove

Location: Audubon, Montgomery County

Relevant issues: Art and architecture, science and technology

Statement of significance: From 1804 to 1808, Mill Grove, a two-and-a-half-story house of native fieldstone, was the home of John James Audubon (1785-1851). The main portion of the house was built in 1762, and its integrity remains high. Audubon began his observations on avian wildlife here; the house now serves as a museum, containing a priceless collection of Audubon's bird paintings.

Minisink Archaeological Site

Location: Bushkill, Pike County

Relevant issues: American Indian history

Statement of significance: Minisink was the most important Munsee Indian community for much of the seventeenth and eighteenth centuries. Archaeological resources located here have yielded information on historic contact between Indian and European people in Munsee Country, a region stretching from southern New York across northern New Jersey to northeastern Pennsylvania. Today, Minisink remains one of the most extensive, best-preserved, and most intensively studied archaeological locales in the Northeast.

Mother Bethel A.M.E. Church

Location: Philadelphia, Philadelphia County

Relevant issues: African American history, religion

Statement of significance: Founded in 1793, Mother Bethel African Methodist Episcopal Church (1889) is a living memorial to Richard Allen (1760-1831), former slave, Methodist minister, preeminent black leader, and founder of the first permanent national association of African Americans.

N. C. Wyeth House and Studio

Location: Chadds Ford Township, Delaware County

Relevant issues: Art and architecture

Statement of significance: N. C. Wyeth's illustrations have excited the imagination of generations of readers. In a career that spanned the first half of the twentieth century, Wyeth illustrated some ninety books and countless stories for such prestigious magazines as *Harpers, McClure's, Saturday Evening Post,* and *Scribner's.* Wyeth lived and worked in the several buildings of this historic district, and planted his roots so deep in the Chadds Ford soil that two succeeding generations of Wyeth artists found nourishment here. His son, Andrew, and grandson, James, both began their art training in his studio. The property is open to the public.

New Century Guild

Location: Philadelphia, Philadelphia County

Relevant issues: Business and industry, women's history

Statement of significance: This building has served as the location for the New Century Guild from 1906 to the present. Founded in 1882, this organization was one of the earliest, largest, and most successful of the many created across the country in the late nineteenth century to deal with the serious problems that arose as more and more women entered the labor force. The New Century Guild explicitly stated from the outset that its goal was to address the specific needs of "self-supporting women," a bold step at a time when many Americans believed no self-respecting woman would work for pay outside the home. The New Century Guild offered women a wide range of comprehensive services, which included a newspaper for working women (founded in 1887 and still published today); a research section that collected statistics on working women; evening classes for pleasure and professional development; a large library with a full-time librarian; a restaurant that offered noonday meals to working women at a modest price; an assembly hall; guest rooms for members; and a health insurance plan.

Oakmont Country Club

Location: Oakmont, Allegheny County

Relevant issues: Sports

Statement of significance: Noted for its nationally significant golf course, this is the oldest top-ranked course in the United States. Its original layout is virtually intact and still in use for club and tournament play. Generally considered to be among the most difficult golf courses in the world, it has hosted major national championships and U.S. Opens.

Olympia

Location: Philadelphia, Philadelphia County

Relevant issues: Naval history

Web site: www.spanam.simplenet.com/olympia .htm

Statement of significance: The oldest steel-hulled American warship afloat, *Olympia* served as Commodore George Dewey's flagship in the Battle of Manila Bay (1898). The cruiser was born out of a program of ships for the "New Navy" of the 1880's and 1890's designed to correct the deficiencies of a weakened and neglected naval force. It is the last remaining ship built during that program and the sole surviving combatant of the Spanish-American War.

Philadelphia School of Design for Women

Location: Philadelphia, Philadelphia County

Relevant issues: Art and architecture, women's history

Statement of significance: From 1880 to 1959, this was the location of the Philadelphia School of Design for Women, which was the first school of industrial design for women in the United States. The school filled a gap in the American vocational, educational, and industrial schema. Led by numerous prominent art educators, and producing innovative and nationally recognized graduates hailing from all over the country, the School of Design excelled in industrial design and art education and helped free American industry from foreign design dependence.

Priestley House

Location: Northumberland, Northumberland County
Relevant issues: Science and technology
Statement of significance: From 1794 until his death, this was the residence of Joseph Priestley (1733-1804). Priestley's research in chemistry enabled him to identify oxygen in 1776 and carbon monoxide in 1794. One wing of this frame house was his laboratory.

The Printzhof

Location: Essington, Delaware County
Relevant issues: European settlement
Statement of significance: Constructed about 1643 of hewn logs, the Printzhof was the residence of Johan Printz (1592-1663), governor of New Sweden, the first permanent European settlement in what was to become Pennsylvania. Today, the only visible remains of the settlement are the stone foundations of this house.

Race Street Meetinghouse

Location: Philadelphia, Philadelphia County
Relevant issues: Religion, social reform, women's history
Statement of significance: Race Street Meetinghouse, which served as the site of the Hicksite Yearly Meeting from 1857 to 1955, was at the forefront of women's involvement both in Quaker religion and in American political activism. Many leaders in the women's movement were associated with this meetinghouse; they included abolitionist and women's activist Lucretia Mott, peace activist Hannah Clothier Hull, and suffrage leader Alice Paul.

Tanner Homesite

Location: Philadelphia, Philadelphia County
Relevant issues: African American history, art and architecture
Statement of significance: This was the boyhood home of Henry O. Tanner (1859-1937), the late nineteenth and early twentieth century African American expatriate painter, whose work earned recognition in Europe and the United States.

Wagner Free Institute of Science

Location: Philadelphia, Philadelphia County
Relevant issues: Science and technology
Statement of significance: Begun in 1860, the Wagner Free Institute of Science is an unparalleled survivor of a virtually extinct institution: the scientific society of the nineteenth century. A two-story, free-standing building containing a gallery for exhibits, offices, classrooms, a library, and large lecture hall, it is characteristic of mid-nineteenth century institutional architecture. The creation of Philadelphia merchant, philanthropist, and amateur scientist William Wagner, the institute is also significant for its association with Dr. Joseph Leidy (1823-1891), one of the most prominent biologists of that century. It was also one of the earliest proponents of adult education in the country.

Walnut Street Theatre

Location: Philadelphia, Philadelphia County
Relevant issues: Cultural history
Statement of significance: This is one of the oldest surviving theaters in the country. Opened in 1809 as the Olympic Theater, the building was originally a circus; legitimate drama was being presented here after 1811. Most of the major figures of the American stage, including Sarah Bernhardt, Ellen Terry, Sir Henry Irving, Richard Mansfield, John Drew, and Maude Adams, appeared on this stage.

Wanamaker Store

Location: Philadelphia, Philadelphia County
Relevant issues: Business and industry
Statement of significance: Constructed in three stages between 1902 and 1910, this twelve-story steel-frame structure is the home store of one of the major merchandising enterprises in retailing history which contributed to the evolution of the department store.

Washington's Crossing

Location: Washington's Crossing, Bucks County

Relevant issues: Military history, Revolutionary War

Web site: gateway.hvrsd.k12.nj.us/stpark.htm

Statement of significance: Here, on Christmas Eve, 1776, forces led by General George Washington landed and prepared to assault Trenton, then held by British forces. By this daring act, Washington carried the war to the enemy and gave the new nation and his oft-defeated army a taste of victory at the war's lowest ebb.

Waynesborough

Location: Paoli, Chester County

Relevant issues: Military history

Statement of significance: From his birth until 1791, this was the residence of Anthony Wayne (1745-1796), American general. The large stone house was originally constructed in 1724 by his grandfather and namesake, Anthony Wayne.

West Birthplace

Location: Swarthmore, Delaware County

Relevant issues: Art and architecture

Statement of significance: Located on the campus of Swarthmore College, this is the birthplace of Benjamin West (1728-1820), who made major contributions to American art through his support for young artists, such as Gilbert Stuart and Charles Willson Peale, as well as through his own painting.

Woodmont

Location: Gladwyne, Montgomery County

Relevant issues: African American history, social reform

Statement of significance: Woodmont was designed by architect William Lightfoot Price, and built in the 1890's for industrialist Alan Wood, Jr. Along with its support buildings, it is a superb example of a large country estate of its time. The house, imitating a medieval French chateau, is replete with turrets and towers, oriels and gargoyles. In 1952, Reverend M. F. Divine, better known as Father Divine, made Woodmont his home and headquarters. A charismatic African American preacher, he had great success in breaking down color lines and fostered integration long before the national Civil Rights movement. Father Divine is buried on the property, which is open to the public.

Rhode Island

For many years, the America's Cup, the world's premier yachting race, was held off the coast of Newport.(Rhode Island Tourism Division)

History of Rhode Island

Though the smallest state in the Union in area, Rhode Island has the longest name: Rhode Island and Providence Plantations. Rhode Island, though it is only 48 miles long and 37 miles wide, has 384 miles of coastline, which earned for it the nickname the Ocean State. The state is practically divided by Narragansett Bay, which extends twenty-eight miles into the interior. As a result, every town in Rhode Island is no more than twenty-five miles from water. The state's geography played a major role in its development, with fishing, boatbuilding, and international trade being its early major industries. The numerous and swift rivers running through the state also shaped industry, being harnessed for power to the nation's first mills. Due to its small size, Rhode Island has always been intimately linked to its neighbors, Connecticut on the west and Massachusetts on the east and north.

Native American Presence

Archaeological evidence shows that Rhode Island has been inhabited for at least eight thousand years. During the 1600's, the area of Rhode Island, Connecticut, and Massachusetts was inhabited by about thirty thousand American Indians of the Algonquian family, roughly split into five tribes: Narragansetts, Wampanoags, Niantics, Nipmucs, and Pequots. They farmed the land for corn, squash, beans, and tobacco.

The first European settlers of the state in the 1630's lived peaceably among the Native Americans; Indians even gave portions of their land to the English. Eventually, however, discord among the groups arose, when whites began taking American Indian land. In the 1637 Pequot War, Pequots unsuccessfully tried to drive out the colonists who had taken over their land. The continued disintegration of ties led to King Philip's War in 1675. The Wampanoags, their leader Philip, and their violent behavior provoked Connecticut and Massachusetts to declare war against them. The Rhode Island Narragansetts joined with the Wampanoags eventually, but the Native Americans were defeated, with thousands of Indians and more than

six hundred whites killed and most of the city of Providence burned. After the war, Indians were shipped to the South or to the West Indies as slaves. Most eventually left the state, and by the year 2000, Native Americans made up less than 0.5 percent of Rhode Island's population.

Discovery and Colonization

Rhode Island may have been visited by Norwegian Vikings as early as 1000 C.E. In 1524 the Italian explorer Giovanni da Verrazano, sailing for France, found Narragansett Bay. He may have named the state, comparing it to the Greek island of Rhodes. The state's name is also often attributed to Dutch trader Adriaen Block, who visited the region in 1614 and called it *roodt eylandt* (red island).

Rhode Island was first settled by Europeans in 1636, when the city of Providence was founded by religious dissenter Roger Williams. Williams was about to be exiled from the Massachusetts Bay Colony to England due to his unpopular views that religion and state should be separate. He escaped, and his Native American friends, the Narragansetts, gave him land that he named Providence. He declared the region "a shelter for persons distressed of conscience."

In 1638 Anne Hutchinson was banished from the Massachusetts Bay Colony for preaching against the established church. She settled in Portsmouth, at the north end of Aquidneck Island. A year later William Coddington broke from Hutchinson's group and founded Newport. After Warwick was founded by Samuel Gorton in 1643, the four towns received a charter from England to become one colony, with freedom of religion guaranteed to all. Soon all those seeking asylum from persecution—Quakers, Jews, Congregationalists, Baptists—made their homes there, and the region became known for its tolerance. Because of its open-mindedness, the colony was considered by outsiders a haven for misfits and was thus scorned.

Although the first antislavery law in the Union was signed in Rhode Island in 1652, Rhode Island, especially Newport and Bristol, was a hub of the so-called "triangle trade" in the 1700's. Rum, which

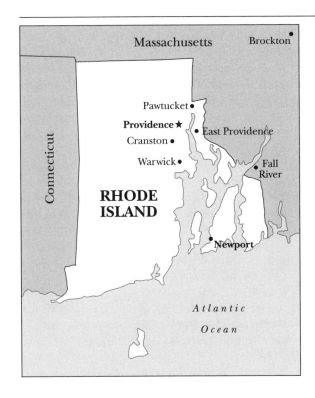

Rhode Islanders manufactured, was traded in Africa for slaves, who were traded in the West Indies for molasses, which was used in New England to make more rum. Slavery was abolished in 1784, and the triangle trade ended by 1800.

Steps to Revolution

By 1750 the main industries in Rhode Island were fishing, rum manufacture, and rum trade. After Great Britain imposed taxes on trade, Rhode Islanders became smugglers to maintain their livelihoods. In 1764 they fired on a British ship, one of the first acts of aggression and rebellion against England. In 1772 the British ship *Gaspee* was burned by Providence residents, in an act thought to be the first of the Revolution.

Always progressive, Rhode Island's general assembly voted to end allegiance to Britain on May 4, 1776—two months before the rest of the colonies. Rhode Island played an active part in the fighting; the Battle of Rhode Island took place in Newport in 1778. A company of freed slaves, known as the Black Regiment, fought with the colonists, becoming the first such regiment to fight in America. After winning independence, Rhode Island was the last of the original thirteen colonies to ratify the Constitution, in 1790, refusing to sign until the Bill of Rights was added. Desiring a balance of power, until 1854 Rhode Island had five capital cities: Providence, Newport, East Greenwich, Bristol, and South Kingstown. From 1854 to 1900, Providence and Newport shared capital status, and in 1900 Providence became the sole capital.

Industry

The American Industrial Revolution began in Pawtucket, Rhode Island, in 1790. Harnessing the power of the mighty Blackstone River, resident Samuel Slater built the first water-powered cotton mill in the Union. Later, in 1827, Slater erected the first steam-powered cotton mill. Rhode Island thrived during the 1800's due to the prosperity of its mills. Though the state's land was arable, by 1860 about 50 percent of Rhode Islanders worked in industrial jobs, while only 10 percent were farmers.

Production remained steady during the Civil War, and after the war the state's industry shifted from production of textiles to that of metals and jewelry. By the second half of the twentieth century an estimated 85 percent of U.S. costume jewelry was produced in Providence, though many factories faced difficulties when low-cost imports from Asia threatened to bankrupt them. Rhode Island is also home to Hasbro, the second-largest toy manufacturer in the world. The three largest employers in the state are industry, tourism, and health care.

Political Makeup

Rhode Island expanded its trend of tolerance into the political arena. In 1842 Thomas Dorr founded the People's Party to try to give all citizens the right to vote. After illegitimately claiming governorship during what is known as Dorr's Rebellion, he was suppressed. However, because of his work, all adult males were given the right to vote, regardless of color. Rhode Island was the only state before the Civil War in which blacks and whites voted as equals.

Until the 1900's, the majority of Rhode Island voters were Republicans. Democrats came into power, however, when diverse immigrants began arriving in the early part of the century. Democrats dominated politics beginning in 1935, never losing control of the General Assembly throughout the century.

During the 1980's, Rhode Island became known as a hotbed of political corruption. After 1986, two mayors in the state were convicted on corruption charges, two chief justices of the state supreme court resigned in disgrace, and a superior court judge was arrested for taking bribes. Possible reasons for the state's scandals include the longtime dominance of one political party, the small size of the state, and the fact that Rhode Island is considered the New England headquarters of the Mafia. Residents hoping for a turn for the better elected Patrick Kennedy to the U.S. House of Representatives in 1988. Although Kennedy was just a twenty-one-year-old attending Providence College, he proved himself worthy of reelection twice.

Ethnic and Religious Heritage

Italian Americans make up a large percentage of the Rhode Island population, second only to Irish Americans. Irish and Italian immigrants helped make Roman Catholicism the prevalent religion in the state. Rhode Island is about 70 percent Catholic, making it the state with the most Catholics.

Revitalization of Providence

Though at the turn of the twentieth century Providence was one of the nation's richest and most thriving cities, after 1925 residents began fleeing to suburban and rural areas. Mayor Vincent "Buddy" Cianci, Jr., was mostly responsible for bringing the city back to life beginning in the 1970's. In the 1990's the two downtown rivers that had been covered by pavement were uncovered, and bridges, walkways, and an amphitheater highlighted the center of the city, replacing unused train tracks and freight yards. Providence became a haven for artists and attracted multitudes with the building of new hotels, a convention center, a giant mall, and an outdoor ice rink. The city experienced a 40 percent drop in crime in the early 1990's, providing more reason for residents to return to the once-empty downtown area. —*Lauren M. Mitchell*

Newport

Date: Founded in 1639
Relevant issues: Colonial America, cultural history, literary history, religion
Significance: Newport is fifteen miles long and four miles across, with a population of thirty thousand. Founded by William Coddington, Newport became a colonial center of trade. It was occupied by the British between December, 1776, and October, 1779. Starting in the early 1800's, the town became a summer retreat for wealthy socialites. Initially, it attracted Charlestonians; later, Bostonians. By the 1890's, Newport was famous for its opulent summer mansions built for New York multimillionaires. These Gilded Age mansions were largely sold or little used following the Great Depression, but several have been restored and opened to the public.

Location: On the southernmost point of Aquidneck Island, on the west connected by Newport Bridge to Jamestown, which is connected to mainland Rhode Island by the Jamestown Bridge; Middletown and Portsmouth are located to the north of Newport

Site Office:
Newport Convention and Visitors' Bureau
23 America's Cup Avenue
Newport, RI 02840
ph.: (401) 849-8098

Newport was settled in 1639 by a group of religious refugees from Boston, including William Coddington and eight other prominent leaders. Coddington's faction had originally settled in Pocasset, a town on the north end of Aquidneck Island, but discovered that its harbor was too shallow for large ships. A perfect harbor was located at the southwest end of Aquidneck, where it would be possible to develop a commercial port and engage in coastal trade. While Coddington established Newport, three men and women established similar communities elsewhere: Roger Williams in Providence, Anne Hutchinson in Pocasset, and William Arnold in Pawtuxet. From 1636 to 1690, these diverse neighbors struggled to maintain unity while providing a refuge for the emigrants who left the rigid churches in Massachusetts, Connecticut, and Plymouth.

Assisted by English merchants, Coddington helped Newport's original settlers build ships and wharves for the purpose of trading goods with the Caribbean colonies. He also set up farms that produced some of the city's leading exports—sheep, cattle, and horses. In 1639, there were ninety-three residents in Newport. The city would become a thriving center of British-American commerce by the late seventeenth century. Newport differed from most American settlements in its cosmopolitan atmosphere, primarily a result of its broad trading practices and religious tolerance. The Quakers and Jews who discovered a haven in Newport during the 1600's made significant contributions to the city's economy and culture.

Prosperity in the Eighteenth Century

Newport's maritime success reached its pinnacle in the mid-eighteenth century when more than five hundred ships used the city's port for trading. Rum was the leading export of Rhode Island. By 1750 the colony had thirty-three distilleries—twenty-two in Newport—which processed molasses imported from the Caribbean. Newport's prosperous image was tainted, however, by smuggling, slavery, and piracy. In a notorious but lucrative system called the triangle trade, molasses, rum, and slaves were shipped between the West Indies, Newport, and West Africa. An import duty of three pounds on each slave was spent on paving the city's streets, though the practice was discontinued in 1720. Thereafter, Newport, like many other colonies, preferred to use public lotteries as a means of raising revenue for urban improvements. In 1764 a lottery paid for more streets; in 1767 the Anglicans paid for their church spire with a lottery, and the Baptists held a lottery to pay for the parsonage of the Reverend James Manning and his pupils. In 1842, after several scandals, the state constitution outlawed lotteries.

Cultural advancements followed the urbanization of Newport. In 1727 James Franklin, nephew to Benjamin, used the city's first printing press to publish a codified version of the colony's laws. In 1732 Franklin created Newport's first newspaper, the *Rhode Island Gazette*, though it failed after several months. By 1758 Newport was prosperous enough to support a weekly newspaper, the *Newport Mercury*. Except for its suspension during the British occupation, the *Mercury* remained in print for well over a century.

Prominent Residents

In 1726 carpenter-architect Richard Munday built Trinity Church, one of the finest colonial churches in America. He modeled the design after the Old North Church in Boston, itself fashioned after Christopher Wren's London churches. Using bricks imported from Britain, Munday also built Colony House in 1739. Rhode Island's first colonial and state government was seated at Colony House, though Newport and Providence alternated as the state capital. From the second-floor balcony, officials read several major proclamations, such as the repeal of the Stamp Act in 1766 and the Declaration of Independence in 1776. During a legislative session at Colony House on May 4, 1776, Rhode Island became the first American colony to renounce allegiance to the king. During the Revolutionary War, British soldiers who were stationed at the building destroyed much of the interior, and the French later converted it into a hospital. In 1780 Colony House served as the location for Rhode Island's first Catholic mass, a funeral for Admiral de Ternay.

In 1729 George Berkeley, dean of Londonderry Cathedral, decided to settle in Newport. Accompanied by a group of distinguished scholars, he intended to build a farm as a means of providing food for a university in Bermuda. Berkeley lived in Middletown, just outside Newport, in a residence called Whitehall, and tried to stir interest in the Church of England through his sermons at Trinity Church. He donated seventy-five books to the public library, founded an intellectual society, and wrote *Alciphron: Or, The Minute Philosopher* (1732) while in Newport. His keen observations regarding America's religious tolerance and increasing independence were recorded in several letters and poems.

Abraham Redwood, a member of Berkeley's literary entourage and a wealthy Quaker merchant, endowed the Redwood Library in 1747. Peter Harrison, Rhode Island's best architect, designed the library's edifice in the manner of Andrea Palladio. It opened in 1750 and is now the oldest library in continuous use in the United States. The Brick Market and Touro Synagogue are also Harrison designs. Built in 1763, Touro Synagogue is the oldest Jewish house of worship in America. Its congregation was established by Sephardic Jews from Spain and Portugal, led by Isaac de Touro of Amsterdam. The synagogue's austere exterior protects an elegant interior, where a gallery is supported by twelve Ionic columns representing the tribes of Israel. The Brick Market was located at the head of Long

Wharf, the busiest Newport wharf throughout the colonial period, and a port for the French fleet during the Revolution. Harrison's British-style design has upper-floor storage rooms above a market area.

For merchants, Thames and Washington Streets were the most popular sites for building waterside homes in the mid-1750's. Though many of these colonial houses were destroyed during the British occupation of Newport, Hunter House remains standing to this day. Completed in the mid-1750's by a merchant named Jonathan Nichols, Hunter House is considered to be one of the finest colonial dwellings in the United States. It is located on Easton's Point, the north end of the harbor where marine trading was heaviest. After Nichols passed away in 1757, the property was sold to Colonel Joseph Wanton, Jr., who added a southern addition and a second chimney. A confirmed Loyalist, Wanton was exiled from Newport after the British occupation of 1776 to 1779, when many homes were destroyed and two-thirds of the residents fled the island. It was believed that Wanton's political ties saved his house. The French used the dwelling as a lodging for two years; thereafter it deteriorated, like much of the town, until William Hunter bought it in 1805.

Coming of the Revolutionary War

Just as Newport was achieving international economic success, Rhode Island began spearheading the revolutionary effort in 1764. Indeed, the colony's strong economy precipitated its urgent call for political freedom. In 1764, the British Parliament passed the Sugar Act, a strict tax on trade with foreign sugar islands. The Crown enforced the duty by patrolling Narragansett Bay with naval ships. The first British vessel, the *Squirrel*, reached the coast of Newport in December, 1763, followed

The Breakers, Newport. (Jim McElholm)

by the *St. John.* In July, 1764, Rhode Island became the first colony to resort to armed resistance when Newport gunners fired on the *St. John.* Several of its crew tried to capture a deserter in Newport but were mobbed, and gunners fired upon the ship again as it tried to leave the harbor.

When Britain threatened to pass another Sugar Act, Stephen Hopkins, the governor of Rhode Island, wrote an argument to the Board of Trade. "The Rights of the Colonies Examined," his remonstrance, was the first official document asserting colonial rights. Newport's citizens emphatically supported Hopkins, although a small group of Tories, "the Newport Junto," defended their king and Parliament. In 1765, the Stamp Act was passed, and the leaders of the Junto, Martin Howard, Jr., and Dr. Thomas Moffat, were hanged in effigy in Newport. The General Assembly of Rhode Island declared the legislation null and void because it violated basic charter rights. After the Stamp Act was repealed in 1766, colonists celebrated the victory under the Newport Liberty Tree. In 1774, Rhode Island became the first colony to call for a Continental Congress, which announced an embargo on all British imports. Britain responded, however, by stationing ten ships off the coast of Newport, an action that virtually eliminated further resistance in Newport. Nonetheless, on May 4, 1776, Rhode Island became the first colony to renounce allegiance to the king, a day now celebrated as "Rhode Island Independence Day."

With revolution, however, came war. In December, 1776, a large British fleet invaded Newport Harbor, and six thousand troops easily captured the city. During Britain's three years of occupation, colonial shipping stopped and half the people of Aquidneck fled the island, most seeking refuge in Providence. In spring 1778, George Washington organized a relief effort that utilized the American force of General John Sullivan and the French fleet of Comte Jean Baptiste d'Estaing. However, the French vessels arrived twelve days before Sullivan's troops landed on Aquidneck. By then, a British fleet of thirteen ships had forced d'Estaing to leave Newport Harbor and withdraw to Boston. Without sufficient strength, Sullivan decided to abort the mission and retreat from Newport. By October, 1779, Britain chose to end the occupation, moving its soldiers to more strategic locations in the south.

Postwar Recovery

After the war, Newport made a slow economic recovery, and it would take one hundred years for the population to reach its former level of eleven thousand people. Continued hostility from England prevented Newport from regaining its dominance in commercial shipping. More important, as the railroads developed, America's reliance on maritime trade gradually waned. During the first half of the nineteenth century, however, Newport regained economic power as a summer resort. Between 1750 and 1850, Newport's first wave of summer visitors consisted of southern slaveholders and Caribbean planters who were attracted to the area's comfortable climate and stimulating social life. Because most of the American families came from Charleston, Newport became known as the "Carolina Hospital."

The Catherine Street Hotel was built in the mid-1820's, and the first summer houses went up in the following decade. In 1839 a cottage was built by Richard Upjohn for George Noble Jones, a plantation owner from Georgia. Later named Kingscote, the Gothic revival home is a symbol of Newport's pre-Civil War architecture, when comfort rather than show predominated. Decorative woodwork, pointed gables, and an aviary over the entrance convey a gentle, airy feel. When the Civil War broke out in 1861, Newport was a center of abolitionism. A slaveowner, Jones had to leave the city and sell his cottage to the King family. In 1881 Stanford White added the dining room; the red slate roof was added in 1886.

Ocean House, the city's first great hotel, was built in 1844, directly across from Kingscote. Between 1825 and 1855, Newport hotels attracted hordes of guests and gossip columnists. By the mid-1850's, however, the summer cottage industry dominated Newport's social scene, causing the larger hotels to close. With the assistance of several property owners and local boosters, a real estate entrepreneur named Alfred Smith bought up several farms, subdivided the land, and constructed dozens of cottages on Bellevue Avenue and Ocean Drive. Smith sold and rented the real estate by searching for clients at hotels. William S. Wetmore, a China-trade merchant from New York, hired Seth Bradford to build the most impressive cottage of the 1850's, Chateau-Sur-Mer, an Italianate stone villa. Wetmore hosted Newport's first great party at the chateau, inviting three thousand guests.

The Literati

In 1840, the second wave of summer residents, the Boston literary set, began rolling into Newport. During the Civil War, many Southerners left the area, selling their property to people from New York and Boston. Among the famous writers and intellectuals who gathered here to socialize were Henry James, Sr., Henry Wadsworth Longfellow, George Bancroft, Thomas Wentworth Higginson, and Julia Ward Howe. The artists included John Singer Sargent, John La Farge, and William Morris Hunt. The Bostonians used Newport as an intellectual retreat rather than a setting for building opulent summer houses. Of Newport's twelve summer houses in 1852, only four were built by Bostonians. Before 1870, the Bostonians' recreational activities centered on the Ocean House Hotel, the Redwood Library, the Art Association of Newport, and the Newport Reading Room.

The Newport cottages developed their eccentricities during the early 1870's. Architect Richard Morris Hunt designed the Henry Marquand House, otherwise known as Bric-a-brac Hall. Hunt also enlarged the 1852 Victorian villa Chateau-Sur-Mer. Hunt added a French ballroom, a roofed carriage entrance on the north side, and replaced the sloping gambrel roof with a steeper mansard roof. The alterations were so dramatic that observers believed the original house had been torn down. The imposing stone structure served as an omen of the massive estates to come, but its rugged style was unique to Newport; one architectural historian described the chateau as a battering ram.

In 1879, James Gordon Bennett, Jr., owner of the *New York Herald*, was rejected from Newport's leading men's club. To regain his stature in Newport society, he built a casino across from his Bellevue Avenue cottage. For decades, cottagers swarmed into the Newport Casino to socialize, dine, listen to concerts, and play tennis. New York architects McKim, Mead, and White designed the establishment, which created a vogue for informal resort architecture modeled after the British Queen Anne style. Within five years, however, the quaint Victorian cottages of the mid- to late nineteenth century would be dwarfed by massive neoclassical mansions unrivaled anywhere in America.

The Gilded Age

Newport became the Queen of Resorts during its third era, known as the Gilded Age (1875-1920). After the Civil War, enormous fortunes were built upon ventures in coal, railroads, oil, and finance. Wealthy New Yorkers tried to model their lifestyle according to European standards set during the Renaissance and Industrial Revolution. Though Americans lacked the status of royal titles and tradition, they created a new aristocracy by living in domestic splendor. According to historian Thomas Gannon, "Much of the opulence . . . of the time was due to a new definition of 'wealth.' Where once the accumulation of a million dollars defined wealth, the new fortunes, built on coal, railroads, oil, and finance, were measured in tens and hundreds of millions."

Samuel Ward McAllister was the driving force behind the movement of New Yorkers to Newport. As a child, McAllister lived in Newport with other southerners. He became a wealthy lawyer in San Francisco, married the daughter of a millionaire in 1853, moved to New York, and bought a summer home in Newport. In the 1870's, as an adviser to Mrs. William Backhouse Astor, McAllister convinced New York's elite (which he dubbed the Four Hundred) to spend the summers in Newport. The cottagers spent money on everything from expensive jewelry to gold-encrusted carriages pulled by English thoroughbreds. Summer wardrobes of well-dressed women consisted of eighty to ninety dresses, one for each social event.

Newport Society

During this era, women dominated the social hierarchy of Newport. While their husbands worked in New York, women like Alice Vanderbilt faced the daunting task of managing palatial estates with enormous summer budgets ($100,000-$300,000). Keeping pace with Newport's complex ceremonial events demanded talented and forceful administrators. Newport society became a symbol of America's second-generation industrial elite, where money alone did not create status. Historian William McLoughlin explains the dilemma: "Class was established by an increasingly rigid code of conduct and behavior that took training and patience. Women's role in this upper echelon of power was to create an aura of taste and refinement in the lavish expenditure of disposable wealth."

Most men, unable to match their wives' grace and charm at Newport's social gatherings, formed men's clubs or went sailing in yachts made by the renowned Herreshoff family of Bristol. The Herreshoffs also built the ships used in the America's Cup races, which took place off the Newport coast after 1930. Their magnificent racing yachts won every cup from 1893 to 1937. Men and women engaged in various other sports: riding, coaching, tennis, and croquet; only women practiced archery, while only men enjoyed fishing, polo, and golf. Women were allowed to swim at Easton's Beach in the morning but had to leave when men arrived in the afternoon. Daytime gatherings on the shoreline included picnics and chowder parties; at night, charades or amateur theatricals.

Marble House

The first celebrated, large-scale cottages, actually mansions, started with several late Gothic houses. More extravagant is the grand scale Marble House, an anniversary present from William K. Vanderbilt to his wife, Alva. The Vanderbilts joined Newport's summer colony in 1888, but shrouded the construction of Marble House in secrecy. To minimize rumors, Vanderbilt kept his French and Italian artisans in isolated quarters and erected high fences around the project. It took four years and eleven million dollars to complete Marble House, which opened on August 19, 1892.

Designed by Richard Morris Hunt, Marble House was modeled after the Petit Trianon at Versailles, and resembles both the White House and the Temple of Apollo. The neoclassical mansion is fronted by a portico of four Corinthian columns that overlook a sweeping circular drive. Hunt used half a million cubic feet of white marble (weighing eighty-four thousand tons) to build Vanderbilt's estate. Like most of the mansions that followed, Marble House was derivative, an imitation of European palaces.

The architecture of Newport's golden age was unparalleled in extravagance, but it lacked an original American identity. Hunt, educated at École des Beaux-Arts in Paris, was well trained in the European tradition, which emphasized neoclassical and neobaroque design. Vanderbilt was so impressed with Hunt's talent that he placed a relief portrait of the architect in the upper hall, right across from a portrait of the Versailles architect

Jules Hardouin-Mansart. The Marble House attractions included a ten-ton, bronze entrance grille and the opulently ornamented Gold Ballroom, featuring carved gilded panels by Karl Bitter, a huge ceiling painting, and Greek figures seated atop a marble mantelpiece.

The Breakers

Completed in 1895, The Breakers is another architectural wonder. Hunt's climactic achievement was designed for Cornelius Vanderbilt, William's older brother and chair of the family's railroad empire. At the time, Cornelius, grandson of the financier of the same name, was worth seventy million dollars, but he began his career earning fifty dollars a month as a bank clerk. A religious man, Vanderbilt spent much of his time on philanthropic activities and donated millions of dollars to charity. In August, 1895, more than three hundred guests were invited to the family's housewarming party, which also served as the coming-out party for his daughter Gertrude Vanderbilt. It took only two years for hundreds of workers to construct The Breakers. Several rooms were designed and built by European craftsmen, then shipped and reassembled in Newport. As a strict precaution against fire, Vanderbilt used no wood and buried the heating plant several hundred feet away.

Covering nearly an acre and containing seventy rooms, The Breakers resembles the Italian Renaissance palaces of Turin and Genoa. Conceived on a monumental scale, the four-story limestone palace is a fitting symbol of the Vanderbilts' vast accomplishments in business. Critics cite the arched double loggia nestled between the colossal end wings as the most striking exterior feature. The Great Hall, rising nearly fifty feet, is the most spacious room in Newport. Framed by Caen stone arches, eight sets of doors lead visitors from this hall to all the family and public rooms. The upstairs bathtub, weighing one ton and carved from a single piece of marble, dispenses hot or cold, fresh or saltwater. A two-story dining room is lined with twelve columns of rose alabaster capped by gilded bronze. Gray ionic pilasters and red velvet draperies decorate the music room.

Other Mansions

Later structures never surpassed the scale of The Breakers, but several mansions are equally interesting. The Elms, the residence of Edward Julius Berwind, is an unusually cool and detached work by Horace Trumbauer, a young architect from Philadelphia. Unlike Newport's leading architects, Trumbauer lacked a Paris education; nevertheless, his 1901 mansion is a faithful recreation of the Chateau d'Asnieres near Paris. The interior, a symmetrical balance of windows, paintings, and mirrors, was filled with period furniture and tapestries from Allard and Sons of Paris. The Elms's most distinctive feature is its grounds, a ten-acre park with manicured shrubs, bushes, and forty species of trees. An ivy-lined path leads visitors to a pair of gazebos that mark the entrance to the sunken gardens—a rich blend of begonias, English boxwood, statues, and fountains.

Stanford White of McKim, Mead and White was commissioned by Theresa Fair Oelrichs to design Rosecliff, a neoclassical masterpiece. Opened in 1900, the light, graceful mansion was modeled after the Grand Trianon at Versailles. Entablature, paired Ionic columns, and arched French doors front the H-shaped exterior. Rosecliff's forty-by-eighty-foot ballroom was the largest in Newport. On August 19, 1904, Oelrichs hosted the White Ball, a lavish extravaganza to celebrate the Astor Cup race. The ballroom and vestibule were completely decorated in white, and the guests arrived in white dresses. To simulate Newport Harbor, a dozen mock ships were moored off the Oelrichs's front lawn and bathed in white light. Scenes for the films *The Great Gatsby* (1974) and *The Betsy* (1978) were filmed in the Rosecliff ballroom.

The Wall Street crash of 1929 officially ended Newport's heyday, though many aristocrats of the Jazz Age had already left the tiny resort, discovering new summer spots that catered to their motorcar lifestyle. Rising property taxes, coupled with the introduction of the income tax, made it impossible for individuals to finance the huge mansions. Moreover, it became bad taste to flaunt one's wealth after the onset of the Great Depression, causing the upper class to seek recreation in foreign lands. The Four Hundred no longer rode the plush cars of the Fall River Steamship Line to Newport. Many Newport mansions were boarded up, vandalized, torn down, or destroyed by fire. The mansion of Mrs. Stuyvesant Fish was converted into middle-income apartments, while the French chateau Ochre Court became Salve Regina Catholic College. By 1950, only a few mansions remained in private hands.

Modern Preservation Efforts

Half a dozen mansions were preserved and restored thanks to the efforts of two women, Doris Duke of the Newport Restoration Foundation and Mrs. G. H. Warren of the Preservation Society of Newport County. The Preservation Society was organized in 1945 to rescue Hunter House, then began acquiring other mansions such as Rosecliff, The Elms, and The Breakers. Today, Preservation Society specialists work full time in maintaining the grandeur of the Gilded Age. Recent efforts have included the restoration of The Breakers's stables, now open to the public.

The breathtaking palaces of Newport can be seen year-round along the rocky southern tip of Aquidneck—Bellevue Avenue, Ochre Point Road, and Ocean Drive. Less grand but more comfortable are the colonial mansions and homes in the old harbor area. Also worth visiting is Green Animals, one of the finest topiary gardens in the United States. Thomas Brayton started the complex in 1880 as a complement to his summer house on Cory Lane in Portsmouth. The garden contains eighty sculptured trees and shrubs, more than two hundred species of flowers, magnolia and grape arbors, and fifty different herbs.   —*Richard Trout*

For Further Information:

Gannon, Thomas. *Newport Mansions: The Gilded Age.* Dublin, N.H.: Foremost, 1982. A large, magnificently illustrated edition with several pages of text and photographs dedicated to each mansion. Gannon also explores the lives of Newport's most distinguished families.

_____. *Newport, Rhode Island: The City by the Sea.* 2d ed. Woodstock, Vt.: Countryman Press, 1992. An ideal publication for anyone planning to visit the island. This comprehensive travel guide covers everything from the historic mansions and colonial houses to nature preserves, specialty shops, and beaches. A revised and expanded edition of Gannon's 1978 *A Guide to Newport, Rhode Island.*

Gavan, Terrance. *The Barons of Newport.* Reprint. Newport, R.I.: Pineapple, 1998. Deals with the Gilded Age, paying close attention to the lifestyle and politics of the upper class. Several pages are devoted to each of the most prominent individuals and families.

Grosvenor, Richard. *Newport, City in Time.* Wakefield, R.I.: Moyer Bell, 1998. A discussion of the buildings, art, and history of Newport.

McLoughlin, William G. *Rhode Island: A History.* New York: W. W. Norton, 1978. Begins in 1636 with a study of Roger Williams and the settlement of Providence. Newport's history is interspersed with stories about Rhode Island's other settlements.

Providence

Date: Incorporated on August 20, 1637

Relevant issues: Colonial America, religion

Significance: Providence, Rhode Island's state capital, was founded by noted colonial politician Roger Williams. It is the site of Brown University, the nation's seventh-oldest college, and the first Baptist church in America, as well as many original colonial homes and buildings.

Location: In the northeast quadrant of Rhode Island, at the northernmost point of Narragansett Bay at the fork of the Providence and Seekonk Rivers

Site Office:

Providence Chamber of Commerce
30 Exchange Terrace
Providence, RI 02903
ph.: (401) 521-5000

The development of Providence is closely linked with the development of the ideas behind the new American republic's basic principles of freedom. The city was founded when noted clergyman and policymaker Roger Williams, expelled by the British colonists of Massachusetts, sought a plot of land on which to engage his strong desire for individual expression of worship. A century and a half later, Williams's ideals were reflected in Rhode Island's refusal to ratify the U.S. Constitution until the Bill of Rights was added, making the state the thirteenth and last state to do so.

Originally an agrarian center whose colonial-era economy lagged behind that of nearby Newport, Providence took its place as Rhode Island's capital of commerce during the shipping boom of the early nineteenth century and cemented that standing with its subsequent shift to industrialism. Schools of higher learning such as Brown University, Providence College, the Rhode Island School of Design, and Johnson and Wales Culinary Institute continue to preserve the city's heritage of educational pursuit, and Providence's unique neighborhoods retain much of their ethnic character, adding to the city's eclecticism. Today, a sustained interest in the city's historic sites contributes to an invigorated tourist industry, and commercial and corporate business thrives.

Early History

The story of Providence begins with the story of Roger Williams, an outspoken and independent-minded Englishman in colonial New England. In 1632 the young man wrote his *Treatise* denouncing King James's land grant to the Massachusetts Bay Colony, arguing that the Indians had sovereign rights to the soil of the New World. At the time, the British were threatening to revoke the patent for the Massachusetts colony, and dissension of Williams's sort was unacceptable to the colony's governor, John Winthrop.

Hired as the teacher of the Salem church, Williams drew further British fire when he asserted that local magistrates should not punish transgressions of the first four Commandments, which he asserted were one's duty not to public office but to God. The magistrates of Boston's General Court sought, and expected to receive, a simple retraction from Williams. When he refused to retract his statements, however, the General Court ordered him exiled from Winthrop's jurisdiction within six weeks.

Before his differences with Winthrop came to a head, Williams had been assigned to inaugurate a trading post in advance of Massachusetts's proposed expansion into the uncharted Narragansett country to the south. Here the fleeing dissident headed.

Founding of the Town

Records of his trip are vague, but it appears Williams and his servant Thomas Angell met four other Salem men by prearrangement at an Indian site in Plymouth patent. Williams and his companions, joined less by ideological reasons than by the necessity to unite against the elements, waited for winter's thaw on the site of what is now Rehoboth,

Massachusetts. The group then set out across the Seekonk River. In spring 1636, in a now-legendary exchange at Slate Rock (a long-buried site to the northwest of the corner of Providence's Williams and Gano Streets, today commemorated with a monument), the canoeing travelers were greeted by an Indian on the bank with the cross-cultural salutation "What cheare, Netop [Friend]?" Most likely, Williams's group continued around Fox Point up the Great Salt (now called Providence) River, to the intersection of the Woonasquatucket and Moshassuck Rivers, where they built their initial settlement.

For squatters' rights to the area of the Indian village known as Mashasuck, Williams negotiated a swap with the Narragansett chieftains Canonicus and Miantunomi (whom he had befriended during previous expeditions), giving the Indians provisions and a sum of money he had obtained when he mortgaged his house in Salem. Williams named the outpost "Providence," thanking "God's mercefull providence" for his find. Contrary to popular assumption, Williams's original intent in settling Providence was to fulfill his own peace of mind, not that of his contemporaries, and he wrote, "It is not true that I . . . desired any to come with me into these parts." Nonetheless, his ideology professed a self-determination of worship for each man, and from the beginning he chose not to deny applicants who sought the same freedom. Within its first year, Providence was a loosely organized community of approximately thirty inhabitants, governed by simple votes of the eight or so "masters of families." Williams's chief priorities were to uphold individual rights and to forge a common bond for the good of the collective, a coupling that would confront the town with many moral dilemmas.

Incorporation

Records show that Providence was officially incorporated as a town on August 20, 1637. In a ceremony on March 24, 1638, the Narragansett chieftains met Williams and other town fathers at Pettaquamscutt Rock to affix their seals to "The Towne Evidence," a deed securing the transaction. Williams also received grants for the Narragansett Bay islands of Aquidneck and Prudence. In his mind, the contracts with the Indians were binding, but to the Massachusetts patents and their ruling

British government, they were without effect—a debate that would take Williams years to resolve.

The Narragansett country wove in and out of channels and coves along Narragansett Bay. Formed by glacial movement, it was a fertile territory previously ignored by European settlers, with a few exceptions: In the first decade of the seventeenth century, the Italian explorer Giovanni da Verrazano spent two weeks at the site of Newport, and in 1614 the Dutch explorer Adriaen Block drew the first accurate map of the region. A few years before Williams's arrival, the minister William Blackstone and his family quietly settled in the area; in later years this solitary figure would come to be a familiar one, as he rode into town on the back of a bull to deliver his sermons.

Rejection of Undesirables

Despite Roger Williams's inclusive idealism, during Providence's infancy he asked Winthrop whether he could veto the acceptance of undesirable newcomers. Providence would tolerate religious nonconformists, but not men and women inclined toward the disruption of its common good. Although Winthrop's responding letter is not in existence, he most likely replied against such a veto power, setting the stage for several decades' worth of agitation from strong-minded people like Samuel Gorton, William Coddington, and Anne Hutchinson. By default, Providence quickly became the destination of social instigators who were unwanted in Boston, giving Providence the nickname "the place where people think otherwise."

In a plight that paralleled Williams's, Hutchinson and her followers were expelled from Massachusetts in 1637 for religious views that were unsettling to the authorities. Williams persuaded Canonicus to let Hutchinson's party move onto Aquidneck Island, where they settled Pocasset (later called Portsmouth, Rhode Island). The rabble-rouser Samuel Gorton's arrival in Pocasset so disturbed the townsfolk that William Coddington and nine others moved to the opposite end of the isle and founded Newport. Gorton then relocated to Providence, where he took sides against William Arnold in a developing furor over the Pawtuxet section of town (incorporated in 1754 as Cranston, Rhode Island). Arnold, in turn, seeking greater plots of land for himself and his followers than Roger Williams had given them, illegally bought the Pawtuxet tract from the rebel Narragansett sachem Saconomoco and aligned it with the Massachusetts Bay Colony, who warned Providence not to interfere.

Despite these conflicts, in its first four years Providence grew to number one hundred inhabitants. Most of their houses were lined along Towne (now South and North Main) Street, to the east of the Providence River. To the north lay the Moshassuck, which was dammed for gristmills and sawmills. Later, the town expanded to build neighborhoods on the west side of the river as well.

Church and State
One of Williams's chief goals was to purify the church by separating its powers from those of the state. He founded the nation's oldest Baptist congregation in 1638, with policies, including rebaptism of the congregation (excluding infants, whose spiritual fates could not yet be determined), that were the source of heated arguments. By many accounts, Providence's townspeople had begun to stray from organized religion.

In 1640, the young town officially organized its system of law with the drafting of its combination. At this time, Williams began to work from the wings, preferring to let other elected officers tend to the business at hand, which was often delicate. In 1643, Gorton purchased a strip of Indian land to the south of Providence called Shawomet (later Warwick), ensuring further land disputes with neighboring Pawtuxet. By 1644, a regional government headed by Nicholas Easton that claimed jurisdiction over both the mainland and the island of Aquidneck had to contend with a rival government set up on the island by William Coddington.

While these crises brewed, Williams traveled to England in 1642 or 1643 to secure a patent for the Providence Plantation, in order to ward off the annexation efforts of Massachusetts and Plymouth. On the voyage overseas, Williams wrote his *Key into the Language of America*, a guide to Indian dialects, which displayed not only his linguistic expertise, but also his political savvy. Despite his opposition to many of England's actions, Williams's book bolstered his reputation among influential parliamentarians, who were impressed by his work in Christianizing the Indians. In 1644 he was awarded with the patent, overturning a verdict that ruled in Massachusetts's favor only three months before.

The *Free Charter of Civil Incorporation and Government for the Providence Plantations in the Narragansett Bay in New England* had been secured for a single colony uniting the mainland and island residents. Unknown to Williams, on the day preceding the award of the charter, the Court of Elections in Newport had proclaimed the island an independent body called Rhode Island, an act that set off still more disputation on his return. Before leaving England, Williams released his treatise *The Bloudy Tenent of Persecution*, a separationist manifesto that was immediately ordered burned.

In a gala ceremony, fourteen canoes turned out on the Seekonk River to greet Williams upon his return. Although records are lost, it is likely he was immediately elected "chiefe office" of the patent, a position he held until 1647, when all four towns (Providence, Portsmouth, Newport, and Warwick) finally accepted the charter and united as one body.

Providence During the Indian Wars
The Providence Plantation's isolation from the United Colonies was repeatedly tested during the ongoing Indian wars of the 1640's. During the course of these conflicts, Boston's Commissioners broke their treaty obligations by secretly advising the Mohegan Indians to kill Narragansett chieftain Miantunomi, whom the Mohegans had captured in battle and whom the Commissioners viewed as a political threat. Miantunomi's murder eventually led to a declaration of open war between the Narragansett and the United Colonies. Much to the dismay of the officials in Boston, Providence declared itself neutral and signed a separate pact with their old Indian allies. (The Narragansett would eventually be wiped out by the combined forces of the Mohegan and the English at the Great Swamp Fight of 1675.)

Meanwhile, the Providence Plantation was itself in danger of fragmentation. Plymouth claimed Aquidneck; both Plymouth and Connecticut claimed the "Gortonist's" Warwick; and Massachusetts, which claimed Pawtuxet, wanted more. On May 18, 1647, however, a delegation consisting of ten representatives from each of the four towns officially accepted the charter and devised a code of laws and a bill of rights. In a broader but equally strategic development, Providence's evolving process of granting land to settlers began to diffuse the power of the town's monopolists and set the stage for renewed growth: Poorer, younger newcomers were now given small "quarter rights" to twenty-five-acre plots, provided they relinquished their right to vote until they were admitted as freemen.

Williams, whose term had run out, sought a peaceful existence as an outpost trader but soon was summoned to act as deputy president to quell another uprising, just one year after the adoption of the charter. After a five-year stay in England to begin the process of reconfirming this charter, Williams returned in 1654 to find that Providence, with 250 inhabitants, was still the smallest of the Plantation's four towns. Lacking an official building, its public meetings were held in a tavern.

When Providence submitted to its citizens an order for mandatory military service, its pacifists were aroused. The incident clearly articulated the town's (and later the nation's) biggest question: how to compromise a desire for free will with a need for collective obligation. This incident inspired Williams's best-known quote on the subject, comparing "human combinations" to "a ship . . . whose weal and woe is common." No one is obliged to attend the ship's prayers, he explained, but they must obey the captain's orders for the good of the whole. Indeed, in 1656 Williams put his ideology into practice as he began to accept the much-maligned Quakers into Providence, provoking the less-tolerant colonies to ridicule the city as the "sewer of New England" and "Rogues' Island."

As Williams's designs lurched toward fruition, many of his detractors began to step aside. In Pawtuxet, William Arnold petitioned Massachusetts to be discharged from their jurisdiction, and the region once again became accountable to what had generally come to be known as Rhode Island. At a General Court session, William Coddington ended years of rebellion by finally acquiescing to Williams. Then in 1663, after a decade and a half of petitions, John Clarke returned from England with a renewed charter for Rhode Island (the original copy of which is currently on display at the Rhode Island State Capitol). Twenty-seven years after the initial settlement, Providence and its affiliated towns could at last claim a unified ambition.

Williams served in public office as one of the assistants of the colony until 1677, when he asked to step down. The year before, Providence had suffered a setback when it was attacked on March 26 by Wampanoag Indian chief Massasoit's son King Philip, who sought revenge for the Boston Commissioners' reckless treatment of the various regional tribes. Williams, who had bargained with Massasoit en route to Providence, was treated with respect by King Philip, but this was not enough to prevent the burning of an estimated 80 of 103 Providence houses to the ground, Williams's among them. Town Clerk John Smith reportedly saved official documents by throwing them out the window of his burning house into a mill brook.

Roughly six years after the burning of his town, Williams died, in 1683. Present-day Providence commemorates the invaluable lifework of its founder at the Roger Williams National Memorial, located at 282 North Main Street.

Providence in the Eighteenth Century

As the eighteenth century began, Providence was looking to finalize its boundaries. By 1714, the thorny Pawtuxet claimants had finally settled for the area spanning modern-day Cranston's west side and Johnston's south side. New towns from within Providence's borders were carved out to appease outlying farmers, for whom the long commute into the center of Providence was a hardship. Between 1723 and 1765, six additional towns were mapped from the area.

Rebuilt after King Philip's attack in 1676, and with many of its inhabitants' lingering land disputes coming to settlements, Providence began to focus internally, on its economy, spirituality, and education. In 1713, Providence opposed a paper money proposal that would have benefited traders but hindered farmers, whose income was better stabilized by trading for silver or gold. Eventually, Rhode Island entered into a New England currency pool. In 1728, during the so-called Great Awakening, Congregationalists in Providence were divided between supporters of Josiah Cotton and Joseph Snow, the latter ministering the first Congregational body in Rhode Island not financially supported by Boston's officials.

By this time, Providence was taking shape as a leader in the commerce of New England. Waterfront lots were granted to those who would build wharves and warehouses, and investors began to see a return on their investment. Access to waterways furnished Providence with the reliable use of

A statue of Roger Williams overlooks downtown Providence. (American Stock Photography)

waterwheels (as opposed to Newport's windmills), and its access to acres of timber provided fuel for iron forging and shipyards, as well as for building and heating. Providence's surrounding Indian villages vanished, and forests fell to make way for churches and meetinghouses, distilleries, tanneries, and ropewalks. Trade with overseas partners brought exotic goods like rum, wine, spices, cocoa, and tropical fruits, all of which contributed to the blooming cosmopolitan atmosphere in the town. Craftspeople engaged in needlework, gadgetry, pickling, and preserving. By 1775 the Market House was completed, providing a center for maritime trade that still stands (now under the care of the Rhode Island School of Design). After the Revolutionary War, during a period of rapid growth, the middle class of shopkeepers and artisans expanded.

Slower in pace was the town's cultural development. In 1762 the Histrionic Academy was closed by the town sheriff for its public presentation of music, considered an extravagance by the townspeople. That same year, the town's first newspaper,

Providence Gazette and Country Journal, began printing, and by 1768 Providence could even boast the services of an Italian dancing master and an elocution teacher.

The Revolutionary War

According to figures from 1774, Providence was still well behind Newport in terms of size, with respective densities of 1,196 and 239 persons per square mile. The Revolutionary War ravaged Newport; its location in the bay attracted British siege, and Newport's economy suffered from losses at sea and from wars among the Caribbean nations with whom it did much of its trading. Providence, on the other hand, saw no combat during the Revolution, mainly due to the construction of nine forts (none of which remain) along the Providence River.

Providence's contributions to the Revolution were largely symbolic, such as the 1772 burning of the *Gaspee*, a British revenue ship that had run aground off present-day Warwick's Gaspee Point, and the Tea Party of March 2, 1775, which mirrored Boston's. On May 4, 1776, two months before the signing of the Declaration of Independence, the Rhode Island Assembly dissolved its ties with Great Britain at the Old State House. Built in 1762, this brick building remains standing at 150 Benefit Street.

After the Revolution, Providence joined Boston in dispatching commercial ships to China, resulting in a lucrative trade in Oriental goods. The versatile and highly successful Brown brothers—John, Joseph, Moses, and Nicholas—were instrumental in directing this and many other ventures crucial to Providence's growth. Brown University is named for Nicholas, who saved the failing Rhode Island College from bankruptcy after it had moved to Providence in 1770. In 1775, Joseph Brown designed the First Baptist Church at 75 North Main Street for followers of Williams's Baptist sect. A Georgian church with a 185-feet steeple, the building also hosts Brown University's commencement activities. In 1786 the architect designed the John Brown House at 52 Power Street. The building, described by John Quincy Adams as the most magnificent he had ever seen, today houses the Rhode Island Historical Society.

The John Brown House rests at the south end of the "Mile of History," a walking tour of preserved buildings that reflects one hundred fifty years of changing architectural styles beginning around 1750. Some of the other structures of note along the route include the 1816 First Unitarian Church, housing the largest bell cast by Paul Revere and Son; the 1838 Providence Athenaeum, established in 1753 and now one of the world's oldest lending libraries; and the former state arsenal, housed in a Gothic castle.

In 1815 the "Great Gale" devastated Providence with flooding that cost the town over one million dollars in repairs. Though thirty-five ships were piled up in its cove and Providence was glutted with debris, this catastrophe was not enough to slow the town's rapid growth. Five years after the storm, Providence's population had soared from 6,300 to 11,745. In 1828, the nation's first indoor shopping center, the Greek revival-style Arcade, was built on Weybosset Street, and is now a National Historic Landmark. In 1831, almost two hundred years after Roger Williams's arrival, Providence incorporated as a city.

After the Civil War, industrialism took root in the city. By 1835, the country's first factory-mutual insurance system had been established, and Providence's economy continued to strengthen with its significant output of textile and jewelry, among other goods. Gradually, the Providence River was filled to accommodate railroad tracks. To staff increasing numbers of factories, the city's immigrant population multiplied, and large communities were formed of Swedes, Portuguese, French-Canadians, and most notably, Italians, whose vibrant culture continues to thrive today on the city's Federal Hill.

Providence in the Twentieth Century

At the turn of the twentieth century, when Providence's population had grown to 175,000, Rhode Island's legislative center of government was relocated there and the state capitol was erected on Smith Hill. The imposing State House is topped by one of the world's three self-supported marble domes, and its outline transformed the appearance of Providence's skyline. Today, after a period of postindustrial hardship, Providence enjoys a diverse culture and economic base of academia on College Hill. Underneath this resurgence lies an ancestral bedrock of religious and political independence.

—*James Sullivan*

For Further Information:

Federal Writers' Project. *Rhode Island.* New York: Houghton Mifflin, 1937. Concise with regard to the city's commercial growth.

James, Sydney V. *Colonial Rhode Island: A History.* New York: Charles Scribner's Sons, 1975. Contains some information on Providence's role in the state's history not found elsewhere.

Winslow, Ola Elizabeth. *Master Roger Williams.* 1957. Reprint. New York: Octagon Books, 1973. An in-depth biographical portrait of the single most important figure in Providence's development.

Roger Williams National Memorial

Date: Established in 1975
Relevant issues: Colonial America, religion
Significance: Roger Williams founded the settlement he called Providence on Narragansett Bay

in 1636 after he was expelled from Massachusetts Bay Colony for insisting that magistrates had no authority to punish people for certain religious violations.

Location: Downtown Providence, one block from the State House on North Main Street

Site Office:
Roger Williams National Memorial
282 North Main Street
Providence, RI 02903
ph.: (401) 521-7266
Web site: www.nps.gov/rowi/

Roger Williams was one of the most significant Puritan leaders to come to America in the seventeenth century. An advocate of freedom of conscience, separation of church and state, and fair negotiation with indigenous Americans, Williams found himself at odds with most other Puritan leaders in North America. His refusal to compromise his principles for personal gain and security brought him scorn from the Puritan establishment, yet his legacy to the eighteenth century Founders of the United States was far greater than that of his tormentors.

Early Life
The year of Roger Williams's birth is uncertain, but most historians believe he was born in the Smithfield district of northwest London in 1603. Smithfield was a thriving center of trade at the time. Williams's father, James, was a successful merchant (tailor) and his mother, Alice (Pemberton) Williams, improved the family's financial circumstances through several properties that she owned. Thus, while not wealthy, the family lived in comfortable surroundings.

Almost nothing is known of Roger Williams's early education, but it is reported that he showed a great interest in religion from a tender age. This is scarcely surprising, as the Smithfield district was alive with Puritan activity. The Puritans were a large "radical" faction within the Anglican Church (Church of England). They believed in the primacy of Scripture over clerical authority and in informal worship—beliefs that were unacceptable to the Anglican hierarchy. They also held controversial political views that included advocacy of limits on the influence of the Crown. During the time of Elizabeth I (1558-1603) the number of Puritans

had greatly increased, as the queen followed a mostly benign policy toward them. In the 1580's some Puritans, led by Robert Browne, insisted that all Puritans break from the Anglican Church and form a separate organization. These Puritans became known as Brownists or Separatists. There were large numbers of Separatists in Smithfield, and Roger Williams attended their meetings as a teenager. Among the many issues discussed was support for Puritan colonists in North America. It is clear that these meetings had a lasting influence on Williams.

In 1617, when he was about fourteen, Williams was employed as a stenographer by Sir Edward Coke, England's most famous jurist of the time. Coke, a staunch defender of the rights of Parliament, considered Williams a protégé. Through Coke's intervention, Williams was admitted to a boys' preparatory school in 1621. In 1624 he was awarded a scholarship to Cambridge, and in 1627 he received his degree. He then began a stint as private chaplain to Sir William Masham in Essex. Through this position he met many prominent Puritan leaders, including Oliver Cromwell.

On December 15, 1629, Williams married Mary Barnard, a marriage that eventually produced six children. In December of 1630 Williams fulfilled a major ambition when he and Mary sailed for America, arriving at Nantasket on February 5, 1631.

Trouble in Massachusetts
Williams's first five years on American soil found him constantly at loggerheads with local Puritan leaders. Between 1631 and 1635 Williams held several clerical positions in Boston, Salem, Plymouth (a Separatist colony), and then Salem again. In each location Williams angered Puritan officials by stating views that were considered dangerous. His notion that all New England Puritan congregations should break from the Anglican Church was unsettling enough, but to this Williams was now adding that there should be a separation of church and state, that the king (Charles I) had no right to grant land that belonged to the Indians, and that magistrates overstepped their authority when they punished people for certain religious "crimes." Not surprisingly, he either left or was sacked from every position he held during this five-year period. Williams, however, did not stop expressing his views in clerical meetings and public gatherings, or

Roger Williams National Memorial. (NPS, Roger Williams National Memorial)

through his many written commentaries.

In 1635 colonial officials in Massachusetts, exasperated by Williams's obduracy and alarmed that he had attracted some loyal followers, decided to take action. On April 30 he was brought before the Massachusetts General Court on charges that he had wrongfully denied the power of magistrates to punish anyone guilty of violating the first four Commandments. The court determined on October 9, 1635, that Williams should be banished from Massachusetts for "new and dangerous opinions against the power of magistrates."

Providence

Banned from Massachusetts Bay Colony, Williams moved with his followers in April, 1636, to a desolate parcel of land owned by the Narragansett tribe. After negotiating with tribal leaders, he purchased the land and established a settlement that he called Providence. True to his conviction that the colonists must appreciate Indian culture and rights, he learned the Narragansett language and urged his followers to create farming and trading ties with the tribe. He had hoped to convert the Narragansetts to Christianity. The Providence settlement, while enduring many difficulties, succeeded to the point where Williams, in 1642, returned to England to seek a colonial charter. That colony would eventually be known as Rhode Island.

Williams spent two years in England during a tumultuous time in the relationship between Crown and Parliament. In the year that Williams arrived, a civil war began involving the forces of Charles I and those of the House of Commons, the latter organized by the great Puritan leader Oliver Cromwell. Obtaining a charter in such unstable circumstances proved difficult, but with the help of Sir Henry Vane, a principal adviser to Cromwell, Parliament granted a charter to Williams in 1643. The document essentially allowed Williams to establish the governance of the colony in any way he wished.

In March, 1644, Williams returned to America as "chief officer" of a democratic colony that was to include the scattered settlements in Narragansett. He intended that freedom of conscience would be rigorously protected. This had been the theme of his best known treatise, *The Bloudy Tenent of Persecution*, which he wrote in 1643 and published in 1644.

Challenges

Williams soon discovered that organization of the colony was going to be difficult and would require some time. There were divisions among those who had settled in the region since 1636, and not all were willing to accept the plans Williams put forward. The followers of Anne Hutchinson, who also had been thrown out of Massachusetts, had ideas somewhat different from Williams's. Hutchinson angered Massachusetts leaders by insisting that the Holy Spirit dwelled in and guided every person. In 1638 she and her followers established a settlement at Portsmouth on Narragansett land.

In addition to some dissent within the colony, there was a constant barrage of criticism toward Williams from Puritans outside the Narragansett region. John Cotton, a prominent Boston clergyman, spoke and wrote vitriolically against Williams's ideas of freedom of conscience and separation of church and state. Indeed, Providence received no support at all from surrounding colonies. Those who settled in Narragansett territory were considered dangerous heretics and even criminals.

Part of Williams's difficulty lay in the vague nature of the 1643 charter. He decided to return to England in 1651 (the civil war was over and Oliver Cromwell had created a Puritan commonwealth) to renew and reconfirm the original charter. As a result, the boundaries for the colony were now more clearly defined. While in England, Williams made an acquaintance with the great Puritan poet and leader John Milton. Williams was well known and highly regarded by English Puritans, particularly for his close association with American Indians. Milton knew of Williams's work in New England and encouraged him to continue to follow his conscience.

In 1654 Williams returned to America with his "improved" charter and served as first president of the Rhode Island colony from 1654 to 1657. The difficulties of cohesiveness and organization remained. By this time Rhode Island had become a refuge for outcast religious factions. A large number of Quakers and various Anabaptist sects poured into the colony. Williams, for a time, seemed swayed by anabaptism (a belief in adult baptism and the absolute adherence to Scripture), but in the end he remained faithful to the Calvinist theology he had followed since his youth.

The Quakers presented Williams with a problem that somewhat tarnished his reputation as a defender of freedom of conscience. The Quakers were pacifists and refused to take up arms in defense of the colony. Williams entered into a long, and often acrimonious, debate with the Quakers over this issue. In 1657 Williams stepped down as president of Rhode Island and gradually drifted from prominence. He continued to serve in various public offices wherever he was needed. His greatest contribution after 1657 was in his ability to converse with New England's Indian leaders. They trusted and respected Williams more than any other colonial spokesman. On many occasions his negotiating skills during contentious times preserved the peace.

Williams was not able to prevent the serious Indian assault of 1675-1676 known as King Philip's War. King Philip was a Wanpanoag tribal leader who convinced the Narragansetts and the Nipmucks to participate in a coalition against the New England colonies. Appropriately enough, Philip first attacked a Quaker settlement at Swansea, Rhode Island. Before the war ended there were heavy losses on both sides, and at least ten towns were totally destroyed. Although he had staunchly supported Indian rights and culture, Williams fought against the Indians on this occasion. The war set back the economic development of Rhode Island and the rest of New England for at least a decade.

From 1636 on, Williams earned his living principally from farming and trade with the Narragansetts. For most of his life, and especially during his last years, he was near poverty. His spirit remained undaunted, and he continued to refer to himself as a "Seeker," that is, one who is devoted to seeking truth and salvation. By the end of his life Williams had fallen into such obscurity that the date of his death, like that of his birth, is uncertain. It is believed that he died sometime during the first three months of 1683.

The Roger Williams National Memorial is on the lot of the original settlement, which is now a park. The site provides historical exhibits and self-guided walking tours of the College Hill Historic District. —*Ronald K. Huch*

For Further Information:

Catton, Bruce, and William B. Catton. *The Bold and Magnificent Dream: America's Years.* Garden City, N.Y.: Doubleday, 1978. A highly readable and interesting account of colonial America.

Chupack, Henry. *Roger Williams.* New York:Twayne, 1969. A brief, compact, and accurate biography.

Ernst, James F. *Roger Williams, New England Firebrand.* New York: Macmillan, 1932. Captures the excitement and turmoil Williams brought to the colonies.

Garrett, John. *Roger Williams, Witness Beyond Christendom, 1603-1683.* New York: Macmillan, 1970. An interesting account of the meshing of Williams's religious and political ideas.

Gilpin, Clark. *The Millenarian Piety of Roger Williams.* Chicago: University of Chicago Press, 1979. Examines the origins and impact of Roger Williams's Christian views. Primarily for academic readers.

Miller, Perry. *Roger Williams: His Contribution to the American Tradition.* New York: Atheneaum, 1970. Essential reading. Written by one of America's most respected historians, it provides an understanding of the importance of Williams's ideas for future Americans.

Morgan, Edmund S. *Roger Williams: The Church and the State.* New York: Harcourt, Brace, and World, 1967. Thoroughly and ably discusses the implications of Williams's position on the relationship of church and state.

Polishook, Irwin H. *Roger Williams, John Cotton, and Religious Freedom. . . .* Englewood Cliffs, N.J.: Prentice-Hall, 1967. Discusses the controversy between Williams and Cotton over the issue of liberty of conscience.

Other Historic Sites

Aldrich House

Location: Providence, Providence County

Relevant issues: Political history

Statement of significance: From 1878 until his death, this three-story clapboard house was the residence of Nelson W. Aldrich (1841-1915), who, as Republican Senate "boss," maintained virtual veto power over legislation, pressing his view that business and government should combine to lead the country, but that business should play the leading role.

Cocumscussoc Archaeological Site

Location: Wickford, Washington County

Relevant issues: American Indian history, colonial America

Statement of significance: Cocumscussoc is the historically chronicled locale of the first trading post established in Narragansett Country by Rhode Island's founder Roger Williams in 1637. Archaeological remains dating to the Historic Contact Period are associated with Richard Smith, Sr., who purchased the site from Williams in 1651, and his son, Richard Smith, Jr., who operated the post from 1662 to 1692.

Crescent Park Looff Carousel

Location: East Providence, Providence County

Relevant issues: Cultural history

Statement of significance: Built about 1895—most of the figures date from 1905 to 1910—this large carousel is the earliest, most elaborate, and probably best preserved of the handful remaining of more than one hundred carousels built by Charles I. D. Looff, one of the foremost manufacturers of carousels in the United States. It is complete with its original shed and early twentieth century band organ and lighting.

Fleur-de-Lys Studios

Location: Providence, Providence County

Relevant issues: Art and architecture

Statement of significance: Fleur-de-Lys Studios, constructed in 1885, is a key architectural monument to the American Arts and Crafts movement. The building's design is the product of a collaboration between painter Sydney R. Burleigh and architect Edmund R. Willson. Both men achieved considerable professional prominence during their lifetimes.

Flying Horse Carousel

Location: Westerly, Washington County
Relevant issues: Cultural history
Statement of significance: Dating from about 1876, this is the oldest carousel of its type, in which the horses are suspended from a center frame, and may be the oldest extant carousel in the United States. It is one of two intact examples of the work of the Charles W. F. Dare Company of New York City, one of the major carousel manufacturers.

Greene Homestead

Location: Coventry, Kent County
Relevant issues: Military history, RevolutionaryWar
Statement of significance: From 1774 to 1783, this two-story clapboard dwelling, which he designed and built, was the residence of General Nathanael Greene (1742-1786), who was among the most important generals in the Continental army.

Old Slater Mill

Location: Pawtucket, Providence County
Relevant issues: Business and industry
Statement of significance: Here, Samuel Slater (1768-1835) perfected America's first successful water-powered spinning machine in 1790, and helped to build the country's first successful cotton mill in 1793. His mill is operated as a museum.

Original U.S. Naval War College

Location: Newport, Newport County
Relevant issues: Military history, naval history
Statement of significance: This institution was established in 1884 to offer advanced courses for naval officers. Alfred Thayer Mahan (1840-1914), a key architect of America's naval policy, became president of the college in 1886.

Site of Battle of Rhode Island

Location: Portsmouth, Newport County
Relevant issues: African American history, military history, Revolutionary War
Statement of significance: On August 29, 1778, in a valley between Lehigh Hill to the north and Turkey and Almy Hills to the south, the British forces which were occupying Newport engaged American forces under Major General John Sullivan in the only Revolutionary War battle in which an all-black unit, the First Rhode Island Regiment, participated on the patriots' side.

Stuart Birthplace

Location: Saunderstown, Washington County
Relevant issues: Art and architecture, colonial America
Statement of significance: From 1755 to 1761, this gambrel-roofed, clapboard house was the home of Gilbert Stuart (1755-1828), best known for his portraits of George Washington and other prominent political figures.

Wanton-Lyman-Hazard House

Location: Newport, Newport County
Relevant issues: Colonial America, political history
Statement of significance: Built probably in 1696, this structure illustrates the architectural transition from seventeenth to eighteenth century styles. It was damaged by Stamp Act riots in 1765 when occupied by a Tory stampmaster.

South Carolina

Drayton Hall, Charleston. (American Stock Photography)

History of South Carolina

South Carolina, known as the Palmetto State, is the smallest of the southeastern states and is one of the richest in history and enduring influence on national events and development. A blend of diverse cultures, including European, Native American, and African American, produced notable social, artistic, political, military, and cultural accomplishments. The state has been among the richest and the poorest in the United States and has known both victory and harsh defeat.

Early History

The first human inhabitants of what is now South Carolina arrived around 13,000 B.C.E. as hunters of the large animals, including elephants, that inhabited the region. During the period from 8000 to 1500 B.C.E., the area's climate changed, bringing hardwood trees and more easily huntable animals such as deer, turkey, and squirrel. Many inhabitants became largely migratory, moving through the seasons to follow their prey. Along the coast, shellfish provided a major diet staple for more settled groups.

Around 1150 B.C.E. a new group, the Mississippians, moved into the area. They built large villages with earthen mounds for temples along river bluffs. These villages established a nation known as Cofitachequi, after its capital, located on the banks of the Wateree River in central South Carolina. In 1540 the Spanish explorer Hernando de Soto was greeted by the "queen" of Cofitachequi during his expedition across the Southeast.

At the time of the arrival of the Europeans, there were thirty to forty separate Native American nations in the region, including Cherokee, Saluda, Catawba, Wateree, Congaree, Wando, Waccamaw, and Coosaw. All these names, and many others, were preserved in place names in South Carolina.

Exploration and Colonization

By 1521 the Spanish had explored the Carolina coast, and on August 18, 1525, Saint Helena's feast day, they sighted and named an island and a sound in her honor; both would retain the name Saint Helena. Lucas Vásquez de Ayllón founded a short-lived Spanish settlement on Winyah Bay near modern Georgetown in 1526, and in 1562, the French under Jean Ribaut challenged the Spanish by establishing a small fort on an island in what they named Port Royal Sound.

The Spanish returned in 1566 and established Santa Elena, also on Port Royal Sound, which grew into a settlement of considerable size and was for a time the capital of all Spanish colonies in North America. However, under increasing pressure from the Native Americans and the English, the Spanish abandoned Santa Elena in 1587 to consolidate their position at St. Augustine in northern Florida.

Colonization and Revolution

In 1663 King Charles II of England granted extensive lands, named "Carolina" after himself, to eight Lord Proprietors, chief among them Anthony Ashley Cooper, earl of Shaftesbury. Cooper, along with English philosopher John Locke, drafted an elaborate Fundamental Constitution for the colony. In April, 1670, the first settlers arrived. Within ten years they had established the city of Charleston at the confluence of the Ashley and Cooper Rivers. Settled largely by English inhabitants of Barbados, the new colony prospered from the production of crops including rice, indigo, and cotton. The wealth of these crops, and the plantation systems they fostered, was gained only through the knowledge and labor of large numbers of African slaves. Long before the American Revolution, there were more blacks than whites in the colony. Along the South Carolina Sea Islands, they created their own distinctive culture, including the Gullah language, a mixture of African, Caribbean, and English languages.

Early threats to the colony included struggles with the Native Americans and raids by pirates such as the notorious Blackbeard (Edward Teach). These dangers were increased by proprietary incompetence, and in 1729 South Carolina became a royal colony. South Carolina was a leader in the move for American independence, and during the American Revolution more than 130 battles and skirmishes were fought in the state. In June, 1776, British naval forces were repulsed from Charleston but returned and captured the city in 1780. The battles of Kings Mountain in 1780 and Cowpens in 1781 helped turn the tide of the war in favor of the Americans. Partisan leaders such as Francis Marion, known as the Swamp Fox, played an essential role in the struggle for independence.

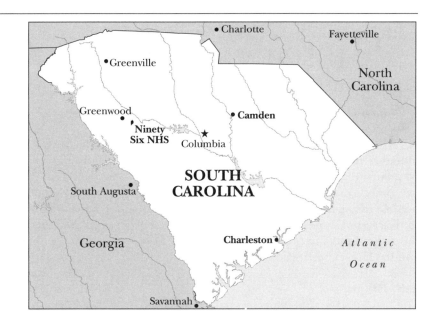

Civil War and Reconstruction
South Carolinians Charles Pinckney and John Rutledge were highly influential in drafting the U.S. Constitution, and they were instrumental in having it adopted by the state legislature in 1788. However, as with many others in the state and throughout the South, they wished to restrain the powers of the federal government, especially regarding the highly sensitive issue of slavery.

It was because of this concern that South Carolina, along with other southern states, increasingly insisted upon the doctrine of state's rights. Senator John C. Calhoun became the chief spokesperson for the South, and while he helped to fashion compromises that kept South Carolina in the Union, he also advocated nullification, the doctrine that a state could declare invalid within its borders an act of the national government. During the Nullification Crisis of 1832-1833 President Andrew Jackson ordered U.S. Navy ships to Charleston to enforce federal law. The election of President Abraham Lincoln in 1860 prompted South Carolina to become the first state to secede from the Union on December 20, 1860.

On April 12, 1861, the Civil War began, when Confederate troops fired on Union-held Fort Sumter in Charleston harbor. During the war, Union troops quickly captured the sea islands around Port Royal Sound, liberating thousands of slaves and placing Charleston under a four-year siege. After General William Tecumseh Sherman's Union army completed its March to the Sea from Atlanta to Savannah, it "let South Carolina howl" as it swept through the state, forcing the Confeder-

ates to abandon Charleston and Columbia, the state capital. Sherman largely blamed South Carolina for the war because it was the first state to secede, and he punished it harshly.

South Carolina was readmitted to the Union in 1868, and a Reconstruction government mingled social and educational reforms with blatant corruption. In 1876, under the leadership of former Confederate general Wade Hampton, white South Carolinians reclaimed their hold on the state. For almost a hundred years, the memory of Civil War and Reconstruction ensured that South Carolina would remain a solidly Democratic state. It was only during the civil rights era of the 1960's, when the Democratic Party became closely associated with that effort, that many white South Carolinians turned to the Republican Party. Senator Strom Thurmond, who had run as a Dixiecrat in 1948 to protest the Democrats' civil rights platform, became a Republican in 1964. In 1974 James Edwards was the first Republican elected governor after Reconstruction.

A Modern Economy
After the Civil War, agriculture remained South Carolina's primary source of income. In the 1880's the textile industry greatly increased, due in large part to the hydroelectric power available upstate. Textile plants drew workers from the farms and rural areas to create a new and thriving industry, until

the Great Depression brought economic disaster in the 1930's. The New Deal of President Franklin Delano Roosevelt sought to remedy these problems in part by the creation of the Santee Cooper Project, one of the largest hydroelectric and navigational efforts in North America, which helped advance South Carolina's economy into the twentieth century. During and after World War II, large military bases throughout the state provided additional economic benefits.

However, agriculture and textiles remained the state's major sources of income until the early 1970's, when modern industry and technology took hold, best exemplified by BMW's 1993 decision to locate its first car-manufacturing plant outside Germany in South Carolina. By that time, manufacturing had become the state's number-one industry in terms of employees and included more than two hundred international companies. Tourism became a major source of income, with visitors flocking to South Carolina's two hundred miles of coastline and beaches; historic cities such as Camden, Charleston, and Beaufort; and three hundred golf courses, many of them world class and the site of prestigious tournaments.

Modernization in the economy brought increased attention to both an old problem and a new concern: the issue of resolving racial differences among the state's population and the need to protect the state's natural environment. South Carolina, with its long and often troubled history, and its abundant natural resources threatened by rapid development and population growth, faced the delicate task of balancing past, present, and future. —*Michael Witkoski*

Camden

Date: Land surveyed for town in 1733
Relevant issues: American Indian history, art and architecture, colonial America, cultural history, military history, Revolutionary War
Significance: The first official English town established in the interior of South Carolina, Camden was the site of a major American defeat in the Revolutionary War. It has become a major center for horse breeding and racing, with many fine homes and buildings from the colonial and antebellum periods.

Location: 27 miles northeast of Columbia on the Wateree River
Site Office:
Kershaw County Chamber of Commerce
724 South Broad Street
Camden, SC 29020
ph.: (803) 432-2525
Web site: www.camden-sc.org
e-mail: camden@camden.net

South Carolina's first inland town, Camden was the site of an American defeat during the Revolutionary War. A flourishing town prior to the Civil War, it has become a premiere area for horse breeding and racing and for tourism.

A Trading Station Becomes a Town
The Wateree Indians, who gave their name to the river, were the first known inhabitants of the area around present-day Camden. To facilitate trade with Native Americans and to expand the borders of South Carolina, King George II of England ordered new townships established in the interior of the colony. In 1733, surveyor James St. Julien laid out a township known as Fredericksburg; it would eventually be known as Camden.

The first settlers came in 1737, and were joined in the early 1750's by Irish Quakers led by Samuel Wyly. Wyly founded a post for trading with the Catawba Indians, the tribe which had supplanted the Wateree. King Haigler, chief of the Catawbas, was a friend of the settlers, and his image is part of the modern town's official seal.

In 1758 Joseph Kershaw of Charleston arrived and built a flour mill, sawmill, indigo works, tobacco warehouse, brewery, and distillery. Kershaw also built Camden's first mansion atop Pine Tree Hill. Kershaw was a dominant figure and a leader in the movement toward independence. In 1765, at Kershaw's urging, the town was renamed Camden in honor of Charles Pratt, Lord Camden, who supported American rights in the British Parliament.

War Comes to Camden
In November, 1774, a grand jury of the Camden District adopted a declaration urging independence from Great Britain. In March, 1776, South Carolina became the first colony to declare itself independent from the Crown.

In May, 1780, British troops under First Marquis Charles Cornwallis (1738-1805) captured Charleston. On June 1 Cornwallis entered Camden, and, with Kershaw's mansion as his residence, imposed harsh military rule. On August 16, 1780, an American force of 3,000 under General Horatio Gates (1728-1806) encountered Cornwallis's 2,300 British regulars outside Camden. Gates, rash and unskilled, placed his militia on Cornwallis's left flank. Cornwallis attacked and routed these inexperienced troops, then drove in the flanks and rear of the Continentals; few escaped, and Johann Baron DeKalb (1721-1780), a European volunteer serving in the American army, was killed. Gates fled more than sixty miles to escape. Camden was one of the most disastrous American defeats of the Revolutionary War.

However, under General Nathanael Greene (1742-1786), Gates's replacement, the American cause revived. On April 25, 1781, Greene faced a British force at Hobkirk's Hill, near Camden. Although defeated, Greene by his presence forced the British to retreat to Charleston.

Prosperity, War, and Renewal

In the new nation, Camden became one of South Carolina's major inland trading centers. George Washington visited in 1791 during his southern tour. By 1802 the town had over two hundred houses and hosted numerous cultural events. In 1813, a great fire destroyed many buildings, while a malaria epidemic in 1816 convinced residents to move inland from the marshy Wateree River. As a result, many houses and shops were built on higher, drier sand hills to the north of the original town. These newer houses often began as small, simple structures that were gradually enlarged into gracious mansions with beautiful gardens.

During the nineteenth century Robert Mills (1781-1855), one of America's most distinguished architects, designed the Kershaw County Court House, Bethesda Presbyterian Church, and a monument to Baron DeKalb. The monument's cornerstone was laid by the Marquis de Lafayette in 1825. During the 1840's and 1850's Camden experienced great prosperity, which ended with the Civil War. By the first year of the war, eighty percent of the county's white male population had joined the Confederate army, and Camden had six generals in gray. Camden was left almost untouched by federal troops when General William Tecumseh Sherman (1820-1891) captured it in February of 1865.

During the 1890's, Camden became a popular destination of northern visitors who delighted in its climate, natural resources, and architecture. Horse breeding, racing, and polo became popular. The "Colonial Cup," one of the nation's richest steeplechase races, is held in the late fall. During the spring, the "Carolina Cup" brings an exciting mix of steeplechase and flat racing.

Places to Visit

A major part of Camden's charm is its architecture. The Kershaw Mansion has been reconstructed on its original site. Many historic houses and buildings remain, ranging from simple log houses to elegant structures with Charleston-style piazzas (porches). Robert Mills, the South Carolina native who designed the Washington Monument, left his mark on Camden. The Kershaw County Court House was designed by Mills in 1825 and revised in 1847. Mills also designed the Bethesda Presbyterian Church. He placed the steeple at the rear of the church and arranged the interior so that the floor and pews gradually rise as they recede from the pulpit.

Steeped in history, Camden also offers the Quaker Cemetery, founded in 1759 and still in use, as well as the 1825 town clockworks. The Revolutionary War park, centered on the Kershaw Mansion, commemorates one of fourteen Revolutionary War battles in this area of South Carolina—battles which helped earn the state its nickname of "Cockpit of the Revolution."

—*Michael Witkoski*

For Further Information:

Buchanan, John. *The Road to Guilford Court House: The American Revolution in the Carolinas.* New York: John Wiley & Sons, 1999. Puts the battle of Camden and its Revolutionary experience in context.

Edgar, Walter. *South Carolina: A History.* Columbia: University of South Carolina Press, 1998. Weaves the story of Camden into the general growth of the state.

Jones, Lewis P. *South Carolina: One of Fifty States.* Orangeburg, S.C.: Sandlapper Press, 1991. Provides a general overview of Camden's role in the state's history.

"Kershaw County Museum." www.camden-sc.org/ museum.html. Excellent site for historical and cultural information about Camden.

Lumpkin, Henry. *From Savannah to Yorktown: The American Revolution in the South.* Columbia: University of South Carolina Press, 1981. Outstanding presentation of the Battle of Camden and its aftermath.

Sweet, Ethel Wylly. *Camden: Homes and Heritage.* Camden: Kershaw County Historical Society, 1978. Local history with excellent color illustrations of houses and other buildings.

Charleston

Date: Settled in April, 1670, as Albermarle Point

Relevant issues: Art and architecture, Civil War, colonial America, Revolutionary War

Significance: South Carolina's oldest city and one of the most historic cities in the country. Its elegant homes, magnificent parks, and beautiful waterfront make the city one of the most visited in the United States.

Location: On a narrow peninsula extending into Charleston Harbor at the confluence of the Cooper and Ashley Rivers

Site Office:

Historic Charleston Foundation
40 E. Bay Street
Charleston, SC 29401-2547
ph.: (803) 723-1623

Since its founding more than three centuries ago, Charleston has had a turbulent history, one marked by earthquakes, tornadoes, hurricanes, devastating fires, and military bombardment and occupation. Yet, the city has managed not only to survive but also to maintain its position as one of the country's most historic sites. Charleston, in fact, has retained a remarkable collection of magnificent gardens, stately churches, and thousands of buildings representing nearly every period of U.S. architectural history.

Early History

Charleston's history as a city began in 1663 when King Charles II of England granted eight loyal friends proprietorship to a large chunk of the future United States, which they named Carolina. (The territory was divided into North and South in 1729.) Seven years later, in April, 1670, 148 settlers landed on the banks of the Ashley River at a spot they named Albermarle Point after the oldest proprietor. Within a few years the name was changed to Charles Towne in honor of King Charles II. Today, Charles Towne Landing, the site of that first permanent settlement, is a state-owned nature preserve and a permanent historic complex that brings to life the experiences of those first settlers.

By the end of the first decade, the settlement moved to a parcel of land between the Ashley and Cooper (then called Etiwan and Wando) Rivers, because the site was better protected against Spaniards, pirates, and Indians. At this time, a group of French Huguenots joined the English colonists. In 1704 Charles Towne became one of the three walled cities on the North American continent.

The settlement site provided an excellent location for trade and commerce. Charles Towne quickly emerged as a thriving seaport and one of the great trading centers in the thirteen colonies and the British Empire. In the 1600's and early 1700's, planters introduced rice, indigo, and cotton, which became the cash crops for much of the wealth accumulated by Charlestonians, allowing them to enjoy the good life and build huge houses and plantations, many of which can be visited today.

Plantation Homes

Magnolia Plantation, for example, is the 250-year-old ancestral home of numerous generations of South Carolina's distinguished Drayton family. The plantation is famous for containing fifty acres of what many consider to be the world's most beautiful garden. Several other Charleston plantations are impressively preserved, including Middleton Place (built in 1755), whose landscaped gardens are the country's oldest; Drayton Hall (built between 1738 and 1742), a landmark preserving some of the oldest and finest Palladian architecture in the United States; and the Boone Hall Plantation (built in 1743), often described as the country's most photographed.

During its formative period, the city established a number of firsts—the first public election in the Carolina territory (1670); the colonies' first planting and exporting of rice (by 1690); the country's first insurance company, the Friendly Society for

Mutual Insurance of Houses (1731); the first newspaper in South Carolina (1732), which after 1739 was edited by America's first female editor; the first opera in the colonies (1735); and the first prescription drugstore, which opened its doors in 1780.

Religious Freedom and Churches

From its beginning, the Carolina colony passed laws that allowed a great degree of religious freedom—freedom that contributed to the colony's rapid growth during the prerevolutionary period. By the early 1700's, many religious denominations—French Huguenot, Anabaptist, and Quaker, among others—were worshipping peacefully together in Charles Towne. Later in the century, they were joined by Presbyterian, Jewish, Lutheran, Methodist, and Roman Catholic congregations.

Today, Charleston can aptly be described as a "City of Churches." Organized in 1681, the Circular Congregational Church established the first Sunday school in South Carolina and today is the only Huguenot church remaining in the United States. The First Baptist Church was founded in 1682, when the congregation of the Anabaptist Church in Kittery, Maine, fled the colony and settled in Charles Towne. Congregated in 1761, St. Michael's Episcopal Church is the city's oldest surviving church building and one of the city's few churches to retain its original design. George Washington worshipped in St. Michael's during his tour of the South in 1791.

In 1791, slaves and free blacks founded the Emmanuel African Methodist Episcopal Church as the "Free African Society." It was here that African American Denmark Vesey laid plans for his famous slave insurrection in 1822. Authorities found out about the rebellion, however, crushed it, and closed down the church. The establishment of The Citadel, the Charleston-based state-supported military academy, resulted from the fear caused by the nearly successful slave revolt.

The Revolutionary War

By 1775 Charles Towne had become one of the wealthiest cities in the colonies. The following year, South Carolina's Provincial Congress established the first independent state government in the colonies and Charles Towne began playing an important role in a series of events leading to the American Revolution. When war broke out, the British attempted to take Charles Towne, but soldiers defending the city repelled the attack. In 1779 Charles Towne successfully defended itself again from the British, but beginning May 12, 1780, the British put the city under siege for six weeks and it fell. The British were able to hold the city until December 14, 1782, when they were forced to evacuate.

In 1783 the city was incorporated and renamed Charleston. It remained the state capital from 1776 until 1786, when Columbia, the present capital, was founded.

During the following century, Charleston continued to be a city of revolutionary ferment. By the early 1830's, tariffs had trebled on iron, salt, all woolen and cotton goods, and some other commodities produced by the South. Charlestonians, like other South Carolinians, were angered. When South Carolina's state legislature met to discuss and debate the issue in 1833, it passed the Ordinance of Nullification and nullified the act increasing the tariffs and declaring no duties should be paid after February 1, 1833.

The Civil War

In December, 1860, Charleston was thrust into the events leading to the Civil War when delegates at a convention in the city decided to sign the Ordinance of Secession. Shortly thereafter, Major Robert Anderson of the Union army sent the women and children from Fort Moultrie on Sullivan's Island to Fort Jackson on James Island and quietly moved his garrison to Fort Sumter, an unfinished federal fort in Charleston Harbor. Confederate leaders sent a commission to Washington, D.C., to negotiate the surrender of Fort Sumter as well as Forts Johnston, Moultrie, and Castle Pinckney.

Then on April 12, 1861, Charleston became the scene of one of the most dramatic events in U.S. history when Confederate troops began shelling Fort Sumter, igniting the Civil War's first military engagement. The skirmish ended quickly, and on April 14, Major Anderson surrendered the fort. One Union soldier was killed during the bombardment, and another died when a gun prematurely exploded during surrender proceedings.

After surrendering Fort Sumter, Union forces regrouped, and soon they controlled the Atlantic coast from Georgetown, South Carolina, to Smyrna, Florida, with the exception of Charleston.

Boone Plantation in Charleston. (PhotoDisc)

They blockaded the city, but the Confederacy remained defiant and determined to defend the city at all costs. In the words of Major General Robert E. Lee, the defenders would, if necessary, "fight street by street and house by house as long as we have a foot of ground to stand on."

Despite four years of deprivation and heavy shelling, Charleston did manage to hold out until late in the war, thanks largely to the blockade runners who brought in vital supplies. On April 14, 1865, four years to the day Confederate troops forced Major Anderson to take down the stars and stripes from the flag staff of Fort Sumter, Anderson, now a general, stood on the spot and raised the same flag over the fort's ruins.

Slow Postwar Recovery

After the war, Charleston's economy was devastated. These hard times, however, were responsible for the preservation of many of Charleston's historic structures. Residents had no money for demolition or rebuilding.

In 1886 the city suffered another catastrophe. At 9:30 in the evening of August 31, Charlestonians were startled by a low rumbling sound followed by a sharp tremor. Then they heard a great roar, increasing in volume and accompanied by violent vibrations. Chimney walls and buildings toppled. This was the second natural disaster to hit Charleston in less than a year. In the fall of 1885, a cyclone had swept the city, causing more than $1.5 million in damage.

Earthquakes in Charleston were nothing new. One hit in 1763, followed by two others in 1811 and 1812, and another in 1843. In 1857 a tremor shook the city so severely many Charlestonians began to hold prayer meetings asking for deliverance. The earthquake of 1886, however, was the worst in the city's history. More than 90 percent of the brick buildings suffered damage to some extent; the wooden buildings fared a little better. Property damage was a staggering five million dollars.

Charleston survived once again, exhibiting the resilience it has shown throughout its long history.

Today, the chief monuments of the earthquake—the plates and bars on the outside of many city homes—form one of the city's most distinctive architectural features. They were inserted through many of the city's houses to steady their upper floors in case the city ever again had to face such a calamity.

At the turn of the century, Charleston made a concerted effort to regain its former position as an important trade center. From December, 1901, until May, 1902, the city held what became known as the South Carolina and West Indian Exposition. To get the project started, Charleston resident F. W. Wagener donated money and a large tract of land. A corporation was established and money solicited.

From its beginning, the exposition suffered a series of setbacks. First, labor troubles almost ended the event. Then came bad weather and rumors that the exposition was closing down. Although the exposition was not as successful as its planners had hoped, Charleston did derive some good from it. Attention was indeed drawn to the city, showing the world its industrial and commercial potential.

Once the expo ended, however, there was little evidence to show any permanent relocation of industry to Charleston.

World War II and Economy Recovery
Charleston's economic fortunes did not change until World War II when the Santee Cooper federal hydroelectric power project, which was completed in 1942, and investment in manufacturing and military installations gave local industry a major boost. By 1984 Charleston was the twelfth largest Atlantic coast port.

Despite its recent economic growth, Charleston has remained linked culturally and historically to the Old South. Indeed, the city has worked hard to strengthen this bond and establish a tradition of respectful care and treatment of its historic structures. This tradition first manifested itself as early as the 1850's, but Charleston's first organized preservation effort did not come until 1920, when the villa that Gabriel Manigault had designed for his brother Joseph about 1803 faced the danger of being replaced by a gas station.

The ruins of Charleston toward the end of the Civil War. (Corbis)

To meet the threat, historically minded citizens organized the Society for the Preservation of Old Dwellings, which was later renamed the Preservation Society of Charleston. The organization is the oldest community-based group of its kind in the United States. After much difficulty, the society successfully preserved the Manigault House. Largely through its efforts, more than seven hundred buildings, or 10 percent of the historic sites built before the 1840's, have been saved.

Modern Preservation Efforts

In 1947 citizens organized the Historic Charleston Foundation as a nonprofit educational organization with the purpose of preserving the nation's architectural and cultural resources as represented in Charleston and the surrounding area. The Foundation's primary efforts have centered in Charleston's Old Historic District, the oldest such district in the city, which encompasses more than 3,600 rated structures and represents approximately 25 percent of the city's land mass.

Included are some of the city's most impressive houses. Built between 1765 and 1769, the Miles Brewton House on King Street is a beautifully proportioned residence that builder/architect Ezra Waite designed. Because of the house's large size, military troops occupied it twice during wartime. British General Sir Henry Clinton used it as his headquarters during the Revolutionary War, and Union general George Meade and Edward Hatch stayed there when Northern troops occupied Charleston during the Civil War in 1865.

In 1772 Thomas Heyward, a wealthy planter, built a three-story Georgian brick house at 87 Church Street where George Washington stayed in 1791. At 76 Church Street is a mid-eighteenth century house occupied by DuBose Heyward in the 1920's. Heyward is best known for his novel *Porgy* (1927), which George Gershwin later set to music as *Porgy and Bess*, America's first folk opera.

Today, these houses and many others that predate the American Revolution are still occupied; some are owned by the families that built them. They are a part of the rich architectural tradition that has experienced every epoch of U.S. history.

—*Ron Chepesiuk*

For Further Information:

The literature on Charleston is voluminous, but the following books provide a good introduction to the historic city:

Davis, Evangeline. *Charleston: Houses and Gardens.* Charleston, S.C.: Preservation Society of Charleston, 1975.

Marion, John Francis. *The Charleston Story: Scenes from a City's History.* Harrisburg, Pa.: Stackpole Books, 1978.

Rosen, Robert R. *A Short History of Charleston.* 2d ed. Columbia: University of South Carolina Press, 1997.

Severens, Kenneth. *Charleston Antebellum Architecture and Civic Destiny.* Knoxville: University of Tennessee, 1988.

Sully, Susan. *Charleston Style: Past and Present.* New York: Rizzoli, 1999. A pictorial study of Charleston's historic buildings.

Ninety Six

Date: Originally merely a geographical term; first European trading post was established there in 1751

Relevant issues: American Indian history, business and industry, colonial America, European settlement, military history, Revolutionary War

Significance: The site sits astride an ancient American Indian trade route known as the Cherokee Path. When Cherokee power was broken during the French and Indian Wars, European settlers flooded the South Carolina backcountry. During the American Revolution, a fort was built by the British army near Ninety Six as part of a defensive network for control of South Carolina. Following a siege by Patriot forces in 1781, the British abandoned the fort and destroyed the town. Reconstructed after the war as Cambridge, the community continued as a business center until the mid-1850's.

Location: East of Greenwood

Site Office:
Ninety Six National Historic Site
P.O. Box 496
Ninety Six, SC 29666
ph.: (864) 543-4068
fax: (864) 543-2058
Web site: www.nps.gov.nisi/

Long before Europeans arrived in backcountry South Carolina, Cherokee Indians had worn a path from their primary town of Keowee in the foothills of the Appalachian Mountains to the coastal region. This ancient American Indian trade route, about eight feet wide and worn to a depth of several feet, was called the Cherokee Path. After the founding of Charles Towne by British settlers in 1670, trappers and traders followed that same trail inland in their search for furs. This commercial artery—running through rich soil, dense forests, and plentiful game—was essential to the opening of the Carolina backcountry to European exploitation. One convenient campsite along the trail was said to be ninety-six miles from Keowee, hence the name "Ninety Six."

In 1751 the first trading post at Ninety Six was built by Robert Gouedy, but few Europeans settled in the area from fear of the Cherokee. During the various colonial wars between the French and the British, the Cherokee allied themselves with the French and fought to defend their lands from the white invaders. Their defeat in 1763 meant the forfeiture of their ancestral lands to the British crown, and European settlers, no longer fearful of the once powerful Cherokee, flooded the South Carolina backcountry. Gouedy's store became a magnet for settlers, and by 1775, Ninety Six was a thriving frontier village of twelve houses surrounded by dozens of farms. The courthouse and jail for the entire Ninety Six Judicial District, which comprised most of western South Carolina, was also sited there.

The American Revolution, or the First American Civil War

The issue of separation from the British crown divided Loyalists and Patriots in the southern backcountry, and a bloody civil war resulted. In 1775, Loyalists and Patriots fought for control of the strategic center at Ninety Six, but an expedition from the low country captured the important town for the Patriots. Over the next six years, a brutal war between the factions took place, with little quarter asked or given. In 1778, the British "Southern Strategy" moved their major military effort from the New England and Middle colonies to the Southern colonies, which they believed they could retain. A defensive network of posts throughout South Carolina was built to control the region and

to protect the Loyalists. At Ninety Six the town stockade was connected to a star-shaped fort and was defended by Loyalist troops.

By 1781, British strategy was in a shambles. Defeats at Cowpens and Kings Mountain, coupled with the departure of General Charles Cornwallis's British army for Yorktown, meant that South Carolina Loyalists were facing elimination. American General Nathanael Greene's strategy was to reduce the various British posts, thereby forcing the British to the coast. In May, 1781, his forces besieged Ninety Six and began constructing a series of parallel and approach trenches. Learning of the approach of a relief column, Greene ordered an assault on Star Fort on June 18 but suffered a bloody repulse. Greene abandoned the siege, the longest of the American Revolution, and withdrew. Within weeks, the British abandoned the fort, destroyed the town, and evacuated over one thousand Loyalists and their families.

Cambridge

Following the American Revolution the town was reconstructed as Cambridge. In 1800 the courthouse was moved, and, although the community continued as a business center, it never regained its political significance. An epidemic in 1815 decimated the population, and thereafter Cambridge was little more than a crossroads. By 1850, the location was but a memory, supplanted by the nearby community of Ninety Six.

Places to Visit

At the historic site a walking loop of about one mile beginning at the visitors' center encompasses a section of the Cherokee Path, the Patriot approach lines to Star Fort, and a reconstructed village with two historic houses. A minimum of one hour should be reserved for a visit. Other places of interest include Park Seed Company in Greenwood and historic Abbeville. —*William S. Brockington*

For Further Information:

Bass, Robert D. *Ninety Six: The Struggle for the South Carolina Back Country.* Lexington, S.C.: Sandlapper Store, 1978. Provides a good analysis of the military importance of the region and of the Loyalist-Patriot bitterness.

Cann, Marvin. *Ninety Six, a Historical Guide: Old Ninety Six in the South Carolina Backcountry, 1700-*

1781. Troy, S.C.: Sleepy Creek, 1996. Brief history of Ninety Six, including excellent maps. Can be ordered from the Ninety Six National Historic Site.

Edgar, Walter B. *South Carolina, a History*. Columbia: University of South Carolina Press, 1998. Best history of South Carolina. Places struggle for Ninety Six and the backcountry into overall context of the history of the state and region.

Hatley, M. Thomas. *The Dividing Paths: Cherokees and South Carolinians through the Era of Revolution*. New York: Oxford University Press, 1995. Analyzes the impact of the collision of two cultures—Native American and European.

Treacy, M. F. *Prelude to Yorktown: The Southern Campaigns of Nathanael Greene, 1780-1781*. Chapel Hill: University of North Carolina Press, 1963. Places Ninety Six into a larger context and analyzes its strategic importance. Gives proper credit to the brilliant strategy of Greene.

Other Historic Sites

Aiken House and Associated Railroad Structures

Location: Charleston, Charleston County

Relevant issues: Business and industry

Statement of significance: These structures are associated with William Aiken, Sr. (1779-1831), who in 1827 founded the South Carolina Canal and Railroad Company. Aiken's Charleston-to-Hamburg railroad was the first to use steam from the beginning of its operations, the first to use an American-made locomotive, and the first to carry the U.S. mail.

Atalaya and Brookgreen Gardens

Location: Murrells Inlet, Georgetown County

Relevant issues: Art and architecture

Statement of significance: Atalaya and Brookgreen Gardens most accurately reflect the distinguished career of Anna Hyatt Huntington (1876-1973), a sculptor whose work spanned a period of seventy years. Huntington specialized in studies of animals, and no other woman of her time period was as accomplished; her work won her international recognition, including the Palmes Académiques of France and the Grand Cross of Alfonso XII of Spain. Her work can be found in public spaces and museums around the world, including the Corcoran Gallery in Washington, D.C. Atalaya served as her winter home and contained a studio in which she created Don Quixote, one of her most important works. When it was founded in 1931, this was the first public sculpture garden in the country. The sculpture gardens at Brookgreen served as a place to display her own works, as well as those of her contemporaries.

Burt-Stark Mansion

Location: Abbeville, Abbeville County

Relevant issues: Civil War, military history, political history

Statement of significance: Here, on the afternoon of May 2, 1865, the final Confederate council of war occurred. Richmond had been evacuated the month before and the Confederate government was in flight; General Robert E. Lee had surrendered the Army of Northern Virginia at Appomattox Court House on April 9; and General Joseph E. Johnston had surrendered Confederate forces in the Southeast on April 26. Still, President Jefferson Davis believed he could rally the troops of Lieutenant General Richard Taylor in the Gulf States, join them with Confederate troops still active across the Mississippi, and continue the struggle for an independent Confederacy. In a meeting in this house, Davis asked his subordinates, among whom were Secretary of War John C. Breckinridge and General Braxton Bragg, for advice on future military plans. His advisers responded that continued resistance was impossible; the war was over. Their unanimous opinion convinced Davis that all had indeed been lost.

Coker Experimental Farms

Location: Hartsville, Darlington County

Relevant issues: Science and technology

Statement of significance: Here, following the example of his father, David Robert Coker (1870-1938) conducted his early crop-improvement experiments on the family plantation. Beginning with thirty experimental cotton selections and methodically applying the latest techniques in the scientific breeding of crops, the work of Coker Experimental Farms played a great role in the agricultural revolution in the South.

Fort Hill

Location: Clemson, Pickens County
Relevant issues: Political history
Statement of significance: From 1825 to 1850, this was the residence of John Caldwell Calhoun (1782-1850), best remembered for his vigorous defense of states' rights. Calhoun penned his "South Carolina Exposition and Protest" at Fort Hill in 1828. His long political career included terms in the U.S. House (1811-1817) and Senate (1832-1843, 1845-1850), service as secretary of war (1817-1825) and secretary of state (1844-1845), and the office of vice president (1825-1832).

Hibernian Hall

Location: Charleston, Charleston County
Relevant issues: Political history
Statement of significance: Completed in 1840, this is the only extant building associated with the Democratic Convention of 1860, one of the most critical political assemblies in the history of the United States. At Charleston, the fate of the old party system was sealed: The Democratic Party was shattered and Republican victory assured in the fall. Hibernian Hall served as headquarters for the faction supporting Stephen A. Douglas, the pivotal personality of the convention.

Ingham

Location: Mount Pleasant, Charleston County
Relevant issues: Naval history, World War II
Statement of significance: Built in 1936, the 327-foot cutter *Ingham* is one of two surviving examples of the Secretary Class, a type significant in the U.S. combat response to the German U-boat threat. *Ingham* escorted convoys across the North Atlantic, Mediterranean, and Caribbean, earning the Presidential Unit Citation; in 1942, it sank U-626. Transferred to duty in the Pacific, *Ingham* spearheaded the liberation of Cor-

regidor and other Philippine territory. In 1968, it returned to combat off Vietnam. When it was decommissioned in 1988, *Ingham* was the oldest commissioned U.S. warship afloat.

Kahal Kadosh Beth Elohim

Location: Charleston, Charleston County
Relevant issues: Religion
Statement of significance: The present Greek revival-style structure (1840) houses a congregation regarded as the birthplace of Reform Judaism in America. It is also the second-oldest synagogue in the United States in continuous use.

Laffey

Location: Charleston, Charleston County
Relevant issues: Naval history, World War II
Statement of significance: The only surviving Allen M. Sumner Class destroyer and the only surviving World War II destroyer that saw service in the Atlantic, *Laffey* acted as escort to convoys to Great Britain, and on D day it bombarded Utah Beach at Normandy. Sent into the Pacific, *Laffey* was involved in one of the most famous destroyer-kamikaze duels of the war. It earned five battle stars and a Presidential Unit Citation for its service.

Mills House

Location: Columbia, Richland County
Relevant issues: Art and architecture
Statement of significance: This classical two-story brick mansion was built for a wealthy merchant by Robert Mills (1781-1855), native South Carolinian, first federal architect, and designer of the Washington Monument.

Penn School Historic District

Location: Frogmore, Beaufort County
Relevant issues: African American history, education, social reform
Statement of significance: In 1862, long before the end of the Civil War, Northern missionaries arrived on St. Helena Island to assist the black population. They organized one of the first southern schools for African Americans here and pioneered health services and self-help programs. The oldest existing structure is the Brick Church (1855), which served as a school for the newly freed slaves.

Powder Magazine

Location: Charleston, Charleston County

Relevant issues: Colonial America, military history, Revolutionary War

Statement of significance: The Powder Magazine is a visible reminder of the era of the Lord Proprietors and their founding government of the Carolinas, of the fortifications which protected the city and made Charleston one of the three fortified cities on the eastern seaboard of British colonial America. Completed in 1713, the Powder Magazine is also associated with the siege of Charleston (1780).

Rainey House

Location: Georgetown, Georgetown County

Relevant issues: African American history, political history

Statement of significance: Joseph H. Rainey (1832-1887), the first black person to serve in the United States House of Representatives (1870-1879), served longer than any of his black contemporaries. The election of Rainey and of Hiram Rhoades Revels, who began a term in the U.S. Senate in the same year, marked the beginning of active African American participation in the federal legislative process. Rainey was born in this house and lived here until 1846. After the Civil War, from 1866 to 1881 and again from 1886 until his death the next year, it was his principal residence.

Rhett House

Location: Charleston, Charleston County

Relevant issues: Political history

Statement of significance: This large clapboard frame dwelling was the residence of Robert Barnwell Rhett (1800-1876), known as the "Great Secessionist" and one of the most effective and prominent of that circle of proslavery "fire-eating" radicals. Beginning in 1850, Rhett launched a carefully programmed campaign to sever the slaveholding states from the Union; he had a major influence on the state's Ordinance of Secession (1860).

Smalls House

Location: Beaufort, Beaufort County

Relevant issues: African American history, Civil War, political history

Statement of significance: This large frame house was the residence of Robert Smalls (1839-1915), former slave, state legislator (1868-1874), U.S. congressman (1875-1881) from South Carolina, and customs collector (1889-1913) for the Port of Beaufort. Smalls first came to national attention when on May 13, 1862, he organized the abduction of the *Planter,* a Confederate steamer based in Charleston Harbor.

Snee Farm

Location: Mount Pleasant, Charleston County

Relevant issues: Political history

Statement of significance: Snee Farm was owned by Charles Pinckney (1757-1824), one of the youngest members of the Continental Congress (1784-1787) and member of the Constitutional Convention, where he presented the "Pinckney Plan." He later served as governor of South Carolina (1789-1792, 1796-1798, 1806-1808), U.S. senator (1798-1801), and minister to Spain (1801-1804).

Snow's Island

Location: Johnsonville, Florence County

Relevant issues: Military history, Revolutionary War

Statement of significance: From approximately December, 1780, to late March, 1781, Snow's Island served as headquarters for forces led by Francis Marion (1732-1795), a South Carolina militia officer who is celebrated as the "Swamp Fox." Employing guerilla war tactics, Marion significantly contributed to the American war effort by conducting numerous raids on British outposts.

South Carolina State House

Location: Columbia, Richland County

Relevant issues: African American history, political history

Statement of significance: Begun in 1851 and completed in 1907, this fine example of neoclassical architecture demonstrates the disruptive effects of the Civil War and Reconstruction eras on Southern development. Here, between 1869 and 1874, the only legislature in American history with a black majority met; it was the setting for *The Prostrate State: South Carolina Under Negro Government,* an influential book which fostered the image of Reconstruction as an era of African

American domination, corruption, and misrule; in 1876, it was the scene of disputes about state elections, which ultimately resulted in the removal of federal troops from the state and the return to power of the Democrats.

Stono River Slave Rebellion Site

Location: Rantowles, Charleston County

Relevant issues: African American history, colonial America, disasters and tragedies, military history

Statement of significance: On September 9, 1739, approximately fifty-one escaped slaves attacked a warehouse located here, killing the guards and seizing the weapons stored within. The group, led by an Angolan called Jemmy, then set off for freedom in the Spanish province of Florida, burning plantations and murdering all whites they encountered along the way. Their attempt was thwarted by a colonial militia, which overtook the swelling band and killed or captured all involved with relative ease.

South Dakota

The State Capitol Building in Pierre. (South Dakota Tourism)

History of South Dakota

One of the plains states in America's Midwest, South Dakota is bounded on the north by North Dakota, on the east by Iowa and Minnesota, on the south by Nebraska, and on the west by Montana and Wyoming. It stretches 360 miles from east to west and 240 miles from north to south. The state is the seventeenth largest of the United States but ranks forty-fifth in population. Its capital is Pierre (pronounced "peer"). Temperatures in South Dakota are extreme—low in winter and high in summer—with minimal precipitation and low humidity.

South Dakota's terrain, with more than three hundred natural lakes and four huge reservoirs created by the damming of its rivers, has considerable variety. Sparsely wooded, it consists largely of rolling plains marked occasionally by buttes rising dramatically from the landscape. In the western part of the plains, well before the towering Black Hills, are the Badlands, with deep canyons and formations carved into the red rocks over eons by wind and water erosion.

Early History

Humans inhabited the Dakotas more than twenty-five thousand years ago. Forty million years ago, dinosaurs roamed the landscape. Dinosaur bones have been unearthed in South Dakota as well as shells of archela, the largest known turtles, which were ten feet long.

The earliest settlers hunted the abundant big game in the area. By 500 C.E., a society of seminomadic Mound Builders thrived in the area and remained for about three hundred years, leaving behind valuable artifacts.

The Arikara Indians moved north from Nebraska in the 1500's and settled along the eastern banks of the Missouri River, where they farmed and fished, prospering to the extent that, by the late 1700's, they had established thirty earth-lodge settlements. In the early nineteenth century, however, the Sioux, a powerful tribe that entered the area from the east, drove the Arikara away.

Exploration and Settlement

The Dakotas became part of France's vast Louisiana Territory in 1682. The first white explorers in the region were French Canadian brothers, François and Louis Joseph de La Vérendrye. While seeking a water route to the Pacific, they entered the area in 1743 and claimed it for France, burying a lead plate near Fort Pierre—the plate was found in 1913.

In 1762 France ceded all its land west of the Mississippi River to Spain, so when the French Canadian fur trader Pierre Dorion became the first permanent white resident in the Dakotas in 1775, the Spanish were in control. The Louisiana Territory was returned to France in 1800 and, in 1803 as a result of the Louisiana Purchase, became the property of the United States.

Explorers Meriwether Lewis and William Clark passed through the area in 1804, bound for the Pacific Northwest, and again in 1806 on their return. A Spanish trader, Manuel Lisa, began trading with the American Indians along the Missouri River in 1809. In 1812 the entire area became part of the Missouri Territory. In the same year, the Sioux Indians, whose property rights were being severely infringed by the United States, sided with the British in the War of 1812.

Relations between the Native Americans and whites in the area were marked by peace treaties that the federal government, with its substantial economic stake in the lands of the Missouri Territory, soon broke. When the Missouri River proved navigable by steamboat in 1831, the commercial viability of the areas along the river became obvious.

Government Relations with the Sioux

In 1857 the modern-day city of Sioux Falls on the Missouri River was planned. Development began in the area, which in 1861 was declared the Dakota Territory, encompassing all of contemporary North and South Dakota, as well as parts of Wyoming and Montana. The southeastern town of Yankton became the territory's capital.

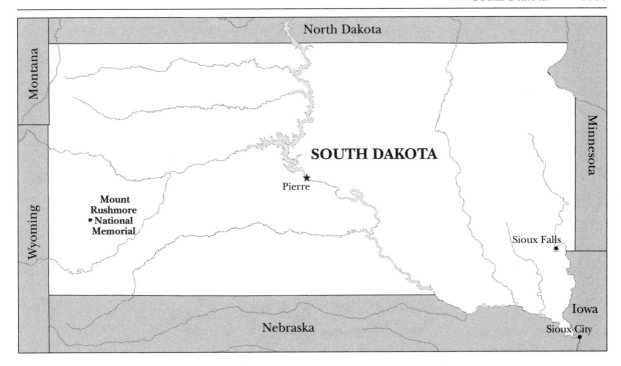

In 1862 the government, frequently warring with the Sioux, forced the Santee Sioux from Minnesota into the Dakota Territory. Strife between the Sioux and the federal government continued until 1890, when, at Wounded Knee, government forces massacred more than two hundred Sioux, including women and children who were attempting to surrender. As late as 1973, two hundred armed members of the American Indian Movement occupied Wounded Knee for seventy-one days demanding reparations.

In 1979 the U.S. Court of Claims ordered the U.S. government to pay the Sioux $100 million for the land it confiscated in 1877. The Sioux, however, refused to accept a monetary settlement, insisting instead on the return of their land, which has great spiritual significance to them.

Moving Toward Statehood

With the formation of the Montana Territory in 1864 and the Wyoming Territory in 1868, the Dakota Territory was downsized to what has become North and South Dakota. In 1872 railroad service began in the territory. In 1874, Lieutenant Colonel George Armstrong Custer discovered gold in the Black Hills, triggering a gold rush. In 1876, when the Sioux attacked prospectors, trying to expel them from Sioux property in the Black Hills, the federal government intervened and, in 1877, confiscated the Black Hills from the Sioux.

Many easterners, eager to obtain land from the government under the Homestead Act of 1862, came to the Dakotas to obtain their allotted 160 acres, for which they filed claims. They cultivated the land and, after living on it for five years, it became theirs. With the discovery of gold, miners flocked into the Black Hills, swelling the population by 1879 to the point that the territory was large enough to warrant consideration for statehood.

The area was wracked by floods in 1881. The devastating blizzard of 1888 killed hundreds of Dakotans. Nevertheless, development continued with the establishment of Yankton College in 1881 and the University of South Dakota at Vermillion in the following year. In 1888 Republicans urged, as part of their platform, the admission of the Dakota Territory as two states.

In 1889 Congress voted to divide the Dakota Territory evenly into North and South Dakota and admitted them as the thirty-ninth and fortieth states in the Union. North Dakota was designated the thirty-ninth state because of its alphabetical preeminence.

South Dakota was plagued by the worst drought in its history for the next nine years. It was another half century before the federal government assisted the state in mounting a concerted effort to build dams to irrigate farms and provide hydroelectric power.

Political Progressivism and the Economy

South Dakota's voters consistently elected reform candidates from the Populist and Progressive Republican Parties. In 1898 South Dakota became the first state to pass initiative and referendum laws, enabling voters to pass any law directly if they obtained enough signatures on petitions to put the matter on the ballot or to reject any laws passed by the legislature if 5 percent of the voters signed petitions requesting that their repeal be placed on the ballot and the repeal is supported by the electorate.

Agriculture and mining were the two most important industries in South Dakota during its early days. In 1909 the Morrell Company opened a large meat processing and packing plant in Sioux Falls, thereby launching an important industry in the state. South Dakota became a major national supplier of meat.

The state needed a dependable railway system to transport its cattle and produce to eastern markets. In 1917 Governor Peter Norbeck spearheaded a movement to end railroad monopolies and to stabilize rates. Under Norbeck's progressive leadership, the legislature voted to extend loans to farmers.

The droughts during the early years of the Great Depression ravaged South Dakota agriculture. Plagues of grasshoppers ate the few crops that survived the drought. The economic situation deteriorated so badly that, in 1932, voters for the first time elected Democratic candidates to every state office in what had long been a Republican state.

In 1954 the state's first productive oil well was drilled in western South Dakota, producing more than two million barrels annually. Strip mining of bituminous coal contributes to the economy of western South Dakota, which also has a large goldmining industry. Despite the mineral wealth of its western region, South Dakota's non-American Indians have settled largely in the eastern region, where manufacturing and service industries flourish.

The electronics industry brings considerable revenue into the state and employs many of its citizens. In 1982 Citicorp, the largest bank holding company in the United States, transferred its credit-card division to Sioux Falls, which underwent a substantial increase in population.

The Native American Population

In the 1990's, more than 7 percent of South Dakotans were Native Americans. Most of them lived on eight major reservations, the largest of them being the Rosebud, the Pine Ridge, the Cheyenne River, and the Standing Rock Indian Reservations in the central or western reaches of the state.

Life for South Dakota's Native Americans remains difficult. Stripped of much of their most fertile and mineral-rich land, they have often been forced during difficult economic times to sell the land remaining to them.   —R. Baird Shuman

Mount Rushmore

Date: Work began in 1927 and was completed in 1941

Relevant issues: Art and architecture, political history

Significance: This monument memorializes critical events in the shaping of United States history: the Declaration of Independence, the Revolutionary War, the preservation of the Union, and the building of the Panama Canal.

Location: Near Keystone, in the southern Black Hills, which are located in the western part of the state; Mount Rushmore is near the geographical center of the country

Site Office:
Mount Rushmore National Memorial
P.O. Box 268
Keystone, SD 57751
ph.: (605) 574-2523
Web sites: www.nps.gov/moru; www.travelsd.com/rushmore/index.htm

The Black Hills' popularity as a tourist destination has combined with the attraction of the Mount Rushmore Memorial to produce an ever-increasing number of visitors who enjoy the natural beauty of the Black Hills and the enshrining of American history. The heads of four United States presidents, each sixty feet high, are carved into the side of the mountain. Each was finished and dedicated at a different time. The National Park Service administers Mount Rushmore and provides guided tours and lectures. Over the years the complex has expanded to include several features: a visitors' center, amphitheater, concession building and staff dormitory, and parking lot.

The Decision to Build

Doane Robinson, a South Dakota historian, conceived the idea of commemorating important events in South Dakota history by carving a gigantic sculpture in the Black Hills featuring Native American tribal leaders and heroes of the old West. In 1923 he suggested this idea to Senator Peter Norbeck as a tourist attraction to bring more people into the Black Hills. These two were instrumental in appealing first to the people of South Dakota for popular support and then to Congress. A federal congressional act authorized the South Dakota state legislature to undertake the memorial project in 1925, but work did not actually begin until 1927 when private contributions were solicited. Federal money became available for the work when a congressional bill was passed in 1929 appropriating $250,000 to be matched on a fifty-fifty basis by private contributions. The first contributors were the three railroads serving the state of South Dakota, Homestake Mine in the Black Hills, and private contributors including Charles Rushmore, a lawyer in New York State. Rushmore had visited the Black Hills around 1883 in connection with checking mining claims. When he first saw the mountain that would bear his name, he asked what it was called. The reply was that it had no name but since he had asked, it could be named for him. The name was not officially recognized by the United States Board of Geographic Names, however, until 1930.

Raising money for the project was always a problem, but fund-raising received a boost in 1927 with the publicity generated by President Calvin Coolidge's summer vacation spent near Mount Rushmore in Custer State Park. He had been persuaded to visit the area by South Dakotans who extolled the region's beauties and who wanted him to visit Mount Rushmore to promote it. At that time, there was only a wagon trail leading from the town of Keystone to the mountain. Visitors had to walk in

or be carried in by mule. President Coolidge arrived at the site to celebrate the first drilling of stone. The sculptor Gutzon Borglum dramatized the event by accepting drills from the president and then lowering himself over the stone face by rope to drill the first point for the face of Washington. Borglum then presented one of the drills to the president to conclude the ceremony. By 1930, when the head of George Washington was dedicated, a road had been built.

Geologically, Mount Rushmore is among the oldest outcroppings in the world. Uncovered by erosion, it is the most exposed part of a granite spine which runs through that part of the Black Hills. This particular spot was chosen because the granite is of a finer texture and therefore more suitable for carving. There are fewer cracks in the stone face, which makes it less subject to weathering.

The Sculptor and the Choice of Subject

Robinson approached the sculptor Gutzon Borglum in 1924 about carving the project and sounded him out about his ideas for it. Borglum, a flamboyant and colorful character, was enthusiastic. From early on, his involvement shaped the conception of the memorial. Borglum had trained as an artist first in San Francisco and then in Paris in the studio of Auguste Rodin. Borglum favored sculpting the human figure and he did many portraits. Before he returned to the United States, he received commissions for sculptures in London.

Borglum had already carved one large-scale project and was enthusiastic about doing another. It was he who suggested that the subject of the memorial be national rather than regional, and he developed the concept of four United States presidents who were instrumental in shaping the destiny of the country. He approved of creating the sculptures on a gigantic scale, equivalent to the huge size of the country. Borglum's choice of subjects to immortalize the United States was accepted. He credited Thomas Jefferson with being the author of the Declaration of Independence and chose him as the first of the four subjects. George Washington was included on the basis of his leading the country militarily at the time of the Revolutionary War and then becoming the country's first president. Abraham Lincoln preserved the union of North and South at the time of the

Mount Rushmore. (Digital Stock)

Civil War. Last, Theodore Roosevelt was a more personal choice by Borglum, who knew him and admired him greatly. Roosevelt was instrumental in the decision to build the Panama Canal, and that was the basis for his inclusion in the list of illustrious contributors to the progress of the United States. Roosevelt had visited the Black Hills. This and his reputation as a leader of the Rough Riders appealed to Borglum and helped win Roosevelt's popular acceptance among the sculpted heads.

The History and Process of the Work

Doane Robinson had originally planned the carving for another area called the Needles, which was a group of narrow vertical granite outcroppings. When Borglum was invited to come to the Black Hills to inspect the site, he found a better one. A major reason for the change was that he found an outcropping more south facing, which offered better light from sun. The sculpture would be more easily seen, and the quality of the stone was better.

Borglum's original conception placed Thomas Jefferson's head on the far left of the group to begin a chronological sequence. Washington's head followed, but then the chronology broke, with Roosevelt and Lincoln following in that order. Carving began on Washington's head in 1927, and it was dedicated in 1930. Jefferson's head was attempted next in the position to the left of Washington's but insufficient good-quality rock and lack of space stopped the work. The carving of Jefferson's head began again to the right of Washington's.

Borglum and his team worked from Borglum's plaster models, which could be hung over the side of the mountain for the workmen to follow. As each head was started, the top center was located. A thirty-foot horizontal arm, which could move in a circular pattern, extended from that central point. A plumb line could be moved along any point of the arm to measure distances out from the surface of the rock. Each model had a miniature version of this arrangement. Comparing the size of any feature on the plaster model with the movement of the plumb line in and out could translate the proportions of the model to the huge size of the finished carving. These measurements were painted on the stone for the workmen to carve away. Pneumatic drills run by compressed air scored parallel lines of holes to within inches of the level of finish. Work done in this manner could be taught to people who were unfamiliar with stone carving. The finish work was then completed by men trained as stone carvers. Slings called "bos'n" chairs were used to lower the workmen over the side of the cliff face, with a loudspeaker system notifying men working winches when to raise and lower the workers as needed. Borglum would view the sculptures through field glasses from four miles away to see what changes and improvements were necessary. Changes would be indicated to the workers by marking a spot with paint.

The original plan as conceived by Borglum was to include a huge entablature carved into the mountain beside the heads which would list the momentous events of United States history and explain the reason for the choices of subject. This part of the concept was still in the planning stage as late as 1935, when an essay contest was held to choose the historical events to be included and to formulate the wording. A winning entry was chosen, but this part of the momentous scheme was never carried out. Borglum's plan included another grandiose idea which was cancelled. He intended to include a huge room carved out of the mountain to serve as a hall containing important records of United States history and sculptured busts of notable Americans. This project actually was begun but never progressed beyond a rudimentary stage before it was abandoned.

The total cost of carving the heads into the mountain was $989,992.32. When that cost is set against the serious economic upheaval of the time, it is a wonder that the project ever progressed beyond the beginning stages. Gutzon Borglum made many trips throughout the region to raise funds when money ran out and work had to stop. To boost his fund-raising efforts, he wrote a small book about the project. The carving took six and a half years of actual working time, which was spread over fourteen years because of the lack of funds. After the Depression hit in 1929, continued funding for nonessential projects was harder and harder to find. Yet this project continued off and on through the Depression decade until it was completed in 1941. If it had not been finished at the time the United States entered World War II, it might not have been finished at all. All available manpower had to go into the war effort, and no one would have been available to work on the carving. Borglum himself died in 1941 before the carving was complete. His son, Lincoln Borglum, who had worked closely with his father, was able to take over the almost complete work and put the finishing touches on it.

—*Ann Stewart Balakier*

For Further Information:

Dean, Robert J. *Living Granite: The Story of Borglum and the Mount Rushmore Memorial.* New York: Viking Press, 1949. A short history of the making of Mount Rushmore, emphasizing Borglum's role in it.

Fite, Gilbert C. *Mount Rushmore.* Norman: University of Oklahoma Press, 1952. The standard history of the project. Includes forty-one photographs; a chronology; a selected bibliography; and maps of the United States, the region, and South Dakota to locate the site.

Olwig, Kenneth R. "Reinventing Common Nature: Yosemite and Mount Rushmore—A Meandering Tale of a Double Nature." In *Uncommon Ground: Toward Reinventing Nature*, edited by William Cronon. New York: W. W. Norton, 1995. Explores the symbolic Eden created at Rushmore, with its attendant environmental issues.

Price, Willadene. *Gutzon Borglum: Artist and Patriot.* Chicago: Rand McNally, 1962. A biography of Borglum with sixty photographs.

Smith, Rex Alan. *The Carving of Mount Rushmore.* New York: Abbeville Press, 1985. Presents a fully illustrated history of the enterprise; contains the text of the winning essay for the entablature contest, and a complete bibliography.

Other Historic Sites

Bear Butte

Location: Sturgis, Meade County

Relevant issues: American Indian history

Statement of significance: Sacred to the Cheyenne, Bear Butte is the place where Maheo imparted to Sweet Medicine (a mythical hero) the knowledge from which the Cheyenne derive their religious, political, social, and economic customs. The site is in Bear Butte State Park.

Deadwood Historic District

Location: Deadwood, Lawrence County

Relevant issues: Business and industry, cultural history

Statement of significance: The site of a rich gold strike in 1875, Deadwood retains its mining town atmosphere. Many original buildings remain. While Deadwood is one of the most highly publicized mining towns of the trans-Mississippi West, much of its fame rests on the famous or infamous characters that passed through.

Fort Pierre Chouteau Site

Location: Fort Pierre, Stanley County

Relevant issues: Business and industry

Statement of significance: Perhaps the most significant fur trade/military fort on the western American frontier, Fort Pierre Chouteau was the largest (almost three hundred feet square) and best-equipped trading post in the northern Great Plains. It was built in 1832 by John Jacob Astor's (1763-1848) American Fur Company as part of its expansion into the Upper Missouri region. The trading activities at the site exemplified the commercial alliance critical to the success of the fur business.

Fort Thompson Mounds

Location: Fort Thompson, Buffalo County

Relevant issues: American Indian history

Statement of significance: This large group of low burial mounds dating from Plains-Woodland times (c. 800 C.E.) contains evidence of the first pottery-making peoples in the area. It is situated on the Crow Creek Indian Reservation.

Frawley Ranch

Location: Spearfish, Lawrence County

Relevant issues: Business and industry, western expansion

Statement of significance: Frawley Ranch represents the development of practical land use for an area unsuited to homestead farming. In the 1890's, lawyer Henry J. Frawley acquired several unsuccessful homestead farms and created a large and prosperous ranch here.

Langdeau Site

Location: Lower Brule, Lyman County

Relevant issues: American Indian history

Statement of significance: Possibly the earliest reliably dated village of the Missouri Trench, Langdeau Site represents the full emergence of the Plains Village traditions in the Middle Missouri cultural area. It is also a cultural intrusion of organized village people with highly adaptive strategies, including horticulture, into an area previously occupied by hunter-gatherers.

Molstad Village

Location: Mobridge, Dewey County

Relevant issues: American Indian history

Statement of significance: A tiny fortified prehistoric village site containing five circular house rings enclosed by a ditch, Molstad appears to represent a period of transition, when Central Plains and Middle Missouri cultural traits were combining to form the basis for Mandan, Hidatsa, and Arikara cultures as they existed at the time of the first contact with Europeans.

Vanderbilt Archaeological Site

Location: Pollock, Campbell County

Relevant issues: American Indian history

Statement of significance: Archaeological information about the earliest culture history of today's Mandan and Hidatsa peoples is preserved in the Vanderbilt Village Site. They began to transform their environment along the Missouri River floodplain near the Cannonball River around 1000 C.E. by expanding their horticultural economy with permanent villages, substantial houses, and more complex technologies. By

1400, the Vanderbilt Village was a dynamic, well-established community within which its people lived comfortably, traded, hunted, fished, and created a highly developed clan tradition with neighboring villages.

Vérendrye Site

Location: Fort Pierre, Stanley County

Relevant issues: European settlement

Statement of significance: Here, in late March, 1743, the Vérendryes, the first Europeans to explore the northern plains region of the present United States, secreted a lead plate beneath a pile of stones. Sixty-one years before Meriwether Lewis and William Clark first arrived in this area, these French explorers, in search of a Northwest Passage to the Pacific, lay the basis for French sovereignty on the Upper Missouri, seeking to define the bounds of French Louisiana to include the entire Mississippi River drainage.

Wounded Knee Battlefield

Location: Batesland, Shannon County

Relevant issues: American Indian history, disasters and tragedies, military history

Statement of significance: On December 29, 1890, this was the scene of the last major clash between Native Americans and U.S. troops in North America. In the period following the introduction of the Ghost Dance among the Lakota and the killing of Sitting Bull, a band of several hundred led by Big Foot left the Cheyenne River Reservation. Intercepted by U.S. troops, they had given themselves up and had been escorted to an army encampment on Pine Ridge Reservation when shooting suddenly started. The ensuing struggle, short but bloody, resulted in seventy-five army casualties and the virtual massacre of Big Foot's band.

Tennessee

Nashville. (Corbis)

History of Tennessee

Tennessee is one of the south central states, strategically located along the Mississippi River on the west and the Unaka range of the Appalachian Mountains on the east. To its north lie Kentucky and Virginia, to its south Georgia, Alabama, and Mississippi, to its east North Carolina, and to its west Arkansas and Missouri. The state, which runs 120 miles from north to south and 430 miles from east to west, has dense forests in the portions that lie within the Great Smoky Mountains. In its lower regions in the west are cypress swamps much like those found in parts of southern Georgia.

Early History

Ancient burial mounds and archaeological artifacts verify the presence of inhabitants in Tennessee prior to recorded history and long before European explorers made their ways into the area. Paleo-Indians are thought to have lived in this region as much as fifteen thousand years ago. These prehistoric inhabitants were followed by other early American Indians.

The early British and Spanish explorers in the area encountered several Indian tribes, notably the Cherokee, the Chickasaw, the Shawnee, the Creek, and the Yuchi. Of these, the Cherokee were the most sophisticated, living in their own well-developed enclaves in the southeastern part of - Tennessee in the Appalachian Mountains. The Chickasaw lived to the west toward the Mississippi River and were considered a belligerent tribe.

By 1714 the Cherokee and the Chickasaw had driven the Shawnee out of the Cumberland Valley, which they inhabited, through the Kentucky area, to north of the Ohio River. At about the same time, these two dominant tribes drove the Creek and Yuchi Indians south to Georgia, leaving the area very much in their hands.

Exploration and Settlement

It is known that a group of explorers led by the Spanish explorer Hernando de Soto, presumably the first Europeans to enter the area, were in southeastern Tennessee in 1540. By the following year, this group had pushed west and had reached the Mississippi River. By 1566-1567, another Spanish group, led by Juan Pardo, had carried out two expeditions in the southeastern part of Tennessee and had erected a fortification near modern Chattanooga.

It was not until 1673 that both French and British explorers arrived, at almost the same time, in the area. Two Virginia traders of British descent, James Needham and Gabriel Arthur, made their way into eastern Tennessee at about this time. In the western extreme of the area, two Frenchmen, Father Jacques Marquette, a missionary, and Louis Jolliet, a fur trader, arrived, having sailed down the Mississippi from the north. A decade later, in 1682, another famous French explorer, René-Robert Cavelier, Sieur de La Salle, and his band of followers constructed Fort Prud'Homme on the Natchez (Hatchie) River.

Early Tennessee

The territory into which many of the explorers pressed was a part of the large Cherokee Nation in eastern Tennessee. The French and British competed for control of the Cherokee, with the French initially emerging as the victors. At the end of the French and Indian War, however, the Treaty of Paris, enacted in 1763, ceded the area to the British.

Daniel Boone explored this territory, and, in 1769, permanent settlement by whites began, with four parts of the state attracting residents. One settlement was in eastern Tennessee near the Virginia border, a town that eventually was to lie partly in Virginia and partly in Tennessee. Another settlement grew up along the Watauga River near Elizabethtown. West of the Holston River near Rogersville, a settlement was established, while a fourth settlement developed near Erwin along the banks of the Nolichuky River.

When it was discovered in 1771 that all the land on which the white inhabitants had settled except that north of the Holston River belonged legally to the Cherokee, the white settlers were forced to lease the land from them. These settlers finally

bought it in 1775 under the Treaty of Sycamore Shoals.

The Revolutionary War

Although this area was remote from the major battlefields of the Revolutionary War, people from the Tennessee region engaged in some combat against the British and the Loyalists. In October, 1780, the Battle of King's Mountain marked the most severe British defeat in the South. Shortly before this battle, North Carolina annexed the eastern region of Tennessee into its western territory and held it until 1784, when it gave the territory over to the U.S. government.

The people in this territory established a separate state, called the state of Franklin, with John Sevier as governor. This state existed for four years. North Carolina, however, attempted to retrieve the territory and finally succeeded in 1789 but soon again ceded it to the United States. In 1790 it officially came to be known as the Territory South of the River Ohio; its governor was William Blount. By 1794 the Tennessee region became the first territory to achieve the representative-government stage under the recently enacted Northwest Ordinance. The first territory to have a delegate in the U.S. Congress, Tennessee, in 1796, became the sixteenth state to enter the Union.

Slavery and the Civil War

Tennessee had few of the sprawling plantations found in parts of the Deep South, although in its eastern lowlands and central area, where cotton was grown, there was considerable slave labor. In eastern Tennessee, however, the agricultural economy was on a small scale. Farmers raised their own food, hunted, and were essentially self-sufficient.

What help they had usually came from their children and other family members.

Before the Civil War, significant road building took place in Tennessee. Turnpikes were constructed, railroad tracks were laid, and waterways were improved for river navigation. Some industry developed, mainly ironworks, but the chief occupation was farming.

Naturally, where slave labor was used, mainly in the western and middle parts of the state, people favored slavery, but in its eastern extremes, Tennesseans were resolutely antislavery. After South Carolina and other southern states left the Union, Tennessee refused to call a convention to consider secession. In April, 1861, however, Tennessee's governor refused to send troops to join the Union army, and on June 8, Tennesseans voted to secede.

Aside from Virginia, Tennessee had more battles fought on its land than any other southern state—more than four hundred. Of its 145,000 soldiers, however, more than 30,000, mostly from eastern Tennessee, joined the Union army. In 1865 Tennesseans voted to abolish slavery, although in 1870 they voted to ban interracial marriages and in 1875 enacted the first Jim Crow laws that strictly limited the freedom of blacks.

Postwar Tennessee

Tennessee was readmitted to the Union on July 25, 1866. It was spared many of the punitive programs that Reconstruction imposed on other southern states. The war left Tennessee impoverished to the point that it was unable to meet its financial obligations and in 1883 settled with its lenders for fifty to eighty cents on the dollar. Farmers were extremely strained financially. In 1891 and 1892, coal miners, protesting the use of convicts leased to Tennessee's coal mines, revolted in the "Coal Miner's War."

Tennessee gained national attention in 1925, when charges were leveled against schoolteacher John Scopes for teaching the theory of evolution in his high school classes. The Scopes trial, known as the Monkey Trial, focused attention on the state, and the outcome, which favored Tennessee's religious conservatives, was decried by much of the nation.

The Tennessee Valley Authority

Rich in natural resources, Tennessee did not profit significantly from its natural wealth until the years following 1933, when Congress established the Tennessee Valley Authority (TVA) as a flood control and power project of President Franklin Roosevelt's New Deal. The TVA harnessed rivers and created lakes. It enhanced the power output that private industry had already begun to finance by building dams on the Little Tennessee, Ocoee, and Pigeon Rivers in the 1920's.

By the mid-1990's, Tennessee was generating some seventy-two billion kilowatt-hours of electricity annually. Besides serving its stated purposes, the TVA created attractive recreational areas in parts of the state. Moreover, the lakes created by the TVA and the Mississippi, Tennessee, and Cumberland Rivers combine to give Tennessee more than a thousand miles of inland waterways. These navigational routes are supplemented by more than 1,100 miles of interstate highways and 154,000 miles of public roads. With 155 airports, Tennessee has ample provision for air transport.

Other Commercial Enterprises

One of the long-standing commercial enterprises in Tennessee is lumbering. The forests of the Appalachian Mountains provide a great deal of hardwood, and the central area of the state is known for its red cedar.

Manufacturing is centered most in eastern Tennessee, which produces grain mill products, inorganic chemicals, drugs, and plastics. A major nuclear research facility at Oak Ridge has brought many scientists into the state, enhancing some of its manufacturing enterprises.

Rich in minerals, Tennessee produces a great deal of gravel, zinc, coal, and clay. It ranks first in the nation for its production of ball clay and gemstones. Although coal production dropped off significantly after 1980, two of the most important zinc-producing operations are in Mascot and Jefferson City, Tennessee. —*R. Baird Shuman*

Beale Street, Memphis

Date: The early nineteenth century

Relevant issues: African American history, business and industry, cultural history, political history, social reform

Significance: Beale Street is referred to as the "home of the blues" because musicians from the region came to Memphis before making their way to Chicago or New York. For African American residents of Memphis, Beale Street was, for nearly a century, the center of commerce, politics, and culture.

Location: Downtown Memphis, running west from the Mississippi River between South Main and South Fourth Streets

Site Office:
Memphis Chamber of Commerce
119 Riverside Drive
Memphis, TN 38103
ph.: (901) 543-5333
fax: (901) 543-5335
Web site: www.memphisguide.com/Beale

Beale Street's place in American history has been ensured by the resurgence in the popularity of blues music. Many performers, such as Arthur "Big Boy" Crudup, "Big Joe" Williams, Lillie May "Big Mama Blues" Glover, and Muddy Waters started their careers in Memphis. Moreover, they inspired countless other musicians like Elvis Presley, Bob Dylan, Bonnie Raitt, and the Rolling Stones to adapt blues music to their own styles. Although much of the original street was demolished in the early 1970's, the city of Memphis has aided in refurbishing the area to form a tourist attraction with several nightclubs and restaurants.

A Thriving Commercial Center

By the 1850's, Beale Street served not only as the southern border of the city, but also as the invisible boundary separating blacks from whites. Although African Americans worked and shopped in Memphis, they were, at first by tradition and later by law, required to use separate side or back entrances. On Beale Street, however, a number of businesses owned by European immigrants catered to a black clientele.

In 1862, during the Civil War, the Union army occupied Memphis. The city became a magnet for increasing numbers of freedmen—formerly enslaved African Americans—who left the plantations in eastern Arkansas, northern Mississippi, and west Tennessee in search of new opportunities. Memphis became so popular a destination that the population swelled to over 27,700, of whom nearly 60 percent were African Americans.

This sudden, massive increase in population created tensions between the black and white communities, especially among recent Irish immigrants, who competed with African Americans for jobs. The result was a violent riot that broke out in May, 1866, and lasted two days. The black community surrounding Beale Street suffered the most as forty-six people died, and many homes and businesses in the African American community were destroyed.

Beale Street and the surrounding community rebounded from the riot, and African Americans continued to move to the city throughout the late 1800's. They opened businesses and enjoyed prosperity for perhaps the first time in their lives. By 1880, in addition to the goods and services provided by European immigrants, at least twenty businesses owned by African Americans inhabited Beale Street. They included barbershops, saloons, carriage operators for both freight and taxi services, and a bank. Thus, by the turn of the century, Beale Street was becoming a thriving commercial center in Memphis.

The Churches of Beale

Beale was not only the center of commercial life for African Americans, but also the center of political life. This was because of two important Memphis institutions. The first, the Beale Street Baptist Church, was started in 1864 and quickly became the largest and most powerful African American church in the city. By 1880, the 2,500-member congregation under the direction of Pastor Taylor Nightingale had grown politically powerful within the African American community.

The Beale Street Baptist Church came to host several prominent visitors, including former U.S. president Ulysses S. Grant, who stopped by in April, 1880. Pastor Nightingale also used the church as his campaign headquarters during a failed bid in 1886 for a seat on the board of education. In 1994 the church earned a place on the National Register of Historic Places.

The second important institution in Memphis at the turn of the century was not a building but a family. The Churches became not only the wealthiest but also the most politically powerful African American family in Memphis. Robert Church, Sr., who was born in Mississippi, came to Memphis during the Civil War when the Union army detained his father's steamboat. Church, whose father was white, left the family business and quickly established himself as a saloon proprietor on Beale Street.

In 1878, Memphis was plagued by a yellow fever epidemic, the second to occur in as many years. Residents who could afford to, fled the city. In the meantime, Church took advantage of low real estate prices by purchasing property, especially in the Beale area. He leased space to other African Americans, who started their own businesses. Church's investments soon made him the first African American millionaire in Memphis, and perhaps even in the South. In the process, he hastened Beale Street's transformation into what one business owner called "the Main Street of Negro America."

His greatest contribution to Beale Street and the African American community of Memphis was the construction of Church's Park and Auditorium. Built on six acres of land Church purchased in 1899, the investment consisted of a landscaped park—the first for blacks in Memphis—and adjacent to it an auditorium seating two thousand people. Church's facilities played host to a number of important Americans including Teddy Roosevelt, who in 1902 addressed a crowd of ten thousand people gathered in the park to hear him speak. The park also is listed on the National Register.

An additional important investment by Robert Church, Sr., was the Solvent Savings Bank and Trust. In 1906 he started the bank, which was located across the street from his park and auditorium. In 1908 Church and the bank came to the rescue of the Beale Street Baptist Church, saving it from foreclosure.

Church died in 1912, but not before establishing his bank as one of the largest African American-owned banks in the country. Control of the bank and his other businesses passed into the hands of his son, Robert Church, Jr. The younger Church was politically active in local and national Republican politics. He also was a founder of the Memphis chapter of the National Association for the Advancement of Colored People (NAACP).

There is no doubt as to the importance of the investments made by the Churches, not just for Beale Street but also for Memphis. The street supported a variety of businesses such as drugstores, theaters, restaurants, insurance agencies, and clothing stores—a trend that continued into the 1960's.

A Night Out on Beale Street

Despite the influence of the Beale Street Baptist Church and the Church family investments, the most famous street in Memphis was notorious for its nightlife. Although a variety of businesses lined Beale, the street also had its share of saloons, and many of them ran illegal gambling operations.

By the early 1900's, Beale became a destination for minstrel shows, vaudeville acts, and musicians who came to play at the growing number of theaters. In 1907, Robert Church, Sr., hired veteran musician and bandleader W. C. Handy to play at his auditorium. By the time Handy arrived in Memphis, he had developed a distinctive form of music, which he had derived from his own experience as a traveling professional musician. Thus Handy, who is known as the "Father of the Blues," did not invent the blues but was instrumental in making the form commercially successful.

The success of the blues musicians led to the opening of other theaters on Beale, including the Daisy, the Savoy, and the Grand. Anselmo Barasso, whose Palace Theater rivaled Church's auditorium in size and attendance, also operated the Theater Owners' Booking Association (TOBA). TOBA had access to more than forty theaters, including the Apollo in New York and the Regal in Chicago. By the start of World War I, when African Americans began migrating to northern cities to find jobs in industry, southern blues musicians stopped over in Memphis. They lived and worked on Beale Street during the day, then played for audiences on Beale at night, hoping to launch their careers.

By the 1940's, blues musicians were reaching wider audiences. Local Memphis radio station WNBR broadcast the *Amateur Night* show held each week at the Palace Theater. In 1949, WDIA Radio, a station owned and operated by whites, switched to a format featuring only African American musicians. It was also WDIA that advanced the career of the "Beale Street Blues Boy," B. B. King. Meanwhile, young men such as Elvis Presley, Carl Perkins, and Jerry Lee Lewis either listened to these radio shows or went to the clubs on Beale to see live performances. By the 1950's, blues music had given birth not only to rock and roll but also to rhythm and blues and soul music.

The End of an Era

Also during the 1950's, African Americans from the South began protesting for equality and an end to segregated public facilities. In Memphis, especially on Beale, there was relatively little protest during the Civil Rights movement. In 1968, however, Memphis sanitation workers went on strike to bring attention to their low pay and poor working conditions. The labor protest soon gained the attention of Dr. Martin Luther King, Jr., who joined the effort and marched down Beale Street in support of the sanitation workers.

Following the assassination of Dr. King, the remaining racial barriers in Memphis collapsed. Ironically the movement to restore civil rights to African Americans was the end of Beale, because black consumers were no longer confined to the shops along that street. By the early 1970's, the city began demolishing the vacant buildings on Beale and in the surrounding neighborhoods, calling them a danger to the public. In the 1980's, however, the city, along with private investors, helped to revive Beale Street into one of the most popular tourist destinations in Memphis.

Places to Visit

Beale Street is now a National Historic Landmark, and several of its institutions are listed on the National Register of Historic Places. However, the majority of businesses on historic Beale are nightclubs and restaurants that typically cater to adults.

The most popular spots are B. B. King's, Elvis Presley's Memphis, the Blues City Cafe, and the Rum Boogie Cafe. Each club features live blues acts and also serves meals. Silky O'Sullivan's is known not only for its live piano bar but also for having the facade of the last building from the original Beale Street. The musical notes embedded in the sidewalks commemorate the blues performers who have passed through Memphis.

Other historic places on Beale include the Orpheum Theater, where traveling Broadway musicals and operas are showcased. Church Park still exists, but the famous auditorium was demolished. W. C. Handy Park, on the other hand, hosts free outdoor concerts during the warm months. The only place on Beale that is not accessible by foot is the Hunt-Phelan Home. It is the last remaining mansion from the pre-Civil War days, a reminder that Beale Street was once the thoroughfare used by white cotton merchants to get to the river.

—*Jonathan M. Jones*

For Further Information:

Church, Annette E., and Roberta Church. *The Robert R. Churches of Memphis: A Father and Son Who Achieved in Spite of Race.* Ann Arbor, Mich.: Edwards Brothers, 1974. Biographies of two important Memphis residents who commercially developed Beale Street.

Dickerson, James. *Goin' Back to Memphis: A Century of Blues, Rock'n Roll, and Glorious Soul.* New York: Schirmer Books, 1996. Explains the connection between the three most prevalent forms of modern music.

Lee, George W. *Beale Street: Where the Blues Began.* College Park, Md.: McGrath, 1969. An anecdotal but nonetheless entertaining look at the earliest days of Beale Street.

McKee, Margaret, and Fred Chisenhall. *Beale Black and Blue: Life and Music on Black America's Main Street.* Baton Rouge: Louisiana State University Press, 1993. Contains both a history of Beale and eleven brief biographical chapters on pioneering blues musicians.

Sigafoos, Robert A. *Cotton Row to Beale Street: A Business History of Memphis.* Memphis: Memphis State University, 1979. Contains several important points about the history of economic development on Beale Street.

Graceland

Date: Built in 1939; bought by Elvis Presley in 1957

Relevant issues: Art and architecture, cultural history

Significance: Graceland was the home of legendary pop singer Elvis Presley (1935-1977), the "King of Rock and Roll" and arguably one of the twentieth century's greatest entertainers.

Location: U.S. Route 51, ten miles from downtown Memphis

Site Office:
Graceland
3764 Elvis Presley Boulevard
Memphis, TN 38116
ph.: (901) 332-3322
Web site: www.elvis-presley.com/HTML/home.html

Admired by millions, Elvis Presley became a cultural icon whose mystique extended to his Memphis mansion, Graceland. One of few entertainers to be intimately associated with a particular house, Elvis turned the luxurious Graceland into a symbol of a poor southern boy who rose to wealth and success, but who at the same time never left his family, his friends, or his roots behind. Built to resemble a traditional antebellum southern plantation house, Graceland helped shape the legend of Elvis Presley and captured the imagination of the public almost from the moment it became his home. After Elvis's untimely death, Graceland became a historic site that would attract not only ordinary tourists, but also fans who continue to be fascinated by Elvis Presley and who gather in Graceland to celebrate his influence on their lives and on American culture.

Elvis Presley's Graceland

A two-story colonial house featuring four columns overlooking the front lawn, set on a hilltop surrounded by oaks and magnolias, Graceland was built in 1939 by Dr. and Mrs. Thomas D. Moore. The fourteen-acre tract of land on which the house was built had been owned by Mrs. Moore's side of the family for nearly a century, and it was named Graceland after Grace Toof, Mrs. Moore's aunt. The house was also called Graceland.

In 1957 Elvis Presley, having achieved tremendous success and renown as a rock-and-roll singer, musician, and film star, affirmed his new status by buying Graceland from Mrs. Moore for $100,000. For the rest of Presley's life, Graceland would be a home for himself and a large circle of people that included his wife, his daughter, his parents, members of his extended family, and friends. After moving into the mansion, Presley constructed a gatehouse as a place in which uncles and cousins could live and work as gatekeepers. He also added iron gates, known as the Melody Gates, which feature twin images of Presley with guitar on a field of musical notes. Presley and his mother Gladys originally furnished the inside of the house with dark blue walls, red carpets, and red satin chairs with rhinestones, and, although over the years the house was redecorated a number of times, the decor continued to reflect Elvis's dramatic taste. The den, which was named the Jungle Room because of its Polynesian motif when the house became a historic site, was where Presley and his friends relaxed and watched football games and movies on television. The exotic decor especially reflected Presley's per-

sonal taste, as did such decorative elements as a striking statue of Venus placed under a plastic waterfall. Other reflections of Presley's personality were his music room, his trophy room, and a small, guitar-shaped swimming pool and fountain. Presley also extended the west and east wings of the house and added a "Meditation Garden," reflecting his interest in New Age philosophy. The Meditation Garden contains a semicircular wall supported by Grecian columns with a stained-glass window in its center, as well as carved figures of angels and other spiritual figures.

Life at Graceland

Presley's life at Graceland demonstrated to his fans that, in spite of his wealth and fame, he never abandoned his family, friends, or, indeed, the South it-

Flowers and mementos adorn Elvis Presley's gravesite at Graceland. (American Stock Photography)

self. Still, fans enjoyed seeing Presley live in style, and saw in Graceland a suitable castle for the man who was known as the "King of Rock and Roll."

There were times when Graceland was the scene for the kind of hedonistic activities associated with the pop music world, but in general it was a place where Presley unwound and lived a private life. Presley also had a home in Hollywood, but Graceland, situated not far from his childhood home in Mississippi, served as a retreat from the pressures of show business and as a way for him to reconnect with his roots and his musical heritage in the South. A man known for his generosity and loyalty, Presley hosted a contingent of friends and family who often lived on the property. Presley was utterly devoted to his mother and father, Gladys and Vernon, who moved into the house in 1957 along with Elvis's paternal grandmother. His beloved mother Gladys died soon after, but his father and eventually his father's second wife Dee Presley continued to live in the mansion. In addition, a retinue of bodyguards, cousins, and friends, happy to be known as Presley's "Memphis Mafia," also more or less lived at Graceland and were an important part of Elvis's social life. The gatehouse was used by many friends and relatives, and eventually Presley brought in mobile homes that were occupied by various uncles, aunts, and cousins. Most of the relatives were also employed at Graceland as staff. However, while Presley provided room and board for his family and friends and lavished gifts on them, he was also warmed and reassured by their protective presence, and when he was at home they all ate meals together at the large dining room table.

Elvis's beautiful wife Priscilla was also an important part of life at Graceland. The former Priscilla Beaulieu moved into Graceland in 1961 when she was sixteen years old and married Presley in 1967. Priscilla and Elvis married in Las Vegas, but soon afterward they held a second wedding reception in the trophy room at Graceland for family and friends. Their daughter, Lisa Marie, was raised at Graceland and continued to visit her father there after his separation and divorce from Priscilla. After Elvis's difficult separation, former beauty queen Linda Thompson lived at Graceland as his companion until a year before his death and helped with Presley's final redecoration of the house.

Although Presley continued to perform and to inspire his admiring fans, in these last years he suffered from obesity, dependence on prescription drugs, and other health problems. He died of cardiac arrest at Graceland at the age of forty-two on August 16, 1977. The sudden and premature death of Elvis Presley at Graceland sent shock waves around the world; his funeral in Memphis attracted international attention and a great outpouring of grief and affection. Along with his mother, father, and grandmother, Presley is buried at a family plot in the Meditation Garden at Graceland.

Graceland Becomes a Historic House
After Presley's death, his daughter Lisa Marie inherited Graceland. Her guardian, Priscilla Presley, replaced the retinue of family and friends with a professional staff and was granted permission to make Graceland a museum. Priscilla also redecorated Graceland in blue and white. Since opening to the public in 1982, Graceland has been visited by millions of people from every state in the Union and nearly every country of the world. It is one of the five most visited home tours in America, and, after the White House, is the most famous home in America. In 1991 Graceland was placed on the National Register of Historic Places.

More than 600,000 visitors tour Graceland each year. It is especially popular during the summer months; in July attendance builds to over 4,000 people each day. Graceland's visitors come from all over the world and from all socioeconomic brackets and age groups, although more than half of the visitors are under the age of thirty-five. Graceland also attracts visiting dignitaries, entertainers, and, especially, musicians.

Graceland has evolved into a mecca for fans of Elvis Presley. As Presley lifted their spirits when he was alive, his music and his Graceland house continue to exert a mystical pull on millions. Many visitors find Graceland an inspirational experience, especially during "Elvis Week," which begins on August 10 and ends on the anniversary of Presley's death, August 16. Elvis Week has taken on aspects of a pilgrimage in which visitors pay tribute to Presley and visit his grave. The event, which has been compared to a family reunion, also includes music, dance, sports, and social and charity events, culminating in a highly emotional candlelight ceremony on August 15. This all-night vigil begins at sunset, when visitors gather in front of the Melody Gates and recite prayers and poems and sing Presley songs while their candles are lit with a torch from the eternal flame from Presley's grave. Led by fan club presidents, participants in this emotional ritual—including some visitors dressed in Elvis costumes—circle Presley's grave with their candles, leaving flowers, notes, and other gifts. The spiritual intensity of Graceland events such as Elvis Week suggests that the house has become to some extent a sacred site for many visitors.

At Christmas, Graceland is decorated with lights and religious images, including a string of blue lights on the winding driveway. These decorations are kept up until around Presley's birthday on January 8, when special times are scheduled for visits to the grave site. While all of the above events draw the ordinary curious tourist, they also attract devoted fans and admirers of the man and his music.

Visiting Graceland

Graceland is open daily from 8:30 A.M. to 5:00 P.M. The tour lasts approximately sixty to ninety minutes and begins when guests take a shuttle bus across Elvis Presley Boulevard to Graceland, where they are supplied with individual headsets that provide narrative, music, commentary from Elvis himself, and personal recollections by Priscilla Presley. The tour of the mansion includes the massive white living room, the music room, Presley's parents' bedroom, the dining room, the kitchen, the pool room, the Jungle Room, and the popular trophy building with its gold records, awards, mementos, dramatic stage costumes, jewelry, and photographs. Visitors are not permitted, however, to view the second floor of the mansion, where Presley had his bedroom and where he died. Behind the main house tourists can view Presley's racquetball building, his swimming pool and fountain, and his business office. The tour ends at the Meditation Garden, where Presley and other family members are buried.

In 1993 Graceland purchased the property now known as Graceland Plaza, directly across Elvis Presley Boulevard, which houses the Elvis Presley Automobile Museum. Visitors walk down a tree-lined mock highway past exhibits of twenty-two cars owned by Presley, including his famous 1955 pink

Cadillac, his 1956 purple Cadillac convertible, his 1973 Stutz Blackhawk, and his motorcycles. Visitors to Graceland Plaza can also enjoy a tour of Presley's two private jet planes: the Hound Dog II and the larger, customized Lisa Marie, which Presley named after his daughter and described as his "flying Graceland." Another section of Graceland Plaza, "Sincerely, Elvis," features personal items such as his offstage wardrobe, sports equipment, home movies, record collection, photographs, his mother's clothing and accessories, his and Priscilla's wedding outfits, and childhood items of Lisa Marie.

Another part of the Graceland experience is Elvis Presley's Heartbreak Hotel, named after Presley's first million-selling record. In keeping with the song's lyrics, the hotel is situated at the end of "Lonely Street," and the desk clerks dress in black. Owned and operated by Graceland, the hotel features decor inspired by Elvis Presley's particular style and taste. —*Margaret Boe Birns*

For Further Information:

Doss, Erika. *Elvis Culture: Fans, Faith and Image.* Lawrence: University Press of Kansas, 1999. Includes discussion of Graceland as a spiritual site and describes Elvis Week. With photographs.

_____. *Elvis Presley's Graceland: The Official Guidebook.* Memphis, Tenn.: Elvis Presley Enterprises, 1993. Provides a history of Graceland and descriptions of the house and grounds.

Hammontree, Patsy Guy. *Elvis Presley, a Bio-Bibliography.* Westport, Conn.: Greenwood Press, 1985. Includes an informative discussion of Graceland and Presley's life with his retinue there.

Marling, Karal Ann. *Graceland: Going Home with Elvis.* Cambridge, Mass.: Harvard University Press, 1996. Free-wheeling examination of Graceland as a cultural phenomenon. Includes drawings of Graceland and a bibliography.

Rodman, Gilbert B. *Elvis After Elvis: The Posthumous Career of a Living Legend.* New York: Routledge, 1996. Includes an insightful discussion of Graceland, emphasizing close association between Presley and the house and its attraction for fans.

Winegardner, Mark. *Elvis Presley Boulevard: From Sea to Shining Sea, Almost.* New York: Atlantic Monthly Press, 1987. Examines Graceland from the perspective of its visitors.

Grand Ole Opry House, Nashville

Date: Radio show first aired on November 28, 1925, as *Barn Dance*; Grand Ole Opry House first occupied in 1974
Relevant issues: African American history, cultural history
Significance: The Grand Ole Opry House, occupied since 1974, succeeded the historic Ryman Auditorium as the sixth home of the long-running country music show *The Grand Ole Opry*.
Location: Seven miles northeast of downtown Nashville
Site Office:
Grand Ole Opry House
2804 Opryland Drive
Nashville, TN 37214
ph.: 615-889-3060
Web site: www.grandoleopry.com

The most famous country music show in American history is *The Grand Ole Opry*. Moreover, inaugurated in 1925, *The Grand Ole Opry* is the nation's longest-running live radio show.

The Birth of the Opry

Originally called *The WSM Barn Dance*, *The Grand Ole Opry* radio show premiered on November 28, 1925, in Nashville. It was the brainchild of George Dewey Hay, program director and announcer for WSM, the radio station of the National Life and Accident Insurance Company. Although he had earlier broadcast a similar show over Chicago's WLS, Hay's trial run in Nashville, which was not yet synonymous with country music, was hardly a sure thing. Frowning on folk culture, the city prided itself as the capital of the state and the location of several colleges and universities, billing itself alternately the "Paris of the South" and the "Athens of the South"—the city was even home of an exact replica of the Greek Parthenon. It is no wonder, then, that Nashville's high-brow cultural elite poured out scorn on *Barn Dance*. Nevertheless, Hay and his employers, who sold policies mainly to working people who appreciated country music, brushed aside criticism and put *Barn Dance* on the schedule the day after Christmas, 1925.

Hay's daring paid off. By the 1970's, the show would be carried by over thirteen hundred stations. From its inception, *Barn Dance* proved so popular that Hay, who remained with the program in some capacity until 1956, remarked that "we soon had a good-natured riot on our hands" as musicians clamored for a spot on the show. Soon a studio had to be built to satisfy the demand of a public flocking uninvited to the broadcasting booth in the National Life Building to see its favorite performers, fiddle-player Uncle Jimmy Thompson and banjo-player and singer Uncle Dave Macon, the *Opry*'s most popular performer for a decade. Another early attraction was "The Harmonica Wizard," Deford Bailey, an African American who performed what he termed black hillbilly music.

Once established as a stage show as well as a radio broadcast, *Barn Dance* became a carefully contrived rural vaudeville show, mixing humor, dancing, music, and skits. Hay required the cast to dress in stereotypical country garb—overalls, floppy hats, and sometimes even bare feet—setting the precedent for the outlandish costuming that would become an inextricable part of country music acts. Hoe-down bands, too, affecting the demeanor of country bumpkins, gave themselves backwoods names (for example, The Dixie Clod Hoppers, The Gully Jumpers, and The Skillet Lickers) and exchanged corny homespun banter between numbers. Most worked for free until around 1930, when weekly salaries were set at five dollars for beginning acts. After two years on the air, it was also time for a name change. Eclectic in its programming, WSM carried the National Broadcasting Company's classical music relay. In December, 1927, Hay, who styled himself "the Solemn Old Judge," gave notice to his listeners that during the previous hour "we have been listening to music taken largely from Grand Opera, but from now on we will present 'the Grand Ole Opry.'"

During the Great Depression, the three-hour program added new personalities, among them Bill Monroe, the father of bluegrass music, and in 1938 Roy Acuff, a powerful singer of authentic mountain music from East Tennessee and country music's first real star. *The Grand Ole Opry* also picked up many new studio audience members and was obliged to move away from the city's center to a larger venue, the Hillsboro Theater and later the Dixie Tabernacle. With a growing audience

The Ryman Auditorium, former home of the Grand Ole Opry. (American Stock Photography)

came prosperity from an ever-expanding list of advertisers, and in 1939, the show moved back downtown to the War Memorial Auditorium. Attempting to keep audience numbers manageable, Hay began charging admission: twenty-five cents, which failed to deter ticket-seekers. The audience continued to grow not only in Nashville but also among nationwide radio listeners when the National Broadcasting Company (NBC) picked up a thirty-minute block. In 1943, the network provided a feed of *The Grand Ole Opry* to 125 stations.

When World War II began in December, 1941, the *Opry* cast members toured military bases as the Grand Ole Opry Camel Caravan. Its members included comedian Minnie Pearl, whose drawn-out hillbilly greeting "How-dy!," hayseed attire, and price tag dangling from her hat perfectly disguised the well-educated, sophisticated woman she actually was offstage. Another of the Caravan's attractions was the courtly Eddy Arnold, who, like Jim

Reeves after him, made few concessions to phony rusticity and crooned in the silken manner of pop singers Bing Crosby and Frank Sinatra.

The Ryman Auditorium

Meanwhile, in 1943, the *Opry* was once again finding its location too confining and moved into its fifth and most-famous home, the Ryman Auditorium, where it would remain for the next thirty-one years. Completed in 1899 by Tom Ryman and originally called the Union Gospel Tabernacle, the Ryman looked like a church and was meant to be a permanent site for religious revival services. It had been built for over a staggering $100,000, however, and to meet the mortgage, Ryman reluctantly agreed to hire out the structure for secular entertainments. In 1901, Lula Naff took on the chore of stirring up business, thus beginning a remarkable era in which the auditorium hosted many of the most famous names in classical music, film, and

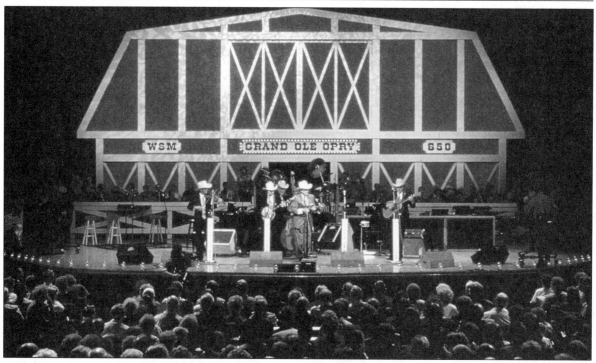

Onstage with the Grand Ole Opry. (American Stock Photography)

politics in the first half of the twentieth century. Tom Ryman would have been appalled to know that in later years parched *Opry*-goers would leave the performance by the side door, cross the ally, and duck into the rear entrance of Tootsie's Orchid Lounge, one of Nashville's most colorful watering holes.

As most of its performances sold out, the *Opry* would need all the Ryman's 3,755 seats. During the warmer months, disappointed patrons who had futilely waited hours in line to buy tickets jostled one another for places outside the open windows. Inside, the lucky ticket-holders crowded together on wooden church pews, fanned themselves in the sweltering hall, passed notes to performers, and stood near the stage with cameras in hand on the chance that an obliging star might pause for a picture. Jammed with milling stagehands, technicians, musicians, and announcers, the stage could be chaotic and cacophonous. The good-natured riot lived on.

Prosperity, Decline, and Renaissance

The *Opry* was more than a popular radio show and a profitable business. Just as Ryman Auditorium became known as the Mother Church of Country Music, *Opry* membership became the union card of country music stardom, the necessary endorsement for virtually all successful country music performers. After World War II, country music's popularity grew dramatically with the infusion of innovative young musicians launched to stardom after Ryman appearances. Membership in the *Opry* ballooned to over 120 in the early 1950's, and with this expansion of its cast came an expanding vision of what necessarily constituted "country music." Hank Williams was arguably the greatest and certainly the most influential of the new breed of singer-songwriters of the late 1940's and early 1950's. A white blues singer of prodigious talent, Williams first appeared at the *Opry* in 1949 promoting his hit song "Lovesick Blues." With his untimely death in 1953 at age twenty-nine, he became the patron saint of country music and was thereafter widely venerated and imitated. To the growing mix of country styles, Ernest Tubb added honky-tonk, Marty Robbins western sophistication, and Chet Atkins virtuoso solo guitar. Gospel music had always been featured at the *Opry*, but no group ever sang it better than the Jordanaires, who recorded and toured with Elvis Presley, a brilliant rock-a-billy singer and visitor to the *Opry* stage in September, 1954. (Afterward, an *Opry* official told him his future lay in truck driving rather than singing.)

Because of country music's financial success, Nashville in the 1950's embraced the *Opry*. Recording studios, publishers, and agents congregated between Vanderbilt University and downtown in an area known as "Music Row," and soon the "Paris of the South" was nicknamed "Music City," country music's hometown. With success, however, came the temptations of complacency and unconscious self-parody. In the late 1960's, country music was ill-prepared for the seismic shift in American popular culture that threatened to shake down the entire edifice of country music, the *Opry* included. In the era of rock and roll and social protest, avaricious promoters and self-satisfied performers appeared at best irrelevant, at worst reactionary. Fortunately, singers from outside country, like Bob Dylan and the Byrds, created a hybrid called country rock, converting a new generation of young fans. Adding considerably to country's rehabilitation in 1972, The Nitty Gritty Dirt Band, in conjunction with old-time country singers and instrumentalists, paid tribute to the *Opry* with an acclaimed triple-record album, *Will the Circle Be Unbroken*. The album's first number, "The Grand Old Opry Song," was a blazing three-minute tribute to forty-seven years of *Opry* history.

Opryland USA

At the moment of country music's renaissance, the long-standing need for a large and comfortable home for the *Opry* became pressing. The venerable Ryman Auditorium was greatly loved, but its declining surroundings in downtown Nashville had become unsavory and sometimes unsafe by the early 1970's. Moreover, the Ryman itself remained as cramped and stifling as always just when the demand for tickets far exceeded its capacity. The *Opry*'s manager, E. W. Wendell, prodded the National Life and Accident Insurance Company to move the show to a new facility. Consequently, March 15, 1974, marked the *Opry*'s valedictory performance at the Ryman Auditorium. Tourists still went on pilgrimage to the auditorium for nearly two decades until its owner, the Gaylord Entertainment Company, spent over eight million dollars to restore the shrine in 1994. In January, 2000, the

Opry returned to the Ryman for four celebratory, worshipful performances.

The *Opry*'s new home in the Pennington Bend of the Cumberland River northeast of Nashville was not just a music hall but a 442-acre conglomerate called Opryland USA, comprising an amusement park, gift shops, a golf course, the *General Jackson* riverboat, a museum, and a three-thousand room hotel and convention center, in addition to the auditorium. (In 2000, the amusement park would be replaced by a 1.2 million-square-foot mall called Opry Mills as a result of declining attendance.) Although lacking the nostalgic charm of the Ryman Auditorium, the air-conditioned and acoustically remarkable Grand Ole Opry House accommodated 4,400 ticket-holders in plush seats and treated them to a show enhanced by the finest sound and light system available. On opening night in 1974, President Richard Nixon pounded out "God Bless America" on the piano to initiate a new day in the *Opry*'s history.

In the last quarter of the twentieth century, *The Grand Ole Opry* changed along with the nation and took country music into diverse and promising directions. One of its most popular artists in the 1970's was Charlie Pride, an African American, and over the next three decades a legion of its best-selling musicians were women building on the pioneering work of Maybelle Carter in the 1930's, Kitty Wells in the 1940's, and Patsy Cline in the 1950's. Dolly Parton, Loretta Lynn, Tammy Wynette, Emmylou Harris, Trisha Yearwood, and many more women took country music into a new millennium.

—David Allen Duncan

For Further Information:

Bedwell, Randall, ed. *Unbroken Circle: A Quotable History of the Grand Ole Opry*. Nashville: Cumberland House, 1999. Delightful anecdotes and quotations from *Opry* stars and others describing events and personalities from the show's past.

Douglas, Susan. *Listening In: Radio and the American Imagination*. New York: Random House, 1999. Argues for the influence of radio in the formation of the American national identity.

Doyle, Don H. *Nashville Since the 1920's*. Knoxville: University of Tennessee Press, 1985. First-rate history of Nashville in the period of the *Opry*'s birth and maturity.

Hagan, Chet. *Grand Ole Opry: The Complete Story of a Great American Institution*. New York: Henry Holt, 1989. The story of the *Opry* from its founding to the late 1980's. Over one hundred impressive photographs.

Kingsbury, Paul. *Grand Ole Opry*. New York: Random House, 1995. Narrative history of the *Opry* carrying the story into the 1990's.

Wolfe, Charles. *A Good Natured Riot: The Birth of the Grand Ole Opry*. Nashville: Vanderbilt University and the Country Music Foundation Press, 1999. Detailed and definitive study of the *Opry*'s origins and quest to gain a national audience in the 1930's.

The Hermitage

Date: Property purchased by Andrew Jackson in 1804; current mansion constructed 1834-1836

Relevant issues: African American history, art and architecture, military history, political history, western expansion

Significance: This is the completely restored plantation home of Andrew Jackson, a legendary general and the seventh president of the United States.

Location: Twelve miles east of downtown Nashville

Site Office:

The Hermitage
4580 Rachel's Lane
Hermitage, TN 37076
ph.: (615) 889-2941
Web site: www.thehermitage.com
e-mail: information@thehermitage.com

The Hermitage historical site consists of the mansion and related buildings that Andrew Jackson built as his home beginning in 1819. It was a working plantation served by over one hundred slaves, whose quarters have been the subject of archaeological excavation. Since the time of Jackson's grandson, the site has been preserved, maintained, and shown by a private foundation as it was in the 1840's.

Jackson Settles in Tennessee

Andrew Jackson was born on March 15, 1767, in the Carolinas, and lived through a brutal occupation by British forces in 1780 and 1781. He studied law in North Carolina, and was admitted to that state's bar in 1787. In 1788 he was sent as a political appointee to serve as prosecuting attorney in the Cumberland region of the western district of North Carolina, which became the state of Tennessee. In Nashville he boarded with Colonel John Donelson, whose widowed daughter, Rachel Robards, married Jackson. Jackson carried on a thriving private practice as well as his public duties, but gave up the law when he was elected to the U.S. House of Representatives from Tennessee in 1796. He resigned in 1797 but was elected to the U.S. Senate by Tennessee's legislature in 1797, only to resign in 1798. He was then appointed to the bench of the superior (supreme) court of Tennessee, a position from which he resigned in 1804, and to the post of major general in the Tennessee militia in 1802.

In March, 1796, Jackson purchased 640 acres at Hunter's Hill east of Nashville, for $700. Entering strictly private life in 1804, he sold this property and house, and for $3,400 purchased 425 acres about two miles away: the heart of what would be The Hermitage. He also engaged in several business ventures, including a distillery, a cotton gin, and several mercantile stores in the area. By 1812 he had 640 acres, and by his death in 1845 about 1,000.

Building on the Site

The original house that Jackson built for himself and his beloved Rachel was a two-story log house, with one large room on the ground floor and two upstairs. Somewhat later he added a second, smaller building, attached to the first by a covered passageway. This was the home of the hero of the Creek Indian War (1813-1814) and the Battle of New Orleans (January 8, 1815), to which Jackson returned after being named Commander of the Southern Military District of the United States. Leaving his military duties to lieutenants, he concentrated on the plantation, and constructed a new house from 1819 to 1821, a place he considered a refuge ("hermitage") from public duty. Local architect Henry Reiff designed and oversaw the construction of the Federal-style brick edifice. The extant kitchen and the smokehouse buildings also date to 1819. The original log buildings were relegated to slave quarters. Bowing to Rachel's piety, Jackson also built a church on the property in 1823, a fine brick structure that still stands.

most immediately on the foundations of the previous structure. It was ready for occupation when Jackson, in a very poor state of health, returned from Washington, D.C., in March, 1837. This is the main structure on the site today. Cedars were planted that summer along the drive up to the house by Ralph E. W. Earl, the "artist-in-residence" at The Hermitage. He died from the exertion and is buried nearby. Many of these cedar trees, and hickory trees that were sent as nuts to "Old Hickory" by an admirer in Ulster, New York, in 1830, were destroyed in a tornado that struck the Nashville area in the spring of 1998.

The Working Plantation

At the apex of its productive life The Hermitage produced corn, wheat, oats, squash, and sweet potatoes, and its major cash crop—cotton. Jackson had as many as 130 acres in cotton, and his was one of the first gins in the region. Jackson also bred cattle, mules, sheep, hogs, and especially horses, some of which he raced in distant competitions. At one point he paid $1,500 for Truxton, a champion Virginian stallion. The farm work was performed by slaves, which Jackson began to acquire in the 1790's. Records show that he and Rachel had ten slaves in 1794, fifteen in 1798, and forty-four after the main house was constructed in 1819—twenty-seven men and seventeen women and girls. During his presidency, 95 slaves worked the place, and in his later years nearly 140 did. His will lists 110 slaves working The Hermitage's 1,000 acres in 1845 and an additional 51 on his Mississippi plantation of 2,700 acres. In the 1990's archaeologists excavated several slave cabins, and began to reconstruct an image of slave life on the site. Families lived in quarters that were twenty by twenty feet square, with fireplaces and attic lofts for sleeping. They were constructed of either log or brick, but only those of log remain standing today. Accounts of slaves on The Hermitage life are rare,

The family cemetery at The Hermitage. The burial site of Andrew Jackson and his wife Rachel is marked by the dome. (AP/Wide World Photos)

In 1828 Jackson won the rollicking presidential election, and prepared to move to Washington, D.C. In December, however, Rachel died, casting a pall over Jackson's life from which he never fully recovered. During his stay in Washington, D.C., The Hermitage was overseen by Andrew, Jr., whom Andrew and Rachel, being childless, had adopted shortly after his birth in December, 1809. Young Jackson received a good deal of advice and guidance from the president, which he apparently ignored. The plantation and other businesses declined as he made poor loans and was generally taken advantage of by the local gentry. In 1834 the mansion burned down, and was rebuilt by Reiff and partner Hume in a grander style, beginning al-but it appears that Jackson was fair by the standards of the day, though he could be harsh if crossed.

The Hermitage After Old Hickory

Jackson left the plantation to Andrew, Jr., in a will that was executed on August 4, 1845. Both he and Rachel are buried on the grounds. In 1856, the state of Tennessee bought the buildings and five hundred acres from Andrew, Jr., for forty-eight thousand dollars and allowed the Jacksons to reside on the property as its custodians. The state offered the site to the federal government as a branch of West Point Military Academy, but the Civil War intervened, and this idea withered. The second-generation Jacksons remained on the property during the war, and it was protected from any destruction by a small army detail. Andrew, Jr., died in 1865, and his widow Sarah remained a tenant until her death in 1888. Their son Andrew Jackson III served as an artillery colonel in the Confederate army, and, as the only surviving member of the family, inherited Sarah's furniture, mementoes, and other heirlooms from the time of Andrew and Rachel. In February, 1889, the state chartered the Ladies' Hermitage Association, which purchased 25 acres and the main structures of The Hermitage two months later. In 1923 the state conveyed an additional 232 acres to the association so that they might "display the respect, love, and affection which a grateful State and people cherish for their illustrious hero and statesman, Andrew Jackson." The remainder of the 500-acre tract in state hands was conveyed to the association in 1935. An additional 125 acres was acquired by the association as a buffer against urban encroachment.

The furnishings—largely in the classical style and purchased in Philadelphia—and relics left to Andrew III were offered to the Ladies' Hermitage Association, but they could not raise the necessary funds. Andrew III then took the collection to Cincinnati and tried to charge admission to view them, but this proved a failure, and he returned them to Tennessee. The association was able to purchase these items, and those in the possession of others, as they could. The Hermitage remains the only nineteenth century historical site of its kind with the original owner's furnishings throughout. Theodore Roosevelt visited The Hermitage in 1907 and arranged for a five thousand-dollar grant to aid preservation, and state funds have supported the site since the early twentieth century. In 1961 the National Park Service designated The Hermitage a Registered National Historic Landmark.

The Mansion and Other Structures on the Site

The centerpiece of the site is the mansion built in Greek revival style between 1834 and 1836. Six two-story Greek columns screen the front of the structure and create a double porch. The fourteen rooms center on the grand entrance hall and the curved staircase at the far end from the front door. This space boasts French wallpaper depicting scenes from the life of Telemachus, son of Odysseus, and is original to the room. Six other rooms retain their original wallpaper, and pains have been taken to ensure authenticity in recreating decoration where replacement has proved necessary. Double parlors served the men and the women guests as they retired from the amply supplied and jovial dinner table. The president took a front bedroom that had a side exit to the portico and a connection directly to his study and library, which housed some six hundred books. Andrew, Jr., and the president's wife occupied back quarters, with a parlor and nursery. The upstairs consisted of four rooms generally reserved for guests, in one of which lived the portrait painter (and tree planter) Ralph Earl, widower of one of Rachel's nieces.

A number of other period buildings occupy The Hermitage site. Apart from the main collection are the 1823 church and nearby Tulip Grove mansion, which was purchased in 1964 and serves as a museum for the Ladies' Hermitage Association. With Rachel's death, Jackson needed someone to serve as hostess in the White House, and his niece Emily Donelson filled the position. When she and her husband Andrew Jackson Donelson returned to Tennessee, Jackson helped pay for construction of the Greek revival mansion of three stories, another Reiff and Hume structure. The couple lived there only during 1836, as she was struck down by tuberculosis in December at the age of twenty-nine. The cabin in which Jackson's personal attendant, Uncle Alfred, lived has been refurnished appropriately, and the carriage house contains the remains of the Jackson phaeton, which was constructed from timbers of the USS *Constitution* and presented to him by the people of Philadelphia. The smokehouse, farm shop, 1804 stone spring house, gardens, and Jackson tombs round out the attractions of the site. —*Joseph P. Byrne*

For Further Information:

Arnold, James E. *Hermitage: Home of Andrew Jackson.* Hermitage, Tenn.: Ladies' Hermitage Association, 1967. Locally produced guide to the site.

Booth, Edward Townsend. *Country Life in America as Lived by Ten Presidents of the United States.* New York: Alfred A. Knopf, 1947. Contains a discussion of life at The Hermitage according to Jackson's accounts and letters.

Coke, Fletch, and John T. Hooper. *The Hermitage Landscape: Before and After the 1998 Tornado.* Nashville: Hillsboro Press, 1999. Well-illustrated descriptions of the grounds and the destruction in the 1998 storm.

Dorris, Mary C. *Preservation of The Hermitage, 1889-1915.* Nashville: Smith and Lamar, 1915. Dorris was one of the early members of the Ladies' Association, and her account is firsthand.

Horn, Stanley F. *The Hermitage: Home of Old Hickory.* New York: Greenberg, 1950. A lengthy narrative and description of the site, Jackson's activities there, and its subsequent history.

Remini, Robert V. *The Life of Andrew Jackson.* New York: Penguin Books, 1990. The shorter version of the standard biography of Jackson.

Shiloh

Date: Established in 1894

Relevant issues: Civil War, American Indian history

Significance: Shiloh is the site of one of the earliest and most decisive full-scale battles in the western theater of operations during the Civil War. On April 6 and 7, 1862, Union and Confederate forces numbering almost 110,000 men fought on the west bank of the Tennessee River between Shiloh Church and Pittsburg Landing. The battle, fought to control the strategic railroad junction of Corinth, Mississippi, resulted in 24,000 casualties and set the stage for the Confederate loss of the upper Mississippi Valley. Within the park also are thirty Indian burial mounds, which were excavated by the Smithsonian Institution in 1934.

Location: If traveling on Interstate 40, south at Jackson, Tennessee, on U.S. 45 and then east on Tennessee Route 142; if traveling east from Memphis, approximately eighty miles on Highway 72 to Corinth, Mississippi, then northeast twenty-five miles on U.S. Highway 45

Site Office:
Shiloh National Military Park
1055 Pittsburg Landing
Shiloh, TN 38376
ph.: (901) 689-5696 (visitors' center), 689-3475 (bookstore)
Web site: www.nps.gov/shil/

The four thousand-acre military park in Shiloh contains a visitors' center, a small theater where a short film introduces the battle, and a bookstore. Visitors can take a self-guided automobile tour to decisive points on the well-marked battlefield, though the looping road does not follow the action of the battle chronologically or geographically. It is also important to note that the vegetation is much denser and the open fields much smaller than at the time of the battle. This is particularly true, for example, at the artillery positions protecting Grant's left flank on the high ground above the Tennessee River, which are now heavily overgrown. The battlefield tour also takes visitors past the Indian mounds.

The Battle of Shiloh
The Battle of Shiloh provides military historians and students of Civil War history with many insights into combat difficulties for leaders, soldiers, and sailors. Inadequacies of transportation, communication, intelligence, training, and experience confronted both leaders and the rank and file.

The strategic problem for the Confederacy in the western theater lay in covering the great distances with adequate forces. Concentration to deliver a decisive blow meant leaving much of Tennessee and Arkansas undefended, while defending along the Confederacy's whole northern border meant being weak everywhere. Western Tennessee provided a particularly difficult problem because the Mississippi sliced north and south through the Confederacy. To the east, the Tennessee and Cumberland Rivers flowed north into the Ohio River, providing the newly forming Union gunboat navy the opportunity to penetrate as far south as Florence, Alabama, and Nashville, Tennessee.

These key rivers were opened to exploitation when General Ulysses S. Grant's forces took Forts Henry and Donelson in February, 1862. As a result, General Albert Sidney Johnston, Commander of the Confederacy's Western District, was compelled to abandon Nashville, the Confederacy's most important regional depot. The loss stunned authorities in Richmond, who finally realized the danger.

General Johnston moved southwest from Nashville and, receiving reinforcements from all directions, was able to concentrate approximately fifty-one thousand men at Corinth, Mississippi. This was the key junction where the major east-west railroad line connecting Memphis to Chattanooga and the East crossed the major north-south link from Mobile, Alabama, through Jackson, Tennessee, to Columbus, Kentucky. It was the strategic linchpin of the region's defense. The Union recognized its significance as well. General Grant's Army of the Tennessee, numbering forty-seven thousand men and supported by Union gunboats, moved up the Tennessee River toward Corinth, while General Don Carlos Buell's Army of the Ohio, numbering almost fifty thousand, moved cross-country from Nashville to join him. Their rendezvous point was Pittsburg Landing, on the west bank of the Tennessee River approximately twenty-five miles northeast of Corinth.

General William Tecumseh Sherman, though only one of Grant's division commanders, commanded the entire force on the ground west of the landing as General Grant stayed at his headquarters at Savannah, Tennessee, several miles upriver and on the opposite bank. The Union troops were in an offensive frame of mind and expected to move forward to attack the defenders of Corinth. Sherman has, therefore, been criticized for the lax security of the troops that poured into the encampment and the administrative, rather than tactical, disposition of his forces.

The Confederates realized that their only hope for success was to defeat Grant before Buell could reinforce him, and they thus moved to attack. The movement out of Corinth to contact was, however, hampered by a poor road network, lack of communications, poor intelligence, and inexperience. These factors delayed the attack until the morning of April 6. Although some of Sherman's subordinates, sensing an enemy presence, sent out patrols, who actually triggered the battle, most of his force was surprised by the early morning attack. The Union defenders were driven back and their camps overrun. Despite this early success the Confederate attack began to suffer from disorganization. General Pierre G. T. Beauregard, the author of the plan, had attacked with two corps on line, one behind the other, with units of two additional corps trailing in column. While the initial attacks were a success, overrunning, as they did, Sherman's command post at Shiloh Church and many Union camps, following Confederate troops began to pile into the lead units. The result was that, despite their success, Confederate units became intermingled, disorganized, and very difficult to control. The fight became one of regiments commanded by whatever senior officer was near at hand whether they were his troops or not.

General Sherman, though he can be faulted for his early lack of alertness and his dispositions, proved his skill as a battlefield commander in what was to be the bloodiest fight of his long career. Under his leadership, his troops and those of General John A. McClernand on the Union right flank reorganized, fought back, and grudgingly gave ground into the middle of the afternoon.

The intermingled troops of Generals Lewis Wallace, Benjamin M. Prentiss, and Stephen A. Hurlbut in the center of the line ultimately saved the Union position. General Grant, who had heard the fighting and rushed to the scene from his headquarters, realized the natural strength of their position and ordered it held at all costs. The key to the defense was a slightly sunken road through a patch of underbrush facing an open field the Rebels had to cross. The dogged defense against repeated Confederate attacks produced some of the bloodiest fighting of the war. The defenders' intense fire so galled the Rebel attackers that they named the position the "Hornet's Nest."

On the Union left, Confederate attacks had more success, though here they suffered a catastrophe. Troops of General John C. Breckinridge, former vice president of the United States, while driving back the Union forces in the vicinity of the Peach Orchard, momentarily lost momentum. General Johnston, attempting to organize a new attack, was mortally wounded. Though command devolved upon General Beauregard, General Braxton Bragg seems at this point to have assumed the role of combat commander.

The Confederate drive on the Union right flank ultimately succeeded, but instead of pushing forward toward the lightly defended Pittsburg Landing, the real objective, they swung left to encircle the Hornet's Nest. The position had endured six hours of attacks and been pounded by concentrated fire of over fifty cannon. In the late afternoon with General Wallace having been killed, General Prentiss surrendered the remaining two thousand defenders. They had held on long enough, however, for Grant to organize a final defensive line on high ground in front of Pittsburg Landing. There in the late afternoon a Union artillery line, supported by gunboats and bolstered by the leading elements of Buell's army, drove off the last Confederate attacks.

Beauregard, believing that General Buell's troops were too far away to assist Grant, assumed that he could complete the victory the following morning. Through the night, however, seventeen thousand of Buell's troops disembarked in a driving rain. In addition General Wallace's division, numbering more than seven thousand men, who had marched and countermarched while the battle raged, now joined the battle line. General Nathan Bedford Forrest had sent scouts into the Union lines and knew of these reinforcements, but he was unable to convey the crucial intelligence to General Beauregard.

Though the element of surprise was gone, the second day of battle was much like the first, but in reverse. Generals Grant and Buell conferred neither during the night nor the next morning and launched their attacks essentially as two separate armies. The result was a soldiers' fight—head-on attacks with little finesse across tangled terrain. Now the Union had the upper hand, and the blue lines surged forward. General James A. Garfield, another future president, led his brigade forward in this advance. A lack of coordination among the attackers allowed the Confederates to give ground slowly in the face of frontal attacks and even deliver occasional counterblows. The battle raged from first light to mid-afternoon when Beauregard, realizing that his force was spent, broke contact and retreated toward Corinth. The Union troops, too bloodied and exhausted to pursue, lost the opportunity that a coordinated attack would have provided to destroy the Confederate's largest western field force.

The cost of the battle had been enormous. Confederate casualties have been estimated at 10,700 of 40,300 engaged (over 25 percent), and Union casualties at 13,000 of 62,700 engaged (20 percent). The enormity of these numbers brought criticism of all involved in the battle. Grant, nevertheless, emerged after several months of eclipse, as a rising star, who would ultimately command all Union forces and win the presidency. The battle also made the career of General Sherman, Grant's trusted subordinate, who as a result of his combat leadership emerged from a cloud of suspicion regarding his mental stability. The Confederacy lost the leadership of General Albert Sidney Johnston, who was killed in action, and General P. G. T. Beauregard, who was never again trusted with a significant field command by Confederate president Jefferson Davis. General Bragg was given command of the Army of Tennessee.

Neither side had been able to deliver a knock-out blow, but Confederate hopes of sustaining their presence in the upper Mississippi Valley were doomed. In May they abandoned Corinth. The loss of Nashville had been followed in rapid succession by the loss of Island Number 10, New Orleans, and Memphis, opening up long stretches of the Mississippi River to Union gunboats. The Confederate army itself survived the Battle of Shiloh, and the Union failure to pursue meant it would fight another day. Nevertheless, Shiloh was a decisive event in the defeat of Confederate hopes in the West.

—*Charles Endress*

For Further Information:

Arnold, James. *Shiloh 1862: The Death of Innocence.* Oxford, England: Osprey, 1988. One of the titles in Osprey's Campaign Series, this short treatment is well illustrated and contains interesting and informative maps.

Daniel, Larry F. *Shiloh: The Battle That Changed the Civil War.* New York: Simon & Schuster, 1997. Sets the battle well within the strategic and operational framework and gives a good tactical account supported by excellent maps.

Espisitio, Vincent J., ed. *The West Point Atlas of American Wars: Vol. 1, 1689-1900.* New York: Praeger, 1959. A short analysis of the campaign accompanies a series of excellent operational and tactical maps.

Frank, Joseph A., and George Reaves. *Seeing the Ele-*

phant: Raw Recruits at the Battle of Shiloh. New York: Greenwood Press, 1989. Contains moving and insightful eyewitness accounts from participants.

Luvaas, Jay, Stephen Bowman, and Leonard Fullenkamp. *Guide to the Battle of Shiloh.* Lawrence: University of Kansas Press, 1996. This is the book for those with an interest in a detailed study of the battle and the ground. The authors take the reader on a self-directed automobile tour of the battlefield, using after-action reports from the Official Record.

Sword, Wiley. *Shiloh: Bloody April.* New York: William Morrow, 1974. A well-written account of the battle, though it lacks the maps that enhance Daniel's book.

Other Historic Sites

Blount Mansion

Location: Knoxville, Knox County

Relevant issues: Political history

Statement of significance: From 1792 until his death, this impressive structure was the residence of William Blount (1749-1800), who had already represented North Carolina in the Continental Congress (1782-1783, 1786-1787) and signed the U.S. Constitution when he moved west to present-day Tennessee in 1790. While governor of the Southwest Territory, Blount was instrumental in Tennessee's admission to the Union and was one of its first U.S. senators.

Chucalissa Site

Location: Memphis, Shelby County

Relevant issues: American Indian history

Statement of significance: Chucalissa is a Walls Phase (1400-1500) prehistoric mound and plaza complex, and the best known and preserved of such sites in the Central Mississippi River Valley. The site is known for its excellent preservation of architectural, floral, faunal, and human skeletal materials.

Fort Pillow

Location: Fort Pillow, Lauderdale County

Relevant issues: African American history, Civil War, military history

Statement of significance: Constructed by Confederate engineers, the fort was occupied by Union troops in June, 1862, and recaptured in April, 1864, by Confederate forces under Major General Nathan Bedford Forrest. Among the approximately 570 Union soldiers were 262 black soldiers—former slaves recruited in Tennessee and Alabama; in the savage, no-quarter fighting, 229 black soldiers were killed by the Confederates. News of the fight—labeled a massacre—had a profound effect: "Remember Fort Pillow" became a battle cry of black soldiers.

Franklin Battlefield

Location: Franklin, Williamson County

Relevant issues: Civil War, military history

Statement of significance: Early on the afternoon of November 30, 1864, General John Bell Hood, against the advice of his staff, ordered his Army of Tennessee to attack Union forces under the command of Major General John M. Schofield. Numerous assaults were made against the entrenched Federals; each assault was repulsed. The enormous losses sustained by Hood's army helped doom his Tennessee campaign.

Franklin Plantation

Location: Gallatin, Sumner County

Relevant issues: African American history, business and industry

Statement of significance: Isaac Franklin (1789-1846) was a principal in the largest slave-trading firm in the antebellum South. At its height, Franklin & Armfield had offices in Alexandria, Virginia; Natchez, Mississippi; and New Orleans, Louisiana, as well as agents in every important southern city and its own fleet of sailing ships. The firm trafficked in thousands of humans annually. Franklin built Fairvue Plantation (1832) when he decided that he would prefer the life of a planter to that of a slave trader. The two-and-a-half-story red brick home with associated outbuildings, such as four slave houses and an overseer's house, reflects the culture of antebellum planters in the upper South.

George Peabody College for Teachers

Location: Nashville, Davidson County

Relevant issues: Education

Statement of significance: The University of Nashville was the first college to receive aid from the Peabody Fund, which had been established in 1867 by philanthropist George Peabody to help rebuild the South's educational system. In 1875, the university began to function as a state normal school; after 1889, it was known as Peabody Normal College and in 1909 incorporated as the George Peabody College for Teachers. Peabody College moved to its present location in 1914.

Hiram Masonic Lodge No. 7

Location: Franklin, Williamson County

Relevant issues: American Indian history, political history

Statement of significance: This was the scene of the signing of the Treaty of Franklin (1830), which provided for the removal of Chickasaw Indians from their eastern homelands to a region beyond the Mississippi. President Andrew Jackson personally opened the meeting, the only time a U.S. president would journey to an Indian council for the purpose of making a treaty.

Jubilee Hall, Fisk University

Location: Nashville, Davidson County

Relevant issues: African American history, education

Statement of significance: Completed in 1876, this Victorian Gothic structure is the oldest building on campus. Fisk University was founded in 1865 by the American Missionary Association to provide a liberal arts education for African Americans after the Civil War.

Long Island of the Holston

Location: Kingsport, Sullivan County

Relevant issues: American Indian history, western expansion

Statement of significance: Located just east of the junction of the North and South Forks of the Holston River, Long Island was a sacred council and treaty ground surrounded by the vast hunting territory of the Cherokee Nation. Starting at Long Island in March, 1775, Daniel Boone (1734-1820) led a team of thirty axmen to open the trail through Cumberland Gap that was to gain fame as the Wilderness Road. Between 1775 and 1795, this trail was used by more than 200,000 emigrants.

Moccasin Bend Archaeological District

Location: Chattanooga, Hamilton County

Relevant issues: American Indian history

Statement of significance: This is the best-preserved and most important compact, yet diverse, sample of archaeological remains known in the Tennessee River Valley, indicative of Chattanooga's pivotal status in trade, communications, economics, and political importance in the interior Southeast. The site includes evidence of occupation by Native American groups of the Archaic, Woodland, and Mississippian periods; because of sixteenth century Spanish trade and gift items found there, the site provides significant opportunities to study the early contact period in the Southeast. Also included are Civil War earthworks associated with the Battle of Chattanooga.

Old First Presbyterian Church

Location: Nashville, Davidson County

Relevant issues: Art and architecture

Statement of significance: The Old First Presbyterian Church was designed very late in William Strickland's career while he was engaged on the construction of the Tennessee State Capitol. Having started his architectural career as an apprentice to Benjamin Henry Latrobe (1764-1820), Strickland (1787-1854) advanced in his knowledge of engineering and became one of the foremost architects in the United States. The Old Presbyterian Church, begun in 1849, is Strickland's largest and only full Egyptian temple, and is known affectionately as "Karnak on the Cumberland."

Polk House

Location: Columbia, Maury County

Relevant issues: Political history

Statement of significance: Constructed in 1816, this two-story brick house was the home of James K. Polk (1795-1849), eleventh president of the United States (1845-1849), who lived here for several years during his youth.

Rhea County Courthouse

Location: Dayton, Rhea County

Relevant issues: Education, legal history, religion, science and technology

Statement of significance: From July 10 to 21, 1925, this was the scene of the controversial and widely publicized trial of John Thomas Scopes (1901-1970) for teaching Charles Darwin's theory of evolution in a Dayton public school. A battle of wits between two great lawyers—William Jennings Bryan, for the prosecution, and Clarence Darrow, for the defense—the trial symbolized the clash between fundamentalist and modernist thought in science, theology, philosophy, and politics.

Sycamore Shoals

Location: Elizabethton, Carter County

Relevant issues: American Indian history, military history, Revolutionary War

Statement of significance: A treaty signed by the Cherokee here in 1775 allowed the United States to purchase twenty million acres of Cherokee land. Also, in 1780, the site served as the rendezvous point for the Overmountain Men on their way to Kings Mountain, where they contributed to the defeat of the British army.

X-10 Reactor, Oak Ridge National Laboratory

Location: Oak Ridge, Roane County

Relevant issues: Science and technology

Statement of significance: When it went into operation on November 4, 1943, this was the world's first full-scale nuclear reactor and the first to produce significant amounts of heat energy and measurable amounts of plutonium; in 1946, it was the first to produce radioactive isotopes for medical therapy. For many years, X-10 was the principal atomic research facility in the United States.

York Farm

Location: Pall Mall, Fentress County

Relevant issues: Military history, World War I

Statement of significance: From 1922 until 1964, this was the residence of Alvin Collum York (1887-1964), highly decorated World War I soldier. On October 8, 1918, during the Battle of the Argonne Forest, Sergeant York fought a virtually one-man battle against the enemy, killing twenty-five enemy soldiers, taking 132 prisoners, and capturing thirty-five machine guns. For his actions, York was awarded the Congressional Medal of Honor and magnified his legend by refusing to capitalize on it.

Texas

Houston. (Corbis)

History of Texas

Until Alaska was admitted as the forty-ninth state in 1959, Texas was the largest of the United States and still is the largest of the contiguous forty-eight states, occupying one-twelfth of the entire American land mass. With a total area of more than a quarter of a million square miles, it stretches almost eight hundred miles from its eastern boundary in Arkansas and Louisiana to its western extremes at Mexico and New Mexico. On the south it is bordered by the Gulf of Mexico and Mexico. Its northern boundary, Oklahoma, lies 730 miles from its southern extreme.

Texas is the only state in the Union ruled under six flags: those of Spain, France, Mexico, the Republic of Texas, the Confederate States of America, and the United States. Early explorers found this vast area intimidating, but modern transportation and a wealth of natural resources, particularly oil and natural gas, helped Texas achieve the third largest population of the United States.

Early History

The earliest settlers in Texas were American Indians who dwelt there before 12,000 B.C.E. By 5000 B.C.E., the early residents were farming and hunting with bows and arrows. In far western Texas, remnants of Pueblo dwellings similar to those found in New Mexico have been unearthed. Indian mounds like those found in the western parts of Illinois, Tennessee, Louisiana, and Mississippi were discovered in east Texas.

Exploration and Colonization

The earliest explorations of Texas were made by Spaniards. In 1519, Alonso de Pineda sailed along the Gulf of Mexico coastline from Florida to Mexico, establishing Spain's claim to the land that lay along it. By 1528, Alvar Nuñez Cabeza de Vaca explored the interior. In the 1840's, Francisco Vásquez de Coronado and Hernando de Soto both led expeditions into Texas, but their reports made the territory sound so forbidding that explorers avoided the area for the next half century.

It was not until 1682, after René-Robert Cavelier, Sieur de La Salle, declared Texas a possession of France, that the Spaniards took a renewed interest in the area. The French were driven out by Native Americans, but in 1690 the Spanish renewed their claim by establishing two missions among the Indians in east Texas. By 1716 they had established five missions in east Texas.

The Native American population of the state ranged from Cherokees in the east, who had been displaced from their lands in other areas, to the Tonkawa, nomadic plains Indians in the central part of the area, to the Coahuitecan and Karankawa tribes, the most primitive of the Native American dwellers, along the Gulf coast. The Lipan Apache, the Comanche, the Kiowa, and the Kiowa Apache inhabited the west.

The U.S. Claim to Texas

Louisiana was ceded to Spain in 1762. By 1800 Texas had established three permanent Spanish settlements, San Antonio, Goliad, and Nacogdoches. In 1800, France took the title to Louisiana, which was sold to the United States in 1803. The boundary between the Spanish and French claims in this area had never been established, so the United States now held a tenuous claim to Texas.

When Texas became part of the new nation of Mexico in 1821, colonization was encouraged. Moses Austin came from Missouri with three hundred families who were given land. Austin's son Stephen brought in more settlers after his father died. Land was plentiful, and land grants were generous and easily obtained.

By 1835 about twenty thousand settlers had arrived in east Texas, bringing with them more than four thousand slaves to work in the cotton fields, thereby establishing Texas as a slave state. In the same year, Mexican general Antonio López de Santa Anna waged war against the Texans during the Texas Revolution, taking about 350 prisoners, who were summarily executed. The following year, he stormed the Alamo, taking control from the few Texans remaining inside.

As Anglo-American immigrants flooded into the area, the United States sought to purchase Texas. The Mexican government, which held

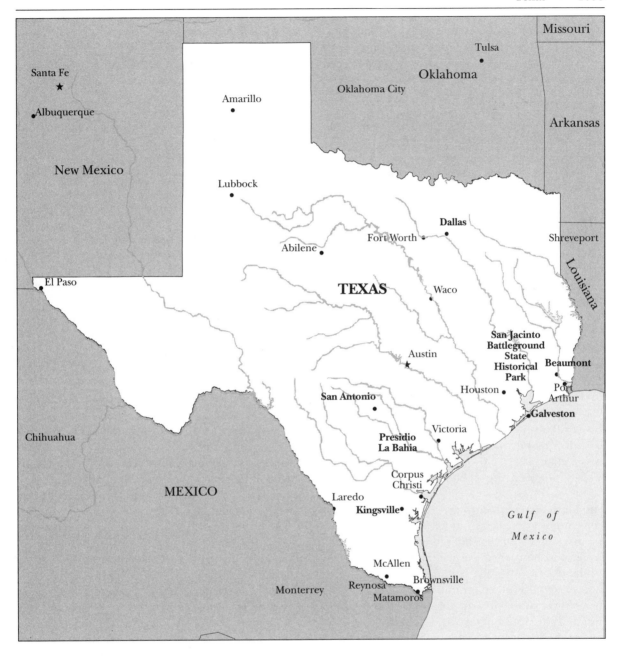

claims to the region, tried unsuccessfully to discourage American immigration. Tensions arose between the United States and Mexico, which objected to the presence of slavery in Texas. In 1836 Texas declared its independence as the Republic of Texas, a status it held until it was annexed as the twenty-eighth state of the United States in 1845.

Cotton, an important crop in eastern Texas during its early settlement, made slave labor attractive to those who raised cotton. With slavery as a part of Texan economy, Texas joined the Confederate States of America in 1861, sixteen years after it had gained admission to the Union.

The Early Texas Economy
Agriculture became a major element in the early economy of Texas, some 85 percent of whose land consists of farms and ranches. Cattle and poultry

production are significant in the state. Citrus fruit was grown early in the southern areas along the Gulf of Mexico and Rio Grande River. Industry was slow to develop in the nineteenth century, largely because Texas did not have sufficient hydroelectric power to drive mechanized industry.

Texas came into its own economically after 1901 when the great Spindletop Oil Field was discovered in southeastern Texas near Beaumont. This discovery triggered a rush to explore other parts of the state for oil, and it was soon found that Texas rested on a huge subterranean sea of oil that extended beyond its land mass into the Gulf of Mexico. Natural gas was also discovered in such quantities that Texas supplied more than a third of the nation's supply.

The oil rush brought enormous revenues into Texas and created hundreds of millionaires almost overnight. The state's population grew from about three million in 1900 to almost four million in 1910, partly because of oil. By 1990, Texas had almost seventeen million residents, making it the third most populous of the United States. By 1998, it was home to slightly less than twenty million.

The sale of oil and natural gas was important to the Texas economy. The discovery of these two fuels spurred the growth of manufacturing industries in the state, which now had the reasonable and ready supply of energy it had previously lacked.

The Move to Manufacturing
Contemporary Texas is one of the ten most productive manufacturing states in the Union. Oil refining and petrochemical companies are among the largest manufacturing industries in the state, most of them centered around the Houston-Beaumont-Port Arthur area in the southeastern portion. In 1961 Houston was chosen as the location of the Manned Spacecraft Center, at which astronauts are trained. It is the control center for the U.S. government's manned space ventures. The establishment of this center brought into Texas considerable other industry that focuses on the manufacture of transportation equipment, including aircraft, automobile assembly plants, and mobile-home manufacturing.

Giant food processing plants grew up to process the livestock, poultry, and vegetables the state produces in abundance. Texas is also preeminent in the manufacturing of machinery, including the com-

plex equipment used in oil exploration and drilling. A thriving mining industry exists, along with extensive textile, clothing, and timber operations.

Transportation
Because of its enormous size, Texas early developed a comprehensive transportation system that, in the early days, involved boat transportation along the Gulf of Mexico and on it rivers, as well as rail transportation served by fourteen thousand miles of track. As the highway system grew to the point that it was the largest in the United States, with sixty-five thousand miles of paved roads, Texans relied more on automobiles than on trains for transportation, so passenger service waned.

In the late twentieth century, Texas had splendid air transportation. The climate is good for flying and the distances make it the most reasonable means of rapid transport. In 1974, the opening of the Dallas-Fort Worth International Airport, the third largest airport in the world, established Texas as an important hub for many national and international airlines. This airport has the second greatest passenger volume in the United States.

Texas Politics
Texas represents an interesting mix of political conservatism and populism. Texans are staunch individualists, yet the state was essentially a one-party state until the election of George W. Bush as its Republican governor in 1994.

Realizing that Texas is a politically important state, with thirty-two electoral votes, national politicians have flocked to it looking for support. Among these was President John F. Kennedy, who went to Texas in November, 1963, to support Democrats running for public office and to help assure his own victory there when he ran for reelection in 1964. Kennedy was assassinated in Dallas by Lee Harvey Oswald. He was succeeded by his vice president, Texan Lyndon Baines Johnson, who remained in office until 1969.

Modern Population
Texas has always had a mix of cultures. In the southern areas along the Rio Grande River live many people of Mexican descent, some of whose families have lived there for two hundred years. These people are technically American citizens, but their ties to Mexico remain strong. The Anglo-American

population includes not only people of British extraction but also large numbers of Germans, in San Antonio, New Braunfels, Seguin, and other towns in central Texas. Eastern and southern Europeans are well represented in the state's population, as are people from the Middle Eastern countries, especially the major oil-producing ones.

In the late twentieth century, about one-third of all Texans were of African American or Hispanic lineage. Spanish is a second language throughout much of Texas and is used along with English in most of its restaurants, hotels, and stores.

—*R. Baird Shuman*

The Alamo

Date: Founded in 1718; under siege from
February 23-March 6, 1836
Relevant issues: Disasters and tragedies, military history
Significance: First founded as a Franciscan mission in 1718, the Alamo was destroyed by a hurricane in 1744. By 1756, the mission church was reconstructed at its present location. In 1836, 180 Texans defended the Alamo for two weeks against a Mexican army numbering 5,000. The three-acre compound was surrounded by stone walls, approximately eleven feet high and three feet thick. A corral and the long barracks were northwest of the church, and the low barracks were behind the southern wall.
Location: Alamo Plaza, downtown San Antonio between Commerce and Houston Streets
Site Office:
The Alamo
P.O. Box 2599
San Antonio, TX 78299
ph.: (210) 225-1391
fax: (210) 229-1343
Web site: www.thealamo.org

The Alamo was the site of one of the most dramatic battles ever fought, but it was never intended to be a military fortress. In 1718, Spanish Franciscans living in Mexico sent Father Antonio Olivares to the San Antonio River with the purpose of starting a mission in what was then Mexican territory. With the authority of Don Martin de Alarcón, military governor of Texas, Olivares estab-

lished a site for a fort and village. Seventy-two settlers, priests, and soldiers migrated to the area from Mexico, and built a mission named after San Antonio de Valero, the viceroy of Mexico.

Early History
The Valero mission was founded in May, 1718, along with the village of San Antonio de Bexar, four hundred yards west, and the smaller Villa Bexar to the south. The mission would not be known as the Alamo until one hundred years later, when Spanish troops from Alamo de Parras named the mission after their hometown. The construction of the present Alamo began in 1756, after a hurricane and fire destroyed the first stone church in 1744.

Between 1680 and 1793, Spain founded thirty-six missions in Texas for the purpose of expanding its religious and political influence. For several decades the Franciscan friars used the Valero mission as a place to convert local Indians to Catholicism. The Payaya and Coahuiltecan tribes faced serious threats from the Apache, who were in turn being pushed south by the Comanche of the high plains. Disease and the Comanche decimated the mission's farming population and livestock, so the Franciscans moved their efforts to a nearby church in 1793. By this date San Antonio had developed into the most important frontier outpost and the provincial capital of Texas.

Texas Independence Movement
A group called the American Volunteers tried to make Texas a republic in 1813, issuing a Declaration of Independence based on the U.S. model. Their efforts were short-lived; a Mexican republican named Bernardo Gutiérrez de Lara rejected the Declaration and issued a Mexican Constitution. During this period before the Texas Revolution, the Spanish army used the mission as a barracks and armory. In December, 1835, a Mexican garrison led by General Martín Perfecto de Cós defended the Alamo against Texans for six weeks, a standoff known as the Siege of Bexar. After Ben Milam called for volunteers, Cós surrendered and Texas held the Alamo until Antonio López de Santa Anna's attack on March 6, 1836.

The story of the stand at the Alamo begins with slavery. Stephen Fuller Austin led U.S. settlers into Texas after Mexican authorities decided this move would help drive Indians out of the territory. By

1830, twenty thousand of these settlers had answered the call to cheap, fertile land in Texas. Many of these Americans owned slaves, however, a practice prohibited by the Mexican government. In 1834, after Austin requested independence for his slaveowning Texans as a prelimary action to joining the United States, he was arrested and jailed by Mexico. President Santa Anna of Mexico then ordered immediate acceptance of his unified constitution for Mexico and its territories.

Until 1835-1836, many Texans were divided over the issue of independence from Mexico. The Consultation of November, 1835, at San Felipe compromised, with delegates electing a legislative council that favored making Texas a self-governing Mexican state, but vesting executive authority in Governor Henry Smith, an advocate of independence. The Texan revolt against Mexico in 1835 was a reaction to the governance of Santa Anna, who revoked several rights of the 1824 Mexican Constitution. After years of disagreement, Texans chose to secede.

In January, 1836, the legislative council of Texas approved a ridiculous plan to invade Matamoros, a small town at the mouth of the Rio Grande. The council believed the action would be a gesture of support for the Constitution of 1824 while advancing statehood as well. Hearing news of a Mexican offensive, Governor Smith and General Sam Houston strongly dissented from the Matamoros expedition. Both men agreed it was logical that Mexico would strike the Alamo first. Smith became outraged after two hundred men left the Alamo for a rendezvous at Goliad, leaving only eighty men to defend the outpost. Although Houston was commander in chief of the Texas army, he could not order the Goliad troops to return since the legislative council had appointed James Fannin as the supreme commander in Goliad.

On January 14, Houston received a letter from Colonel James Neill that complained about problems at the Alamo: "We are in a torpid, defenseless situation, we have not horses enough to send out a patrole or spy." The poor conditions and morale convinced Houston to abandon the outpost. He sent Colonel Jim Bowie and thirty men to Neill's aid, with orders to blow up and evacuate the mission. Bowie was a respected frontiersman, and his daring escapades with a double-edged knife were recounted all over Texas, but he was not a military strategist. After arriving at the Alamo on January 19, Bowie challenged Houston's orders by deciding to defend the mission. The few defenders would have the advantage of a well-stocked armory left behind by General Cós.

Green B. Jameson, a twenty-nine-year-old lawyer from San Felipe and a military engineer, noted the Alamo's glaring weaknesses. Jameson wrote to Sam Houston on January 18, "You can plainly see that the Alamo never was built by a military people for a fortress." The old mission was built around a rectangular courtyard that ran north and south. This three-acre space was surrounded by stone walls, twelve feet high in some areas, with a thickness between two and three feet. The church, located at the southeast corner of the mission,

The Alamo. (PhotoDisc)

was damaged by now. Its towers and dome had collapsed into the nave, but the stone walls remained. The church itself was sturdy, but it was set back from the compound, leaving a fifty-yard space in the southeast corner. A two-story structure called the long barracks stood slightly northwest of the church, and the one-story low barracks were located behind the southern wall. Two corrals were nestled between the long barracks and the church.

Fortification of the Alamo

As the Texans learned that the Mexican cavalry was heading for San Antonio, Jameson led the fortification effort. The mission walls lacked the embrasures and barbettes of a fortress, but makeshift defenses were quickly installed. Jameson closed the space in the southeast corner with a palisade of stakes and dirt, created parapets and gun mounts made from earth and timber, and stationed their most powerful cannon, an eighteen-pounder, in the southwest corner, facing the town. Captain Almeron Dickinson organized the mounting of twenty guns.

As Bowie's determination to defend the Alamo increased, his physical condition deteriorated from a disease later diagnosed as tuberculosis. Having learned that Mexican General Ramirez y Sesma's force was approaching, with five thousand Mexicans following close behind, Bowie wrote a letter to Governor Smith

> The salvation of Texas depends in great measure on keeping Bexar out of the hands of the enemy. It serves as the frontier picquet guard, and if it were in the possession of Santa Anna, there is no stronghold from which to repel him in his march toward the Sabine. Colonel Neill and myself have come to the solemn resolution that we will rather die in these ditches than give it up to the enemy.

On February 3, the day after Bowie sent his letter, Colonel William B. Travis arrived at the Alamo with thirty volunteers, ranging from a Baptist minister to a medical student. Next to arrive were Davy Crockett and a group of twelve men. Reputed as a vicious Indian fighter and an excellent marksman, Crockett had spent time in the Tennessee legislature and U.S. Congress. After failing to get re-elected to Congress in 1835, Crockett reportedly told his constituents that he was going to Texas and they could go to hell.

Members of the Garrison

By February 10, an assortment of other volunteers had trickled in. The Alamo's garrison numbered 142. They differed in nationality and profession; some were city dwellers, others roamed the frontier. The youngest man of the garrison was eighteen-year-old William Malone, who had recently run away from his home in Georgia. Robert Moore, a fifty-five-year-old private from Virginia, was the oldest. The New Orleans Greys, who arrived in Texas in November, 1835, were the only formal military group. In his diary, a member of Santa Anna's force had recorded seeing a blue flag—the flag of the New Orleans Greys—flying above the Alamo's church.

After receiving months of training near Saltillo, Mexico, Santa Anna's army had departed for Texas on January 26. Three infantry brigades were commanded by Generals Urrea, Gaona, and Tolsa; General Andrade headed the cavalry. About 4,100 men and a dozen cannon reached the Rio Grande on February 12, where General Sesma and 1,500 men joined the Mexican advance. Sam Houston feared for the Texans in San Antonio.

During a party to celebrate Crockett's arrival, a courier arrived with news of Santa Anna's progress. Bowie, Travis, and Crockett gathered to discuss their options, but Neill was excluded from the gathering. Neill's stint as commander was over; he appointed Travis as the new commander and left the compound on "sick leave." Since Travis was only twenty-six, most of the volunteers voiced their preference for Bowie. Travis settled the conflict with a vote, and Bowie won by a landslide. By February 14, however, Bowie allowed Travis equal share of the Alamo's command; Travis would assume a greater share as Bowie's illness progressed.

Santa Ana Advances on San Antonio

After increasing reports of an advancing Mexican army, civilians began fleeing San Antonio on the morning of February 23. A disbelieving Travis sent two men, John Sutherland and John Smith, to investigate. The Texans rode their horses to a hill south of town and spotted a fully equipped cavalry of nearly four hundred soldiers, assembled in battle formation. As the men galloped back to town, shouting warnings, Sutherland's horse fell and landed on his legs. Hearing the cries of the Texans, a lookout in San Antonio began ringing the bell of the San Fernando Church.

Panicked townspeople fled their houses and stores, gathering whatever possessions they could. Texans raced up Potrero Street, seizing grain and military equipment from surrounding huts and herding thirty cattle into the Alamo's corral. Bowie guided the two sisters of his late wife into the Alamo. Other friends and relatives of the Texan volunteers huddled in the rooms of the church, a haven save for the stores of gunpowder. Several black slaves were brought in as servants.

Travis assigned Crockett to the Alamo's weakest position, the southeast gap between the church and the low barracks. The young commander decided there was time to call for volunteers. He scrawled a desperate letter: "The enemy in large force is in sight. We want men and provisions. Send them to us. We have 150 men and are determined to defend the Alamo to the last. Give us assistance." Travis addressed the note "To any of the inhabitants of Texas" and ordered an injured John Sutherland and John Smith to deliver it to Gonzales, Texas.

After arriving in San Antonio, Santa Anna's troops hung a red banner, the Mexican symbol for no surrender, from the San Fernando church. This told the Texans, eight hundred yards away, that they would have to fight to the death. Travis responded by firing a shot from the eighteen-pounder. East of the Alamo, James Butler Bonham heard the cannon as he returned from Goliad, where Colonel James Fannin had refused to send reinforcements. Interpreting the shot as a last call for help, Bonham stepped up his progress. On the morning of March 3, he would be the last man to enter the Alamo, raising the number of defenders to 183.

Call for Unconditional Surrender

Inside, the Texans heard a Mexican bugle call and some thought it meant a chance to negotiate. Without consulting Travis, Bowie sent a messenger to ask if the Texans could surrender and reestablish residence in San Antonio. Under a white flag, Jameson carried the message but returned with the news that the Mexicans demanded an unconditional surrender. Another cannon shot resounded

from the Alamo, and both sides made final preparations for war.

At dawn on February 24 the Mexicans began their assault with sporadic artillery fire from a riverbank four hundred yards away. For the rest of the day, two nine-pounders bombarded the fort while a five-inch howitzer scattered shots into the courtyard. Travis, unshaken, wrote a second message that would eventually focus the world's attention on the rout in San Antonio:

> Fellow citizens & compatriots—I am besieged, by a thousand or more of the Mexicans under Santa Anna—I have sustained a continual Bombardment & cannonade for 24 hours & have not lost a man—The enemy has demanded a surrender at discretion, otherwise, the garrison are to be put to the sword, if the fort is taken—I have answered the demand with a cannon shot, & our flag still waves proudly from the walls—I shall never surrender or retreat. Then, I call on you in the name of liberty, of patriotism & everything dear to the American character, to come to our aid, with all dispatch—The enemy is receiving reinforcements daily & will no doubt increase to three or four thousand in four or five days. If this call is neglected, I am determined to sustain myself as long as possible & die like a soldier who never forgets what is due to his own honor & that of his country—Victory or Death.

Though the note itself was sent to Gonzales, Texas, addressed "To the People of Texas & all Americans in the world," its message spread to New Orleans, New York, Boston, and Europe. Travis's passionate plea would eventually unite the country behind Texas and inspire U.S. troops to avenge the Texans' deaths at the Alamo.

Travis sent his request with Captain Albert Martin while a second courier went southeast to Goliad, arriving on February 26. Here, Colonel Fannin finally responded, leaving his outpost and heading west with 320 men. Led by a reluctant Fannin, the relief expedition encountered several problems. First the group's supply wagon broke down, and the entire garrison was ordered to wait until the wagon could be repaired. By dusk, Fannin decided to delay the trek until morning, but during the night several oxen wandered off and it took his men all day to recapture them. Late in the afternoon of February 27, Fannin's doubts got the best of him. Intimidated at the prospect of facing thousands of Mexican troops, he rationalized that Goliad would be defenseless if they proceeded.

As Fannin's men returned to Fort Defiance in Goliad, Mexican forces led by General Urrea annihilated the Matamoros expedition at San Patricio, fifty miles south. On February 24, the message sent with Sutherland and Smith arrived at Gonzales, seventy miles east of San Antonio. With Smith as a guide, a twenty-five-man militia company under George Kimbell departed on the 27th. Before leaving town, the soldiers stopped at the residence of John G. King, where fifteen-year-old William King asked to go in place of his father. Kimbell agreed to the trade.

On the night of February 29, the Gonzales company secretly crept through the Mexican lines and arrived at the Alamo walls by 3 A.M. on March 1. A Texan sentry, assuming they were Mexicans, began firing on them, shooting one man in the foot. When a militiaman from Gonzales shouted a familiar oath, the main gate was opened and the men entered before Mexican patrols could respond. Though the reinforcements were immediately welcomed with boisterous approval, Travis was disheartened by the meager number.

Not one Texan was killed during the first week of fighting. The initial melee occurred when a Mexican scouting party was driven back with heavy rifle and cannon fire. The next day, Texans set fire to several wooden shacks near the mission after the Mexicans tried to use the area for a gun emplacement.

During the night, the enemy's gun batteries drew closer as Santa Anna gradually compressed his encirclement. Mexican soldiers dug trenches behind shacks and constructed battery emplacements, avoiding the deadly area within two hundred yards of the fortress. When Travis sent another call for assistance, the messenger escaped by pretending to be a Mexican soldier.

The Second Week of the Siege

In between the sporadic Mexican advances, the Texans worked hard at strengthening the Alamo's walls, digging trenches, and remounting guns. Sometimes the ailing Bowie had his cot carried among the soldiers so he could continue his command. One of the Mexican officers, Captain Rafael Soldana, recalled a man who fought bravely from the Alamo's palisade. Most likely, it is Davy Crockett, as he describes "a tall man, with flowing hair" who

> wore a buckskin suit and a cap all of a pattern entirely different from those worn by his comrades. This man would rest his long gun and fire, and we all learned to keep at a good distance when he was seen to make ready to shoot. He rarely missed his mark, and when he fired he always rose to his feet and calmly reloaded his gun, seemingly indifferent to the shots fired at him by our men. He had a strong, resonant voice and often railed at us.

A cold snap hit San Antonio for two days. The Texans struggled to keep warm while protecting themselves from the Mexican bombardment. Trying to destroy his foes psychologically, Santa Anna ordered his men to maintain their taunts, bugle calls, and nightly shelling. As a morale booster, Crockett entertained the men with his fiddle while John McGregor played his bagpipes; the two men even contested to see who could play loudest. Only one defender, Henry Warnell, expressed the confining dread most of the men felt: "I'd much rather be out in that open prairie. . . . I don't like to be penned up like this."

On March 3, Santa Anna's army of 2,500 men received more reinforcements, and the Mexicans drew closer. Travis sent a final grim message: "I feel confident that the determined valor and desperate courage of my men will not fail them. . . . Although they may be sacrificed to the vengeance of a Gothic enemy, the victory will cost the enemy so dear, it will be worse for him than a defeat."

A burst of renewed shelling bombarded the crumbling Alamo on the dawn of March 4. The Texans had withstood an eleven-day siege thus far, but Travis became aware their time was running out. On March 5, he called a meeting and offered the following terms to his men: Anyone who wanted to leave could do so, but whoever stayed had to fight to the death. Legend has it that Travis drew a line in the dirt with his sword and asked those who wanted to stay to cross the line. Only one man chose to leave.

The Final Mexican Assault

March 5 also found Santa Anna completing a plan of attack. The next morning his army would simultaneously converge on all sides of the Alamo. Colonel Morales and one hundred men would storm Crockett's palisade, Colonel Duque and three hundred men would storm the northeast, Romero would attack the area by the corrals with another three hundred, and General Cós would strike the northwest side with four hundred. East of the Alamo, Sesma's cavalry would patrol for anyone attempting to escape.

At 5:00 in the morning on March 6, the Mexicans began their charge with bugle calls and a cry of "Viva Santa Anna." The Mexican army band played the Degnello, a death march. Duque's men hit first, assailing the north wall carrying twenty-eight ladders. Texans raced to their positions, where five guns lay ready by each man, and immediately fired upon the mass of climbing bodies. Santa Anna watched the smoky confusion from the north. His rear column tried to aim for the Texans, but killed dozens of Mexicans near the walls as others dove for cover. On the north parapet, next to the fourteen-pounder, a bullet struck Travis in the middle of the forehead, immediately killing him.

Waves of Mexicans charged the east, south, and west sides, but steady rifle and artillery fire repulsed the initial assault. The Mexican columns regrouped and started a second assault, suffering scores of fatalities as they were driven back once again. The third attempt at overtaking the Alamo proved deadly. Santa Anna dispatched his reserves to help with Duque's column, and Romero's eastern column merged with the northern attack just as they managed to breach a fortified hole of timbers.

General Cós and his northwestern column shifted east, joining the two columns surging into the fort. The Texans turned their cannon around and blasted the swarming intruders, but their numbers were overwhelming. Crockett's men retreated as Morales's southern attack breached the makeshift palisade and took the eighteen-pounder. His troops opened the main gate, allowing entrance to a swirling tide of Mexicans.

Surrounded on all four sides, with no time to reload, the Texans engaged in desperate hand-to-hand combat as they struggled across the plaza to the long and low barracks. As planned, the defenders made their last stand within these fortified shelters. Earthen barricades had been constructed in front of all five doors to block the flood of bodies, and newly created loopholes allowed the Texans to let loose a cascade of bullets, killing countless Mexicans.

Crockett's Tennesseans, cut off from the barracks, viciously retaliated, one man killing eight Mexicans. From the north wall, near Travis's body, Mexicans trained the fourteen-pounder on the barracks; Mexicans on the south wall did the same with the eighteen-pounder. Cannon fire obliterated the parapets, followed by a volley of rifle fire while Mexicans stormed the buildings. The remaining Texans were clubbed or stabbed with bayonets, including Bowie as he lay on his cot.

With only minutes left, Captain Dickinson and thirteen men continued fighting from within the church, hitting their foe with grapeshot. Once again, the eighteen-pounder was used, this time to blast the church. Brandishing a torch, defender Robert Evans attempted to light the powder magazine before getting cut down. Clutching her daughter, Susannah Dickinson sat mourning by her dead husband. A desperate Jacob Walker burst into the room searching for a hiding place but was immediately killed.

Surrender of the Last Defenders

General Castrillón confronted the last seven defenders inside the church. He ordered his men to cease their attack and allowed the Texans to surrender. Castrillón pleaded on the captives' behalf, but Santa Anna ordered their immediate execution. Ten noncombatants were spared: Bowie's two sisters-in-law; the widow of Gregorio Esparza and her four children; other Mexican women and children; and Joe, Travis's servant.

The number of Mexican casualties is uncertain, as no two sources agree. Although the majority of Texan sources claim one thousand casualties, the best estimate is two hundred killed and four hundred wounded, or six hundred total casualties. Many of the wounded later died as a result of poor medical treatment.

Legacy of the Battle

A giant funeral fire in the Alamo's plaza served as the burial ground for 183 Texans. Though Santa Anna tried to conceal the modest number of men who had resisted his forces, claiming six hundred Texans and seventy Mexicans were killed, the harm inflicted at the Alamo would soon be evident. Regardless of the Mexican casualties, a small group of Texans had delayed Santa Anna's advancing army for two weeks. Their stand provided General Sam Houston with enough time to mobilize his army.

Also, the slaughter in San Antonio enraged Americans as no victory could have. News of Travis's messages for help inflamed emotions and guilt. Soldiers from Goliad and elsewhere were shamed by their failure to answer the call. William Gray predicted that "Texas will take honor to herself for defense of the Alamo and will call it a second Thermopylae, but it will be an everlasting monument of national disgrace."

Texan Reprisals Against the Mexicans

Seven weeks after the Alamo, Gray's prophesy rang true as four hundred Texans avenged their brethren with a massacre of Mexican forces at the San Jacinto River. Late in the afternoon of April 21, as they swept the ranks of Santa Anna, Houston's army finally responded to Travis with the battle cry, "Remember the Alamo." After a battle that killed six hundred Mexicans and only nine Texans, Santa Anna and six hundred fifty soldiers were taken prisoner. Some four thousand Mexican troops retreated to Mexico and Texas won its independence. Texas remained independent for nearly a decade, with its entrance into the United States delayed by controversy surrounding admission of another slave state. Finally, on December 29, 1845, it became the twenty-eighth state of the Union.

The Alamo in Later Years

The U.S. Army renovated the buildings at the Alamo in 1849. They went through a variety of uses in subsequent years. A store was built over the long barracks in 1876, and the church, sold to the state of Texas in 1883, was used as a warehouse. In 1903 the long barracks property was put up for sale as a hotel site. To prevent the sale, Clara Driscoll, a member of the Daughters of the Republic of Texas, bought the property.

In 1905, the state repaid Driscoll and turned all the Alamo buildings and grounds over to the Daughters of the Republic of Texas, to maintain and operate as long as the group could do so at no cost to the state. The group has turned the former church into a shrine to those who died in the battle, and made the long barracks into a museum. These are the only original structures remaining, but the Alamo grounds also house the Texas Historical Research Library of the Daughters of the Republic of Texas.   —*Richard Trout*

For Further Information:

Davis, William C. "Remember the Alamo!" *American History Illustrated*, October, 1967. A short, less descriptive article than the one by Hutton below.

Hoyt, Edwin P. *The Alamo: An Illustrated History*. Dallas: Taylor, 1999. A pictorial work about the history behind and siege of the Alamo.

Hutton, Paul Andrew. "The Alamo: An American Epic." *American History Illustrated*, March, 1986. This thorough article features interspersed biographies of Travis, Bowie, and Crockett.

Lord, Walter. *A Time to Stand: The Epic of the Alamo*. Lincoln: University of Nebraska Press, 1961. A book that maintains an excellent balance between facts and narration. Lord has drawn from an extensive array of sources—accounts by participants, contemporary letters, and land office records. Remarkably detailed, the story is engagingly told from the perspective of the major players—Travis, Bowie, Santa Anna, and even Colonel Fannin.

Nevins, David. *Texans*. New York: Time-Life Books, 1975. Provides a thirty-page chapter, "The Alamo: Victory in Death," which effectively summarizes the major events. The beautiful color illustrations include Santa Anna's map of the battlefield, an easily comprehensible drawing of the Alamo, and paintings of the defenders.

Beaumont

Date: Established on December 16, 1838

Relevant issues: Business and industry

Significance: This town is the site of the Lucas Gusher at Spindletop on January 10, 1901, making Beaumont the birthplace of the Texas oil industry. It features the Lucas Gusher Monument, dedicated on January 10, 1951, and now designated a National Historic Landmark.

Location: Thirty-five miles from the Gulf of Mexico, on the shores of the Neches River, in Jefferson County

Site Office:
Beaumont Convention and Visitors' Bureau
801 Main Street #100
Beaumont, TX 77701-3548
ph.: (409) 880-3749

Beaumont traces its roots back to the settlement started by Noah and Nancy Tevis on the banks of the Neches River around 1825. The settlement of Tevis Bluff soon became a fur trading center for the area. In 1835, Henry Millard bought fifty acres from Noah Tevis and began planning the community of Beaumont. According to one account, the town was named for his wife, Mary Warren Beaumont. According to another account, Beaumont was the name of a pioneer family in the area. A third version indicates that the name derived from the French words "beautiful hill" and referred to Big Hill (now known as Spindletop), to the southeast of town.

The town was formally established on December 16, 1838, and became the seat of what is today Jefferson County. By 1840 Beaumont's major industry was lumber. The market for lumber grew significantly as the South began rebuilding after the U.S. Civil War. Four sawmills were built between 1876 and 1878, and within twenty years these mills had an average daily output of 200,000 feet. Beaumont's other major industry was rice. Local cultivation of the crop had begun as early as the 1840's, and with advances in irrigation toward the end of the century, the harvests grew rapidly. A large rice mill was opened in 1892, and by 1900 nearly six thousand acres were being cultivated.

Discovery of Oil
The town's population was then eighty-five hundred, and it probably would have remained at that level had oil not been discovered a year later. The story of the Texas oil industry began with a one-armed mechanic, brick maker, and Sunday school teacher named Patillo Higgins. During business trips associated with his brick plant, Higgins first came into contact with oil drilling. His knowledge

The McFaddin-Ward House in Beaumont. (Beaumont Convention & Visitors Bureau)

of geology was limited to what he had picked up through reading and during his travels, but he soon became convinced that the Gulf coast contained large oil deposits. Higgins quit the brick business and took up real estate.

While leading a Sunday school outing to Big Hill, Higgins found what he had been looking for: five springs, eight feet deep, with multicolored water and gas bubbling to the surface. Based on what he had taught himself of geology, he believed that Big Hill was sitting on a huge pool of oil. Higgins began looking for ways to acquire land on the site, and in 1892 he lined up several local investors to form the Gladys City Oil, Gas, and Manufacturing Company (named for one of the girls from the Sunday school outing). The company acquired more than 2,500 acres and began drilling. Unfortunately, little was known at this time of the drilling techniques needed for the Gulf coast's soft strata, and the wells they drilled proved failures.

His funds exhausted, Higgins began searching for new capital to continue. The civic leaders in Beaumont had given up on him—some even said he was insane—and such notable contemporary geologists as William Kennedy had declared that there was no oil to be found anywhere on the Gulf coast, let alone in Beaumont. Ultimately, Higgins resorted to placing an advertisement in a manufacturing journal.

The advertisement was seen by Anthony F. Lucas, an engineer who supervised the drilling operations at several Louisiana salt mines. He had frequently found oil in these salt domes, and he felt that the dome beneath Big Hill might also cover such deposits. In June, 1899, Lucas put $31,150 into the operation and became the major investor; Higgins was left with only a 10 percent share.

Difficulties of Drilling
Lucas's initial drilling attempts were promising. Traces of gas and oil were discovered, but he had to stop at 575 feet due to gas pressure that was too great for his light equipment. By this time, however, he had run out of funds and was unable to purchase heavy equipment he needed. Lucas sought backing from Standard Oil but was turned away empty-handed. Finally, Professor William Battle Phillips of the University of Texas heard of the attempts to drill for oil on Big Hill. Phillips became the country's first leading geologist to approve of

the project, and his influence won Lucas a hearing with the nation's premier wildcatters: the Pittsburgh partnership of James McClurg Guffey and John H. Galey.

Guffey was a flamboyant promoter and businessman; Galey was a wildcatter so skilled at locating drilling sites that some said he could smell oil. Together they were responsible for the successful wells at Corsicana, Texas, in 1896. They knew there was oil on the Gulf coast and agreed to drill three 1,200-foot wells for Lucas. As part of the financing agreement, however, Lucas's share was cut to a mere one-eighth. Higgins retained his thirty-three-acre holding on Spindletop, but he was cut out of the new deal altogether. (Higgins eventually sued the others and reached a settlement out of court.)

To drill the well, Galey contacted Jim Hamill, who had pioneered rotary drilling techniques at Corsicana. Hamill, along with his brothers Curt and Al, came to Beaumont and began drilling on October 27, 1900. The drill site that Galey had chosen was not far from the bubbling springs seen by Patillo Higgins on the Sunday school picnic. Galey promised "the biggest oil well this side of Baku" (the oil-rich city on the Caspian Sea).

Adoption of the Name "Spindletop"
By this time, Big Hill was known as Spindletop. Once again, there are several explanations for the name: It derived either from a pine tree that had grown like an inverted top; from the effect of heat waves on the hill, which made the trees look from a distance as if they were spinning; or from the bare masts of schooners visible above the trees of a nearby spring.

In early December, the Hamills had drilled to 870 feet and found the first traces of oil. Soon thereafter, however, they encountered problems with sand washing up through the pipe and were ready to abandon the well. According to one source, Lucas's wife personally persuaded Galey to continue drilling. By January, 1901, Al Hamill, along with his brother Curt and fellow driller Peck Byrd, were manning the rig twenty-four hours a day. At 10:00 A.M. on January 10, while they were running a new drill bit into the well, mud began pumping furiously out of the hole. Seven hundred feet of pipe suddenly shot out, smashing through the top of the derrick and breaking apart in midair. Curt Hamill, who was standing atop the derrick, was lucky to have escaped with his life. With mud blinding his eyes and six tons of pipe falling all around him, he somehow hurried down a ladder and scrambled for safety with the other men.

When the mud and rocks stopped shooting from the well, gas briefly flowed out, and then all was quiet. The men ventured back to assess the damage. According to Al Hamill,

> Naturally we were all disgusted. We started shoveling away the mud—when, without warning, a lot of heavy mud shot out of the well with the report of a cannon. It was followed for a short time with gas, then oil showed up in head flows. In a very short time oil was going up through the top of the derrick and rocks were being shot hundreds of feet into the air. Within a very few minutes the oil was holding a steady flow at more than twice the height of the derrick.

They immediately sent for Lucas. As Lucas approached the drill site, he became so excited that he jumped out of his horse-drawn buggy and ran up to the well, shouting "Al! Al! What is it?" When he learned it was oil, Lucas hugged Al Hamill and exclaimed "Thank God, thank God!"

An Unstoppable Gusher
Oil was flowing from the gusher at an estimated rate of 70,000 to 100,000 barrels per day. The Hamills were unprepared for such a flow—they had no tanks to hold the oil and no way to shut it off. It was ten days before they were finally able to cap the well, working from plans drawn by Peck Byrd on a brown paper bag. In the meantime, up to 800,000 barrels of oil had soaked into the ground surrounding Spindletop. A minor fire broke out on January 12, and a more serious one erupted a month later. Sulfuric gas fumes from the oil spray stained all the houses in Beaumont.

The town soon had plenty of money for repainting. News of the well spread quickly throughout the country and the world. Within two days a thousand people had descended on the town. In a few months, the town's population went from eighty-five hundred to fifty thousand. All these people wanted land for drilling, and the price of real estate skyrocketed. Land that had once sold for $10 an acre now went for up to $900,000. Many of the land deals were fraudulent, and the area soon became known as "Swindletop." According to one witness, so much money changed hands that the town's sole bank was overwhelmed: "They just shipped money in there by the sackfuls. Got where the bank wouldn't accept any deposits, because they had it piled up in sacks around the lobby."

A writer from *Harper's Weekly* reported that Beaumont had been transformed into "the dirtiest, noisiest, busiest, and most interesting town on the continent to-day." Crime was rampant. The town averaged two or three murders a night, and sixteen men were found one morning floating in the Neches River with their throats cut. The police chief advised citizens who traveled at night to walk in the middle of the street and carry a gun: "An' tote 'em in your hands, not on your hips, so everybody can see you're loaded." Prostitutes were ubiquitous; according to historian Daniel Yergin, the police began holding public hearings in which "each woman's fine was announced, and the man who paid it could keep her for twenty-four hours."

Competition for Control
Because Texas politicians were openly hostile toward Standard Oil, the giant company was largely kept out of open deals at Spindletop. This cleared the way for other oil companies. James Hogg, the former governor of Texas, together with Joe Cullinan, a leading figure in the Corsicana oil industry, and John W. "Bet-a-Million" Gates, a New York businessman who reputedly would bet on anything, formed the Texas Fuel Company, later known as Texaco, to tap Spindletop's riches. The Sun Oil Company, of Pennsylvania, also invested in Beaumont. Standard Oil itself made several secret investments in the region, including the creation of the Magnolia Petroleum Company, a predecessor of Mobil Oil.

Meanwhile, Guffey entered into a contract with Sir Marcus Samuel, the head of Shell Transport and Trading Company in Britain. Upon reading of the Lucas Gusher, Samuel immediately saw the opportunity to beat out his chief competitor, Standard Oil, and to achieve his dream of converting the shipping industry from coal to petroleum fuel. In June, 1901, Samuel agreed to buy half of Guffey's annual production at twenty-five cents a barrel. The deal was to last for twenty-one years and include a minimum of 14.7 million barrels. As the output from Spindletop in 1902 was 17,420,949 barrels, there seemed little danger of supply falling short.

By 1902, however, there were 285 wells on Spindletop. Mineral rights in the United States were at this time governed by the "law of capture," by which oil belonged to whoever owned the drilling site. If several wells were tapping the same oil deposit, it became crucial for each owner to pump as much and as fast as possible. This they did at Spindletop, with disastrous results. Not understanding the importance of maintaining gas pressure to extract the oil, they overproduced; by 1903 the site was becoming depleted. At the same time, Guffey was still under contract with Shell to deliver his quota. Guffey had already bought out partners Galey and Lucas, and he now turned to the Mellon family, who had originally backed his efforts. The Mellons renegotiated the deal with Shell and took over Guffey's company, creating Gulf Oil. Shell's financial difficulties led it into a merger with Royal Dutch Petroleum in 1906.

Bust and Boom

With the boom at Spindletop over, Beaumont became a ghost town. Lucas visited in 1904 and commented "The cow was milked too hard, and moreover, she was not milked intelligently." The Beaumont lumber industry, which had experienced a boom with the demand for derricks and housing, soon slumped. The rice industry continued to grow, however. In 1908 the Neches River was dredged for shipping, and in 1916 a canal was completed to the Gulf of Mexico. Beaumont soon became a major port. The waterways were widened and extended repeatedly over the next twenty years.

In November, 1925, Spindletop shocked the oil industry for a second time. New technology allowed deeper drilling, and a large oil pool was discovered on the flanks of the salt dome. This time production was more carefully managed, and the new pool went on to surpass the first. More than seventy-five million barrels had been produced by 1935. When the owners of the field sold out to Standard Oil in August of that year, they were paid $41.6 million in cash, at that time the third-largest private cash transaction in U.S. history. The site continued as a productive oil field until the 1950's, when it was cleared for sulfur mining.

Modern Beaumont

Today, Beaumont is home to more than 114,000 citizens and continues as a center for the oil, lumber, agriculture, chemical, and mining industries. Visitors to the city can stop at the John Jay French Museum to gain an understanding of life in the town during the mid-nineteenth century. The opulent lifestyle of the early Texas oil elite has been preserved in the McFaddin-Ward House. The Lucas Gusher Monument, a fifty-eight-foot granite obelisk on the site of Lucas's well, was dedicated on January 10, 1951, and has since been designated a National Historic Landmark. A reconstruction of the Gladys City Boomtown was dedicated on January 10, 1976.

The significance of the Lucas Gusher cannot be overstated. It created the Texas oil boom and quite literally fueled the growth of nearby Houston. More important, it ushered in what historian Daniel Yergin has called the "hydrocarbon society." Prior to Spindletop, oil was used mainly to produce kerosene for illumination. Gasoline was a mere byproduct, little valued by refineries. The crude from Spindletop was of too poor a quality to produce kerosene. It therefore was used for heating and to power engines. By the fall of 1901, the massive oil glut in Texas had driven the price down to three cents a barrel, offering huge incentives for industry to convert to oil for fuel. The cheap oil also spurred the popularity of automobiles with internal combustion engines, forever changing the way people lived, worked, and traveled.

—*Robert M. Salkin*

For Further Information:

Dooley-Awbrey, Betty, and Claude Dooley, and the Texas Historical Commission. *Why Stop? A Guide to Texas Historical Roadside Markers.* 4th ed. Houston: Lone Star Books, 1999. A guide to the historical markers and legends of Texas.

Hansen, Harry. *Texas: A Guide to the Lone Star State.* Rev. ed. New York: Hastings House, 1969. Originally compiled by the Federal Writers' Program of the Work Projects Administration in the state of Texas. A good general history of the early days of Beaumont.

Moore, Judy. *Texas Guide.* 2d ed. New York: Open Road, 2000. A guidebook which includes maps.

Presley, James. *A Saga of Wealth: The Rise of the Texas Oilmen.* New York: G. P. Putnam's Sons, 1978. A more detailed description of the events leading up to the discovery of the Lucas Gusher.

Yergin, Daniel. *The Prize: The Epic Quest for Oil, Money, and Power.* New York: Simon & Schuster, 1991. The standard popular history of the oil industry. Its treatment of the oil companies that sprung up in Beaumont is particularly insightful.

Dealey Plaza, Dallas

Date: Assassination of President John F. Kennedy on November 22, 1963

Relevant issues: Disasters and tragedies, political history

Significance: This National Landmark District was the site of the assassination of U.S. president John Fitzgerald Kennedy. In addition to 3.07-acre Dealey Plaza, the district includes the Dallas County Administration Building (formerly the Texas School Book Depository) from which Lee Harvey Oswald allegedly fired the fatal shots; the triple underpass created by the convergence of Commerce, Elm, and Main Streets; and a portion of the railyards just north of Elm Street, including the railroad switching tower.

Location: Dallas; a rectangular park in the westernmost portion of the West End Historic District bounded by Commercial Street on the south and Elm Street on the north

Site Office:
The Sixth Floor
Dallas County Historical Foundation
411 Elm Street
Dallas, TX 75202-3317
ph.: (214) 653-6666

Before U.S. president John F. Kennedy was assassinated in Dallas on November 22, 1963, the small rectangular park named in honor of George Bannerman Dealey was known primarily as part of a plan to create a gateway to the city from the west and to relieve traffic congestion at the railroad tracks leading in and out of Union Station. An advocate of city planning, Dealey was the publisher of the *Dallas Morning News*. He was also president of the West of Commerce Realty Company, which had donated most of the right-of-way west of the underpass to the city. Construction began in 1934 and was completed in 1940. The park included extensive landscaping, Art Deco-style garden structures, and reflecting pools. Felix de Weldon, who sculpted the Iwo Jima Memorial at Arlington National Cemetery, was commissioned to create a twelve-foot bronze statue of George Bannerman Dealey. The statue was dedicated in 1949.

Early History of the Site
The land occupied by Dealey Plaza and the rest of the historic district is part of the original town of Dallas, settled in the early 1840's by John Neely Bryan. In 1849, Bryan sold this land to a homesteader for fifty dollars. The land's ownership had changed twice before it was sold in 1894 to the Southern Rock Island Plow Company. Four years later the company built a five-story warehouse on the corner of Elm and Houston Streets. After the warehouse was struck by lightning and burned to the ground, the company built the current seven-story building in its place. The Carraway-Byrd Corporation purchased the building in 1937 but soon defaulted on the loan. Two years later, local businessman Colonel D. Harold Byrd bought the building at a public auction for thirty-five thousand dollars. In 1963, Byrd was leasing the building to the Texas School Book Depository Company, a textbook brokerage firm.

Three years earlier, John Fitzgerald Kennedy had been elected to the presidency by one of the smallest margins in U.S. history, beating Richard M. Nixon by 34,227,096 to 34,108,546 votes. At age forty-three, Kennedy was the youngest president ever elected; he was also the first Roman Catholic to hold the nation's highest office. His youth and vitality seemed to capture the imagination of the nation. Handsome and witty, Kennedy was also perfectly suited to the new medium of television. His wife, Jackie, and their two young children, Caroline and John Jr., were admired and cherished.

Kennedy's Political Problems in Texas
In spite of the country's fascination with the First Family, not everyone was enamored of Kennedy's political views. His liberal stance on civil rights, his pledge to return civilian control to the Central Intelligence Agency (CIA), and his willingness to communicate with communist nations angered many Americans. Kennedy and his supporters knew that they would have to work hard to earn re-

Dealey Plaza in 1964, a year after President John F. Kennedy was assassinated there. The arrow points to the sixth floor of the former Texas School Book Depository from which Lee Harvey Oswald allegedly fired the fatal shots. (AP/Wide World Photos)

election in 1964. Texas was considered a pivotal state in the election. Kennedy had narrowly carried Texas in 1960, largely as the result of the influence of his running mate, Lyndon Baines Johnson, a native of the state and powerful politician.

In November, 1963, President Kennedy traveled to Texas for a two-day campaign trip. So important was this trip that the administration decided to capitalize on Jackie's popularity by having her accompany him. As an additional show of support, Vice President Johnson and his wife, Lady Bird, as well as Texas governor John Connally and his wife, and Texas senator Ralph Yarborough joined the Kennedys for a ride through Dallas in an open-car motorcade.

Kennedy's Motorcade Through Dallas

After a visit to Fort Worth, the Kennedys arrived at Dallas's Love Field on the morning of Friday, November 22, and drove through the streets of the city on their way to a luncheon at the Trade Mart. An estimated 200,000 people lined the streets to greet the president and his wife. Mrs. Connally turned from her seat in the front of the limousine and remarked, "You can't say the people of Dallas don't love you, Mr. President." Moments later, as the motorcade passed by the Texas School Book Depository and headed for the triple underpass, shots were fired. President Kennedy and Governor Connally slumped in their seats and mass confusion reigned for several moments before the limousine rushed to Parkland Memorial Hospital. There, the president was pronounced dead at 1:00 P.M., Central Standard Time. Although seriously injured, Governor Connally recovered from his wounds.

Eyewitness reports that the shots had been fired from the Texas School Book Depository and from behind the fence above the grassy knoll at Dealey Plaza sent police officers and Secret Service agents in both directions. A depository employee, Lee Harvey Oswald, was stopped in the building's kitchen but released after being identified by a fellow employee. Forty minutes later, police entered the sixth floor of the building and found a barricade constructed of cardboard boxes in the southeast corner where the windows overlooked Dealey Plaza. They also found three spent bullet cartridges and a paper bag. Near the staircase, police found a rifle.

After leaving the Texas School Book Depository, Oswald traveled by bus and taxi to his rooming house but left again quickly. By now, a description of the employee seen in the building's kitchen was being broadcast over police radios. Dallas patrolman J. D. Tippit apparently spotted Oswald and attempted to arrest him. Oswald allegedly killed Tippit and then hid in the Texas Theater where he was apprehended at 1:45 P.M. By the next day, November 23, Oswald was formally charged with the murder of President Kennedy.

Accused Assassin Lee Harvey Oswald

Born in 1939 in New Orleans, Oswald had dropped out of high school and joined the U.S. Marine Corps. In the corps, he learned to be a skilled marksman. He also began to voice support for the Soviet Union and its policies. In September, 1959, Oswald was released from the Marine Corps. He soon left for the Soviet Union where he spent two and one-half years trying, unsuccessfully, to become a Russian citizen. While working in Minsk, Oswald met and married a Soviet woman named Marina Nikolayevna Prusakova. In June, 1962, Oswald was permitted to return to the United States with his wife and their daughter, June Lee.

During the investigations that followed the assassination, officials found that between the summer of 1962 and the fall of 1963, Oswald purchased a .38 caliber revolver, a rifle, and a telescopic sight through the mail; attempted to shoot an ultrarightist, former U.S. Army general named Edwin A. Walker in Dallas; and set up a branch of the Fair Play for Cuba Committee in New Orleans. He also traveled to Mexico City in an attempt to obtain a visa to go to Cuba and to lobby the Soviet Union for permission to return. In October, 1963, he started work at the Texas School Book Depository as an order clerk.

Reaction to Kennedy's Assassination

Many people in the United States and thousands around the world were plunged into shock and disbelief at Kennedy's assassination. In the United States, workers and schoolchildren were sent home early. Schools, government offices, and businesses remained closed all Friday afternoon. Millions spent the weekend in front of their television sets. Certain images would become indelibly imprinted in the public's memory: Jacqueline Kennedy's blood-stained pink suit and stunned face as she witnessed Johnson's hastily arranged oath of office aboard Air Force One; the endless lines of grief-stricken citizens as they filed past the slain president's casket in the rotunda of the Capitol; Kennedy's three-year-old son "John-John" saluting the casket during the funeral procession.

Millions also were watching on November 24 as Dallas policemen transferred Oswald from the City Jail to the County Jail. Jack Ruby, a local nightclub owner, pushed forward from the crowd and shot Oswald once, fatally. Ruby was convicted of murder in March, 1964, and sentenced to death. The verdict was overturned on appeal in 1966, but Ruby would succumb to cancer the following year before the case came to trial.

Creation of the Warren Commission

Seven days after Kennedy's assassination, recently sworn in President Johnson appointed a national commission, headed by Supreme Court Chief Justice Earl Warren, and charged it with determining who was responsible. Rumors of a conspiracy were already circulating. On September 24, 1964, the Warren Commission issued its report, stating that Oswald acted alone. In spite of the report, talk of a conspiracy continued. In the late 1970's, a House of Representatives' Select Committee on Assassinations (by then, civil rights activist Martin Luther King, Jr., and President Kennedy's brother Robert had also been killed by assassins) conducted an investigation based on acoustical information gathered in Dallas. The committee concluded that, while Oswald fired the shots that killed John F. Kennedy, a 95 percent probability existed that a second gunman had fired from behind a grassy knoll in Dealey Plaza. The committee went so far as to concede that a conspiracy "probably" existed.

Further studies based on the acoustical evidence, conducted in 1980 and 1982, resulted in a repudiation of the House Committee's conclusions. In 1988, the Justice Department officially closed its investigation and stated that Oswald acted alone. However, a vast majority of Americans still believe that a conspiracy existed.

Legacy of the Assassination in Dallas

In the years that followed the assassination, the nation's perception of Dallas was tainted by the events of November, 1963. Some civic leaders blamed the media for perpetuating the idea that the assassination was somehow Dallas's fault. The sixth floor of the Texas School Book Depository remained untouched from 1963 to 1977 as city residents tried to forget what had happened there. In 1970, Colonel Byrd sold the building to Aubrey Mayhew, a Nashville promoter with plans to convert the structure into a museum honoring the slain president. The Texas School Book Depository moved out of the building in 1971, and the following year an arson fire caused five thousand dollars in damages. Mayhew was struggling in his museum fund-raising efforts at the time, and his bank was threatening foreclosure proceedings. In August, 1972, the building was reclaimed by Byrd, who put it up for sale a year later.

It was not an easy building to sell. Some members of the community called for the city to tear it down, but city officials refused to issue a demolition permit. Paradoxically, no one wanted to move into the building, but the city could not condone its destruction. The site continued to attract visitors, who usually stood on some part of Dealey Plaza and pointed to the sixth floor window. The city fielded constant requests for information about the assassination site.

An option to purchase the building reverted to Dallas County in 1977, and that same year voters approved a $1.8 million bond package that included $400 million dollars to purchase the building. All floors except the sixth were then converted to county office space. In 1977 and 1978, the Dallas County Commissioners Court, the Dallas County Historical Commission, and the Texas Historical Commission worked out a solution to the nagging problem of what to do with the sixth floor. In 1979, a panel funded by the National Endowment for the Humanities recommended that the floor be converted into a cultural exhibit on the Kennedy assassination and its legacy, a recommendation

that was approved by the Dallas County Commissioners.

In 1981 the exterior of the building was restored and the first two floors were renovated by the firm of Burson, Hendricks and Walls. The building was then renamed the Dallas County Administration Building.

Modern Preservation Efforts

In 1983, the Dallas County Historical Foundation was formed in order to raise $3.5 million for the creation of the exhibit and to guide its operation. Initially, the foundation met with opposition. The city of Dallas was preparing to host the 1984 Republican National Convention, and a general attitude prevailed that Dallas should focus on more positive images. The observance of the twentieth anniversary of the assassination in 1983 and the intense news coverage during the convention the following year actually worked to the foundation's advantage, however. The foundation used the access to a wide audience that both events provided to publicize its goals, often invoking the words of President Kennedy himself: "History is the memory of a nation." Consequently $1.3 million was donated from citizens, private corporations, and foundations. In 1985, the county commissioners advanced the foundation the remaining $2.2 million, to be repaid from admission fees.

The building continued to evoke strong emotions—a second arson attempt had been made during the Republican Convention. The fire caused minimal damage to the building's basement.

The Sixth Floor exhibit was opened to the public on Presidents' Day, February 20, 1989, and is described by the foundation as "an educational exhibition examining the life, death and legacy of John F. Kennedy within the context of American history." Simple in design, the floor still resembles a warehouse. Instead of books, the walls are lined with plain, white display boards that present photos illustrating the Kennedy era.

The beginning sections depict the social and cultural milieu in which Kennedy came to office. Visitors can view print and video samples of his speeches and legendary wit. The achievements and challenges of his short presidency are presented: the space program, the Peace Corps, the Bay of Pigs disaster, and the Cuban Missile Crisis. A television monitor tells the story of the Kennedy's arrival in Texas. As visitors move toward the southeast window, stills from the films taken by onlookers slowly reveal the assassination. Behind glass, the southeast corner of the floor is piled with book cartons, in much the same way that it appeared on November 22, 1963. The next step brings the visitor to a window overlooking Dealey Plaza and the spot where Kennedy was shot.

Another television monitor shows reporter Walter Cronkite breaking the news of the assassination. In a small, darkened theater, a videotape of the funeral and the reaction around the world plays every few minutes. Further on, the various conspiracy theories are discussed, involving organized crime, the CIA, the Federal Bureau of Investigation, the U.S. military, the Dallas Police Department, even aliens from outer space. The final video presentation, narrated by Cronkite, presents possible reasons behind the ongoing fascination with John F. Kennedy.

The district was designated a National Historic Landmark on October 12, 1993, and was formally dedicated on November 22 of the same year, thirty years after the assassination of President Kennedy. According to national historical landmark guidelines, landmark status is not usually granted for at least fifty years after the historic event, unless special circumstances of "extraordinary national importance" exist.
— *Mary F. McNulty*

For Further Information:

Hundreds of documents, articles, and books have been published regarding the assassination of President Kennedy. The following is a small, select list.

Belin, David W. *Final Disclosure*. New York: Charles Scribner's Sons, 1988. Written by the counsel to the Warren Commission, and supports the commission's findings and rebuts conspiracy theories.

Groden, Robert J., and Harrison Edward Livingston. *High Treason*. Baltimore: Conservatory Press, 1989. Advances a conspiracy theory.

Manchester, William. *The Death of a President*. New York: Harper, 1967. Details the assassination and its effect on the nation.

Marrs, Jim. *Crossfire: The Plot That Killed Kennedy*. New York: Carroll and Graf, 1989. Supports the theory that there was a conspiracy to kill Kennedy.

Morrow, Robert D. *Betrayal*. Chicago: Henry Regnery, 1976. Written by an operative who worked for the CIA in the late 1950's and early 1960's. Morrow implicates the CIA in a plot that killed Kennedy.

Report of the President's Commission on the Assassination of President John F. Kennedy. Washington, D.C.: U.S. Government Printing Office, 1964. The Warren Commission's report on the incident.

Report of the Select Committee on Assassinations, U.S. House of Representatives. Washington, D.C.: General Printing Office, 1979. Another official government inquiry.

Simon, Art. *Dangerous Knowledge: The JFK Assassination in Art and Film*. Philadelphia: Temple University Press, 1996. This title in the series Culture and the Moving Image examines artistic representations of the events in Dealey Plaza.

Galveston

Date: First surveyed by Europeans in the 1780's

Relevant issues: Civil War, disasters and tragedies, naval history

Significance: Galveston Island is about twenty-seven miles long and three miles wide at its widest point. The city of Galveston lies at the extreme eastern end of the island. A major port in the nineteenth century, the wealth of which allowed its citizens to create luxurious and often highly unusual residences and public buildings, Galveston declined in the twentieth century as Houston, its inland neighbor, prospered. Its eclipse as an economic power served to preserve its architectural grandeur virtually intact.

Location: Two miles off the northeast end of Texas's Gulf coast

Site Office:
Galveston Historical Foundation
2016 Strand Street
Galveston Island, TX 77550-1631
ph.: (409) 765-7834

Galveston Island's most notable events suggest an inauspicious history involving social outcasts and natural disasters. In the sixteenth century, a group of shipwrecked Spanish conquistadores named the island Malhado (misfortune). The island's regular inhabitants apparently were the scourge among Native American tribes in the area. Then there was a reign of pirates in the early nineteenth century and plagues of deadly yellow fever. The hurricane of 1900 surely devastated Galveston the most.

There is also the Galveston that served proudly as port of entry for Texas (both the republic and the state), and which was known throughout the latter half of the nineteenth century as "Queen of the Gulf," one of the most prosperous ports in the nation. Galveston remained a key port well into the twentieth century, until its eclipse by inland rival Houston. Since then the island has capitalized on its history and access to the Gulf to develop a resort economy.

Early History

Before the coming of Europeans, Galveston Island—actually two islands until a storm in the early nineteenth century closed the pass between them—had been occupied, on a seasonal basis, since at least 1400 by the Karankawas, a group of nomadic Native American tribes who lived in the coastal areas of Texas. They were rumored to practice ritualistic cannibalism, but their first encounters with Spaniards were amicable. The Karankawas even shared their meager resources with the Spaniards when the latter lost their provisions to the surf. As elsewhere in the New World, though, the Europeans eventually alienated their hosts, and a mutual wariness marked by sporadic hostilities developed between the natives and the Spaniards. The Karankawas survived into the nineteenth century and survived a battle with the island's pirate residents in 1821. By 1844, however, the aggressive policies of the Anglo-Americans who came to control Galveston Island and Texas had driven most of the Karankawas south to Mexico.

Galveston Island might have figured incidentally in at least one Spanish investigation of the Texas coastline. In 1519, navy lieutenant Alonso Alvarez de Piñeda sailed from Jamaica and followed the northern Gulf coast to the Rio Grande, a route that would have taken him past the island. Making a much more consequential visit in 1528 were the survivors of the Pánfilo de Narváez expedition, which had sailed from Spain with the intention of conquering Florida. Instead, the four hundred soldiers lost track of their fleet and were attacked by hostile natives; soon they were starving

and determined to sail farther west on crude barges with sails made from their clothing. One barge after another disappeared in the Gulf storms, and only about eighty survivors made it to Galveston Island. Chief among these survivors was Álvar Nuñez Cabeza de Vaca, second in command of the party, and eventually the first European to see the interior of present-day Texas. It was he and his companions who called the island Malhado, but after their escape from the Karankawas and his published account of his journey, the land was renamed Isla de las Culebras (Island of the Snakes).

The next major record of the Galveston area resulted from Spanish navigator José de Evia's survey of the island, bay, and harbor in the 1780's. He named the bay for Bernardo de Gálvez, the Spanish governor of Louisiana (and later viceroy of Mexico) who had ordered the survey.

The Pirate Lafitte

A succession of privateers and other opportunists who had been driven out of Louisiana set the stage for Galveston's role as a trading post. The first to establish a long-term settlement on the site of the present city was Jean Lafitte, the pirate who had helped Andrew Jackson defeat the British in the Battle of New Orleans as the War of 1812 drew to a close. For this patriotism he was pardoned for the piracy he had practiced around New Orleans, and he briefly enjoyed the company of legitimate society there. He soon returned to smuggling, slave trading, and privateering, and when threatened with arrest in Louisiana in 1817, he headed for Galveston Island.

He arrived there in the wake of other adventurers; Henry Perry, Louis-Michel Aury, and Francisco Xavier Mina had become active on the island in the previous year or two, recruiting mercenaries to help Mexico fight its revolution against Spain. On one incursion into Mexico, Perry and Mina's rebel forces were routed, and the two men were killed by royalist troops. When Aury returned to Galveston, he found his authority there had been usurped by the pirate Lafitte, who had sailed into Galveston Bay in May, 1817, and taken over the nearly deserted settlement.

Lafitte renamed the colony Campeachy (or Campeche), flew the Mexican flag, and encouraged the immigration of other renegades and adventurers. Lafitte ruled the slave markets, saloons,

Visitors to Galveston can tour the widow's walk of the Samuel May Williams Home. (Jim Cruz)

and gambling dens from a fortified building called the Maison Rouge (red house). The settlement was a pirate's mecca, a market to dispose of contraband and slaves captured from Spanish ships. Lafitte in turn shipped the goods overland by mule to New Orleans and sold slaves for one dollar per pound. Importation of slaves had been outlawed by this time in U.S. history, and slaves had become a valuable commodity among pirates and their agents in the United States.

Lafitte's protocol was to attack only Spanish ships, and he looted more than one hundred during his four years on Galveston Island. He knew that the Spanish could not ably defend themselves and that Spain would not ask the United States for assistance, because doing so might establish precedent for American authority in Texas. Lafitte was careful not to attack U.S. vessels, and when in 1819

a rogue captain attacked a U.S. cutter, Lafitte hanged the offender. A second incident, though, prompted the United States in 1821 to deliver an ultimatum to Lafitte to leave Galveston Island. In a grand parting gesture, Lafitte left Campeachy in flames as he boarded his ship, *Pride*, and sailed off into the Gulf of Mexico. Presumably he was headed for the newly independent Mexico, and he may have died of fever in the Yucatán in the 1820's.

Galveston Becomes a Texas Port
Only a few years after Lafitte's departure, Galveston commenced its history in legitimate commerce when the legislature of Coahuila and Texas (by then a Mexican state) made Galveston a port in 1825. This act was in response to a petition by Stephen Fuller Austin, the founder of Anglo-American Texas, whose business at the time involved helping some three hundred families get settled in Texas. Austin persuaded the Mexican government to believe that a Texas-based coastal trade would benefit both his colonists and Mexico, and that Mexico would be able to balance its imports from England by exporting Texas cotton. Traffic was sufficient for Mexico to send a garrison to guard the customhouse in about 1830. Anglo-Americans had begun to locate at the site of the future town (there were about three hundred settlers in 1832), and the settlement gained importance as commercial traffic increased throughout the 1830's.

A French Canadian Indian trader, Michel Branamour Menard, who had signed the Texas Declaration of Independence in 1836, bought about 4,600 acres on Galveston Island with nine associates on December 8, 1836, from the First Congress of the Republic. He subsequently formed the Galveston City Company to sell lots to settlers.

The Texas Independence Movement
The ensuing years of turmoil between Texas and Mexico, and between Mexico and the United States, only enhanced Galveston's strategic impor-

tance. On November 25, 1835, with the Texan revolt impending against Mexico, the provisional government of Texas authorized the establishment of a navy, with Galveston as the base of operations. In January, 1836, they purchased the vessels *Liberty*, *Invincible*, *Independence*, and *Brutus*, and this navy of four ships effectively prevented a Mexican blockade of the Texas coast, allowing trade with the United States to continue throughout the Texas Revolution.

Galveston achieved even greater prominence in the revolutionary effort when it became temporary capital of the fledgling Republic of Texas. Just before the Texan victory in the Battle of San Jacinto on April 21, 1836, Texan president ad interim David Burnet and his cabinet—fleeing from the Mexican army's sack of Harrisburg—arrived in Galveston, leaving open the possibility of escaping to New Orleans by sea.

Already a port of call, Galveston became port of entry for the Republic of Texas in 1837, and customs duties provided substantial support for the young republic. The next year, Galveston County was organized, and the city of Galveston was incorporated in 1839. Six years later, Texas was admitted into the United States. As Texas's official port, Galveston served as entry point for thousands of American and European immigrants. Between 1844 and 1847 the German and Alsatian immigrants alone numbered about 9,500. Most new arrivals passed through to inland destinations in the new state of Texas, but many remained to settle in Galveston.

With an eye on Galveston's bright prospects as a port, Texas's state legislature passed an act for harbor improvement in 1856, but the required federal funds were not immediately forthcoming. There were some timely transportation improvements, however, including the construction of a fourteen-mile canal—part of the eventual Gulf Intracoastal Waterway—begun in 1857; in 1859 the first bridge to the mainland opened, a wooden railway trestle for the Galveston, Houston, and Henderson Railroad. When Texas seceded from the Union in 1861, Galveston was a well-connected city with a population of more than ten thousand people.

Civil War Blockade

Texas experienced the Civil War firsthand when the USS *South Carolina* appeared off the port of Galveston in July, 1861, to enforce President Abraham Lincoln's order to blockade the Southern coastline. Business as usual ceased, but blockade runners in small boats began to transport cotton to neutral ports in the Caribbean. The Confederates erected several small forts on the eastern end of the island to respond to the occasional bombardment of the city.

The blockade continued for more than a year, until Union Commander William B. Renshaw demanded the surrender of the city on October 4, 1862. Though Texas's governor urged Galvestonians to burn "every spear of grass" as they departed the city, the Union occupation of the harbor on October 9 was not resisted, and marines raised the Union flag over the customhouse.

Shortly after the city's capitulation, General John B. Magruder took over as Confederate commander of Texas. He planned to drive the Union forces out of Galveston by having "cotton-clad" steamboats attack federal ships in the harbor while Confederate soldiers attacked the Union soldiers stationed on the wharf. The Confederate forces carefully rolled their cannons into position, and with a booming salvo commenced the Battle of Galveston at 5:00 A.M. on New Year's morning of 1863.

The Confederate assault on the wharf went awry, however, when the ladders with which they planned to scale the dock proved to be too short. The two steamers, armed at Houston and protected by bales of cotton, arrived just in time to engage the federal ships. Though the Union guns sank one of the steamers and seriously disabled the other, the Confederate sailors managed to board and take control of the USS *Harriet Lane*. Meanwhile, the Northern command vessel ran aground, and the remaining federal gunboats retreated from Galveston, leaving the troops on the wharf unprotected. The Confederates captured more than six hundred federal troops, and thus won the Battle of Galveston. Southern casualties numbered 26 killed and 117 wounded, and the Union lost about 50 soldiers total. Galveston flew the Confederate flag until the South's capitulation at the end of the war.

After being informed of the fall of Richmond and the surrender of Robert E. Lee, Magruder boarded a federal ship and signed the surrender papers on June 2, 1865. On June 5 the U.S. flag was raised over the courthouse. Union troops under General Gordon Granger landed on June 19, and he announced that the Emancipation Proclamation was in effect. African Americans in Texas have since celebrated this as their day of emancipation, familiarly known as Juneteenth.

Post-Civil War Prosperity
After the war, Galveston began to enjoy renewed prosperity, as trade channels reopened and demand for cotton shipments increased. Nature intervened again in 1867, when a malaria epidemic ravaged the city; similar epidemics had been recorded in 1839, 1844, 1847, 1853, 1854, 1858, 1859, and 1864. About three-fourths of the city's residents caught the disease, and more than one thousand people perished. Fortunate medical advances soon eradicated the disease, and this last epidemic proved only a temporary setback for Galveston.

When Texas was readmitted to the Union in 1870, Galveston, with its population of fourteen thousand, still ranked as the state's largest city. Galveston bustled as the state's uncontested main port, with Houston, some fifty miles inland, serving as the transfer point for shipments through Galveston to inland Texas.

The city's prosperity continued unabated—in 1874 a visiting reporter from the *New York Herald* called Galveston "the New York of the Gulf"—and it ranked behind only Providence, Rhode Island, in per capita wealth among American cities. Thus Galveston was able to recover relatively quickly from a nighttime fire that swept through the city in 1885 and destroyed forty-two blocks of homes and businesses.

Creation of Deep-Water Port
In 1889 Congress agreed to make Galveston a deep-water port, capable of serving the world's largest cargo ships, which otherwise could not dock in Texas. The resulting channel and harbor improvements, costing $6.2 million and completed in 1896, included two jetties of immense Texas granite blocks; one jetty extended five miles and the other seven miles into the Gulf of Mexico.

Even this vibrant economy was no match for the disaster that befell the city in 1900. There had been eight major Gulf storms recorded in Galveston since 1818, but the hurricane of September 8, 1900, remains the worst natural disaster in U.S. history in terms of human lives lost.

The 1900 Hurricane
Despite notice of threatening weather, most residents remained in Galveston. When the storm finally broke on the morning of September 8, many fled to the mainland, but by night those who remained were unable to leave. The island's highest elevation was barely eight feet above sea level, and there was nothing to break the force of the gale. By 4:00 P.M., the entire city of Galveston was under one to five feet of water, and by 5:15 P.M., with the wind velocity clocked at ninety-six miles per hour, all communications with the mainland were cut off. The hurricane built to a climax at about 8:00 P.M., when winds of an estimated 120 miles per hour swept a tidal wave four to six feet high across the city.

All told, the winds, raging waves, and flooding left six thousand people dead. There were so many corpses, mostly unidentifiable, that barges of them were towed out to sea and burned. Fifteen hundred acres of houses—more than thirty-six hundred dwellings—were destroyed, leaving eight thousand people homeless. The estimated property loss was twenty million dollars, with one-third of the island entirely stripped.

To avoid future losses of such magnitude, the city began two large-scale engineering projects: a massive sea wall and the raising of the city's surface level. The new sea wall comprised ten miles of steel-reinforced concrete. It was sixteen feet wide at its base and five at its top, which was seventeen feet above mean low tide. The engineers added an immense granite breakwater for further protection. They raised the city as high as the sea wall on the vulnerable Gulf side and allowed the land to slope down to the natural level at Galveston Bay. All across the city, thousands of acres were elevated anywhere from eight to fifteen feet. The protective measures have been tested by serious hurricanes since, including a major storm in August, 1915, and another in September, 1961. Damage and loss of life were minimal in both instances.

Galveston Is Eclipsed by Houston
Galveston suffered not only physical losses in 1900, but also long-term economic disadvantages. The devastation precluded a timely role for Galveston

in the early twentieth century oil bonanza. Indeed, it was not until 1922 that oil production began in Galveston. While its chief rival was sidelined, the port of Houston began to encroach on Galveston's commercial territory by sending barges out to the Bolivar Roads pass into Galveston Bay, where merchants could transfer cotton and other goods without paying Galveston's wharfage fees.

During the 1920's, the port of Houston was well on the way to bypassing the port of Galveston in tonnage, thanks to Houston's oil shipments. Galveston still held on as a major cotton port, shipping one-third of the nation's cotton through the 1960's. By 1990, when Houston ranked as the nation's third-largest port by tonnage, Galveston no longer ranked even close to the top.

Galveston benefited in one respect from its decline as a port: Its lackluster shipping economy meant that much of the town's original architecture did not fall prey to developers' interests. Today, Galveston boasts a historic charm that distinguishes it from its industrial neighbors. Among the more famous private residences are the Creole-Greek revival-style Samuel May Williams Home, built between 1838 and 1839, and the Victorian-style Bishop's Palace, designed by Galveston architect Nicholas J. Clayton and constructed between 1886 and 1893. Clayton also designed many of the Victorian buildings lining "the Strand," once Galveston's major commercial street. As the home to dozens of preserved historical buildings such as these, Galveston is considered by many to be the most beautiful city in Texas.

—*Randall J. Van Vynckt*

For Further Information:

Barnstone, Howard. *The Galveston That Was.* Reprint. College Station: Texas A&M University Press, 1999. Largely of architectural interest, with historic photographs by Henri Cartier-Bresson and Ezra Stoller.

Fornell, Earl Wesley. *The Galveston Era: The Texas Crescent on the Eve of Secession.* Austin: University of Texas Press, 1961. Details the social and economic issues that led to secession.

McComb, David. *Galveston: A History.* Austin: University of Texas Press, 1986. Even more to the point than his book *Texas* below.

———. *Texas: A Modern History.* Austin: University of Texas Press, 1989. A highly readable, fast-paced account of the state's history, including anecdotes about Galveston.

Webb, Walter Prescott, ed. *The Handbook of Texas.* Austin: Texas State Historical Association, 1952. This book and its 1976 supplement edited by Eldon Stephen Branda constitute a whopping 3,075 pages of exhaustive history.

King Ranch

Date: Established in 1853
Relevant issues: Business and industry
Significance: Developed by Henrietta M. King and her son-in-law Robert Justus Kleberg along a railroad right-of-way, King Ranch covers some 825,000 acres and is engaged in cattle ranching and oil producing.
Location: Fifty miles southwest of Corpus Christi, along Route 77
Site Office:
King Ranch Visitor Center
P.O. Box 1090
W. Highway 141
Kingsville, TX 78363
ph.: (512) 592-8055

An agricultural and oil-producing town in southeast Texas, Kingsville began its existence in 1904, when Henrietta M. King and her son-in-law Robert Justus Kleberg developed it along a newly built railroad running from St. Louis through Brownsville to Mexico. Originally a farming town, Kingsville grew and adapted as the nearby mammoth King Ranch developed oil fields.

Kingsville contains Texas A&M University; the Henrietta Memorial Museum, which houses memorabilia from the King Ranch and the King and Kleberg families; and the John E. Conner Museum, which contains ranching memorabilia as well as displays of natural history and Indian and Mexican artifacts.

The King Ranch

The town's most interesting facet is its intimate relationship with King Ranch. The 825,000-acre ranch covers an area larger than the state of Rhode Island and is the largest beef cattle operation in the United States. The ranching and oil-producing behemoth contains much of Kleberg, Nueces,

The main house of King Ranch in 1949. (The Institute of Texan Cultures/courtesy Belton Kleberg Johnson)

Brooks, Kenedy, and Jim Wells Counties. The ranch began in 1853 when Richard King, a brash Rio Grande steamboat captain, recognized the beef-producing potential of the Wild Horse Desert and began buying old Spanish land grants in the area.

King was a rough sort of man who drank whiskey and liked to fight. He was born on July 10, 1824, to Irish immigrants in New York City. Apprenticed early to a jeweler, he stowed away on the steamship *Desdemona* when he was eleven years old and was made a cabin boy. His captain taught him to read and handle numbers, and he even sent King back to Connecticut to attend school for eight months.

In the late 1830's, King signed on to serve aboard a steamboat during the Seminole War in Florida. After the war, he worked on the steamboats that carried freight up and down the Apalachicola and Chattahoochee Rivers in Florida. At the tender age of nineteen, he became a ship's pilot.

In 1843, King met Mifflin Kenedy, master of the *Champion*. In 1846, Kenedy was recruited for the Mexican War and became captain of the *Corvette*, which plied the Rio Grande. On Kenedy's advice, in 1847, King also signed on for government service. By the summer of 1847, King had become first pilot on the *Corvette* and was working under Kenedy carrying supplies eight miles from Brazos Santiago across the open sea and then up the Rio Grande. By November, 1847, King, then twenty-three, had become captain of the steamer *Colonel Cross*.

At the end of the Mexican War, King set up an inn at Boca del Rio and waited for new steamship opportunities to arise. In April, 1848, he paid $750 for the *Colonel Cross*, a boat for which the government had paid $14,000 only three years previously. As captain of the *Colonel Cross*, he hauled cargo for the merchants of Matamoros, Mexico. Business was not good and despite cutting his crew to a minimum he barely made his expenses.

In 1850, Charles Stillman, King's chief competitor, brought King and Kenedy into a partnership to revive Stillman's own ailing steamboat business. With firmer financial backing, King devised a plan to have larger boats to carry cargo from Brazos across the open sea and smaller ones negotiate the shallow Rio Grande. This plan was so successful that in less than two years, the partnership, M. Kenedy and Company of Brownsville, Texas, drove every other freight hauler from the river.

Beginnings of the King Ranch

Richard King first got interested in ranching in April of 1952, when he rode through the Wild Horse Desert on a trip inland to attend Texas's first state fair at Corpus Christi. At the fair, King made friends with Richard "Legs" Lewis, and in the course of their association they decided to build a cow camp in the Wild Horse Desert.

King and Lewis made a good pair. King knew of Mexican families that held grants in the area. Lewis, a captain of the Texas Mounted Volunteers, could protect the stock. Together, they built a camp along a spring that fed into Santa Gertrudis Creek. Lewis tended and protected the herd from outlaws and Indians, while King provided the funds, which he drew from his successful freight operation.

On July 25, 1853, King paid $300 for the Rincón de Santa Gertrudis, a grant of 15,500 acres in which the town of Kingsville now stands. Next, he spent $1,800 for the Big Santa Gertrudis grant, which covered 53,000 more acres, contained several streams, and touched the earlier purchase at one point.

King built dams to capture water for mass watering of cattle, while Lewis engaged in livestock deals and the delivery of herds. Together they upbred the local stock of mustangs by mixing them with the blood of good studs. As for cattle, King chose only the best available Mexican bulls and range cows for his breed herd. The horse business was good from the beginning, but with cows there were problems of transportation and markets. Overall outlays for stocking his cow and horse herds topped $12,000 in 1854 alone.

A notorious womanizer, Lewis was shot and killed by an irate husband on April 14, 1855. To prevent Lewis's shares from falling into unfriendly hands, King joined with his friend Major W. W. Chapman and bought them at auction on July 1, 1856, for $1,575. Chapman himself was soon forced to withdraw from the partnership. For stability, King then turned to his old friend and partner, Mifflin Kenedy. Along with fellow steamboater Captain James Walworth, they formed a new corpo-

ration, R. King and Company, to hold the ranch. King and Kenedy each held three-eighths of the shares, and Walworth owned two-eighths.

The Civil War

During the Civil War, King and his ranch played important roles for the Confederacy. He had known General Robert E. Lee well during that officer's service in Texas, though the story that King first bought land on Lee's advice is untrue. What Lee actually told King is "buy land and never sell."

Early in the war, Northern ships blockaded many Southern ports. Desperate for imported munitions and medical supplies, the Confederacy moved cotton through its "back door" at Brownsville, where M. Kenedy and Company steamers made huge profits on wartime shipments. When the North blockaded Brownsville, the South, along with smugglers across the river in Matamoros, used Mexico's neutrality to evade the blockade. M. Kenedy and Company steamers, under the guise of Mexican ownership, continued to carry freight.

King's ranch was another important link in the cotton trade. Since the ranch stood along cotton's overland route, approximately one hundred fifty miles north of Brownsville, King naturally became involved in brokering cotton. In fact he and Kenedy contracted to supply the Southern force with cotton to export for gold, weapons, and supplies for the latter part of the war. The profits King made on the deal may have reached sixty thousand dollars.

By the war's end Stillman had withdrawn from the steamboat partnership and Walworth had died. King and Kenedy bought Walworth's shares for fifty thousand dollars, and flush with cash from the war, ordered four brand-new steamboats. Trade on the Rio Grande declined after the war. Chaos hit Mexico, depression hit the South, a hurricane damaged both Brownsville and Matamoros, and the railroad began to compete with the river trade. In May, 1874, both Kenedy and King sold out of the shipping business.

In 1868 King and Kenedy, who remained close friends all their lives, divided their land and livestock holdings and began fencing in their lands. As sole possessor of the Santa Gertrudis, King registered his famous brand, the "Running W" the following year. Called the viborita, or little snake, by King's workers, that brand would mark more than

58,000 head of cattle and 4,400 head of horse stock by November of 1869.

The Great Cattle Drives

In 1869, King began sending his now immense cattle herds on long drives to Kansas City and St. Louis, where they were shipped to northern centers like Chicago. These cattle drives were sometimes as long as a thousand miles, and King would often supervise the actual selling himself. It has been calculated that King made an average of fity thousand dollars per drive and repeated this type of venture scores of times through the booming 1870's.

Flush with money from these drives, King bought land in the Carricitas region. Often the titles of these lands were divided among the descendants of the original holders of the Spanish land grants. Sometimes these grants overlapped. Other times they contained separate and conflicting grants made by the Republic of Texas. King and his lawyers patiently bought up these rights, called "derechos," sometimes paying for the same piece of land twice or more. By the end of the 1870's, King's holdings covered more than 600,000 acres.

Robert Justus Kleberg

In 1881 Robert Justus Kleberg, a lawyer, soundly beat King in a minor law suit in Corpus Christi. King recognized Kleberg's talent and put him on retainer. Kleberg soon became an important factor in ranch management and a frequent visitor to Santa Gertrudis, where he courted King's daughter, Alice Gertrudis King. By the time Richard King died of stomach cancer, on April 14, 1885, King's wife and heir, Henrietta M. King, had enough confidence in Kleberg to appoint him ranch manager.

Robert Justus Kleberg was born to Prussian immigrants on his family's farm near Meyersville, Texas, on December 5, 1853. His father, also named Robert Justus Kleberg, was a judge in DeWitt County, Texas, and had been a hero in the Texas Revolution and prominent in the Confederacy. The younger Kleberg was a stocky man a little below medium stature. His complexion was ruddy and he wore a bushy mustache.

Kleberg, who married Alice Gertrudis King in June of 1886, became manager at a time when the King Ranch's debts equaled its huge assets. He faced a collapse in cattle prices and a drought in south Texas that lasted from 1886 to 1893.

He kept the ranch going by selling some land and pursuing a more methodical, business-like approach. He rid the Santa Gertrudis of mustangs, added barbed wire to the board fences King had erected, and hired a professional livestock manager named Sam Ragland. Not one to neglect expansion, he also bought land as discouraged ranchers gave up and sold cheap. By 1895 the Santa Gertrudis was one of the world's largest commercial producers of horses and mules.

Kleberg had a scientific bent and was always ready to invest in new technologies to advance the ranch. He helped finance a cure for southern cattle fever, and in the early 1890's he invented the first cattle dipping vat. In 1898 he hired Theodore L. Herring, who solved the ranch's fresh water problem by using heavy equipment to drill artesian wells.

At the turn of the century, Kleberg began negotiating for the Laureles property, which would extend the Santa Gertrudis holdings east to the shores of the Laguna Madre. In two separate transactions, one in 1901 and the other in 1906, Henrietta King paid almost $700,000 for 170,000 acres. These purchases brought the ranch's area to the million-acre mark.

Beginnings of Kingsville

Kleberg, like Richard King, was constantly in search of better ways to bring cattle to market. In 1903, he and his fellow ranchers were finally able to bring the railroad to southeast Texas. That year, the St. Louis, Brownsville and Mexico Railway was incorporated, with Kleberg as president. On July 4, 1904, the railroad's inaugural train ran from Brownsville to Corpus Christi, passing about three miles from the ranch's main house at a site that would soon become Kingsville.

To build the town, Kleberg organized Kleberg Town and Improvement Company in 1903. Led by Kleberg and owned by Henrietta King and the Johnston Brothers (the firm that built the railroad in exchange for land grants), the Kleberg Town and Improvement Company installed waterworks, built an ice factory, set up a weekly newspaper, and constructed the Kingsville Power Company. A separate company, Algodon Land and Irrigation, was organized for farmers growing tropical and citrus plants. In deference to Henrietta King's religious beliefs, the sale of alcohol was prohibited in Kingsville. On February 27, 1913, Kingsville became the seat of the new Kleberg County.

On January 4, 1912, the original King Ranch house burnt to the ground. In two years, at a cost of $350,000, a new house was built with twenty-five rooms (each with a fireplace) and nearly as many baths, a veranda, a grand salon, and a dining hall for fifty guests. The architectural style included "scrambled elements of Mexican, Moorish, and California Mission of Long Island and Wild Horse Desert," according to historian Tom Lea.

By the time of World War I, the King Ranch had established large herds of shorthorn and Hereford cattle. These English cattle produced better beef than Texas longhorns but were too fragile for the hot Texas climate. Searching for a better breed, Kleberg in 1910 began crossing shorthorns with Brahman cattle from India.

After the war, he arrived at a breed about five-eighths Shorthorn and three-eighths Brahman. Using a bull named Monkey, the ranch developed a herd that was astutely developed and carefully watched. In 1940 the United States Department of Agriculture officially recognized the Santa Gertrudis as a new and separate breed of cattle.

The raising of horses was also an important element of the ranch's business. Initially King and Kleberg had tried to improve their stocks by crossing the native mustangs with thoroughbred stock. These mounts, however, were too nervous to be useful on the range. Eventually Robert Kleberg's younger son, Robert "Bob" Kleberg, Jr., found an ideal mare named Old Sorrel. From this mare, the King Ranch developed its own distinctive American quarter horse, alert but not nervous, strong, agile, fast, yet compact enough to handle. King horses became prize-winners often used in circuses.

At the start of World War I, Robert Kleberg was attacked by palsy and Bob took over active management of the nation's biggest beef ranch. After the war, the younger Kleberg, who had been schooled in agriculture, cut back his father's pet project of agricultural development and made several large land purchases. More than forty thousand acres had been sold to meet a postwar slump, but Bob Kleberg more than made up for those losses by ac-

quiring almost thirty-five thousand acres of Stillman property south of Falfurrias.

On March 31, 1925, Henrietta King died at the age of ninety-two. In her declining years she had given the Santa Gertrudis main house to her daughter Alice and made a will to divide her properties among her children after a ten-year trusteeship. Appraisers of her estate indicated that, at her death, she owned 94,347 head of cattle, 3,782 horses, 802 mules, 47 jennies, 355 goats, 595 sheep, and 997,444.56 acres of land not including what she had willed to her daughter. Her assets totaled $7.1 million, while her liabilities reached $1.7 million.

Financial Threats to the Ranch

In the mid-1920's, the country's deflationary environment caused the ranch to lose money consistently. Furthermore, estate taxes from Henrietta King's will were high enough to imperil the ranch's financial integrity. By 1933 Bob Kleberg, the ranch's manager and the estate's trustee, was desperate for money.

A savior came in the form of the Humble Oil and Gas Company (later known as Exxon U.S.A.). In exchange for exclusive drilling rights on the land, Humble obligated itself to make annual bonus payments large enough to cover the interest on the debts owed by King's estate. The ranch also got a yearly bonus of thirteen cents an acre and retained a one-eighth royalty on the gross proceeds of oil production.

With at least his interest payments guaranteed, Bob Kleberg consolidated the family debts under a $3,223,645 first mortgage. He also moved to bring as much of the ranch as he could under the control of his branch of the family. He was able to buy some land from more distant heirs but one estranged element of the family, the Atwoods of Chicago, brought suit in 1933 over the trusteeship and division of the estate. These suits were not brought to a close until after World War II.

Incorporation of the Ranch

On December 14, 1934, the Klebergs incorporated their part of the ranch under the name King Ranch. They controlled more than 802,000 acres, including the original Santa Gertrudis and Laureles grants, as well as Norias and Encino.

In the 1930's Bob Kleberg became fascinated with the world of thoroughbred racing. Working with his nephew Richard "Dick" Kleberg, Jr., who later managed the ranch, he bought many expensive horses and began a breeding program that rapidly brought great success to the ranch, including a Triple Crown winner.

Meanwhile in the oil fields, Humble worked conservatively. It sought extensions of existing fields, and in May, 1939, it tapped the edge of the Luby Field in Nueces County. It was not until 1945, however, that Humble drilled the ranch's first successful wildcat well and hit the second-largest reserve of oil and gas in Texas.

In the 1950's, oil activity expanded as Humble and the Klebergs negotiated two lease extensions. In exchange for a one-sixth royalty they added first ten years and then fifty years to the lease. All this drilling created the necessity for roads to carry heavy equipment, roads that brought the motor vehicle into use for transporting cattle.

As the King Ranch entered the mid-1970's, schisms began to develop among the descendants of Henrietta and Richard King. Arguments over how much each member of the family should be paid led to the departure of former managers Robert Shelton and Belton Kleberg Johnson. Though oil and gas royalties peaked at $100 million dollars in 1979, in the early 1980's Shelton and Johnson sued their relatives, claiming their failure to police the oil company resulted in lost revenues.

In August, 1988, the family chose former Kimberly-Clark chief executive Darwin E. Smith as the ranch's first outside chairman. At the time, *Fortune* described the ranch as "suffering falling revenues from its oil leases, a decline in beef consumption, a troubled shrimp farming venture and captious family members anxious to liquidate their holdings."

In August, 1989, the *Texas Monthly* estimated that Helen "Helenita" Kleberg Groves, Bob Kleberg's only daughter, was believed to control one-third of the ranch, worth $400 million. Her cousins Ida "Illa" Larkin Clement and Katherine Kleberg Yarborough split their branches' fortunes with siblings or their heirs. In 1993, the ranch was estimated to have seven hundred employees and revenues of $250 million. —*Jordan Wankoff*

For Further Information:

Dehnhardt, Robert Moorman. *The King Ranch Quarter Horses*. Reprint. Norman: University of Oklahoma Press, 1995. Contains a capsule history of the ranch but is primarily concerned with horse breeding.

Lea, Tom. *The King Ranch*. Boston: Little, Brown, 1957. The most complete history of the ranch. It contains facsimiles of many early documents but is marred by Lea's somewhat romantic tone. It was commissioned by the ranch to celebrate its one-hundredth anniversary.

Sizer, Mona D. *The King Ranch Story: Truth and Myth—A History of the Oldest and Greatest Ranch in Texas*. Plano: Republic of Texas Press, 1999. A history of King Ranch. Includes bibliographical references.

La Villita

Date: European settlement began in the mid-eighteenth century

Relevant issues: European settlement, Latino history, religion

Significance: The twenty-seven restored buildings in the National Historic District of La Villita chronicle settlement over a period of two hundred years. From private homes to churches to commercial buildings, this area is rich in the history of San Antonio. The area was restored beginning in 1939.

Location: On the east bank of the San Antonio River in the heart of the old city, a square block enclosed by Nueva Street, Alamo Street, Villita Street, and South Presa Street; the area of La Villita is directly adjacent to the Alamo

Site Office:

La Villita Tourist Information Center
418 Villita Street
San Antonio, TX 78205
ph.: (210) 207-8619

La Villita is a charming area that mirrors the history of San Antonio in a large group of historic structures dating from the early nineteenth to the early twentieth century. The area was first settled by the Coahuiltecan Indians. European settlement began in the middle of the eighteenth century, primarily because the area was adjacent to the Mission San Antonio de Valero (later known as the Alamo), which was founded in 1718. There was another Spanish settlement on the west side of the river,

The Cós House, La Villita. (San Antonio Convention and Visitors Bureau/Doug Wilson)

Other observers at the time described the settlers as nothing more than "squatters." Many of the poor Spanish settlers had intermarried with the native peoples who worked at the mission. So by the late eighteenth century, the polyglot style of this area had already begun.

The mission was secularized in 1793, and the land it had controlled was distributed to the Native American and European settlers. The mission then became a military stronghold, and the soldiers stationed there lived in the La Villita area.

San Antonio During the Mexican Independence Movement

When Mexico's struggle for independence from Spain began in 1810, the San Antonio area was a hotbed of revolutionary fever. It was the policy of the Spanish to confiscate the homes and property of those engaging in independence activity. Under this policy, a number of homes in the La Villita area owned by soldiers and civilians were taken by the government. The Spanish then issued land grants to others more sympathetic to the government, and the confiscated property was given away. The oldest extant land grants issued under this policy date to 1818. Some other confiscated homes served as quarters for Spanish soldiers, who occupied them rent-free.

The forces of nature proved far more influential on the development of La Villita than did the local politics. A flood on July 5, 1819, wiped out virtually everything on the west bank of the river. La Villita, on the east side, was virtually untouched, as it was on higher ground. Within days of this disaster, residents of the devastated area began to petition the government for land grants on the previously undesirable east side of the river. The structures erected by those wealthier families form the majority of the restored structures still standing today in La Villita.

Mexico became independent from Spain in 1821, but in a few years there came a movement for Texan independence from Mexico. Being adjacent to the Alamo, the La Villita area was the scene of numerous battles in 1835 and 1836. After the Mexi-

and four missions to the south. Because this area was at the northern end of the Spanish domain in the New World, the settlers were often in danger of attack from hostile Indian tribes, although relations with the Coahuiltecans were peaceful. The settlements experienced frequent cholera epidemics as well.

By the late eighteenth century, the area now known as La Villita was hardly the showplace it later became. The residents lived in a primitive collection of ramshackle structures. A visitor, Fray Juan Augustin Morfi, described it thus in 1778: "The town consists of fifty houses of stone and mud and seventy-nine of wood, all poorly built . . . so that the whole resembles more a poor village than a villa. . . . "

can defeat at the Storming of Bexar in December, 1835, the surrender was signed by General Martín Perfecto de Cós in a home in La Villita. This house, now known as the Cós House, still stands.

Many of the earlier, more primitive structures in the area were damaged during the Texas Revolution, and even after Texas won its independence, La Villita was under threat of Mexican invasion. This danger passed only after Texas joined the United States in 1846.

San Antonio Under American Rule

The mid-nineteenth century saw much of the area change hands from the original Spanish and Native American owners, to non-Hispanics. The architecture of the area reflected this change. The older homes made of adobe or mesquite wood and clay were replaced by limestone structures with a Victorian flavor. These new owners also brought with them construction and decorative styles from such homelands as Germany and France, making La Villita the interesting and diverse collection of architecture it is today. African Americans also were an important element in this mixture of peoples.

By the early twentieth century, La Villita was still primarily residential. By the 1930's, the area had become more industrial and commercial, with a scattering of rooming houses. Many old adobe houses were demolished to make way for new structures. By 1939, a utility company, the Public Service Company and Water Board, owned much of the area and had allowed it to deteriorate badly.

Louis Lipscomb, San Antonio police and fire commissioner under Mayor Maury Maverick, described what he saw in 1939 as follows: "The area around La Villita was one of the worst slum districts in San Antonio . . . it was a hangout for winos, all sorts of vice, and a terrible looking, dirty neighborhood." The mayor, upon urging from Lipscomb, visited the area and decided to try to gain control of it for the city. He traded some city land to the Public Service Company and the city took over La Villita.

Maverick then contacted a friend in Washington, D.C., who ran the National Youth Administration (NYA), a federal New Deal work program. After some preliminary cleaning and the demolition of some twentieth century commercial structures, the NYA began restoration of the first seven houses on October 9, 1939.

Buildings in La Villita

The Carnegie Corporation soon granted the city fifteen thousand dollars for a library, museum, and community center building. This building was named Bolívar Hall, after the early nineteenth century South American independence leader Simón Bolívar. This, along with a few other new structures, was dedicated in May, 1941.

After World War II, other buildings were acquired and restored, and the La Villita area was expanded. The area became a city historic district on October 2, 1969, and later was named a national one.

Among the historic structures of La Villita, the Cós House is one of the oldest; it predates 1835. Other buildings of particular interest include the Florian House, built in 1855 with an addition in the late nineteenth century (thereby illustrating the contrast between antebellum and Victorian design), and the Esquida-Downs-Dietrich House, an adobe structure that was found intact inside the cinder-block walls of a candy company's warehouse in the late 1960's. These and the other buildings of La Villita form a monument to the history of San Antonio and the various cultures that contributed to it. Many of the buildings house arts and crafts shops. Interpretive markers, placed by the La Villita Tenants Association and the San Antonio Conservation Society, guide visitors through walking tours of the area.

—*Steve Palmer*

For Further Information:

There is little in book form on La Villita. A variety of literature, however, is available by contacting the La Villita Tourist Information Center.

Federal Writer's Project, Texas. *Old Villita*. San Antonio, Tex.: City of San Antonio, 1939.

Presidio La Bahia

Date: Built in 1721; moved to its present site in 1749

Relevant issues: Disasters and tragedies, European settlement, military history

Significance: Presidio La Bahia is the only fully reconstructed Spanish colonial fort in the Western Hemisphere. Strategically situated on the route connecting the province of Texas with Mexico, this Spanish frontier fort was established to protect nearby missions. It subsequently played a key role in the history of the area and was the site of the Goliad Massacre and other events of the Texas Revolution.

Location: On Texas Route 183 off Route 59, one hundred fifty miles southwest of Houston and eighty miles east-southeast of San Antonio

Site Office:
Presidio La Bahia
P.O. Box 57
Highway 183
Goliad, TX 77963
ph.: (512) 645-3752

The European settlement of Texas was spurred by conquistadores such as Francisco Vásquez de Coronado, who sought gold and instead found a new country that they called (variously) Amichel, the New Philippines, and Tejas (the origin of the name "Texas"). The ensuing development of the area produced a melting pot of Spanish, Mexican, Indian, and Anglo-American cultures that in the late 1700's and early 1800's was stirred to conflict. The result, after first Texas independence and then Texas statehood, was a deep cultural rift between the Mexicans and Anglo-Americans.

Early European Exploration
There were over ninety European expeditions into the area by the early 1700's. Most were conducted by the Spanish, but when the French founded Fort St. Louis, the Spanish perceived it as a threat to their undisputed control of the area. Franciscan monks proposed to establish missions in Texas, and the Spanish quickly agreed, leading to the founding of San Francisco de los Tejas on May 25, 1690. By 1731, there were a dozen missions in the area. Strategically situated on the route connecting the province of Texas with Mexico, Presidio Nuestra Señora de Loreto de La Bahia was established in 1721 as a Spanish frontier fort to protect nearby missions and subsequently played a key role in the history of the area; in 1749, it was moved to its present site.

The nearby mission—Espíritu Santo—was created to Christianize the Karankawa Indians on Matagorda Bay. It was called Mission La Bahia (Bay Mission) even after it moved inland in 1726 to the Mission Valley area of Victoria and finally to the present-day site in 1749. Another mission, Mission

Nuestra Señora del Rosario, was established nearby by Franciscans in 1754.

The missions had some difficulty in winning converts, but they, along with the presidio, were successful in another effort—developing the cattle-ranching industry of Texas. By 1770 Espíritu Santo had forty thousand head of cattle, while Rosario claimed thirty thousand. The missions also had herds of sheep, raised primarily for their wool, which the missionaries used to make clothing and blankets. Soldiers of the presidio oversaw the herds of the missions and provided troop escorts for cattle drives to other Spanish settlements.

The presidio played a role in the American and Mexican wars for independence. During the American Revolution, the presidio's troops assisted the armies of Bernardo de Gálvez, a Spanish ally of the American colonists. The combined Spanish and Continental forces won victories over the British at Baton Rouge, Natchez, Mobile, and Pensacola.

The Mexican Independence Movement
In 1812, during the Mexican fight for independence from Spain, the presidio was seized by a group of Mexican revolutionaries and their French, Indian, and American allies, under the command of Bernardo Gutiérrez de Lara and Augustus Magee. The revolutionary army held the fortress through a lengthy siege and pushed the Spanish forces back to San Antonio. At this time the Americans decided to declare the first Republic of Texas, but Gutiérrez insisted that Texas remain part of Mexico.

In 1819, an army assembled by James Long in Mississippi invaded Texas and again declared the colony an independent republic. Long and his forces occupied La Bahia in October, 1821, but Spanish troops surrounded them and forced their surrender. When Mexico won its independence that same year, its army took control of the presidio.

The Texan Independence Movement
The Texan independence movement did not disappear, however, and it was this movement that would result in the most historic events at the presidio. During the 1820's and 1830's, Mexico was engaged in an ongoing debate over just how powerful its central government should be. Many of those living in Texas favored a decentralized govern-

ment, which was endorsed by the liberal Mexican constitution of 1824. When Antonio López de Santa Anna became president in 1833, he at first pledged to uphold the constitution, but then voided it in 1835. That year, Texan activist Stephen Fuller Austin, who had been imprisoned in Mexico for a year and a half because he was suspected of revolutionary activities, was released and appealed to Texans—and their allies in the United States— to take arms in the cause of Texan independence.

When Mexican troops came to quash the Texas rebellion, the presidio was the first military installation they secured, early in October, 1835. Within days, however, a Texan revolutionary force captured the presidio, in the first offensive operation of the Texas Revolution. On December 20, the presidio was the site of the first signing of the Declaration of Texas Independence from Mexico.

A fresco by Antonio Garcia inside Our Lady of Loreto Chapel at Presidio La Bahia. (Newton M. Warzecha)

Siege of the Alamo

During the siege of the Alamo at San Antonio early in 1836, the presidio at Goliad was manned by a force of between four hundred and five hundred; some were from Texas, but mostly the men were from the United States, under the command of Colonel James W. Fannin, Jr. Fannin's actions during this time were controversial. William B. Travis asked Fannin to come to the aid of the Texan forces at the Alamo. Fannin refused Travis's first request, but when the second came Fannin and most of his troops set out for the Alamo. They left on February 26 and spent the night on the banks of the San Antonio River, but they backtracked to Goliad the next day. For this action, some have called Fannin a coward; others have said he was merely being prudent, and undoubtedly saved his troops from being wiped out at the Alamo. Fannin justified the action by explaining that not only had his ammunition wagons broken down, he had also received word that Mexican forces under General José Urrea were nearby. Fannin said,

> It was apparent to all that the evacuation of Goliad . . . would leave the whole frontier from [San Antonio] to the coast open to the incursions of the enemy. . . . Everyone felt an anxiety to relieve our friends . . . yet everyone saw the impropriety, if not the impossibility, of our proceeding under existing circumstances.

On March 14, Fannin received an order from Sam Houston, commander in chief of the Texas forces. Urrea and his men were on the way to Goliad; Fannin was to abandon the presidio for the nearby settlement of Victoria. Because of transportation difficulties, and possibly his own reservations, Fannin did not begin his retreat until March 19. By then Urrea's forces were very close indeed. Near Coleto Creek, a few miles east of Goliad, the Mexican army surrounded Fannin's troops. After a day and a half of fighting, and unable to stand up to Urrea's artillery reinforcements, Fannin and his soldiers surrendered and became the Mexicans' prisoners.

The Mexican government had decreed that any foreigners who aided the rebellion were to be executed. As most of Fannin's soldiers were from the United States, they were eligible for this penalty. Urrea promised to intercede with Santa Anna, so that prisoners who asked for clemency would be spared. Urrea moved on with his army, taking some of the captured troops with him to serve as medical attendants to his wounded. Fannin and his remaining troops—about four hundred men—were locked up in the presidio, under the supervision of Mexican Lieutenant Colonel José Nicolás de la Portilla.

The Goliad Massacre

Santa Anna refused Urrea's plea for mercy and ordered Portilla to execute the prisoners. On March 27, 1836—Palm Sunday—all but twenty-seven were killed, in an episode that became known as the Goliad Massacre. Fannin was the last to die. Some of the bodies were burned, but others remained where they fell and created a feast for wolves and vultures. Urrea was outraged and wrote in his diary:

> I never thought that the horrible spectacle of that massacre could take place in cold blood . . . a deed proscribed by the laws of war and condemned by the civilization of our country. . . . [The Texan and U.S. troops] surrendered confident that Mexican generosity would not make their sacrifice useless, for under any other circumstances they would have sold their lives dearly, fighting to the last.

The massacre served to solidify support for the Texan cause. "Remember Goliad!" joined "Remember the Alamo!" as the Texans' rallying cry the following month at the Battle of San Jacinto, where Texas finally won its independence. Texas became part of the United States in 1845.

The presidio fell into disrepair after the Texas Revolution, but in the 1960's it was restored to 1836 appearance. The graves of Fannin and his men are on the grounds. The compound is administered by the Catholic Diocese of Victoria. The two hundred-year-old Our Lady of Loreto Chapel at the presidio continues to host religious services. The chapel features a striking fresco by Corpus Christi artist Antonio Garcia, and a statue of Our Lady of Loreto by Gutzon Borglum, the sculptor of Mount Rushmore.

The Mission Espíritu Santo was secularized in 1831 and rebuilt in 1848 by the Goliad City Council. It subsequently became Aranama College, a college for Spanish-speaking Texans. The college shut down in 1861 when its entire student body joined the Confederate army. The mission was left to ruin but was meticulously rebuilt in the 1930's. The ruins of Mission Rosario also may be viewed within Goliad State Historical Park.

Historic Buildings

There are several notable historic structures within the town of Goliad. The Second Empire Goliad County Courthouse was built in 1894 by the San Antonio architect Alfred Giles and was expanded in 1964. It is the focal point of a group of turn-of-the-century commercial, public, and residential buildings that covers portions of nine blocks. On the courthouse's lawn is the oak Hanging Tree. From 1846 to 1870 court was held under the tree, and those found guilty were hanged on the spot.

The Old Market House Museum opened in the early 1870's as a market for meat and produce vendors. In 1886 it became a firehouse and meeting hall. The museum features documents and artifacts relating to farming and ranching in the Goliad area from the mid-nineteenth century to the early twentieth century.

The Captain Barton Peck House is a stuccoed limestone home built by an easterner who arrived too late to fight for Texas independence and went home but was so attracted by Goliad that he returned in 1842. The Greek revival house took ten years to build and remains one of the finest early examples of that style in Texas.   —*Bob Lange*

For Further Information:

Castaneda, Carlos E. *The Mexican Side of the Texas Revolution.* Salem, N.H.: Ayer, 1976. The Mexicans' view of the Texas Revolution is presented through excerpts from memoirs and diaries of the Mexican officers.

Fehrenbach, T. R. *Lone Star: A History of Texas and the Texans.* 1968. Reprint. New York: Da Capo Press, 2000. Though every bit as thorough in research and presentation of the facts as Hansen (below), uses a more contemporary tone.

Habig, Marion A. *The Alamo Chain of Missions: A History of San Antonio's Five Old Missions.* Rev. ed. Livingston, Tex.: Pioneer Press, 1997. A discussion of the missions in the San Antonio area.

Haley, James L. *Texas: An Album of History.* New York: Doubleday, 1985. Contains an account of the revolution and the Goliad Massacre.

Hansen, Harry. *Texas: A Guide to the Lone Star State.* Rev. ed. New York: Hastings House, 1969. Originally compiled by the Federal Writers' Program. Thorough, well researched, and scholarly in its presentation, the book contains a calendar of annual events across the state, twenty-nine driving tours (including one through Goliad and mission country), maps, and selected readings about Texas.

McDonald, Archie P., ed. *The Texas Experience.* College Station: Texas A&M University Press, 1986. An anthology that presents Texas in mosaic; it is a collection of many writers from Texas schools who offer insights on a variety of topics from history to popular culture.

San Antonio Missions

Date: Established as a National Historical Park in 1978

Relevant issues: American Indian history, art and architecture, European settlement, Latino history, religion

Significance: This site consists of four Spanish missions: Mission Concepción, Mission San José, Mission San Juan, and Mission Espada. All four are prime examples of Spanish Mission architecture as adapted for use in the New World. The construction of these historic missions was a joint effort of skilled craftsmen from Spain and Mexico and the local Coahuiltecan Indians.

Location: On the Mission Trail in the south central portion of San Antonio, south of Interstate 35, west of Interstate 37, and north of the south section of Interstate 410

Site Offices:

San Antonio Missions National Historical Park Headquarters
2202 Roosevelt Avenue
San Antonio, TX 78210
ph.: (210) 534-8833

Visitor Center
6701 San José Drive
San Antonio, TX 78214
ph.: (210) 932-1001
Web site: www.nps.gov/saan/

The Spanish conquests in the New World were accomplished by both political and religious means. The mission was instrumental in the achievement of both of these goals. Once an area was conquered by the military, the Catholic Church followed immediately. While the Spanish withdrew, some 140 years after they arrived, the work of the church continued, and its influence is still felt today.

The Franciscans

The San Antonio Missions were all established and maintained by members of the Franciscan order, who countered the sometimes brutal military treatment of the Native Americans with respect and concern. This attitude caused the conversion of a high percentage of Native Americans to Catholicism, a result highly applauded by the Spanish rulers.

Each mission was a nearly self-contained community usually consisting of a church, a school, stores, and small workshop areas, along with pueblos in which the natives lived. There would also be a presidio—military base—nearby, for protection as well as soldiers' quarters, often located inside the mission near the friars' cloisters. The surrounding area would be primarily farmland, which was worked by the natives under the direction of the friars. The natives were encouraged to govern themselves democratically and were taught farming methods and other skills such as blacksmithing. The missions eased the Coahuiltecan Indians' transition to European culture and formed the basis for present-day San Antonio.

The San Antonio Missions National Historical Park consists of more than forty structures, restored and unrestored, which together form the most outstanding grouping of Spanish colonial architecture in the United States. The greatest treasures are in the four missions that stand within the park.

Mission Espada

The oldest of these is Mission San Francisco de la Espada, originally founded in eastern Texas in 1690. It was moved to its current location on the San Antonio River and dedicated March 5, 1731. This name can be translated as "Saint Francis of the sword," an appropriate name since, as the most exposed of the San Antonio missions, it was often subject to Apache raids.

Mission San José, part of the San Antonio Missions. (PhotoDisc)

In a quiet location, Espada suffers little from encroachment of anything modern. Espada's design is one of massive simplicity though some areas, such as the door, exhibit striking Moorish-style beauty. The mission has been partially restored, and the random use of different stones in its original construction makes for a decidedly rustic appearance.

As is usually the case with surviving missions, the wall that originally surrounded Espada is long gone, but the foundation of the wall is still evident amidst the grass and overgrowth. The original wall was about 350 feet square, and enclosed within it were a granary, monastery, workshops, and sleeping areas for the natives, all of which are now gone. Still standing is a circular wall two feet thick that served as fortification and lookout for the mission.

The primary reason San Antonio was chosen for the site of important missions was the deep, swift, and clear San Antonio River, which was essential for irrigation of crops. Mission Espada in particular was located in an area believed perfect for irrigation. Later, the missionaries found that the river bed was too low for this purpose. Undaunted, the friars designed and built an aqueduct system to solve this problem. This system is still operational today, providing water to neighboring farms.

It was the policy of the Catholic Church to secularize missions once church leaders felt that the friars' missionary work was completed. For Mission Espada, secularization was complete in 1794. From this point on, the mission began to deteriorate and became home for criminals and transients until restoration began in the 1920's.

Mission San Juan

Mission San Juan, the second oldest of the group, also was originally founded in east Texas, in 1716. It was first moved to the Colorado River, near Austin, and in 1731 was relocated to its present site on the east bank of the San Antonio River.

San Juan was not as successful as many of the other missions. Much of its failure was due to the lack of sufficient space for livestock and farming. Like Mission Espada, it was also in an exposed area and subject to attack by the indigeneous people. Nevertheless, at its height, 51 families, totaling nearly 203 persons, lived at this mission.

As is the case with Mission Espada, the original foundation of the mission wall is visible today, and some parts of this wall are still standing to their original height of three hundred feet. The restored chapel still exhibits much of its original Moorish and Romanesque effects. The entrance is an early example of "open gable" design common in subsequent Texas missions. The two-foot thick front wall has no bell tower but, instead, has three arched openings (two side by side and one above) in which bells were hung.

The interior rectangle of the chapel exhibits faint drawings on the walls. As described in the last century by a Father Bouchu, these decorations show a mixture of Spanish and Native American styles:

A painted rail about four feet high running around the chapel first attracted the eye, then the elaborately painted Roman arch in red and orange over the doorway. The design of this decoration is decidedly of a Moorish cast with corkscrew and tile work, and pillars of red and orange squares. These pillars are about twelve feet high and support another line or rail of color and upon this upper line are a series of figures of musicians each playing a different instrument. The figures are for some reason more indistinct than their instruments, the latter being accurately drawn and easy to distinguish. One of the figures over the frescoed arch of the door is a mandolin player, the best example of them all, the violin bow and features of his face being distinct: his hair is black, his lips red, face and legs orange, feet black, the body of the violin orange and the rest of him and the bow red. To the right of him is a guitar player dressed in a bluish green color, sitting in a red chair.

Time and the elements have faded these brilliant artworks.

It is said that at this mission, Mexican General Antonio López de Santa Anna, on his way to the Alamo, staged a mock wedding to a local young woman whom he wished to make his mistress.

This mission began to decline earlier than many of the others in the area, and its population decreased. It was secularized in 1784 and continued its deterioration until the restoration era of the 1920's.

Mission Concepción

Mission Nuestra Señora de la Purisima Concepción was another transfer from east Texas, where it was founded in 1716. Moved to San Antonio in 1730, it is located about two and a half miles south of the Alamo. It was erected on the site of the former Mission San Francisco Xavier.

It took a number of years to build this mission, and, when finished, it included two small chapels, instead of the single standard large one. Mission Concepción is of great interest today because it has received no restoration at all, save some minor cleaning in the late nineteenth century. The architecture is simple but imposing, exhibiting primarily Romanesque styling. The interior walls, however, were anything but plain, and much of the original artwork, though faded, is still evident to-

day. Much of the appeal of the Catholic Church to the indigenous tribes was the pageantry of the ceremonies and the striking beauty of the chapels. These wall paintings, many of them created by the natives themselves, played a large part in the majestic effect that greeted them when they entered the chapel.

The door of this mission is also of great interest. It is six feet wide and ten feet tall, and above it is a triangular arch, representing the trinity. All along the perimeter of the outside of the door is an ornately knotted rope representing the girdle of the Franciscan friars. Over the door is a small scroll which, translated, says "With these arms be mindful of the mission's patroness and princess, and defend the state of her purity."

As with the other missions, parts of the exterior wall remain visible. As is usually the case, the living quarters, blacksmith shop, granary, and other nonreligious buildings are long gone.

This mission is the only one, other than the Alamo, that was used as a fort during the Texan battle for independence from Mexico. On October 28, 1835, Colonel Jim Bowie and ninety Texans were surrounded by four hundred Mexicans there. During the fierce battle that followed, the Texans routed the much larger Mexican force and suffered only one casualty. This was the first fight the Texans won against the Mexicans.

Mission San José

The last mission of this group of four to be founded was the Mission San José y Miguel de Aguayo. It became the largest and most successful of the San Antonio missions, and became known as the "Queen of the Missions" because of its extraordinary beauty. It has been carefully restored and, today, is probably the most outstanding old Spanish mission from the viewpoint of the historian or the tourist.

This mission was founded in 1720, two years after the establishment of Mission San Antonio de Valero, later known as the Alamo. It was the second mission located on the San Antonio River and is five miles southeast of the Alamo. This original building, however, is not the one that stands today. A fierce storm in 1768 caused the collapse of the dome of the church. In addition, treasure hunters had dug at the base of the original building to such an extent that the building was now unstable; the friars decided to erect a new structure. The cornerstone was laid late in 1768. The building thus dates from forty to fifty years later that those of the other missions, and that difference in time may well account for the more elaborate and outstanding features of this mission.

The building itself exhibits Gothic, Romanesque, and Moorish characteristics. Though the church has been restored to much of its former glory, we must go to a firsthand description from 1777 by a Father Juan Augustin Morfi to discover how it looked when new:

> The convent has two stories with spacious galleries. The one on the second floor opens out on the flat roofs of the Indian quarters and is very convenient. . . . The figures of the facade of the church, the bannisters of the stairway of the convent, and the image of Saint Joseph that is on the pedestal, all were made more beautiful by the ease with which the stone is worked. There are enough rooms for the missionaries and for the convenience of a few guests, as well as the necessary offices for the religious, a large and well-ordered kitchen, a comfortable refectory, and a pantry. There is an armory, where the guns, bows and arrows, and lances are kept. . . in a separate room are kept the decorations and dress with which the Indians bedeck themselves for their dances.

The soldiers' quarters were located opposite the church. As was often the case, inside the mission was a granary, a carpenter shop, spinning and weaving areas, and also a place where sugarcane was made into brown sugar and molasses. This was the first recorded instance of sugarcane being processed in Texas. The outer wall, in typical fashion, was in the shape of a square. The interior perimeter of this wall was lined with the homes of the native families.

A unique feature of this mission was the two swimming pools, one for the natives, and one for the soldiers. The pools were filled with water by use of a gravity canal that also served farmers as an irrigation outlet.

This largest of the missions boasted miles of fields under cultivation, as well as a ranch with thousands of head of cattle, sheep, goats, and other animals. The native tribes worked the farm and ranch, and prospered accordingly. It is said that the community at this mission was more harmonious than most, with less soldier abuse of the natives than was normally the case.

More so than is the case with the three other missions, an intense effort was made to restore San José. This restoration was accomplished, with mostly positive results, by Harvey P. Smith in the 1930's. As a result, it is the most rewarding and instructive mission to the historian and the tourist, and shows well how the natives, friars, and Spanish soldiers lived nearly two centuries ago.

The church itself is famous for its beautifully carved portal and rose window, but there are many other glorious sights as well. Among these are the parapet and carved spouts (to carry off rainwater) and the two stairways that lead to the second story of the tower. Each step of the stairway is a hand-hewn block of oak wood. The famous rose window is the crowning beauty of the church and is part of the front facade. The facade has been called the peak achievement of Spanish mission design, and remains stunning more than two hundred years after its construction.

Local Legends

There are two legends surrounding this historic mission. According to one, Pedro Huizar, the young artist who designed and carved the facade, was waiting for his girlfriend, Rosa, to arrive from Spain so they could be married. Just as he was finishing his work, he received notice that her ship had been lost at sea. In memory of her, he created the rose window and, it is said, just as he finished it he heard her calling him and soon afterward he died.

The second legend concerns an adventurer from Spain who was killed by Apaches and buried in the Mission San José. His fiancé, back in Spain, begged to go to the mission to see his burial place, but was unable to do so. It so happened that the bells for the mission were to be cast in her hometown and so, in front of the crowd that had gathered to witness the casting, she threw her ring and golden cross into the molten material. Others in the crowd did the same, and she hoped this would bring her message of love to her dead lover.

Another unusual feature of this mission is an underground chamber which appears to have been partially sealed by bricks and which was decorated with various wall paintings. It has never been determined what this chamber was used for.

Written birth, marriage, baptism, and death records exist at this mission covering the period from 1777 to 1884; it is one of the few missions where such materials survive.

Mission San José was secularized in 1792 and began to deteriorate quickly. As was the case with some of the other missions, the nineteenth century brought mostly thieves and souvenir hunters who damaged the buildings. From 1835 to 1844 Santa Anna used it as barracks for his soldiers, as later did those fighting for Texan independence. The 1920's and 1930's brought restoration, and Mission San José stands as a stunning monument to the artistic abilities of the Native Americans and the Franciscan friars.

The Missions National Historical Park hosts festivals throughout the year. Many of these are staged with the help of the local churches. Catholic services are still held in all four of these missions. The first week in August is the annual Semana de las Missiones, the Week of the Missions, which features lectures, performances of dance and music, food booths, and demonstrations of Indian crafts.

—*Steve Palmer*

For Further Information:

Ashford, Gerald. *Spanish Texas: Yesterday and Today.* Austin, Texas: Jenkins, 1971. Provides an overview.

Burke, James Wakefield. *Missions of Old Texas.* Cranbury, N.J.: A. S. Barnes, 1971. By far the most comprehensive and best presented discussion of these four missions, along with many others. His description of mission life is extremely interesting.

Fisher, Lewis F. *The Spanish Missions of San Antonio.* San Antonio, Tex.: Maverick, 1998. A history of the Catholic Church and its missions in San Antonio. Includes bibliographical references.

Haley, James L. *Texas: An Album of History.* Garden City, N.Y.: Doubleday, 1984. This worthwhile text gives a more general overview.

San Jacinto

Date: Battle fought in April, 1836
Relevant issues: Military history
Significance: This is the site of the battle in which General Sam Houston defeated the Mexicans

under President Antonio López de Santa Anna and won independence for the Republic of Texas. Today the site is a one thousand-acre State Historic Park marked by the San Jacinto Monument, a 570-foot reinforced concrete tower constructed between 1936 and 1939. The park is also home to the battleship *Texas*, which was active in both world wars.

Location: The San Jacinto Battleground State Historical Park is twenty-two miles east of downtown Houston, off Highway 225 and a few miles north off Highway 134, in southeastern Texas

Site Office:
San Jacinto Battleground State Historical Park
3523 Battleground Road
Le Port, TX 77571
ph.: (713) 479-2421
Web site: www.sanjacinto-museum.org

Since its admission into the United States, Texas has been known for things done on a grand scale. Ironically, a tiny plot of land is the place that Texans hold most dear in their history. This plot is the battlefield of San Jacinto, where, in 1836, a band of men led by Sam Houston defeated Mexican president and general Antonio López de Santa Anna's men, thereby winning independence for the upstart Republic of Texas.

Texan Independence Movement

After Texas declared its secession from Mexico in 1835, Santa Anna led troops into the area to quell the uprising. His men were superior both in training and number to the Texans, and this became increasingly apparent in early 1836. Texan forces under William B. Travis were slaughtered at the Alamo in San Antonio on March 6 by invading forces sixteen times their number. On March 20, about four hundred Texans led by James Walker Fannin were surrounded, captured, and later massacred (along with Fannin himself) at Goliad by order of Santa Anna. The message that followed from Santa Anna to the Texas residents urged them to return to the Mexican fold or face complete destruction.

Meanwhile, Texas general Sam Houston had been desperately trying to assemble troops east of San Antonio at Gonzales to come to Travis's aid. With the fall of San Antonio and a report that Santa Anna was near with perhaps as many as two thousand troops, Houston felt there was no choice but to abandon Gonzales and begin a retreat across eastern Texas that would come to be known as the "Runaway Scrape." He forced the town's residents to set fire to their homes; they joined Houston's 375 men for protection, as soldiers and citizens alike moved away from the burning city. With the Alamo captured and Houston's comparatively tiny army on the run, an overconfident Santa Anna believed it would only be a matter of time before the revolution was over.

Provisional Government

Texas's provisional government was elected on March 17 and led by President David G. Burnet, who publicly castigated Houston for fleeing from confrontation. Oddly enough, Burnet offered this public censure as he himself fled east to Harrisburg (present-day Houston), trying to find someplace safe from which to rule. Houston understood from the disaster at the Alamo that his force was undermanned and untrained—it needed seasoning and reinforcements. So for a month, Houston's soldiers would retreat eastward, all the while picking up more civilians seeking protection from the Mexican troops. Santa Anna's men were pillaging and burning anything of value they found. They were also freeing enslaved blacks as they tracked Houston's men to the north.

The Texans were hampered by the increasing numbers of tagalongs and by their lack of adequate supplies and wagons; although Santa Anna was moving toward them at a rate of twenty-five miles per day, they were finally about to get some good news. An unusually dry spring had slowed the growth of prairie grass; the subsequent lack of grazing lands for the Mexicans' horses slowed Santa Anna's pursuit and allowed the Texans to retain their small lead in the race for the Louisiana border. A rainy period came shortly afterward, flooding the lands and making a muddy mess of the marching territory.

The good news was short-lived; just a few days later, after passing the Navidad River, the Texans received word of the outcome at Goliad. Though the news was tragic, Houston used both the Goliad and Alamo Massacres throughout their march to stoke the emotions of his men; when some of the survivors of Goliad joined the other soldiers, they spoke of horrors that served only to incense their counterparts. For one reason or another, every man in Houston's army hated Santa Anna with a burning passion.

Destructiveness of the Mexican Army

As Houston moved east picking up more men, the Mexicans moved from town to town, destroying everything in their path. One of Santa Anna's field generals, José Urrea, was having particular success as he moved to the south of the Mexican president. Not wanting to be shown up by one in his command, Santa Anna quickly swung his own men toward Harrisburg and the provisional government. His plan was to capture Burnet and then head northward to destroy Houston, who was rumored to be in the area.

It was now April, and Houston had increased the size of his army to nearly one thousand. After crossing the Brazos River on April 12, Houston had a decision to make. Would he turn north toward Nacogdoches and keep fleeing, or head south to finally have a showdown with Santa Anna? To the cheers of his troops and the disdain of the civilians, Houston decided it was time for battle. The civilians, who were to continue on toward Nacogdoches, demanded protection, however, and when three hundred men volunteered, Houston had no choice but to let them go. The defections left him with a fighting force of somewhere between seven hundred and eight hundred.

Santa Anna entered Harrisburg on the night of April 15, only to find most of the city burning and Burnet nowhere to be found. Not only were the city's two newspaper buildings still standing, the editors were still putting out newspapers; when Santa Anna questioned them, they told him that Burnet and his government had fled further east to New Washington, a city on Galveston Bay. Wanting the glory of capturing the rebel president, Santa Anna took a five hundred-man contingent and pursued them. As Santa Anna arrived in New Washington, Burnet, his wife, and his cabinet members were caught trying to row across the bay to safety. Santa Anna refused to fire on a boat that carried a woman, thereby letting Burnet slip through his fingers once again.

While the Mexicans were spending their time on futile pursuits, Houston was marching his men through burned-out Harrisburg on April 19 to keep emotions at a high level. There the Texans re-

The San Jacinto Monument. (AP/Wide World Photos)

ceived word that Santa Anna had moved toward New Washington and that his next goal was to control Lynch's Ferry at the San Jacinto River in an effort to trap the rebels. Houston also was informed that Santa Anna had left most of his force behind in the hope of a hasty capture of Burnet.

Houston's Strategy

Houston knew that his best chance at victory was to meet the smaller Mexican force at the ferry; indeed, getting there first and controlling it would be his best chance at escape should the battle not go in his favor. It would also be important to engage the Mexicans quickly, before their one thousand reinforcements waiting at the Brazos River arrived. So, for the rest of the day of April 19, the Texans moved toward the ferry at the confluence of the San Jacinto River and Buffalo Bayou, a forty-five-mile-long stream. The tone of the conflict had changed—it was Houston who was now on the offensive.

Houston won the foot race to the ferry, arriving on the morning of April 20 just three hours before the Mexicans. Though the Texans had control of the ferry, it would not be long before Santa Anna's

troops arrived in battle formation. Immediately, the Mexicans moved toward the Texans, firing the one cannon they had in their possession. The Texans responded with two cannon of their own, sending the Mexicans retreating into a grove of trees at the south end of the battlefield.

Santa Anna certainly was in no hurry to attack again; he had Houston's back pinned against the fifteen-foot-deep Buffalo Bayou, and his own right covered by the San Jacinto River. He expected five hundred more troops led by General Martín Perfecto de Cós by morning, which would give him a nearly two-to-one advantage over the Texans. The confident Mexican general ordered his troops to set up camp and build barriers, in case Houston tried to launch an attack early the next morning. Around sunset, eighty-five Texan calvalrymen tried to capture the Mexican cannon, but were quickly driven back at the cost of two minor injuries and several downed horses. This incident and some sporadic rifle fire ended a relatively uneventful first day of fighting.

Houston's men set up camp in their own grove of trees on the bank of the Buffalo Bayou, awaiting orders to attack, but Houston would not let them engage, even as April 21 dawned. Cós arrived with reinforcements from the west via Vince's Ferry at 9:00 A.M.; Houston sent one of his best men, Erastus Smith, to destroy Vince's Ferry before any more Mexicans could cross. Smith succeeded, and by doing so effectively trapped the two armies between the waters. Conflict at San Jacinto was then inevitable.

At noon, Houston met with his field generals and debated whether or not to launch an offensive; his two junior officers voted to attack, while his four senior officers voted to lie in wait. The final decision was to wait, though Houston knew he would attack that afternoon. Meanwhile, Santa Anna and Cós waited in their camp, unable to understand why the Texans had not attacked. With their soldiers tired from a long night of marching and building entrenchments, and believing that no man would dare attack in broad daylight over an open field, the Mexican generals allowed their men to take an afternoon nap. Santa Anna himself was still supremely confident that the conflict would begin and end as soon as he decided to launch his own attack.

Throughout the early afternoon, as the Mexicans either meandered around their camp or slept, Houston finally began to prepare his men for an advance. To create an illusion of inactivity, he made sure all movements took place within a clump of covering trees. This secrecy was not needed, however; the Texans' lookouts posted in the trees could not even locate any Mexican sentries in the camp across the plain; Santa Anna's men were not suspecting a thing.

The Battle Begins

With only seven hundred men to organize, Houston was ready within an hour. He placed himself at the center of his men; to the left were two infantry regiments and to the right the two cannon and four more infantry companies. The cavalrymen, led by Mirabeau Lamar, were sent to the far right to cut off the only easy escape route for the Mexicans. At four o'clock, Houston gave the order, and his men advanced in unison toward Santa Anna's troops.

With cries of "Remember the Alamo!" and "Remember Goliad!" the Texans swarmed furiously toward the Mexican line. When they were within six hundred feet of the barricades, they opened fire with the two cannon, sending grapeshot into the camp of the bewildered Mexicans. After softening up the defenses, Houston's men opened with musket fire as they mounted and surged over the barriers. While driving across the field, Houston was wounded in the ankle by a musket shot.

After only eighteen minutes, the Texans were in total control of the Mexican camp. The battle was over in a heartbeat, but the senseless slaughter of surrendering Mexican troops would continue for the next several hours. Houston's generals tried to control their men, but the soldiers were resolved to make Santa Anna's men pay for the Texans' months of hardship. The atrocities were particularly brutal: A Mexican drummer boy with two broken legs who begged a Texan to spare his life was shot in the head. Many other Mexican soldiers who jumped into Peggy Lake, a bog off the river, were picked off by sharpshooters as they surfaced for air. Finally, nearly four hundred Mexican troops banded together to surrender en masse in the hope that they would escape the fate of their compatriots who were captured individually. The strategy worked; they were spared and were taken prisoner.

Santa Anna's Escape

Santa Anna realized early in the battle what its outcome would be, and he managed to slip away as the commotion raged around him. He trekked south toward Fort Bend where General Antonio Gaona and reinforcements waited, in the hope of regrouping and launching another assault on San Jacinto. The general evaded the search parties for a while, but was picked up the next morning by scouts who did not know who he was. When they marched him back into the camp at San Jacinto, his own men identified him by calling out "El Presidente!" as he walked by. He finally revealed his identity and asked to be brought to Houston, who was then recovering from his wound.

The Texans wanted Santa Anna executed for his war crimes, but Houston knew he was more valuable alive than dead. Two more Mexican generals, Vincente Filisola and José Urrea, were reported to be nearby with more than seven thousand troops at their disposal; killing their leader would only provoke them to attack and continue a war that, if prolonged, would be certain disaster for the Texans. In exchange for his life, Santa Anna agreed to order all his troops to retreat beyond the Rio Grande.

When this retreat had ended, Texas was finally free from Mexican rule. Houston and Stephen F. Austin would be nominated for the presidency of the republic the following November, with Houston riding the tide of San Jacinto to a landslide victory.

When the dust at San Jacinto finally settled, the disparity in casualties was astonishing. Only nine of Houston's men were killed or mortally wounded, as compared to more than six hundred dead and seven hundred prisoners on the other side. Though his men were greatly outnumbered, Houston effectively used surprise to defeat his overconfident enemy. However, the massacre that ensued has been branded one of the worst U.S. war atrocities ever, a blight on what is otherwise regarded by Texans as the greatest day in their history.

Visiting the Site

Visitors to the battlefield site can walk across the battlegrounds, and they can browse in the San Jacinto Museum of History at the base of the San Jacinto Monument, a 570-foot concrete tower with an observation floor at the top that offers views of the battlefield and nearby Houston. One other attraction of note to the west of the site in the Houston Ship Channel is the battleship *Texas*, which in 1948 was given to the people of the state after it had seen action in both World War I and World War II.

—*Tony Jaros*

For Further Information:

Bruhl, Marshall de. *Sword of San Jacinto: A Life of Sam Houston.* New York: Random House, 1993. A complete biography of the general who led Texas to freedom, and then became the republic's first president.

Haley, James L. *Texas: From the Frontier to the Spindletop.* New York: St. Martin's Press, 1985. Gives an overview of the main events in the state's history until roughly 1910.

Long, Jeff. *Duel of Eagles.* New York: William Morrow, 1990. Chronicles the Texas-Mexico conflict, with particular emphasis on the siege at the Alamo.

San Jacinto Museum. www.sanjacinto-mueum.org. This site contains information for the State Historical Park, the museum, and the battleship *Texas.*

Other Historic Sites

Apollo Mission Control Center

Location: Houston, Harris County

Relevant issues: Aviation history, science and technology

Statement of significance: This site represents the importance of the Johnson Space Center in the U.S. manned spaceflight program. This control center was used to monitor nine Gemini and all Apollo flights, Apollo-Soyuz, and space shuttle flights.

Cabot

Location: Port Isabel, Cameron County

Relevant issues: Military history, naval history, World War II

Statement of significance: Reflecting the exigencies of World War II, *Cabot* (1943) is the sole survivor of a unique class of light carriers built atop the incomplete hulls of cruisers of the President Class. Built as hasty replacements for the carriers lost early in the war, the Independence Class carriers served with distinction in nearly every major naval engagement of the war in the Pacific from 1943 on. *Cabot* earned nine battle stars and the prestigious Presidential Unit Citation. In 1967, it was turned over to Spain and recommissioned SNS *Dedalo*; in 1989, *Cabot* was returned to the United States. Essentially unmodified, *Cabot* is now a museum of World War II naval technology.

Elissa

Location: Pier 21, The Strand, Galveston, Galveston County

Relevant issues: Naval history

Statement of significance: Built in 1877, the bark *Elissa* is the second-oldest operational sailing vessel in the world and one of the three oldest merchant vessels still afloat. Open and accessible to the public, *Elissa* allows visitors to participate as working crew members, providing a firsthand perspective on square-riggers, maritime culture, seafaring, and maritime preservation.

Fort Belknap

Location: Newcastle, Young County

Relevant issues: American Indian history, Military history, western expansion

Statement of significance: Established in 1851 following the Mexican War when the Texas frontier was being ravished by Comanche-Kiowa raids, Fort Belknap was the anchor of a chain of outer border posts stretching from the Red River to the Rio Grande. Until 1865, it was the key post in the protection of the exposed frontier; it bore the brunt of Comanche-Kiowa assault, and during the Civil War it served as a base for campaigns against these raiders.

Fort Brown

Location: Brownsville, Cameron County

Relevant issues: Civil War, Latino history, military history

Statement of significance: Established in April, 1846, by Brigadier General Zachary Taylor, Fort Brown was under siege at the time of the battle of Palo Alto, and its siege was raised by the Americans' defeat of the Mexican army at Resaca de la Palma. Troops stationed here fought the last battle of the Civil War; the fort was the center for troop activity during the Mexican bandit trouble of 1913 to 1917.

Fort Richardson

Location: Jacksboro, Jack County

Relevant issues: American Indian history, military history, western expansion

Statement of significance: Established in 1867 to replace the recently abandoned Fort Belknap as the northernmost fort in the Texas chain of fortifications, the fort played an important role in the protection of American lives and property during the days of the Kiowa-Comanche conflict of the post-Civil War period, particularly the Red River War of 1874.

Fort Sam Houston

Location: San Antonio, Bexar County

Relevant issues: Aviation history, Latino history, military history

Statement of significance: Authorized in 1875 and completed in 1879, this was the U.S. Army's principal supply base in the Southwest; the fort supplied the Rough Riders in 1898 and John J.

Pershing's Mexican campaign in 1916. Experiments with the Wright biplane here led to the establishment of the Signal Corps Aviation Section in 1914.

Hangar 9, Brooks Air Force Base

Location: San Antonio, Bexar County

Relevant issues: Aviation history, military history

Statement of significance: Erected in 1918 for the U.S Army Signal Corps Aviation Section on one of its hastily established World War I training fields, this wood-trussed frame structure is the country's oldest Air Force aircraft storage and repair facility and symbolizes the early Army effort to create an effective air force.

J A Ranch

Location: Palo Duro, Armstrong County

Relevant issues: Business and industry

Statement of significance: Between 1879 and 1889, under the direction of Charles Goodnight (1836-1929), the J A Ranch grew to encompass 700,000 acres of grassland supporting forty thousand head of cattle. Goodnight, a pioneer cattleman and the first rancher in the Texas Panhandle, is recognized for his scientific cattle breeding.

Johnson Boyhood Home

Location: Johnson City, Blanco County

Relevant issues: Political history

Statement of significance: From 1913 to 1920, and again from 1922 to 1930, this small, one-story frame house was the family home of Lyndon Baines Johnson (1908-1973), thirty-sixth president of the United States (1963-1969).

Landergin Mesa

Location: Vega, Oldham County

Relevant issues: American Indian history

Statement of significance: A ruin consisting of a series of buildings atop a steep-sided mesa on the east side of East Alamosa Creek, this is one of the largest, best-stratified, least-damaged, and most spectacularly located ruins of Panhandle culture.

Lubbock Lake Site

Location: Lubbock, Lubbock County

Relevant issues: American Indian history

Statement of significance: Excavations at the site in Yellow House Canyon, discovered in the 1930's, have revealed a stratified sequence of human habitation spanning eleven thousand to twelve thousand years and providing evidence for occupation during Clovis, Folsom, Plainview, Late Paleo-Indian, Archaic, Ceramic, and historic periods.

Majestic Theatre

Location: San Antonio, Bexar County
Relevant issues: Cultural history
Statement of significance: The great film palaces gradually replaced burlesque as entertainment within everyone's reach, rich and poor alike. In the 1920's and 1930's, the picture palace flourished in big cities and small towns as fantasy worlds into which anyone could escape for a few hours. When the boom was over, it left remnants of this glittering age across America; a handful of these theaters have been reused and restored. The Majestic Theatre, which opened in 1929, is one of the few remaining atmospheric/fantasy palaces in the United States and one of the most remarkable and faithfully restored in the Southwest.

Palo Alto Battlefield

Location: Brownsville, Cameron County
Relevant issues: Latino history, military history
Statement of significance: Here, on May 8, 1846, 2,300 U.S. Army soldiers led by Brigadier General Zachary Taylor engaged 3,300 Mexican troops under the command of Major General Mariano Arista in the first of two important battles of the Mexican War fought on American soil. Galling fire from Taylor's artillery kept Mexican forces from reaching the American line. After the battle, the Mexican troops began their retreat to behind the Resaca de la Palma; Taylor's victory here made the invasion of Mexico possible.

Porter Farm

Location: Terrell, Kaufman County
Relevant issues: Cultural history, political history
Statement of significance: Here, in 1903, Dr. Seaman A. Knapp (1833-1911), special agent of the U.S. Department of Agriculture, organized the first cooperative farm demonstration, which was designed to help local cotton farmers deal with the boll weevil. From this one highly successful demonstration, the entire nationwide Agricultural Extension Service has developed: Boy's Corn Clubs, Ladies' Canning Societies, 4-H Clubs, and intensified county fair activities all stem from the extension work begun on the Porter Farm.

Rayburn House

Location: Bonham, Fannin County
Relevant issues: Political history
Statement of significance: From 1916 until his death, this farm house—known as the Home Place—was the residence of Samuel T. Rayburn (1882-1961). "Mr. Sam" served in the U.S. House of Representatives from 1913 until his death in 1961 and was Speaker (1940-1947, 1949-1953, 1955-1961) twice as long as any other individual to hold that office. His astute political sense preserved the delicate balance between factions of the Democratic Party.

Resaca de la Palma Battlefield

Location: Brownsville, Cameron County
Relevant issues: Latino history, military history
Statement of significance: In the early hours of May 9, 1846, after the battle of Palo Alto, Mexican forces under Major General Mariano Arista retreated to Resaca de la Palma; Brigadier General Zachary Taylor and his army gave pursuit and the fighting resumed. Taylor ordered his cavalry to charge the Mexican position, sending the enemy into disarray. The Mexican commander narrowly escaped capture, his tent and all of his personal effects falling into the hands of the attackers; his forces fled across the Rio Grande while all the Mexican artillery and supplies fell to the victorious Americans.

Roma Historic District

Location: Roma, Starr County
Relevant issues: European settlement, Latino history
Statement of significance: Roma's architectural fabric represents the evolution of a key town in the border region during the nineteenth century. Roma is the only intact U.S. settlement that derives from the mid-eighteenth century colonization and town planning efforts of José de Escandon; the Escandon town planning, coloni-

zation, and land grant system are of key historic significance in the development of the Spanish empire and in the unfolding of the Mexican Northeast and the American Southwest from 1748 to 1835. Roma's buildings form a virtual "living catalog" of the different building technologies uses along the lower Rio Grande in the nineteenth century. The brickwork of a number of residences and commercial structures in the district that were designed by Henrique Portscheller is strikingly elegant, featuring rounded corners and finely carved classical motifs.

Trevino-Uribe Rancho

Location: San Ygnacio, Philadelphia County
Relevant issues: Latino history
Statement of significance: The Jesús Trevino-Blas Uribe Rancho is an exceptional survivor of vernacular Mexican architectural and ranching traditions on the northern, or American, side of the Rio Grande. Evolving from a simple one-room stone shelter, built c. 1830 by Jesús Trevino, who maintained his principal residence in Mexico, the complex grew in four, possibly five, building campaigns, into a large ranch headquarters forming an enclosed quadrangle. Although the last addition dates from 1871, traditional building patterns were maintained, illustrating the persistence of Hispanic culture along the borderlands long after Texas had become part of the United States. Largely in original condition, the complex vividly portrays the Mexican-Texan frontier experience.

USS Texas

Location: Houston, Harris County
Relevant issues: Military history, naval history, World War I, World War II
Statement of significance: Sole survivor of six American dreadnoughts, *Texas* was completed in time to participate in the American landings at Veracruz. It served during World War I as a member of the Atlantic Fleet, hunting down German warships; between the wars, it was the first battleship to launch an aircraft from its decks. During World War II, *Texas* served on Atlantic convoy duty, bombarding shore positions during the invasions of North Africa, Normandy, and Southern France; in late 1944, it proceeded to the Pacific, where it participated in the bombardment of Iwo Jima and Okinawa.

Woodland

Location: Huntsville, Walker County
Relevant issues: Military history, political history
Statement of significance: From 1847 to 1859, Woodland, a typical Texas hill country cottage of clapboard over logs, was the residence of Sam Houston (1793-1863), who led the Texas army to victory at San Jacinto, was president of the Republic of Texas (1836-1838, 1841-1844), and represented the new state in the U.S. Senate (1846-1859). His last public post was as governor (1859-1861); he was removed from office for refusing to support Texas's secession from the Union.

Utah

Arches National Park. (PhotoDisc)

History of Utah

As attested by archaeological evidence, Utah's territory has been continuously inhabited for the past eleven thousand years. The earliest indigenous peoples hunted with spears, used baskets to gather wild foods, and made stone tools. Later peoples, besides hunting and gathering, grew maize. Utes and Paiutes arrived about six hundred years ago, followed later by Navajos. When Anglo-Americans began settling the Utah region, these American Indians, together with the Shoshones and Bannocks, were most numerous.

The first people other than American Indians to enter the region were Spaniards and Mexicans. Juan Maria Rivera made two expeditions to the area in 1765. In 1776 two priests of the Franciscan Order, Fathers Francisco Atanasio Domínguez and Francisco Silvestre Vélez de Escalante, led an expedition from Santa Fe, now in New Mexico, seeking passage to Monterey, California. No further expeditions were recorded until the early nineteenth century, when trade between Santa Fe and Indians of the Utah region became common. From then until the 1840's, numerous fur traders and other mountain men visited the area for varying lengths of time, and many pioneers and adventurers on their way to California traveled across it, but no permanent settlements were established. In 1824 the famous scout Jim Bridger came upon the Great Salt Lake and, tasting its briny water, believed it an ocean.

In its formative period, Utah's inhospitable terrain and geographically remote location far from both the populous East and the growing Pacific region were principal factors in its destiny. On the one hand, its arid and mountainous landscape dissuaded early travelers from settling, but on the other, its remoteness attracted the people whose predominance most influenced its character from first settlement to the present day. Those were the Mormons, hearty, closely knit, deeply religious, hardworking folk, who adapted well to Utah's harsh topography.

Arrival of the Mormons

Numbering about three million today, Mormons are formally members of the Church of Jesus Christ of Latter-day Saints. They take their name from the title the Book of Mormon, an important holy book along with the Bible. A principal belief is that Jesus appeared in the New World after the Crucifixion. After their church was founded in 1830 by Joseph Smith in Fayette, New York, Mormons were persecuted wherever they settled. Non-Mormons feared their aloofness from society and what appeared as strange ways, such as their communal economy and theocratic organizational structure, in which religious and civic affairs were intertwined. What antagonized others most, however, was the Mormon belief in polygamy, families with several wives, a church doctrine that emerged in the 1850's.

Leaving New York in 1831, Smith and his followers moved to Ohio, but trouble there led to expulsion in 1838-1839. Settling in the Illinois town of Nauvoo, by 1842 they had aroused deep resentment in that state. Arrested in 1844, Smith and his brother were murdered by a mob. Two years later, led by Brigham Young, a man of exceptional leadership qualities, the Mormons fled Illinois, venturing west into unsettled territory in search of secure autonomy. Young, traveling with an advance party, upon sighting the Great Salt Lake Valley in 1847, is said to have declared, "This is the place."

Since their beginnings the Mormons had sent missionaries to other states and western European countries to gain adherents. Now in their new desert home, they called their followers to join them, and Mormons began arriving in the thousands, especially from northern Europe. By 1850 a number of towns had been founded; within Brigham Young's lifetime, some 350 settlements were established. By 1900 the number had grown to 500 settlements in Utah and the surrounding states, the result of the Mormon policy of colonization. The towns, based on communal ownership, were planned communities of farmers and tradesmen.

Becoming a Territory

Meanwhile, after the Mexican War of 1846, the Mormon territory became part of the United

States, and the community's autonomy was once more put in jeopardy. Mormons had participated in the war on the American side, sending a volunteer battalion on a famous march from Kansas to San Diego. In 1849-1850, Brigham Young declared the Mormon settlement a new state of Deseret, after the word for honeybee in the Book of Mormon. With Young as governor, church leaders filled all offices. Deseret encompassed an immense area extending to San Diego in Southern California, giving access to a port for Mormon immigration and trade. Congress, however, suspicious of the proposed state's huge size and theocratic polity, rejected it, setting up instead the smaller, but still large, territory of Utah, including Nevada, Wyoming, and parts of Colorado. Utah Territory's size was progressively pared, until 1868, when the future state's present borders were drawn. Brigham Young was the first territorial governor.

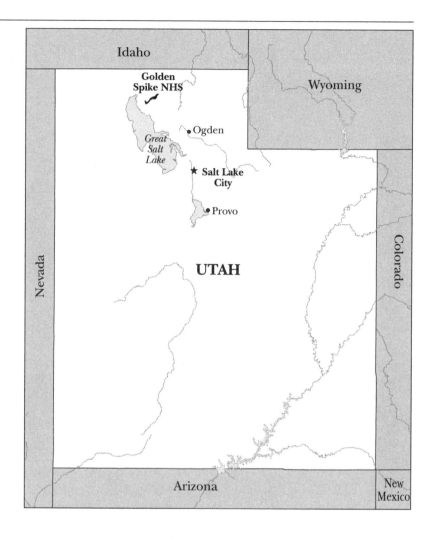

The Mormon Church did its utmost to populate its territory, issuing a call for members to gather there. In 1849 the church set up a Perpetual Emigrating Fund, used to bring poor members from distant places. Mormons soon began arriving in the thousands from northern Europe, including many from the British Isles. In the end, the fund raised hundreds of thousands of dollars for Mormon emigration.

Conflicts with Non-Mormons
Relations between Mormons and non-Mormons were tense, and conflicts frequent. Outsiders were excluded from positions of power and influence, and mutual suspicion abounded. Mormons recalled persecution; non-Mormons questioned Mormon loyalty to American democracy. In 1857 rumors of Mormon rebellion against the United States led the administration of President James Buchanan to send some 2,500 troops to occupy Salt Lake City and its environs—events known as the Utah War. Mormon attacks on the troops' supply trains did little to relieve federal anxieties.

Later, the church's official neutrality in the Civil War had a similar effect. Young was stripped of his office, and a non-Mormon was installed as governor by the U.S. government. Then, in the darkest chapter of Utah's history, Mormons slaughtered more than one hundred non-Mormon civilian men, women, and children traveling through southern Utah from Missouri and Arkansas. However, after some negotiation, peace was achieved in 1858, though further incidents recurred in the 1860's, when federal soldiers returned.

Besides trouble with non-Mormons and with Washington, D.C., the new territory also experienced conflicts with American Indians. At first Brigham Young's Indian policy was successful in securing peace. American Indian resentment over settler occupation of their lands soon led to hostilities, however. In 1853 the Walker War, named for a Ute chief, broke out, but it ended the next year when Young persuaded the Utes to lay down their arms. Bannock and Shoshone raids continued in northern Utah until 1863, when U.S. Army troops defeated them. Peace was restored in 1867, but raids continued until late 1872. More conflicts occurred in the twentieth century, but by the mid-1920's the Indians had receded. By century's end, however, Native Americans used the legal system to further their interests.

While these events were taking place, others occurred that would have far-reaching effects on Mormon-dominated Utah. Non-Mormons were arriving in significant numbers to work mines, after silver and lead were discovered in Bingham Canyon, near Salt Lake City. Mormons had previously made such discoveries, but were discouraged from exploiting them for fear of attracting outsiders and losing labor needed to produce necessities. Other non-Mormons opened stores or other businesses.

At this time, the nation's communications were progressing. For a scant nineteen months in 1860-1861, the Pony Express road across Utah carried mail from St. Joseph, Missouri, to Sacramento, California. The arrival of the telegraph linking the nation from coast to coast and the completion of a transcontinental railroad in 1869 opened Utah's products to national markets, and a boom began in railroad feeder lines to transport them.

From Territory to State
As the territory progressed economically, it sought entrance to the Union as a state. This proved a formidable task, since distrust of Mormons was prevalent. In 1852 Brigham Young had publicly acknowledged Mormon polygamy. In the 1870's and 1880's, Congress passed acts prohibiting this practice. Utah petitioned for statehood seven times before it was successful. Opposition to statehood receded only after 1890, when Mormon leader Wilford Woodruff issued a manifesto renouncing polygamy. In 1895 a constitution was ratified outlawing this practice and separating church and state; the following year Utah became the nation's forty-fifth state.

Utah's new constitution called for several elected officials in the executive branch, some of whom cannot be reelected. In keeping with a tradition of strong leadership authority, governors have more power than those of nearby states. Most judges are elected, however, and the legislature is bicameral.

Into the American Mainstream
The old ways of the original Mormon settlers died hard. When the last survivor of the 1847 trek from Illinois died in Idaho in the 1920's, thousands of Mormons trooped north to pay their final respects. By then, Utah had begun decisive change that would transform it into a modern society. By World War I Utah was entering the American mainstream. The social landscape was increasingly urbanized, and the economy was developing. New ores, especially copper, were mined, and smelting became a large industry. Labor unions emerged, and with them labor conflict appeared. The Depression hit the state particularly hard, and severe droughts in 1931 and 1934 did not help matters. However, as elsewhere in the nation, the coming of World War II eased economic hardship, as federal defense dollars combined with conscription to lessen unemployment.

Postwar Developments
After World War II, Utah passed from being an agricultural and mining state to an industrial state. A Geneva steel plant opened in 1943, and federal investment in defense industries during the decades that followed spurred industrialization. Utah became a principal site of missile development, and other defense industries took root.

By the 1980's and 1990's a number of high-tech industries that were growing in importance were located in Utah. The state was becoming more politically and culturally sophisticated. Environmental politics entered the scene, and figures such as Utah senator Orrin Hatch became important in Washington politics. As the end of the century approached, Utah had moved from a predominantly industrial to a service economy, as tourism and other service industries expanded. While the position of the Mormon Church remained strong, barely more than a century of statehood had seen Utah move squarely into the modern world.

—*Charles F. Bahmueller*

Golden Spike

Date: Railway completed on May 10, 1869; National Historic Site authorized on July 30, 1965

Relevant issues: Business and industry, western expansion

Significance: This is where the transcontinental railway line was completed. The line was disassembled and contributed as scrap for the metal drives of World War II. The site is now a National Historic Site.

Location: Brigham City, seventy-five miles northwest of Salt Lake City

Site Office:
Golden Spike National Historic Site
P.O. Box 897
Brigham City, UT 84302-0923
ph.: (435) 471-2209
Web site: www.nps.gov/gosp

When the Founders of the United States first envisioned the nation, they probably did not realize that eventually it would border the world's two largest oceans. They certainly could not have imagined that, less than a century later, citizens would be able to traverse the three thousand-mile width of the continent in the span of days. The struggle to achieve that feat came to a conclusion in a little Utah town called Promontory.

Development of the Railroads

As in Great Britain and continental Europe, the development of railroad transportation in the United States heralded a new era of exploration and commerce. In fact, railroads were most likely the single largest economic spark the young nation had ever known. Whereas the Mississippi and Missouri Rivers were open deep into the Midwest for ship traffic, much of the nation, particularly the newly settled areas in the Rocky Mountains and along the Pacific coast, was virtually inaccessible. While settlers had reached these areas by horse and wagon, supplies could not be delivered quickly via that method. Therefore, the penetration of the railroad into these areas changed the new economies

dramatically. The agricultural products and mineral ores of the West could now be transported to the manufacturing centers of the East. In addition, food, supplies, and other raw materials could be sent to the West over the railways, helping to bolster the fledgling industries there.

However, the railroads into the West reached only so far. A great natural barrier in the form of the Cascade Range and the Rocky Mountains had, until the mid-nineteenth century, precluded any rapid travel directly from the East to the Pacific coast. While the pioneers had been able to cross the mountains via horse and wagon, the trip was difficult and often deadly during searing summer heat and the bitter winter snows. Even so, the admission of California to the Union in 1850 and the news of its bounty of natural resources enticed many easterners. In that year, the U.S. House of Representatives' Committee on Roads and Canals issued a statement that a transcontinental railroad would "cement the commercial, social and political relations of the East and West [and be] a highway over which will pass the commerce of Europe and Asia." Previously, commerce across the country had been almost entirely dependent on the long journey around South America's Cape Horn or across the dense jungles of Central America. Many congressmen believed a railroad link would reduce time and expense in transporting goods, as well as the mail and government troops to Pacific coast defense posts.

Plans for a Transcontinental Railroad

Soon, the Republican and Democratic political parties each had written the development of a transcontinental railroad route into their party platforms. Congress began to debate where the eastern terminus of the line would be located, with many lawmakers arguing that their particular city offered the most political and economic benefits. To help settle the dispute, the army's Corps of Topographical Engineers was commissioned by Congress to determine the most practical railroad route from the Mississippi to the Pacific. By 1855, the engineers had decided that there were four possible routes: two in the North and two in the South. The transcontinental link that finally was built followed none of those routes, however.

Theodore D. Judah, a Sacramento Valley railroad engineer, became obsessed with the idea for

A reenactment of the completion of the transcontinental railroad at Promontory Point. (courtesy of the Utah Travel Council)

the railway. He mapped out a route of his own that would pass through California's Sierra Nevada at Donner Pass, the famed crossing where many settlers had died in winter snows on their way west. Judah lobbied politicians in Washington, D.C., but his most sympathetic supporters turned out to be four Sacramento merchants: Charles Crocker, Mark Hopkins, Collis P. Huntington, and Leland Stanford. As they were interested in promoting their businesses, the four investors wanted the line to pass by several Nevada mining towns once it had surmounted the Sierra Nevada. In June, 1861, the four incorporated the Central Pacific Railroad Company of California, while Judah worked with the nation's lawmakers to secure funding for the route's construction.

The Civil War and the Railroads

The Civil War had already erupted in April, 1861, and so the railway line took on new, military significance for the North. The Union also hoped to so-

lidify ties with California, which had threatened to secede with the Confederacy. With the backing of President Abraham Lincoln, the Railroad Act of 1862 was passed by Congress in June, 1862, and signed into law in July of that year. The act created the Union Pacific Railroad and authorized it to build a railway westward from the Missouri River to the California border or at whatever point it met the Central Pacific Railroad tracks being built eastward. Without the congressmen from the seceded states to lobby for a southern route, the northern route was chosen. Omaha was selected as the Union Pacific's terminus. The federal government gave land grants and subsidies along a four hundred-foot right-of-way beside the railroad that cut through public domain land in the intermountain West, allowing for homesteading and the creation of towns.

The 1864 Railroad Act earmarked more government subsidies for the project. Even with that, federal loans provided no more than half the transcontinental railway's needed capital. It was hoped that land grants or private investment would make up the rest. The success of the proposed transcontinental railroad was far from certain, and few investors appeared. As a result, the Central Pacific and the Union Pacific formed dummy construction companies that funneled business back to themselves, free from government regulation. Consequently, the Central Pacific and the Union Pacific reaped large profits.

Construction on the Transcontinental Railroad Begins

When actual construction began on each end of the railway in 1865, the logistics of the undertaking became even more complicated. The Central Pacific had to ship all equipment, tools, rails, and bolts around South America's Cape Horn or across the Panamanian Isthmus in Central America to San Francisco, delaying work for weeks. The Union Pacific could ship supplies more easily to Omaha, but both companies expended great amounts of money and effort relaying supplies from the terminal points to the ends-of-track, where the construction workers made camp. Then, supplies were shipped by wagon train even farther into the wilderness to the surveying parties and grading crews, who prepared the trackbed. In the Great Plains, Union Pacific graders prepared trackbed about one hundred miles ahead of the track being laid by the construction crews; in the mountains, the graders tried to stay two hundred to three hundred miles in advance of the track.

Tent cities sprang up adjacent to each of the railroad workers' base camps along the Union Pacific line. Brothels, saloons, and gambling houses proliferated in these cities as a diversion for tired workers. Many of them developed into full-fledged towns. North Platte, Nebraska; Cheyenne, Wyoming; Laramie, Wyoming; and Green River, Wyoming, all began as raucous railroad boomtowns. On the Central Pacific line, tent camps were nonexistent. Most of the workers were Chinese laborers, not known to be drinkers or gamblers. In addition, Charles Crocker, who headed Central Pacific's construction firm, imposed law and order, outlawing liquor and vice in his workers' camps.

Construction Difficulties

Strict discipline was necessary among Central Pa-

cific workers as they faced nearly insurmountable construction obstacles from the start. Their Union Pacific counterparts were laying track through the flat Platte Valley in Nebraska. Central Pacific crews, on the other hand, encountered their toughest work immediately. The ominous Sierra Nevada mountains loomed only a few miles east of Sacramento, their starting point. At one point, the Central Pacific was forced to construct nearly thirty-seven miles of snowsheds over the mountains to shelter the track from avalanches during the winter. Many men died in the winters of 1866-1867 and 1867-1868 when unusually heavy snowfall buried base camps overnight. It took nearly two years for the Central Pacific line to be laid to the Sierra Nevada summit, only one hundred miles east of Sacramento.

Union Pacific work crews, while working on flat land, faced danger of a different kind: Indian attacks. Sioux and Cheyenne Indian tribes attacked Union Pacific workers repeatedly. Soon, several U.S. military battalions were stationed along the route in new forts constructed to protect the railroad workers. Work progressed on the Union Pacific line quickly; from 1865 to 1868, crews laid 350 miles of track.

As Central Pacific crews descended the Sierra Nevada into the Nevada desert, Union Pacific crews began to work feverishly. It became a race to see which company first would reach the Great Salt Lake Basin in Utah. Both companies wanted to control as much of the rail route and the Great Basin trade as possible. Moreover, both wanted to be able to retire the debt on the government loans they had used to build the line before the loans' due date in 1875. Central Pacific and Union Pacific leaders also became convinced that whichever company built the longest portion of the transcontinental railway would enjoy greater prestige in the eyes of the nation.

Conflicting Union Pacific-Central Pacific Plans

By the spring of 1868, Central Pacific and Union Pacific survey teams were working side by side near Fort Bridger, Wyoming, but it soon became apparent that the two survey parties were planning to lay lines in different places that would not connect. The Central Pacific submitted its planned line to the U.S. Department of the Interior. Secretary of the Interior Orville Browning approved the Central Pacific line because he was hostile to the Union Pacific. The Union Pacific protested Browning's ruling. Browning, therefore, appointed a special commission to hear the two companies' complaints and determine the most equitable line. As a result, the meeting point of the railways was set forty-eight miles west of Ogden, Utah, in a circular basin at the summit of the Promontory Mountains. Building the lines to this terminus proved to be even more challenging. On the eastern flank of the Promontory Mountains, the ten-mile grade was very steep, averaging a climb of eighty feet to the mile. The Union Pacific brought in extra workers, many of them Irishmen and Mormons from the surrounding areas.

By mid-April, 1869, the two railheads were only fifty miles apart. Central Pacific and Union Pacific company officials set May 8 as the day for the ceremony to unite the rails. About that time, officials from both companies began traveling toward the terminus in trains on their respective tracks. Central Pacific officials were the first to arrive. They carried a $350 golden spike engraved with the words "The Last Spike" and presented it to officials in San Francisco by David Hewes, a construction magnate from the city. The train with Union Pacific officials aboard was stopped at Piedmont, Wyoming, when five hundred workers demanding back wages surrounded the car. The workers chained the car's wheels to the rails and vowed not to release the officials until they were paid. The officials wired the Union Pacific's offices in Boston for money and the train was allowed to pass.

Joining of the Railroad Lines

On May 7, Central Pacific crews had reached the summit, but Union Pacific crews had not. It was not until two days later that the Union Pacific laid its final 2,500 feet of track. Crews left one rail length between the Union Pacific and Central Pacific railheads. On May 10, 1869, two days after the ceremony had been scheduled to take place, some five hundred to six hundred dignitaries, railroad officials, guests, construction workers, and local spectators gathered in the chilly mountain air, squinting in the spring sun.

Excited by the impending event, the crowd quickly became unruly, pressing forward to get a view of the last spike being driven. In the end, only about twenty people were able to see the uniting of the rails. Telegraph companies attached a wire to the last spike in order to transmit the sound of the final blows to an expectant nation. The golden spike was one of many pounded into the last railroad tie. The actual "last spike" was an ordinary iron one. At exactly 12:47 P.M., officials from both the Central Pacific and the Union Pacific took turns swinging at the wired spike and celebrations broke out across the country. After the ceremony, locomotives from each line advanced over the connected rails. Engineers from both engines joined hands across the divide and a bottle of champagne was broken over the final tie to christen the new transcontinental link. The actual completion of the railroad occurred later in the afternoon as the special spikes and ties were lifted up and replaced with ordinary spikes and ties. For the first time, American citizens could cross the young nation directly and rapidly.

The Rise of Promontory

The town of Promontory, Utah, grew up around the terminus point. For about a year, the town and the rail station boomed, providing a transfer point between the Central Pacific and Union Pacific lines. Rows of tents (many with false fronts) housed hotels, lunch counters, saloons, gambling dens, and several shops. However, the prosperous days of Promontory, like those of many other railroad boomtowns, were limited. In early 1870, the terminus of the two lines was moved east to Ogden.

The first transcontinental route hastened the development of several others. In 1883, three other lines were completed: the Northern Pacific line from Minneapolis, Minnesota, to Portland, Oregon; the Atchison, Topeka and Santa Fe from Kansas to Los Angeles, California; and the Southern Pacific from New Orleans, Louisiana, to San Francisco, California. Ten years later, the Great Northern line from St. Paul, Minnesota, to Seattle, Washington, was opened.

Decline of the Transcontinental Route

Soon after the turn of the twentieth century, the Promontory transcontinental route began to fall into disfavor. The steep grade on the eastern slope of the Promontory Mountains forced the railroad companies to run helper engines on the line to push the cargo uphill. These extra engines cost nearly $1,500 per day to run. Consequently, the companies began looking for a more economical route. In 1902, the Southern Pacific Railroad, which had absorbed the Central Pacific, chose to shorten the line through the Great Basin by building a railroad trestle south of the existing line that would run directly across the Great Salt Lake.

The Lucin Cutoff, as it was called, decreased shipping expenses across the Great Basin for the Southern Pacific by nearly sixty thousand dollars per month. For almost forty years, the Promontory line was used only when bad weather threatened a crossing on the cutoff. In 1942, the Southern Pacific decided to tear up the Promontory line and contribute the scrap iron to efforts in World War II. The "undriving" of the last spike received as much fanfare of the initial ceremony seventy-three years before. One of those in attendance at the "undriving" was Mary Ipsen, an eighty-five-year-old woman who lived in nearby Bear River City, Utah. At age twelve, she had worked as a waitress on the mess car of a work train involved in building the Central Pacific-Union Pacific line over the Promontory Mountains.

In the late 1960's, the Department of the Interior built a visitors' center, marker, and replica locomotives and rails at the spot where the two rail lines were united more than a hundred years ago. Although air travel now makes it possible to span the nation's coasts in a matter of hours, the Golden Spike National Historic Site is a tribute to America's nineteenth century railway visionaries and the laborers who made their vision a reality.

—*S. Marshall Poindexter and Sharon M. Poindexter*

For Further Information:

Dowty, Robert R. *Rebirth of the Jupiter and the 119: Building the Replica Locomotives at Golden Spike.* Tucson, Ariz.: Southwest Parks and Monuments Association, 1994. Discusses the construction of replica locomotives for the site by the Department of the Interior in the late 1960's.

Utah Historical Quarterly 37, no. 1 (Winter, 1969). In commemoration of the hundredth anniversary of the railway's completion, this entire issue is devoted to the subject of the railway, its construction, and its impact.

Utley, Robert M., and Francis A. Ketterson, Jr. *Golden Spike.* Washington, D.C.: National Park Service, 1982. Presents an excellent overview of the creation of the transcontinental railway.

Temple Square, Salt Lake City

Date: Cornerstone laid on April 6, 1853

Relevant issues: Religion

Significance: On this ten-acre city block stand three historic buildings of the Church of Jesus Christ of Latter-day Saints: the Temple, the Tabernacle, and the Assemble Hall. A much-visited tourist attraction, Temple Square is also home to two visitors' centers.

Location: In the heart of Salt Lake City, bounded by Main Street, West Temple, North Temple, and South Temple Streets

Site Office:

Church of Jesus Christ of Latter-day Saints
50 East North Temple Street
Salt Lake City, UT 84150-0002
ph.: (801) 240-2640

The Church of Jesus Christ of Latter-day Saints, known commonly as the Mormon Church, has a worldwide membership of some nine million people. While it is organized in more than one hundred thirty countries, the church is most commonly associated with the state of Utah and especially Salt Lake City, its international headquarters. Located at the heart of Salt Lake City is Temple Square, a ten-acre city block that takes its name from the fact that the most famous of the church's temples stands there. Perhaps as well known as the Temple itself is the Salt Lake City Tabernacle, the original home of the Mormon Tabernacle Choir, and located directly west of the Temple on Temple Square. The Assemble Hall, which is directly south of the Tabernacle, is another historic building on Temple Square, and there are two visitors' centers also located at the site.

Origins of the Mormon Church

Although the Mormon Church is most closely associated with Utah, it had its origins in upstate New York in 1830, when Joseph Smith organized the church. Smith, regarded by church faithful as a modern-day prophet, had received a series of revelations including those that led him to translate a purportedly ancient text that he published as the Book of Mormon. The Mormon Church accepts the Book of Mormon, along with the Bible, as scripture.

The church was began with only six members but grew quickly, largely because of active missionary work by the early members. Missionary work has long been a hallmark of the Church of Jesus Christ of Latter-day Saints, and young men and women serve throughout the world as volunteer lay missionaries.

The growth of the church in those early years was accompanied by severe mistrust and misunderstanding of the Mormons throughout the eastern United States. After joining the church, members gathered to be with Smith and other members of the church but could not find a place where they could establish a community free of persecution. They were forced out of Ohio, Missouri, and Illinois. Their settlement known as Nauvoo, on the banks of the Mississippi River in Illinois, was the largest city in the state in the 1840's. It was in Illinois in 1844 that Joseph Smith and his brother Hyrum were imprisoned and murdered by an angry mob. No longer able to remain in the state, Smith's followers abandoned Nauvoo in 1847 and began the long journey across the plains to find a new home far away from their persecutors.

Led by Brigham Young, later Joseph Smith's successor as prophet and president of the church, the first group of Mormon pioneers arrived in the Salt Lake Valley on July 24, 1847. Upon entering the valley, Brigham Young is said to have stated, "This is the place." July 24 was later made a Utah state holiday.

Brigham Young Selects the Temple's Site

Only four days after his arrival in the Salt Lake Valley, Brigham Young designated the place where the Temple should be built. A stake was driven into the ground, and that has become the traditional center of the Temple. It was not until six years later that ground was broken for the structure. On April 6, 1853, the cornerstone was laid. It took forty years for the Temple to be completed.

Young made the first rough sketches of the structure based on a building he had seen in a vision. The assignment to actually plan the Temple fell to Truman Angell, a church member who was sent to England to increase his skills as an architect. The design of the Temple includes six non-matching spires, three on the east and three on the west, with a gold-leafed angel holding a trumpet mounted on the tallest eastern spire.

The Utah War

The foundations for the Temple were nearly in place by 1858, when the U.S. government sent troops against the Mormons. President James Buchanan had dispatched 2,500 men to the Salt Lake Valley to forcibly replace Young as governor of the territory. Upon learning of the government's plans, the Mormons buried the foundation of the Temple to make it appear as a freshly plowed field and then fled Salt Lake City. After a diplomatic resolution to the confrontation, the Mormons returned to Salt Lake City but were unable to do any work on the Temple for another two years.

Finally in 1860, Young directed that the foundation be uncovered. That process lasted for two more years and when the task was finally completed large cracks were revealed in the foundation. The original foundation was completely removed and a new one was begun with better quality stones that would be cut to fit without mortar. Thus it was not until 1867 that the structure began to rise above the ground.

The Tabernacle

In the meantime just west of the Temple another structure was nearing completion. The Tabernacle, begun in 1864, was first used for meetings in 1867. With its characteristic domed roof, the Tabernacle is 250 feet long and 150 feet wide. The roof is 80 feet high and is the result of a latticework construction of timbers held together with wooden dowels and leather straps. There are no supporting columns in the interior. The building is famous for its outstanding acoustics and magnificent organ. It was long home to the Mormon Tabernacle Choir, which performed there regularly after 1867, although it had been formed twenty years earlier in the very year that the Mormons first arrived in Salt Lake City.

The Tabernacle is used twice each year for the general conference of the Church of Jesus Christ of Latter-day Saints and is the site of numerous meetings and recitals throughout the year. Visitors can enjoy daily tours and organ recitals and can hear the choir rehearse each week as well as perform every Sunday morning. The design of the Tabernacle

The Mormon Temple, Salt Lake City. (courtesy of Utah Travel Council)

tracks were laid in 1873, allowing the blocks to be moved by steam engine. Shortly thereafter, steam derricks were used to raise the blocks of granite into place on the structure, also increasing the speed and ease of construction.

By 1877 the walls of the Temple stood some forty feet high, but in that same year construction began on another structure, the Assemble Hall, also on Temple Square. Used for meetings, concerts, and other gatherings, the Assemble Hall stands directly south of the Tabernacle and was completed in 1882. Built of rough-cut granite with white spires, the structure was completely restored from 1979 to 1981. The Assemble Hall was designed by Obed Taylor.

During the 1880's, work on the Temple continued, but it was frequently threatened as the Mormons came under increasing pressure from the federal government to abandon the practice of plural marriage. During this period three other temples of the church were completed and dedicated in other parts of Utah, but it was the "Great Temple" that had so consumed the early Mormon pioneers and it was still not finished. After the church abandoned polygamy in 1890, the threat to the Temple disappeared and by 1893 the capstone was laid.

has been attributed to Brigham Young but its construction was supervised by William Folsom and by a bridge builder named Henry Grow, who was responsible for the wooden lattice truss construction.

Building of the Temple

After the problems experienced with the first foundation of the Temple, it was decided that the structure should be built of the finest stone available in the region. Little Cottonwood Canyon, twenty miles from the construction site, was chosen as the quarry for the granite that was to be used for the Temple. Originally the large blocks were moved by oxen teams out of the canyon to the Temple site but the work was greatly accelerated after railroad

Dedication of the Temple

On April 6, 1893, exactly forty years after the start of construction, the Temple was finally dedicated. The Temple is 186 feet long and 99 feet wide, and its tallest spire rises more than 222 feet. The walls of the building are 9 feet thick at the bottom and taper to a thickness of 6 feet at the top. The interior of the Temple is adorned with fine woodwork, plaster ornamentation, murals, paintings, and elegant furnishings. Shortly before its dedication, nonmember guests were invited to take a tour of the building since it would not be open to them once it had been dedicated. Reports concerning the Temple and its dedication appeared in newspapers throughout the country. On April 7, 1893, *The New York Times* reported: "Brigham Young conceived the design, presumably through inspiration of some unnatural power, for no such building is to be seen elsewhere in any quarter of the globe."

On the same day, the *Chicago Tribune* reported the event of the Temple's dedication and attempted to also explain something about the purpose and use of the edifice: "These temples are not, as might be supposed, analogous to the churches of other denominations, but are used for private rites or ceremonies, to which, of course, only the initiated are allowed admission." Commenting on the structure itself the newspaper reported: "It is universally conceded that for general effect, both interior and exterior, there is no finer church edifice in the whole of America."

These reports contrast with the cynical prognostication of a writer for *Harper's Weekly* who visited Salt Lake City in 1857 and wrote concerning the Temple project: "quite a stupendous undertaking. . . . Its foundations, which are foolishly costly, are of solid rock. . . . [The Saints] have now resolved to erect it entirely of cut stone. Its plans are publicly exhibited, and, should it ever be completed, it will form a very magnificent pile."

In celebration of its centennial, the Salt Lake Temple underwent a complete renovation and stands today as a symbol of the enormous sacrifice and faith of those early Mormon pioneers. It also remains a working temple that can only be entered by faithful members of the church. While entrance to the Temple is limited, the site is visited by thousands each year who come to see the magnificent exterior of the building and visit the other structures on this historic square.

Visitors' Center

In addition to the Temple, the Tabernacle, and the Assemble Hall, there are also two visitors' centers located on Temple Square, where presentations about the Mormon Church are given. Of particular interest is the Christus statue located in the rotunda of the north visitors' center. The square is surrounded by a fifteen-foot wall and is beautifully landscaped with gigantic elms, seasonal plantings, and fountains. During the Christmas season the square is decorated with hundreds of thousands of lights.

Directly to the east of Temple Square is another entire city block housing administrative buildings of the Church of Jesus Christ of Latter-day Saints as well as historic Hotel Utah, recently renovated as another visitors' center, and the Beehive House, which was a home for some of Brigham Young's many wives. Across the street to the west of the square is the church's museum of art, as well as its world-renowned genealogical library, which is open to all who are interested in researching their ancestry.

For more than one hundred years, Temple Square in Salt Lake City has been a sanctuary for members of the Church of Jesus Christ of Latter-day Saints. The beautifully manicured grounds and historic buildings make the square a top tourist destination as well. The towering spires of the Temple and the gleaming domed roof of the Tabernacle stand in quiet grandeur as a monument to the perserverance of the Utah Mormon pioneers and as a symbol of faith to the current members of a worldwide church. —*Michael D. Phillips*

For Further Information:

Arrington, Leonard. *Brigham Young: American Moses.* New York: Alfred A. Knopf, 1985. A complete account of the life of Brigham Young.

Arrington, Leonard, and Davis Britton. *The Mormon Experience: A History of the Latter-day Saints.* New York: Alfred A. Knopf, 1979. A more complete overview of Mormon history from the church's foundation until the present.

Holzapfel, Richard N. *Every Stone a Sermon: The Magnificent Story of the Construction and Dedication of the Salt Lake Temple.* Salt Lake City: Bookcraft, 1992. The most complete historical account of the construction of the Salt Lake Temple. Painstakingly researched, the book is rich in scholarly detail.

Nash, Carol Rust. *The Mormon Trail and the Latter-Day Saints in American History.* Springfield, N.J.: Enslow, 1999. Explores the founding of the Latter-day Saints by Joseph Smith, their persecution, the migration west led by Brigham Young, and the church's legacy and its present role in society.

Ostling, Richard N., and Joan K. Ostling. *Mormon America: The Power and the Promise.* San Francisco: HarperSanFrancisco, 1999. Revealing look at church history and practices, with special attention given to the church's rapid growth, worldwide missionary program, and accelerated temple-building program.

Other Historic Sites

Alkali Ridge

Location: Monticello, San Juan County

Relevant issues: American Indian history

Statement of significance: This is a series of thirteen habitation sites along Alkali Mesa. Excavations helped clarify the development of Anasazi culture in the San Juan drainage, by defining the Pueblo II period (c. 900-1100). Local development from Basketmaker III (400-700) through Pueblo III (1100-1300) periods was shown to be a continuous growth influenced by neighboring peoples.

Danger Cave

Location: Wendover, Tooele County

Relevant issues: American Indian history

Statement of significance: Results of excavations at this site formed the basis for definition of a long-lived Desert culture which existed in the Great Basin area. The earliest cave stratus (c. 9500-9000 B.C.E.) is characterized by crude chipped stone artifacts; Zone II (c. 8000-7000 B.C.E.) by milling stones, basketry, and notched projectile points characteristic of the Desert culture; and Zones III, IV, and V (c. 7000 B.C.E.-500 C.E.) by materials showing an elaboration of the same culture.

Desolation Canyon

Location: Green River, Carbon County

Relevant issues: Western expansion

Statement of significance: John Wesley Powell (1834-1902), naturalist and explorer, led a Smithsonian expedition down the Colorado River in 1869 to the previously unexplored canyon, giving names to the natural features along the way.

Emigration Canyon

Location: Salt Lake City, Salt Lake County

Relevant issues: Religion, western expansion

Statement of significance: Forms the natural passage through the Wasatch Mountains to Salt Lake Valley traversed by Brigham Young and his Mormon followers on the last leg of their journey from the Missouri Valley in 1847.

Fort Douglas

Location: Salt Lake City, Salt Lake County

Relevant issues: Military history, western expansion

Statement of significance: This fort was established in 1862 on a site occupied by the army stationed here to maintain federal authority in the Mormon territory in the 1860's. It also represented an effort to protect transcontinental telegraph lines, mail, and transportation routes.

Old City Hall

Location: Salt Lake City, Salt Lake County

Relevant issues: Political history

Statement of significance: Erected between 1864 and 1866, it served both as a municipal building and Utah territorial capitol until 1894. This site was a focal point for confrontations between federal officials and Mormon leaders.

Smoot House

Location: Provo, Utah County

Relevant issues: Political history

Statement of significance: This was the residence of Reed O. Smoot (1862-1941) from 1892 until his death. Smoot, a United States senator (1903-1933), was a staunch advocate of protective tariffs. The Hawley-Smoot Tariff (1930) raised import duties to an all-time high and invited retaliation by other nations, actions which most scholars believe exacerbated the Great Depression.

Young Complex

Location: Salt Lake City, Salt Lake County

Relevant issues: Political history, religion, western expansion

Statement of significance: Brigham Young (1801-1877), was the second president of the Mormon Church and colonizer of Utah. From 1852, when their construction began, until Young's death, these buildings were closely associated with events in western expansion and settlement, and political, social, and religious movements of the era. During this time, Young was the predominant political and religious figure in Utah Territory. Young joined the Mormon

Church in 1832 and by 1835 had become one of Joseph Smith's Twelve Apostles; after Smith's murder at the hands of a mob in 1844, Young became leader of the church. In 1846, he led the Mormons out of Nauvoo, Illinois, and ultimately conducted a group of his followers to a site near Great Salt Lake, then in Mexican Territory.

Vermont

Burlington. (Vermont Department of Travel & Tourism)

History of Vermont

Vermont is the seventh smallest state. The only New England state not bordered by the Atlantic Ocean, Vermont is bordered by New Hampshire in the east, New York on the west, Massachusetts in the south, and Quebec, Canada, in the north. Vermont owns more than half of Lake Champlain, which makes up the half of the state's western border.

Vermont's terrain has a little of everything, from the Taconic Mountains, with good granite quarries, to the Champlain Valley, with the flattest land and best soil in the state, to the Green Mountains, which run through the middle of the state. There are about 430 lakes and ponds in Vermont, 420 named peaks, and forests on about 80 percent of the land. The waterways in the state provide trade routes to Canada and New York, and the forests produce hardwood, paper, and the nation's largest supply of maple syrup.

Native American Lands

Until the 1500's, Vermont land was inhabited by Abenaki, Mahican, and Pennacook Indians, all members of the Algonquian tribe. Then the land was overtaken by tribes of the powerful Iroquois Confederacy. When French settlers arrived in the 1600's, they allied themselves with the Algonquians, because they wanted to trade furs with them. The first permanent white settlement in Vermont was Fort Dummer in the southeast, built by the English to protect Massachusetts residents from French and American Indian raids. There were never any major battles between Native Americans and Europeans over land, as there were in the rest of New England. Still, American Indians were made unwelcome in the state, and they made up less than 2 percent of Vermont's population in the late twentieth century.

Settlement of Vermont

After French explorer Samuel de Champlain settled Quebec and Montreal, he traveled south on the Richelieu River into the lake named for him. In 1609 he claimed the Vermont area for France, naming the mountains Verd Mont (green mountains). The French built a few military posts to protect their land and established a fur trade with the Algonquians, but Vermont, unlike the other New England states and New York, was not settled for a long time.

In 1724 Dutch newcomers moved into the southwest of the state, and in 1750 Vermont began to attract settlers. Benning Wentworth, the royal governor of New Hampshire, sold pieces of land west of the Connecticut River to pay off his debts, though he had no claims to the region. Between 1750 and 1764, 138 towns on three million acres were established, and the area was called the New Hampshire Grants.

From 1754 to 1763, the French and Indian War raged because of land disputes between the French and British. Fighting in the Lake Champlain area ended with the British, with Iroquois allies, defeating the French and Algonquians. The 1763 Treaty of Paris, ending the war, gave control of Vermont to Great Britain.

The governor of New York, George Clinton, had also been making claims on the New Hampshire Grants. After he decreed that settlers in the Grants should pay New York for their land, the landowners in the Grants went to King George III of England with their cause. The king sided with the Grants residents, ordering Clinton not to bother them or to issue any land grants for land that was not his. However, in 1769-1770 Clinton gave titles to 600,000 acres in the Grants and tried to evict those who lived there. Some Vermonters, called the Bennington Nine, fought New York's claims to the area and formed a regiment, the Green Mountain Boys, led by Ethan Allen. The group drove the New York settlers out of the region.

The American Revolution

The Green Mountain Boys were active in the American Revolution (1775-1783), capturing Britain's Fort Ticonderoga and a British ship in 1775. Even though they logically should have sided with the British for supporting their claims to the Vermont land, they were more interested in liberty for the United States. American Indians fought on the

British side, hoping to be able to keep some of their rightful land, in vain. The only Revolutionary battle fought for Vermont took place in July of 1777 at the Battle of Bennington. Although the battle took place on New York land, the fight remains significant to Vermonters because Vermont won, leading to the defeat of the British at Saratoga, a turning point in the war.

Independence

In 1777 the residents of the New Hampshire Grants declared their independence from England and New York and called their state New Connecticut. Five months later, they changed the name to Vermont. In 1777 they drafted a constitution; the Bill of Rights from that year would be used for more than two hundred years. In 1778 Vermont declared itself independent of the Continental Congress, because the region believed the Congress was a danger to Vermont's liberty; the area made a separate peace treaty with Britain.

Although the Congress wanted to invade Vermont, General George Washington warned against it, but he advised Vermont governor Thomas Chittenden to relinquish his claims to thirty-five New Hampshire and fourteen New York towns. In 1790 Vermont paid New York thirty thousand dollars for disputed land. In 1791 it became the fourteenth state, but its people never forgot its tradition of independence and the fact that it was, unlike the rest of New England, never an English colony.

Industry

Vermont's early industry depended on water and timber, of which the state had plenty. Gristmills, sawmills, and paper mills were built on the state's fast streams. In 1805 Brattleboro became a printing center, and cities such as Brandon became iron-mining hubs. The first canal built in the United States was at Bellows Falls in the Connecticut River in 1802, and steamboats began operating on Lake Champlain in 1808, carrying goods to and from Canada. The Embargo Act of 1807 mandated against trade between the United States and foreign countries, so Vermonters had to smuggle food and lumber into Canada in order to maintain their livelihoods.

A special breed of horse, the Justin Morgan, was bred to plow hilly farms in the state, and Spanish merino sheep were imported for the manufacture of wool, leading to the opening of tanneries, carding mills, and finally textile factories. In the 1870's and 1880's industries and cities grew, but Vermont never became fully industrialized, like the rest of New England, with huge cities and numerous factories. The state stayed mostly rural. In fact, the Great Depression of the 1930's did not really affect Vermont because the state was so rural.

Economy

During the War of 1812 the economy boomed, because the production of wool was essential for troops fighting Britain. However, after the war, in 1814, trade with Britain resumed, lowering wool prices. By 1820 the economy was doing poorly, and thousands of people left the state. The construction of the Champlain-Hudson Canal in 1823 and the Erie Canal in 1825 helped trade, but by the 1840's Vermonters were leaving again because of cheaper land in the West and depleted resources and topsoil in the state. The residents who stayed behind turned to dairy farming, which would be Vermont's main industry for more than one hundred years.

Although from the 1820's to the 1850's the population was declining, more so-called summer people were visiting the state for the refreshing air and spring waters. Tourism became a big business, and Vermont was the first state to open a state publicity service to encourage tourism, in 1891. After the Civil War (1861-1865) agriculture stayed in decline, and more Vermonters took the federal government's offer of cheap land in the West. However, immigrants began flocking to the state, from Ireland, Scotland, Italy, Spain, and Sweden. In the late twentieth century most immigrants, about 9 percent, were from Quebec.

World War II

The Vermont General Assembly declared war on Germany in September of 1941, three months before Pearl Harbor was attacked. Because Vermont men in training for the war returned fire under attack at sea, they declared war. The state sent fifty thousand soldiers to the war. Vermont experienced a huge population growth after the 1940's, with people looking to return to a quieter, simpler way of life. The state was still two-thirds rural, with the highest proportion of rural residents in the country.

Independent Thinkers

Vermont never followed the religious movements of the rest of New England, such as the Puritan or Congregationalist faiths. For this they were deemed atheistic sinners by the surrounding communities.

Vermont was very antislavery, providing numerous stops on the Underground Railroad, the escape route for slaves out of the South. Vermonters were so antislavery that more than 75 percent voted for Abraham Lincoln in 1860 against opponent Stephen A. Douglas, who was a native Vermonter. Vermont contributed more than nine million dollars and thirty-five thousand men to the Civil War effort on the Union side.

After the Civil War the state became notoriously Republican-minded, and it remained that way until 1958. During the 1950's and 1960's it became more liberal, electing a Democrat, William H. Meyer, to the House of Representatives for the first time in more than one hundred years. In 1974 Patrick Leahy became the first Democratic senator from Vermont since the inception of the Republican Party in 1854.

Environment and Industry

Soon after World War II, Vermont became a huge ski attraction, due to the invention of the mechanized rope tow to pull skiers up a mountain. The downside of this technology and influx of people is that the environment suffered. In 1970 the Environmental Control Law was passed to cut down on pollution and development. It stated that developers would have to prove their projects would have no adverse effects on the surrounding environment.

By the 1990's, the service industry was the largest in the state, accounting for 67 percent of the workforce and 62 percent of the gross state product (GSP), mostly in the tourism and leisure fields. Manufacturing accounted for 21 percent of the workers and 26 percent of the GSP, and agriculture applied to only 6 percent of the workers and 1 percent of the GSP. However, 40 percent of the dairy in New England comes from Vermont, and it is the leading producer of maple syrup in the United States.

—*Lauren M. Mitchell*

Marsh-Billings-Rockefeller National Historical Park

Date: Opened in June, 1998

Relevant issues: Art and architecture, cultural history, political history, western expansion

Significance: Marsh-Billings-Rockefeller National Historical Park is the only site in the National Park System of the United States that is dedicated to an idea: that of the evolving conception of the conservation of natural resources.

Location: Immediately north of the town center in Woodstock, approximately ninety miles south and east of Burlington

Site Offices:

Marsh-Billings-Rockefeller National Historical Park
P.O. Box 178
54 Elm Street
Woodstock, VT 05091
ph: (802) 457-3368
Web site: www.nps.gov/mabi/

Billings Farm and Museum
P.O. Box 489

Route 12 and River Road
Woodstock, VT 05091
ph: (802) 457-2355
Web site: www.billingsfarm.org

Marsh-Billings-Rockefeller National Historical Park was created from a gift of the Rockefeller family in 1992 and opened to the public in 1998. The property includes the historic home of George Perkins Marsh, Frederick Billings, and Mary French and Laurance Spelman Rockefeller. The property includes the grounds associated with the mansion and a managed forest of about six hundred acres. As the home of successive generations of Americans concerned with the conservation of natural resources, Marsh-Billings-Rockefeller is the first national park dedicated to the idea of conservation. Adjacent to the park is the Billings Farm Museum, an eighty-eight-acre working farm and educational institution operated by a private, non-profit foundation.

George Perkins Marsh

George Perkins Marsh was born to a prominent family in Woodstock, Vermont, in 1801 and spent his early childhood in a family home nearby. The mansion that was to become the centerpiece of the

The Marsh-Billings-Rockefeller Mansion. (Marsh-Billings-Rockefeller National Historical Park)

Marsh-Billings-Rockefeller National Historical Park was built for his growing family during the period 1805 to 1807. Marsh learned to read as a young child and read with such intensity that his physician ordered him to stop reading at the age of seven, so that his eyesight might recover from the strain. During the four years that he was forbidden to read books, he learned to read the landscape, including the identification of all the native trees.

In 1820, Marsh graduated at the top of his class at Dartmouth College. He went on to practice law in Burlington, Vermont, but eventually turned his attention toward other pursuits, including raising sheep, investing in a woolen mill and railroads, and lecturing and writing on a variety of topics. He served in the Vermont legislature and in the U.S. Congress (1843-1849). In Congress, he worked for the establishment of the Smithsonian Institution and against slavery and the Mexican War.

From 1849 to 1854, he served as a diplomat in Turkey and Greece. On his return to Vermont, he began to speak about the consequences of unchecked logging activity and lamented the changes in the land and water that had resulted. In 1861, he became the U.S. Minister to the Kingdom of Italy, where he would serve until shortly before his death in 1881. In 1864, he published his most influential work, *Man and Nature: Physical Geography as Modified by Human Action*, in which he described the relationship between humans and the natural environment. He decried the destruction of the North American landscape and promoted a new ethic of responsible stewardship. The book became an important early work in American conservation thought.

Frederick Billings

Woodstock native Frederick Billings was born in 1823 and spent his early career in the American West. He made a fortune first as a lawyer in California during the Gold Rush and later as a developer of railroads. His railroads required a constant supply of timber to replace ties, and Billings began the practice of replanting trees along the railroads as they were used in order to create a renewable supply. This was both a prudent business practice and a progressive conservation practice for the time.

On returning to Vermont in the 1860's, Billings was alarmed to find that substantial clear-cutting had damaged the land, causing severe soil erosion and flooding. In 1869, he purchased the childhood home of George Perkins Marsh, deciding to make it a model of resource conservation. On the uplands of the property he planted selected species of trees and managed them for sustainable harvest. He opened more than twenty miles of carriage trails to make these forests accessible to the public. On the lowlands, he established a dairy farm to demonstrate responsible land stewardship. After his death in 1890, his wife Julia Billings and their three daughters continued the careful management of the entire property.

Mary and Laurance Rockefeller

In 1954, the property came into the hands of Laurance Rockefeller and Mary French Rockefeller, a granddaughter of Frederick Billings. Laurance Rockefeller's strong interest in conservation resulted in his appointment to environmental posts by several presidents. He is known both for his vacation resorts in areas of extraordinary natural beauty and for his gifts of land to the public in many of those areas. In Woodstock, Laurance and Mary Rockefeller continued the conservation practices of Frederick Billings on both the farm and the forest, which is one of the oldest continuously managed forests in the United States. The Rockefellers also added to a collection of conservation art that includes paintings and prints by Thomas Cole, Albert Bierstadt, and Asher B. Durand.

Visiting the Park

Marsh-Billings-Rockefeller National Historical Park is open from late spring through early autumn. More than twenty miles of carriage road are available for hiking; other uses are restricted. The houses and grounds of the park—including the collection of conservation paintings and prints—may be accessed only as part of guided tours. Separate visitors' centers at the National Historical Park and the Billings Farm Museum provide interpretive materials and special programs. Visitors should expect to spend a half day to a full day touring the house and grounds. The park and museum offices should be contacted for information about seasonal park hours (the park is not open year-round), details of tour offerings, tour reservations (strongly recommended), and special programs.

—*James Hayes-Bohanan*

For Further Information:

Bridges, Peter. "The Polymath from Vermont." *Virginia Quarterly Review* 75, no. 1 (1999): 82.

Harr, John Ensor, and Peter J. Johnson. *The Rockefeller Conscience: An American Family in Public and Private.* New York: Charles Scribner's Sons, 1991.

Marsh, George Perkins. *Man and Nature: Physical Geography as Modified by Human Action.* Edited by David Lowenthal. Cambridge, Mass.: Harvard University Press, 1973.

Winks, Robin W. *Frederick Billings: A Life.* Berkeley: University of California Press, 1998.

_____. *Laurance S. Rockefeller: Catalyst for Conservation.* Washington, D.C.: Island Press, 1997.

SS Ticonderoga

Date: Built in 1906

Relevant issues: Business and industry, cultural history, military history, naval history, science and technology

Significance: The *Ticonderoga* is the last surviving example of the hundreds of walking-beam-powered steamboats that plied the nation's waters from the nineteenth century into the early decades of the twentieth. It played a significant role in both trade and tourism throughout its long working life.

Location: At the Shelburne Museum in Shelburne, seven miles south of Burlington

Site Office:
Shelburne Museum
U.S. Route 7
P.O. Box 10
Shelburne, VT 05482
ph.: (802) 985-3346; TTYRelay: (800) 251-0191
fax: (802) 985-2331
Web site: www.shelburnemuseum.org
e-mail: museinfo@together.net

The *Ticonderoga* was built for passenger service on Lake Champlain by the Champlain Transportation Company, a firm that owned and operated two other steamers on the lake. Ironically, the *Ticonderoga*—which was the last such steamboat to be constructed on the lake—was in fact intended as a replacement for the last wooden steamer on Lake Champlain, the *Maquam*. The W & A Fletcher Company of Hoboken, New Jersey, was contracted to build the vessel at a cost of $95,500. In actuality, Fletcher only manufactured the *Ticonderoga*'s engines, since the fabrication of the steel hull was subcontracted to a Newburgh, New York, firm, the T. S. Marvel Shipbuilding Company. The *Ticonderoga*'s hull was "built" twice. First, Marvel fashioned the necessary sections of the hull and put them together as they would fit in the finished vessel. Then the hull was taken apart to facilitate shipping through the Champlain Canal. It was at Shelburne Harbor, Vermont, that final assembly was completed when a work gang from Marvel riveted the various sections back together. With its steel hull securely riveted together, the *Ticonderoga* was launched on April 18, 1906, at 3:08 P.M., in the presence of some two thousand spectators. The vessel was not yet complete, however. It was only after work was finished on the wooden superstructure that the steamboat could begin regular service; this occurred on August 6, 1906.

The completed steamboat was an odd combination of old and new aspects of industrial technology. On one hand, there was nothing remarkable regarding its dimensions. With its 220-foot length, 57.5-foot beam (width), and 7-foot draft (depth), the *Ticonderoga* was dwarfed by its 262-foot sister ship, the *Vermont III*. Further, while its one-cylinder, coal-powered, vertical-beam engine could drive the vessel from a cruising speed of seventeen miles per hour to a maximum speed of twenty-three miles per hour, Robert Fulton had proven this technology nearly a century earlier. On the other hand, that nearly obsolete steam-engine design provided the necessary power for the vessel's two General Electric dynamos (generators). These dynamos allowed the *Ticonderoga* to boast electric lighting and a two-million-candlepower searchlight when such items were still novelties to many people. Though not conceived as an overnight vessel, the *Ticonderoga* nevertheless had five staterooms, and its plush stateroom hall was generously finished in such fine woods as butternut and cherry. With such impressive features, it comes as no surprise that the final cost of the steamboat came to $162,232.65.

The *Ticonderoga* in Its Prime: 1906-1932

With its wide beam and shallow draft, the *Ticonderoga* was the ideal passenger vessel for plying the waters of Lake Champlain. Its capacity was 1,070 persons, but in a limited sense the *Ticonderoga* was also a freighter of sorts. Due to the importance of farming to the local economy, the vessel carried shipments of livestock (horses, sheep, and cattle) and apples when they were in season. The steamboat could also ferry up to twenty automobiles, even though it was not built for this purpose. Its most unusual cargo was a three-ton elephant named Minnie, which the *Ticonderoga* transported from Burlington to Plattsburgh in 1913 as part of the Aborn Comic Opera Company.

For its first ten years, the vessel followed a route that ran from St. Albans down to Port Henry. A typical season would begin in April and last into November; the steamer was docked for the duration of winter. In order to ensure its safe operation as a passenger vessel, the *Ticonderoga* was inspected prior to each season by the U.S. Steamboat Service. In addition, the master, the pilots, and the engineers all had to be recertified for their licenses each year. The twenty-nine-member crew, who lived on board the vessel, maintained safety standards throughout the season with weekly fire and lifeboat drills. However, even with such constant vigilance, steaming through this mountain lake was not without its hazards, and the *Ticonderoga* had its share of accidents. The first was relatively minor, a lightning strike in 1912 that damaged the electrical circuit, the stern staff, and some decking. By far the worst occurred in August of 1919, when the vessel became stranded on Point au Fer Reef and began to leak. The three hundred passengers, who were taken to shore in lifeboats, were uninjured, but the *Ticonderoga* suffered serious damage in the accident. Its seams opened up, and it sank until it settled onto the reef. Repairs cost $5,395, and the vessel was out of service until the following year.

The *Ticonderoga* was built to fill a specific economic niche: Because of the scarcity of roads, automobiles, and bridges in the Lake Champlain area, the steamboat could count on a ready supply of its main cargo—people. It was a successful vessel, and this is attested by the fact that in its best season (1917) it carried some 80,896 passengers and 2,762 cars. What its owners could not control, though, were forces that were rapidly altering the world at large and the economic conditions that had made the *Ticonderoga* possible. The first economic jolt in the *Ticonderoga*'s long career occurred during World War I, when the Federal Railroad Administration took control of the vessel. Because of this, the *Ticonderoga*'s owners were forced to suspend excursions throughout 1918. While this enabled the vessel to shuttle weapons and soldiers between army bases in Plattsburgh, New York, and Colchester, Vermont, it decimated passenger business on the lake. In 1918, the passenger total plummeted to 49,457.

More lasting and, ultimately, more damaging consequences ensued from two events that occurred in 1929. The first was the August opening of the Champlain Bridge, which joined Crown Point, New York, and Chimney Point, Vermont. With the increasing availability of the automobile, driving represented a significant saving in time over steamboat travel. The second economic milestone of that year was the stock market crash of October, an event that heralded the long economic decline that came to be known as the Great Depression. Due to the combined effects of the new bridge and the economic collapse, passenger totals for the *Ticonderoga* sank from 45,855 in 1929 to just 26,611 in 1932. Because a steamboat was so costly to operate—with expenses for fuel, maintenance, and personnel—the *Ticonderoga* became less and less profitable. Economic conditions deteriorated to such an extent that both the *Ticonderoga* and the *Vermont III* were taken out of service from 1933 through 1935.

The Later Years: 1936-1953
The economy eventually improved enough for the *Ticonderoga* to resume regular service on July 2, 1936, but the steamboat era on Lake Champlain was quickly passing. The Delaware and Hudson Railroad, the parent firm of the Champlain Transportation Company, sold the latter to Horace Corbin on February 25, 1937. Under the new owner-

The S.S. Ticonderoga. (Vermont Department of Tourism)

ship, the *Ticonderoga* was transformed into a showboat. More bars were added, the once-elegant dining room became a dance floor, and dance bands performed on the aging vessel. When the nation entered World War II, business increased because the *Ticonderoga*'s main competitor—the automobile—was severely hampered by gasoline rationing and limited production. On the other hand, coal, the fuel for the steamer's huge engine, was restricted much less stringently and thus was more easily obtained. Such wartime conditions, though, were by their very nature emergency measures, and the familiar financial woes reasserted themselves with the end of the war. Cheap and available gasoline and a vigorous automobile industry had returned, along with one new problem: a critical shortage of engineers skilled in the operation and maintenance of the vertical walking-beam engine.

With increased competition came the inevitable decline in business, and the venerable steamer found itself changing hands several times over the next few years. When, in 1948, Corbin could no longer make the steamboat pay, he sold it and his other vessels to James G. Wolcott, Lewis P. Evans, Jr., and Richard H. Walhams. However, they were more concerned with the ferry business than with an obsolete steamer, so the *Ticonderoga* saw little activity that year. The usual fate for old steamers was either conversion to some other use or a one-way trip to the scrap yard. Fortunately, intervention came in the form of Martin Fisher, who bought the vessel at auction in May, 1949. His father, Alanson, had once been master of the *Ticonderoga*, and his hope was to tap into nostalgia for the lake excursions of the past. Yet even with his determination to keep the old steamer in operation, business continued to decline. Diesel-powered ferries transported more than a quarter million people on Lake Champlain in 1948, and they were also able to move more than eighty thousand cars. The *Ticonderoga*, with its expensive appetite for coal and limited space for automobiles, now had to contend with docking fees so exorbitant that it frequently had to shuttle between different docks.

Once again, however, the *Ticonderoga* was saved from the scrap heap. Community concern for the vessel was demonstrated by the Burlington Junior Chamber of Commerce, which created a Civic Betterment Fund to help pay off the vessel's debts and began a campaign to raise ten thousand dollars to ready the vessel for the upcoming season. The Junior Chamber of Commerce was instrumental in having a new dock constructed for the *Ticonderoga*, and its members even volunteered their time to paint the vessel. Even the best intentions, though, were not enough to sustain this relic from Lake Champlain's past. It was only through the intercession of philanthropists Electra Webb and her husband James Watson Webb that the *Ticonderoga* survived. On January 21, 1951, the Webbs purchased the old steamer from the Fisher Steamboat Company to add to their growing collection of Americana at the Shelburne Museum. The Webbs bought the vessel with the intention of maintaining it as the last active steamboat on Lake Champlain, and for a time the *Ticonderoga* continued in this guise, as well as serving as a floating museum for some items from their collections. Passenger totals nearly doubled during the three seasons of operation under the new owner, from 17,500 in 1951 to 30,000 in 1953. This increased business, however, was not sufficient to offset rising expenses and the lack of people skilled in the operation of steamboats.

Its Final Voyage

Once the decision was made to cease operation of the vessel on the lake, the question became a matter of how to maintain the *Ticonderoga* and integrate it with the rest of the museum collection. The museum eventually made the momentous decision to move the steamboat, in one piece, two miles overland from the lake to the museum grounds. Merritt-Chapman and Scot, an engineering firm, began the process at Shelburne Harbor by excavating a 450-foot-long basin, at the bottom of which sat a large cradle. A tugboat maneuvered the old vessel into position on November 6, 1954, and as the water was pumped out of the basin the steamer came to rest on the cradle. W. B. Hill Company was subcontracted to do the actual moving of the boat, which began on January 31, 1955. With the *Ticonderoga* placed on sixteen flatbed railroad cars, a winch mounted on a large truck slowly pulled the steamer over dual tracks that were laid out in front. The "*Ti*"—as the vessel was now affectionately called—reached its final berth on April 6, 1955. Thanks to a major restoration in the 1990's, visitors boarding the *Ticonderoga* will discover the charm and elegance of steamer travel in the 1920's. This popular museum attraction is open year-round, with reduced hours from late October to late May.

—*Cliff Prewencki*

For Further Information:

Brouwer, Norman J. *International Register of Historic Ships*. Annapolis, Md.: Naval Institute Press, 1985. Gives the steamer's specifications and a brief history.

Strum, Richard M. *"Ticonderoga": Lake Champlain Steamboat*. Shelburne, Vt.: Shelburne Museum, 1998. Provides a detailed account of the vessel and its times. Includes both color and black-and-white illustrations.

Other Historic Sites

Coolidge Homestead District

Location: Plymouth Notch, Windsor County

Relevant issues: Political history

Web site: www.cit.state.vt.us/dca/hp_sites.htm

Statement of significance: Calvin Coolidge (1872-1933) was born in Plymouth Notch in the house attached to his father's general store. In 1876, the family moved across the street and it was there in 1923 that Coolidge was sworn in as president by his father, a justice of the peace, after word of President Warren G. Harding's death had been received. The president and six generations of the Coolidge family are buried here. The district consists of twelve buildings and is a state-owned historic site.

Frost Farm

Location: Ripton, Addison County

Relevant issues: Literary history

Statement of significance: A distinguished twentieth century poet and winner of four Pulitzer Prizes, Robert Frost (1874-1963) lived and wrote at this farm in the summer and fall months from 1940 until his death.

Morrill Homestead

Location: Strafford, Orange County

Relevant issues: Political history

Web site: www.cit.state.vt.us/dca/historic/hp_sites .htm

Statement of significance: Justin S. Morrill (1810-1898) was responsible for the Morrill Acts (1862, 1890), which provided for land grant colleges. He designed and constructed this Gothic Revival house from 1848 to 1851, and he retained ownership while in the Congress as a representative (1855-1867) and senator (1867-1898), until his death in 1898.

Mount Independence

Location: Orwell, Addison County

Relevant issues: Military history, Revolutionary War

Web site: www.middlebury.edu/~mtindep

Statement of significance: This site, on Lake Champlain opposite Fort Ticonderoga, was fortified by colonial troops in 1776 to prevent the British from penetrating to the Hudson River through the Champlain Valley.

Naulakha

Location: Dummerston, Windham County

Relevant issues: Literary history

Statement of significance: Rudyard Kipling (1865-1936), the first English-language author to win the Nobel Prize in Literature (1907), had this house and outbuildings built for his American bride. Despite their brief residence in the house (1893-1896), Kipling wrote several of his best-known books here, including *The Jungle Book* (1894) and *Captains Courageous* (1897).

Robbins and Lawrence Armory and Machine Shop

Location: Windsor, Windsor County

Relevant issues: Business and industry

Statement of significance: Shop employees here made significant improvements in the design and production of machine tools in the 1840's. Their efforts helped to accelerate the Industrial Revolution in America. (This building now houses the American Precision Museum.)

Rokeby

Location: US Route 7, Ferrisburgh, Addison County

Relevant issues: African American history, social reform

Web site: www.cr.nps.gov/nr/underground/vt1 .htm

Statement of significance: Rokeby, a Robinson family farmstead for four generations, is significant for its role in the Underground Railroad. Rare surviving documentation that the Robinson family kept attests to its use as a stop and provides accurate insights into an understandably shadowy segment of American history. In 1851, one former slave who escaped to Canada wrote that he was "at work at my trade getting a living looking through the glasses you gave me for which I never shall forget to be thankful. I think that I shall soon be able to send for my family if I conclude to stay here." Of all the known Underground Railroad sites, Rokeby is unrivaled in its historical integrity and in the poignancy of the stories its documents tell. It is open to the public as a museum.

St. Johnsbury Athenaeum

Location: St. Johnsbury, Caledonia County

Relevant issues: Art and architecture

Statement of significance: The Athenaeum's construction (1868-1873), its collection of American landscape paintings and books, its original role as a public library and free art gallery, and the industrial origins of the fortune that provided it all contribute to the national significance of the building. The art collection contains a number of Hudson River School paintings. This unaltered building retains a strong, elegant Victorian flavor of the nineteenth century.

Stellafane Observatory

Location: North Springfield, Windsor County

Relevant issues: Science and technology

Statement of significance: Stellafane Observatory played a pioneering role in the development of amateur telescope-making and popular astronomy in the United States. The site contains the original clubhouse of the Springfield Telescope Makers (1924) and the first large optical telescope (1930) built and owned by that kind of amateur society; since their construction, both clubhouse and telescope have remained in continuous use and have been preserved essentially in original condition. Annual conventions held on the site attract thousands of amateur telescope makers and astronomers from many countries.

Willard House

Location: Middlebury, Addison County

Relevant issues: Education, women's history

Statement of significance: This two-story brick structure was, from 1809 until 1819, the home of Emma Willard (1787-1870), an influential pioneer in the development of women's education in the United States. It is now used as the admissions office for Middlebury College, which was known as the Middlebury Female Seminary when it was founded in 1814 by Willard.

Virginia

The State Capitol Building in Richmond. (PhotoDisc)

History of Virginia

One of the most historic of all the fifty United States, Virginia played pivotal roles during the colonial period, the American Revolution, and the Civil War. Following the adoption of the Constitution, Virginians had a major influence in shaping the direction and destiny of the early nation, and four of the first five American presidents, from George Washington through James Monroe, were from Virginia. In fact, a Virginian held the presidency for twenty-four out of the first twenty-eight years of the United States.

Early Inhabitants and European Settlement

Compared to other portions of the East Coast, Native Americans seem to have arrived fairly late in the Virginia area, settling there after 8000 B.C.E. In the Piedmont area to the west, the tribes of the Sioux language family included Manahoac, Monacan, and Tutelo. In the southwestern portion were the Cherokee, while the Nottoway were found in the southeast; both of these were part of the Iroquoian language community. To the north, along the upper portions of Chesapeake Bay, the Susquehanna had migrated into the region from the area which is now Pennsylvania. These were also Iroquoian speakers. Along the lower portions of the Chesapeake Bay coast itself, including the area where the first English settlers arrived, the dominant Native Americans were the Algonquian speaking members of the group known as the Powhatan Confederacy, named after its powerful chieftain.

In addition to hunting and fishing, especially along the bountiful coastal waters of the Chesapeake Bay, the tribes turned to agriculture, which flourished in the excellent soil and long, warm growing season of the area. One of their major innovations was the growth and cultivation of tobacco, which the Native Americans passed on to English settlers shortly after their arrival in 1607.

The English colony of Jamestown, founded on a peninsula jutting into the Chesapeake Bay, was part of a grandiose land grant from the English King James I which stretched from what is now southern Maine to California and included both the island of Bermuda and the modern Canadian province of Ontario. However, despite the imperial designs, during its early days Jamestown was hard pressed to simply survive and barely weathered internal division, attacks by the Native Americans, disease, and near starvation. Under the leadership of Captain John Smith, the new colony endured and by the 1620's was exporting tobacco to England as a cash crop. The cultivation of tobacco and other crops was transformed in 1619 when the first Africans arrived in the colony as indentured servants; by the 1630's slavery had been introduced, and in 1661 it was legalized. Slavery was to remain an essential part of Virginia's plantation economy until the end of the American Civil War.

A Rich Colony Leads a Revolution

The first legislative assembly in the English colonies gathered in Jamestown in 1619. Even though Virginia became a royal colony in 1624, the House of Burgesses, as the assembly was known, remained a potent force in colonial affairs, including encouraging growth and development, including expansion beyond the Blue Ridge Mountains to the west. In eastern Virginia, especially along the rich lands of the tidewater, tobacco farming brought enormous wealth to planters, merchants, and traders. By the middle of the 1700's, Virginia was among the richest of the American colonies.

It was also among the most independently minded. In 1676 Virginian Nathaniel Bacon led a popular revolt against despotic colonial governor Sir William Berkeley. As early as 1765 the Virginia House of Burgesses had officially opposed the Stamp Act, and in 1769 Virginia launched a boycott of all British goods to protest additional taxes which the colonists regarded as unfair and illegal. It was at the Virginia Convention of 1775 that Patrick Henry delivered the speech which included his famous words, "Give me liberty, or give me death." Henry's sentiment was given more practical form in June, 1776, when Virginia officially declared itself independent from Great Britain. On July 4, 1776, the Declaration of Independence,

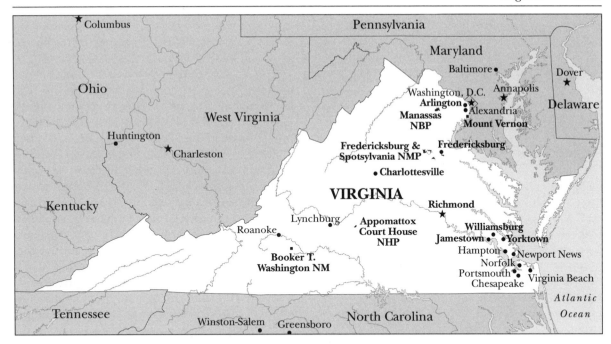

largely written by Virginian Thomas Jefferson, extended this freedom to all thirteen colonies.

Virginia provided both leaders and a battleground for the American Revolution. George Washington was named commander of the Continental army, while other military leaders included George Rogers Clark, Daniel Morgan, and "Light-Horse Harry" Lee, father of Robert E. Lee. The founder of the American navy, John Paul Jones, was a Virginian, although born in Scotland. The climactic battle of the Revolution came with the combined American and French defeat of British forces under Lord Cornwallis at the siege of Yorktown. This victory ensured final victory for the American cause.

A New Nation and Civil War

Virginians were active in the creation and growth of the new United States. The Constitution, which replaced the ineffective Articles of Confederation, was largely drafted by James Madison, who later became the fourth president of the United States. He shared that office with a number of others from his state, including George Washington, the country's first president; Thomas Jefferson, the third; and James Monroe, the fifth. In all, Virginians held the position of president for twenty-four of the first twenty-eight years of the new nation. In addition,

the most influential chief justice of the United States, John Marshall, was a Virginian. He served from 1801 through 1835 and established the independent judiciary as an essential branch of the American federal government.

Although a southern, slaveholding state, Virginia had not taken the radical position held by others such as South Carolina during the intense national debate over slavery. The seizure of the federal arsenal at Harpers Ferry in 1859 by abolitionist John Brown, who hoped to spark a slave revolt, was put down by Colonel Robert E. Lee of the U.S. Army. When the first seven states seceded from the Union after the election of Abraham Lincoln in 1860, Virginia refrained from action. It did not leave the Union until April, 1861, after Lincoln had called up volunteers to suppress the rebellion. Richmond, less than a hundred miles from Washington, D.C., was named capital of the Confederacy, ensuring that the major battles of the Civil War would be fought in Virginia.

Over the next four years, Robert E. Lee and the Confederate Army of Northern Virginia repulsed repeated attacks by federal forces. Aided by generals such as Jeb Stuart and "Stonewall" Jackson, Lee defeated Union forces that greatly outnumbered his home. In his classic 1863 victory at Chancellorsville, however, Lee lost his best lieutenant when

Stonewall Jackson was accidentally killed by his own troops, and later that summer Lee and his army were defeated at Gettysburg. During the bloody campaigns of 1864 Union general Ulysses S. Grant wore down Lee's troops and brought about the Confederate surrender at Appomattox Courthouse in April, 1865, effectively ending the Civil War.

A Modern State

During the Civil, War Virginia had lost the western part of its territory when counties beyond the mountains loyal to the Union formed a new state, West Virginia, which entered the Union in 1863. Following the Civil War, Virginia went through the harsh period of Reconstruction imposed on the other states of the defeated Confederacy. During this time, Robert E. Lee lost his U.S. citizenship and Jefferson Davis was imprisoned at Fort Monroe on Chesapeake Bay. Virginia was readmitted to the Union on January 26, 1870.

Prior to the war, Virginia had been an industrial and manufacturing leader in the South. Its Tredegar Ironworks in Richmond, for example, was the Confederacy's most important supplier of metal and weapons. However, following the devastation brought by the war, Virginia reverted to a primarily agricultural economy, based largely on crops such as tobacco, cotton, peanuts, and forestry products. It was not until the early years of the twentieth century that the state began to recover its industrial and manufacturing capabilities. By the middle of the century, thanks in large part to the stimulus of production during World War II, these again had become important aspects of the state's economic base.

During the 1970's and 1980's Virginia, in cooperation with Maryland and other neighboring states, made a concentrated effort to clean up and restore Chesapeake Bay, whose environment had been severely damaged by decades of neglect and pollution. More than one hundred rivers flow into the Bay, some of them originating as far away as New York and West Virginia, but many of them rising in Virginia itself. Excess nutrients from agricultural fertilizer and organic chemicals have been two of the major elements damaging conditions in the Bay. However, by 1992 efforts at environmental stewardship had reached the point where more than three-quarters of Chesapeake Bay (78 percent) was reported as being in "excellent" condition. This was good news for Virginia's seafood industry, in particular for the fishers who harvest world-famous Virginia oysters and blue crabs.

Fishing is indeed important to the state, but the modern Virginia economy is a diverse one. Agriculture, much of it located in the fertile Shenandoah Valley and in the southwestern portion of the state, remains a mainstay, with tobacco, corn, and other grains as significant crops. Shipbuilding and ship repair remain important along the coast, especially in the Hampton-Norfolk-Portsmouth area, which also is the site of a major U.S. naval base. Manufacturing, including electronic equipment and other technologically sophisticated products, is important; Virginia is one of the nation's major producers of synthetic fibers. In northern Virginia, many residents are employed by the federal government. Because of the state's great natural beauty and multitude of historical sites, Virginia's tourism industry is a key part of its economy. This economic diversity means that the state retains a position it has long held in its history—that of being one of the leading states in the nation.

—*Michael Witkoski*

Appomattox Court House

Date: Confederate army surrendered there on April 9, 1865; designated a National Historical Park on April 15, 1954

Relevant issues: Civil War, military history

Significance: The tiny village of Appomattox Courthouse, where Confederate general Robert E. Lee surrendered the Army of Northern Virginia to federal general Ulysses S. Grant, has been restored to its 1865 appearance. Thirteen of the original buildings remain and have been restored by the National Park Service, while nine other structures have been rebuilt on their original sites. The latter include the McLean House, site of the surrender, which effectively ended the Civil War.

Location: On Virginia Route 24 in south-central Virginia about ninety-two miles west of Richmond, eighteen miles east of Lynchburg, and three miles northeast of the town of Appomattox

Site Office:
Appomattox Court House National Historical
Park
Superintendent's Office
P.O. Box 218
Appomattox, VA 24522
ph.: (804) 352-8987
Web site: www.nps.gov/apco/

The Civil War between the industrial North and the mainly agricultural South was fought over the issues of slavery and states' rights. During early 1861 the Southern states seceded from the Union, and on April 12, 1861, the war began when Confederate troops attacked Fort Sumter in the harbor of Charleston, South Carolina. For three years the war dragged on indecisively, characterized by large, bloody battles such as Gettysburg, First and Second Manassas (Bull Run), and Antietam.

Grant Becomes Commander of the Union Armies
Dissatisfied with Northern military leadership, President Abraham Lincoln appointed Ulysses S. Grant general in chief of the Northern army in March, 1864. Grant decided that the Army of the Potomac, which had been defending Washington,

Appomattox Court House. (Corbis)

D.C., should cross the Rapidan River in Virginia and attack the Confederate forces under the great Southern general, Robert E. Lee. Led personally by Grant, the campaign began in May with the battles of the Wilderness and Spotsylvania Court House, followed in June by a bloody clash at Cold Harbor.

After Cold Harbor, Grant led his forces past Richmond to assault the industrial and transportation center of Petersburg, about twenty-five miles to the south. Success would have cut off Lee's sources of supply and led to the fall of Richmond, the capital of the Confederacy. Uncharacteristic hesitation on the North's part forced the two sides to settle into siege warfare, which dragged on for ten disastrous months beginning in June, 1864. The siege finally ended on April 1, 1865, when the Confederate right flank fell and Lee withdrew his starving and disease-ridden troops to the west.

On April 2 Union forces broke through the Confederate lines near Fort Fisher, southwest of Petersburg. That night Lee abandoned the last southern defenses of Petersburg while his army trudged to Amelia Court House about thirty miles to the west. He hoped to reorganize and find supplies urgently needed by his starving troops. Grant sent General Philip Sheridan's cavalry and a strong corps under General George Meade on a forced march parallel to Lee's army. On April 3 news came that Richmond had fallen. Lee found no food rations at Amelia Court House, so he continued to move west, the only direction open to his army.

Defeat of the Confederate Army
The Northern army caught up with the Confederates at Sayler's Creek and inflicted a stinging defeat. The Union troops captured nearly eight thousand southern soldiers and eight Confederate generals. The remnants of two Confederate corps were sent fleeing across the fields. Lee's weary army crossed the Appomattox River and continued marching in the direction of Appomattox Station (later the town of Appomat-

tox). Sheridan's cavalry leapfrogged ahead to block the way while Union infantry closed a ring around the Confederate army. By April 8 Lee's Army of Northern Virginia was at the end of its tether, its morale extinguished and its organization shattered.

The negotiations for surrender that now developed between the two generals were remarkably polite. Many Northern politicians had called for a severe and punitive peace to be imposed on the south, although Lincoln was in favor of a peace leading to reconciliation as well as reunion. General Grant was a harsh and, when necessary, ruthless war leader whose objective had been to fight and destroy the Confederate army. During the negotiations with Lee, however, he showed an unexpected and statesmanlike awareness of the need for an amicable peace.

Lee and Grant's Historic Meeting

During the night of April 8, Lee sent a letter through the lines to Grant offering to meet him to discuss the restoration of peace. Grant replied that he was authorized only to set the terms for military surrender. On the morning of April 9, Lee, who realized surrender was inevitable, wrote to Grant again requesting a meeting to discuss surrender terms. Grant's emissary found Lee sitting under an apple tree by the side of the road just northeast of the village of Appomattox Courthouse. Lee then sent his aide, Colonel Charles Marshall, into Appomattox Courthouse to find a suitable location for the meeting. The first person Marshall encountered there was a businessman, Wilmer McLean. It was a Sunday, and the courthouse was closed and locked. McLean showed Marshall a somewhat run-down house, which Marshall considered unsuitable. McLean then offered his own house. By early afternoon of April 9 both Lee and Grant were at the McLean House. Their historic meeting took place in the front parlor on the left of the central hall.

Accompanied by members of their staffs, Lee and Grant conversed cordially about their service in the Mexican War and mutual friends (both were West Point graduates). Finally, Lee asked Grant to put the surrender terms in writing. The document required the Army of Northern Virginia to surrender unconditionally; the officers and men to swear not to take up arms against the U.S. govern-

ment; arms and artillery to be turned over to Union officers, except for officers' side arms, private horses, and personal baggage; and officers and men to be allowed to return home without interference by U.S. authorities. Grant also allowed the private Confederate soldiers to retain their horses to help work their farms, and he ordered rations to be provided for the near-starving Southern army. Lee praised Grant's generosity, saying it would do much toward conciliating the southern people.

The formal surrender ceremony was set for April 12, four years to the day after the Confederate assault on Fort Sumter, which began the war. The generals then left the McLean House but later had one more meeting on horseback between the lines, described as a pleasant conversation of more than half an hour. Grant then broke up his field headquarters just west of Appomattox Courthouse and left for Washington, D.C.; General Joshua Lawrence Chamberlain accepted the surrender. Lee avoided the surrender ceremony but waited for it to be over before leaving for Richmond; General John Gordon led Confederate forces at the ceremony at which Chamberlain ordered his men to salute the Confederates. In this dramatic and historic fashion, the Civil War effectively concluded in such a manner that a federal regimental historian at the scene wrote that this most stupendous of struggles was brought to an end in the most compassionate manner.

The McLean House

The two-story McLean House was the finest home in the tiny village of Appomattox Courthouse. It was built, as was the courthouse itself, of brick with stone chimneys and a comfortable wooden porch extending across the front. Two smaller wooden buildings behind the main structure served as the kitchen and the slave quarters, although the latter had lost its function by the time of the surrender. The house faced the Richmond-Lynchburg Stage Road close to the Appomattox County Courthouse and just down and across the road from Meeks's Store and the Clover Hill Tavern. The latter had a separate guesthouse and catered to locals as well as to stagecoach passengers interrupting their journey between Richmond and Lynchburg. A few miles south was Appomattox Station, which actually was a station on the Southside Railroad.

Wilmer McLean's presence in Appomattox Courthouse was the ironic result of a series of events. McLean and his family were actually war refugees. McLean's home had been in northern Virginia near Manassas, where the first major battle of the Civil War—also called the First Battle of Bull Run—was fought in July, 1861. His house was on the battlefield, and at one point a shell crashed through his window. A year later the second Battle of Bull Run was fought in the same area. McLean had had enough and decided to move to a quieter and safer location where there would be little likelihood of either army ever appearing. He ended up purchasing the Raine House, built in 1848 in Appomattox Courthouse, and in 1863 moved his family to this seemingly obscure village, which had fewer than one hundred fifty residents. The village had been given its name by the state legislature in 1845, when it was designated the county seat for the new county of Appomattox. Before that, it was an even smaller settlement called Clover Hill.

McLean had been right to hesitate to offer his house for the surrender negotiations because the aftermath was disastrous for his property. No sooner had Grant and Lee left than souvenir hunters descended on the McLean home. Union general Edward Ord bought the table on which the surrender was signed for ten dollars. General George Armstrong Custer purchased the table on which the terms were written out by Grant for twenty-five dollars. McLean tried to keep the parlor chairs which had been occupied by the two generals, but two cavalry officers seized them by force, thrust ten dollars in McLean's hand, and rode off. Some chairs and sofas in the house were cut to pieces and parceled out to relic hunters, pictures were taken from the walls, and much that was movable was taken away with McLean receiving little or no compensation for many items. Besides losing many of his furnishings to souvenir hunters, McLean, whose business was trading in sugar, wound up in financial difficulties after the war. Attempting to earn something himself from the surrender, he borrowed heavily to finance the printing of thousands of copies of a lithograph depicting the historic scene in his parlor. There proved to be little demand for the pictures, and McLean went bankrupt.

The Village of Appomattox

The tiny village where McLean had intended to wait out the war now had a place in history. Situated in a shallow valley with rich slopes of cultivated land rising above it on every side, the village had only two streets and about twenty-five dwellings. Despite its small size, the village was at the time the only place in the county that could be called a town. Appomattox County was mainly rural and agricultural, and to this day it has remained a region of moderate-size farms.

After the surrender, Appomattox Courthouse was largely forgotten, and the few schemes to commemorate it failed. In 1889 some Union veterans organized the Appomattox Land Company and made plans to develop the area, but their plans came to nothing. The McLean house was bought by promoters who intended to move it to Washington as an exhibit. The historic house was torn down, but the project failed financially and the remains of the house were left in a pile to rot. In 1892 the courthouse burned to the ground and the county seat was moved to Appomattox Station, now called Appomattox, a few miles to the southwest. Thanks to its location on the railroad Appomattox enjoyed economic success while Appomattox Courthouse declined into a sorry place of abandoned and decayed buildings. This proved to be an advantage, however, when the country was ready to memorialize the place of the surrender because the original character of the site was more easily recoverable.

Modern Preservation Efforts

The restoration efforts were set in motion when Congress passed a bill on June 18, 1930, calling for the erection of a monument on the site of the old courthouse. In July, 1933, this responsibility was taken over by the National Park Service, which suggested restoring the entire village. The idea quickly won local and national support. The proposal was referred to Congress, and on August 3, 1935, President Franklin D. Roosevelt signed a bill into law creating the Appomattox Court House National Monument. The Resettlement Administration began acquiring land, and the park was proclaimed established on April 10, 1940. Work on the buildings was soon interrupted by the country's entry into World War II. After the war, reconstruction and restoration resumed, and gradually the buildings were opened. The building program is now mostly completed and, aside from minor changes in restored structures, the village appears much as it did on the day when Grant and Lee met there.

On April 6, 1954, the village's designation was changed to Appomattox Court House National Historical Park. The courthouse was reconstructed in 1963-1964 and now contains the park's visitor center as well as exhibits relating to the historic events. The Clover Hill Tavern, which dates from 1819, has been restored and contains a model of the village as it was at the time of the surrender. The tavern kitchen, the jail, and several other buildings have been restored or reconstructed, and most are open to the public. The McLean House has been reconstructed and refurnished with furniture similar to McLean's, but the furnishings are not believed to be originals. The reconstructed house was dedicated on April 16, 1950, with descendants of Grant and Lee as guests of honor.

—*Bernard A. Block*

For Further Information:

Catton, Bruce. *A Stillness at Appomattox.* New York: Doubleday, 1953. The third and last volume of Catton's Pulitzer Prize-winning history of the Civil War.

Foote, Shelby. *The Civil War: A Narrative.* Vol. 3. 40th anniversary ed. Alexandria, Va.: Time-Life Books, 1999. A much more exhaustive recounting of the closing years of the war.

National Park Service. *Appomattox Court House National Historical Park, Virginia.* Washington, D.C.: National Park Service, 1980. A compact, informative, and very well illustrated review of the important events relating to the historic site.

Arlington National Cemetery

Date: Established on June 15, 1864
Relevant issues: Civil War, cultural history, military history, Revolutionary War, Vietnam War, World War II
Significance: Of the more than one hundred national cemeteries in the United States, Arlington is one of only two administered by the U.S. Army and has the second largest number of people buried within its boundaries, over 260,000 persons. Veterans from all the nation's wars, from the American Revolution onward, are buried there. The remains of those now at Arlington National Cemetery who were killed before the Civil War were reinterred there after 1900.

Location: Arlington, across the Potomac River on a hill overlooking the nation's capital, Washington, D.C.

Site Office:
Superintendent
Arlington National Cemetery
Arlington, VA 22211-5003
ph.: (703) 289-2500
fax: (703) 697-4967
Web site: www.mdw.army.mil/cemetery.htm

Every year, between four and five million people visit Arlington National Cemetery to tour the grounds and pay homage to those who served their nation in the armed forces, government, or public office. The land constituting the cemetery was first established as a place to bury the nation's military dead during the Civil War, when a 200-acre plot was set aside for that purpose. Since that time the land dedicated has been expanded to over three times its original size.

Arlington House

The 612-acre property now containing Arlington National Cemetery was once part of an 1,100-acre plantation owned by George Washington Parke Custis, grandson of Martha Washington by her first husband, Daniel Parke Custis. Young George Custis was raised by his grandmother and her second husband, George Washington, at Mount Vernon, and when he reached adulthood he became determined to perpetuate the memory and principles of the first U.S. president. He was only three years old when he inherited the 1,100-acre plantation upon the death of his own father. At one point he thought about naming the estate Mount Washington, but he finally chose Arlington because it was the name of the Custis family ancestral estate in the Tidewater area (eastern shore) of Virginia.

Custis hired an English architect named George Hadfield to design the mansion on his estate. Hadfield had come to Washington in 1785 to help build the U.S. Capitol. Begun in 1802 but not completed until 1818, Arlington House was constructed in the Greek revival style and was completed in stages. The central section contained a formal dining room, a sitting room, and a large hall. One of the most recognizable features of the mansion's central section is the exterior portico displaying eight large columns, each approximately five feet in diameter at the base.

George Washington Parke Custis married Mary Lee Fitzhugh in 1804, and the two lived in Arlington House until their deaths in 1857 and 1853, respectively. They were buried close to each other on the property. Over the years their mansion home became a treasury of Washington heirlooms, including portraits, Washington's personal papers and clothes, and the command tent which the great commander in chief had used at the Battle of Yorktown.

The plantation was next inherited by the couple's only surviving child, Mary Ann Randolph Custis, who was born in 1808. On June 30, 1831, Mary Ann married a recent graduate of West Point, Lieutenant Robert E. Lee, and they also lived at Arlington House for the next thirty years. Though the Lees spent much of their time traveling between U.S. Army duty stations and Arlington, six of

their seven children were born at Arlington. Lee was at home on April 20, 1861, when he resigned his commission in the U.S. Army in the wake of Virginia's secession from the Union just three days before. On April 22, Lee left Arlington for Richmond to accept command of Virginia's military forces. He never returned to Arlington. About one month later, with the occupation of Arlington House by Union forces imminent, Mary Ann Lee also left the home, managing to save only some family valuables.

As Union troops under the command of Brigadier General Irvin McDowell crossed the Potomac and took up positions around Arlington House, fortifications were erected at several locations around the 1,100-acre estate, including Fort Whipple, which became Fort Myer. Arlington House became a headquarters for Union officers supervising the defenses of Washington, D.C., and though many of the Lee family possessions were moved to the U.S. Patent Office for safekeeping, some items, including Mount Vernon heirlooms, were looted.

The National Cemetery

Wartime law required property owners in areas occupied by Union troops to pay their property taxes in person. Because the Lees failed to appear to pay their $92.07 tax bill, Arlington House and the accompanying estate were confiscated by the federal government, offered for sale on January 11, 1864, and purchased by a tax commissioner for government, military, charitable, and educational purposes. Six months later, Arlington National Cemetery was established when a portion of the Arlington estate was appropriated for use as a military burial ground by Brigadier General Montgomery C. Meigs, commander of the garrison at Arlington House. On June 15, 1864, Secretary of War Edwin M. Stanton officially declared the Arlington mansion and two hundred acres of surrounding land a military cemetery, and sixty-five Union soldiers were in-

Arlington National Cemetery. (PhotoDisc)

terred there. By the end of the Civil War, more than sixteen thousand headstones dotted the cemetery's landscape. Among the first monuments erected on the estate to honor the Union dead was a stone and masonry vault containing the remains of some eighteen hundred casualties from the Battle of Bull Run, built by order of General Meigs. Later Meigs himself was buried on the grounds within one hundred yards of Arlington House, along with his father, mother, and wife.

Neither Robert E. Lee nor his wife (the official titleholder of the estate) ever attempted to recover their lost property. After Lee's death in 1870, George Washington Custis Lee, the oldest son of General and Mrs. Lee, filed suit to regain the Arlington estate, claiming the land had been confiscated illegally and that he was the legal owner. In December, 1882, the U.S. Supreme Court, in a 5-4 decision, returned the property to Lee, agreeing that the property had been confiscated without due process. However, in March, 1883, Lee accepted a congressional settlement of $150,000 as compensation for the property.

For several years the superintendent and staff of the cemetery used Arlington House for office space and living quarters. In 1925 the War Department began restoring the mansion to its original condition. In 1933 oversight responsibilities for the mansion were transferred to the National Park Service, and in 1955 it was designated as a memorial to Robert E. Lee. Arlington House may be visited during designated operating hours; brochures are available for self-guided tours.

Tomb of the Unknowns
The Tomb of the Unknowns, originally known as the Tomb of the Unknown Soldier, is is one of the most-visited places at Arlington National Cemetery. On March 4, 1921, the U.S. Congress approved the burial of an unidentified American soldier from World War I at Arlington. On Memorial Day of that year, four unknowns were exhumed from American cemeteries in France, and one was selected to be transported to the United States for reinterment. President Warren G. Harding officiated at the interment ceremonies at Arlington on November 11, 1921.

The tomb is a sarcophagus of white marble quarried in Colorado. It consists of seven pieces weighing seventy-nine tons. The north and south sides of the tomb are divided into three panels each by Doric pilasters or columns carved into the sides. Sculpted into the east side, which faces Washington, D.C., are three Greek figures representing Peace, Victory, and Valor. Inscribed on the west, or back, side are the words "Here rests in honored glory an American soldier known but to God." The tomb was completed and opened to the public on April 9, 1932.

On August 3, 1956, President Dwight D. Eisenhower signed a bill to select and memorialize unknowns of World War II and the Korean War. President Eisenhower presided over reinterment ceremonies on May 30, 1958. An unknown soldier of the Vietnam conflict was reburied at Arlington on May 28, 1984, under the direction of President Ronald Reagan. The U.S. Army began guarding the Tomb of the Unknowns on April 6, 1948, and it is now guarded twenty-four hours a day, 365 days a year.

Memorial Amphitheater
Another important site on the grounds of Arlington National Cemetery is the Memorial Amphitheater, which was the dream of Judge Ivory G. Kimball, who wanted visitors to have a place to meet and honor America's defenders and fallen heroes. Because of Kimball's efforts, Congress authorized the construction of the amphitheater in March, 1913. Groundbreaking for the structure took place on March 1, 1915; President Woodrow Wilson laid its cornerstone on October 15, 1915, and the amphitheater was dedicated on May 15, 1920. Items placed within a box inside the cornerstone included a copy of the Bible, the Declaration of Independence, the U.S. Constitution, a U.S. flag from 1915, and several other items. The amphitheater is constructed of marble quarried in Vermont. A Memorial Display Room, situated between the Memorial Amphitheater and Tomb of the Unknowns, is made of marble imported from Italy and houses plaques and tributes presented in honor of those buried in the tomb. Among the many inscriptions found in various locations around the amphitheater is a quotation from the Roman poet, Horace, etched above the west entrance: *Dulce et decorum est pro patria mori* (it is sweet and fitting to die for one's country).

About five thousand visitors attend each of the three major memorial services held every year on

Easter, Memorial Day, and Veterans Day. The services are sponsored by the U.S. Army Military District of Washington, though several other military organizations also conduct memorial services in the amphitheater.

On December 4, 1863, near where the Memorial Amphitheater now stands, the federal government established a community for freed slaves, the Freedman's Village, which provided food, housing, medical care, employment training, and education for former slaves who migrated to the area; the village operated for more than thirty years. Over eleven hundred freed slaves were given some land by the government, where they farmed and lived; however, they were removed in 1890, when that portion of the Arlington estate was dedicated as a military installation.

Visiting Arlington

Arlington National Cemetery is an active military cemetery, conducting about fifty-four hundred burials each year (between twenty-two and twenty-four funerals Monday through Friday). Because of limited space, eligibility for burial at Arlington is restricted to specific categories of honorably discharged U.S. servicemen and servicewomen. More information can be obtained from the Superintendent of Arlington National Cemetery. In addition to subterranean interment, Arlington also has a large columbarium for housing cremated remains—ultimately a total of 50,000 niches capable of holding 100,000 remains. Any honorably discharged veteran is eligible for inurnment in the columbarium.

A new cemetery visitors' center was opened in January, 1990. Situated near the cemetery entrance, it provides parking, historical information, and gravesite location information. Removal of the old visitors' center allowed for expansion of the cemetery, making 9,500 additional grave sites available. An atrium inside the visitors' center contains exhibits and an information hall. Arlington National Cemetery is a sobering reminder of those who have served their country.

—*Andrew C. Skinner*

For Further Information:

Ashabranner, Brent. *A Grateful Nation: The Story of Arlington National Cemetery.* New York: George Putnam's Sons, 1990. Written with younger audiences in mind, this work traces the history of the national cemetery and shrine to American heroes.

Hinkel, John Vincent. *Arlington: Monument to Heroes.* New and enlarged ed. Englewood Cliffs, N.J.: Prentice Hall, 1970. An excellent resource, which lays out the history of the cemetery and highlights stories of some of the men and women buried at Arlington who served in the armed forces. Some maps are included.

National Park Service, Division of Publications. *Arlington House: A Guide to Arlington House, the Robert E. Lee Memorial, Virginia.* Washington, D.C.: U.S. Department of the Interior, 1985. A succinct, helpful guide to the Arlington estate mansion, containing history, photographs, and illustrations.

Peters, James Edward. *Arlington National Cemetery, Shrine to America's Heroes.* Kensington, Md.: Woodbine House, 1986. Perhaps the most helpful and comprehensive book for both historians and tourists. Contains histories and descriptions of the cemetery's many monuments.

Reef, Catherine. *Arlington National Cemetery.* New York: Dillon Press, 1991. For juvenile audiences. This work examines the history and current activities of the most famous of our national burial places.

Booker T. Washington National Monument

Date: Established in 1956

Relevant issues: African American history, education

Significance: Born into slavery on this 207-acre former tobacco farm, Booker T. Washington (1856-1915) rose to become a famous educator and African American spokesman during the trying period following the end of Reconstruction in the South. From 1895 to 1915, he was the most famous and influential African American in the United States. Visitors to this living historical farm learn about Washington's early life as a slave through exhibits, living history demonstrations, audiovisual programs, and historic trails.

Location: In the town of Hardy, sixteen miles northeast of Rocky Mount via Virginia Route

122, twenty miles southeast of Roanoke, and twenty-one miles south of Bedford

Site Office:

Superintendent
Booker T. Washington National Monument
12130 Booker T. Washington Highway
Hardy, VA 24101-9997
ph.: (540) 721-2094
Web sites: www.nps.gov/bowa/; www.nationalparks
.org/guide/parks/booker-t-was-1957.htm

James Boroughs's tobacco plantation was typical of the small plantations in the area. Boroughs owned ten slaves to produce his labor-intensive cash crop on 5 of his 207 acres and to help make the plantation as self-sufficient as possible, supporting his wife and fourteen children. The "big house" on the plantation had five rooms, luxurious compared to the one-room log cabin in which Booker T. Washington grew up but still rather basic.

Booker T. Washington. (Library of Congress)

Booker, his older brother, and his sister lived in their dirt-floor and windowless one-room cabin, which also served as a kitchen for the "big house." Today one can see re-creations of many of the plantation's buildings, Booker's kitchen-cabin, the tobacco and horse barns, the corn crib, the smokehouse, the blacksmith shed, and the chicken lot. One can walk the grounds, absorbing the upbringing of self-sufficiency and manual labor that provided a background for Washington to later found the famous Tuskegee Institute of Alabama (1881), which stressed education in agriculture and industry as a first step toward African American economic viability. The sights, sounds, and smells of Boroughs's plantation as experienced by Booker await the visitor, along with crops, wild plants, and farm animals similar to those of Booker's youth.

Up from Slavery

Booker T. Washington's first nine years of life were spent in abject poverty as a slave on the Boroughs Plantation. His bed was a few old rags spread out on the dirt floor of a one-room cabin measuring fourteen by sixteen feet. His mother served as cook for the Boroughs family, and the one room served also as a kitchen for the plantation. Since there was no stove, food had to be cooked over an open fireplace. In his memoirs, Washington could not recall a single time that the family sat down to eat together in a civilized manner and viewed his early life in the Piedmont region of Virginia as taking place "in the midst of the most miserable, desolate, and discouraging surroundings." He did recall his mother cooking a chicken for the family in the middle of the night and rationalized the covert action. In general food was parceled out at various times, whenever it was available. Washington's only shoes during slavery were wooden ones that were uncomfortable and clumsy to wear. The height of discomfort was the homegrown flax, turned into shirts for slaves, which felt like thorns and bristles when new.

Washington's father, a white man from a nearby farm, played absolutely no role in his life. Washington claimed, in fact, that he did not even know his father's name. Washington's early education came from working in various capacities on the farm, helping to maintain the few livestock, vegetable gardens, and industries which served to make the plantation largely self-sufficient. He recalls in his autobiography, *Up from Slavery* (1901), that his early life was completely occupied by labor, leaving little time for play. What he learned was that hard work and self-reliance were primary ideals. Formal education was not permitted for slaves. The closest Washington got to a schoolhouse was carrying the books for one of his master's daughters.

While uneducated, Washington recalls that slaves were remarkably well informed about national developments as the Civil War began. While intensely loyal to their masters and sincerely mourning the death or wounding of the masters' sons in battle, slaves also followed the progress of battles through word of mouth and were very much aware that slavery was a major issue. Frequent conversations were held at night, in whispers, about the latest developments in the Civil War, picked up from the post office or from family conversations in the "big houses." Washington recalls that he never met a slave who did not want freedom, nor would he ever meet an African American who wanted a return to slavery. He also recalls that while living conditions seriously declined for the masters as the war progressed, the already low quality of life for slaves did not seriously decline. Finally, in April, 1865, a proclamation was read on the Boroughs Plantation announcing that slavery was at an end. Soon Washington left with his family for Malden, West Virginia, to join his stepfather. The family moved into another rundown shack. As deprived as Washington's life under slavery may have been, he points out that it was not much different from that of many thousands of other slaves. He was also thankful that slaves learned how to do many things on the plantation, and he pitied the poor slave owners and their families left behind who had mastered no special industry necessary for survival.

More Hard Work and an Education
Life in Malden for the nine-year-old Washington meant work in the salt furnace and coal mines, often in shifts beginning at 4:00 A.M. A little bit of schooling took place in the afternoon, whenever possible. An opportunity for some improvement came when he was selected as a houseboy for a wealthy townswoman who encouraged Washington to further his education. According to Washington, this experience also provided him with the values of frugality, cleanliness, and personal morality, which he would carry with him for the rest of his life. In 1872 he left for a new school for black students, the Hampton Institute, which was one of the earliest freedmen's schools directed toward industrial education. According to Washington's memoirs, most of his journey from Malden to Hampton was made by foot. Like many Hampton students, he paid his tuition by working. Most of his responsibilities were those of janitor.

Graduating with honors in 1875, Washington taught school in Malden for two years, then attended Wayland Seminary in Washington, D.C. He returned to Hampton in 1879 as an instructor, where he organized a night program to train seventy-five American Indian students. This program was used as a model for his founding of Tuskegee Institute in Tuskegee, Alabama, in 1881, with help from northern philanthropists such as Andrew Carnegie and John D. Rockefeller as well as southern philanthropic organizations.

The school reflected the Booker T. Washington credo of self-reliance born of hard work. His students made the brick and built most of the buildings on the original campus. The school, which stressed industrial training rather than traditional academic learning, also embodied Washington's willingness to accommodate contemporary segregationist policies and lack of voting rights. For Washington, freedom from economic slavery was the first step before later civil rights could be achieved. His position was stated in his Atlanta Compromise Address of 1895, which accepted temporary segregation and voting rights restrictions if whites would support African American economic and educational advancement. As he said, "In all things that are purely social we can be as separate as the fingers, yet one as the hand in all things essential to mutual progress." Washington was a handsome individual and a dynamic speaker, and this speech at an exposition in Atlanta catapulted him into the national spotlight and gained for him fame as the leading spokesperson for African Americans.

The Nation's Most Influential African American

Few whites were threatened by Washington's accommodationist attitudes, and most African Americans were highly respectful of his rising national prestige. He helped found the National Negro Business League in 1900. Washington was a celebrated dinner guest of Theodore Roosevelt at the White House in 1901, the same year that his autobiography *Up from Slavery* became a widely read work. Soon he became a political adviser to Roosevelt and William H. Taft, influencing a multitude of political patronage positions. He also served on the board of trustees for both Fisk and Howard Universities. In the meantime the Tuskegee Institute, under his guidance, emerged as a national center for industrial and agricultural training as well as a center for training black teachers.

As new African American leadership came to the fore in the Niagara Movement (1905-1909) and under the auspices of the National Association for the Advancement of Colored People (NAACP), beginning in 1909, Washington's ideas were openly challenged. A chief critic was the Harvard sociologist and writer W. E. B. Du Bois, who found Washington's silence on racial oppression and disenfranchisement to be reprehensible. The Washington-Du Bois clash of ideas became one of the great debates in American political life. In his later years Washington denounced the increasing number of lynchings in the South and advocated making "separate but equal" facilities more equal. He also wrote under code names to denounce Jim Crow laws and racial violence directed toward blacks.

Booker T. Washington died at Tuskegee on November 14, 1915, at the beginning of both the Great Migration from the rural South to the urban North and World War I, two events that would transform the remainder of the twentieth century. He rose from slavery to become the nation's most influential African American and remains a pioneer on the long journey toward racial equality. In the American epic he was one of the great self-made men who rose from the lowest of circumstances to achieve positions of national stature. His theme of self-reliance would be repeated for many succeeding generations.

Places to Visit

The scenic Blue Ridge Parkway is only twenty-five miles west of the Booker T. Washington National Monument. Appomattox Court House National Historical Park is 75 miles east. The Virginia Museum of American Frontier Culture is seventy-five miles northwest, and the Guilford Court House National Military Park is sixty miles south.

Visitors to the Booker T. Washington National Monument should plan two hours to view exhibits and audiovisual programs in the visitors' center and to see the re-creation of historic buildings on the Plantation Trail—a one-quarter-mile loop. An additional hour is needed to walk the Jack-O-Lantern Branch Trail, a half-mile loop through woods and fields. Visitors are advised to keep their distance from animals and not to enter pastures or pens. The site is open daily from 9:00 A.M. to 4:30 P.M., except Thanksgiving Day, Christmas, and New Year's Day. In the winter months, the area may be closed due to icy conditions.

—Irwin Halfond

For Further Information:

Bontemps, Arna W. *Young Booker: Booker T. Washington's Early Days.* New York: Dodd and Mead, 1972. Traces the events of Washington's youth and early career that were a driving force behind his emergence as a famous educator.

Drinker, Frederick E. *Booker T. Washington: The Master Mind of a Child of Slavery.* New York: Negro Universities Press, 1970. This work, first published in 1915, is splendidly illustrated and describes Washington's life in a somewhat romanticized manner.

Harlan, Louis R. *Booker T. Washington: The Making of a Black Leader, 1856-1901.* New York: Oxford University Press, 1972. A scholarly study of Washington's life and the development of his career to a position of national leadership.

Thornbrough, Emma. *Booker T. Washington.* Englewood Cliffs, N.J.: Prentice Hall, 1969. A standard biography of Washington.

Washington, Booker T. *My Larger Education: Being Chapters from My Experience.* Miami: Mnemosyne, 1969. The author's account and reflections on the formative influences in his life.

_____. *Up from Slavery: An Autobiography.* Reprint. Garden City, N.Y.: Doubleday, 1951. The landmark autobiography of Booker T. Washington, first published in 1901.

_____. *Working with the Hands.* New York: Arno

Press, 1969. This sequel to *Up from Slavery* describes the author's experiences in industrial training at Tuskegee Institute.

Fredericksburg

Date: Town incorporated in 1782; established as a National Battlefield in 1927

Relevant issues: Civil War, military history

Significance: Part of Fredericksburg and Spotsylvania National Military Park, this site includes the battlefields of Fredericksburg, Chancellorsville, Spotsylvania Court House, and the Wilderness.

Location: In northeastern Virginia, approximately forty-one miles from Alexandria and fifty miles from Washington, D.C., on the Rappahannock River

Site Offices:

Fredericksburg and Spotsylvania National Military Park
120 Chatham Lane
Fredericksburg, VA 22405
Web site: www.nps.gov/frsp/

Fredericksburg Battlefield Visitor Center
706 Caroline Street
Fredericksburg, VA 22401
ph.: (800) 678-4748; (540) 373-6122

Although small in both area and population, Fredericksburg has always stood near the center of national history. Because of its strategic position on the Rappahannock River, the city has been a chief river port for the Shenandoah Valley, a home for colonial forefathers, and a critical Civil War battle site that changed hands no less than seven times from 1861 to 1865. Indeed, the city's most important day remembers not the living but those who died during one of those clashes to take the area surrounding Fredericksburg when Confederate troops led by General Robert E. Lee routed Union troops led by Ambrose E. Burnside.

Early History

Fredericksburg was settled in 1671 and named for the father of King George III. The site was laid out in 1728 but was not incorporated as a town until 1782. It became a city in 1879.

Members of George Washington's family have as many ties to Fredericksburg as they do to Mount Vernon. From ages six to sixteen, Washington lived at Ferry Farm, across the Rappahannock from the city limits. He later bought a house for his mother in the city, where she lived for seventeen years before her death. Washington's only sister, Betty, married businessman Fielding Lewis in 1750 and built Kenmore, one of the city's most famous residences, which still stands today. Around 1760, Washington's brother Charles built a home where Patrick Henry, Thomas Jefferson, and George Washington would come to discuss politics. The home later became the Rising Sun Tavern, the name it bears today.

In addition to the Washingtons, Fredericksburg was home to James Monroe, who had a law office in Fredericksburg from 1787 to 1789 and later became the fifth president of the United States. Preserved at the site of his Fredericksburg office is the desk Monroe used to sign the Monroe Doctrine, the policy which stated the United States would frown upon European intervention in the affairs of the Western Hemisphere.

The Civil War

The city that was famous early in its existence for its permanent inhabitants became even more famous for its transient inhabitants, the soldiers, during the Civil War. Northern Virginia, because of its placement between the Union capital of Washington, D.C., and the Confederate capital of Richmond, saw frequent and bloody fighting, particularly in the area of Fredericksburg, where four battles were fought within only seventeen miles of the city limits.

In late 1862, the Union army lay staggered and weary. After a series of unsuccessful battles with high casualties, highlighted by what could at best be called a September standoff at Antietam (Sharpsburg), Maryland, President Abraham Lincoln dismissed General George McClellan as commander of the Union Army of the Potomac on November 5. He replaced him with Ambrose E. Burnside.

Following the Antietam battle, Confederate commander (of the Army of Northern Virginia) Robert E. Lee withdrew to the Shenandoah Valley to refit his troops. When the refitting was finished, Lee took a gamble, splitting his forces and sending

Stonewall Jackson south into the Shenandoah Valley in the hope that McClellan would attack and Jackson would be able to outflank and crush the Union army. At one point, the Confederate forces were divided over Virginia by a marching time of two days. Prior to his dismissal, McClellan had planned to exploit this mistake by driving his forces southwestward, hoping to split, cut off, and destroy at least one part of the fractionalized force.

General Burnside's Campaign Against Fredericksburg

With Burnside in command, however, plans changed. Despite the fact that on the day he took command he outnumbered Lee and James Longstreet, directly in front of him at Culpeper, Virginia, by three to one, he scrapped McClellan's plan. He instead preferred to drive toward the Confederate capital of Richmond via the southeast, crossing the Rappahannock River at Fredericksburg. If he took Richmond, he believed, the Confederates would crumble. Burnside's plan was to cross the river, take the hills west of town, and set up a stronghold on the way, surprising Lee.

Burnside submitted his plan to Washington, D.C., and it was approved by Lincoln, who cautioned that for it to work, it had to be carried out quickly and efficiently, as Confederate intelligence was well known for its accuracy and speed. Still weary and miserable from the Antietam battle, Burnside's troops began the march south and east through the cold November rain toward Fredericksburg on November 15. True to Burnside's prediction, Lee was surprised, but poor planning by the Union War Department and subsequent poor judgment on Burnside's part doomed this attack as the final of the Union disasters of 1862.

Union forces reached the town of Falmouth, across the Rappahannock from Fredericksburg, on November 17. Burnside had covertly marched his troops down the eastern shore of the Rappahannock—in order to cross to Fredericksburg, he needed materials for pontoon bridges from the War Department in Washington. Although other supplies had met the arriving the army, materials for the pontoon bridges were nowhere to be seen. Either the message was never delivered, or the War Department did not understand the importance of having the bridge material in Falmouth exactly when Burnside arrived. Because of the oversight, the Union soldiers hunkered down in Falmouth waiting for the pontoons to arrive.

On the day Burnside arrived at Falmouth, Lee received the first intelligence of Burnside's movements. Further investigation revealed that the entire Army of the Potomac had stationed itself near Fredericksburg, and on November 19 Lee ordered his division under James Longstreet to go there immediately. Lee's troops moved toward Fredericksburg from the west. Other Confederate forces led by Stonewall Jackson and A. P. Hill rushed to the site.

A Snag in the Union Plans

The same November 19 found Ambrose Burnside worrying, as his bridge material had still not arrived. He wrote a letter to the War Department, saying the supplies must be sent at once. Despite the initial error by the War Department, the town and surrounding area could have been taken easily had the supplies arrived within even three days of when they were supposed to, as Longstreet's men did not arrive until November 21. The bridge material did not begin arriving, however, until November 25. While the Union army waited, Lee and his men dug into the hills that studded the landscape to the west of town in an area known as Marye's Heights, preparing themselves for the Union onslaught.

Burnside could fault no one but himself for the second grave error. To protect his men crossing the river, he stationed cannon at the top of the heights on his side. Not wanting his men to face the shelling, Lee hid his men and in turn hid their numbers, fooling Burnside into believing the main Confederate force was south of the actual town. He had purposely left the town lightly guarded to lull Union commanders into a false sense of security.

Four days after arriving, on November 21, Union general Edwin Sumner notified Fredericksburg officials that they must surrender by five o'clock that afternoon. More than six thousand citizens were displaced from their homes, taking only what possessions they could carry.

Longstreet and the rest of the Confederate army did not want to see the town destroyed by Union artillery. They were able to persuade Burnside not to use cannon under the provision that the town would not be used as a Confederate stronghold. During the ten days that followed, the waiting continued. Burnside first chose Skinker's Neck, a site fourteen miles south of Fredericksburg, as one of his main crossing points, but Lee put a division there and Burnside reluctantly retreated to form a new plan. As the Union army dawdled, Lee's forces kept preparing—digging trenches, placing guns, and stationing groups of forces. Burnside grew increasingly worried as he watched Jackson's and Longstreet's forces join Lee, but he refused to abort his battle plan, as pressure from Washington for a Union victory grew.

Burnside finally decided he wanted five pontoon bridges built at various sites up and down the river. At 3 A.M. on December 11, construction finally began, nearly one month late. Work on the lower two bridges went without incident, but others that were built closer to the town faced constant fire from sharpshooters holed up in the buildings. Burnside saw this aggression as a violation of the agreement he had made with Longstreet and thus saw the town as fair game for an artillery assault. On the same day, December 11, the shelling of Fredericksburg began. Under the protection of the artillery fire, the remaining pontoon bridges were finished, and the Union army prepared to enter the town.

By the next day, the last of the sharpshooters had been driven out, and the town was in the hands of the Union. Soldiers advanced into the town and, while waiting for orders to attack Confederate positions, looted, ravaged, and destroyed what they could find. Burnside had nearly 113,000 men and Lee about 85,000—the largest number of men to ever clash on a Civil War battlefield.

Between the town and Marye's Heights lay an open field that the Union soldiers would have to cross in order to climb the hill. Between that field and the hills stood a stone wall, where four divisions of Confederate infantry stood, waiting to repel any Union charges against the Heights. Lee could not believe that anyone would be so foolish as to attack such a fortified position. Still, Burnside marched on, disregarding warnings given to him by his field commanders.

The Assault Begins

On the morning of December 13, Burnside gave the order for the full-scale assault to begin. Four divisions under the command of William Franklin attacked Stonewall Jackson's troops, which were on the left. Another Union division led by George Gordon Meade was able to penetrate Jackson's force briefly but was driven back by artillery fire. Burnside wanted to use this left attack to distract Lee before his central assault began with Sumner and Joseph Hooker. After Meade and Franklin battled with Jackson for nearly two hours, Burnside finally gave the order for Sumner to attack the heart of the Confederates—Lee, the grassy field, the stone wall, and Marye's Heights.

As wave after wave of troops headed toward the stone wall, Confederate gunners stopped their charge. Hundreds, then thousands of Union troops fell under heavy artillery and rifle fire. Reinforcements waited in the town to join the assault, trying not to notice the scores of mangled men being brought to the field hospitals. After Sumner's men had been decimated, Burnside ordered Hooker to lead the next major charge. Hooker balked, but Burnside forced him into action. In all, Burnside ordered sixteen assaults on the Heights before deciding they could not be taken. More than nine thousand Union troops lay dead on the field—they never got any closer than twenty-five yards in front of the stone wall that guarded the Heights.

Under the barrage of gunfire, hundreds of soldiers lay in trenches in the ground, waiting for night to fall so they could escape back to the Union lines under the cover of darkness. Wounded soldiers bled and froze to death in the December cold. Those who were alive waited more than twenty-four hours for the truce signed on December 14, which allowed the Union troops to gather their dead and wounded and to retreat across the river.

Burnside sat in shock at the camp, weeping. He decided that he would lead another charge of the wall himself but was talked out of it by other officers. He could not persuade any of his other generals to launch a new attack the next morning. Confederate troops drifted back into the town after it had been abandoned, to salvage what was left.

In all, the Union lost 12,600 men, while the Confederates suffered 5,300 losses, but many of those were assumed missing, having returned home for Christmas. The Union army set up camp near Falmouth for the winter.

Destruction of Burnside's Reputation

Burnside was looked upon as a fool by both Washington, D.C., and his troops. Even the lowest-ranking soldier knew that after the bridge materials had arrived late, the situation was an impossible one for the Union army and should have been abandoned. Burnside, by his stubbornness and his underestimation of the strength of the Confederate forces, managed to make the stone wall a place that no one in the Union army would soon forget.

Shortly after the December disaster, Burnside was replaced as commander of the Army of the Potomac by Joseph Hooker. Hooker spent the next few months rebuilding his army, preparing for another attack against Lee that would see the infamous stone wall once again playing a role, albeit a small one.

General Hooker's Campaign

Hooker's spring plan involved keeping a portion of his troops near Fredericksburg to fool Lee while secretly moving his main force toward Chancellorsville, ten miles to the north and west. This main force would circle around Lee and trap him against the river. The movement began on April 27, 1863.

Lee's intelligence informed him of the plan, and he rushed all but ten thousand of his troops northward to meet Hooker. As Hooker and Lee clashed to the north, a Union brigade under John Sedgwick stormed across the river into Fredericksburg, trying yet again to take Marye's Heights in order to attack Lee's rear. Because the Confederate force was smaller and less entrenched, they were able to succeed in surging over the stone wall and climbing the ridge.

Their celebration was short-lived, though; as Lee was routing Hooker to the north, the Confederate force under Jubal T. Early was able to knock the Union troops off the ridge and again back across the river by May 3. In all, the Union lost an additional seventeen thousand troops at this battle, which would become known as Chancellorsville, while the Confederates lost thirteen thousand, one-fourth of their fighting force. One of the greatest casualties for the Confederates was Stonewall Jackson, who developed pneumonia and died following the amputation of his arm after being wounded by his own forces.

Other Civil War Battles

Later in the Civil War, the Fredericksburg area saw two other battles, the Wilderness and Spotsylvania

Court House. They marked the beginning of a year-long struggle that culminated in the Confederate surrender at Appomattox on April 9, 1865.

In the Battle of the Wilderness, May 5 and 6, 1864, Lee met Ulysses S. Grant in combat for the first time. Grant was by then the commander of all the Union armies. Grant crossed the Rapidan River, an upper branch of the Rappahannock, hoping to confront Lee's forces in open country rather than in the densely forested area called the Wilderness, just west of the Chancellorsville Battlefield. The Union soldiers, however, did encounter Confederate troops in the Wilderness, and there ensued chaotic fighting with neither side gaining an advantage. During the battle, the dry forest caught fire, raising the number of casualties. Those killed, wounded, or missing totaled nearly 15,400 for the Union, out of a force of 118,000, and 11,400 for the Confederates, out of 62,000.

From the Wilderness, Grant moved to the southeast, hoping to capture the crossroads at Spotsylvania. A Confederate unit arrived there first, however, strictly by chance: The soldiers had had to leave their position in the Wilderness because of the fire. They stopped the Union advance on May 8. The Union and Confederate forces engaged in a series of attacks and counterattacks. One part of the battlefield became known as the "Bloody Angle" because water in the trenches was stained red. Also in this area, the gunfire was so intense that it felled an oak tree. The battle featured fierce hand-to-hand combat. In the end, the Union forces were unable to break through Confederate lines, so Grant moved around the Confederates, southward and closer to Richmond. The siege of Petersburg began in June.

Modern Preservation Efforts

The Fredericksburg and Spotsylvania National Military Park contains all four battlefields. At each one, there are numerous exhibits and markers to outline the historic facts. The Fredericksburg Battlefield includes the Marye's Heights National Cemetery, and the Spotsylvania Court House site has a Confederate cemetery. In nearby Guinea, Virginia, also part of the National Military Park, is the Stonewall Jackson Shrine. Jackson died in this small house, which served as the office for a plantation called Fairfield.

Following the war, the ravaged town rebuilt and later gained city status. Today, though still sporting only a modest population of around fifteen thousand, Fredericksburg remains an important farm and industrial shipping city on the Rappahannock. Its monuments, cemeteries, and fields of battle serve as a memorial to the thousands of men who gave their lives in the American Civil War.

—Tony Jaros

For Further Information:

Davis, William C. *Stand in the Day of Battle.* New York: Doubleday, 1983. A detailed account of the early years of the war, with complete quotes from eyewitnesses and battle diagrams.

Ward, Geoffrey C. *The Civil War.* Reprint. New York: Alfred A. Knopf, 1997. A colorful and complete history of the conflict. The book formed the basis for a popular multipart television series.

Wheeler, Richard. *Lee's Terrible Swift Sword.* New York: Harper, 1992. Another detailed account of the early years of the war.

Jamestown

Date: James Fort founded in 1607

Relevant issues: Colonial America, cultural history, European settlement, political history

Significance: James Fort was the first permanent English settlement in North America. The first Anglican congregation in North America met here in 1607. The settlement grew to become Jamestown, the first capital of the Virginia colony. In 1619, America's oldest legislative body, the House of Burgesses (later the General Assembly), held its first session in Jamestown. In that same year, the arrival of both Africans and a substantial number of women from England helped ensure the colony's survival.

Location: Jamestown Island, on the James River, nine miles from Williamsburg via the Colonial Parkway

Site Office:

Colonial National Historical Park
P.O. Box 210
Yorktown, VA 23690-0210
ph.: (757) 898-2410
Web site: www.nps.gov/colo/

Jamestown's place in American history is ensured by its being the first successful English settlement, as well as by the number of political, religious, and cultural events originating on this small island site. Here three cultures—Native American, European, and African—met and began the creation of a new nation.

Founding of the Fort

In June, 1606, the Virginia Company, a group of London merchants, received a charter from King James I of England, authorizing them to explore and colonize a large North American area, from what would become North Carolina to the southern part of the future state of New York. The first group of 104 men and boys sailed from London in December, and on May 13, 1607, reached the swampy island which they would name for their king. (An order proclaiming the anniversary of that day as a day of thanksgiving would be issued by the colonial government in 1619.) The land itself was called Virginia, in memory of Elizabeth I, the "Virgin Queen."

The site was chosen for its military value—the island was secluded but provided a good view of any Spanish ships that might arrive—and the colony's goals included searching for gold and a trade route to Asia, not particularly settling and farming. The first settlers included artisans and laborers, but about half, according to Captain John Smith (1580-1631), who soon assumed leadership of the colony, were gentlemen, unaccustomed to manual labor. The absence of women and families also indicated a desire to acquire wealth as quickly as possible, partly through trade with Native Americans, rather than a desire to establish a new place to live.

The Englishmen encountered a number of Algonquian Indians who initially offered them corn and furs, but no gold, and had no intention of working for the intruders. Relations quickly deteriorated, leading the colonists to built a triangular wooden fort, which protected their church and storehouse, as well as several houses.

Indian attacks were but one of many trials faced by the English. Jamestown Island was marshy and disease-ridden; the water was bad, and in the summer the heat became intense. The fort was accidentally burned in 1608. Unwilling or unable to successfully imitate Native American cultivation methods, many colonists died of starvation as well as disease, and their numbers dropped to thirty-eight in less than a year. Following the so-called Starving Time, by 1609 to 1610 only sixty of five hundred settlers still survived.

Although the extent of John Smith's role in Virginia's early history has been debated by scholars, there is no doubt that his robust energy kept Jamestown functioning during its first two years, until he was injured in a gunpowder accident in October, 1609, and returned to England. While exploring the interior and trading with local tribes, Smith met a formidable counterpart in Powhatan (c. 1550-1618), the leading chief of approximately twenty-four tribal units near the settlement. Powhatan, whom Smith described as possessing "such a Majestie as I cannot expresse," had no illusions about the English and distrusted them, as their numbers continued to increase.

Smith's brief captivity at the hands of the Indians in December, 1607, led to his meeting with Powhatan's favorite daughter, Pocahontas (c. 1596-1617). There are varying interpretations of Smith's story that she intervened to save his life, but clearly she became fascinated with the colonists, visited them on a number of occasions, and perhaps interceded on their behalf. In 1613 she was captured and held in Jamestown; after accepting Christianity, she married a planter, John Rolfe (1585-1622), in 1614. Their union fostered a brief peace between the two cultures. In 1616 Pocahontas accompanied Rolfe and the colony's governor, Sir Thomas Dale (d. 1619), to London, where she was presented at court and had a brief emotional reunion with Smith. She died at Plymouth early in 1617, leaving one son from whom many Virginians have claimed descent.

Life in the Colony

Until his death in 1622, John Rolfe played a vital role in the colony's success through his importation of tobacco, beginning in 1612, from the West Indies. Smoking tobacco became fashionable despite King James's disapproval of the "noxious weed," and it ensured the Virginia colony's economic survival. Until the land wore out and the market declined in the 1660's, tobacco was supposedly planted everywhere in Jamestown, including its unpaved streets.

The labor-intensive nature of tobacco cultivation led to a demand for more workers. Despite an influx of poor white servants, many of whom sold their labor as indentures for between five and seven years, the labor shortage fueled the importation of African workers. It is not known whether the twenty Africans sold by the Dutch in 1619 were indentured or permanently enslaved, since a number of African Americans managed to acquire freedom and property during the seventeenth century. However, opportunities for poor men, both white and black, became increasingly limited by the 1670's, as Virginia's class structure became more fully developed. By contrast, many of the women who survived the occasional Indian attacks, disease, and primitive conditions fared well in Virginia. The colony's gender imbalance meant that the one hundred white women sent by the Virginia Company in 1619 and those who followed them, including servants, had more opportunities to improve their status through marriage than did females in England. Less is known about African women, but 1619 census records indicate that in addition to the men on the Dutch ship, seventeen black females and fifteen black males were living in the colony.

Still another vital component of Virginia life arrived in 1619 with Governor Sir George Yeardley, who was empowered by the Company to summon an assembly of "burgesses"—two elected representatives from each of eleven settlements—who first met with him and his council on July 30, 1619, in the church at Jamestown. In the early 1640's, the General Assembly became a bicameral legislature.

Despite this establishment of representative government on the parliamentary model, Virginia was increasingly dominated socially and economically by a few relatively wealthy men, who were usually friends of the governor. Faced with falling tobacco prices and convinced that the rich planters and merchants who met in Jamestown were keeping them from acquiring the acres they needed to become gentry, a growing number of poor farmers sought more Indian land, by force if necessary.

Indian Attacks, Governor Berkeley, and Nathaniel Bacon

The truce that began with Pocahontas's marriage to John Rolfe had deteriorated by 1620. A growing number of confrontations and murders on both sides inspired Powhatan's brother and successor, Opechancanough (c. 1544-1644), to organize a

Ships in the Jamestown harbor. (PhotoDisc)

who were outside Berkeley's inner circle. Both groups found a leader in Nathaniel Bacon (1647-1676), a member of the gentry who came to Virginia in 1674. Portraying himself as a deliverer from both the Indians and the governor, Bacon soon quarrelled with Berkeley, massacred a peaceful tribe, and by 1675 led a four hundred-man army of white and black servants in a brief rebellion which culminated in Bacon's burning of Jamestown. After Bacon's death from dysentery in 1676, Berkeley briefly resumed power, but his arbitrary methods led to some limitations being placed on the governor's power, decreased taxes, and access to more Indian land for poor white farmers. To forestall a future rebellion by lower-class whites, the African slave trade also increased.

surprise attack on the English settlements on March 22, 1622. Although 347 out of 1,240 settlers were killed, Jamestown escaped destruction, according to tradition, because of a warning by Chanco, a Christian Indian. Over the next two years the English retaliated, killing more than one thousand native people, regardless of their tribal affiliation. This destruction and the growing ineffectiveness of the Virginia Company led King James to revoke its charter in 1624 and make Virginia a royal colony.

Twenty years later, a second raid by Opechancanough also failed to eradicate the settlement. Captured and brought to Jamestown in 1646, the aged chief was shot by one of his guards, despite the efforts of Governor William Berkeley (1606-1677) to keep him alive as a potential hostage or trophy. Virginia's Native Americans were forced to recognize English sovereignty and became increasingly marginalized as they were pushed farther west.

By the early 1670's the elderly and increasingly unpopular Berkeley could not satisfy both the demands of Virginia's lower classes for land, decreased taxes, and protection from the Indians and the desire for power of prosperous men

Jamestown's Decline and Rebirth

Jamestown's statehouse burned in 1698, and the government moved to Williamsburg in 1699. No longer a colonial capital, Jamestown gradually declined, and by the nineteenth century little remained except the 1639 church tower, a graveyard, a 1697 brick powder magazine, and the ruins of an eighteenth century plantation house. At the beginning of the Civil War, Confederate troops built an earthwork fort near the church, and in 1862 the island was occupied by Union forces. As the James River claimed more and more of the site, including the magazine, the 1607 fort appeared to be lost forever.

Following the acquisition of 22.5 acres of the island by the Association for the Preservation of Virginia Antiquities (APVA) in 1893, excavations near the church began to rescue Jamestown's remains from oblivion. A protective seawall was also built by the state and national governments in 1901.

To celebrate Jamestown's three hundredth anniversary in 1907, a memorial church was constructed on the 1639 foundations, and bronze statues of Smith and Pocahontas were commissioned. After 1934, when the National Park Service acquired the remainder of Jamestown Island, excavations continued through the 1950's around the five-acre site of the town. The theory that James Fort had washed into the river was disproved in 1994, after the Jamestown Rediscovery Project, mounted by the APVA, found numerous artifacts and evidence of the triangular structure.

Areas of Interest

Exhibition galleries, maintained by the National Park Service, and a brief video presentation illustrate Jamestown's early existence. There is a also six-mile loop trail which includes a reconstructed glasshouse where craftsmen re-create Jamestown's first industry. Continuing work on the 1607 fort site provides visitors with a unique archaeological experience.

In 1957 the state of Virginia constructed the Jamestown Festival Park four miles from the original settlement; it houses exhibition galleries, the reconstructed fort, an Indian village similar to Powhatan's, and reproductions of the three ships that brought the first settlers to Virginia. Various public events are held at this site.

—*Dorothy Potter*

For Further Information:

Gleach, Frederic W. *Powhatan's World and Colonial Virginia: A Conflict of Cultures.* Lincoln: University of Nebraska Press, 1997. Describes the interaction of Powhatan's tribes and the early colonists from a Native American perspective.

Hume, Ivor Noel. *The Virginia Adventure.* New York: Alfred A. Knopf, 1994. A fascinating account which includes information about Tudor England and Roanoke island, as well as Jamestown.

Kelso, William M. *Jamestown Rediscovery I: Search for 1607 James Fort.* Jamestown: Association for the Preservation of Virginia Antiquities, 1995. Details the rediscovery and excavations of the James Fort, including more than thirty color photographs of items found on-site.

Kupperman, Karen Ordahl. "The Founding Years of Virginia—and the United States." *The Virginia Magazine of History and Biography* 104, no. 1 (Winter, 1996): 103-112.

Lindgren, James M. *Preserving the Old Dominion:*

Historic Preservation and Virginia Traditionalism. Charlottesville: University Press of Virginia, 1993. Describes efforts of preservationists to save historic structures and also maintain traditional values. Focuses on the APVA, America's first state preservation organization.

Molineux, Will. "Jamestown Rediscovered." *Colonial Williamsburg: Journal of the Colonial Williamsburg Foundation,* December, 1999/January, 2000, 38-43. Discusses the progress of the Jamestown Rediscovery team.

Vaughan, Alden. *American Genesis: Captain John Smith and the Founding of Virginia.* Boston: Little, Brown, 1975. Includes Smith's achievements before and after his Jamestown adventures.

Manassas

Date: Established on May 10, 1940
Relevant issues: Civil War, military history
Significance: This park commemorates two important Civil War battles fought at different times in the same location. The 1861 First Battle of Manassas (also called First Bull Run) was the Civil War's first major engagement. The 1862 Second Battle of Manassas (or Second Bull Run) was a Southern victory and a springboard for Confederate general Robert E. Lee's Maryland campaign.
Location: Twenty-five miles west of Washington, D.C., one-half mile north of Interstate Highway 66, Exit 47 (Manassas-Sudley Road/Highway 234)
Site Office:
Manassas National Battlefield Park
12521 Lee Highway
Manassas, VA 22110
ph.: (703) 361-1339
fax: (703) 754-1861
Web site: www.nps.gov/mana/

Neither battle at Manassas was a decisive encounter, but each was significant. The First Battle of Manassas was the Civil War's first major battle and a hard-fought Confederate victory. Its intensity and outcome portended the upcoming long, hard war. It was also where the legendary Confederate general Thomas Jackson became "Stonewall" Jackson. The Second Battle of Manassas completed one of Confederate general Robert E. Lee's greatest tactical successes, while subordinates such as Stonewall Jackson and General James Longstreet performed brilliantly. It spurred Lee to undertake one of his two wartime campaigns outside Southern territory.

The Manassas National Battlefield Park has weathered controversies that make its existence seem as tumultuous as the battles it consecrates. Many years passed before the U.S. government recognized the battlefield's historical worth and created a park. After World War II, Washington, D.C.'s exploding suburban growth into northeastern Virginia sparked debates over use of neighboring land—and also over the larger issues of preserving and respecting historic places.

First Battle of Manassas

As the Civil War began in 1861, Manassas town did not yet exist, but two strategically important railroads met at a place called Manassas Junction. One went west to Virginia's Shenandoah Valley, the "Breadbasket of the Confederacy." The other proceeded south toward the Confederate capital of Richmond, Virginia. In June, 1861, the Confederates resolved to hold the junction against an expected Union attack or, if the opportunity arose, to advance from it against the Union capital in Washington, D.C.

The Union moved first. The general commanding the Union army in northeastern Virginia, Irvin McDowell, knew that his mostly volunteer force was not combat ready, but both the Union government and the general public wanted quick military action. Further, the volunteers' ninety-day enlistments faced imminent expiration. The Southern forces gathering at Manassas were an obvious objective, and McDowell's army marched against them on July 16, 1861.

McDowell also acted because the Confederate forces were then split between those at Manassas under General Pierre G. T. Beauregard and those farther west, near Harpers Ferry, under General Joseph E. Johnston. If McDowell and the Union general opposing Johnston, Robert Patterson, moved in concert, they might defeat the Rebels decisively. However, Patterson did not act, and when Beauregard detected McDowell's advance, Johnston began transferring reinforcements via the western rail line.

By July 20, 1861, the two armies obliquely faced each other across a creek which gave the upcoming battle another name, Bull Run. Beauregard expected a Union move toward the actual railroad junction and concentrated most of his army of twenty thousand near that spot for his own planned advance. McDowell's twenty-nine thousand troops moved along Warrenton Turnpike, north of the railroad, and massed along the stream north of the main Rebel lines. McDowell planned to feint against the northern end of the Rebel forces at the Warrenton Turnpike's stone bridge across Bull Run, swing a large force north and west along that creek, and then move it south across the creek behind Beauregard's left flank.

McDowell's plan exceeded the abilities of his untrained force, which could not execute it quickly enough. The flanking units commenced marching at 2:00 A.M. on July 21 but did not cross Bull Run at Sudley Springs ford until well after daybreak. Meanwhile, alert Rebels detected the Union move, and Colonel Nathan Evans's small force moved north against it. Other Rebel units under General Bernard Bee and Colonel Francis Bartow joined Evans as the Yankees advanced southward amid hard fighting to a small ridge called Matthews Hill.

The Union assault pushed the Rebels a mile farther south and up another eminence called Henry House Hill. Beauregard and Johnston (now present on the field) frantically transferred their forces from previous positions and from arriving trains to stop the Yankees. Brigadier General Thomas Jackson commanded one of the reinforcing brigades, and both he and his men remained steady as the Rebel line wavered under Union pressure all along the hill's crest. Nearly all accounts recall that General Bee steadied his faltering unit by calling, just before he was fatally wounded, "There is Jackson standing like a stone wall!"

The battle climaxed on Henry House Hill as the lines seesawed through the afternoon. More Union forces arrived to press the Rebels, including two artillery batteries which applied extra force against the Rebel left flank's far end. However, train-borne Rebel reserves in turn flanked the Union assault from the west, forcing a Union retreat in the late afternoon.

Lack of training produced confusion among commanders and soldiers on both sides, and this factor also adversely affected the Yankees' retreat.

The Henry House on the Manassas Battlefield. (National Park Service)

Their withdrawal rapidly became disorderly, and when Confederate shelling created a traffic snarl at a stone bridge, the retreat became a panicky rout. For their part, the Rebels were too disorganized to exploit the victory, and Union forces reconstituted themselves behind Washington's defenses.

The First Manassas Union and Confederate casualty totals were 2,700 and 2,000, respectively. The battle buoyed Southern morale and showed an overconfident North that the Rebels were in earnest. It highlighted Union troop unreadiness, and before 1861 ended, General George McClellan relieved McDowell and started an intense training regimen. Many officers who became famous Civil War leaders fought in the battle. Among these were the Union's William Tecumseh Sherman and Ambrose Burnside, and the Confederacy's James Longstreet and Jeb Stuart. Most prominent was the South's Thomas Jackson, whose steadiness on Henry House Hill earned him the nickname "Stonewall" and marked his potential for greater feats.

Second Battle of Manassas

McClellan's spring 1862 advance up the James Peninsula toward Richmond foundered upon his own caution and the brilliance of the Confederate Army of Northern Virginia's new leader, General Robert E. Lee. In response, the Union created a new army of seventy thousand troops, led by General John Pope, to push toward Richmond from Washington. In August, 1862, the Union government also directed General McClellan to transfer his forces to support Pope.

Aware of these developments, Lee did not rest in his defenses outside Richmond. In July, he sent Stonewall Jackson's corps against Pope. On August 9, Jackson halted Pope's advance units at Cedar Mountain. Since both McClellan and Pope moved very slowly, Lee transferred most of his Army north in mid-August to strike Pope before McClellan fully reinforced him. Attempts to trap and destroy Pope's Army between the Rapidan and Rappahannock Rivers having failed, Lee split his task force of fifty-five thousand by sending Jackson's corps on a fast march far around Pope's right flank to the Union supply depot at Manassas Junction.

Jackson's force seized the junction and its supplies on August 27. Jackson then organized a hidden defensive line on an unfinished railroad about a mile northwest of Henry House Hill on the old Manassas battlefield. As Pope sent forces to find him, he ambushed some of them in a hard but inconclusive fight on August 28. Now knowing Jackson's position, Pope moved to crush him.

However, Pope did not concentrate his attack, and he also ignored the rest of Lee's army. As Union forces unsuccessfully charged Jackson's line in furious but uncoordinated assaults on July 29, Lee's other corps under General James Longstreet moved up against Pope's left flank south of the unfinished rail line. Disregarding evidence of this buildup, Pope attacked Jackson again on August 30. As this assault wavered in the afternoon, Lee ordered Longstreet to strike.

Longstreet's attack crumpled the Yankees' left flank and forced Pope's precipitate withdrawal.

Hastily assembled Union forces delayed the Confederates long enough at Chinn Ridge and Henry House Hill to prevent a rout and allow the rest of the Union army to escape to good defensive positions east of Bull Run. Confederate attempts on July 31 to exploit the victory failed due to bad logistics, exhausted troops, nasty weather, and McClellan's reinforcements. Both sides' battle losses were high, though the Rebels suffered about half as many casualties as the Union's sixteen thousand.

Lee decided to further his success by invading Maryland and hopefully fomenting an uprising by local sympathizers. Also, Lee wanted his army to leave war-ravaged northern Virginia and perhaps inspire foreign support by winning battles in Union territory. General Pope was relieved of command, and McClellan took command of the forces pursuing Lee. President Abraham Lincoln delayed announcing his Emancipation Proclamation until Union battlefield fortunes improved. This occurred with the September 17, 1862, battle fought at Sharpsburg (Antietam Creek), Maryland.

The Battlefield Park
From months after the first battle through later years, private groups erected monuments on spots commemorating various actions and sacrifices. Hugh Henry, owner of the house that gave the embattled hill its name, used his residence as an informal museum through the early 1900's. During the same time, the U.S. government considered Manassas as a potential park site, but budget constraints and lack of sustained interest prevented fruition of the plan. Meanwhile, interested locals tried to create a Manassas Battlefield Confederate Park in the 1920's and 1930's.

President Franklin D. Roosevelt's New Deal changed the site's fortunes. The government created a Recreational Demonstration Area at the site for families. This bureaucratic move helped secure the funding, developmental effort, and interest to create a national battlefield park in 1940.

As Washington, D.C.'s suburbs spread into northeast Virginia after World War II, the park encountered several controversies involving land use on or near its property. There was a 1950's plan to route Interstate Highway 66 through it. The 1970's featured attempts to locate a national military cemetery on it and to build an amusement theme park nearby. The 1980's witnessed moves to enlarge its patrol horse stables and to create an adjoining shopping mall complex. Perhaps most famous was Disney Corporation's early 1990's plan to build a theme park near the site.

Opponents of these measures defeated all of them. Altering the park or its surroundings pitted those who prized the battlefield's significance against those concerned with the local area's economic welfare. Also, the shopping mall and both amusement park actions sparked national debate over heritage preservation versus urban development. Thus, these initiatives often created powerful antidevelopment coalitions of citizens' groups, Civil War enthusiasts, U.S. representatives, news reporters, and even National Park Service staff, which overwhelmed their opponents. Indeed, the shopping mall enterprise and 1970's amusement park plan led the government to expand the park boundaries.

What to See
The preservation efforts have yielded rewards. The visitors' center resides on the hotly contested Henry House Hill, and from there one sees relatively few signs of modern urban life. Open daily except Christmas, the visitors' center has a museum as well as guide material for touring the battlefield. Battlefield landmarks can be reached by car or walking trail, and historical markers support understanding of them. Sudley Springs ford is on the park's north boundary, and the Bull Run stone bridge is on the park's eastern edge. The unfinished railroad is still visible on the park's west side. The scene of Longstreet's flanking assault underlies both the original park territory and land acquired in the shopping mall and amusement park debates.

Outside the park are Washington, D.C.'s obvious attractions. The Blue Ridge mountains are thirty miles west. Other Civil War National Battlefield Parks such as Gettysburg, Antietam, Fredericksburg, and Spotsylvania are each within a day's travel.   —*Douglas Campbell*

For Further Information:
Davis, William. *Battle at Bull Run*. Baton Rouge: Louisiana State University Press, 1977. Examines the First Battle of Manassas and preceding actions.

Hanson, Joseph Mills. *Bull Run Remembers.* Manassas, Va.: Prince William County Historical Commission, 1957. Author's essays about the area's Civil War events and people.

Hennessy, John. *The First Battle of Manassas: An End to Innocence.* Lynchburg, Va.: H. E. Howard, 1989. Former Manassas National Battlefield Park historian focuses upon the battle itself and makes extensive use of primary sources.

_____. *Return to Bull Run: The Campaign and Battle of Second Manassas.* New York: Touchstone, 1993. Focuses more upon the second battle than the campaign. Again, the former park historian makes heavy use of primary sources.

Martin, David. *Second Bull Run Campaign.* Conshohocken, Pa.: Combined Books, 1997. Overall account of the campaign and battle.

Naisawald, L. Van Loan. *Manassas Junction and the Doctor.* Manassas, Va.: Lake Lithograph, 1981. Covers the area's overall history.

Zenzen, Joan. *Battling for Manassas.* University Park: Pennsylvania State University Press, 1998. Comprehensive, well-documented history of the park and its controversies up through the Disney theme park debate.

Monticello

Date: Built from 1770 to 1782

Relevant issues: Art and architecture, colonial America, political history

Significance: The house and grounds of Thomas Jefferson's estate were designed by Jefferson himself as his main residence. Construction of the main house began in 1770 and was completed in 1782; reconstruction of the main house began in 1793 and was largely completed by 1809. The construction of additional buildings continued for twenty years. The estate was sold in 1831 to James L. Barclay and converted to a silkworm farm; in 1834, it was sold to Uriah Phillips Levy. Monticello was acquired in 1923 by the Thomas Jefferson Memorial Foundation.

Location: Route 53, three miles southeast of Charlottesville

Site Office:

Monticello, Department of Public Affairs
P.O. Box 316
Charlottesville, VA 22902

ph.: (804) 984-9822, 984-9800
Web site: www.monticello.org

The third president of the United States, Thomas Jefferson, contributed perhaps more than any other person of his time to the shaping of the United States. He drafted not only the Declaration of Independence in 1776 but also the Territorial Ordinance of 1784, which provided for new states to be created west of the original thirteen, and the 1786 Virginia Statute for Religious Freedom. In 1803 he bought the Louisiana Territory from Napoleon for fifteen million dollars and thereby doubled the size of the country, and in that same year he also commissioned the Lewis and Clark Expedition into the unexplored lands of the West. He even saw to the creation of the U.S. dollar and decimal currency. In these and other ways Jefferson undoubtedly had an enormous impact on American history; accordingly, he has secured a place in the national mythology.

Jefferson's Home

Something of that impact can still be felt today at his home, Monticello, on the "little mountain" from which Jefferson derived its Italian name. He designed the house and its grounds himself, and they stand now as a memorial to his fascinating and contradictory personality.

Born in 1743, Jefferson included architecture among the many interests he pursued as a young man while managing the property he inherited from his father. His father, who died when Jefferson was fourteen years old, had also bequeathed him surveying equipment, and his education at the College of William and Mary had included mathematics and classics. By 1768 or 1770 he was ready to start work on his first plans for buildings at Monticello, a site on the edge of one of his estates commanding spectacular views of the Blue Ridge Mountains and what was then unsettled wilderness.

The first building at Monticello, the south pavilion known as Honeymoon Cottage, was an adaptation of a conventional western Virginia farmhouse. In contrast, the first version of the main house, begun in 1770 and completed in 1782, featured classical columns forming a double loggia that covered both the first and second floors of the front of the house. Throughout the changes Jefferson was to

Monticello. (Virginia Tourism Corporation)

he helped to write the first of the new state constitutions and became governor under its terms. It was from Monticello that he had to flee in 1781, when British troops arrived to try to capture him. His wife, Martha, died there in 1782, only ten years after their marriage.

In 1784 Jefferson became U.S. minister to France. By 1789, when he returned home, he had collected enough works of art, pieces of furniture, and other effects to fill eighty-six crates. He had also further refined both his appreciation of European architecture and his revulsion against existing American architectural practices. In his *Notes on the State of Virginia*, first published in 1785, he had dismissed the famous colonial buildings of Williamsburg, the former state capital, as a "shapeless pile of bricks" built in "the most wretched style I ever saw."

Building Monticello

Soon after returning he was able to see the newly built state capitol at Richmond, which was based on his own adaptation of a Roman building, the Maison Carrée in the French city of Nîmes. In 1792 he decided to rebuild Monticello on a larger scale. He retired from public life and began making changes to the house in 1793, residing there until 1797. His second plan called for a new entrance hall, the doubling of the floor space of the house, the building of an extra story, the extension of the front windows to form continuous verticals across all three floors, and, to the astonishment of his workmen, the addition of the first dome in Virginia. (A similar dome can be seen on the Thomas Jefferson Memorial in Washington, D.C., dedicated in 1943 to mark the bicentennial of his birth.) He decided to leave the Honeymoon Cottage unchanged alongside this home fit for a European aristocrat.

The project took twenty years to complete, and once again Jefferson was absent for much of the time. He served as the first secretary of state, under George Washington, from 1789 to 1793; as vice president to John Adams, from 1797 to 1801; and as president himself for two terms, from 1801 to 1809, during which he used Monticello as his an-

make in its design, the external symmetry and the classical styling of the main house at Monticello reflected the influence of the sixteenth century Italian architect Andrea Palladio, whose *I quattro libri dell' architettura* (1570; four books of architecture) were referred to by Jefferson as his "Bible." Even so, Jefferson made some innovations. For example, in both versions of the main house he placed the kitchens and other service rooms in the basement and in extensions, known as "dependencies," under the terraces on either side of the house, rather than in the wings customarily added above ground, and he gave the rooms varying shapes, sizes, and heights.

It was at Monticello in 1774 that Jefferson, prevented by illness from attending the first Virginia convention on new British laws for the colonies, wrote *A Summary of the Rights of British America*, one of the first and most influential pamphlets to claim that the British Parliament's right to govern the colonies was not merely limited but in fact was nonexistent, for the colonies were new societies, self-created and self-governing. Yet at that stage Jefferson still believed that the colonies were subject to the king, and he did not expect them to become independent. After 1774, as the movement toward independence grew into war against the British, Jefferson spent little time at Monticello, dividing his time between the Continental Congress in Philadelphia and state politics in Williamsburg, where

nual summer residence. He retired at last, aged sixty-six, after taking on this unique succession of public offices, and went to live at Monticello once again, this time with his daughter Martha, her husband, and their children. Jefferson continued to make modifications at Monticello, telling a visitor in 1809 that he hoped it would go on being unfinished while he lived, since he greatly enjoyed putting up buildings and pulling them down. Between 1806 and 1823 he also saw to the building of an octagonal house at Poplar Forest, eighty miles from Monticello, as a retreat, and his last major project was the creation of the University of Virginia at Charlottesville. He himself designed the university's buildings, which were put up between 1819 and 1826 and were arranged as separate units on a campus instead of as a set of traditional courtyards. He died on July 4, 1826—the same day his rival John Adams died and the fiftieth anniversary of the Declaration of Independence. He was buried in the family graveyard that he had placed on the western edge of the Monticello site in 1773.

Jefferson was not the only prominent Virginian of his day to enlarge his house and remodel it along European aristocratic lines. In the 1770's, George Washington had already doubled the size of Mount Vernon and added a portico along the entire front of the house. James Madison, too, enlarged his home at Montpelier. Together, Montpelier, Mount Vernon, and Monticello, with their large, columned entrance porticoes, contributed to what has since become known as the "Federal" style.

Features of Monticello

No other house has an interior quite like Monticello's. The entrance hall, on the eastern side of the house, was used to exhibit Jefferson's collection of curiosities, including Native American artifacts collected by Meriwether Lewis and William Clark on their expedition, the remains of a mastodon and other animals, several maps, and a clock designed by Jefferson himself that indicated not only hours and minutes but also the days of the week by a system of weights and pulleys. To the west of the hall, and balancing it architecturally with its own portico opening onto the flower garden, is the parlor, with its collection of thirty-five portraits and other works of art. The northern wing contains the tea room, decorated with busts of American leaders and Roman emperors; the dining room, sepa-

rated from the tea room by sliding glass doors, where food was brought in through revolving shelves and wine through a dumb waiter; and two guest bedrooms.

In Jefferson's time, visitors were usually not permitted to enter the private southern wing. The sitting room here became the schoolroom for Jefferson's grandchildren after 1809. Jefferson's bedroom, his "cabinet" or study, and his book room or library are also located in this wing. (After the British had burned down the original Library of Congress, along with the other federal buildings in Washington, D.C., in 1814, Jefferson sold his collection of about 6,500 books to the federal government to form the nucleus of what is now the world's largest library.) On the south side of the first floor is a glass-walled greenhouse, where Jefferson cultivated seeds and practiced carpentry. While Jefferson worked, slept, and received visitors on the first floor, the relatives who lived with him occupied the nursery and bedrooms on the second and third floors. Fire regulations require that these floors are now closed to visitors.

Jefferson paid close attention to the landscape as well as to the house. A terraced vegetable garden, two vineyards, beds of figs and other fruit known as "berry squares," and orchards were laid out on the southeastern slopes below the main house, and a small brick pavilion was built on the edge of the vegetable garden. (All these features were restored or reconstructed during the 1980's.) In 1808, assisted by one of his granddaughters, he laid out flowerbeds at the corners of the main house and planted floral borders along the smallest and highest of the four curving paths that run concentrically around the mountaintop. (The gardens were restored in 1939.) Further down the mountain to the west, beyond the graveyard, Jefferson left the woods to grow untended. He also took an active interest in the plantation of five thousand acres that supported the life of the homestead, converting from tobacco to wheat after 1794 and experimenting with crop rotation and contour plowing.

Condition of Monticello at Jefferson's Death

The magnificence of the main house and its grounds, now that they have been restored, makes it difficult to envisage the condition of Monticello after Jefferson's death in 1826. The financial problems of the estate had begun even before that point. A lottery and a voluntary subscription scheme to help the aged former president had raised $6,000, yet at his death Jefferson's debts still totaled more than $100,000. In 1827 his family was forced to sell all his remaining personal property. The empty house and deserted grounds of Monticello were sold in 1831, to be converted into a silkworm farm. Only three years later, after silk production had proven unprofitable, Monticello was sold again, this time to the Levy family, who owned it up until 1923. In that year the Thomas Jefferson Memorial Foundation bought it and began the work of restoration.

Monticello was the place Jefferson loved more than any other. As he wrote, "I am as happy nowhere else, and in no other society, and all my wishes end, where I hope my days will, at Monticello." It was also the place where most of Jefferson's slaves lived. By 1796 this revolutionary champion of life, liberty, and the pursuit of happiness, who had described slavery as "an abominable crime," nevertheless owned one hundred seventy of his fellow human beings, and he still owned one hundred thirty when he died thirty years later. It was mainly their labor that provided the capital for the construction and maintenance of Monticello and helped Jefferson to keep up the way of life of a country gentleman.

Jefferson and Slavery

At Monticello, the slaves were housed in log cabins along Mulberry Row, a thousand-foot road laid out between the flower garden and the vegetable garden and hidden from the house by the mulberry trees for which it was named. Here some of them worked iron and wood; raised poultry; slaughtered livestock; operated the dairy, the washhouse, and the stable; and (from 1815) made woolen, hemp, and cotton cloth. Others went to work in the house, the gardens, or the plantation. Many historians have concluded that Jefferson fathered at least one child by Sally Hemings, one of the house slaves.

Like most white people of his day Jefferson believed that blacks were naturally inferior to whites. This prejudice led him to assume that his slaves needed his protection and that the only long-term solution would be to emancipate all the slaves at once and expel them from the United States. It proved impossible even to begin to put such a pol-

icy into practice. His condemnation of the slave trade was struck out of the Declaration of Independence, and his proposal to prohibit slavery altogether was defeated—though by only one vote—in the Continental Congress in 1784. In later years he was less able, or less willing, to challenge the institution. As president he banned the slave trade, but not slavery itself, from the Louisiana Territory; in 1807 he signed a law that banned the Atlantic slave trade but left it to the states to enforce the ban (or, in the South, turn a blind eye to smuggling). Monticello is a memorial to a great American whose principles of democracy and liberty can still inspire people all over the world, but it is also a reminder of slavery and of Jefferson's ambivalence to it.

—*Patrick Heenan*

For Further Information:

Adams, William Howard. *Jefferson's Monticello.* New York: Abbeville Press, 1983. Among the thousands of books on various aspects of Jefferson's life and times, this appears to have been the first study of Monticello itself. This beautifully illustrated and absorbingly detailed account of Jefferson's plans for the site, his life there, and its fate after his death

Bear, James A., Jr., ed. *Jefferson at Monticello.* Charlottesville: University of Virginia Press, 1967. The life of the slaves at Monticello and their relations with their owner as glimpsed through the memoirs of one of these slaves, Isaac Jefferson, and of their overseer, Edmund Bacon.

Betts, Edwin M., ed. *Thomas Jefferson's Farm Book.* Charlottesville: University of Virginia Press, 1987. Includes Jefferson's letters about slaves and slavery.

Jones, Veda Poyd. *Thomas Jefferson: Author of the Declaration of Independence.* Philadelphia: Chelsea House, 2000. A biography of Jefferson that discusses his childhood, education, involvement in colonial politics, writings, and career as a statesman.

Langhorne, Elizabeth C. *Monticello: A Family Story.* Chapel Hill: University of North Carolina Press, 1987. Concentrates on Jefferson's family and slaves.

McLaughlin, Jack. *Jefferson and Monticello: The Biography of a Builder.* New York: Henry Holt, 1990. Highlights the men and techniques involved in the construction of the house.

Mount Vernon

Date: Sold to Washington in 1754

Relevant issues: Art and architecture, colonial America, political history

Significance: This estate of George Washington, the first president of the United States, is where he died on December 14, 1799, and where he and his wife Martha are buried. It was purchased by the Mount Vernon Ladies' Association in 1858, then restored and renovated. A National Historic Landmark, it consists of the twenty-room, two-and-a-half-story mansion and numerous outbuildings, including original slave quarters, situated on five hundred acres.

Location: Sixteen miles from downtown Washington, D.C., and eight miles south of Alexandria, Virginia, located at the end of the George Washington Memorial Parkway, overlooking the Potomac River

Site Office:

The Mount Vernon Ladies' Association of the Union
Mount Vernon, VA 22121
ph.: (703) 780-2000

Five years before he died in 1799, George Washington wrote to a friend extolling the beauties of Mount Vernon, yet if he returned to his estate today he would be astounded at its appearance. Although he would recognize the mansion, the outbuildings, the pathways, and even some of the landscaping, the most striking change to him would be the improvements visible everywhere, the very ones he had sought in his own lifetime and might have achieved had he lived longer than sixty-seven years.

The noxious marsh that lay a half mile from Mount Vernon, to which Washington attributed the cause of the spring and summer fevers in the area, is gone, drained and turned into a nursery for the flower and vegetable gardens of Mount Vernon; the embankment on which the mansion is situated, and which threatened to crumble under the force of the Potomac River, has been strengthened by army engineers more than once; the grasses, meadows, and fields surrounding the estate are immaculately kept, not as they appeared when George Washington lived at Mount Vernon but undoubtedly as he would have dreamed them

to be. In his lifetime, George Washington was known far and wide as an excellent farmer who employed the most progressive methods of his day and whose sprawling, beautiful eight thousand-acre estate reflected ceaseless care and attention.

The Life of George Washington

George Washington was not born at Mount Vernon. Not until he was three and one-half years old, in 1735, did his father Augustine bring him and his older half brother Lawrence to Little Hunting Creek Plantation, the future Mount Vernon. He lived there until he was seven. What the estate looked like then is a matter of conjecture, except that it was much smaller (at most sixteen hundred acres) than the Mount Vernon where George Washington died. There is a record of George Washington's great-grandfather, John Washington, who in 1674 purchased the property that would eventually become Mount Vernon. John Washington was not a wealthy man; he purchased his property, consisting of five thousand acres, jointly with a friend and fellow colonist, Nicholas Spencer. The farmland was excellent and, when properly tended, yielded rich crops. By 1690, both John Washington and Nicholas Spencer were dead, and their property was divided among their descendants. In time, George Washington's father came to inherit several properties, one of which was the future Mount Vernon.

Why the whole family left Little Hunting Creek Plantation when George was seven, after only four years' residence, has not been established. If George Washington's great-grandfather John had been a struggling colonist who had left England to seek his fortune, he certainly, at his death, bequeathed a considerable estate to his descendants.

George Washington's father, Augustine, died in 1743, leaving Lawrence, the older half brother, to act as surrogate father to George, who was eleven. By then Lawrence was married and living at Little Hunting Creek, which he had decided to rename Mount Vernon to honor the memory of his former commanding officer, Admiral Edward Vernon. The death of this older half brother in 1752 at age thirty-four, probably of the same tuberculosis that had killed their father, was a deep personal loss for the young George Washington. When Lawrence's infant daughter Sarah died two years later, Lawrence's widow sold Mount Vernon to George. It was

1754, and he was a tall, handsome, very well-liked young man of twenty-two. Even at that young age, he was the commanding officer of the Virginia militia, had little time to spend at Mount Vernon, and, perhaps because he was still a bachelor, had little incentive to stay put.

Not until after his marriage to the wealthiest heiress in Virginia, Martha Dandridge Custis, when he was twenty-six, did he begin to turn serious attention to improvements at Mount Vernon. He longed to "retire" there permanently (become a gentleman farmer) after his marriage, but the French and Indian War intervened. Until the early 1760's, Washington was away often; after the war ended, he quit the militia and returned to Mount Vernon with relief, although public affairs frequently called him away.

In 1775, he accepted the command of the Continental army, and the war between the colonies and Great Britain meant that he would not return to Mount Vernon to live until 1783. A few years later, he was elected president, and then reelected, which necessitated living in the temporary capitals of New York and Philadelphia. It is little wonder that Washington, who tried in these years to return to Mount Vernon at every opportunity, was delighted when Congress approved the site of the new "federal city" just sixteen miles from his scenic estate. Not until the late 1780's, barely a decade before his death in 1799, did Mount Vernon assume the appearance that it has at present. This fact is known from the detailed records Washington kept of his estate. As a young man he had been trained as a surveyor, and his plans of Mount Vernon have survived the ravages of time. They are marvels of detail, indicating where every single tree had been planted, where every single path of his estate lay, the exact location of all the buildings, and the sizes of the fields and meadows. How the interiors of his mansion and other buildings appeared, and what they contained, can be ascertained in

part from his voluminous correspondence as well as from his diaries.

Mount Vernon's Original Condition

It is known that when he became owner of Mount Vernon in 1754, it hardly resembled today's imposing plantation. The estate consisted at most of a couple thousand acres, and the family resided on the first floor of the house, which contained four small rooms around a central hall, and perhaps a room or two upstairs (there was a half floor above the first floor). Mount Vernon technically consisted of five farms. The mansion itself and the outbuildings surrounding it stood on five hundred acres. Compared to most people living in the colonies in the late eighteenth century, the Washingtons lived in a roomy house on a grand scale.

George Washington had a decided flair for interior design and architecture. He supervised the construction of the beautiful columned piazza at the back of the mansion, which extended the full length of the house. There his innumerable visitors could recline on comfortable chairs and enjoy the gorgeous setting. (A full set of these chairs has been reconstructed based on the one chair that survived the decades of neglect after Washington's death.) The flagstones of the piazza came from a quarry in England, and when they became thor-

Mount Vernon. (PhotoDisc)

oughly worn out in the early twentieth century, they were replaced by exact replicas made from the same stone from the same English quarry.

Washington kept up with the latest trends in interior design and decorating. He loved wallpaper and ordered most of it from England. A tiny scrap of the original green wallpaper in the dining room was used as a guide for its reproduction. The size of the mansion nearly doubled under his ownership, from one and one-half to two and one-half floors. The large dining room was entirely of his design. The ceiling and the mantel have won high praise for their workmanship and intricate design (the mantel was a gift from an English admirer). Another beautiful room was the west parlor, the center of family life and social gatherings. The walls were painted in an expensive Prussian blue, and above the mantel hung family portraits and the family coat of arms.

In 1775, the year Washington became commander in chief of the Continental Army, his library was under construction. Washington was not known to be bookish, but a library was a common feature among gentlemen farmers, and his library was where Washington engaged in his correspondence and planning. His desk stood there as well as his globe, one of the very few original objects that remained in the house when it became a museum just prior to the Civil War.

Washington in Retirement

Upon his retirement from the presidency in 1797, Washington lived in Mount Vernon for another two and one-half years. He died in the upstairs bedroom in 1799, of a throat infection caught after spending time outdoors in cold and snowy December weather, planning an improvement on his estate. At his death, his estate had been enlarged from two thousand to eight thousand acres. His mansion was nearly twice the size that it had been when he acquired Mount Vernon in 1754; in addition, there were now a dozen outbuildings. Ever the planner and designer, he had selected a site for his and his wife's tombs, at the bottom of his property, along the Potomac; their tomb is usually the first site visited by tourists who come to Mount Vernon by boat.

Washington left a thriving, prosperous estate when he died. He was a professional farmer and kept up with the latest advances in the science of agriculture, such as the use of fertilizers, crop rotation, and even experimental crops. After his death, Mount Vernon entered into a slow and sad decline. Martha Washington survived her husband by two years. It was she who began the habit, continued by subsequent heirs to Mount Vernon, of giving away objects that had once belonged to Washington, or to the estate, to visiting friends or relatives. Almost all of George Washington's and the house's belongings and furnishings disappeared in this way. Their recovery took decades and will never be complete.

Mount Vernon After Washington

Fifty years after George Washington's death, Mount Vernon had been altered shockingly. The estate itself was considerably smaller, having been subdivided into five farms after Washington's death. The land no longer yielded the abundant crops that it had produced under George Washington's careful management; the estate's income had dwindled to the point where even the most necessary repairs could not be made. When fire destroyed some of the outbuildings, not only were they unrestored but their gutted remains also were left standing, visible to passengers traveling past the estate by boat. One of these, a wealthy planter's wife from South Carolina, was saddened at the desecration of Mount Vernon. What this woman did not know was that the owner, John Augustine Washington, Jr., had tried to interest both Congress and the Virginia legislature in purchasing the estate for $200,000, but both turned a deaf ear to his appeal. Meanwhile, southern hospitality demanded of him that he feed and entertain the many visitors who came to Mount Vernon to pay their respects, and this was a serious drain on his finances.

When the woman, Mrs. Robert Cunningham, returned home, she described the plight of the house and property to her invalid daughter, Ann Pamela Cunningham. The younger woman was galvanized into action. It was then 1853, and within ten years the Mount Vernon Ladies' Association of the Union, which she founded, had rescued Mount Vernon for posterity.

She was roundly criticized by men and women alike for her unladylike conduct—organizing fund-raisers, hiring a lawyer, and chartering an all-women's organization that would actually restore and operate an important historic site. In spring

1858, the owner of Mount Vernon finally sold the estate to the Mount Vernon Ladies' Association for $200,000. He and his wife stayed on until George Washington's birthday in 1860. He left behind, on behalf of the future restoration of the house and grounds, the only personal possessions of George Washington still left at Mount Vernon: his globe, the key to the Bastille sent him by General Lafayette, and an original clay bust of George Washington himself.

Preservation Efforts

Ann Cunningham and her assistant, Sarah Tracy, moved into the mansion. This would be a temporary arrangement until the basic restoration of the house and grounds was complete. As it turned out, the U.S. Civil War broke out before much could be accomplished. Ann Cunningham returned to her home in South Carolina, but her assistant stayed on in the hope that her presence in the house would spare it from the worst ravages of the war. Apparently it did, although the estate was situated between battle lines of both armies and shelling in the area was heavy at times. Even during the war, however, Mount Vernon had visitors. Mary Lincoln sailed to Mount Vernon with a group of friends, among the first visitors to pay admission to tour the house and grounds. In 1866, Ann Cunningham returned to take up where she had left off. With Mount Vernon's restoration under way, she retired from the regency of the association in 1873 and died a year later.

Although the repair of the buildings and grounds of Mount Vernon were well in hand by then, the recovery and restoration of the interior had barely begun. The effort to reacquire the many original pieces from Washington's day spanned decades. In the first decade of Mount Vernon's restoration, many individuals came forward, claiming to possess an object that had once belonged to Washington. These objects were often difficult to authenticate. Gradually, major items were returned to Mount Vernon, such as the harpsichord that had belonged to Martha Washington's granddaughter Nellie Custis, the sundial that stands in front of the house, the lantern that had hung in the main hallway, and the bed in which George Washington died. Some of the refurbishing was based on guesswork, from letters and other documents that have survived. A dining room table of mahogany was constructed based on eyewitness descriptions. There were no clues whatsoever about the particular wallpaper that had hung in some of the rooms, so more general research into eighteenth century wallpaper led to the creation of a hand-printed reproduction.

Although the aim of the Mount Vernon Ladies' Association has been the authentic restoration and preservation of Mount Vernon, ultimately a few concessions had to be made to modernity. As early as 1878, a burglar alarm was installed. Later, Thomas Edison designed an electric power system for the house and grounds, although the mansion rarely is lit by electricity. In 1924, Henry Ford donated a fire-fighting system.

Today, only pleasure boats cruise by Mount Vernon. Instead of glimpsing a sad wreckage, they glide by a beautiful eighteenth century estate, one of the finest specimens of that era's architecture and furnishings.

—*Sina Dubovoy*

For Further Information:

Alden, John Richard. *George Washington: A Biography.* Reprint. Baton Rouge: Louisiana State University Press, 1996. A well-regarded, well-written biography of George Washington.

Griswold, Mac. *Washington's Gardens at Mount Vernon: Landscape of the Inner Man.* Boston: Houghton Mifflin, 1999. This pictorial work discusses the character and contributions of Washington through gardening.

Johnson, Gerald W. *Mount Vernon: The Story of a Shrine.* New York: Random House, 1952. A fascinating account of the decline of Mount Vernon after Washington's death. It is also the story of Ann Pamela Cunningham, the woman who saved Mount Vernon for posterity.

Mount Vernon Ladies' Association. *Mount Vernon: A Handbook.* Rev. ed. Mount Vernon, Va.: Author, 1985. Contains a detailed, heavily illustrated account of Mount Vernon's history and describes the evolution of the estate to the present, including the gardens and outbuildings.

Smith, Richard Norton. *Patriarch: George Washington and the New American Nation.* Boston: Houghton Mifflin, 1993. Both this biography and the one by Alden (above) approach Mount Vernon less from the standpoint of the evolution of an estate than as a reflection of the man who lived and died there.

Richmond

Date: Incorporated in 1742

Relevant issues: Civil War, colonial America, political history, Revolutionary War

Significance: Richmond, the capital of Virginia, is a city rich in American history. It served as a site of several encounters during the American Revolution. As the capital of the Confederacy during the Civil War, it was a central target for the Union army. Richmond today is a vibrant city, offering a multitude of interesting sites and side trips, and is surrounded by the Richmond National Battlefield Park.

Location: On the eastern side of the state along the James River; approximately sixty miles farther east lie the Chesapeake Bay and the Atlantic Ocean, while Washington, D.C., is 105 miles due north and the Blue Ridge Mountains lie about 50 miles to the west

Site Office:

Metropolitan Richmond Convention and Visitors Bureau

Sixth Street Marketplace

550 East Marshall Street

Box C-250

Richmond, VA 23219-1852

ph.: (804) 782-2777

One of the oldest cities of the United States, Richmond has survived many tribulations in American history, from the early 1600's through modern times. It has served as the capital of Virginia since 1779, when Thomas Jefferson succeeded Patrick Henry as governor and the state's seat was moved from Williamsburg. Benedict Arnold led British forces into Richmond in 1781, embarrassing the colonists' cause with his easy victory. Many famous statesmen and artists have spent time in the city over its long life. It was the Civil War that many believe defined the modern character of Richmond. For four arduous years, the city was the capital of the Confederacy, and the world watched the city with more attention than ever before or since. "On to Richmond!" became the North's battle cry as it struggled to hold the Union together.

Early History

The site for Richmond was discovered long before it became a center of commerce and politics. On May 24, 1607, Captain Christopher Newport and a small group of men reconnoitering the area planted a wooden cross near the Falls, then a thundering waterfall in the James River, before they returned to the Jamestown settlement, some sixty miles away. The cross was used, most likely, to mark the territory for King James I, though efforts to further settle the area then met with fierce Indian resistance. The site would later become the heart of downtown Richmond. In 1645, the British built Fort Charles on the north side of the river. One year later they dismantled it and rebuilt it on the south side of the river, where land was easier to cultivate.

Ongoing disagreements with Indians over the territory led to a fierce battle in 1656. The colonists, under Colonel Edward Hill, suffered a huge defeat in the fighting and had to sue for peace. In 1659, Thomas Stegg, Jr., son of a wealthy Virginian merchant, contracted one thousand acres at the Falls, south of the river. By 1661, Stegg had purchased a total of eighteen hundred acres of land in the vicinity, an area later to be known as Falls Plantation. When Stegg died childless in 1671, he left most of his properties to his nephew, William Byrd, who immediately moved into his uncle's stone house and began laying plans for his inheritance. Though the site was isolated and dangerous, particularly due to the roving bands of Indians still vying for the land, Byrd established a trading post at the Falls. Trading was hampered by the continual conflicts with the Indians, and when colonists determined to fight under leader Nathaniel Bacon in 1675, without the support of government officials, Byrd led several companies against the Indians.

Conflict finally died down several years later, when a treaty was signed with area tribes, and Byrd expanded his trading post, traveling as far as North and South Carolina to trade cloth, kettles, hatchets, beads, rum, arms, and deerskins for beaver and other furs, herbs, and minerals. Byrd was also involved in trading African slaves, and he managed large tobacco warehouses near the Falls. He also continued to acquire more land in the area. In 1688, he bought Westover Plantation, an area of twelve hundred acres about twenty miles downstream from the Falls. He and his wife and children moved into a house there in 1689. When Byrd died in 1704, his son, William Byrd II, inherited Westover as well as another twenty-six thousand acres of land. Erudite, London-educated, and well-connected, this Byrd relished his role as a promising young leader of eighteenth century Virginia, though he spent much time in London and only occasionally inspected his extensive tracts of land on either side of the James River.

Laying Out of Richmond

By the 1720's, the area around the Falls was becoming more thickly settled, not only because of steady commerce with the Indians but also because of the growth of the tobacco trade, of which the Falls was a center. Members of the Virginia House of Burgesses—the lower house of the Virginia General Assembly—asked Byrd to sell them approximately fifty acres of riverside property, for the purposes of building a town. Byrd vehemently opposed the idea of being "forced" to sell and was loath to give up some of his most profitable holdings to potential competitors. Reluctantly, and not without a legal fight, Byrd finally gave in, and by 1737 a town was laid out and lots were sold with the stipulation that purchasers would build houses within three years. Byrd donated land along the banks of the river to be used as a common area, where town fairs would be held, as well as land for a church, and he named the town Richmond, because the new town reminded him of the English village of Richmond on Thames. In 1742, the Virginia General Assembly incorporated Richmond as a town, with 250 inhabitants, covering one-fifth of a square mile. The town was well situated for steady development, and by 1769 Richmond's population had increased to 574.

Colonial displeasure with British rule was running high by 1770. Patrick Henry's anti-Stamp Act speech in Williamsburg had raised eyebrows in 1765, but by 1773 the Boston Tea Party fed a growing fervor for independence. A Virginia Convention was called—without the governor's permission—to discuss the chances of arming against Great Britain, and Richmond was chosen as the site, since it was felt that Williamsburg, then the capital, lay under threat of British attack. The convention was held in March, 1775, in the town's church, later known as St. John's. Delegates from all parts of Virginia arrived in Richmond for the meeting; they included George Washington, Thomas Jefferson, Richard Henry Lee, and Patrick Henry. The weeklong debate brought heavy discussion of war and of breaking with Great Britain, based on the new Declaration of Rights, which the first Continental Congress of 1774 had drafted in Philadelphia. During the convention, Patrick Henry spoke with passion: "We must fight! I repeat it, sir, we must fight!" He expounded, "Why stand we here idle . . . I know not what course others may take; but as for me, give me liberty or give me death!" His resolution calling for organization of militia caused great debate and was carried by only a narrow margin. Henry headed up the committee created to arm and train the militia. Hence, when the "shot heard round the world" was fired in April, 1775, at Concord, Massachusetts, the Virginians were prepared.

Richmond Becomes Capital of Virginia

The long-debated issue of moving the seat of state government from Williamsburg to somewhere more central and safe was decided in 1779, when the general assembly voted in favor of Richmond. Governor Thomas Jefferson, who had recently succeeded Patrick Henry in the position, moved to the state capital in 1780, and land was set aside for public buildings. Jefferson himself designed the architecturally famous Virginia State Capitol. The American Revolution was nearing its end when Benedict Arnold raided Richmond with his British troops early in 1781. Arnold, who had been an officer in the Continental Army before going over to the British, advanced up the James River with the British Navy to within twelve miles of the city, then marched on the town, taking it almost unopposed. Richmond was not heavily protected at the time; its best soldiers had been sent to colonies where there was heavier fighting. Jefferson recognized quickly that his small militia was no match for the British regulars, and he ordered much of the city's stock of arms and important records to a safer place across the river, but Arnold's troops discovered and destroyed most of the stock.

The British burned many of the city's buildings and destroyed large reserves of tobacco as well as additional records kept in the Henrico County Courthouse. Arnold withdrew his troops the next day, after much damage had been done. He tried again to attack Richmond several months later but was thwarted by a force led by the Marquis de Lafayette. The General Assembly had fled from Richmond to Charlottesville, only to be driven from

Historical figures on the base of the George Washington equestrian monument in Richmond depict the role of Virginia in the Revolutionary War. (American Stock Photography)

there to Staunton by the British cavalry. The British then returned to take unprotected Richmond a second time, where they remained for several days to rest and pillage the stores that the city had replenished after Arnold's first assault. At last, in the autumn of 1781, British General Lord Cornwallis surrendered his army to Washington at Yorktown, and thus began the closure of the conflict.

Richmond spent the remainder of the century rebuilding and expanding as a city. By 1786, the city boasted a population of about 1,800. The influx of immigrants from France and Germany particularly influenced Richmond during those decades, as did immigrants from Scotland, Ireland, Spain, and the Netherlands. This mix of people lent the city a cosmopolitan air. The tobacco industry also flourished, aided by slavery, although slaves in Virginia were becoming increasingly restless and resentful. By 1800, the city's population had reached 5,737, half of whom were black.

Richmond in the Nineteenth Century

When a canal was completed around the Falls, Richmond became a significant manufacturing center, starting with numerous flour mills. With the extension of the James River westward and the growth of the railroads during the 1830's and 1840's, Richmond mills were producing large quantities of flour and shipping them to California and South America. Tobacco also became a large export industry, mainly in the form of chewing tobacco (cigarettes were not produced until after the Civil War). Iron and gunpowder also were increasingly important industries and were of vast significance to the Confederacy during the Civil War. Richmond also served as a bustling port for cargo ships during the early 1800's.

As a capital city, Richmond was a center of politics and law. In 1807, former vice president Aaron Burr's trial for treason took place in Richmond, with U.S. Supreme Court Justice John Marshall, a Richmond resident, presiding. Burr had killed Alexander Hamilton in a duel in 1804 and hence was considered a fugitive. Burr also stood accused of trying to set up a separate government, posing a threat to the United States. After a highly political and irregular trial, Burr was pronounced not guilty, but he lived under suspicion for the rest of his life.

The capital city also enjoyed a reputation as a leading cultural and theatrical center during the early nineteenth century. One of its favorite young actresses, Elizabeth Arnold Poe, was playing at the Richmond Theatre in 1811 when she fell ill and died, leaving three young children. After she was buried in St. John's churchyard, Edgar, her two-year-old son, was taken into the John Allan household. The childless Allans, who were associated with Richmond's mercantile firm of Ellis and Allan, gave Edgar the middle name of Allan, and thus he became Edgar Allan Poe. Poe became a familiar figure in Richmond during the 1830's, working for the *Southern Literary Messenger* magazine, writing book reviews, critical articles, poems, and short stories, all of which gave both him and the publication national acclaim. He resigned his position with the *Southern Literary Messenger* in 1837 and moved to New York, returning to Richmond for brief visits until his death in 1849.

The Civil War

The 1850's brought increasing debate over slavery in Virginia and the state's role in the South. In 1860 and 1861, the secession of several neighboring states and the formation of a provisional government of the Confederate States of America, led by Jefferson Davis as president, raised many questions and fueled debates in the pubs and press of Richmond. Richmond mirrored the state in its opposition to secession, although an increasing number of people were in favor of it. Most of Richmond was politically conservative, and when Virginia called a convention at Richmond to debate the issue, delegates voted firmly against secession. Sentiments changed when southern forces attacked Fort Sumter in South Carolina in April, 1861, and U.S. president Abraham Lincoln called for volunteers, including eight thousand from Virginia, to fight against the Southern rebels. Richmonders had to face the choice of fighting fellow Southerners or breaking from the Union, and the tide turned strongly in favor of secession. Convention delegates, reluctant to break all ties with the Union but equally reluctant to turn against their Southern neighbors and still firmly committed to slavery, voted to secede two days after Lincoln's call for volunteers.

The celebration in Richmond was wildly jubilant. Then, the realization sunk in that Virginia had much preparation ahead before it could fight a battle. Governor John Letcher invited Colonel Robert E. Lee, who had just declined an offer to command the Northern armies, to accept the post of major general in charge of Virginia's forces, and Lee arrived in Richmond on April 22, 1861. Eager recruits from throughout the South poured into Richmond, where Lee supervised their training and organization. In late April, Virginia invited President Davis to move the Confederate capital from Montgomery, Alabama, to Richmond, citing various reasons, the most compelling of which were the ready supply of food and the existence of the Tredegar Ironworks, the South's largest manufacturing concern, maker of guns, ammunition,

and rails. (Tredegar would go on to produce the armor for the ironclad ship CSS *Virginia*.)

Because Richmond was the capital of the Confederacy, many Northerners expected that the rebellion would be over once the city, only about one hundred miles from Washington, D.C., was taken. The principal Union rallying cry at the beginning of the war was "On to Richmond!" The Union's first drive toward Richmond ended in July, 1861, at the battle of first Bull Run near Manassas, in northern Virginia. Although it was a Southern victory, Richmond's jubilation was short-lived, as its hospitals were quickly filled with the wounded from both sides. The next Union invasion of Virginia occurred eight months later, in the spring of 1862. Union general George McClellan, a thorough planner but an overly cautious field commander, moved on Richmond from the southeast, via the peninsula between the York and James Rivers. In March, 1862, seventy thousand Union men from the Army of the Potomac landed at Fort Monroe on the southeastern tip of the peninsula. Initially, they were opposed by only three thousand Confederate soldiers stationed near Yorktown. McClellan, however, was convinced during every phase of this operation, now called the Peninsula Campaign, that he faced a numerically superior enemy. He wasted valuable time, giving the Confederates a chance to organize themselves and to build fortifications.

By late May, 1862, a 60,000-man Southern force had been pushed to the eastern outskirts of Richmond by about 110,000 Northerners. At one point, Union lines were within five miles of Richmond, and gunfire could be heard in the city. With their backs literally against the wall, the Confederate troops under General Joseph E. Johnston counterattacked on May 31 at the Battle of Fair Oaks, also known as Seven Pines. The most significant outcome of the battle was that Johnston was wounded and replaced by General Robert E. Lee, who intensified the offensive. Lee called in Stonewall Jackson and his army from the successful Shenandoah Valley campaign.

The Seven Days Battle

Leaving only twenty-five thousand men in Richmond's defense lines, the Confederate army counterattacked with fifty thousand troops and fought a week of nearly continuous battle now known as the

The ruins of Richmond during the Civil War. (Corbis)

Seven Days. First, the Confederates attacked at Mechanicsville, about five miles northeast of Richmond, but lack of tight coordination gave the Union army an edge, and the Northerners held the field. McClellan was rattled by the aggressiveness of the Confederates, however, so he pulled back to Gaines's Mill, farther east of Richmond. The next day, Jackson's and General James Longstreet's Southerners attacked the Northerners at Gaines's Mill and achieved a victory despite heavy losses, driving the Union forces south across the Chickahominy River. These two great battles in two days convinced McClellan to abandon his drive on Richmond and to shift his operations farther south, toward the James River. Over the ensuing five days, battles were fought at Savage Station, Frayser's Farm, and Malvern Hill (all in the vicinity of Richmond), and the Union Army of the Potomac was driven down to Harrison's Landing, farther south along the James River. Richmond would not experience a direct threat of attack for another two years.

Richmond was changed drastically by the Civil War. Almost overnight, the city was transformed from a graceful provincial capital into the seat of government for the Confederate States of America and the principal target for invading Union armies. Richmond became crowded, dangerous, and expensive, as everything worth having was in short supply. People suffered in the cold months from lack of warm clothing, food, and fuel. The city, which had a population of only about forty thousand before the war, was filled with wounded troops, prisoners, deserters, and refugees. Nearly everyone was involved in some manner in caring for the sick and wounded. Horses and vehicles were commandeered for use as ambulances, and housewives were urged to supply food and medicine to the many hospitals. During the war, Chimborazo Hospital, with two hundred fifty buildings and tents, was the largest hospital in the world and tended some seventy-six thousand men. Several of the Civil War's most notorious military prisons were located in and around the city: Belle Isle housed approximately ten thousand enlisted men on an island in the James River; Libby Prison, an old tobacco warehouse, confined one thousand Union officers under squalid conditions; and Castle Thunder incarcerated political prisoners. The Richmond Arsenal, of which Tredegar Ironworks was the most important component, accounted for half of the cannon, rifles, pistols, and ammunition manufactured by the South during the war.

By 1864, the Confederates had strengthened Richmond's defenses by building many fortifications on all sides of the city. Although city alarms were raised several times during the spring of 1864, Richmond was no longer the main Union objective. Under General Ulysses S. Grant, the Army of the Potomac's purpose was to destroy Lee's Army of Northern Virginia; the fall of Richmond would occur naturally once Lee was defeated. Grant and Lee fought battles to the north (Wilderness Campaign), the east (Cold Harbor), and the south (Siege of Petersburg) of the city. When Lee was finally flanked and forced out of his defensive positions around Petersburg, only twenty-five miles to the south, on April 1, 1865, Richmond's fate was sealed. Roads and bridges out of the city were clogged with refugees. The evacuating Confederate soldiers and government officials set fire to arsenals and military stores to prevent their falling into Union hands. In the chaos, the fires raged out of control, and eventually an estimated seven hundred buildings in the city were consumed by flames.

Union Occupation

Union troops entered Richmond early on the morning of April 3, 1865, and played a major role in putting out the fires and restoring order. President Abraham Lincoln, who had been visiting nearby Union forces, entered the smoldering city on the afternoon of the following day. With a small escort of only ten sailors, he visited Jefferson Davis's office and Libby Prison, and was enthusiastically greeted by hundreds of newly freed slaves. Along on the visit was Union Admiral David Porter, who later recalled: "I don't think I ever looked upon a scene where there were so many passionately happy faces."

The people of Richmond struggled to slowly rebuild their city, and whites and blacks had to learn to coexist. Many Richmonders could not bring themselves to celebrate the Fourth of July until 1871, so bitter were they about the course of history and the Union's triumph. The city's renewal was

slowed in the 1870's by deep financial and business panics that affected the entire nation. The city persevered, however, and continued to grow. Today its skyline is dominated by skyscrapers, and it is home to several large corporations, Philip Morris, Universal Corporation, CSX, and Reynolds Metals among them. Many agree, however, that modern Richmond's character and special mystique derive from the tempering influence that its rich history—in particular, the Civil War—left for later generations.

Modern Preservation Efforts

That history is illustrated by a multitude of sites within the city and on its outskirts. The White House of the Confederacy, at Twelfth and Clay Streets, has been restored to its appearance during the Civil War and is furnished with many of the Davis family's belongings. Adjacent to it is the Museum of the Confederacy, housing the world's largest collection of Confederate artifacts, including Robert E. Lee's tent, field glasses, and writing desk; Stonewall Jackson's musket; and Jeb Stuart's trademark plumed hat.

Richmond National Battlefield Park covers major Civil War battle sites to the north, east, and south of Richmond; the park is headquartered at 3215 East Broad Street, the site of Chimborazo Hospital. Monument Avenue, in the west end of Richmond, features statues of Lee, Jackson, Stuart, Davis, and scientist-oceanographer Matthew Fontaine Maury. Hollywood Cemetery, in the south end of Richmond near the James River, is the site of the graves of Stuart, Davis, and Maury, along with U.S. presidents James Monroe and John Tyler, novelist Ellen Glasgow, historian Douglas Southall Freeman, and more than eighteen thousand Confederate soldiers, including the first one to die in the Civil War.

Sites commemorating Richmond's colonial and revolutionary history include St. John's Church. During the summer at the church, actors re-create the events of the Virginia Convention, including Patrick Henry's "give me liberty or give me death" speech. The Thomas Jefferson-designed Virginia State Capitol in downtown Richmond is still in use and offers tours. Also open for tours is the Virginia Executive Mansion, the oldest continuously occupied governor's mansion in the United States. Jackson Ward, a neighborhood northeast of downtown, is rich in African American history; the area became home to a thriving black community shortly after the Civil War. Sites there include the home of entrepreneur and bank president Maggie Lena Walker, a monument to dancer Bill "Bojangles" Robinson, and the Black History Museum and Cultural Center of Virginia. Another aspect of Richmond's history is showcased in the Edgar Allan Poe Museum, southeast of downtown.

Southeast of Richmond along the James River lie numerous historic plantations, including William Byrd II's Westover Plantation; Berkeley Plantation, the birthplace of U.S. president William Henry Harrison; and Sherwood Forest Plantation, the home of John Tyler, who became president upon Harrison's death. West of Richmond is Tuckahoe Plantation, the boyhood home of Thomas Jefferson.
— *Christine Walker Martin*

For Further Information:

Dabney, Virginius. *Richmond: The Story of a City.* Rev. ed. Charlottesville: University Press of Virginia, 1990. Dabney, a native Richmonder and past editor of the *Richmond Times-Dispatch*, provides a colorful narrative of the history of Virginia's capital. From his enthusiastically Southern viewpoint, he recounts many details of the sites and personalities of the city, beginning with early colonial times.

Hoehling, A. A., and Mary Hoehling. *The Day Richmond Died.* San Diego: A. S. Barnes, 1981. An interesting, entertaining perspective on Richmond during the Civil War. Offers many details of daily life in the city and important characters of Richmond society during the four years of war; it lends a realistic flavor to events by relying for quotations on numerous entries from journals that have survived.

Sears, Stephen W. *To the Gates of Richmond.* New York: Ticknor & Fields, 1992. A well-written, in-depth account of the events and tactics of the Peninsula Campaign at the outset of the Civil War.

Takagi, Midori. *Rearing Wolves to Our Own Destruction: Slavery in Richmond, Virginia, 1782-1865.* Charlottesville: University Press of Virginia, 1999. Examines slavery in the urban setting of Richmond from the early United States to the end of the Civil War.

Williamsburg

Date: Built in 1699
Relevant issues: Colonial America, cultural history, political history, Revolutionary War
Significance: This city forms part of the Historic Triangle, which consists of Williamsburg, Jamestown (the first permanent English settlement in America), and Yorktown. Williamsburg's 173-acre Historic Area has been restored to conform to its appearance on the eve of the American Revolution.
Location: City in southeastern Virginia, seven miles from Jamestown on the James River and twelve miles from Yorktown on the York River
Site Office:
Colonial Williamsburg Foundation
P.O. Box 1776
Williamsburg, VA 23187-1776
ph.: (800) HISTORY [447-8679]; (804) 229-1000
Web site: www.history.org

Williamsburg was the center of Virginia's social, cultural, and political life in colonial America. Even today, with its broad boulevards and well-planned streets, the historic part of the old town exudes a particular eighteenth century orderliness. Named in honor of King William III of England, Williamsburg depended for its existence on three basis concepts—education, religion, and government. It was a city built on ideas, albeit one that developed more or less from scratch. As capital of the Virginia colony from 1699 to 1776 and of the Commonwealth of Virginia from 1776 to 1779, the town was intended to reflect Virginia's growing prominence among the British colonies and its status as the jewel of the Crown. Many prominent Americans either lived or worked in Williamsburg. Patrick Henry delivered his famous "Caesar-Brutus" speech opposing the Stamp Act in the House of Burgesses in the Capitol building. Other important statesmen associated with Williamsburg include Thomas Jefferson, George Washington, and Richard Henry Lee.

Virginia's Capital Cities

Williamsburg was not the first capital of the Virginia colony. That honor belongs to Jamestown, which was founded on May 26, 1607, as the first permanent English settlement in the American colonies. The first legislative assembly of 1619 was also organized in Jamestown. The location of the capital was problematic from the beginning, however, for Jamestown was located on a swamp-infested, disease-ridden island that was vulnerable to attack. When Jamestown's state house burned down in 1698 for the fourth time, Governor Francis Nicholson suggested it was time to move the capital to a new location. Several sites were considered. Ultimately, the House of Burgesses, the lower house of the colony's legislature, chose an area known as Middle Plantation, situated between the York and James Rivers some five miles away. It had several advantages over Jamestown: It was located on high ground, was relatively free of disease, and was the home of the College of William and Mary.

Middle Plantation had been founded in the early seventeenth century as a defense against possible Indian raids. The sparsely populated settlement grew gradually; by 1690 it had developed into only a small village. Middle Plantation had served as a temporary capital on several occasions—for instance, during Bacon's Rebellion in 1676 and again in 1677, when Jamestown suffered a devastating conflagration.

The Building of Williamsburg

In 1699 the colonial government passed an act that ordered the building of the capital city of Williamsburg. The act, written primarily by Governor Nicholson, contained specific provisions, such as dividing the town into half-acre lots and setting houses back six feet from the main thoroughfares. A survey map of the proposed town was completed on June 2, 1699.

Government was Williamsburg's major activity, and many businesses were formed to serve the needs of persons in government. In 1736, William Parks established in Williamsburg the weekly *Virginia Gazette*, the colony's first newspaper. Entertainment also became an important attraction. Taverns functioned as year-round social centers. The Raleigh Tavern, which opened around 1717, hosted both social and political activities.

Although loyal subjects of the Crown, Virginians were not averse to expressing their opinions. This independent spirit soon led to conflict with the mother country. The end of the French and Indian War in 1763 set the stage for trouble. Although Britain emerged victorious and gained some significant territory from the dispute—including Canada from France and Florida from Spain—the great expense of running the war contributed to hard economic times, forcing Parliament to seek additional sources of revenue. A number of duties were levied on various goods in the colonies, but the most odious of them all, at least in the colonists' minds, was the Stamp Act of 1765, which placed a tax on deeds, licenses, newspapers, and various other documents. This piece of legislation prompted Patrick Henry, in the Virginia House of Burgesses, to utter the words: "Caesar had his Brutus, Charles the First, his Cromwell, and George III may profit by their example. If this be treason, make the most of it." Tensions ran so high that Virginia governor Francis Fauquier dissolved the legislature for challenging the authority of Parliament. The continual protests made an impact, for the Stamp Act was repealed the following year. There was much celebration in the streets of Williamsburg, as elsewhere in the colonies.

Undaunted, Parliament tried other measures of raising revenue in the colonies. In 1767 it passed the Townshend Acts, which placed a tax on tea, paper, lead, and paint imported into the colonies. Further conflicts ensued between Parliament and the colonies, including Virginia, where legislators in 1769 proclaimed that they alone had the legal authority to tax their fellow Virginians. The new governor, Norborne Berkely, Baron de Botetourt, once again dissolved the legislature. In defiance, the burgesses met at the Raleigh Tavern and resumed their discussion in the tavern's Apollo Room. On May 17, 1769, eighty-nine members, including Thomas Jefferson, Patrick Henry, and Richard Henry Lee, signed a document banning British goods and, in so doing, declared their right to self-determination.

Botetourt died in September, 1770, and was replaced by the unpopular John Murray, Earl of Dunmore. Meanwhile, the voices of protest grew more vociferous throughout the colonies. The Virginia legislature established a Committee of Correspondence to keep in touch with the other colonies regarding events in Britain. Following the Boston Tea Party on December 16, 1773, when a group of Bostonians disguised as Indians boarded a British ship and dumped tea into Boston Harbor, Dunmore sought to avert trouble in Virginia by dissolving the legislature. Once again, the burgesses chose to defy the law. They gathered at Bruton Parish Church to discuss their options. They scheduled a state convention and encouraged other colonies to send representatives to the First Continental Congress, where Virginians played a key role in protestations against British rule.

The Revolutionary War

Events continued to move quickly. The Revolutionary War began on April 19, 1775, when shots were fired in Lexington, Massachusetts. By the following year, on May 15, 1776, the Virginians had issued their Resolution for Independence, declaring their freedom from England and establishing the independent Commonwealth of Virginia. The resolution was adopted unanimously. Patrick Henry was elected the first governor of the Commonwealth of Virginia. Meanwhile, George Washington, a Virginia planter and hero of the French and Indian War, had been named commander of the Continental Army. Finally, on July 4, 1776, the Continental Congress adopted the Declaration of Independence. By then, the Revolutionary War was in full swing.

Williamsburg played a significant role on both sides during the war. The British commander, Lord Charles Cornwallis, occupied the capital for a time and converted the Governor's Palace into a hospital for British troops. The Marquis de Lafayette, the young Frenchman who fought on the colonists' side, and Washington used the capital as their headquarters during the last days of the war. Washington stayed at George Wythe's house on the Palace Green. He marched south from Williamsburg and, on October 19, 1781, soundly defeated Cornwallis at the Battle of Yorktown—the battle that won independence for the colonies.

In 1779, Thomas Jefferson succeeded Patrick Henry as governor of Virginia. By then, authorities had decided that, due to its proximity to the York and James Rivers, Williamsburg posed a security risk. For this reason, Richmond was chosen as the new capital, both for its better climate and for its less vulnerable, more central locale. After the move to Richmond, Williamsburg continued to serve some governmental functions, although in an admittedly lesser capacity. It was still a county seat, for example. It also continued to be the home of two major institutions, the College of William and Mary and the Public Hospital. The latter, originally

proposed by Governor Fauquier in 1766 and opened in 1773, was the first hospital for the mentally ill in the colonies. Even so, Williamsburg had lost its primary reason for existence. With little industry or commerce, the former capital began a slow decline. In all likelihood, Williamsburg would have remained a quiet, small town—albeit one with a glorious past—were it not for the arrival of the Reverend W. A. R. Goodwin in 1902 as rector of Bruton Parish Church. Goodwin, for better or worse, changed the town's destiny.

The Restoration of Colonial Williamsburg

William Archer Rutherford Goodwin was born in Richmond on June 18, 1869. He studied at Roanoke College in Salem, Virginia, and worked as a door-to-door book salesman. Among the reading materials he peddled was the Bible. For a while he considered the law as a profession, but in 1889 he decided to enter the ministry.

In 1907, Goodwin persuaded the congregation of Bruton Parish Church to restore the old church's sanctuary in celebration of the three hundredth anniversary of the founding of Jamestown. There was nothing left at Jamestown, and Goodwin wanted to see that Williamsburg played an important role in the observance of the anniversary. He also worked toward restoring other Williamsburg structures. With help from the Colonial Dames of America, Goodwin acquired the George Wythe House, an early and important Williamsburg residence that had been abandoned. He eventually became determined to restore the town to its original eighteenth century splendor.

In the mid-1920's, Goodwin met John D. Rockefeller, Jr., then one of the richest men in the world, through the Phi Beta Kappa society at William and Mary. By the time Goodwin made his acquaintance, Rockefeller had already contributed money toward the preservation of European churches and created Acadia National Park in Maine. He also donated funds to many universities and medical institutions.

Goodwin discussed his vision with Rockefeller, persuading the multimillionaire to contribute two million dollars to the restoration of Williamsburg. The rector then proceeded to buy up the town, lot by lot. Goodwin hired the Boston architectural firm of Perry, Shaw, and Hepburn, and an advisory committee of architects was formed. Architect Wil-

The Governor's Mansion in Williamsburg. (American Stock Photography)

liam G. Perry was assigned to map out the town while Goodwin continued to buy individual houses as they became available. Rockefeller agreed to finance all purchases and expenditures associated with the venture, but he insisted on complete anonymity.

In early 1928, an official announcement appeared in the press: Williamsburg was to be rebuilt "as nearly as possible" to reflect its pre-Revolutionary past. Immediately, plans to renovate the Wren Building on the William and Mary campus got under way. Meanwhile, everyone in town had his or her own ideas about the identity of Goodwin's mysterious benefactor. Some mentioned Henry Ford; others thought it could be George Eastman or J. P. Morgan. Finally, on June 12, 1928, the identity of the generous donor was revealed at a mass meeting in the auditorium of a Williamsburg high school.

As the restoration work began in the late 1920's, historical accuracy was emphasized. Colonial records and newspapers were combed, descriptions of original buildings meticulously searched, colonial building techniques studied, and architectural details precisely marked down. Teams of researchers scoured the Virginia countryside for any remnants of regional architecture. Old buildings were

bought and dismantled, and their eighteenth century materials stored and cataloged for future reference.

The local zoning ordinance authorized the restoration or reconstruction of pre-1800 buildings to be located in a part of town designated the Historic Area. The Historic Area is bisected by Duke of Gloucester Street and is bounded roughly by Henry Street on the west, Waller Street on the east, Lafayette Street on the north, and Francis Street on the south. It is divided into eight geographical areas: Market Square, from Market Square to the Capitol, the Capitol and environs, the area around Palace Street, from Palace Street to the College of William and Mary, North England and Nicholson Back Streets, and Waller and Francis Back Streets. Structures that were erected in the colonial era were to be either rebuilt or restored; postcolonial structures were, for the most part, demolished or removed from the area. One by one, the intrusions of modern-day life began to disappear. Utility lines were buried under the ground. Modern stores were removed from Duke of Gloucester Street and relocated to the new business district of Merchants Square. In 1934 President Franklin D. Roosevelt attended the reopening of Duke of Gloucester Street, which he called "the most historic avenue in America." Williamsburg now officially belonged to the public.

Goodwin died on September 7, 1939. The rector's initial goal was simply to restore and duplicate the original buildings. That vision grew and expanded beyond mere physical duplication to try to include an explanation of what life in colonial Williamsburg was really like. The effort involved not only architects and engineers but also historians and archaeologists. Rutherfoord Goodwin, the rector's son, created the idea of hiring local women, dressed up in colonial finery, to act as the town's unofficial ambassadors. Goodwin's vision has grown more sophisticated over the years. Now costumed actors, well versed in colonial history and customs, assume the roles of eighteenth century Williamsburg residents. The restoration also cost far more than originally anticipated. By the time of his death in 1960, Rockefeller had put sixty-eight million dollars into Williamsburg, and members of his family continued to donate funds.

Modern Preservation Efforts

Today, Williamsburg's Historic Area includes eighty-eight original colonial-era structures and fifty major reconstructions. Some of the original buildings are the Bruton Parish Church, in continuous use since 1715; the Wren Building, the President's House, and the Brafferton at the College of William and Mary; and the homes of George Wythe (host to George Washington) and Peyton Randolph, who led the Virginia delegation to the First Continental Congress and was elected the Congress's president. Reconstructed buildings include the Governor's Palace, the Capitol, the Public Hospital, and the Raleigh Tavern. Eight miles east of Williamsburg is Carter's Grove, an eight hundred-acre plantation with extensive historical exhibits. The slave quarters at the plantation are part of Williamsburg's expanded efforts to convey information about the lives of African Americans in colonial times. Half the population of eighteenth century Williamsburg was black.

Williamsburg is part tourist spot and part living history site, attracting more than one million tourists a year. The Historic Area forms the heart of the modern city of Williamsburg with its ten thousand or so residents. Colonial Williamsburg is operated by the Colonial Williamsburg Foundation, a nonprofit organization formed in 1928. A commercial subsidiary was established in 1984 to operate hotels and colonial-style taverns and to manufacture everything from crafts to colonial-style furniture. Here, in the fulcrum of America's colonial past, history and pleasure live amiably side by side.

—*June Skinner Sawyers*

For Further Information:

Beney, Peter. *The Majesty of Colonial Williamsburg.* Gretna, La.: Pelican, 1997. A pictorial work featuring magnificent color photographs.

Cease, Cheryl J., and Susan Bruno. *The Insiders' Guide to Williamsburg: Jamestown-Yorktown.* Rev. 9th ed. Helena, Mont.: Falcon, 1999. A practical, comprehensive, and up-to-date source of information.

Kopper, Philip. *Colonial Williamsburg.* New York: Harry N. Abrams, in association with the Colonial Williamsburg Foundation, 1986. An in-depth study. Despite its coffee table veneer, it is both well written and lavishly illustrated.

Olmert, Michael, Suzanne E. Coffman, and the Colonial Williamsburg Foundation. *Official Guide to Colonial Williamsburg.* Rev. ed. Williamsburg, Va.: Colonial Williamsburg Foundation, 1998. Part guide book and part history book. As such, it functions as a serviceable introduction to the town. It also contains practical information, complete descriptions of the buildings open to the public, and easy-to-follow maps of the Historic Area.

Yorktown

Date: Established in 1691

Relevant issues: Colonial America, political history, Revolutionary War

Significance: This town had a population of twenty-five hundred in 1750 and was larger than Williamsburg. Three hundred years after its founding, it had become a backwater village of five hundred. Today, the earthworks for the 1781 siege of Yorktown have been reconstructed, and several eighteenth century buildings have been restored in the town.

Location: The west bank of the York River, on U.S. 17, about thirteen miles east of Williamsburg and thirty-two miles north of Norfolk

Site Office:

Colonial National Historical Park
P.O. Box 210
Yorktown, VA 23690-0210
ph.: (757) 898-2410
Web site: www.nps.gov/colo/

Yorktown, on a bluff above the York River, is the site of the most decisive military operation of the American Revolution. British and Hessian forces under the command of Lieutenant General Charles Cornwallis captured the town in August, 1781, to secure the York River as a harbor on the Chesapeake Bay for British warships and as a base for regaining British control of Virginia. The American commander in chief, George Washington, had learned in May that the French, allies for the past three years, were sending another fleet across the Atlantic. Later that month he met in Connecticut with the commander of the French army in America, the Comte de Rochambeau, to plan where to strike a crippling blow at the British war effort. The two armies marched overland from New England in late August and surrounded Yorktown a month later.

British warships were turned back before the siege by French ships, which blockaded the entrance to Chesapeake Bay. The French fleet then sealed the entrance to the York River, preventing reinforcements from the main British army from reaching Yorktown. Cornwallis surrendered October 19, 1781. The British public and a majority of the members of Parliament wanted the war to end, and in 1782, after the humiliating defeat at Yorktown, peace negotiations began. The Treaty of Paris that formally ended the war was signed September 3, 1783, but not ratified by both Britain and the United States until May 12, 1784.

Modern Restoration Work

The earthworks of the Yorktown Battlefield have been reconstructed. Immediately after the siege, Washington had the allied French and Continental forces destroy its earthen siege lines so they could not be used against the French troops that occupied the town that winter. The official battlefield tour includes the British inner defense line, which was modified and strengthened eighty years later by Confederate forces during the Civil War; the grand French battery; the second Allied siege line; redoubts nine and ten, where there was fierce hand-to-hand fighting between the Allies and the British on October 14, 1781; and the surrender field. Visitors can tour the Moore House, where the Articles of Capitulation were completed on October 18.

Several eighteenth century buildings have been restored in the town. The Georgian home of Thomas Nelson, Jr., a signer of the Declaration of Independence, was built around 1711, and there are still cannon balls in the wall facing Nelson Street from the siege of 1781. This building is not to be confused with the Nelson House that Cornwallis made his headquarters; that was the home of Nelson's uncle and was razed in the nineteenth century. A marker was placed on the site of the Nelson House in 1927 by the Association for the Preservation of Virginia Antiquities.

In the more than two centuries since the siege of Yorktown, "in fully chronicling the moves of the various pieces in this martial chess game, historians have exhausted reams of paper without giving a very clear picture," said Clyde Trudell, who for several years served as restoration architect for the National Park Service at Yorktown. Was it by chance that Yorktown was the site of such a historic event? Why did Cornwallis move into a location so easy to surround? Did the British simply want to bring the six-year war to an end—even if it meant defeat?

Early History

Yorktown was laid out in 1691 after the Virginia House of Burgesses passed the Act for Ports. The act established fifteen ports to ensure collection of the customs due from the tobacco trade. Yorktown had "the best harbor in the State for vessels of the largest size," the recently retired governor of Virginia, Thomas Jefferson, wrote in fall of 1781. "The river there narrows to the width of a mile, and is contained within very high banks, close under which vessels may ride."

In August, 1781, a Hessian soldier serving with Cornwallis described his initial impression of Yorktown:

> This Yorktown, or Little-York, is a small city of approximately 300 houses; it has, moreover, considerable circumference. It is located on the bank of the York River, somewhat high on a sandy but level ground. . . . There was a garrison of 300 militia men here, but upon our arrival they marched away without firing a shot back to Williamsburg, which is 16 English miles from here. We found few inhabitants here, as they had mostly gone with bag and baggage into the country beyond.

The American Revolution was fought a long way from tidewater Virginia until the spring of 1781. In the early years of the war the important battles took place in the northern colonies. Sir Henry Clinton, the British commander in chief starting in 1778, moved the British military headquarters from Philadelphia to New York, and General Washington used most of the revolutionary army to keep watch around New York. Fighting in that part of the country developed into a stalemate that continued to the end of the war.

A captured British gun in Yorktown. (American Stock Photography)

General Cornwallis and the Revolutionary War

In July, 1779, Cornwallis, returning from his wife's funeral in England and six months of mourning, sailed into New York Harbor to assume the post of second in command of the British forces in America. A military professional for a quarter of a century, Cornwallis had played a key role in defeating the Continental Army at Long Island, New York, in August, 1776, and led the column of 7,500 British troops that crushed Washington at Brandywine, Pennsylvania, in September, 1777. Clinton, disappointed that Cornwallis was not accompanied by promised reinforcements, sent his resignation to London. He himself could not return to London, of course, until he knew whether the ministry accepted the resignation.

Cornwallis wanted action. The British had taken Savannah, Georgia, in December, 1778, and a combined Continental and French effort to retake that coastal city failed in October, 1779. That winter, the time seemed opportune for moving the theater of operations to the south. Clinton and Cornwallis made two assumptions: first, that control of the sea would make it possible to move British troops up and down the coast with ease while revolutionary forces faced the difficulties of overland travel; and second, that many southern colonists were still loyal to the king and would join with their British liberators to end the war.

The southern campaign at first lived up to British expectations. The British captured Charleston, South Carolina, in May, 1780. After Clinton learned that the ministry did not accept his resignation, he returned to New York. Cornwallis moved into the interior of South Carolina and crushed General Horatio Gates at Camden in August, 1780. It was an especially sweet victory because Gates had been the general who gave the British their first major defeat at Saratoga, New York, in October, 1777. More loyalists were casting their lot with the British, but it soon became apparent that a Tory column was not going to give Cornwallis the support he needed to subdue the Carolinas. In October, 1780, at Kings Mountain, near the North Carolina border, a band of revolutionary riflemen from the backwoods killed, wounded, or captured an entire force of 1,100 Tories.

Cornwallis's Southern Strategy

After a costly March, 1781, victory by British forces at Guilford Courthouse, North Carolina, Cornwallis decided it was time to devise his own southern strategy, with Virginia as its key. Cornwallis was already in Virginia when he received Clinton's May 29 letter that said. "In the disordered state of Carolina and Georgia, I shall dread what may be the consequences of your Lordship's move."

That summer, while letters crossed back and forth between Virginia and New York with ever changing instructions from his commanding officer, Cornwallis skirmished around Williamsburg with the Marquis de Lafayette, the young French-man commanding the small revolutionary force sent to harrass the British. The only significant engagement occurred in July at Green Spring, near Jamestown, where Lafayette escaped a trap that would have decimated his troops.

At that point no one knew that the decisive battle would be at Yorktown. Clinton and Cornwallis had been debating the merits of several options when a packet of eleven letters arrived from London addressed to Clinton. The letters, dated January 31 to May 2, 1781, were from Lord George Germain, the secretary for the American colonies and the man in charge of prosecuting the British side of the war. Germain's May 2 letter approved Cornwallis's plan to execute his part of the war from Virginia. Clinton ordered him to position his forces where they could protect British battleships, frigates, and smaller vessels in Chesapeake Bay.

On July 27, Cornwallis wrote to Clinton, "I shall, in obedience to the spirit of Your Excellency's orders, take measures with as much despatch as possible to seize and fortify York and Gloucester, being the only harbor in which we can hope to give effective protection to line of battle ships." On July 30, Cornwallis sailed for Yorktown from Portsmouth Harbor on the Elizabeth River, Virginia's largest harbor with room for three hundred or more ships. From Portsmouth, Cornwallis had been able to keep an eye on Lafayette's forces in Williamsburg, just to the north on the James River, while waiting to see how serious Clinton was about a proposed military mission to solidify the British position in Pennsylvania.

Cornwallis had gone to Portsmouth after receiving scathing criticism from Clinton, who had usually been tactful in his letters because of the higher position Cornwallis occupied in English society. (Cornwallis had served in the House of Lords since 1762, when he assumed his late father's title as sixth earl of Eyre). Clinton wrote,

Experience ought to convince us that there is no possibility of re-establishing order in any rebellious province on this continent without the hearty assistance of numerous friends. These, my Lord, are not, I think to be found in Virginia . . . but I believe there is a greater probability of finding them in Pennsylvania than in any, except the southern provinces. In these your Lordship has already made the experiment; it has there failed—they are gone from us, and I fear not to be recovered. . . .

Cornwallis Lands at Yorktown

On August 2, Cornwallis landed at Yorktown and selected as his headquarters a house with a view of the harbor and the rest of the town. The owner was Thomas Nelson, secretary to the former colony, who was still in residence. Then in his seventies, Nelson had remained neutral in the conflict and was allowed to remain in his home by Cornwallis, who is reported to have treated his host with courtesy.

Yorktown, which had never been of such strategic importance before, was not strongly fortified. Ten transport ships were sunk to form a barrier on the east that would discourage an attack from the river. A ravine to the north of Yorktown and a swamp to the south were natural barriers. Ten redoubts (earthen barriers with stakes pointed outward discouraging an assault) completed the protective ring. Three of these redoubts were constructed on the most vulnerable half-mile throat of land, where the road from Williamsburg to the northwest and Hampton to the south came into Yorktown. Many of the sixty-five guns installed in the fourteen batteries were cannibalized from the frigate *Charon* tied up in the river.

While the British built up the Yorktown fortifications, Lafayette kept a watchful eye and sent word to Washington that Cornwallis seemed to be planning to stay there awhile. Also in mid-August, Washington learned from the Comte de Rochambeau, commander of the French army in New England, that the French fleet commanded by Admiral de Grasse had left the West Indies headed for the Chesapeake Bay and could stay there only until October 15. Washington and Rochambeau had previously been considering an attack on Clinton in New York, but Washington had managed to round up only six thousand of the ten thousand troops needed for that action; Rochambeau had only five thousand men. That would be enough, however, to take on Cornwallis in Virginia. When the Continental and French armies left New England in late August and passed by New York, Clinton thought they were practicing an elaborate deception to lure him from his stronghold.

The French Fleet

British admiral Samuel Hood tailed Admiral de Grasse's French fleet as it headed north from the West Indies. Then he lost sight of the French and reached the Virginia capes ahead of them. Assuming that de Grasse had continued north, possibly as far north as Newport, where de Grasse's compatriot Admiral de Barras had been locked in for three years by the British navy, Hood headed for New York. There Hood conferred with Clinton and Rear Admiral Thomas Graves, who knew by then that de Grasse's destination had been Virginia. Hood and Graves led a fleet of nineteen British ships from New York Harbor headed for the Chesapeake August 31. That same day de Grasse's fleet sailed into the Chesapeake. The next day forty French ships went up the James River with three thousand reinforcements for Lafayette in Williamsburg. Four French ships anchored at the entrance to the York River.

The British fleet intercepted de Grasse's French fleet September 5 just outside the Virginia capes. The British lost the advantage of surprise by waiting to attack until late afternoon when both sides were lined up in battle formation. When the twenty-four French ships and nineteen British vessels stopped firing at each other at dusk, the British fleet had suffered the most damage, but the battle was a draw. The French had the strategic position they wanted, however, and did not risk any more damage to their fleet. They were between the British navy and Yorktown; Cornwallis would have to stay there. Four days later the British ships headed back to New York. While they were en route, Commodore Edmund Affleck, still in New York, wrote to the Board of Admiralty in London,

> I am making every preparation possible for the supply of the fleet in masts, yards & rigging as well as provisions for their return, but the deficiency of all these articles are not to be described and without the arrival of supplies from England and a mast ship from Halifax which the Warwick is gone for, the demands of the fleet cannot be complied with.

On September 23, Clinton learned that the French had thirty-six ships blockading the entrance to Chesapeake Bay, ten more than he had been told in earlier intelligence reports. With the smaller number he had thought it would be possible for a few British ships to run past the French and get into the bay. He would now have to wait until the British fleet in New York Harbor, waiting for supplies from England, could at least match the strength of the French fleet in Virginia. That day he wrote down his thoughts on the situation. He realized that if the army under Cornwallis was lost, "there will be little hope of British dominion in America—except by an exertion of which I fear our country is not capable." Later he sent a message to Cornwallis that the British fleet might be able to sail from New York October 5 to come to his rescue.

While the French fleet continued to control access to Chesapeake Bay, the allied armies began closing in on Cornwallis. Washington reached Williamsburg, Lafayette's headquarters located fifteen miles northwest of Yorktown, on September 14. When Rochambeau arrived a few days later, the allies had more than fifteen thousand troops for the siege. On September 28, they marched on Yorktown.

Inside the Yorktown fortifications were most of the seventy-five hundred British and Hessian troops commanded by Cornwallis. A smaller contingent was defending Gloucester Point, a mile across the York River on the east bank. Cornwallis began withdrawing from his outer defenses at Yorktown on September 29 when he received the message from Clinton that the British fleet would soon be returning to break the siege. The Continental and French forces moved forward to occupy the vacated British outer defenses and strengthened them for their assault.

Battle of Yorktown Begins

The first shots were fired at the British on October 9. The first siege line—begun the night of October 6—was established about eight hundred yards from the British defenses. Two nights later a second, closer siege line was begun. The allied forces then set their sights on the two British redoubts that blocked them from establishing a second parallel. On October 14, four hundred French soldiers attacked redoubt nine, which was manned by about one hundred twenty British and Hessian troops. The fortification fell in less than thirty minutes. Redoubt ten, held by about seventy defenders, was overpowered in ten minutes by four hun-

Moore House, the site on the Yorktown Battlefield where the British surrendered and signed the Articles of Capitulation. (American Stock Photography)

dred Continentals led by Alexander Hamilton.

On October 15, Cornwallis wrote to Clinton:

> Last evening the enemy carried my two advanced redoubts on the left by storm, and during the night have included them in the second parallel, which they are at present busy perfecting. . . . The safety of the place is therefore so precarious that I cannot recommend that the fleet and army should run great risk in endeavoring to save us.

At a midnight conference on October 15, Cornwallis and his officers decided to send 350 men on a surprise mission to disable some of the allied cannon in the second parallel batteries. They chose as their point of attack the junction of the French and Continental sections of the trenches. When challenged by sentries, they would pretend to be Continental reinforcements to the French and French reinforcements to the Continentals. The first part of the plan worked, as they rushed onto the redoubts, bayoneting the defenders but not pursuing them. Their mission was to spike the cannons' touchholes with their bayonet points, rendering the cannon useless. While they were thus engaged,

they were surprised by French grenadiers under Lafayette's brother-in-law, the Vicomte de Noailles, who had been aroused by the commotion. A fierce bayonet fight continued until dawn. By noon on October 16, every cannon had been cleared. The renewed bombardment of Yorktown was even more vigorous than before.

On the night of October 16, Cornwallis decided to escape from the siege by crossing the York River to Gloucester. It would take three trips to get all of his men across. The first contingent made it across to Gloucester, but it took two hours before the boats returned for the second group to embark. Ten minutes after the boats had pushed off again, rain began to fall. It soon developed into a torrential storm, and the boats were forced to return to the Yorktown shore.

Cornwallis Surrenders

About 7:00 A.M., October 17, Cornwallis called a council of war. After all the other setbacks, the report on the ammunition supply—only a hundred mortar shells left—made the decision unanimous: surrender. It was a coincidence that October 17 was the anniversary of General John Burgoyne's 1777 surrender to the revolutionary forces at Saratoga, which had led directly to the alliance with France.

Fourteen Articles of Capitulation for the surrender were drafted at the Augustine Moore House on October 18. Article Three called for the British York garrison to march out at two o'clock, October 19, "with shouldered arms, colours cased and drums beating a British or German march." The surrendering army chose an old English air, "Down Derry Down," with several sets of lyrics ranging from "When the King Enjoys His Own Again" to "The World Turned Upside Down."

When the surrender ceremony was ready to take place, Cornwallis was not there. According to historian Thomas Fleming, Cornwallis "had found, at the last moment, he could not endure the mortification of surrender and [gave] the task to his deputy," General Charles O'Hara. When O'Hara explained to Washington "that Lord Cornwallis was indisposed, . . . Washington coolly directed O'Hara to receive his orders from General Benjamin Lincoln, the American second in command."

The same day the British surrendered at Yorktown, the British fleet that could have broken the siege left New York. They did not find out they were too late until October 24, when they reached Chesapeake Bay.   —*Carolyn J. Daily*

For Further Information:

Fleming, Thomas J. *Beat the Last Drum: The Siege of Yorktown, 1781.* New York: St. Martin's Press, 1963. Gives a clear and detailed explanation of why Yorktown became the site of the last battle of the American Revolution. There are extensive direct quotes from both the British and American military leaders.

Manceron, Claude. *The Winds from America, 1778-1781.* Translated by Nancy Amphoux. New York: Alfred A. Knopf, 1978. Gives a fascinating account of the French view of events at Yorktown.

Sands, John O. *Yorktown's Captive Fleet.* Charlottesville: University Press of Virginia, 1983. Discusses the significance of sea power in the American Revolution and explains why the British, who had controlled the seas, did not break through the French blockade in time.

Stevens, Benjamin Franklin, ed. *The Campaign in Virginia, 1781: An Exact Reprint of Six Rare Pamphlets on the Clinton-Cornwallis Controversy.* 2 vols. London, 1888. Contains the full text of letters to and from Sir Henry Clinton, commander in chief of the British forces in America, including Clinton's notes. Clinton, who seldom left New York during the forty-one months between taking the top command and the siege of Yorktown, spent much of his time explaining his inaction.

Wheat, Thomas Adrian. *A Guide to Civil War Yorktown.* Knoxville, Tenn.: Bohemian Brigade Bookshop, 1997. Discusses the experience of Yorktown residents from 1861 to 1865.

Other Historic Sites

Bacon's Castle

Location: Bacon's Castle, Surry County

Relevant issues: Colonial America, military history

Statement of significance: Built probably in the 1660's, this structure is among the earliest Virginia cross-plan houses, distinguished by its curvilinear gables and two-end chimney units of three stacks each. In 1676, it was used as a fortress by rebel troops during Bacon's Rebellion (1676-1677), the first instance of violent resistance to British colonial exploitation in America. Led by Nathaniel Bacon (1647-1676), a young nobleman, rebels seized and fortified this house.

Ball's Bluff Battlefield and National Cemetery

Location: Leesburg vicinity, Loudoun County

Relevant issues: Civil War, military history

Statement of significance: In October, 1861, to quiet his critics, Major General George B. McClellan ordered Union troops stationed along the Potomac between Edwards Ferry and Harpers Ferry to make "a slight demonstration" and draw out the Confederate force based in Leesburg. The resultant Union defeat here on October 21, 1861, led to the creation of the Joint Committee on the Conduct of the War, the first major exercise of congressional authority to oversee and investigate operations of the federal executive branch.

Banneker SW-9 Intermediate Boundary Stone

Location: 18th and Van Buren Streets, Arlington, Arlington County

Relevant issues: African American history, colonial America, science and technology

Statement of significance: This boundary stone commemorates the accomplishments of Benjamin Banneker (1731-1806), farmer, mathematician, inventor, astronomer, writer, surveyor, scientist, and humanitarian. Perhaps the most famous black man in colonial America, Banneker helped survey the District of Columbia.

Camp Hoover

Location: Graves Mill, Madison County

Relevant issues: Political history

Statement of significance: Secluded among the hemlocks at the base of Fork Mountain is what remains of the retreat developed between 1929 and 1932 as a "Summer White House" for President Herbert Hoover. Three of the thirteen original buildings are still extant, as are trails, stone bridges, man-made trout pools, a stone fountain, and a massive outdoor stone fireplace. Originally built on a parcel owned by Hoover and his wife Lou Henry Hoover, the camp is now within the boundaries of Shenandoah National Park, and, as requested by Hoover, it is administered and equipped as a summer weekend retreat for the president of the United States.

Cedar Creek Battlefield and Belle Grove

Location: Middletown, Frederick County

Relevant issues: Civil War, military history

Statement of significance: General Philip Sheridan defeated Confederate General Jubal T. Early here, climaxing the struggle for the Shenandoah Valley. Belle Grove, a one-and-a-half-story stone house built by James Madison's brother-in-law in 1790, served as Sheridan's headquarters.

Drew House

Location: Arlington, Arlington County

Relevant issues: African American history, health and medicine

Statement of significance: From 1920 to 1939, this two-story clapboard structure was the residence of Charles Richard Drew (1904-1950), the noted black physician and teacher, who is best remembered for his pioneer work in discovering the means to preserve blood plasma. Drew had the distinction of being the first African American to receive the Doctor of Science in Medicine degree.

Drydock No. 1

Location: Portsmouth, Portsmouth County

Relevant issues: Civil War, naval history

Statement of significance: The shipyard, established in 1767, is the oldest in the country; the drydock was constructed from 1827 to 1834. During the Civil War, the Union frigate USS *Merrimack* was rebuilt by the Confederates in this drydock, becoming the ironclad CSS *Virginia.*

Five Forks Battlefield

Location: Petersburg, Dinwiddie County

Relevant issues: Civil War, military history

Statement of significance: This battle ensured success for Ulysses S. Grant in his campaign to force Robert E. Lee from the Richmond-Petersburg defenses.

Ford House

Location: Alexandria, Alexandria County

Relevant issues: Political history

Statement of significance: From 1955 to 1974, this was the home of Gerald R. Ford, Jr., the thirty-eighth president of the United States. These years constitute the major part of Ford's long congressional career, as well as his service as vice president and the first ten days after his assumption of the presidency following President Richard Nixon's resignation.

Fort Monroe

Location: Hampton, Hampton County

Relevant issues: Civil War, military history

Statement of significance: Constructed between 1819 and 1834, Fort Monroe was one of the country's major military posts from the time of its establishment; Robert E. Lee, then a lieutenant, played a prominent role in the final stages of its construction. During the Civil War, the fort was a staging area for Union land and naval expeditions. On March 9, 1862, thousands of spectators stood on the ramparts of Fort Monroe to watch the momentous battle between USS *Monitor* and CSS *Virginia*, the first battle in history between ironclad vessels. From May, 1865, to May, 1867, the fort was the site for the imprisonment of Confederate president Jefferson Davis.

Fort Myer Historic District

Location: Arlington, Arlington County
Relevant issues: Aviation history, military history
Statement of significance: Dating from the late nineteenth century, Fort Myer was the site of the earliest experiments in military aviation conducted by the Wright Brothers in 1908. Since 1909, Quarters 1 (1899) on "Generals Row" has been the home of the Chiefs of Staff of the U.S. Army.

Franklin and Armfield Office

Location: Alexandria, Alexandria County
Relevant issues: African American history, business and industry
Statement of significance: Between 1828 and 1836, Isaac Franklin, in partnership with John Armfield, created the largest-scale slave trading operation in the antebellum South. They established their headquarters in Alexandria (then a part of the District of Columbia), adjacent to an area with a surplus of slaves available at low prices. This building served as the firm's Alexandria office, where Franklin purchased slaves who were then transported New Orleans and Natchez, where Armfield handled sales. At its peak, their firm had agents in almost every important Southern city, owned a fleet of sailing ships, and trafficked in thousands of slaves annually. In the process, both partners became enormously wealthy. After Franklin and Armfield sold the building, the house continued as a center for slave trading until 1861; during the Civil War, it housed captured Confederate soldiers.

Gadsby's Tavern

Location: Alexandria, Alexandria County
Relevant issues: Colonial America
Statement of significance: Comprising two adjoining tavern buildings, the smaller of which dates from 1752, this is one of the best-known eighteenth century inns in the country. George

Washington recruited men here in 1754 for the French and Indian War, and the first celebration of the federal Constitution took place here on June 28, 1788.

General George C. Marshall House

Location: Leesburg, Loudoun County
Relevant issues: Military history, World War II
Statement of significance: General George Catlett Marshall, Jr. (1880-1959), who lived here eighteen years from 1941 until his death, called this house Dodona Manor, after the Greek oracle of the whispering oak leaves on the Hill of Dodona. During these years, Marshall rose from being an Army officer held in professional respect, but without celebrity, to one of the most important and respected figures of the twentieth century. Winston Churchill, recalling the years of World War II, said that the only individual on whom all the leaders conferred unqualified praise and admiration was General Marshall.

Glass House

Location: Lynchburg, Lynchburg County
Relevant issues: Business and industry, political history
Statement of significance: From 1907 to 1923, this was the residence of Carter Glass (1858-1946), one of the most influential shapers of U.S. financial policy in the first half of the twentieth century. Glass served in the U.S. House of Representatives (1902-1918), as secretary of the Treasury (1918-1920), and as U.S. senator (1920-1946). He authored the Glass-Owen Act (1913), which established the Federal Reserve System.

Greenway Court

Location: White Post, Clarke County
Relevant issues: Colonial America
Statement of significance: From 1751 to 1781, this was the estate of Thomas Lord Fairfax (1693-1781), the only English peer residing in the colonies and the proprietor of a five million-acre land grant in Virginia. Fairfax employed George Washington as a surveyor.

Gunston Hall

Location: Lorton, Fairfax County
Relevant issues: Political history

Web site: visit.gunstonhall.org/gunstonhall/wel
come

Statement of significance: Notable for its interior carved details and formal gardens, Gunston Hall was built (1755-1758) for George Mason (1725-1792), a leading Revolutionary figure, author of the Virginia Declaration of Rights (1776), and member of the Constitutional Convention whose refusal to sign the document without a Bill of Rights was vindicated by events.

Hampton Institute

Location: Hampton, Hampton County

Relevant issues: African American history, education

Statement of significance: Founded by the American Missionary Association to train selected young black men and women to "teach and lead their people, first by example," Hampton Normal and Industrial Institute opened in April, 1868, with two teachers and fifteen students; today, it is a fully accredited liberal arts college with an international faculty and student body. The institute served as a model for numerous African American industrial schools subsequently founded to aid the freedmen; Booker T. Washington, founder of Tuskegee Institute, was himself a graduate of this school.

Hanover County Courthouse

Location: Hanover Court House, Hanover County

Relevant issues: Colonial America, legal history

Statement of significance: This Georgian courthouse has been used continuously since its completion around 1735. It was here that, in 1763, Patrick Henry argued and won "The Parson's Cause," a case involving religious liberty in the colony.

Jackson's Headquarters

Location: Winchester, Winchester County

Relevant issues: Civil War, military history

Statement of significance: In the months preceding his famous Shenandoah Valley campaign (March-June, 1862), Confederate major general Thomas J. "Stonewall" Jackson (1824-1863) used this Gothic Revival house as his headquarters. Jackson's rapid maneuvering in the valley kept valuable federal forces from joining the well-conceived Peninsular assault on Richmond by the Army of the Potomac and contributed to the failure of Union major general George B. McClellan's strategy.

Lee Chapel, Washington and Lee University

Location: Lexington, Lexington County

Relevant issues: Education, military history

Statement of significance: Built in 1867 under his supervision, this Victorian Gothic brick building commemorates the years Robert E. Lee (1807-1870) served as president (1865-1870) of the college, then known as Washington College. Lee is buried in a chapel vault.

Lightship No. 101 "Portsmouth"

Location: Portsmouth, Portsmouth County

Relevant issues: Naval history

Statement of significance: Now known as *Portsmouth*, Lightship No. 101 is one of a small number of preserved American lightships. Essential partners with lighthouses as aids to navigation along the coast of the United States, American lightships date to the 1820's. Built as one of two vessels from the same plan, No. 101 served at least five stations in the middle Atlantic states guiding coastal, intercoastal, and international vessels into Chesapeake and Delaware Bays and within Nantucket Bay.

Lunar Landing Research Facility

Location: Hampton, Hampton County

Relevant issues: Aviation history, science and technology

Statement of significance: Constructed in 1965, this facility was used to prepare U.S. astronauts to land on the moon. It employed a mock Lunar Excursion Module (LEM) attached to a fixed facility. The experience gained showed that astronauts could master skills needed to land the LEM on the moon.

McCormick Farm and Workshop

Location: Steele's Tavern, Rockbridge County

Relevant issues: Science and technology

Statement of significance: Cyrus McCormick (1809-1884), inventor, manufacturer, and philanthropist, lived and worked here. McCormick's invention of the mechanical reaper in 1834 helped revolutionize agriculture. Both his workshop and his farmhouse have been preserved.

Marlbourne

Location: Richmond, Hanover County

Relevant issues: Civil War, science and technology

Statement of significance: This was the property of Edmund Ruffin (1794-1865), who used his plantation as a laboratory for agricultural experiments in an effort to improve on the soil-depleting agricultural practices of the antebellum South. An ardent secessionist, he fired the first shot against Fort Sumter from Morris Island in Charleston, South Carolina, in 1861. After the collapse of the Confederacy, he took his own life at Marlbourne.

Marshall House

Location: Richmond, Richmond County

Relevant issues: Legal history

Web site: www.apva.org/apva/marshall.html

Statement of significance: From 1790 until his death, this was the property of John Marshall (1755-1835). After brief service as secretary of state (1800-1801), Marshall became the fourth chief justice of the United States, in which office he remained until his death.

Mitchell House

Location: Middleburg, Loudoun County

Relevant issues: Aviation history, military history

Statement of significance: From 1926 until his death, this was the residence of General William "Billy" Mitchell (1879-1936), the dominant figure in American military aviation between the world wars. Mitchell foresaw the strategic value of air power; his advocacy of his ideas led to his 1925 court-martial.

Monroe Law Office

Location: Fredericksburg, Fredericksburg County

Relevant issues: Legal history, political history

Statement of significance: James Monroe (1758-1831), who would be the fifth president of the United States (1817-1825), used this structure as a law office from 1786 to 1789, after studying law with Thomas Jefferson.

Montpelier

Location: Orange, Orange County

Relevant issues: Political history

Statement of significance: For seventy-six years, this was the residence of James Madison (1751-1836), fourth president of the United States (1809-1817). Madison was dubbed the "Father of the Constitution" for his preeminent role at the Constitutional Convention. He is buried here with his wife Dolley.

Moton House

Location: Capahosic, Gloucester County

Relevant issues: African American history, education, social reform

Statement of significance: From 1935 until his death, this two-and-a-half-story Georgian Revival structure was the residence of Robert Russa Moton (1867-1940), influential African American educator. Moton began his career in education at Hampton Institute, from which he had graduated in 1890. In 1915, he was chosen to succeed Booker T. Washington as the principal of Tuskegee Institute; during the next twenty years, Moton guided the school's transition from a vocational and agricultural school to a fully accredited collegiate and professional institution. He received the Harmon Award in Race Relations in 1930 and the Spingarn Medal in 1932.

NS Savannah

Location: Newport News, York County

Relevant issues: Naval history, science and technology

Statement of significance: Designed and constructed in the late 1950's as the first nuclear merchant ship, this combination cargo-passenger vessel was developed as part of President Dwight Eisenhower's Atoms for Peace initiative. Even though the market for such vessels never materialized, the design, construction, and operation of a new type of pressurized water reactor, utilizing low-enriched uranium, represented a major technological success. NS *Savannah* was also a success in accomplishing its unique public relations role as a floating exhibit on the peaceful use of nuclear energy. It sailed a half million miles around the world and was visited by a half million people. This exposure, unprecedented for a nuclear facility, is credited with easing anxieties over nuclear energy.

Oak Hill

Location: Leesburg, Loudoun County

Relevant issues: Political history

Statement of significance: From 1808 to 1830, Oak Hill, a two-story brick house, was a residence of James Monroe (1758-1831), fifth president of the United States (1817-1825). He built the mansion here in 1820. He first outlined the Monroe Doctrine in a letter written here.

Pentagon

Location: Arlington, Arlington County

Relevant issues: Military history

Statement of significance: Completed in 1943, the Pentagon is associated with events and people that have shaped America's geopolitical role in the post-World War II period. In the decades since its construction, the Pentagon has become an internationally recognized symbol for the emergence of the United States as a military "superpower" and is closely linked to the nation's national defense establishment.

Pittsylvania County Courthouse

Location: Chatham, Pittsylvania County

Relevant issues: African American history, legal history

Statement of significance: Here, in 1878, Judge J. D. Coles excluded black citizens from serving as grand and petit jurors in Pittsylvania County. Arrested and charged with a violation of the Civil Rights Act of 1875, Judge Coles filed a petition with the United States Supreme Court, asking that he be released and that all charges be dropped. The Supreme Court held that his action had been a clear violation of the law and denied his petition for release. The Supreme Court's ruling in *Ex Parte Virginia* (1878) demonstrated that as a result of the Fourteenth Amendment to the Constitution, the federal government had a qualified but potentially effective power to protect the rights of all American citizens and represents one of the few victories for African Americans in the federal courts in the generation after 1865.

Pocahontas Exhibition Coal Mine

Location: Pocahontas, Tazewell County

Relevant issues: Business and industry

Statement of significance: Located in the low hills of northeastern Tazewell County, this mine was opened in Spring, 1882, to exploit the extraor- dinarily thick seam of very high quality semi- bituminous coal. To get the coal to market, a branch line of the Norfolk and Western Rail- road was built to the new town of Pocahontas and the mine; soon after this development, nu- merous other mines were operating in what came to be known as the Pocahontas-Flat Top coalfield. The quality of the coal, the relative ease of accessibility to the thick seam, and the development of a coke industry combined to make coal from this region highly sought after for the manufacture of steel and for steam gen- eration.

Randolph Cottage

Location: Glen Allen, Henrico County

Relevant issues: African American history, education

Statement of significance: This structure commemo- rates Virginia E. Randolph (1874-1958), a nota- ble African American teacher who, because of her exemplary work at Henrico County's Moun- tain Road School, in 1908 was asked to become the country's first Jeanes Supervising Industrial Worker, or instructor, under the sponsorship of the Negro Rural School Fund. Her task was to improve vocational training in elementary and secondary schools throughout the county; her success in that role made her the model for thousands of others in a program that was insti- tuted throughout the South.

Reynolds Homestead

Location: Critz, Patrick County

Relevant issues: Business and industry

Statement of significance: From 1850 to 1874, this property was the home of Richard Joshua Reynolds (1850-1918), whose company was re- sponsible for both Prince Albert Smoking To- bacco (1907) and "Camels" (1913) cigarettes. With the Camels brand, the R. J. Reynolds To- bacco Company conquered a market and trans- formed an industry.

Ripshin Farm

Location: Trout Dale, Grayson County

Relevant issues: Literary history

Statement of significance: From 1927 until his death, this rustic stone-and-log structure was the sum- mer home of author Sherwood Anderson (1876-

1941), who is generally credited with reintroducing subjectivity into American literature through his frankly self-revealing works.

Rising Sun Tavern

Location: Fredericksburg, Fredericksburg County

Relevant issues: Revolutionary War

Web site: www.apva.org/apva/rising.html

Statement of significance: Built in 1760 by Charles Washington, the youngest brother of George Washington, the tavern was a meeting place for Southern leaders on their way to the Continental Congress in Philadelphia. It was also the scene of a Peace Ball celebrating the victory at Yorktown in 1781.

Sayler's Creek Battlefield

Location: Farmville, Amelia County

Relevant issues: Civil War

Statement of significance: After the April 2-3, 1865, evacuation of Richmond and Petersburg and the flight of the Confederate government, General Robert E. Lee attempted to move his Army of Northern Virginia to North Carolina, where he hoped to join forces with General Joseph E. Johnston. A logistical mix-up caused a one-day delay at Amelia Courthouse, during which time Union forces moved to his front and cut off his line of retreat. The three distinct battles fought on April 6, 1865, in the valley of Sayler's Creek form the last major engagement between the armies commanded by Lee and Ulysses S. Grant and led to the surrender at Appomattox Courthouse.

Scotchtown

Location: Ashland, Hanover County

Relevant issues: Colonial America, political history, Revolutionary War

Web site: www.apva.org/apva/scotchtwn.html

Statement of significance: From 1771 to 1777, this large one-and-a-half-story frame house was the residence of Patrick Henry (1736-1799), the Revolutionary leader and fiery orator. During these years, Henry made his most-famous speeches and served in the Continental Congress and in his first term as governor of Virginia.

Semple House

Location: Williamsburg, Williamsburg County

Relevant issues: Political history

Statement of significance: Constructed about 1770, this structure is believed to have been designed by Thomas Jefferson. It is an example of a Roman country house style adapted for a frame townhouse. John Tyler (1790-1862), tenth president of the United States (1841-1845), resided here while attending grammar school and the College of William and Mary (1802-1807); he was related to the Semples.

Spence's Point

Location: Westmoreland, Westmoreland County

Relevant issues: Literary history

Statement of significance: For much of his life, this property was associated with John Dos Passos (1896-1970), acclaimed as one of the major and most influential of modern American writers. His early works, based on his experiences in World War I, stripped war and military life of the romanticism with which they were traditionally viewed; in the *U.S.A.* trilogy (1930-1936), Dos Passos invented a new form of storytelling in which social history itself became the dynamic drive of the work, instead of merely its framework.

University of Virginia Historic District

Location: Charlottesville, Charlottesville County

Relevant issues: Art and architecture, education

Statement of significance: The district includes Thomas Jefferson's original "academical village" (constructed 1817-1827) with its classrooms and quarters, as well as the Rotunda—the focal point of Jefferson's design—and several buildings added by Stanford White. Jefferson's brilliant arrangement of the University buildings in the European neoclassical tradition of the period produced a collegiate complex that is among the most beautiful in the world.

Virginia Military Institute Historic District

Location: Lexington, Lexington County

Relevant issues: Education, military history

Statement of significance: The first state-supported military college, VMI was formally organized in 1839. Often called the "West Point of the

South," the institute has provided leaders for the Confederate Army, including "Stonewall" Jackson, and for the two world wars, including George S. Marshall.

Waterford Historic District

Location: Waterford, Loudoun County

Relevant issues: Colonial America, European settlement

Statement of significance: The oldest settlement in Loudoun County, Waterford was established by Pennsylvania Quakers about 1730. By 1840, Waterford had about three hundred settlers, housed in Georgian brick-and-frame row houses. It is a rare example of a little-altered early Anglo-American village with an almost pristine setting.

Wilson Birthplace

Location: Staunton, Staunton County

Relevant issues: Political history

Statement of significance: Woodrow Wilson (1856-1924), educator, author, and the twenty-eighth president of the United States (1913-1921), was born in this two-story Greek revival brick house late in 1856. The structure was then the parsonage of Staunton's First Presbyterian Church, where Wilson's father was serving as pastor. The next year, the family left for Augusta, Georgia, where the Reverend Wilson had accepted a new pulpit.

Woodlawn

Location: Richmond Highway, Alexandria, Fairfax County

Relevant issues: Art and architecture, cultural history

Statement of significance: Woodlawn was built between 1800 and 1805 for Major Lawrence Lewis and his wife Eleanor (Nelly) Parke Custis, on land that George Washington, his uncle and her stepgrandfather, willed them. The brick house, designed by Dr. William Thornton, architect of the U.S. Capitol, integrates Georgian and Federal features in its design. Woodlawn is also a pivotal monument in the evolution of historic preservation in America. In 1948, a group was formed specifically to save it and soon served as a prime example of the purposes for which the National Trust for Historic Preservation was created. In 1951, the trust accepted Woodlawn as its flagship property. The mansion is open to the public.

Washington

The State Capitol Building in Olympia. (State of Washington Tourism Division)

History of Washington

Like its southern neighbor Oregon, Washington is divided into two distinct geographical parts, a wet, forested western portion and a semiarid east. Washington's forests made it one of the nation's great timber producers, while its dry eastern portion requires extensive irrigation for agricultural productivity. While it shares geographical features with Oregon and Idaho, making up the Pacific Northwest region, Washington's social and political complexion has its own unique qualities. On reason is that unlike Oregon, Washington was not first settled by farmers.

After the earliest period, in which its white inhabitants were predominantly trappers, Washington's early history was dominated by extraction industries, such as gold mining and logging. Later, toward the end of the nineteenth century, large industry brought with it conflict between big business and big labor, which affected the state's social character. Later still, after the middle of the twentieth century, industries that prospered in the state on account of the Cold War left their own indelible imprint on the state's economy, society, and politics.

Early History

The early history of the area that became Washington was dominated by the struggle for control of the region by Great Britain, Russia, and Spain, followed by the United States. By 1775 Spain was sending expeditions up the Pacific coast, mainly to secure a buffer zone between Russian and British claims and its Mexican territory. Russia asserted claims far distant from Alaska, sending landing parties as far south as California. While Spain and Russia dropped out of the competition by the end of the eighteenth century, Britain opposed its former colonies, now a scrappy young republic. The Americans, for their part, strengthened their claims to the region when, after the 1803 Louisiana Purchase, the expedition of Meriwether Lewis and William Clark arrived and wintered by the Pacific at Fort Clatsop.

In 1792, the Americans sent Captain Robert Gray to the northwest, where he discovered the Co-lumbia River and named it after his ship. In the same year, Britain sent an expedition led by George Vancouver to the region. Members of the expedition of British Captain James Cook had already discovered the value of sea otter pelts bought from American Indians and sold profitably in China. By 1818 the two nations agreed to share the region. The Pacific North West Company dominated the fur trade until 1821, when it merged with Hudson's Bay Company, which remained the most influential non-Indian power in the area until 1846.

Native American peoples occupied a key position in the fur trade, especially in the beginning, before white trappers appeared in any numbers and before Indian populations became depleted. Native Americans provided sea otter pelts and other furs to white traders in exchange for manufactured goods, especially those made of metal, unknown in Indian cultures. These included tools that added to the Native Americans' ability to produce goods for themselves. Indians benefited from material goods, but their contact with whites proved catastrophic, since they contracted smallpox and other diseases that decimated their numbers. It has been estimated that the population of Native American peoples on the northwest coast declined during the century following 1774 from about 200,000 to about 40,000, or some 80 percent. Moreover, by the 1820's sea otters were nearly extinct.

By 1810 a second phase of the fur trade began, increasingly dominated by Europeans and centered on beaver and similar mammals. This trade was focused on inland areas and required European trading companies to establish forts and interior avenues of transportation. News of the area finally took hold of the American imagination in the East and Midwest after the success of fur-trading companies illustrated the possibilities of internal development. The stage was set for the arrival of immigrants in large numbers.

The Anglo-American condominium begun in 1818 lasted into the 1840's. By then, however, the U.S. westward expansion, with its drive to possess the continent as its manifest destiny, brought hun-

dreds, then thousands of American settlers to the region. In the early 1840's, Hudson's Bay Company, which was interested in commerce, not settlement, moved its base of operations northward, focusing on the area that became British Columbia. Although American nationalists sought lands north of the fifty-fourth parallel, the United States, negotiating in 1846 with far-stronger Britain, settled for the forty-eighth parallel as a boundary. Two years later Oregon Territory, including what became Washington, was established.

From Territory to State

After the establishment of Oregon Territory in 1848, the population north of the Columbia River grew rapidly. Accordingly, in 1853 the Territory of Washington was formed. A decade later, gold strikes in the eastern portion led to its breaking off to become separately organized as Idaho Territory. Except for adjustments in Puget Sound's San Juan Islands, Washington's boundaries were now fixed. Sentiment for statehood strengthened during the Civil War, and in 1867 the territorial legislature urged Congress to admit a new state. Not until 1889, however, did Congress pass the required legislation for statehood, admitting Washington into the Union.

As it was growing toward statehood, Washington experienced an ugly social and moral pathology, in the form of anti-Chinese racism. When economic downturns arrived, labor unions made scapegoats of Chinese laborers, who arrived after 1840. Chinese were reviled for driving down wages, and serious incidents occurred, especially in the mid-1880's in Seattle, Tacoma, and other cities, when Chinese workers were driven out. As a result, the Chinese population in the Pacific Northwest dropped sharply.

If few Chinese could resist ill treatment, the same was not always true of the state's Native American peoples. Prophetic religious visions encouraging American Indians to live by their old customs were one form of resistance. Suing in the courts was another. Such attempts at peaceful resolution of disputes followed the armed conflicts that occurred, for example, between 1855 and 1859, when the influx of miners after gold strikes alarmed the Indians. Relations between settlers and Indians were complicated by the fact that there were different points of view not only among federal government, settlers, and the Indians, but within each group as well. Tribes or subtribal bands sometimes fought among themselves over policy toward white society.

Policy toward the American Indians reflected both idealism and self-interest, resulting in the reservation system. Reservations were designed both to separate tribal societies from the settlers and to "civilize" them, that is, to adapt them to the European ways, "detribalizing" and assimilating them to American society. Native American children were taken to boarding schools for this purpose. The treaty system that reflected this policy was unreliable, however, partly because the U.S. Senate frequently rejected treaties. Moreover, not all tribal members agreed with the treaties as negotiated, and discontent and confusion sometimes followed their signing. Treaties signed in 1854 and 1855 failed to prevent the conflicts of 1855-1858. Both wars and considerable crime broke out between American Indians and settlers between 1850 and 1880. Efforts were made to reform the reservation system and assimilation policy, to little effect. After the 1930's, however, the goal of assimilation was reconsidered. By the 1970's, Native Americans were having considerable success defending tribal rights in the courts.

The 1880's to 1945

Washington inaugurated its statehood with a government that reflected its past as a frontier society. As the frontier distrusted political power, especially executive power, so did the state. Accordingly, Washington's constitution called for a plural executive, with a number of elected offices, rather than a single, all-powerful governor. These included, besides governor and lieutenant governor, a secretary of state (chief elections officer), an attorney general, a treasurer, an auditor, and others.

The state's politics in the next decades followed national trends as well as homegrown movements. Populism and radical parties and sects arose between 1880 and 1920, making a lasting impact. Reformers were influential because the state saw itself in a formative, malleable stage of collective life. The state's constitution showed strong Populist influence, distrusting big business by banning gifts or loans of public money and credit to private enterprise. The constitution's bill of rights protected individual rights even more than the federal Bill of Rights. Not surprisingly, the People's Party candidate for president received 22 percent of the vote in 1892.

The Progressive movement also deeply affected Washington, as it did its southern neighbor. Around the turn of the century, like Oregon, Washington voters gained the powers of initiative, referendum, and, later, recall elections. Municipal ownership of utilities and urban planning became public policy, and nature conservation, a recurring feature of the state's politics, appeared. In addition, radicalism and utopianism had some influence; the Industrial Workers of the World (IWW), a Marxist party founded in Chicago in 1905, was active on the political fringes prior to and just after World War I.

By the Depression years of the 1930's, radicalism was a spent force, and, as elsewhere in the nation, federal policies attempted to come to the state's rescue. In building dams and in other projects, federal spending became an essential element in the state's economy, prefiguring what was to come. The most important single project was the Grand Coulee Dam, but other dams were constructed. In addition, the Civilian Conservation Corps (CCC) was active in parks and forests; and there existed public housing and irrigation projects, among other federal programs.

Power generated from the Columbia River Basin was essential for the defense industries that sprang up during the war years. Among them were atomic development works at Hanford, where the plutonium for the nation's first atomic weapons was produced. Later it was discovered that the Hanford nuclear reactor also produced much radioactive waste that endangered both people and the natural world.

Postwar Economy and Politics

After World War II, many thought the state's economy would suffer badly from the nation's military stand down, but they were mistaken. The advent of the Cold War brought further defense spending to Washington, including additional development of the Hanford atomic facility. By the 1950's the Boeing Company near Seattle was receiving large contracts from the Pentagon. Federal spending also helped the state with the continuing development of hydroelectric power and crop-irrigation facilities through dam construction. Thanks to voter loyalty, the state was gaining influence in Washington, D.C., through the reelection of its senators Warren Magnuson and Henry "Scoop" Jackson, sometimes called "the senator from Boeing." Later, Representative Tom Foley became Speaker of the U.S. House of Representatives.

To celebrate the success of the state and its principal city, a world's fair was held in Seattle in 1962. Its futuristic free-standing tower, known as a Space Needle, became an icon of forward-thrusting technological prowess and self-confidence and was widely imitated around the world. As might be expected, the influence of the Boeing Company on the exposition was widely noticeable.

Later decades, however, saw a different side of Washington's success, as environmentally conscious activists sought to counterbalance the influence of timber and other industries. This was especially evident as the state's nuclear-power board defaulted on bonds used to build nuclear reactors, all but one of which were never completed. This was also evident as early as 1974, when Spokane opened Expo'74, the world's first environmental world's fair. By the end of the century, Washington was economically thriving on a balance of "high-tech" industries such as Boeing and Microsoft, tourism, and agriculture. Although anti-Asian sentiment was long outdated, civil rights issues for African Americans remained. Environmental problems, such as the decline of salmon, a state icon, also remained, and there was marked resistance to further economic development that would endanger the state's natural environment.

—*R. Baird Shuman*

Mount St. Helens

Date: At least eighty thousand years old; erupted on May 18, 1980

Relevant issues: American Indian history, disasters and tragedies, science and technology

Significance: Mount St. Helens exploded violently in May, 1980, causing the worst volcanic disaster in the recorded history of the United States. The cataclysmic eruption and related events rank among the most significant geologic events in the United States during the twentieth century.

Location: About fifty miles northeast of Portland, Oregon, and about sixty-one miles southeast of Olympia, Washington

Site Office:
Mount St. Helens Visitors' Center
3029 Spirit Lake Highway
Castle Rock, WA 98611
ph.: (360) 274-2100
fax: (360) 274-2101
Web site: www.fs.fed.us/gpnf/mshnvm/attractions/west.html

The 1980 eruption of Mount St. Helens ensures its place in American history. It was the first volcanic eruption to occur in the continental United States outside Alaska since 1921, when Lassen Peak in northern California erupted. The processes, effects, and products of the chain of events in 1980 were the most intensively studied and photographed of any explosive volcanic eruption in the history of the world. Mount St. Helens has provided an unprecedented opportunity for scientific research on the dynamics and potential hazards associated with an active composite volcano.

Historical Background

Based upon the age of windblown deposits associated with Mount St. Helens, it is estimated that volcanic eruptions from the mountain may have occurred as long as eighty thousand years ago. The oldest rocks found at Mount St. Helens are between forty thousand and fifty thousand years old. The mountain was probably first discovered by Native American people who crossed the Bering Strait land bridge and colonized part of the North American continent. Northwest Indians referred to the mountain as *La-wa-la-clough*, meaning "smoking mountain," or *Tah-one-lay-clak*, which means "fire mountain."

According to Indian legend, the mountain was once a beautiful maiden known as Loo-wit. When Wy'east and Klickitat, two brave sons of the Great Spirit Sahale, fell in love with Loo-wit, she had difficulty choosing between them. The two braves fought over her, burying villages and forests as they threw fiery rocks at each other, causing many earthquakes. Sahale became furious, smote the three lovers, and erected a mighty mountain from which all three fell. Because Loo-wit was so beautiful, the mountain (Mount St. Helens) dedicated to her was a symmetrical cone of dazzling white. Wy'east (Mount Hood) lifts his head in pride, but Klickitat (Mount Adams) weeps to see the beautiful maiden wrapped in snow, so he bends his head as he gazes on Mount St. Helens.

The name "Mount St. Helens" was given to the mountain by George Vancouver while he supervised the surveying of the northern Pacific coast between 1792 and 1794. He named it on October 20, 1792, in honor of British diplomat Alleyne Fitzherbert (1753-1839), whose title was Baron St. Helens. Meriwether Lewis and William Clark sighted the mountain from the Columbia River between 1805 and 1806. Although they reported no evidence of eruptive volcanism, reports from the Sanpoil Indians of eastern Washington indicated that a major eruption had occurred around 1800.

Meredith Gairdner, a physician at Fort Vancouver, wrote about darkness and haze during possible eruptive activity at Mount St. Helens in 1831 and in 1835. On November 22, 1842, the Reverend Josiah Parrish reported an eruption of Mount St. Helens, which was corroborated by missionaries who reported ash fallout at The Dalles, Oregon, forty-five miles southeast of the volcano. Based on contemporary sketches and paintings by Paul Kane, as well as a number of other reported observations, scientists think that eruptive activity at Mount St. Helens occurred intermittently between 1847 and 1857. Although minor steam explosions and large rock falls were reported in 1898, 1903, and 1921, Mount St. Helens gave little or no evidence of being a volcanic hazard for over a century after 1857.

Geographic and Geologic Setting
Surrounded by the Gifford Pinchot National Forest, Mount St. Helens is part of the Cascade Range, which extends from British Columbia, Canada, to Lassen Peak in northern California, a distance of about 930 miles. Being the youngest of the fifteen major volcanoes in the Cascade Range, it consists of several coalesced dacite domes, lava, and interlayered ash deposits. Volcanic cones with this internal structure are known as composite cones or stratovolcanoes. Mount St. Helens is located about thirty-five miles almost due west of Mount Adams, which is in the eastern part of the Cascade Range, about fifty miles from Mount Rainier, the giant of Cascade volcanoes, and about sixty miles southeast of Mount Hood.

Mount St. Helens was generated along an ocean-continent subduction boundary, where the Juan de Fuca Plate is subducting under the North American Plate. The subduction zone has existed for approximately 20 million years. In the 1990's, the Juan de Fuca Plate was moving east-southeast at about 1.2 inches per year, while the North American Plate was moving to the southwest at 0.91 inches per year. The pre-1980 landscape of Mount St. Helens was dominated by dense coniferous forests, clear streams, and lakes. The elevation at the summit was 9,677 feet. Following the 1980 eruption, the elevation at the summit was reduced to 8,363 feet. During the 1980's and 1990's, more than a dozen extrusions of thick, pasty lava built a mound-shaped lava dome in the mountain's crater. This dome is 3,609 feet in diameter and 886 feet tall.

The 1980 Eruption
Including the 1980 eruption, Mount St. Helens has erupted at least forty-five times. Four major eruptions, each with at least 0.27 cubic miles of resulting deposits, are known to have occurred. The largest was probably the one in 1480, which was about five times larger than the 1980 eruption. After lying dormant for about 123 years, Mount St. Helens began to stir with a series of small earthquakes initiated on March 20, 1980. After a week of increasing local seismicity, the mountain began to eject steam and ash. In April, the U.S. Forest Service and Washington state officials closed all areas near the mountain, which ultimately saved thousands of lives.

During April and May, numerous geologists gathered at Mount St. Helens to conduct a wide variety of studies. By the end of April, a large bulge on the northern flank of the mountain had developed, 1.24 miles long and 0.62 miles wide, expanding horizontally at a steady rate of 4.9 feet per day. Geologists carefully monitored the bulge, seismic activity, and gas emissions, hoping to detect any significant change that would indicate an imminent large eruption. However, no anomalous activity occurred, and seismic activity actually decreased. On May 15, thirty-nine earthquakes were reported, but only eighteen on May 17.

On Sunday morning, May 18, the mountain was silent. Only minor plumes of steam rose from two vents. At 8:32 A.M., a complex earthquake of 5.1 on the Richter scale shook the volcano, removing the confining pressure and causing a huge, 0.64-cubic-mile landslide that removed the bulge and the upper 1,312 feet of the volcano, leaving a 1,969-

foot-deep crater with a width of 1.25 miles. The landslide quickly developed into a debris avalanche that sped at 68 to 87 miles per hour down the North Fork Toutle River. In addition, melting snow and ice from the mountain produced flooding and aided the movement of debris.

Parts of the avalanche entered Spirit Lake, eight miles from the summit, blocking the lake's outlet, causing the water level to rise 197 feet. The debris buried Toutle Valley to a depth of nearly 165 feet. It swallowed up 200 homes and cabins, as well as cars, logging trucks, and timber, carrying them downstream, destroying bridges, highways, and other construction. More than 186 miles of highways and roads and 15 miles of railways were destroyed or extensively damaged. Trees amounting to more than 4 billion board feet of salable timber were damaged or destroyed. A thick layer of volcanic ash deposited over a wide area destroyed many agricultural crops, including wheat, apples, potatoes, and alfalfa. All birds, most small mammals, many big game animals, and millions of salmon and other fish in the area perished.

When the top of the mountain was blown away at about 8:45 A.M., some observers described the noise and shaking as similar to being next to ground zero in an atomic bomb blast. Visibility dropped to zero as the thick volcanic dust hid the sun, and day became night as far away as 500 miles. Over 250 miles away, Spokane, Washington, was in complete darkness at 3:00 P.M. Bolts of lightning flashed from Mount St. Helens, sparking numer-

Mount St. Helens after the 1980 eruption. (PhotoDisc)

ous forest fires. The air was so full of smoke and pumice that people could not survive outside. The volcanic ash and gases irritated skin, eyes, and lungs, making breathing extremely difficult. As the eruption spread horizontally outward across the collapsing slope, rock, ash, and suffocating gases caused numerous injuries and the deaths of fifty-seven people. Lighting fires was impossible in the thick ash fall and volcanic gases. The ash cloud rose to an altitude of eleven miles, fanned out eastward, then moved in a broad arc across the United States, completely circling the earth by June 5. Many earthquakes and aftershocks accompanied the eruption, and the volcanic activity completely changed the surrounding landscape for miles. The total damage from the eruption rose to over $1.1 billion. The closing of the eruption episode was marked by the slow rise of magma through the central chamber to form a new lava dome in the summit crater.

Since the 1980 eruption, there have been smaller explosive eruptions. They have been smaller in terms of lesser amounts of magma involved, as well as less mountain in which to allow the pressure to accumulate. Consequently, eruptions can occur after smaller amounts of gas have exsolved.

Places to Visit
Despite the troubled economy due to unemployment, and reduced tourism caused by the 1980 eruption, thousands of visitors began flocking back to the area to marvel at the effects of the eruption. On August 27, 1982, President Ronald Reagan signed a law that set aside 110,000 acres around the volcano as the Mount St. Helens National Volcanic Monument, the nation's first such monument, managed by the United States Forest Service. Many trails, view points, information stations, campgrounds, and picnic areas have been established to accommodate the increasing number of visitors each year. Since the summer of 1983, visitors have been able to drive to Windy Ridge, only four miles northeast of the crater. This spectacular vantage point, which overlooks Spirit Lake, offers a firsthand view of the awesome evidence of the volcano's destruction, as well as a picture of the remarkable, gradual recovery of the land as revegetation proceeds and wildlife returns.

Since 1986, mountain climbing to the summit of the volcano has been allowed. Winter exploration

of the crater is a very difficult but rewarding adventure. The majestic Mount St. Helens Visitors' Center was completed in December, 1986, at Silver Lake, about thirty miles west of Mount St. Helens and a few miles east of Highway 5. It is open between May 1 and December 6 of each year. During the mid-1990's, an interpretation complex about five miles northwest of Mount St. Helens was opened in the Coldwater Lake area, from which visitors can see inside the crater and its dome.

Although Mount St. Helens has not erupted for many years, its lava dome is still warm and steaming. Volcanologists who study Mount St. Helens believe that it is likely to erupt again within a few decades or a century at most. The volcanic activity is carefully monitored in an effort to provide ample warning and mitigate the effects of any future eruption.

—Alvin K. Benson

For Further Information:

Aylesworth, Thomas G., and Virginia L. Aylesworth. *The Mount St. Helens Disaster.* New York: Franklin Watts, 1983. Describes the sequence of events associated with the 1980 Mount St. Helens eruption.

Decker, R. W., and Barbara Decker. *Volcanoes.* New York: W. H. Freeman, 1989. An information-packed introduction to the study of volcanoes, written in an easy-to-read style.

Goldner, Kathryn A., and Carole G. Vogel. *Why Mount St. Helens Blew Its Top.* Minneapolis: Dillion Press, 1981. Explores basic scientific insights into what caused the 1980 Mount St. Helens eruption.

Hamblin, W. Kenneth, and Eric H. Christiansen. *Earth's Dynamic Systems.* 8th ed. Upper Saddle River, N.J.: Prentice Hall, 1998. Excellent overview of how volcanoes work, including a summary of the major events that transpired during the 1980 Mount St. Helens eruption.

Harris, S. L. *Fire Mountains of the West.* Missoula, Mont.: Mountain Press, 1988. A classic summary of the volcanoes of the Cascade Range, including Mount St. Helens.

Montgomery, Carla. *Fundamentals of Geology.* 3d ed. Dubuque, Iowa: Wm. C. Brown, 1997. Includes a fundamental description of volcanoes and scientific aspects of the 1980 Mount St. Helens eruption.

Perry, Ronald W., and Michael K. Lindell. *Living*

with Mt. St. Helens. Pullman: Washington State University Press, 1990. Describes the hazards associated with living near Mount St. Helens and how humans can adjust to and live with such hazards.

Whitman Mission

Date: 1836-1847

Relevant issues: American Indian history, disasters and tragedies, European settlement, religion

Significance: Whitman Mission was an early Presbyterian mission to the Cayuse Indians and an important stop on the Oregon Trail. It is a National Historic Site that serves as a memorial to Dr. Marcus and Narcissa Prentiss Whitman, who, along with nine others, were killed by members of the Cayuse tribe on November 29, 1847.

Location: Seven miles west of Walla Walla, six miles north of the Oregon border, and about twenty miles west of Umatilla National Forest

Site Office:

Whitman Mission National Historic Site
328 Whitman Mission Road
Walla Walla, WA 99362-9699
ph.: (509) 522-6360
fax: (509) 522-6355
Web site: www.nps.gov/whmi/

Marcus Whitman was born in Rushville, New York, in 1802. In his teens, he attended a Congregational school taught by Moses Hallock in Plainfield, Massachusetts. He had decided by 1820 to become a minister, but it was not until 1834 that he was able to realize this ambition. Between 1820 and 1824, he worked in his stepfather's tannery and served a medical apprenticeship to a Rushville doctor, enrolling in the College of Physicians and Surgeons in Fairfield, New York, in 1825. Whitman received an M.D. in 1831 and worked as a physician in Wheeler, New York, until 1835. In 1834, a Rushville, New York, clergy member recommended him to the American Board of Commissioners of Foreign Missions (ABCFM), a combined agency of the Presbyterian and Congregational churches, located in Boston.

From this agency Whitman received an appointment in January, 1835, as a missionary doctor to the native population of the American West. Before setting forth with fellow missionary Samuel Parker, he became engaged to Narcissa Prentiss of Angelica, New York. In 1836 he established a mission to the Cayuse near Fort Walla Walla in the Oregon Territory and returned to New York to marry Narcissa. On their trip west to the mission, they met Henry and Eliza Spalding, who were planning to set up a mission among the Osages, but the Whitmans persuaded them to continue to Oregon with them. Narcissa Whitman was the first white woman to cross the Blue Mountains, and the cart in which she rode was the first wheeled vehicle to enter the Oregon territory from the East.

The Establishment of the Missions

The Whitmans and Spaldings were responding to what the missionary Protestant sects of the 1830's regarded as a call for spiritual help from Native Americans living in the West. In March, 1833, the *Christian Advocate* published a letter attributed to a group of Flathead Indians from Clark's Fork of the Columbia River, requesting "The White Man's Book of Heaven." This letter, reportedly brought to the home of General William Clark in St. Louis in the fall of 1832, was widely reprinted and discussed in the eastern Protestant press. Missionaries were sent to the Indian tribes in the Columbia Plateau by both Catholics and Protestants. The latter counted among the goals of Christianization the establishment of Indian agricultural communities centered on the missions. The missions of both the Whitmans among the Cayuse at Waiilatpu near Walla Walla and the Spaldings at Lapwai, Idaho, were of this type. At Waiilatpu ("place of the rye grass") the mission included medical services, a school, and a gristmill as well as a church.

The Oregon Trail and the Settlement of the Pacific Northwest

In February, 1842, Marcus Whitman was informed that the ABCFM, disappointed by the small number of Indian converts, was planning to close the missions at Waiilatpu and Lapwai. The following fall, he set out for Boston with two objectives: to change the ABCFM's mind in favor of continuing both missions and to bring back with him a group of new immigrants whose presence would help to establish a permanent Caucasian settlement in the Oregon Territory. A few later historians, including

A monument to those killed at the Whitman Mission in 1847. (Whitman Mission National Historic Site)

along the Columbia River Valley. They made it clear to the federal government that it was possible to settle the inland Northwest, and to maintain trade and communications with it. During the 1840's, the Whitman Mission became an important stop on the Oregon Trail, with increasing numbers of settlers coming across the mountains by wagon to look for farmland in the Territory. The Cayuse and other Columbia Plateau tribes looked on this trend with considerable disquiet, especially when white colonists brought diseases such as measles, which decimated the tribes. Dr. Whitman's medical efforts helped many whites recover from the measles epidemic, but he was unable to alleviate the suffering of the Indians, to whom this was a new disease. The Cayuse and some of their neighbors began to regard the mission as a source of trouble and danger.

The Whitman Tragedy

On November 29 and 30, 1847, Cayuse tribe members led by Tiloukaikt attacked and killed thirteen persons at the Whitman Mission: Marcus and Narcissa Whitman, Andrew Rogers, Jr., Lucien Saunders, Nathan Kimball, Crockett A. Bewley, Isaac Gilliland, John Sager, Francis Sager, Jacob Hoffman, Amos Sales, Peter D. Hall, and a man named Marsh. All are buried in the Great Grave at the Whitman Mission National Historic Site, on the spot where the bodies were interred by the Oregon Volunteers militia in 1848. The Indians alleged to have been involved in the assault were tried in Oregon City in 1850. Many of the witnesses were survivors of the 1847 tragedy. Whitman Seminary, now Marcus Whitman College in Walla Walla, was originally built by fellow missionary Cushing Eells as a memorial to the Whit-

Oliver Nixon, created a century-long controversy by arguing that this action on Whitman's part prevented the federal government from ceding the Oregon Territory to Great Britain, and that this too was one of Whitman's objectives.

It is clear, at any rate, that the settlers who returned with Whitman in the spring of 1843 were significant as a vanguard for additional settlement

mans on the site of the mission. There is a statue of Marcus Whitman in the Statuary Hall of the Capitol Building in Washington, D.C.

—*Rachel Maines*

For Further Information:

Bell, James Christy. *Opening a Highway to the Pacific, 1838-1846.* New York: Columbia University Press, 1921. Describes the opening of the Oregon Trail and the role of the missionary colonists in European settlement of the Pacific Northwest.

Drury, Clifford M. *Marcus and Narcissa Whitman and the Opening of Old Oregon.* Glendale, Calif.: Arthur H. Clark, 1973. Two-volume illustrated work with detailed discussions of the relations between Christian missionaries and the Indian tribes in Old Oregon.

Lansing, Ronald B. *Juggernaut: the Whitman Massacre Trial, 1850.* Pasadena, Calif.: Ninth Judicial Circuit Historical Society, 1993. Account of the trial of the Cayuse tribe members accused of the Whitman killings.

Nixon, Oliver W. *How Marcus Whitman Saved Oregon: A True Romance of Patriotic Heroism, Christian Devotion, and Final Martyrdom.* Chicago: Star, 1895. Controversial tribute to Whitman's memory which argues that the missionary was responsible for saving what is now the Pacific Northwest for the United States.

Whitman, Narcissa Prentiss. *Where Wagons Could Go: Narcissa Whitman and Eliza Spalding.* Lincoln: University of Nebraska Press, 1997. Letters and journal accounts edited, and with an introduction by, Clifford Merrill Drury.

Other Historic Sites

Adventuress

Location: Seattle, King County

Relevant issues: Naval history

Statement of significance: A schooner yacht and pilot boat, *Adventuress* is a significant example of the "fisherman profile" design of the yachts of Bowdoin B. Crowninshield, a noted early twentieth century American naval architect whose work was influential in the development of American yachts and fishing schooners. Built (1913) for the purpose of private Arctic exploration and hunting, *Adventuress* was acquired by the San Francisco Bar Pilots in 1914 and worked until 1952 as a pilot boat, guiding maritime traffic across the treacherous San Francisco Bar into the internationally important and busy port of San Francisco.

American and English Camps, San Juan Island

Location: Friday Harbor vicinity, San Juan County

Relevant issues: Political history, western expansion

Statement of significance: These sites are associated with the conflict about the water boundary between Vancouver Island, British Columbia, and the U.S. Oregon Territory, including the "Pig War of 1859," when hostilities almost began between Americans and the British. The 1871 Treaty of Washington provided for a peaceful settlement of this dispute.

Arthur Foss

Location: Kirkland, King County

Relevant issues: Business and industry, military history, naval history, World War II

Statement of significance: Built in 1889, *Arthur Foss* is the only known wooden-hulled nineteenth century tugboat left afloat and in operating condition in the United States. It towed lumber and grain-laden square-rigged ships across the treacherous Columbia River and hence was a key participant in the Pacific coast lumber trade and the international grain trade. While under charter to the U.S. Navy, *Arthur Foss* was the last vessel to escape Wake Island successfully before Imperial Japanese forces attacked and captured that Pacific outpost in 1942.

Chinook Point

Location: Chinook, Pacific County

Relevant issues: Western expansion

Statement of significance: Captain Robert Gray's May, 1792, discovery of the Columbia River at Chinook Point gave the United States a strong claim to the Pacific Northwest, a claim which was long disputed by Great Britain.

Fireboat No. 1

Location: Tacoma, Pierce County
Relevant issues: Naval history
Statement of significance: Fireboat No. 1, built (1929) and operated only on Puget Sound, is representative of most fireboats built prior to World War II throughout the United States. One of ten fireboats greater than fifty years of age left in the United States and one of the few remaining 1920's fireboats, it is the least modified, has not undergone extensive modernization, and is well preserved. Today it is a monument and museum.

Fort Nisqually Granary

Location: Tacoma, Pierce County
Relevant issues: Western expansion
Statement of significance: The fort was the first permanent Anglo-American settlement on Puget Sound, serving as a communications and supply center for other trading posts. The fort's one-story granary, built in 1843 of log construction, and the Factor's House are the only surviving original examples of Hudson's Bay Company buildings still standing in the United States. Moved in 1934 from their original site to Point Defiance Park, today both the granary and Factor's House are restored and open to the public.

Lightship No. 83 "Relief"

Location: Kirkland, King County
Relevant issues: Naval history
Statement of significance: Known by its last official designation, *Relief,* No. 83 was built (1905) to serve as one of the first four lightships on the Pacific coast. It served to guide mariners to three major ports—Eureka on Humboldt Bay, San Francisco, and Seattle. No. 83 and its sister are the earliest surviving examples of American lightships.

Marmes Rockshelter

Location: Lyons Ferry, Franklin County
Relevant issues: American Indian history

Statement of significance: This is the most outstanding archaeological site yet discovered in the Northwest. Excavations at the site have revealed the earliest burials in the Pacific Northwest (c. 5500-4500 B.C.E.) and possibly the oldest human remains yet encountered in the Western Hemisphere (c. 11,000-9,000 B.C.E.). The eight strata at the site all contain cultural materials.

Paradise Inn

Location: Mount Rainier National Park, Pierce County
Relevant issues: Art and architecture, cultural history
Statement of significance: A rustic hotel with furnishings in the lobby that have a handcrafted artistry and Gothic feeling reminiscent of northern European woodwork. Built in 1916 on a smaller scale than the Old Faithful Inn in Yellowstone National Park, it was part of one of the earliest ski resorts in the United States.

Puget Sound Naval Shipyard

Location: Bremerton, Kitsap County
Relevant issues: Military history, naval history, World War II
Statement of significance: Puget Sound Naval Shipyard was the principal repair establishment for the U.S. Navy's battle-damaged battleships and aircraft carriers, as well as smaller warships, of the Pacific Fleet during World War II. Five of the eight battleships bombed at Pearl Harbor on December 7, 1941, were repaired at the shipyard and returned to duty. During the war, the shipyard repaired twenty-six battleships (some more than once), eighteen aircraft carriers, thirteen cruisers, and seventy-nine destroyers; in addition, fifty ships were built or fitted out at the yard. More than thirty thousand workers built, fitted out, repaired, overhauled, or modernized nearly four hundred fighting ships here between 1941 and 1945.

Seattle Electric Company Georgetown Steam Plant

Location: Seattle, King County
Relevant issues: Business and industry, science and technology
Statement of significance: Erected from 1906 to 1908, this reinforced concrete building houses the last

operational examples of the Curtis vertical steam turbogenerator, the first type of large-scale steam turbine developed. This new technology established General Electric as a leader in the manufacture of steam turbines. The plant also exemplifies facets of the history of urban power use and development.

West Virginia

The Wheeling Suspension Bridge. (West Virginia Division of Tourism/Steve Shaluta, Jr.)

History of West Virginia

More than most states, West Virginia has been shaped in its development and its history by its geography. Although part of Virginia for almost a century, it was separated from the coastal and central portions of Virginia by the Allegheny Mountains and was thus removed from the sources of political and economic power and influence. Lying completely within the Appalachian Highlands, the state is mountainous and rugged, and although it is blessed with abundant mineral resources such as coal and natural gas, it has little land available for large-scale agriculture. Travel and transportation have often been extremely difficult and even hazardous, fostering a sense of isolation in the state, which in turn fostered a high degree of independence expressed in the state's official motto, *Montani semper liberi* (mountaineers are always free).

Early Times

Although Native Americans entered the West Virginia area as early as fifteen thousand years ago, most of them regarded the territory as unfit for permanent settlement and good only as hunting and battle grounds. Later, when the Cherokee, Iroquois, and Shawnee arrived to establish villages, they located them near the major rivers; instead of developing agriculture, these tribes relied on hunting. The tradition of tribal warfare continued, including fights over the springs found throughout the area that were a source of valuable salt, used in food preservation and for trading.

Colonization

The original grant of Virginia by King James I of England included what is now West Virginia. The colonists first explored the western portion of their territory in 1669, when an expedition under John Lederer reached the Blue Ridge Mountains. Thomas Batts and Robert Fallam followed in 1671, striking along the New River and claiming the Ohio Valley for England, a claim that was disputed both by France and by Native Americans. Morgan Morgan, a Welshman, is traditionally considered the first European settler in the West Virginia area, having established Bunker Hill in 1726. Morgan was followed by other colonists, including Germans from Pennsylvania and Scotch-Irish from northern Ireland. Although King George III prohibited American colonists from crossing the Allegheny Mountains, this ban was largely ignored, and during the period from 1722 through 1740, the Iroquois and Cherokee ceded their lands to advancing settlers.

The distance and physical barriers between the western settlements and the rest of Virginia began to cause difficulties. In addition, the planters and traders along the Virginia tidewater and eastern rivers exerted a monopoly on the state's political

and economic life. Settlers beyond the Allegheny Mountains grew restive, and by 1776, when the American colonies were ready to break with Great Britain, western Virginia was asking the Continental Congress for independence from Virginia. The necessities of the ensuing American Revolution put this request on hold, however. As part of Virginia, it joined the Union in 1788.

Independence and Civil War

Following American independence, political and economic power in Virginia shifted more than ever toward the tidewater and eastern section, where slaveholders were dominant. The west was unsuccessful in its requests for fairness during the revision of the state constitution in 1829, and it continued to suffer from neglect by the Richmond state government. Poor roads, inadequate schools, higher taxes, neglected economic development, and lack of representation in the state legislature were among the west's major complaints. Some, but not all, were addressed in a new state constitution adopted in 1851, but the movement toward separate statehood continued.

In 1859, John Brown, a militant abolitionist from Kansas, seized the federal armory at Harpers Ferry as the first step in a revolt. He was soon captured, tried, and hanged for treason. Soon the nation was in the throes of the Civil War, and Virginia joined other southern states in seceding from the Union. The largely non-slave-holding and pro-Union western counties summoned a convention in Wheeling in August, 1861, and formed a government for a new state to be known as Kanawha. In November of that year a second convention at Wheeling adopted the name "West Virginia" and began drafting a constitution. In December, 1862, President Abraham Lincoln approved an act admitting the new state.

In the aftermath of the Civil War arose one of the most famous feuds in American history, that of the Hatfields and the McCoys. Both families lived along both banks of the Tug River, which forms the border between Kentucky and West Virginia. The precise cause of the feud is unknown. Some have suggested the theft of a McCoy hog by a Hatfield; others, a forbidden romance between a McCoy girl and a Hatfield boy. Whatever the underlying reasons, the feud began in earnest during 1882, when a West Virginia Hatfield was killed by Kentucky McCoys. As the feud escalated, West Virginia authorities sought to suppress it by legal action, even taking their case to the U.S. Supreme Court. When the feud finally came to an end in the late 1880's, more than a dozen people had been killed.

Coal Mining and Coal Strikes

Following the Civil War, West Virginia advanced in exploitation of its major resources, primarily timber, coal, and natural gas. Coal had been discovered as early as 1742, but the deposits were not effectively mined until after the Civil War, primarily because of transportation difficulties. When these difficulties were solved by the spread of the railroads, West Virginia became the leading producer of bituminous, or soft, coal in North America. In addition to its abundance and relative ease of mining, the state's coal proved to be remarkably free from sulfur and other impurities, making it even more valuable.

Although coal was the chief source of West Virginia's revenues, it was also a major cause of internal problems. Coal mining was hard and dangerous work, and mine owners insisted on long hours and low pay for their workers. Deaths in mine disasters were frequent, and the toll was often high: In 1907, 537 persons died in mining accidents, 362 of them in one mine alone in Monongah, the worst single mining disaster in U.S. history.

Efforts to organize and unionize the miners to fight for better pay and working conditions were met with bitter hostility by mine owners, other businesses, and even the state and federal governments. Time and again, West Virginia governors declared martial law and called up the National Guard to put down strikes and other union-organizing efforts. The struggles reached a peak of violence in the years between the end of World War I and the Great Depression. In 1920, the Matewan Massacre led to the deaths of more than ten people during a confrontation between miners and their supporters in the community and mine owners and their forces. As a result, the United Mine Workers of America saw an increase in its membership, but its work toward better conditions was smothered when federal troops were ordered into the area. The strikes and conflicts continued until New Deal programs and the need for increased coal supplies for defense production during World War II brought better conditions to the mines.

Into the Future

The market for coal was often uncertain, and prices for the product could fall to low levels. Because of this, its isolation, its poor economic base, and inadequate schools, West Virginia suffered from a high degree of poverty, which reached its depth during the Great Depression. As part of Appalachia, the mountainous region stretching from Pennsylvania to upper Alabama, West Virginia was among the prime targets for massive federal assistance, especially during the Great Society's War on Poverty during the administration of President Lyndon Johnson. Funding was made available for roads, schools, retraining for workers, forest restoration, and the fight against rural poverty. Entire communities, especially in the more remote areas of the state, were aided by these efforts. In addition, the state's private sector began to revive.

Following World War II, coal production proved uncertain, largely because it was linked to the availability of other energy sources, such as oil, and to environmental concerns about matters such as strip mining. The timber industry, which had been a source of income for the area since the mid-1700's, expanded greatly after steam power replaced hydroelectric power in the late nineteenth century. Natural gas, which had been discovered in 1815, was also plentiful in the state. However, manufacturing became the major source of income for the state, ahead of mining and timbering combined. Chief products were first steel and later chemicals and allied products.

In 1960, West Virginia played a major role in U.S. presidential politics when its Democratic presidential primary pitted John F. Kennedy against Hubert Humphrey. Kennedy's landslide victory over Humphrey (almost 61 percent of the vote) caused Humphrey to withdraw from the race and, more important, demonstrated that a Catholic such as Kennedy could have a chance at victory. In the November presidential election Kennedy won the presidency. Political analysts regarded the West Virginia primary as a turning point in Kennedy's campaign and its results among the most important in American politics.

As the twentieth century ended, West Virginia continued to diversify its economic base, adding to mining, forestry, and manufacturing and drawing increasingly on recreation and tourism. The completion of major interstate highways through the state made travel easier and faster and encouraged development of the southern portion of the state, where vast areas of largely untouched natural beauty lured visitors, campers, and nature enthusiasts. Once an isolated and difficult-to-reach territory, West Virginia was rapidly becoming a destination for a variety of travelers.

—*Michael Witkoski*

Harpers Ferry

Date: Ferry service established in 1733; antislavery raid led in 1859; became part of the National Park System in 1944

Relevant issues: African American history, Civil War, disasters and tragedies, social reform

Significance: This National Historical Park in one of the first industrial towns in the United States is the site of the ill-fated raid led by abolitionist John Brown in 1859. It is also the site of numerous activities during the Civil War and the former home of Storer College, one of the earliest racially integrated institutions of higher education in the United States.

Location: Northeastern edge of West Virginia, just west of the Maryland state line on U.S. Highway 340, at the confluence of the Potomac and Shenandoah Rivers, seventy-five miles northwest of Baltimore

Site Office:
Harpers Ferry National Historical Park
P.O. Box 65
Harpers Ferry, WV 25425
ph.: (304) 535-6298
Web site: www.nps.gov/hafe/

Nestled between the Potomac and Shenandoah Rivers, Harpers Ferry in the nineteenth century was a growing industrial town that could have earned a reputation for technological innovations; however, the raid led by abolitionist John Brown and the Civil War that followed brought Harpers Ferry another kind of notoriety entirely. Harpers Ferry's origins go back to 1733, when a trader named Peter Stephens established a ferry service at the junction of the two rivers. Stephens ran the service until 1747, when he sold it to Robert Harper, a millwright who had left Philadelphia to settle in the Shenandoah Valley. Harper erected a water-powered gristmill on the Shenandoah River, and the two businesses were so successful that he was able to purchase the land from Thomas Lord Fairfax in 1751.

The abundance of natural resources such as water power, wood, fertile farm land, and iron ore in combination with the stunning physical beauty of the area made Harpers Ferry an ideal location for industry, and by the turn of the century the town boasted flour mills, sawmills, machine shops, cotton mills, forges, and furnaces. When the Chesapeake and Ohio Canal along the Potomac and the Baltimore and Ohio (B&O) Railroad were built in the 1830's, Harpers Ferry became a transportation center as well.

George Washington Makes Harpers Ferry an Armory

In the late 1700's, Harpers Ferry caught the eye of President George Washington, who was looking for a site on which to built a federal armory. Washington was impressed with the town's convenient access to water power and raw materials, its secure position protected by the Blue Ridge Mountains, and its proximity to the nation's capital in Washington, D.C. He also saw the potential for the valley to become a major industrial and transportation center that would, in turn, create a foundation for the new nation's financial development. The Armory Act of 1794 provided for the establishment of an armory at Harpers Ferry, and the federal government purchased the land from John Wager, Sr., whose wife had inherited the land from Robert Harper. By 1801, the first weapons were produced. The weapons that were carried on the Lewis and Clark 1804-1806 transcontinental expedition were manufactured at Harpers Ferry. By 1810, the armory was producing ten thousand muskets a year.

By 1821, the armory employed 271 people. The armory consisted of three parts. The main component included twenty buildings along the Potomac in which the weapons were made. Opposite this, on Shenandoah Street, stood the arsenal where arms were stored and displayed. The third section, Hall's Rifle Works, was built on Virginius Island, located upstream in the Shenandoah River. In 1819, a craftsman named John H. Hall had successfully employed the concept of interchangeable parts in the manufacture of rifles. This innovation replaced the time-consuming process of making unique parts for each type of weapon and simplified weapon repair. This procedure was eventually used to make a wide variety of products including sewing machines, watches, clocks, and even railroad cars. Although several inventors, including Eli Whitney, had been experimenting with the idea for several years, Hall was the first to put the theory into practice. Hall patented the breech-loading interchangeable flintlock rifle and was awarded a government contract in 1819 to make rifles for the military on Virginius Island.

Harpers Ferry in the Early Nineteenth Century

Other industries grew in the area as well, especially after a canal that had been built to circumvent the Shenandoah River's rapids in 1806 was modified in 1823 into a network of canals and millraces to harness the water power. By 1859, industries on Virginius Island included an iron foundry, a machine shop, a cotton mill, a flour mill, and a carriage manufacturing shop. The town of Harpers Ferry and the surrounding communities of Virginius Island and Bolivar Heights reached their growth peak in the mid-1800's. Harpers Ferry was incorporated as a town in 1851, when more than four thousand people were living and working amid the Blue Ridge Mountains. In Harpers Ferry tailors, wheelwrights, blacksmiths, carpenters, and shoemakers plied their trades. Shops, pharmacies, saloons, and inns catered to the residents and visitors.

The Antislavery Movement

The forces that would bring Harpers Ferry its greatest fame came together in the mid-1800's. The debate over the existence of slavery was causing unrest in the country. The abolitionist movement was growing, and its supporters were becoming more and more vocal. In 1831, William Lloyd Garrison, a New England printer, started an antislavery newspaper called *The Liberator,* which advocated immediate emancipation for slaves. The newspaper, circulated in both the United States and England, brought more activists to the abolitionist movement. The Mexican War of 1846 further exacerbated the controversy. Abolitionists saw the war as an attempt to preserve slavery; when the war brought the United States 850,000 square miles from the Atlantic to the Pacific that Southerners claimed for slaveholders, the gulf widened between proslavery and antislavery forces. Slaveholders for their part were angered by the abolitionist movement and feared slave uprisings. Antislavery meetings were often the scenes of violence.

Pockets of antislavery societies appeared throughout the north, including Ohio's Western Reserve, an area that encompassed the banks of Lake Erie on the north, Cleveland and Hudson on the east, Akron on the south, and Sandusky on the west. One of the Western Reserve's most prominent citizens was John Brown, a frontiersman and shepherd, who was an ardent abolitionist. Brown was from an intensely religious family and he echoed his father's belief that slavery was wrong in the eyes of God. In spite of the demands of a growing family and business, John Brown spent much of his adult life traveling throughout the country participating in antislavery demonstrations and activities. When at home, he often incurred disfavor from his neighbors for aiding Native Americans who came to the area to hunt. Secretly, he harbored fugitive slaves and provided them with arms before they continued on their flight to freedom.

The abolitionist movement was divided on the means for accomplishing emancipation. William Lloyd Garrison led the pacifist faction, which believed that influencing public opinion and changing racist attitudes would result in freedom for slaves. Another group, led by James G. Birney, advocated the organization of an antislavery political party. John Brown was part of a small faction that believed that force was the only solution. Brown wanted to arm escaping slaves and their supporters to enable the slaves to resist recapture. Initially he did not intend to attack slaveholders. When the Fugitive Slave Act was enacted by Congress in 1850 to appease Southerners incensed over the admittance of California as a free state, Brown joined with other abolitionists to organize resistance to the act. People were urged to arm themselves and to refuse to cooperate with authorities who were tracking runaway slaves.

John Brown's Abolitionist Vision
Brown became more militant in his beliefs, especially during the struggles in the Kansas Territory between southern slaveholders and northern abolitionists. By 1859, he had formed the idea of establishing a free state in the South and decided to start his campaign in Harpers Ferry. Brown chose Harpers Ferry for several reasons. First, the town was centrally located between the slaveholding plantations and farms of the South and the free states of the North. Second, the Virginia mountains were ideal for guerrilla warfare and for establishing a stronghold. Some historians also believe that Brown wanted access to the weapons at the armory. Others, however, note that Brown already had more than enough weapons to equip a small army.

In July, 1859, three months before his raid, Brown and three of his sons set up a base at Kennedy Farm in Maryland, five miles from Harpers Ferry. They spent the remainder of the summer collecting supplies and arms and recruiting men to join them in their cause. In truth, the men did not know Brown's real intent. They had joined with him in the belief that they were going to establish a haven for runaway slaves. When he informed them, on the eve of the raid, that he intended to invade and capture Harpers Ferry, many were vehemently opposed to the plan; however, he was able to gain their support.

The Raid on Harpers Ferry
Late on the night of Sunday, October 16, 1859, Brown and his band of twenty-one men (sixteen white and five black) stole into Harpers Ferry. First, they captured the night watchman on the Potomac River toll bridge. They then moved to the armory. To Brown's surprise, the townspeople reacted quickly once they were alerted to the invasion. The militia and U.S. Marines were called in, and by the next afternoon the raiders found themselves barricaded in the armory fire engine and guard house. To Brown's dismay, the town's slaves never rallied behind him.

The raid so infuriated the townspeople that each time one of Brown's men was sent out into the streets to signal surrender he was immediately killed. When Fountain Beckham, the mayor of Harpers Ferry, was killed during one barrage of gunfire, mob hysteria took over. One of Brown's men, William Thompson, who had been taken prisoner earlier, was dragged into the street and shot repeatedly. His body was then tossed into the Potomac River. On Tuesday morning, the leader of the Marine unit, Colonel Robert E. Lee, demanded Brown's unconditional surrender. When Brown refused, Lieutenant Jeb Stuart ordered his men to knock down the door of the guard house. Two more of Brown's men and a Marine were killed in the ensuing battle. An injured John Brown was taken to the paymaster's office.

On October 31, John Brown was convicted of treason against the Commonwealth of Virginia, of inciting a slave rebellion, and of murder. Throughout the trial, Brown stood by his belief that what he had done was right. He refused to enter a plea of insanity and warned that bloodshed would surely occur if the country refused to emancipate the slaves. On December 2, Brown was hanged in the Jefferson County seat of Charles Town. John Wilkes Booth and Thomas "Stonewall" Jackson were among those in the crowd.

Aftermath of the Raid

The Harpers Ferry raid sparked further outrage among southern slaveholders, who saw it as proof that abolitionists would stop at nothing to achieve the emancipation of the slaves. Eighteen months later, Brown's prediction came true when the Civil War broke out. The war meant more hardship for Harpers Ferry. Because of its geographical position, its role as a transportation center, and the existence of the armory, the town was a valuable location for both the Union and the Confederacy. Consequently, control of Harpers Ferry changed hands eight times during the war. The population dropped to three hundred after the first six months of the war as men went off to serve in the army and as families fled for safer surroundings.

In April, 1861, as Confederate troops were approaching Harpers Ferry, Union lieutenant Roger Jones decided that the forty-two soldiers under his command would not be able to hold off the attack. He gave orders for the arsenal and the armory to be set on fire, then led his contingent to safety in the north. The armory was saved from destruction by the townspeople. For the next seven weeks, General Stonewall Jackson supervised the removal of the armory's machinery and tools, which were

Harpers Ferry in the nineteenth century. (Corbis)

then sent to Richmond, Virginia, and Fayetteville, North Carolina, to make weapons for the Confederate army. In June, as word reached Harpers Ferry that Union troops were advancing, the Confederate forces set fire to the railroad bridge and the armory building. Two weeks later they burned Hall's Rifle Works and the Shenandoah River bridge.

The Union occupation lasted only three weeks, and for the next six months Harpers Ferry remained unoccupied. In February, 1862, Union forces again moved in to protect communication and supply lines along the B&O Railroad. The government also wanted to prevent a Confederate invasion into the Shenandoah Valley. The Union forces were able to maintain control of the town until September, when Confederate general Robert E. Lee sent troops, under the leadership of Stonewall Jackson, with specific orders to capture or destroy the garrison at Harpers Ferry. On September 15, after being surrounded on three sides, 12,500 Union soldiers surrendered, constituting the largest surrender of Union troops during the war.

Jackson then left for Sharpsburg, Maryland, to reinforce Lee at the Battle of Antietam. Union troops were able to move back into Harpers Ferry five days later and stayed in the town until June of 1863. Forces were ordered back on July 14 to provide protection after the Confederate retreat from Gettysburg ten days earlier. A year later, the Confederates again moved into the town, prompting Union general Philip Sheridan to mount a major offense to claim the Shenandoah Valley once and for all. In three quick battles occurring in September and October, Sheridan was able to defeat General Jubal Early and put an end to Confederate resistance in the area.

Postwar Developments

After the war, a small group of former residents returned. Together with the few people who had remained in Harpers Ferry, they tried to rebuild their once-prosperous town. However, the increased use of the steam engine in industry diminished the need for water power to run machinery. Then a trio of devastating floods in 1870, 1889, and 1896 virtually wiped out the town. By the end of the 1800's, Harpers Ferry was all but abandoned.

The one bright spot in Harpers Ferry's post-Civil War history was the establishment of Storer College, one of the country's first racially integrated institutions of higher education. During Reconstruction, northern missionaries, backed by aid from churches and the federal government, journeyed to southern towns to help newly freed blacks adjust to their new lives. One of these missionaries was Reverend Nathan Brackett of the Freewill Baptists, a Protestant denomination from New England. He came to Harpers Ferry to establish a school to provide basic education. With help from a federal agency called the Freedmen's Bureau, Brackett was able to open the school in the Lockwood House, one of the homes that had been built in the 1840's to house armory supervisors. The school got further assistance from a Maine businessman named John Storer, who pledged ten thousand dollars if the Freewill Baptist Church was able to match it within a year and agreed to open the school to both sexes of all races. This was accomplished. The next challenge was to obtain a state charter and control of the land. Postwar bitterness was inhibiting such endeavors in the state legislatures and in the U.S. Congress. Brackett persevered and eventually obtained the state charter in 1868 and gained control of the land in 1869.

The school faced more hurdles because many townspeople were opposed to the presence of free blacks in Harpers Ferry. Students and teachers were verbally harassed and threatened with physical violence. In spite of this opposition, the school grew to become a teachers' college, another of John Storer's goals. At the time, it was the only college in the region in which blacks could obtain an education above the primary level. In addition to college-credit courses, Storer offered a four-year high school program and courses in industrial arts and home economics.

By 1881, racial tensions had eased enough that when Frederick Douglass came to speak at the dedication of the school's Anthony Hall and spoke admirably of John Brown, his words were met with applause. Storer College was also the site, in 1906, of the second conference of the Niagara Movement, a group of black intellectuals led by W. E. B. Du Bois. Four years later, several of the participants went on to create the National Association for the Advancement of Colored People (NAACP).

Eventually, the work of the NAACP and others made Storer's existence unnecessary. In 1954 the U.S. Supreme Court issued its landmark ruling in

Brown v. Board of Education of Topeka, Kansas. Racial segregation in American public education was declared unconstitutional. The ruling gave blacks access to a wider variety of colleges, and Storer closed its doors in 1955.

Modern Preservation Efforts

Harpers Ferry is now a small village with little more than 350 residents, most of whom serve the tourists who visit each year. As much as was possible, the town has been restored to its original condition. Robert Harper's house, built from 1775 to 1782, is the oldest surviving building. Harper died the year it was completed, and the home was converted to an inn. The armory fire engine and guard house, which came to be known as John Brown's Fort, has been preserved. The brick fire engine house was dismantled and set up as an exhibit at the Chicago World's Fair but was repurchased and returned to Harpers Ferry in 1895.

The Episcopal Church, which was used as a barracks and a hospital during the Civil War, now stands in ruins. However, St. Peter's Catholic Church, which was built in the 1830's for the Irish Catholic immigrants who came to build the Chesapeake and Ohio Canal, is still in use. During the Civil War, the church declared its neutrality and therefore did not suffer any damage. Visitors to Harpers Ferry also may tour the John Brown Museum and a Civil War Museum, as well as several Storer College buildings.   *—Mary F. McNulty*

For Further Information:

DeVillers, David. *The John Brown Slavery Revolt Trial: A Headline Court Case.* Berkeley Heights, N.J.: Enslow, 2000. Focuses on the trial of the abolitionist who was hanged for treason and murder following his attempt to capture the military arsenal in Harpers Ferry.

Hearn, Chester G. *Six Years of Hell: Harpers Ferry During the Civil War.* Baton Rouge: Louisiana State University Press, 1999. An account of the impact of the Civil War on Harpers Ferry.

Scott, John Anthony, and Robert Alan Scott. *John Brown of Harpers Ferry.* Reprint. New York: Facts on File, 1993. A thorough description and analysis of John Brown and the United States in the years preceding the Civil War. A fairly extensive bibliography is included.

Other Historic Sites

Andrews Methodist Episcopal Church

Location: Grafton, Taylor County

Relevant issues: Cultural history

Statement of significance: This was the site of the first Mother's Day service, held on May 10, 1908. The result of the effort of Anna M. Jarvis (1864-1948) in the early part of the twentieth century, the observance of Mother's Day is internationally celebrated. Mother's Day was never intended to be a commercial holiday; rather, it was intended to be a serious and religious tribute to American motherhood.

Campbell Mansion

Location: Bethany, Brooke County

Relevant issues: Education, religion

Statement of significance: From 1811 until his death, this was the home of Alexander Campbell (1788-1866), founder of Bethany College and the leading influence in America's largest indigenous religious movement. Campbell, called the "Sage of Bethany," was an educational pioneer, renowned debater, political reformer and philosopher, prolific author, successful businessman, and agricultural leader, and was the leading spokesperson for the denomination now known as the Disciples of Christ. Bethany College, which was chartered by the State of Virginia in 1840, embodied Campbell's educational philosophy, which was welded out of his experience at the University of Glasgow, where he was introduced to the leading currents of thought in his day, and his acquaintance with Thomas Jefferson's pedagogic principles at the University of Virginia. Campbell's example influenced more than two hundred institutions of higher learning and some two hundred academies and institutes across America.

Clover Site

Location: Lesage, Cabell County

Relevant issues: American Indian history

Statement of significance: These are the extraordinarily well preserved remains of an Indian town dating to about four hundred years ago. The site pertains to the Fort Ancient culture, descendants of the cosmopolitan Hopewell trading societies and related to the other great urbanizing mound builders of the Mississippian period.

Davis and Elkins Historic District

Location: Elkins, Randolph County

Relevant issues: Business and industry, political history

Statement of significance: Halliehurst and Graceland, a pair of mansions on the grounds of Davis and Elkins College, are the key surviving buildings associated respectively with two of the Gilded Age's most important business and political figures, Stephen Benton Elkins and Henry Gassaway Davis. United personally by Elkins's marriage to Davis's daughter, they became partners in business and, though titular political opponents, shared a common interest in shaping federal legislation that favored the interests of those such as themselves who were "captains of industry."

Grave Creek Mound

Location: Moundsville, Marshall County

Relevant issues: American Indian history

Statement of significance: Dating to c. 500 B.C.E., this is one of the largest and oldest mounds in the United States representative of the burial mound tradition of the Adena culture, which preceded the Hopewell culture.

The Greenbrier

Location: White Sulphur Springs, Greenbrier County

Relevant issues: Cultural history

Statement of significance: One of the country's oldest resorts, the Greenbrier (1820) was originally built to cater to wealthy Southerners. Known from its beginnings as the "Queen of the Southern Spas," the large complex of sulphur springs, luxury accommodations, formal gardens, and golf courses is still a primary symbol of gracious Southern entertaining. The center building has been added to over the years, but the fashionable resort, as a whole, is in excellent condition.

Matewan Historic District

Location: Matewan, Mingo County

Relevant issues: Business and industry, social reform

Statement of significance: The Matewan Historic District is exceptionally significant in the history of labor organization in America. It was the scene of the "Matewan Massacre" of May 19, 1920, in which coal company officials tried to remove union workers from company housing. The conflict was precipitated by striking coal miners who demanded the company recognize the legitimacy of the United Mine Workers of America. The coal companies retaliated by bringing in armed guards to evict miners from local mines and their families from company housing. The ensuing conflict left ten people dead. The episode was a pivotal event in the eventual end of coal company control in West Virginia.

Old Main, Bethany College

Location: Bethany, Brooke County

Relevant issues: Education

Web site: www.bethanywv.edu/tourcampus/oldmain.html

Statement of significance: Old Main has been the dominant building at this small, rural college in West Virginia's panhandle since it was erected between 1858 and 1871. The building also represents the college's pivotal historical role as the headquarters of Alexander Campbell, a principal founder of the Christian Church (the Disciples of Christ); the college is the fountainhead institution of more than one hundred colleges and universities established in the United States by the church. The phenomenon is intimately linked to the Scots-Irish ethnic settlement of the American frontier. Additionally, Old Main is one of the country's earliest intact large-scale examples of collegiate Gothic architecture.

Reber Radio Telescope

Location: Green Bank, Pocahontas County

Relevant issues: Science and technology

Statement of significance: Designed and built in 1937 by Grote Reber, this is the first parabolic antenna specifically designed and built to do research in the newly emerging field of radio astronomy. An amateur astronomer and electronics expert, Reber was from 1937 until after World War II the world's only active radio astronomer. His telescope design is the forerunner of the majority of present-day radio telescopes.

Traveller's Rest

Location: Kearneysville, Jefferson County

Relevant issues: Military history, Revolutionary War

Statement of significance: A limestone house built by Continental army general Horatio Gates (c. 1728-1806), this was his permanent residence until 1790. Patriot forces led by General Gates compelled the surrender of General John Burgoyne's army at Saratoga in October, 1777. American troops under Gates were, in turn, defeated by First Marquess Cornwallis at the Battle of Camden, South Carolina, on August 16, 1780.

West Virginia Independence Hall

Location: Wheeling, Ohio County

Relevant issues: Civil War, political history

Statement of significance: Originally constructed as a U.S. customhouse in the spring and summer of 1861, the building was the home of the pro-Union state conventions of Virginia. It served as the capitol of the Restored (Unionist) Government of Virginia between 1861 and 1863. The first constitutional convention for the new state of West Virginia also took place here, earning it the name of Independence Hall.

Wheeling Suspension Bridge

Location: Wheeling, Ohio County

Relevant issues: Art and architecture, science and technology

Statement of significance: This is the oldest major long-span suspension bridge in the world, with a span of more than one thousand feet. This bridge is possibly the nation's most significant extant antebellum engineering structure. Its construction established American leadership in the building of suspension bridges.

Wisconsin

The State Capitol Building in Madison. (Wisconsin Department of Tourism/Bob Queen)

History of Wisconsin

Influenced by a landscape shaped by ancient glaciers, Wisconsin developed into a state with three distinct regions. The southeast corner of Wisconsin, along the shore of Lake Michigan, is an urban, industrial area, dominated by Milwaukee, the state's largest city. The northern third of the state is a sparsely populated area of forests and lakes, primarily used for tourism and recreation. Between these two regions, the southern, western, and central areas of the state are productive agricultural lands, particularly in dairy farming.

Early History

During the last two million years, glaciers advanced and retreated over much of North America. The last major advance began about twenty-five thousand years ago and reached its greatest extent around fifteen thousand years ago. At this time, it covered nearly two-thirds of Wisconsin. A smaller advance, about ten thousand years ago, covered only the northern part of the state. As a result of this glacial activity, this area now contains numerous streams and marshes, as well as more than fourteen thousand lakes. The areas of older glacial activity, which have been subjected to erosion, now contain flat plains and rolling hills. The southwest part of the state, which was not covered by glaciers, is an area of ridges and valleys carved by rivers.

The first humans to inhabit the area arrived about twelve thousand years ago, when much of northern Wisconsin was still covered with glaciers. These people, known as the Paleo-Indian culture, hunted bison and other large animals. About ten thousand years ago, as the climate warmed, the people of the Archaic culture hunted large and small animals and gathered wild plants for food. About three thousand years ago, the people of the Woodland culture used bows and arrows to hunt, made pottery, and built large mounds. About one thousand years ago, the people of the Mississippian culture lived in large, permanent villages and cultivated corn, beans, and squash.

In the early seventeenth century, just before Europeans arrived in the area, the major Native American peoples living in Wisconsin included the Santee Dakota in the northwest, the Menominee in the northeast, the Iowa in the southwest, and the Winnebago in the southeast. In addition to crops associated with the Mississippian culture, the peoples of northern Wisconsin also subsisted on wild rice growing in wetlands.

During the 1640's, the Iroquois, a powerful confederation of Native Americans living in the New York area, launched a series of wars against Native

Americans living to the west. The Iroquois were enemies of the French, while the peoples living in the Great Lakes region were generally allied with the French and participated in the French fur trade. The wars drove many Native American peoples westward into Wisconsin, including the Potawatomi, the Ojibwa, the Sauk, the Fox, the Ottawa, the Huron, the Miami, the Mascouten, and the Kickapoo. Many of these peoples later moved farther west, but the Ojibwa, the Menominee, the Winnebago, and the Potawatomi remained in the state. Other Native American peoples moved westward into Wisconsin in the 1820's, including the Oneida, the Stockbridge, the Munsee, and the Brotherton. Most Native Americans in Wisconsin now live in reservations in the northern part of the state or in Milwaukee.

European Exploration and Settlement

The first European known to reach Wisconsin was the French explorer Jean Nicolet. In 1634 Nicolet journeyed from Lake Huron through the strait between the Upper and Lower Peninsulas of Michigan, becoming the first European to reach Lake Michigan. He then sailed into Green Bay, a narrow inlet of Lake Michigan, and reached Wisconsin. Here he negotiated a peace treaty with the Winnebago. In 1671, the French missionary Claude-Jean Allouez founded a mission at Green Bay. A fort was built on the site in 1717, and Green Bay served as the center of the fur trade in the area for one hundred years.

At the end of the French and Indian War, a struggle between France and Great Britain for control of North America, the area was acquired by the British. At the end of the American Revolution, twenty years later, the area was acquired by the United States. Wisconsin was part of the Northwest Territory from 1787 to 1800, part of the Indiana Territory from 1800 to 1809, part of the Illinois Territory from 1809 to 1818, and part of the Michigan Territory from 1818 to 1836. The Wisconsin Territory was created in 1836.

American settlement of the area began slowly. Although the future site of Milwaukee was settled as early as 1800, it did not develop into a town for thirty years. The United States built Fort Howard at Green Bay in 1816 and began building the town of Green Bay in 1829. The opening of the Erie Canal in 1825, linking the Hudson River with Lake Erie,

made travel between the heavily populated eastern states and the sparsely populated Great Lakes region much easier. The discovery of lead ores in southwestern Wisconsin in the 1820's also encouraged settlers. Mineral Point, established in the area of the lead mines in 1827, quickly became the most important settlement in the area and served as the first territorial capital.

Statehood and Economic Growth

At first, the Wisconsin Territory was settled mostly by Americans from eastern states. The lead mines brought immigrants from Cornwall, a region of southwestern England famous for mines, in the 1830's. These were soon followed by immigrants from Germany, Ireland, and Italy moving into southwestern Wisconsin. German immigrants also settled in Milwaukee in the 1840's. After losing a large part of its western lands to the newly created Iowa Territory in 1838, the Wisconsin Territory became the thirtieth state ten years later.

After statehood, settlers entered Wisconsin from eastern and southern states, Germany, Poland, Scandinavia, and the British Isles. As lead mining played a less important role in the state, dairy farming and other forms of agriculture came to dominate the economy. Several institutes of higher learning were founded in the late 1840's, and the nation's first kindergarten was opened in Watertown in 1856.

The national crisis over slavery led to the creation of the Republican Party of Wisconsin in Ripon in 1854. During the Civil War, Wisconsin was firmly on the side of the Union. The Republican Party continued to dominate state politics for a century. The war brought industrial development to Milwaukee, and the city went on to be an important center of labor-union activity.

In the 1870's, zinc ores were discovered in southwestern Wisconsin. Zinc mining remained an important industry in the state for more than one hundred years. The 1870's also saw the rise of the production of lumber in the northern part of the state. Lumber resources were nearly depleted by the 1920's, so the forestry industry turned from lumber to the production of woodpulp for papermaking. This would remain an important part of the economy. Iron mining developed in northern Wisconsin in the 1880's and continued into the 1960's.

The Twentieth Century

Wisconsin played an important role in the Progressive movement of the early twentieth century, as political reformers fought corruption and the influence of the railroads and other powerful business interests. A national leader in the Progressive movement, Wisconsin native Robert M. La Follette, Sr., served as governor of the state from 1900 to 1906, and as a U.S. senator from 1906 until his death in 1925. The Progressive movement remained a faction within the Republican Party until 1934, when the Wisconsin Progressive Party was created. The party rejoined the Republicans in 1946, but many of its members joined the Democratic Party instead.

Influenced by the Progressive movement and labor unions, Milwaukee elected Socialist mayors in 1910, 1916, and 1948. Despite the state's reputation for reformist and radical politics, it also produced numerous conservative politicians. One of the most controversial was Wisconsin native Joseph R. McCarthy, who served as a U.S. senator from 1946 until his death in 1957. McCarthy drew national attention with accusations that a large number of Communists had infiltrated the government of the United States.

During the Great Depression of the 1930's, Wisconsin's economy, balanced between manufacturing and agriculture, suffered less than those of most states. Agriculture in particular remained remarkably stable, with Wisconsin leading the nation in dairy farming after 1920. Despite this stability, Wisconsin, like the rest of the nation, saw a shift in its population from farmlands to cities. In the 1920's about half of the state's residents lived in rural areas; by the 1980's, about two-thirds of the population lived in urban areas.

The need for military equipment during World War II greatly increased industrial production in the southeastern part of Wisconsin and made it one of the leading manufacturing states in the nation. The rise in the tourism industry in the second half of the twentieth century also greatly benefited the economy. Wisconsin's economy was slowed by a nationwide recession in the late 1980's, but to a lesser extent than most other states. During the 1990's, Wisconsin maintained a reputation for economic stability; an honest, efficient state government; and innovative, if controversial, public policies.

—*Rose Secrest*

Circus World Museum

Date: Established in 1959

Relevant issues: Cultural history

Significance: The Ringling Brothers Circus began in Baraboo in 1884 and continued to use the site for its winter quarters until 1918. The Circus World Museum, opened in 1959, gives visitors the opportunity to examine circus memorabilia as well as to enjoy live circus acts.

Location: 426 Water Street (State Highway 113) in Baraboo, south-central Wisconsin

Site Office:

Circus World Museum
550 Water Street
Baraboo, WI 53913-2597
ph.: (608) 356-8341, 356-0800
fax: (608) 356-1800
Web site: www.circusworldmuseum.com
e-mail: ringmaster@circusworldmuseum.com

Almost seven million people visited the Circus World Museum between 1959 and 1999. The museum is owned by the State Historical Society of Wisconsin and operated by the nonprofit Circus World Museum Foundation. It is recognized worldwide for its unrivaled collection of circus wagons, its educational programs, and its archival collection devoted to the history of the American circus. Designated a National Historic Landmark, the Museum preserves eight buildings and barns that once were a part of the original quarters.

Beginning of the Ringling Brothers Circus

Albrecht (Al) Ringling was the oldest son of a German immigrant who operated a modest harness shop in the small community of Baraboo. After Ringling observed a circus in his youth, he and four of his brothers began giving amateur performances for the local citizens, and he obtained a job traveling as a juggler and a ropewalker. A person with both strength and dexterity, Ringling's specialty was the innovative balancing of a heavy plow over his head. In 1882, he and his four brothers organized a variety show, the Carnival of Fun, which toured the small towns of the Midwest.

In 1884, the brothers joined with Yankee Robinson, a retired circus operator, to establish a small circus with a tent that would hold six hundred people. On May 19, the troupe gave its first show, in

Baraboo. They had twenty-one performers, including Al Ringling's wife, a snake charmer. Their summer tour of southern Wisconsin was moderately successful. Each year, the performances became bigger and more spectacular. The purchase of their first elephant in 1888 was a milestone. By 1890, they were operating a railroad train of eighteen cars. The next year they expanded from one ring to three rings and took the name The Ringling Brothers World's Greatest Shows.

Growth and Departure from Baraboo

By the turn of the century, the circus was giving shows primarily in the larger cities of North America, and it no longer played in Baraboo. Its only serious rival was Barnum & Bailey. After James Bailey died, the Panic of 1907 forced his widow to sell the circus to the Ringling Brothers for the small sum of $41,000. For the next decade, the brothers ran the two shows separately. The Barnum & Bailey circus had its winter quarters in Bridgeport, Connecticut, while the Ringling Brothers Circus continued to have its winter quarters in Baraboo. With its many animal shelters along the Baraboo River, the circus was one of the largest employers of the region.

By the early 1900's, the brothers were quite wealthy, and they owned large houses in Baraboo. Al Ringling continued to be devoted to the city, but his younger brothers preferred to spend most of the winter in Florida. Ringling built an opera house, which he intended to donate to Baraboo. In 1916, however, he died before signing the will, and his brothers decided not to make the gift.

In 1918, the Ringling Brothers and Barnum & Bailey merged into a single operation, which they called "The Greatest Show on Earth." This was was very bad news for the community of Baraboo, because the brothers decided to make their winter quarters in Connecticut. Nine years later, the great circus moved from Connecticut to Florida. For its fiftieth anniversary in 1933, the circus held a performance in Baraboo, the first such performance in almost forty years. By this time, all the brothers but one had died.

The Museum

By the 1950's, circus shows were becoming much less common than before. John Kelley, an attorney for the Ringlings, had the idea of establishing a lo-

cation to preserve as much of the past as possible. He suggested that the most logical location was Baraboo. The idea was enthusiastically supported by the city, its local organizations, and the state historical society. In 1959, the Circus World Museum held its grand opening. Since then, the museum has assembled the world's largest collection of antique circus wagons, including many that cannot be seen anywhere else.

In 1965, the Robert L. Parkinson Library and Research Center was added to preserve the paper, photographic, and sound materials which had been donated to the museum. The mission of the library is to collect, preserve, and interpret circus history. Its holdings have grown to more than fifty thousand photographs, eight thousand posters, three thousand books, six hundred films, and thousands of other items related to the history of the American circus. The professional staff includes an archivist and a curator of artifacts. The library is free and open to the public the entire year.

Also in the late 1960's, the museum erected the Moeller Hippodrome in order to present live circus performances. In 1972, these were expanded to include big-top performances with international award-winning casts. In 1985, the museum presented its first magic show. In 1998, visitors were first allowed to observe circus wagon restoration. Each year about 200,000 people visit the museum for a family experience that is both fun and educational.

—*Thomas T. Lewis*

For Further Information:

Conover, Richard. *The Circus: Wisconsin's Unique Heritage.* Baraboo, Wis.: Circus World Museum, 1967. Especially appealing for people interested in the local history of Wisconsin.

Eckley, Wilton. *The American Circus.* Boston: Twayne, 1984. An excellent general introduction to circus history, with an excellent bibliography.

Jansen, Dean. *The Biggest, the Smallest, the Longest, the Shortest: A Chronicle of the American Circus from Its Heartland.* Madison: Wisconsin House, 1975. The best source for the role of Wisconsin in circus history.

May, Earl Chapin. *Circus: From Rome to Ringling.* New York: Dover, 1963. A very interesting historical work, with much information about the Ringling brothers.

North, Henry Ringling, and Alden Hatch. *The Circus Kings: Our Ringling Family Story*. Garden City, N.Y.: Doubleday, 1960. A personal account from a member of the family.

Plowden, Gene. *Those Amazing Ringlings and Their Circus*. Caldwell, Idaho: Caxton Printers, 1967. An interesting and informative book with many anecdotes about the Ringling brothers and their career.

Taliesin

Date: Built in 1911

Relevant issues: Art and architecture, education

Significance: A National Historic Landmark, this is the home and studio of architect Frank Lloyd Wright, designed by the architect himself. The six hundred-acre estate also includes the Hillside Home School, built in 1902 and now home of the Frank Lloyd Wright School of Architecture, founded as the Taliesin Fellowship by Wright and his wife Olgivanna in 1932. The site also features Midway Farm, built in 1938; the Romeo and Juliet Windmill, built in 1897; and Tan-y-deri, the home that Wright designed in 1907 for his sister, Jane Porter.

Location: Spring Green, in the south central part of the state, 40 miles northwest of Madison and 180 miles northwest of Chicago

Site Office:

Taliesin Preservation Commission
Spring Green, WI 53588-0397
ph.: (608) 588-7900
Web site: www.talisenpreservation.org
e-mail: visitctr@mhtc.net

In 1911, American architect Frank Lloyd Wright built a home for himself in the Helena Valley of Wisconsin, where his Welsh ancestors had settled a century before. Since then, Taliesin has come to symbolize the genius as well as the eccentricity of one of America's greatest architects. Known as much for his flamboyant lifestyle as for his revolutionary architectural designs, Wright fell in love with one of his clients. In fact, Mamah Borthwick Cheney and her husband, Edwin, were friends of the Wrights in Oak Park, Illinois. The liaison between Wright and Cheney scandalized the community, and when the two traveled to Europe together

in 1909, the newspapers covered the tryst with delight.

When Wright returned to the home he shared with his wife, Catherine, and their six children, he found that his unorthodox behavior was costing him customers. Faced with debts incurred by his growing family and his extravagant spending habits, he decided to convert half of his Oak Park home and studio into rental property. He also persuaded his mother to sell her home in Oak Park and purchase property in Spring Green, Wisconsin, on which he planned build a home with the understanding that she could live there as well. Because Wright was also planning to divorce his wife and bring Mamah Cheney to Taliesin, he tried to keep the construction site a secret. The media fascination with his private life was too intense, however, and a Chicago newspaper exposed his plan in 1911. Although Catherine Wright refused to agree to a divorce, the architect moved into his new home with Cheney.

"Taliesin" in Welsh Mythology

Named for a poet-prophet in Welsh mythology, Taliesin means "shining brow" and was built into the side of a hill using limestone from a nearby quarry. In Taliesin Wright found the perfect palette on which to practice his theory of "organic architecture." Overlooking the Wisconsin River and surrounded by garden walls, stone pavements, terraces and open porches, Taliesin was built, in Wright's words, "the way nature builds." It has been suggested that Wright was inspired by Villa Medici, a beautifully terraced home in the Tuscan countryside outside Florence, Italy. Built low to the ground in Wright's trademark Prairie Style, the limestone and stucco structure is accentuated with dark cypress trim and hundreds of casement windows that flood the rooms with light. Inside, the combination of stone and wood dominates the fifty-one rooms. Many of the rooms were designed with secluded terraces and balconies so that their inhabitants could enjoy nature in private. Pools and fountains are fed from the stream below, and flower beds are in abundance.

Wright had spent his childhood in the valley outside Spring Green working on his uncles' farms. There he acquired his love for nature and began to develop his idea that buildings should blend in with their surroundings. By the time he built

Taliesin, he already had designed other structures in the valley, including the Romeo and Juliet Windmill and the Hillside Home School for his aunts, Jane and Nell Lloyd Jones. Built in 1902, Hillside Home School was one of the first coeducational boarding schools in the United States and was considered progressive for its time. The sixty-foot windmill was part of the school's water system and used a diamond and octagon configuration, hence the name "Romeo and Juliet." Wright described it this way: "Each is indispensable to the other . . . neither could stand without the other." In 1907 he designed a house called Tan-y-deri (Welsh for "under the oaks") for his sister Jane and her husband.

Murder, Fire, and Rebuilding
In the summer of 1914, Mamah Cheney, her two children, and five members of Taliesin's building crew were murdered by the estate's gardener, who then set the living quarters on fire. Wright was in Chicago supervising the construction of Midway Gardens, an elaborate European-style cafe and entertainment restaurant, and returned home to find his love and his dream destroyed. Only his studio and a small bedroom behind it survived. Cheney was buried in the Unity Chapel on the grounds of Taliesin. Wright overcame his grief by rebuilding immediately. Taliesin's second phase included an enlarged studio, new living quarters for draftsmen, farm buildings, stables, guest quarters, servants' quarters, and a new residence for Wright that boasted immense roofs and massive fireplaces.

The costs of building and rebuilding Taliesin as well as those of maintaining the residence in Oak Park for Catherine and the children were mounting rapidly. Wright's refusal to check his reckless spending habits exacerbated the problem. The buildings at Taliesin contained his extensive collection of furniture, expensive carpets, and artifacts. The estate was a showcase of Japanese screens, sculptures, and prints, and the rooms were kept filled with fresh flowers.

Wright's Marital Problems
A year after Cheney's death, Wright began a stormy romance with Miriam Noel. Over the next nine years, the relationship was marked by explosive fights and tearful reunions. Wright's mother, Anna, did not like Noel and would not stay at

Taliesin when Noel was there. Wright's housekeeper at the time, Nellie Breen, also disapproved of Noel's presence at the house and charged him with violating the Mann Act, which prohibited transporting a woman across state lines for immoral purposes. Wright hired Clarence Darrow to act on his behalf, and the charges were ultimately dropped. The gossip, however, continued. Noel, for her part, did not like the plainness of Taliesin's furnishings and insisted on adding embellishments of her own. In spite of it all, the relationship continued and Noel accompanied Wright to Japan to assist him in the supervision of the Imperial Hotel construction from 1919 to 1922.

In 1923 Catherine Wright finally agreed to a divorce, and Frank Lloyd Wright married Miriam Noel in November of that year. The marriage was short-lived: The Wrights were separated six months later. In the meantime, Wright met Olgivanna Lazovich Hinzenberg, the daughter of the chief justice of Montenegro, part of what is now Bosnia-Hercegovina. Once again, Wright brought his lover to Taliesin and more scandal into his life. During this time, in 1925, parts of Taliesin were again destroyed by fire. This one was blamed on faulty electrical wiring. Wright rebuilt, incorporating elements of the previous construction.

By mid-1925, Olgivanna was pregnant and Miriam Noel was contesting the divorce. Miriam held press conferences, hired private detectives, and appeared at Taliesin demanding admittance. The publicity did not help Wright's image or income, and he feared that Olgivanna could be deported.

In August, 1926, Wright and Olgivanna, their baby daughter Iovanna, and Olgivanna's daughter Svetlana retreated to Minnesota, where Wright began to work on his autobiography. By October, Miriam had tracked them down and they were arrested. Ironically, Miriam charged Wright with violating the Mann Act and demanded that Olgivanna and Svetlana be deported. Wright and Olgivanna were released from jail as the investigations continued. At the same time, the Bank of Wisconsin was threatening foreclosure on Taliesin. Wright arranged for many of his valuable prints to be sold, but the profits were disappointing. He then devised a plan to sell shares in his own future and set about to find ten investors with $7,500 each. With these investors, the Frank Lloyd Wright Corporation was created. Taliesin suffered still an-

Taliesin. (©2000 Pedro E. Guerrero)

hotel, and they were married in La Jolla, California, in August, 1928. Upon returning home to Taliesin, the Wrights found the home in disarray and damaged by water. Wright himself accused the Bank of Wisconsin of holding parties at Taliesin and causing extensive damage.

The Depression Years
The 1929 stock market crash and the ensuing Great Depression resulted in a dearth of architectural work. Wright sought to make a living by writing and lecturing. Hillside Home School had fallen into disrepair after Wright's aunts died, and Olgivanna seized on the idea to create the Taliesin Fellowship, a school for aspiring architects. The first class of students was put to work rebuilding the Hillside Home School. The drafting studio was designed with the stone fireplaces and oak trusses that are characteristic of Wright's architecture. Wright said he wanted the studio to be "an abstract forest with light pouring from the ceiling." The leaded glass windows that had been part of the original structure were replaced with plate glass donated by the Pittsburgh Plate Glass Company. New roofing tiles were also laid. The gymnasium was converted to a theater. After a fire in the late 1940's, Wright rebuilt the theater and lowered the stage.

Wright's fervent need to create and revise meant that Taliesin was constantly in a stage of reconstruction. The architectural apprentices who came to study with Frank Lloyd Wright found that they were expected to learn by doing. In his book *Apprentice to Genius*, Edgar Tafel, who spent ten years at Taliesin, recalled the building of the drafting studio:

> We apprentices furnished much of the labor. We dug foundations, brought sand from the river bottom, felled trees and cut them into lumber, burned the lime and mixed plaster, laid the roof, did all the millwork, built the furniture, laid the

other fire, albeit a minor one, in the midst of the chaos.

Wright hired another well-known attorney, Philip F. La Follette, to defend him against the legal charges and to help him save Taliesin. La Follette was a member of a prominent Wisconsin family and later served two terms as governor of the state. He negotiated an agreement with the bank that allowed Wright to work in his studio so that he could meet his financial obligations and provided him with a year's grace on the loan. La Follette also negotiated a divorce settlement with Miriam and worked to get the deportation investigation halted. The ownership of Taliesin was divided between Wright's major benefactor, Darwin Martin, and Chicago businessman Benjamin Aldridge Page. Martin and Page also agreed to meet the cash payment requirement of fifteen thousand dollars. As co-owners, they were responsible for the mortgage payments, taxes, and interest on the property.

Wright and Olgivanna spent the next year in Arizona while he was working on the construction of a

floors, stained the trusses, did finished grading and cleaned away the debris.

In addition to Tafel, early Fellowship students included Herbert Fritz, the son of one of the survivors of the 1914 massacre; Karl Jensen; Henry Klumb, who designed the University of Puerto Rico; and William Wesley Peters, who later married Olgivanna's daughter Svetlana.

Fellowship members also were expected to help with the day-to-day running of Taliesin. During the years of the Great Depression, Taliesin was virtually self-sustaining. The grounds included Midway Farm, where food was grown organically; a facility to generate electricity; a fuel yard; and a water works.

Fallingwater

While cash flow continued to be a problem, Wright's success with the Imperial Hotel in Japan brought much-needed commissions. In 1935 Wright designed Fallingwater, a weekend home cantilevered over a waterfall, for Mr. and Mrs. Edgar J. Kaufmann in Bear Run, Pennsylvania. Edgar Kaufmann had made a fortune in department stores and soon became Wright's primary benefactor. This development was providential because Darwin Martin died later that same year. Wright then convinced Benjamin Page to sell his interest in Taliesin for one dollar; however, Martin's family refused to surrender their share. Once again, fate stepped in. Wes Peters was by this time married to Svetlana and had recently come into a substantial inheritance from his father. Some of the money was used to buy out Martin's share, and the mortgage was put in Peters's name. After another threat of foreclosure in 1939, the mortgage and all of Wright's possessions were transferred to The Frank Lloyd Wright Foundation, a nonprofit educational corporation. Martin's family continued to seek compensation for another decade but ultimately admitted defeat in 1949. Once the financial arrangements were settled, Wright and Peters began to purchase much of the original Lloyd family holdings in the valley. They managed to acquire three thousand acres, including three miles of waterfront property.

Wright's Interest in Communal Living

Throughout his life, Wright believed in a commu-

nal way of living. In fact, the community at Taliesin was very close to the socialistic ideal that was espoused by many intellectuals of the time. Wright's pacifism had never been a secret either, and in the 1930's his opposition to the growing war in Europe was evident in his public appearances. This opposition was shared by the Fellowship apprentices who consequently applied for draft exemption when the United States entered World War II in 1941. The applications were denied; three apprentices served prison terms for refusing to report for active duty, and two others spent time in camps for conscientious objectors. The Federal Bureau of Investigation (FBI) initiated an investigation into Wright and the Fellowship in an attempt to prove that he had exerted undue influence on his young students and that he was guilty of sedition. The federal government, however, refused to prosecute.

During the war years, the market for architectural commissions came to a grinding halt. Most of the other apprentices were serving in the armed forces. Wright spent his time revising his autobiography and working on a winter home for the Fellowship, Taliesin West, near Scottsdale, Arizona. Work on Taliesin West had begun in 1937 and the first phase was finished by 1940, but Wright continued to expand and modify his western site until his death in 1959. The Fellowship divided its time between the two locations; a small group of apprentices stayed in Wisconsin during the winter months to tend farm animals. Olgivanna's aunt and uncle, Vlado and Sophie Lazovich, stayed at Taliesin West in the summer to supervise the maintenance and care of the buildings. When the war ended, aspiring architects flocked to Taliesin for the chance to study with Wright.

Wright's Problems with the FBI

The FBI continued its probe into the Fellowship, and in 1951 Wright's name was placed on the House Committee on Un-American Activities' blacklist. This time the target was the school itself. Taliesin had been awarded G.I. Bill accreditation, and the FBI investigated reports that the school was more a religious cult that a genuine school. Once again, however, the federal government declined to take legal action. At the same time, Wright was embroiled in a fight with the city of Spring Green over the issue of tax-exempt status for Taliesin. He

The Romeo and Juliet Windmill. (©2000 Pedro E. Guerrero)

After Wright's death, Taliesin Associated Architects was formed to carry on the work already under way. The Fellowship became the Frank Lloyd Wright School of Architecture, which continues to use both Taliesin and Taliesin West as campuses.

Modern Preservation Efforts

The entire Taliesin estate was given National Historic Landmark status in 1976. A commission created by Wisconsin governor Tommy Thompson in 1989 rebuilt the Romeo and Juliet Windmill. The Hillside drafting studio is currently used by the Taliesin Associated Architects and the students of The Frank Lloyd Wright School of Architecture. Hillside also houses an extensive collection of photographs and models, including a twelve-foot-square model of Broadacre City, Wright's idea of a utopian community. Wright's Wisconsin residence is now home to the students and architects of Taliesin who still gather in the 28-by-32-foot living room for evening concerts. Taliesin West, also a national historic landmark, houses The Frank Lloyd Wright Foundation and The Frank Lloyd Wright Archives.   —*Mary F. McNulty*

For Further Information:

Kruger, Marilyn. "Taliesin." *Gourmet*, February, 1991. A beautifully written piece that traces Wright's professional and personal life while evoking clear images of the Wisconsin estate.

Secrest, Meryle. *Frank Lloyd Wright*. Reprint. Chicago: University of Chicago Press, 1998. A comprehensive examination of the architect that balances his genius with his idiosyncracies. The book covers his ancestry and his childhood years as well as the more than seventy years of his architectural career.

Tafel, Edgar. *Apprentice to Genius*. Reprint. Baltimore: The Johns Hopkins University Press, 1993. An account of the author's years as an apprentice in the Taliesin Fellowship. Although Tafel is clearly a ardent supporter of Wright, the author does touch on some of the more contro-

lost the case and was ordered to pay more than eighteen thousand dollars in back taxes. Infuriated, Wright threatened to burn Taliesin to the ground, a thought that horrified his friends and supporters to the extent that they raised the money to pay the outstanding tax bill.

When Wright died in 1959 in Arizona, he was working on plans to build Unity Temple at Taliesin as the site of his final resting place. His body was brought back to Spring Green, and he was buried temporarily in the Unity Chapel. The apprentices vowed to complete the temple, but it never came to fruition. Just before Olgivanna died in 1985, she made known her desire that Wright's body and hers be cremated and the ashes kept in Arizona. Iovanna signed the necessary papers, and Wright's body was quickly exhumed and cremated. The cremation caused an uproar among some members of the family and the Fellowship who believed that Wright's remains belonged in Wisconsin. Others observed that after Svetlana's death, Oglivanna spent less and less time at Taliesin and seemed to feel more at ease in the home in Arizona that she and Wright had built together. Svetlana had been killed in a traffic accident in 1946.

versial aspects of his time at Taliesin, including his decision to leave to start his own practice. Also noteworthy for its abundance of photographs.

Wright, Frank Lloyd. *An Autobiography.* Reprint. New York: Horizon Press, 1977. Written in 1932 and revised in the 1940's.

_____. *Letters to Apprentices.* Fresno: Press at Cali-fornia State University, Fresno, 1982. Also recommended.

Wright, Olgivanna Lloyd. *Our House.* New York: Horizon Press, 1959. Written by Wright's third and last wife. While obviously a loving tribute to her husband, it presents an insider's perspective on life at Taliesin. It is written in an easy-to-read story form and contains many anecdotes.

Other Historic Sites

Administration Building and Research Tower, S. C. Johnson Company

Location: Racine, Racine County

Relevant issues: Art and architecture

Statement of significance: One of three notable commissions executed by architect Frank Lloyd Wright (1867-1959) during the Great Depression, these structures employ a highly original system of cantilever-slab construction in a classic of modern office design. Wright's imaginative approach to structure is seen in his use of rounded, organic forms and in the T-shaped columns and treelike tower.

Astor Fur Warehouse

Location: Prairie du Chien, Crawford County

Relevant issues: Business and industry

Statement of significance: Constructed c. 1828, this stone building, one of the American Fur Company's principal establishments, recalls the Astor empire and Prairie du Chien's prominence as a fur trading center.

Aztalan

Location: Aztalan State Park, near Lake Mills on Wisconsin 89, Jefferson County

Relevant issues: American Indian history

Statement of significance: This large, stockaded temple mound site, first discovered in 1836, is the northernmost of the major Mississippian culture archaeological sites. It now forms Aztalan State Park. It represents an important northern extension of the Cahokia phase of the Middle Mississippi culture.

Dousman Hotel

Location: Prairie du Chien, Crawford County

Relevant issues: Cultural history, western expansion

Statement of significance: Constructed 1864-1865, this three-story, buff-colored brick structure is the largest, most luxurious, and last built of several large hotels in Prairie du Chien during the nineteenth century, while the town was an important river steamboat and railroad terminus. It was used as a stopping point by thousands of emigrants to the West after the Civil War.

Fountain Lake Farm

Location: Montello, Marquette County

Relevant issues: Education, social reform

Statement of significance: John Muir (1838-1914), pioneering advocate of natural preservation, lived at Fountain Lake Farm from 1849 to 1856, during his early teens, and periodically between 1862 and 1864. Late in life he traced the formation of his conservation philosophy to the years he spent at Fountain Lake Farm. Though no structures associated with Muir's period of residence are extant, a natural meadow, spring, and lake remain.

Fourth Street School

Location: 333 West Galena Street, Milwaukee, Milwaukee County

Relevant issues: Education, political history

Statement of significance: Milwaukee's Fourth Street School is the only surviving structure in America associated with Golda Meir (1898-1978), who from 1967 to 1974 was prime minister of Israel. Fleeing the pogroms of their native Russia, Meir's family came to this city and settled on Walnut Street. In 1906, the young Golda attended the Fourth Street School, where she learned English and exhibited a talent for leadership; in 1912, she graduated valedictorian. The school continues to serve the students of Milwaukee.

Garland House

Location: West Salem, La Crosse County

Relevant issues: Literary history

Statement of significance: This rambling, nondescript structure is associated with author Hamlin Garland (1860-1940). Garland's early work exploded the romantic myths of the West, exposing the hard lot of the pioneers and frontiersmen; his later, more romantic novels—one of which brought him the Pulitzer Prize (1922)—celebrated the strength of the individual rather than the oppressive environment. Garland bought this house for his parents in 1893; he visited regularly, doing much of his writing during his lengthy stays.

Greene Memorial Museum

Location: Milwaukee, Milwaukee County

Relevant issues: Science and technology

Statement of significance: Amateur naturalists played a crucial role in the development of nineteenth century science by assembling extensive collections of natural history specimens. From 1878 to 1894, Thomas A. Greene assembled a comprehensive collection of minerals from around the world, as well as an unparalleled collection of fossils from the classic ancient reefs of the Milwaukee-Chicago, stimulating further research on these structures by eminent geologists of the day and providing abundant material for future paleontological research. The entire collection was originally donated to Milwaukee-Downer College, a women's college, where Greene's heirs built a fireproof museum building to house it in 1913. The museum, along with the rest of the campus, was later sold to the University of Wisconsin, Milwaukee.

Johnson House

Location: 33 East Four Mile Road, Racine, Racine County

Relevant issues: Art and architecture

Statement of significance: Built in 1937-1938 for Herbert Johnson, president of Johnson's Wax Company, this large house was considered by its architect the finest (and most expensive) house he had built up to that date. Frank Lloyd Wright's design is so completely wedded to its site—rolling grassy slopes and shallow ravines—that it seems to grow naturally from the earth. Displaying what its author called the "eloquence of materials"—beautifully finished and integrated surfaces of wood, concrete, and brick put together with respect and taste—it is the last of Wright's Prairie Houses. Currently, it is one of the most important educational and cultural conference centers in the Midwest.

La Follette Home

Location: Maple Bluff, Dane County

Relevant issues: Political history, social reform

Statement of significance: From 1905 until his death, this was the residence of Robert M. La Follette (1855-1925). La Follette served in the House of Representatives (1885-1891) but did not emerge as a major force in governmental reform until his service as governor of Wisconsin (1901-1906). As a U.S. senator (1906-1925), he continued to champion "progressive" causes and was the Progressive Party candidate for president in 1924, the year before his death.

Little White Schoolhouse

Location: Ripon, Fond Du Lac County

Relevant issues: Political history

Statement of significance: A meeting in this simple, one-story clapboard and frame schoolhouse on March 20, 1854, and another in Jackson, Michigan, on July 6, to protest passage of the Kansas-Nebraska Act, which permitted the extension of slavery beyond the limits of the Missouri Compromise, drew dissatisfied Whigs, Free-Soilers, and Democrats. These meetings were the first of those that led to the formation of the Republican Party.

Milton House

Location: 18 South Janesville Street, Milton, Rock County

Relevant issues: African American history, social reform

Statement of significance: This tall, hexagonal building, constructed of concrete grout and covered with plaster, is nationally significant not because of its unusual shape and construction but because of its antebellum usage. Built as a hotel, it and the nearby log Goodrich Cabin served as stops on the Underground Railroad. Fugitive slaves could enter the cabin, open a trapdoor, and make their way through a tunnel to the Milton House, where the Goodrich family provided food, shelter, and assistance to reach their next stop on their way to Canada and freedom. This property, open to the public as a museum, also illustrates the westward spread of abolition and its transformation from a moral to a political issue. Joseph Goodrich, founder of Milton and proprietor of the hotel, moved from New York State to Wisconsin and was one of many who brought the reform movement and its ideals westward.

Namur Historic District

Location: Namur, Door County
Relevant issues: Cultural history
Statement of significance: Located in northeastern Wisconsin, this area contains the nation's largest known concentration of Belgian-influenced farmsteads, other rural buildings, and landscape features. Namur is a lively ethnic enclave where French is still spoken with a Walloon accent and where the heritage of the area is evident in food and ethnic festivals. Although Belgian settlement of the area dates to the 1850's, most of the buildings were constructed after the Great Peshtigo Fire of 1871.

Oconto Site

Location: Oconto, Oconto County
Relevant issues: American Indian history
Statement of significance: At this prehistoric burial ground, implements of the Old Copper Culture people, who occupied the northern Midwest about 2500 B.C.E., have been found in association with human burials. The site forms the Copper Culture State Park.

Soldiers' Home Reef

Location: Milwaukee, Milwaukee County
Relevant issues: Science and technology
Statement of significance: This rock mound in the Menomonee River Valley near Milwaukee was discovered by Increase A. Lapham, Wisconsin's first scientist, in the 1830's. In 1862, James Hall was the first to recognize and interpret this and several other early mounds as fossil reefs, making them the first ancient reefs described in North America and among the first described anywhere in the world. Thomas C. Chamberlin used this and other reefs in formulating his paleoecological and sedimentological model of reef development, which was published in his classic 1877 work *Geology of Eastern Wisconsin.*

Turner Hall

Location: Milwaukee, Milwaukee County
Relevant issues: Cultural history
Statement of significance: Milwaukee Turner Hall, built in 1882, is among the few surviving nineteenth century historic buildings associated with the American Turners, a very influential organization of German Americans. The last Turner clubhouse in Milwaukee, the "German Athens" of America, it exemplifies the major place and multifaceted role the Milwaukee Turners have held in this national organization. The buildings also represents the Milwaukee Turners' unheralded role in political reform from the antislavery movement in the 1850's through the era of progressive municipal reform.

University of Wisconsin Armory and Gymnasium

Location: Madison, Dane County
Relevant issues: Political history, social reform
Statement of significance: This was the site of the 1904 Wisconsin Republican Convention, a seminal event in the history of the Progressive movement. At this convention, Robert M. La Follette's Progressives defeated the Stalwarts for control of the Wisconsin Republican Party. Widespread favorable publicity launched La Follette on the national scene. The controversy and legal suit engendered by the "Gymnasium Convention" and La Follette's subsequent vindication by the Supreme Court of Wisconsin led the Progressives to victory that November, giving them a majority in the state legislature the following year. This allowed the enactment of substantial reforms, many of which were subsequently adopted by many states across the nation.

University of Wisconsin Science Hall

Location: Madison, Dane County
Relevant issues: Education, science and technology
Statement of significance: Science Hall is associated with Charles R. Van Hise (1857-1918), who was the first geologist in the nation to apply microscopic lithology to the extensive study of crystalline rocks and to use those results in the formulation of geological principles. Van Hise's emphasis on the quantitative application of physical and chemical laws to geological problems was one of his greatest contributions to the science of geology. His influential 1904 monograph *A Treatise on Metamorphism* moved geology out of the science of classification and into formulating principles. As a teacher, Van Hise earned a reputation for training geologists who matched his own high standards in scientific research.

Villa Louis

Location: Prairie du Chien, Crawford County
Relevant issues: Business and industry
Statement of significance: Hercules Louis Dousman I (1800-1868), prominent fur agent for the American Fur Company, adviser to the government on matters ranging from Indian affairs to land surveys, and owner of river steamboats and a proponent of the railroads, built a large brick Georgian style house here in 1843. In 1870, it was replaced by his son with this villa complex with outbuildings. The house stands on a mound—believed to be a Hopewell site—which was also the site of two early forts.

Wyoming

Devil's Tower. (Digital Stock)

History of Wyoming

Wyoming is an expansive, arid land of high sweeping plains punctuated by series of mountain ranges. Its average elevation is some 6,700 feet above sea level. Travelers have frequently remarked on the state's austere beauty: "Nature has collected all of her beauties together," explorer John C. Frémont wrote of the region in 1842, "in one chosen place." Passing through the state's southern tier at night, travelers are mesmerized by multiple, simultaneous lightning storms illuminating vast plains, jagged mountains silhouetted in the background.

For all its magnificence, however, for much of its history Wyoming has been only the path to somewhere else. Today, Wyoming's immense emptiness supports fewer than half a million people, a diminishing portion of whom are destined to lead rugged lives employed in mining, livestock grazing, and agriculture. Memory of the state's colorful past is kept alive by frequent rodeos, roundups, and frontier celebrations. Each summer tourists flock to its spectacular scenery—to Jackson Hole, the Grand Tetons, and incomparable Yellowstone, the world's first national park.

Early History

According to archaeological evidence, the earliest immigrants to Wyoming arrived about eleven thousand years ago, leaving various traces. In 1965 two dwellings testifying to the habitation of the earliest peoples were discovered near Guernsey, on the North Platte River, southeast of Casper. For many years immense herds of buffalo roamed the midwestern plains. They attracted many migrating peoples from Asia who traversed the Bering Straits, many of them inhabiting the Wyoming region—tribes such as the Arapaho, Bannock, Crow, Cheyenne, Sioux, and Shoshone.

Earliest contact between these peoples and whites may have occurred in the mid-eighteenth century, when French trappers entered the area. Extensive exploration did not begin until the following century, however, after the United States concluded the Louisiana Purchase in 1803 and President Thomas Jefferson sent Meriwether Lewis and William Clark to chart what the nation had bought. By then, parts of Wyoming had been claimed by Spain, France, and Great Britain. It required several more acquisitions for Wyoming's modern territory to be completed. The 1819 Treaty with Spain, the partition of Texas after the Lone Star Republic joined the Union in 1845, the agreement with Britain over the Columbia River country in 1846, and the Treaty of Guadalupe Hidalgo in 1848 all included land within the state's modern borders.

Exploration

Fur trading was the initial stimulus to exploring Wyoming. The first American to do so was a former member of the Lewis and Clark Expedition, John Colter. In 1807, Colter traveled across the Yellowstone area, where he sighted its geothermal activity. Other fur traders crossed Wyoming going to and from Astoria, Oregon. In the 1820's more fur trappers and traders made their way west, many of them to Wyoming. In 1825, an annual gathering of these men, who included Indians, was inaugurated that lasted for fifteen years. In 1834 traders founded Fort Williams, later renamed Fort Laramie, which became the area's first permanent trading post. In 1843 famous scout Jim Bridger founded a second trading post near the western end of the state, east of Evanston.

At about the same time, John C. Frémont led a party through the region guided by scout Kit Carson. Frémont's reports to Congress on his explorations spurred provision for protection of migrants on the Oregon Trail, and in 1849, the government purchased Fort Williams. Wyoming had become a pathway for tens of thousands of migrants and adventurers using several trails leading west, including the Oregon, California, and Mormon Trails. These trails traversed the South Pass through the Rocky Mountains, continued to Fort Bridger, then divided. The first Mormon party passed through in 1847. A Mormon colony established near the Utah border perished in a blizzard in 1856. A succession of outposts was established in the 1860's, including telegraph stations and state coach and freight line

along the great trails. By 1870 Wyoming had more than nine thousand white inhabitants. Discovery of gold in the Black Hills of the Dakotas led to fierce Indian resistance, when thousands of settlers ignored treaty provisions and moved into territory the Sioux considered sacred. Bloody battles were fought with the U.S. Army. Peace was finally restored in 1876, when the last of the Indian warriors fled or surrendered and settled on reservations.

By then Wyoming had undergone development as a separate society. The coming of the railroad led to the formation of Wyoming Territory in 1868. Population jumped to more than twenty thousand in 1880 and to some sixty-two thousand in 1890. Mining was supplemented by cattle grazing and shipments of longhorns from Texas on their way to market. Sheep also made their appearance, setting the stage for protracted struggle between sheepmen and cattlemen later immortalized in Hollywood films. Oil had been known to exist in the region since the 1830's, when it was used to grease wagon wheels. In 1883 the first well was drilled in the Dallas Field, in the Wind River region.

Politically, Wyoming Territory was growing up quickly. In 1869 it became the first territorial legislature to allow women to vote, serve on juries, and hold office. In 1924 it was first to elect a female governor. However, in certain respects it remained primitive. The Wyoming Stock Growers Association, formed as a local association in 1873, grew powerful enough to enforce its own vigilante law in defense of its interests. In the 1890's matters deteriorated with the decline of the cattle industry and ruinous cattle rustling by groups such as the notorious Hole-in-the-Wall Gang. Homesteaders, who fenced off the open range, arrived. In 1892 the association decided to act, embarking on the Johnson County Cattle War. Texas gunmen, hired to murder a list of enemies, killed two men before the law stepped in. Later in the 1890's more violence

stops. In 1860-1861, Pony Express riders crossed Wyoming in their epic journey from Missouri to California.

From the late 1840's onward, Native Americans viewed these developments with suspicion. The opening of the Bozeman Trail in 1864 after gold was discovered in Montana particularly alarmed them, as settlers streamed in. Native Americans and settlers made and broke treaties, and fighting continued throughout the decade. Settlers began to arrive in greater numbers when gold was discovered in the South Pass area in 1867 and later when coal was found. To keep the Bozeman Trail operating, the U.S. Army opened Fort Phil Kearny in 1866. The Sioux, led by Chief Red Cloud, detested the fort and determined to raze it. More than 150 white men were killed in its defense, including 81, led by Captain W. J. Fetterman, killed in a single battle. The army closed the fort in 1868 after concluding a treaty with the Sioux, who agreed not to oppose the building of a railroad in the south.

Becoming a Territory

The greatest influx of settlers occurred with railroads, beginning with the Union Pacific, which crossed Wyoming in 1868. Construction camps that sprang up became towns, such as Rawlins, Green River, and Rock Springs; more towns arose

occurred with the influx of sheepherders, blamed for the inability of cattle to find sufficient food.

Statehood

These events aside, by the turn of the century Wyoming was fast becoming part of the nation. In 1889, without waiting for passage of a congressional enabling act, a proposed state constitution was drawn up. The following year Wyoming became the nation's forty-fourth state. It arrived into the Union with a progressive constitution that included a provision for women's suffrage. The constitution also included fulsome support for popular sovereignty and freedom of religion. Judges would be elected, not appointed, on a nonpartisan basis. The constitution was made difficult to amend.

The state's politics have been marked by both conservative and maverick tendencies. In the 1980's one of its senators, Dick Cheney, was selected secretary of defense, and another, Alan Simpson, was widely admired by political opponents for his candor and civility. Wyoming has also been noted for its patriotism. Despite its small size, it contributed to the Spanish-American War of 1898, surpassing its quota of volunteers. It also sent twelve thousand men and women to World War I.

Economically, Wyoming was able to increase its agriculture after the turn of the century through irrigation, as homesteaders continued to arrive. In addition, tourism became more economically significant for the state, as better roads and railroad service made it easier for people to reach scenic areas such as Yellowstone. The Depression, however, hit the state hard, though an increase in oil production and New Deal projects helped hard-pressed wage earners.

World War II and Postwar Developments

World War II found Wyoming's patriotic spirit intact, as tens of thousands of men and hundreds of women went off to war. At home the economy bustled with government's demands for food and mineral deposits for the war effort. After the war, the state continued to prosper, when the Cold War brought more federal government spending. Atomic weapons production brought lucrative mining ventures when uranium was discovered in the state, and military spending increased when Wyoming was chosen as a primary site for testing of intercontinental missiles.

The state's population continued to grow, from 92,000 at the turn of the century to 290,000 in 1950 and 40,000 more a decade later. After that time, however, growth was uneven, advancing only 2,000 from 1960 to 1970 and actually losing ground from 1980 to 1990. By then, although it had grown to more than 450,000, comparatively little manufacturing in the state and the difficulty of agriculture still placed it at the bottom of the list of state populations. Economically, although services provide some 60 percent of the state's income, it is heavily dependent on the land, through mining, grazing, and construction. By the 1990's, the state was attempting to broaden its economic base, especially by developing tourism. Politically, the state was divided between those who favored economic development and those who looked to the conservation of the state's natural resources.

—*Charles F. Bahmueller*

Fort Laramie

Date: Built in 1834; proclaimed a National Monument on July 16, 1938, and a National Historic Site on April 29, 1960

Relevant issues: Business and industry, European settlement, military history, western expansion

Significance: This National Historic Site was originally a trading post built by fur traders William Sublette and Robert Campbell. It was purchased by the American Fur Company in 1836, then sold to the U.S. Army on June 6, 1849. The post was ordered to be abandoned in August, 1889.

Location: The National Historic Site is three miles southwest of the town of Fort Laramie, off U.S. Route 26

Site Office:
Fort Laramie National Historic Site
HC 72, Box 389
Fort Laramie, WY 82212
ph.: (307) 837-2221
fax: (307) 837-2120
Web site: www.nps.gov/fola/

Until the coming of the railroad, Fort Laramie was the capital of a vast domain extending from the northern Missouri River posts to Denver and Sante Fe. For more than fifty years, first as a trading post and later as a military fort, Laramie served in the advance of an epic westward migration across the plains to Oregon and California. The post's key location compelled it to play a leading role in the fur trade, the Oregon and Overland Trails, the Pony Express, the transcontinental telegraph line, and the U.S. military campaigns against the Plains Indians.

Early History

Fort Laramie was originally built by fur trader and pioneer William Sublette. In the early 1830's, Sublette and his partner, Robert Campbell, established a trading post near the mouth of Yellowstone River, a few miles from Fort Union, which was owned by John Jacob Astor's American Fur Company. The new trading fort posed an immediate threat to Astor's monopoly over the upper Missouri fur trade and led to an agreement providing for Sublette and Campbell to abandon their post and Astor's company to retreat from the central Rocky region for one year. In 1834 Sublette and Campbell withdrew from the upper Missouri and built a new trading fort at the river junction of the North Platte and Laramie's Fork. The strategic and commercial advantages of the post became immediately apparent, as it was located at the intersection of the Great Plains route to the mountain fur areas and the Trappers Trail south to Taos, as well as within trading distance of various Indian tribes.

Originally named Fort William, the post hastened the decline of the fur rendezvous in the central Rockies, an annual trading fair among trappers, Indians, and traders, in favor of the buffalo robe trade based in settlements and fixed outposts. Also, the fort marked the first permanent outpost of white society in Indian country in the central Rocky region. Within a year of the fort's beginnings, Sublette lured the nomadic Oglala Sioux south from the Dakota trading posts in the Black Hills to the North Platte with inducements of better trading goods, richer grasslands, and numerous buffalo.

In years following, the Oglala Sioux, more than any other tribe, made the trading post its home base. Other tribes also followed, including the Arapaho, the Cheyenne, and the Crow. The new fort signaled the expansion of permanent trading posts that had started on the upper Missouri following the War of 1812. A booming market for buffalo robes in the 1830's had developed in the American

East, and traders offered every enticement to involve the Indians in the expanding robe trade. As a result, the Plains Indians slaughtered buffalo, trading the robes for guns, powder, ammunition, knives, blankets, whiskey, and other goods. Trading at the annual rendezvous and at river posts became a vitally important event each year, often leading the Indians to satisfy both their need for trade goods and the huge market for buffalo robes.

In 1835, Sublette and Campbell sold the fort to the Rocky Mountain Fur Company run by Thomas Fitzpatrick, Jim Bridger, and Milton Sublette (younger brother of William), who in 1836 sold it to their archrival, the American Fur Company. In the late 1830's, the company considerably expanded Fort William into a major center of trade with the Plains Indians—the Sioux, the Arapaho, the Cheyenne, and the Crow. The post consisted mostly of trading and repair rooms, small living quarters, and, in the middle of the central open area, a large tree that served as a flagpole on special occasions.

In 1841, Lieutenant Lancaster P. Lupton established a new trading post, named Fort Platte, about a mile and a half from Fort William on the North Platte River above the mouth of the Laramie River. The appearance of Lupton's post and the rotting condition of old Fort William compelled the American Fur Company to construct a new adobe fort on higher ground a mile upstream. The company christened the new post Fort John after John B. Sarpy, a partner in the American Fur Company, but it was soon commonly called Fort Laramie. With competition from Fort Platte also came the explosive liquor trade, wreaking degradation on Indian tribes in spite of its suppression by the Bureau of Indian Affairs starting in 1842.

The Oregon Trail

William Sublette not only had built the original fort but also pioneered the trail that would reinforce Fort Laramie's importance as a major way station for emigrants headed to Oregon and California. From 1830 to 1838, Sublette helped forge a wagon trail up the Platte and over South Pass to the fur rendezvous. Thomas Fitzpatrick followed this same path on his treks to the West Coast. In 1841, Fitzpatrick led a small band of settlers on the first westward journey across the plains to the Pacific coast, starting a tide that would soon rise to flood proportions and cast Fort Laramie in the forefront of the mass western migration. In 1842, Fitzpatrick guided another group of settlers to the Oregon Territory in the face of Indian hostility. Although the trail over the Continental Divide was already well known among many fur trappers and wilderness guides, publicity generated by Lieutenant John C. Frémont's expedition to South Pass opened the way for mass migration to the Pacific coast. To protect emigrants along the Oregon Trail, Frémont also advocated the establishment of a military post at Fort Laramie.

With the Democratic presidential victory of 1844, expansionists were determined to claim Oregon and California as U.S. soil. As a result, President James K. Polk recommended that a chain of forts be built on the route between the frontier settlements on the Missouri and the Rocky Mountains, and in 1846 Congress legislated the establishment of such military posts along the Oregon Trail. The outbreak of hostilities with Mexico, however, delayed action. At the war's conclusion in 1848, the United States had won California and the vast southwestern territory beyond the Rocky Mountains. In addition, Great Britain had ceded Oregon Territory up to the forty-ninth parallel to the United States in 1846. The Far West became U.S. soil awaiting settlement by eastern emigrants. The compelling need to turn Fort Laramie into a mili-

tary post became even more apparent with the discovery of gold in California in 1848, igniting a frantic gold rush across the Overland Trails and reinforcing Fort Laramie's role as a major provisioning station and safe haven for emigrants headed west. At the height of the California gold rush, it was reported that more than nine thousand wagons passed by Fort Laramie in a single day.

The Oregon and California (Overland) Trails started out as nothing more than a crude network of rutted traces across the western United States. Starting from Independence, Missouri, the trails ran together across the plains of Kansas and Nebraska into North Platte River country to Fort Laramie. From Fort Laramie emigrants crossed the Continental Divide at South Pass and normally headed for Fort Bridger on the edge of present-day Wyoming. At Soda Springs, Idaho, the California Trail split off heading southwest while the Oregon Trail turned northwest toward the Snake River valley. Travelers could take alternative routes, including Sublette's Cutoff just west of South Pass, which crossed a fifty-mile stretch of barren country devoid of water and grassland. Those who successfully made the arduous trek saved eighty-five miles and a week of travel to Oregon. Western-bound emigrants usually started in the spring when the land along the trail provided them with abundant water and grass for livestock. If they began the journey early enough in the year, the waterholes and grasslands would not be fouled or overgrazed. Most emigrant deaths resulted from disease, especially cholera. At Fort Laramie and other depots along the way, emigrants could replenish dwindling stocks of food and other staples, repair wagons, and allow livestock to graze before grasslands became scarce farther on.

Erection of Fort Laramie

During the gold rush stampede, the U.S. War Department sent Brevet Major Winslow F. Sanderson heading a company of mounted riflemen to reconnoiter the sur-

Fort Laramie. (National Park Service)

rounding country around Fort Laramie to determine the best site for a military outpost. Given Fort Laramie's strategic location, Sanderson ordered its purchase from the American Fur Company for four thousand dollars. On June 26, 1849, the U.S. Army assumed ownership of the old fort that had served as the main trading station for the central Rockies. By mid-August, a second company of mounted riflemen and a company of infantry along with wagonloads of supplies and equipment joined Sanderson at Fort Laramie. After being fully garrisoned, the fort underwent immediate and continual improvements with the building of the first officers' quarters, a two-story edifice known as "Old Bedlam," quartermaster and commissary storehouses, warehouses, stone guardhouses, the magazine, a hospital, a permanent bakery, stables, additional quarters for officers and enlisted men, and a post trader's store. Following its fur trade phase, the fort never stood as a fortified post even after the Indian troubles of 1854. The Fort Laramie garrison typically ranged in strength from sixty to two hundred soldiers until the Utah War of 1858. Troop strength was again reduced during the U.S. Civil War, despite the Sioux uprisings along the Powder River.

In the spring of 1850, the tide of emigration past Fort Laramie swelled to more than fifty thousand in search of gold, causing widespread destruction of grasslands and loss of buffalo along the trail. The vast devastation prompted bitter complaints among various Indian tribes and led to increasing tensions on the plains. Thomas Fitzpatrick, who had led the first emigrant party over the Continental Divide and was now an Indian agent for the Bureau of Indian Affairs, recognized the need to alleviate a potentially explosive situation. He advocated a general treaty with the Plains Indians to compensate them for the mass despoiling of grasslands and the disappearance of the buffalo.

Consequently, Congress appropriated $100,000 to support Fitzpatrick's treaty plans, and in 1851 a grand council was held in the vicinity of Fort Laramie, thirty-five miles downstream on the North Platte at Horse Creek, where more than ten thousand Sioux, Cheyenne, Assiniboin, Shoshone, Arikara, Gros Ventre, Mandan, Arapaho, and Crow gathered for the mass assembly. The greatest gathering of Indians ever held on the Plains was moved from the original site of Fort Laramie to Horse Creek to provide better foraging grounds for the Indians' horses.

Colonel David D. Mitchell, superintendent of the western Indian country, proposed the terms of the treaty—that the Indian nations cease warring among themselves and that the nations agree to delineate the boundaries of their territories. Within these boundaries each tribe would be responsible for maintaining peace and order. Furthermore, each tribe was to elect one chief to conduct the transaction of business with the U.S. government. In return, the Indian nations were promised an annual annuity of fifty thousand dollars for fifty years to be given in the form of merchandise and provisions. The U.S. Senate later reduced the time period to ten years but increased the annuity to seventy thousand dollars as compensation. The patronizing terms of the Fort Laramie Treaty signaled the beginning of the end of Plains Indian independence as tribes grew increasingly reliant on trade goods and government benevolence.

Conflict on the North Platte

Tensions mounted on the North Platte. The ever-growing Overland traffic continued to destroy grasslands and reduce the buffalo herds, increasing the impoverishment and desperation of the Indians. The stationing of regular troops who were unsympathetic to Indian ways at Fort Laramie exacerbated tensions still further. A skirmish between Fort Laramie troops and the Miniconjou group of the Sioux in June, 1853, resulting in the death of three Indians, presaged more troublesome times ahead. On August 18, 1854, open hostilities broke out following an incident eight miles east of Fort Laramie near a trading post. More than one thousand hungry Sioux had gathered in the vicinity of the fort to receive their annual annuities when one of them killed a lame cow that strayed into their camp from a Mormon wagon train. After the Mormons reported the incident at Fort Laramie, Lieutenant John L. Grattan led a detachment of twenty-eight volunteer soldiers, field guns, and an interpreter on an expedition to capture the accused Miniconjou. A drunken interpreter and Grattan's rash orders to fire peremptorily on the Sioux resulted in the wounding of Chief Conquering Bear, a signer of the 1851 Fort Laramie Treaty, and sparked the massacre of the entire Fort Laramie detachment, beginning a twenty-five-year period of intermittent warfare.

In 1854, Congress created the territories of Kansas and Nebraska and passed the Preemption Law to enable farmers to settle the land at nominal prices. The great land rush that ensued at first had little effect on the Plains Indians, but the new territories stretched all the way to the Rockies, including tribal hunting grounds and Fort Laramie. One year later, the Army Corps of Engineers and the Department of the Interior began constructing roads to the Rockies and beyond, soon traversed by thousands more emigrants going west to Utah, California, and Oregon; stage coach lines; and the Pony Express. In the early 1860's, Western Union began building the first transcontinental telegraph line. The mass of relentless white advancement mainly followed the Oregon and Overland trails, along which stood the military post of Fort Laramie. As in previous years since 1849, the fort continued to protect transportation and communication lines from Indian hostilities and to serve as an important way station for supply, intelligence, reinforcement, and diplomacy for the military campaigns against the Sioux.

Wars with the Sioux

As a result of the Grattan incident and Chief Conquering Bear's subsequent death, the Sioux began attacking emigrants on the Oregon-California Trail. On November 13, 1854, a small band of Brule Sioux attacked the monthly mail wagon to Salt Lake, killing three, wounding one, and making off with ten thousand dollars in gold. By that time, Indian hostilities spread from the Platte to the Missouri as other Sioux tribes joined the war. In retaliation for the Grattan massacre and the continuing Indian insurgency, Brevet Brigadier General William C. Harney was ordered to deal with the Sioux emergency. An experienced soldier who had fought Indians from Florida to Wisconsin, Harney led an expedition of some seven hundred cavalry, infantry, and light artillery soldiers to pacify the central plains and secure the military post of Fort Laramie. The punitive expedition culminated in 1855 when Harney massacred one hundred Brule Sioux at Ash Hollow after tracking them down one hundred fifty miles south of Fort Laramie. On March 1, 1856, Harney forced the Sioux to sign a peace treaty at Fort Pierre, essentially restating the terms of the Fort Laramie Treaty of 1851.

The Civil War Years

The years during the Civil War marked some of the most dangerous in the fort's history. The exigencies of the southern rebellion compelled the reduction of the Fort Laramie garrison to skeletal strength. Under the command of Colonel William O. Collins, the Eleventh Ohio Volunteer Cavalry was spread thin for hundreds of miles at outposts from Mud Springs to South Pass to protect the new telegraph line from Sioux attack. The discovery of gold in 1862 in Montana territory prompted another gold rush along the Oregon Trail, and in 1864 John Bozeman pioneered a new road to Montana, which split off from the Oregon Trail west of Fort Laramie through Powder River country, the heart of Sioux territory. The flood of prospectors and the continuing mass emigration to California and Oregon ignited the Powder River War.

In 1866, as peace negotiations were under way with the Sioux at Fort Laramie, Colonel Henry B. Carrington led an expedition to establish two military posts along the Bozeman Trail. Despite warnings from the Sioux, Carrington proceeded with the expedition, prompting Red Cloud to declare war and lay siege to the Bozeman Trail. Ironically, Fort Laramie not only supplied the U.S. Army with weapons, intelligence, and communications, but also filled a similar role for the warring Sioux. Fort Laramie was never without ostensibly friendly Indian bands who traded and camped near the post, providing needed arms and intelligence to the hostile tribes. In 1868, an uneasy peace ensued with the signing of the second Fort Laramie Treaty. It lasted until the discovery of gold in the Black Hills and the subsequent eruption of the Sioux Black Hills campaign of 1876-1877, in which the fort again played a central military role.

Coming of the Railroad

In the 1860's and 1870's, the construction of the Union Pacific Railroad seventy miles to the south and the Chicago and Northwestern Railroad fifty miles to the north effectively bypassed Fort Laramie and signaled the beginning of its decline in importance. The military post continued to field expeditions and patrols but was ordered to be abandoned in 1889. The last troops left the fort in March, 1890, months before the last military action against the Plains Indians, the Massacre at Wounded Knee.

A year later, the buildings at Fort Laramie were sold at public auction and subsequently razed or moved, leaving mostly archaeological remains. Three purchasers, however, bought the fort and preserved a substantial part of the historic post. Through the efforts of John Hunton, the last post trader, most of "officers' row," including Old Bedlam, two officers' quarters, and the trader's store, was preserved. Others converted the cavalry barracks to a hotel and the nearby commissary warehouse and bakery to barns. The captain's quarters of 1870 and the 1866 guardhouse were preserved in their original state. Ten principal buildings survived, albeit in a dilapidated condition, until 1938, when the National Park Service received the site from the state of Wyoming and subsequently declared it a National Historic Site.

Modern Preservation Efforts

Since 1950, the site has undergone a continuing program of stabilization and restoration of historic structures. Today, the restored buildings include the trader's store and complex comprising the officers' club, enlisted soldiers' bar, and post office; Old Bedlam, complete with commanding officer's headquarters and bachelor officers' quarters; two additional concrete officers' quarters; and bakery, guardhouse, magazine, commissary, and cavalry barracks. The site also encompasses remains of the hospital, administration building, several officers' quarters, and other structures. The old 1876 bridge across the North Platte has been preserved, as well as sections of the Oregon-California Trail, deep ruts carved into the land by the passage of thousands of wagon wheels. The contemporary historic site celebrates Fort Laramie as an outpost of empire which played an important role in the fur trade, the Oregon and Overland Trails, and the Plains Indian Wars.   —*Bruce P. Montgomery*

For Further Information:
DeVoto, Bernard. *Across the Wide Missouri.* 1947. Reprint. Boston: Houghton Mifflin, 1998. Contains a description of Fort Laramie. Deals with the Rocky Mountain fur trade.

_____. *The Year of Decision, 1846.* 1943. Reprint. Boston: Little, Brown, 1989. A narrative story of the pre-Civil War, far western frontier that describes Fort Laramie.

Frazer, Robert W. *Forts of the West.* Norman: University of Oklahoma Press, 1963. Offers a brief description of the fort.

Hart, Herbert M. *Old Forts of the Northwest.* Seattle: Superior, 1963. Contains a brief description of the fort.

Mattes, Merrill J. *The Great Platte River Road: The Covered Wagon Mainline Via Fort Kearny to Fort Laramie.* Reprint. Lincoln: University of Nebraska Press, 1988. A comprehensive study of the pioneer trail on the Great Platte River Road, including two chapters on Fort Laramie dealing with the 1849 California gold rush and the fort's role as the gateway to the mountains.

Nadeau, Remi. *Fort Laramie and the Sioux.* New rev. ed. Santa Barbara, Calif.: Crest, 1997. A readable account of the effect of Fort Laramie as a trading and military outpost of the American frontier on the high Plains Indians—the Sioux, Cheyenne, and Arapaho. The book's major theme concerns Fort Laramie's role in advancing the settlement of the West and precipitating the decline and fall of the those Indian nations.

Yellowstone

Date: Founded in 1872

Relevant issues: American Indian history, cultural history, military history, political history, western expansion

Significance: Yellowstone National Park, dedicated by Congress on March 1, 1872, was the first national park in the United States and the first step toward the creation of a National Park Service. Cultural sites show human occupation dating back twelve thousand years. The park embraces the area traversed by the fleeing Nez Perce Indians in 1877.

Location: Northwestern Wyoming, extending into Montana and Idaho

Site Office:
Yellowstone National Park
P.O. Box 168
Yellowstone National Park, WY 82190-0168
ph.: (307) 344-7381; TDD: (307) 344-2386
Web site: www.nps.gov/yell/

With almost 3,500 square miles, Yellowstone is the largest wilderness in the lower forty-eight states. Five years after it was dedicated, visitors saw

Chief Joseph and his band of Nez Perce Indians fleeing through the park toward Canada. Caught just short of the border by General Nelson Miles, Chief Joseph surrendered with his famous speech, "From where the sun now stands, I will fight no more forever."

As the nation's first park, it served as a laboratory for administration of the nation's natural, historical, and cultural resources. The stone arch entrance, where the cornerstone was laid by President Theodore Roosevelt in 1903, bears his name and the legend, "For the benefit and enjoyment of the people," taken from the Dedication Act of 1872.

The National Park Idea

Stirred by mountaineers' tales of the geysers, boiling mud, hot springs, and steam vents, scientists began to organize expeditions into the Yellowstone wilderness after the Civil War. Two expeditions gave birth to the concept of a national park. In the fall of 1870, the Washburn-Langford-Doane Expe-

dition explored the watershed of the Yellowstone River. While sitting around a campfire, members agreed that the wilderness should be placed in the public domain for the people to enjoy and preserved from spoliation by unscrupulous speculators and commercial developers.

In 1871, Colonel F. V. Hayden led a U.S. Geological Survey team of scientists, artists, and photographers, who mapped and documented the natural habitat, geothermal sites, and landscape of Yellowstone. Hayden joined with the Washburn team in proposing that Congress reserve the lands as a national park. He used the sketches and paintings made by team artist Thomas Moran to convince Congress that Yellowstone was unique and should be preserved for future generations. Congress enacted the legislation creating Yellowstone National Park on March 1, 1872, and placed the park under the exclusive control of the secretary of the interior.

Congress mandated that the park be operated for the benefit and enjoyment of the people, and

Buffalo still roam Yellowstone National Park. (PhotoDisc)

that the natural and scenic environment be preserved in an undisturbed condition. The secretary of the interior was empowered to make rules and regulations to preserve the timber, mineral deposits, and natural curiosities, and to protect the wildlife from destruction.

Civilian superintendents managed the park from 1872 to 1886, but they had little expertise in handling public demands, in dealing with concessionaires, or in conserving wildlife. Rather than appropriating funds to hire qualified personnel, Congress expected the park to pay its operating costs from revenue collected on site. However, enough money was never collected in public utility fees, taxes on concessions, vehicle permits, and sales of timber, stone, and animal hides to maintain public services and enforce conservation as well. Without sufficient funding and training, the superintendents were overwhelmed, and park operations were in chaos.

In 1886, Congress eliminated the civilian superintendent's job and told the secretary of the interior to invoke the Sundry Civil Act of 1883 and request troops from the War Department to protect the park.

Fort Yellowstone
That same year, Company M of the First United States Cavalry, with Captain Moses Harris in command, moved into temporary quarters in frame buildings at Camp Sheridan near the foot of Mammoth Hot Springs Terraces. After five harsh winters, the cavalry realized that the assignment was not temporary and requested permanent quarters. Congress approved fifty thousand dollars to build Fort Yellowstone. The original fort buildings included headquarters, officers' quarters, barracks, a guardhouse, and horse stables.

In 1909, new buildings of native sandstone were added to the fort, including the Scottish Rite Cha-

Old Faithful geyser, which erupts about every half hour. (PhotoDisc)

pel. These red-roofed multiple-chimney buildings are part of the Fort Yellowstone-Mammoth Hot Springs Historic District. By 1910, 324 soldiers were stationed at Fort Yellowstone, accompanied by a number of families and civilian employees.

The Army also built log cabins in the backcountry for use by troops on patrol against poachers, vandals, and forest fires. These outposts, four of which still stand, were a day's journey (sixteen to twenty miles) apart. They were outfitted with bunk beds, a table, desk, bookcases, and wood-burning stoves. A soldier station at Norris (c. 1886) was rebuilt and modified after it burned in 1897. After the Park Service took over, Norris Station was used as a park ranger station and residence until the 1959 earthquake. Restored in 1991, the station houses the Museum of the National Park Ranger.

The Army served as park rangers and policemen for thirty years, until the National Park Service took control of all national parks and monuments then under the Interior Department's jurisdiction.

The National Park Service

On August 25, 1916, Congress passed the National Park Service Organic Act and transferred Yellowstone National Park to the new agency's supervision. The Organic Act defined the fundamental purposes of the Park Service: to provide for public enjoyment; to preserve the natural, cultural, and historical features and objects in unimpaired condition; and to protect the wildlife and habitat.

In 1918, when the Army transferred control to the Park Service, some of the soldiers stayed on as park rangers. The Park Service reorganized Yellowstone into three ranger districts, each supervised by an assistant chief ranger. The Park Service adopted distinctive uniforms in 1922. Though few women were park rangers until the 1960's, the women's uniforms in the 1920's had long skirts held up by galluses, worn with buttoned-up jackets similar to the men's uniforms. By 1925, all permanent rangers were qualified under Civil Service Rules, and seasonal rangers were appointed as needed. Colorado A&M College became known as the "Ranger Factory" because so many of the students worked as seasonal rangers at Yellowstone.

The automobile brought tremendous changes to Yellowstone. The facilities had to be reorganized to accommodate the traveling public's shift to motorized vehicles. National Park Service Director Stephen Mather called a conference of concessionaires in Washington, D.C., to make these decisions. Yellowstone Park Transportation Company was given exclusive rights to provide public transportation, on condition that it be fully motorized. The company ordered 116 motor buses, with spare parts and tires, at a cost of $427,104.67. Frank V. Haynes retained the photographic concession but surrendered his stagecoach and bus lines. The park also suspended boat operations on the lake.

Control of permanent camping at the park was simplified into a single system. The two camping companies merged, closing old camps and lunch stations, and opening five new camps at locations that were convenient for automobiles: Mammoth Hot Springs, Old Faithful, Yellowstone Lake, Canyon, and Tower Junction. The Yellowstone Park Hotel Company remained in charge of hotel operations but closed two stopover hotels. The reorganization activities were interrupted when the United States entered World War I and resources were shifted to the war effort.

Under the Park Service, the parks began interpretative programs and museums to enhance visitors' experience. Yellowstone's staff naturalist had charge of the educational program. He installed museums and trailside exhibits at stopping points throughout the park, and trained rangers as interpreters. They conducted public lectures, group singing, and storytelling at each of the ranger stations.

In the off-season, park rangers manage the elk and buffalo herds. They cut hay for winter feed and killed coyotes until 1934, when the director ordered that practice stopped. The rangers maintain the elk and buffalo herds at a level the parklands can sustain, killing off any surplus. To protect Wyoming cattle herds, the rangers test the buffalo herds for brucellosis, a disease that is transmissible to humans. Rangers also worked at the Lake Fish Hatchery until it closed in 1958, and the Lake Hatchery Historic District became the headquarters for the southern Yellowstone Lake Maintenance District.

Not all Wyoming citizens celebrate the park's existence. Stockmen, farmers, and lumbermen want the rights to graze sheep and harvest timber on lands that are not being used. In 1927, proposed changes that would extend the park boundaries sparked a controversy. The state of Wyoming asked the federal government to return the Teton Mountains and part of Teton National Forest for a state park. Senator Tom Cooper of Wyoming asked that three million acres be ceded back to Wyoming to provide income to the public school system.

In the face of protests, the Park Service dropped its request to add to the park the headwaters of Yellowstone River and reservoir sites in the Falls River Basin. On March 1, 1929, Congress enlarged the park by 78 square miles through an exchange of two tracts between the U.S. Forest Service and the National Park Service.

In reorganizing his administration in 1933, President Franklin D. Roosevelt issued executive orders giving the Park Service control of all national parks, monuments, and historic sites. During his administration, millions of dollars and hundreds of workers flowed to the Park Service from the Civilian Conservation Corps and other New Deal programs, to build roads, museums, and administration and visitors' centers, and to improve facilities at the national parks. In 1941, after these improvements, Yellowstone attracted a record visitation of 581,761 people.

However, with the advent of World War II and rationing of gasoline and tires, park visitation plummeted. Many park concessions and services were suspended for the duration. After the war, Yellowstone was inundated with war-weary pleasure seekers, all in automobiles. Yellowstone Park's facilities were again overwhelmed.

To cope with the problem, the Park Service proposed "Mission 66," a ten-year project to upgrade all national parks and public services by the year 1966. Yellowstone's objectives were improved road and trail systems, public facilities for visitors, effective interpretation, and protection of park resources. Projected costs for ten years exceeded two million dollars. Inadequate funding slowed Yellowstone's renovation even while visitation increased. Mission 66 was incomplete when it was replaced by the Interior Department's "Road to the Future," a less ambitious plan oriented toward recreation.

Yellowstone, the nation's historic pioneer park, has been a showcase for the National Park Service's mandated challenges—to create an enjoyable experience for visitors and simultaneously preserve the historical and natural treasures for future generations.

Visiting Yellowstone

Yellowstone Park is replete with historic districts, buildings, museums, and trails that tell the history of the park and the land it encompasses.

Historic highlights of each area and descriptions of historic districts and landmarks are available on-line, as are guides to the Thomas Moran paintings and other museum exhibits. Visitors need a week to see all areas. For a visit of one or two days, select one or two areas for enjoyment. Park headquarters and the Fort Yellowstone-Mammoth Hot Springs Historic District are accessible year-round. The *Visitor Guide to Accessible Features in Yellowstone National Park* is available free on-line and at all visitors' centers. Visitors should contact the park for information about fees, lodging, camping, rules, reservations, and permits.

—*Marguerite R. Plummer*

For Further Information:

Fishbein, Seymour L. *Yellowstone Country: The Enduring Wonder.* Washington, D.C.: National Geographic Society, 1989. A photographic overview of the park.

Frantz, Joe B. *Aspects of the American West.* College Station: Texas A&M University Press, 1976. Examines the role of Yellowstone in relation to the National Park Service.

Haines, Aubrey L. *Yellowstone National Park: Its Exploration and Establishment.* Washington, D.C.: Government Printing Office, 1974. Historical sketches of early explorations and the creation of Yellowstone Park.

_____. *The Yellowstone Story: A History of Our First National Park.* 2 vols. Yellowstone National Park, Wyo.: Colorado Associated University Press, 1977. A richly detailed history inspired by people who made the history of Yellowstone Park.

Murphy, Thomas D. *Three Wonderlands of the American West.* Boston: Page, 1919. Features copies of Hayden expedition maps, Thomas Moran paintings, and photographs of the Yellowstone area.

National Park Service. *Beyond Road's End: A Backcountry User's Guide to Yellowstone National Park.* Washington, D.C.: Government Printing Office, 1988. Guide for exploring the backcountry.

Other Historic Sites

Expedition Island

Location: Green River, Sweetwater County

Relevant issues: Western expansion

Statement of significance: This was the embarkation point of Major John Wesley Powell (1834-1902) for his 1871 expedition down the Green and Colorado Rivers and possibly for his 1869 trip as well. On these trips, Major Powell explored the last large land area unknown to European Americans in the mainland United States.

Fort Phil Kearny and Associated Sites

Location: Story, Johnson County

Relevant issues: American Indian history, western expansion

Web site: www.wavecom.net/philkearny/index.html

Statement of significance: Established in 1866 to protect travelers along the Bozeman Trail, the fort was under virtual siege (1866-1868) in the "Red Cloud War" as Sioux groups fought successfully to prevent white invasion of their hunting grounds. This was one of the few times when the Army was forced to abandon a region it had occupied.

Horner Site

Location: Cody, Park County

Relevant issues: American Indian history

Statement of significance: This site has yielded evidence that several distinctive weapons and tools found in the Plains region were all part of a single prehistoric flint tool industry of Early Hunter origin. Initial age estimates place occupation of this site at approximately 5000 B.C.E.

Independence Rock

Location: Casper, Natrona County

Relevant issues: Western expansion

Statement of significance: This is a well-known natural landmark on the Oregon Trail, 1,900 feet long and 850 feet wide. Numerous travelers painted, carved, or wrote their names on its surface over the years.

Medicine Wheel

Location: Kane, Big Horn County

Relevant issues: American Indian history

Statement of significance: This represents one of the most interesting and mysterious remains of late period aboriginal culture. Its builders and function are unknown. Composed of loose, irregularly shaped, whitish flat stones placed in a circle, it is apparently little modified since its construction (c. 1800); twenty-eight linear spokes, seventy to seventy-five feet in length, radiate from the hub.

Obsidian Cliff

Location: Mammoth, Park County

Relevant issues: American Indian history

Statement of significance: Obsidian Cliff occupies a unique position in national prehistory as a singularly important source of lithic materials for prehistoric peoples of interior western North America. It is recognized as an exceptionally well preserved, heavily utilized lithic source that served the utilitarian needs and ceremonial requirements or early indigenous peoples over a large area of North America for twelve thousand years.

Oregon Trail Ruts

Location: Guernsey, Platte County

Relevant issues: Western expansion

Statement of significance: Worn from two to six feet into an eroded sandstone ridge on the south side of the North Platte River, this roadbed gives clear physical evidence of the route followed by those who migrated westward across the Plains in the mid-nineteenth century.

Penney Historic District

Location: Kemmerer, Lincoln County

Relevant issues: Business and industry

Statement of significance: This district includes the Golden Rule Store and the home of James Cash (J. C.) Penney (1875-1971), who began here, in 1902, the retail chain that still bears his name.

Sheridan Inn

Location: Sheridan, Sheridan County

Relevant issues: Cultural history

Statement of significance: William F. ("Buffalo Bill") Cody (1846-1917) operated this hotel from

1894 to 1896, catering principally to sportsmen. The frame building has a piazza on two sides.

South Pass

Location: South Pass City, Fremont County
Relevant issues: Western expansion
Statement of significance: This was the easiest passage through the Rocky Mountains, heavily used by westbound settlers, fur traders, and miners in the nineteenth century. The traffic through the pass helped establish an effective U.S. claim to the Pacific Northwest.

Upper Green River Rendezvous Site

Location: Daniel, Sublette County
Relevant issues: Business and industry, western expansion
Statement of significance: Of the fifteen annual meetings held by mountain men of the Rocky Mountain fur trade from 1825 to 1840, this was the most popular rendezvous site. The annual spring trading fair held here attracted Anglo-American traders and trappers, including Kit Carson and Jim Bridger, and Native Americans.

Wyoming State Capitol

Location: Cheyenne, Laramie County
Relevant issues: Political history, women's history
Statement of significance: As a territory, Wyoming was the first major jurisdiction in the United States where women had full suffrage, and in 1889, an all-male group drafted a state constitution that included woman suffrage. When Wyoming Territory applied for statehood in 1890, Congress, after a close vote, passed the Wyoming statehood bill. This building represents that symbolic victory for the woman suffrage movement which commanded national attention.

AMERICA'S
HISTORIC SITES

Category Index

American Indian history

Art and architecture

Asian American history

Aviation history

Business and industry

European settlement

Health and medicine

Latino history

Legal history

Naval history

Revolutionary War

Science and technology

Women's history

World War I

World War II

Subject Index

A&P, 750
Abaco, 322
Abbe, Cleveland, 305
Abbe House, 305
Abbot, Charles Greeley, 288
Abbott, Edith, 415
Abbott, Grace, 415
Abbott, Robert Sengstacke, 433
Abbott (Robert Sengstacke) House, 433
Abenakis, 510
Abercromby, James, 828
Abernathy, Ralph, 7
Abilene, Kansas, 477
Abó, 783-784
Abolitionist movement, 264, 436, 874, 948, 1237
Academy of Music, Philadelphia, 986
Acadia, 495, 513
Acadian Cultural Center, 503
Acadians, 513; in Louisiana, 495, 503; in Maine, 513
Acheson, Edward G., 1014
Acheson House, 1014
Ácoma Pueblo, 757-760
Actors, 128, 229-230
Acuff, Roy, 1078
Adams, Henry, 562
Adams, John, 597, 1000; and the White House, 301-302
Adams, John Quincy, 258, 597; and the White House, 302
Adams, Robert McCormick, 289
Adams, Samuel, 585, 1000
Adams National Historic Site, 597
Addams, Jane, 414, 416-418
Adventures of Tom Sawyer, The (Twain), 659
Adventuress, 1230
African Americans; in Alabama, 3, 8, 12; in California, 182; in Delaware, 247-248; in the District of Columbia, 253, 270; education of, 12, 81, 277, 473, 645, 1175, 1215, 1240; in Georgia, 350; in Illinois, 399; in Indiana, 441; in Louisiana, 497; in Massachusetts, 560; in Mississippi, 633, 636; in Missouri, 648; in New York, 839, 847; in Oklahoma, 964; in Pennsylvania, 997; in South Carolina, 1045; in Tennessee, 1071; in the Union army, 264; in Virginia, 1173, 1202; and woman suffrage, 285; in World War I, 467
African Burial Ground, New York City, 901
African Meeting House, Boston, 560
Afro-American Realty Company, 849
Agriculture; in California, 88, 112; in Florida, 313

Aguilar, Isidro, 152
Aiken, William, 1055
Aiken House, 1055
Air Force, U.S., 7, 214, 382
Aircraft carriers, 194
Airplanes, 922, 947
Airships, 750
Alabama, 1-16
Alamo, the, 1092, 1095-1101, 1121, 1124, 1131
Alaska, 17-35; U.S. purchase of, 18, 29
Alaska gold rush, 24, 30
Albacore, 722
Albany, New York, 796
Alcatraz Island, 89-93
Alcorn University, 645
Alcott, Bronson, 586, 598
Alcott, Louisa May, 561-562, 586
Aldrich, Nelson W., 1042
Aldrich House, 1042
Aleuts, 18, 28, 34
Alfred P. Murrah Federal Building, 954-955
Alger, Horatio, 599
Algonquians, 556, 1153
Alice Mine, 673
Alien land laws, 136, 189
Alkali Ridge, 1150
Allegheny Mountains, 1234
Allegheny Portage Railroad National Historic Site, 1006
Allen, Ethan, 829
Allen, Richard, 1020
Allenswood, 816
Allouez, Claude-Jean, 609, 1246
Alta California, 143, 176
Altgeld, John P., 411
Altimira, José, 170
Alvarado, Juan B., 175
Amadas, Philip, 924
Amalgamated Copper Mining Company, 675
Amana Colonies, 459, 460-464
Amana Society, 463
Ambrose, Lightship No. 87 , 905
Amelung, Johann Friedrich, 549
"America the Beautiful," 214
American Antiquarian Society, 597
American Federation of Labor Building, 305
American Fur Company, 201, 614, 1066, 1254, 1262
American Indian treaties, 92, 391, 482, 643, 1089, 1264